A Portrait of

ISAAC
NEWTON

THE DA CAPO SERIES IN SCIENCE

A Portrait of

ISAAC NEWTON

FRANK E. MANUEL

A DA CAPO PAPERBACK

Library of Congress Cataloging in Publication Data

Manuel, Frank Edward.
  A portrait of Isaac Newton / Frank E. Manuel.
    p.   c. – (A Da Capo paperback)
  Reprint. Originally published: Cambridge: Belknap Press of Harvard University
Press. 1968.
  ISBN 0-306-80400-X
  1. Newton, Isaac, 1642-1727. 2. Physicists – Great Britain-Biography. I. Title.
QC16.N7M3 1990
530′.092 – dc20   89-71431
[B]   CIP

This Da Capo Press paperback edition of *A Portrait of Isaac Newton* is
an unabridged republication of the edition published in Cambridge, Massachusetts
in 1968. It is reprinted by arrangement with Frank E. Manuel.

Published by Da Capo Press, Inc.
A Subsidiary of Plenum Publishing Corporation
233 Spring Street, New York, New York 10013

Fritzie her Booke

PREFACE

Among early attempts at a biography of Isaac Newton were eighteenth-century academic eulogies—Fontenelle's delicate, balanced performance before the Académie des Sciences, in the course of which he discreetly praised the deceased associate member without incurring the resentment of the disciples of Descartes and Leibniz, and Paolo Frisi's enraptured *Elogio* of 1778, which depicted Newton as the descendant of one of the most ancient families in the realm and constantly dwelt upon the Olympian serenity of his existence. The best eighteenth-century account was probably the one incorporated in the *Biographia Britannica* (1760), whose author had inspected papers in the possession of the Earl of Macclesfield and had garnered bits of evidence from conversation with men who had known the living Newton. Charles Hutton still had access to the oral tradition for the article on Newton in the *Mathematical and Philosophical Dictionary*. In the next century, the rather malevolent sketch by the French astronomer Jean-Baptiste Biot, who stressed Newton's madness, was answered by an official portrait of heroic dimensions, the *Memoirs of the Life, Writings, and Discoveries of Sir Isaac Newton* (1855), by the Scottish scientist Sir David Brewster. He was the first biographer to plough through the mass of personal documents in the possession of the Portsmouth family and to return with a rich harvest—despite his repugnance to a serious examination of Newton's unitarian religious beliefs, his alchemical papers, his chronological studies, his commentaries on prophecy, and his complex psychic nature. Disconcerting revelations about Newton's personality by two other Victorian scientists, the astronomer Francis Baily and the mathematician Augustus de Morgan, were, after an initial shudder, forgotten by most of their contemporaries. In 1931 Richard de Villamil published a not altogether accurate version of the catalogue of Newton's library, part of which he had discovered, along with sundry personal documents. And in 1934 Louis Trenchard More went over much of the same ground that Brewster had and produced an eminently respectworthy biography; but though he raised several knotty questions and reflected about Newton's character and behavior during critical episodes, he had not really been divested of the conventional blinders of his predecessor. The celebration of the tercentenary of Newton's birth, postponed to the end of World War II, brought forth a rich collection of papers from major figures in the scientific world of the Grand Alliance—a worthy sequel to the 1927 commemoration of his death. The Sotheby sale of Portsmouth papers in 1936 had dispersed many of Newton's manuscripts, but at the same time it had brought others into the public eye. John Maynard Keynes, who had purchased quantities of Newton's personal, theological, and alchemical manuscripts that were later presented to King's College, Cambridge, would read them in taxis, it is said, and the result of his perusal was an impish address full of shocking innuendoes, read after his death by his brother Geoffrey L. Keynes at the tercentenary. Coming after Baily and de Morgan, he was the third to uncover the nakedness of the father.

In the past two decades we have entered upon a new period in Newtonian studies. Historians of science have been inquiring into Newton's methods and the sequence of his discoveries with more painstaking scrutiny than has ever been bestowed upon any other scientist. The eight volumes that Derek T. Whiteside is devoting to the mathematical papers alone is some measure of the scope of the Newtonian enterprise—an international scholarly industry. Today even a scribble by Isaac Newton is reproduced with the care and reverence once reserved for the *Codex Sinaiticus*. The Cambridge University Press publication for the Royal Society of Newton's *Correspondence,* now through its fourth volume, is a major undertaking, and permission to quote from this source is gratefully acknowledged. If in my transcriptions I have lowered superior letters, allowed *ye* to be printed as *the,* failed to indicate every scratched-out syllable and variant, and even adhered to nineteenth-century orthography when the printed version did not depart substantively from the manuscript, this looseness should not be construed as a denigration of the purism of contemporary learned journals and their contributors.

The historians of science to whose work I am indebted is an illustrious roster: Sir E. N. da C. Andrade, I. Bernard Cohen, R. J. Forbes, Charles C. Gillispie, Henry Guerlac, A. Rupert Hall, Marie Boas Hall, John W. Herivel, Robert Kargon, Alexandre Koyré, David Kubrin, Thomas S. Kuhn, J. A. Lohne, J. E. McGuire, Douglas McKie, L. D. Patterson, P. M. Rattansi, Leon Rosenfeld, J. F. Scott, F. Sherwood Taylor, H. W. Turnbull, Richard S. Westfall, Derek T. Whiteside. A kind reception accorded to a preliminary draft of portions of the early chapters of this book by the historians of science who participated in the international tercentenary celebration of the *annus mirabilis* 1666, at the University of Texas in Austin, encouraged me to complete this portrait. The pot of Newtonian studies is bubbling vigorously, and I have sometimes had to choose—albeit with misgivings—among divergent interpretations of a document or an event by rival specialists who have devoted themselves to one or another aspect of Newton's thought.

It will quickly become plain to the reader that on more than one occasion I steered my way between a Scylla of historians of science and a Charybdis of psychoanalysts. The existence of an unconscious with a symbolic language different from that of conscious everyday life and of the great rational systems of Western thought is a fundamental assumption of this study. Should the unconscious perchance not exist, one of the underpinnings of the book collapses. I owe a large debt to the psychoanalysts, psychologists, and sociologists from whom I have learned: Rose and Lewis Coser, Abraham H. Maslow, Ricardo Morant, Dr. Harry Rand, Dr. Frederick Wyatt. I have profited from discussion of parts of the book at New York University —in the post-doctoral colloquium headed by Dr. Bernard N. Kalinkowitz and in the seminar of the Research Center for Mental Health under Dr. George S. Klein. In 1963, at the Center for Advanced Study in the Behavioral Sciences, Erik H. Erikson discussed with me my first queries about Newton, and through the years I have been deeply moved by Erikson's works and thought, in particular during two week-long seminars sponsored by the American Academy of Arts and Sciences in the summers of 1966 and 1967. Though I can by no means claim the privilege of true discipleship, perhaps he may allow me the more dubious epithet of fellow traveler.

For assistance indispensable to the progress of my research and for permission to quote from manuscripts in their keeping I express gratitude to the librarians of the following institutions: the Fitzwilliam Museum, King's College Library, Trinity College Library, and the University Library in Cambridge; the Royal Greenwich Observatory at Herstmonceux; the British Museum, the Royal Society of London, and the Royal Mint; the Bodleian Library in Oxford; the Bibliothèque Publique et Universitaire in Geneva; the Bibliothèque Nationale in Paris; the Sir Isaac Newton Library in Babson Park, Massachusetts; and the Pierpont Morgan Library in New York. Use of the collections of the Boston Athenaeum, the New York Public Library, and the libraries of Harvard, Yale, and Columbia Universities and of the General Theological Seminary of New York is a benefit I have long enjoyed, and I tender my thanks to their staffs for their unfailing helpfulness. A private collector, Mr. Joseph Halle Schaffner of New York, kindly allowed me to study and to excerpt manuscripts that he owns.

I especially appreciate the willingness of friends and colleagues to read the manuscript in whole or in part: Ida and Leo Gershoy, Leo Goldberger, Albert B. Novikoff, Dr. Samuel F. Tabbat. David Carrithers helped prepare the typescript, and New York University generously gave me a grant for technical assistance.

PREFACE

I wish to thank the editors of *Daedalus* for allowing me to use here material that appeared in the Summer 1968 issue. In addition, chapters 16 and 17 draw upon two of my previous works—*The Eighteenth Century Confronts the Gods* (Harvard University Press, 1959) and *Isaac Newton, Historian* (Harvard University Press, 1963).

Frank E. Manuel

Washington Square
New York

CONTENTS

PART THREE

In London Town

ILLUSTRATIONS

A Portrait of
ISAAC
NEWTON

INTRODUCTION

Say, ye who best can tell, ye happy few,
Who saw him in the softest lights of life,
All unwith-held, indulging to his friends
The vast unborrow'd treasures of his mind,
O speak the wondrous man! how mild, how calm,
How greatly humble, how divinely good;
How firm establish'd on eternal truth;
Fervent in doing well, with every nerve
Still pressing on, forgetful of the past,
And panting for perfection: far above
Those little cares, and visionary joys,
That so perplex the fond impassion'd heart
Of ever-cheated, ever-trusting man.
This, *Conduitt,* from thy rural hours we hope;
As thro' the pleasing shade, where Nature pours
Her every sweet, in studious ease you walk;
The social passions smiling at thy heart,
That glows with all the recollected sage.
  —James Thomson, *A Poem to the Memory of*
        Sir Isaac Newton

Newton's long life from 1642 to 1727 divides itself neatly into
three parts, each of which is largely confined to a particular locality
—the county of Lincolnshire, Cambridge, and London. He virtually
never strayed outside the triangle. The first eighteen years, as well
as the marvelously creative period when he was about twenty-three,
the *annus mirabilis,* were spent in Lincolnshire, and he returned
there for brief sojourns until he was a very old man. From his entry

into Trinity College in 1661 until he was elevated to the wardenship of the Mint in 1696 and moved away to the capital, thirty-five
years passed. He lived in London for thirty-one years longer. On
his personality and behavior during the Cambridge and London
phases, the full and the waning, there are many documents in his
own hand and the recorded testimony of numerous eyewitnesses,
though irksome questions remain unsolved. But Newton's underlying character was already shaped before he went up to Trinity,
and for the early years the evidence is scanty and cries for interpretation.

Before unveiling the portrait, a few disclaimers. This is *a* portrait
of Isaac Newton and it does not pretend to encompass the whole
man and his multifarious works—assuredly not the detail of his inventions in optics, mathematics, and mechanics, or his alchemy,
chemistry, revision of chronology, and interpretation of Scripture.[1]
Having contributed a share to the elucidation of Newton's chronological, mythological, and what are sometimes called his theological
manuscripts in an earlier volume,[2] in this book I am turning to
Newton the man—his person, his world outlook, and his style of
life. Without presuming to unlock the secret of Newton's genius or
its mysterious energy, I aim to depict and to analyze aspects of his
conduct, primarily in situations of love and hate, and to probe for
the forces that shaped his character. In his studies of the great, Freud
forthrightly disavowed any intention of explaining their extraordinary powers. The essays on Leonardo and Dostoevsky examined
critical episodes in their life histories and searched for the origins of
neuroses, but refrained from establishing a facile causal relationship
between the passions and fixations that sometimes drove them to
distraction and their creativity. At most, Freud would point out the
signs of struggle with destructive impulses in their natures, clues
left behind, proof that a battle had been waged; he could not account for the victory. We stand in awe before genius, and wonder
the more because its works are achieved in the face of odds that
have crushed lesser men. When the magnitude of the forces that
might have led to disintegration is recognized, the acts of sheer will

2

and overcoming astound. There have doubtless been others with psychic configurations similar to Newton's who have never been heard of since. Elements of quiet strength in men of genius are naturally harder to identify than those of weakness or uncontrolled violence, for we are more prone to remark upon the turbulence of the waters than to notice their stillness; but that is perhaps true of our observation of all life processes that may be isolated.

There have been many attempts in Western thought to characterize if not explain the extraordinary men whom society has called geniuses. That the first inventors of arts and sciences were godlike heroes or demigods is part of the mythic tradition of which we have never been divested. A Greek perception of poetic genius as divine madness has, through the centuries, been stretched to cover the powers of the artist and the scientist, and Plato's idea is still relevant, if only as ancient witness to the belief that such men often teeter on the verge of chaos. The daemonic in genius, symbolized in the medieval Faust legend, has been kept alive in a long line of literary adaptations. Romantic portrayals of the genius introduced Christian elements that rendered poignant the sacrifices and martyrdom of his person.

Many present-day theories are knowingly or unknowingly related to these older views. With the extension of clinical studies in psychology there has been an understandable tendency to stress the pathological in men of genius—and since they are often great, and articulate, sufferers, the materials are plentiful. The establishment of a connection between specific neurotic symptoms and the gifts of genius remains, however, far more problematical, though many of the formulas that have been advanced are founded on deep insight and long experience. The birth of creativity has sometimes been thought of as restitution for a traumatic loss either of a physical or a psychic character—a sophistication of an ancient belief that sensed in genius a gigantic expenditure of effort to overcome the challenge of handicaps and deprivation. Today hereditary factors are assigned less weight in the scientific analysis of genius than they were in the nineteenth century, though there may be some empirical evidence for the inheritance of musical and mathematical talent. Other theories that cast light on the nature of genius are equally credible, as long as they do not presume to pre-empt the whole field, and the historian profits from these illuminations when they have direct and immediate bearing on his documents. The recent literature on genius is vast, provocative, respectworthy, and necessarily inconclusive.

To reduce the enigma of genius to superior native energy merely begs the question, since latent powers can be stifled or fostered. But vast fonts of plain physical energy, keen sensory responsiveness, and a phenomenal memory are common attributes, though not absolute conditions, of genius that apply to Newton. His longevity is an index of stamina, and there were no protracted physical illnesses that we know of, even though he was somewhat hypochondriac. He lost only one tooth, he kept his hair to an old age, and his nearsightedness was corrected with time. All witnesses agree that he had a prodigious capacity for many hours of continuous intellectual labor with little sleep. We hear nothing of his need for rest and relaxation. Yet after an expression of wonderment at the flowering of his genius and the multiplicity of creative forms in which it manifested itself, I can offer no explanation of what appears to be a grand sport of nature. Of the magnificence of his mathematical inventiveness, perhaps his most spectacular "genius" in the seventeenth-century sense of the word, I have least to say.

The tendency for men of genius to form clusters limited in time and place is an intriguing phenomenon that has long provoked historical inquiry. One cannot but remark the efflorescence of scientific achievement in England of the second half of the seventeenth century, the world of Boyle, Barrow, Hooke, Flamsteed, Halley, Wren, Wallis, and Isaac Newton. Why that extraordinary concentration in an offshore island of the European continent during this particular period? The benign conditions in the environment—in the broadest sense—will be dwelt upon whenever reasonable correspondences can be established between the world of science, contemporary religious and philosophical belief, and social and political practice, though a simple relationship between economic substructure and intellectual superstructure in what Leibniz called the "golden age of English science" is dubious.

There is no implication that the young man delineated in the early chapters of this book had to develop by an ineluctable destiny into the Cambridge recluse who constructed a system of the world, the psychically disturbed middle-aged man of the black year 1693, the authoritarian Master of the Mint, the dictatorial President of the Royal Society, and the fierce, often ruthless, combatant in five or six great wars of truth. Such determinism is alien to me. But while life experiences modify and alter a basic structure, the earliest impressions and traumas are the most potent and pervasive—a rather old notion, to be sure, already part of the wisdom of Descartes and Locke, not to speak of Plato. Contemporary psychology has formalized many observations on human development and I intend to make free use of its science, though not always its vocabulary. Admittedly, only an acquaintance with the adult Newton provokes one to raise basic queries about beginnings, to delve in the junior part of his life for the roots of the consuming passions of the mature man. There was early instilled in Newton a complex of attitudes and beliefs common to many others of his time, status, and religion. Through an educational process that began in infancy, social forces were internalized and became a part of his being. The interplay of his own creative personality, that which was uniquely Isaac Newton, a man of genius who lived in the illusion and the truth of his singularity, with what the society around him nurtured, repressed, or tolerated is the essential drama of his life. The historical study of great dead men has both advantages and disadvantages over the efforts of those who cure souls. Historians can rarely check their intuitive guesses with the subject, but on the other hand they have a completed life before them, and the end always tells much about the beginnings. The focus, too, is different: the point of departure is not a malaise, but a far more general question, the nature of a genius in a moment of time.

Conventional sources of knowledge about Newton's history

through the *annus mirabilis* 1666 are meager. In the church at Colsterworth in Lincolnshire there is an entry of his birth and a sundial he is said to have fashioned; his name is carved on a window ledge in the Grammar School at Grantham a few miles away;[3] and Trinity College preserves a record of his scholastic career, including notations of his comings and goings in the Buttery Book, which scholars and fellows signed when absenting themselves and re-entering. The Lincolnshire antiquary, Canon C. W. Foster, has compiled an impeccable genealogy of Isaac Newton and his collateral relations, based upon wills probated in Lincoln and entries of marriages, births, and deaths in various parish registers of the area.[4] More open to question is Newton's own reconstruction of his genealogy for the College of Heralds when he was knighted in 1705, though the very errors are pregnant with meaning. Such are the hard facts of his early biography.

Miscellaneous documents reveal something about the persons with whom Newton was living during this period, even though much of the material is of a later date. There are a tiny burnt fragment of a letter from his mother, a few notes from his half sister, a mammoth commonplace book that once belonged to his stepfather, evidence about the ejection of Puritan divines who were his teachers at Grantham, a few notices of college friends identifiable in the registry of Cambridge graduates. Little more is known about his tutor at Trinity, Benjamin Pulleyn, than that he was a Greek scholar. Isaac Barrow, Newton's eminent predecessor in the Lucasian Chair of Mathematics, and Henry More, the renowned Cambridge Platonist who originally came from Grantham, were attracted to the young genius in their midst, but their personal remarks about him, though noteworthy, are sparse.

Two rather extensive memoirs were drafted by friends who aspired to write Newton's life. (There was a third pretender to the role of Newton's biographer, his distant relative Sir Michael Newton, but he died before he got started.) The more complete one, prepared by Dr. William Stukeley, drew upon conversations with Newton in the 1720's and upon interviews with a few elderly people in Lincolnshire, primarily a Mrs. Vincent, the childhood sweetheart of the Newton legend. Stukeley was capable of being matter-of-fact. A medical doctor, a divine, and a major antiquarian—one of the great eighteenth-century scholars of British prehistory and an authority on the Druids—he was bold enough to differ with Newton on such delicate subjects as the revision of world chronology, the interpretation of Scripture, and the history of ancient architecture. On his admission to the Royal Society in 1718 for his knowledge of medicine, the President took a fancy to the new Fellow forty-five years his junior. Like any old man, he was pleased on occasion to talk about his youth and it was easier with a person from the same county. Newton was invariably more open with younger men than with his coevals or his seniors. When Dr. Stukeley, who had decided to leave London and settle in Grantham because of violent seizures of gout, took leave of Newton in 1726, Sir Isaac desired him to "carry his service" to a Mr. Richard Chrisloe, who, apart from Mrs. Vincent, was the "chief acquaintance he had left in that place."[5] Unhappily, by the time Stukeley got there, the apothecary Chrisloe, a boyhood friend whom Newton held in high esteem, had died; though Stukeley learned of several other aged folk in the neighborhood of Colsterworth, most of them were dead before he could hear their stories. His record is thus almost entirely a rehearsal of the reminiscences of Mrs. Vincent, all that remained of Newton's past in Lincolnshire.

The full text of Stukeley's *Memoirs of Sir Isaac Newton's Life* was first published in 1936 from a manuscript now preserved in the Royal Society. Though it was not completed until 1752, there are earlier versions of roughly the same material, notably long letters written in 1727 to Newton's physician Dr. Mead, for transmission to John Conduitt,[6] the wealthy member of Parliament who had married the daughter of Newton's half sister. These letters ultimately became a part of the Portsmouth Collection of Newton's manuscripts and were drawn upon by Newton's editors and biographers from the eighteenth century onward. The same data are included in the Surtees Society publication in the 1880's of Stukeley's

Family Memoirs and Correspondence.[7] The Royal Society manuscript is embellished with Stukeley's engraving of Colsterworth Church, a sketch of Newton's birthplace at Woolsthorpe, and a monstrous allegorical figure holding a shield with a profile drawing of Newton made from life, his hair encircled by an antique fillet. The many-breasted naked woman sitting on a globe virtually clawing the shield tells us more about Stukeley than about Newton.

Stukeley defined his mission as a search for the origins of Isaac Newton, "the preparation and presages of his extraordinary abilitys." By his own admission Stukeley suppressed some stories, since his primary purpose was "to show the signs of a rising genius."[8] In 1752 he was an old man, proud of his former association with great figures of science and literature, a doctor who had fallen into country obscurity. On a number of points Stukeley's early letters to Dr. Mead are more vivid than the long reflected-upon and revised memoir.

John Conduitt, the second memorialist, was an awestruck admirer of Newton, and shortly after his hero's death sent inquiries to various friends from whom he hoped to gather information. His purpose was twofold: to supply material to Fontenelle for a formal eulogy before the French Académie des Sciences, of which Newton had been an associate member, and to assemble facts for a full-scale biography that he himself proposed to write some day. A pompous Plutarchian fragment of what he hoped to do, now in King's College Library, hardly moves one to regret the failure of his literary ambitions,[9] but in Conduitt Newton found the great adulator of his life. If he could not impress with the weight of his intelligence, he compensated for the lack with the warmth of his affection. Conduitt was sufficiently imbued with the Bollandist spirit to maintain that there was some worth in printing any manuscript from Newton's hand, and the preservation of Newton's papers owes much to his care.

The memoir that John Conduitt delivered to Fontenelle is largely based on Stukeley's letters and a few other responses to the round robin inquiry. Since Conduitt was also the repository of

Newton's recollections during the years they lived together in the same London house, his manuscript notes, based upon Newton's reminiscences and upon observations made by his wife, Catherine, enliven the picture; they were reproduced in part by Edmund Turnor in the early nineteenth century, but many minor details are still unprinted. Though the hand that wrote the notes is Conduitt's, the voice is the voice of the aged Newton.

No correspondence has survived from the period of Newton's youth—his first extant dated letter is of February 23, 1669, when he was past twenty-six—but we possess four notebooks covering the last years in Lincolnshire and the first in Trinity College—one each in the Pierpont Morgan Library of New York, the Fitzwilliam Museum, Trinity College, and the University Library in Cambridge.[10] In addition, there is a Latin exercise book from a somewhat earlier period now in Los Angeles, and the famous Waste Book, as his stepfather's commonplace book is now called, in which Newton wrote mathematical and dynamical notes. Supplementing these materials are scattered marginalia in books that Newton owned as a youth and a few stray sheets of his proposal for a new philosophical language. These notebooks and manuscripts, the best guides to an understanding of his personality and superior in many ways to the worshipful memoirs of Stukeley and Conduitt pieced together after his death, have only been touched upon by Newton's biographers. They allow us to make conjectures about his temper, his moods, his emotions, his character. They may even be a window into his fantasy world. The notebooks can be read with different prepossessions. Students of his mathematics, the *Principia,* and the *Opticks* have found among these papers his earliest scientific intuitions; but they are documents that also pose perplexing psychological questions, and suggest some answers. The materials in the notebooks require interpretation and structuring, a more hazardous venture than mere repetition of the anecdotes of Stukeley and Conduitt, telling though they may be. If the data are read with an awareness that theorizing about them involves speculative leaps and analogical thinking, a new dimension in the understanding of young

Newton can be explored. For some historians such readings may be soft currency or even false coin. While conscious of recent abuses in the interpretive extension of the boundaries of meaning in historical scholarship, a man of the late-Freudian era cannot put on blinders, refraining from an examination of psychological facts and from making hypotheses about them merely because they are not subject to traditional forms of verification.

The dating of the early manuscript materials presents problems that cannot always be resolved. John Conduitt remarks in one of his papers in King's College that Newton early learned to write in different hands, a not uncommon practice—Sir William Petty even recommends it in one of his educational schemes. Attempts to set the documents in chronological sequence on the basis of handwriting alone are therefore not wholly successful. During this period there was a trend away from the ornate "secretary" to a simpler, flowing Roman hand that could be written more speedily. Penmanship books were published that offered examples of various combinations of scripts for adoption by young scholars.[11] The dates on the flyleaves of Newton's notebooks and printed books that he owned do not, moreover, preclude the possibility of earlier or later entries. In 1659 he signed a good number of his belongings as a sort of juvenile act of taking possession. "Quisquis in hunc librum/ teneros conjecit ocellos/ Nomen subscriptum perlegat/ ipse meum/ Isaac Newton/ Martij 19/ 1659" is the caution inscribed in the Trinity notebook.[12] Such an affirmation of his person by the sixteen-year-old dates the signature but does not date the contents of the notebook.

The oldest writings in Newton's hand are probably ten leaves once in the Portsmouth Collection of his manuscripts and now in private possession in the United States, containing about three hundred and fifty phrases, each of them written in English and Latin in parallel columns, a language exercise of no apparent significance. There were in mid-seventeenth-century England many printed school texts of this character in which brief "sentences," as they were called, were used to develop a speaking and writing knowledge of Latin. Usually the colloquies between master and pupil in textbooks such as Comenius' *Orbis sensualium pictus* or Culman's *Sententiae pueriles* were concentrated around single topics;[13] Newton's "sentences" are random and therefore more revealing of his person. The handwriting of Newton's exercises is the "secretary" that he was taught at school—so flowery that it resembles drawing —and we shall call it "Old Barley" in honor of his writing-master in Grantham. Though the Portsmouth catalogue of Newton's manuscripts describes this piece as "not in Newton's hand," in my judgment the nineteenth-century compilers were probably in error.[14] On internal evidence one can conclude that many of the "sentences" were free inventions and not assigned by a schoolmaster. The contents of the exercise book might have been written by a boy of about fifteen—a mere surmise. Some of the "sentences" may conceivably have been copied out of a printed book, in which case their worth would be diminished though not destroyed.

In chronological order the next manuscript is probably the tiny notebook in the Pierpont Morgan Library in New York, which bears an inscription not in Newton's hand: "Isacus Newton hunc librum possidet. teste Edvardo Secker. pret: 2^d ob. 1659." It includes long excerpts and paraphrases from the writings of John Bate and John Wilkins, contemporary popularizers of science,[15] as well as an ecclesiastical calendar for the years 1662 through 1689, all in "Old Barley," and a passage translated into a modified Shelton shorthand beginning "When Jesus saw the Crosse," a remedy for the ague if carried around as an amulet.[16] In the same basic "Old Barley" but somewhat less elaborate, there is a list of about twenty-four hundred words under the title, "The several things contained under these generall heads," broken down into sixteen chapters in alphabetical order with titles such as Artes, Trades, & Sciences; Of Kindred, & Titles; Of Man, his Affections, & Senses. Each of the chapters in turn has words arranged under a letter of the alphabet, though within the subsections an alphabetical sequence is only occasionally followed. Three of the general heads make reference to pages of a *nomenclatura* which is beyond question Francis Gregory's *Nomenclatura brevis anglo-Latino,* a book that was long used in grammar schools in both England and America. Newton alphabetized and copied many sequences directly from this *Nomenclatura;* but often enough he departed from its text, disregarding the alphabet and inserting his own additions, and then the document becomes provocative—a series of words that are free associations around a subject and can be interpreted for their psychological content.[17] The Morgan notebook also contains entries in Newton's new script, which he acquired sometime after coming up to the University. In this definitive, elegant, rather free, Roman hand, which we shall call "Trinity," he wrote pieces on dialing, the dissection of the triangle, the Copernican theory, and a system of phonetic orthography that introduces a few Hebrew signs.[18] The system is illustrated on the last leaf by a brief letter in duplicate, both in ordinary English spelling and in the new manner, an exhortation to a friend to stop drinking that sounds like a transcript from a sample letter book. Both versions are for some reason signed "T.N."[19] Of greater interest are the leaves of the Morgan notebook that cite a few hundred words to illustrate the new orthography, a choice again suggesting free association.

A stray document in private possession, in "Trinity" script, contains notations for a philosophical language which, like numerals, was meant to serve as the basis for universal, visual communication while men of all nations preserved their own idiosyncratic speech. Here again the selection of word and idea illustrations appears to be a random one. The top sheet of this notational system is decorated by a minuscule genealogical table of Newton's ancestry, as well as of the brood of his mother's second husband, and—to add to the confusion—by an enigmatic rhyme in "Old Barley": "the site of this is as a kiss."

The notebook in the Fitzwilliam Museum in Cambridge contains Newton's account of receipts and expenditures at the University from May 23, 1665, through April 1669, written in the "Trinity" hand. One sheet of the notebook is a complicated exercise in connection with the learning of Hebrew entitled *Nova Cubi Haebraei Tabella,* in which the Hebrew words are rendered into Latin in "Old Barley" script. (Some of the letters on this page help to confirm the authenticity of the Latin-English exercise book, which is in a similar hand.) There are in addition stray alphabetical letters in "Old Barley" on the flyleaf. Of paramount importance in the Fitzwilliam notebook are two lists of sins to which Newton confessed, one list of forty-nine headed "before Whitsunday 1662," the other list of nine headed "after Whitsunday," both written in Shelton shorthand, a variant of the kind Pepys used in his diary. Shorthand was learned by young men primarily in order to record sermons lest they forget them. In his examination of conscience in 1662 Newton probably resorted to shorthand for secrecy's sake, though there may have been another reason: devoutly religious Puritans would refrain from writing down a particularly horrible crime in ordinary script because this act was in some sense akin to a repetition of the sin.

The Cambridge University Library notebook, in which "Old Barley" and "Trinity" are sometimes intermingled on the same page, is the most famous personal record of Newton's early university career and has been exploited brilliantly by historians of science for dating the origins of Newton's major conceptions. The extended table of contents of this serious commonplace book is an index to the manifold philosophical, mathematical, physical, and religious problems with which he was preoccupied. The long passages quoted from Aristotle and his commentators are a reminder that, though Newton was an early convert to the new philosophy, he was first educated in the traditional philosophic disciplines.[20] References in the notebook to Newton's interest in problems that today would be called psychological have not attracted commentators; many show an acquaintance either at first or at second hand with the reflections of that erratic philosopher and adventurer

Kenelm Digby, of Descartes, of Henry More, of Joseph Glanvill the apologist for the new science and believer in witches, and of Hobbes. Newton's entries are for the most part queries rather than conclusions. Of equal if not superior worth for historians of science is the Waste Book in the Cambridge University Library, whose earliest dated notation is November 1664.

The tiny Trinity College notebook, which contains Latin word lists entitled *Utilissimum Prosodiae Supplementum,* another running expense account, and a shorthand inscription on the flyleaf, is among the less rewarding early documents, as are a few other manuscripts of this period that are particularly difficult to place. A Latin oration on Henricus Sextus, now at Babson Park in Massachusetts, is written in a hand intermediate between "Old Barley" and "Trinity"; and so is a puzzling sheet on the origins of the signs of the zodiac buried among the thousand-odd New College folios at Oxford that are of a later date.

Since individual sections of the four notebooks and early manuscripts differ in handwriting and a date on a flyleaf does not establish the time of composition of the several parts, our notions about the precise year of a specific passage have to be tentative, except of course where it is explicitly dated—though a manuscript that is exclusively "Old Barley" is probably anterior to Newton's twentieth birthday. In any event, for purposes of the early part of this portrait, exact dating has not been feasible and the most I can say is that we are dealing with documents of the young Newton.

The notebooks constitute only a minor portion of Newton's total manuscript legacy covering commonplace books, correspondence, working notes and drafts of his mathematical discoveries, optics, dynamics, and alchemical experiments; shipbuilding blueprints; educational projects; ecclesiastical calendars; historical theology, interpretations of mythology, and world geography; economic treatises; records of the Royal Mint and of estates for which he acted as executor; chronological and historical studies of ancient kingdoms; commentaries on Daniel and the Apocalypse; medical abstracts and potions.[21] On virtually all of these "foul and waste papers" Newton's executor, Thomas Pellet, once wrote in a bold hand "not fit to be printed." The confusion of some of the manuscripts is difficult to describe. Newton wrote from left to right, then turned the page and wrote from top to bottom over the same sheet. The chance juxtaposition of ideas is delightfully surrealistic. On a receipt of two pounds two shillings dated January 31, 1721, "towards the Relief of Poor Proseleytes, for the Year 1722," there is a computation of the year of the return of the Heraclidae. Stray notes for the *Principia* collide with reckonings of the precession of the equinox, lists of kings of Israel, summonses to meetings at the Mint, drafts of letters to eminent scientists, chits addressed to himself on his chances of re-election to Parliament, lists of books, letters begging for charity. The subjects run into each other, and one must be wary lest Chiron the Centaur appear as a worker at the Mint for whom a raise (delayed sixty years) is being requested by the new Master. But these manuscripts amounting to millions of words, which are now the object of careful examination by historians of science, also yield bits of psychological information. Newton kept all sorts of scraps of paper, though the absence of any letters from his mother beyond a single charred fragment is strange. There is only a handful of letters from other members of his family. Did he burn them or were they destroyed in chance fires? The testimony of the German divine Samuel Crell that a few weeks before his death Newton consigned many manuscripts to the flames may or may not be accurate[22]—thousands of folios were left behind and the selection seems random. There is also a note in Conduitt's papers that he helped Newton burn "boxfulls of informations" in his own handwriting taken at the Mint.[23] After one has scrutinized the twelfth version, with minor variants, of a reply to the Huguenot scholar Des Maizeaux on the Leibniz controversy, or the twentieth copy of a world chronological table, the adjective "obsessive" does not seem too strong. The hoarding of pieces of paper, scribbled on all sides, from boyhood exercise books and youthful expenditure accounts through drafts of his denunciation of the French scholars before the Royal Society when he was eighty-three bespeaks a certain parsimoniousness and, to say the least, retentiveness.

Though records about the person of the mature and aged scientist are richer than materials on the Lincolnshire lad, they are not as plentiful as might be expected for a man of his fame. His correspondence, with one major exception during the crisis of 1693, reveals him only by indirection; he kept no diaries, wrote no autobiography, left no intimate private notes about individuals among the millions of words of manuscript on all aspects of creation. Conduitt caught a few personal comments, but he was no Boswell. Notations Newton made about his early discoveries were written down late in life when they were needed to plead a case of priority. There is far more about God than man in these papers. Those that do touch on human beings are usually drafts of letters and official documents, and here microanalysis—watching the minute changes of feeling as he moves from one version of a statement to another—occasionally reveals a hidden truth.[24]

In the end we know Newton primarily through the intervention of others: those who painted his likeness, those who admired his genius, or those who abominated him. When he became the cynosure of many eyes there were ample references to him in contemporary diaries and in the scientific correspondence of the age. Men close to him tended to be sharply divided in their reactions—there were idolizers and there were enemies—even as he himself was rarely neutral to a creature whose existence he deigned to recognize. His countryman Dr. Stukeley writes of the "natural dignity and politeness in his manner in common life," and of "a spirit of beneficence and philanthropy [that] was, as it were, the basis of his composition."[25] His friend Locke said he was "a nice man to deal with [meaning touchy, hypersensitive] and a little too apt to raise in himself suspicions where there is no ground," and he therefore advised his kinsman not to approach him too directly lest he give offense.[26] In the secret diary of Robert Hooke, an enemy, he figures as the "veryest Knave in all the Ho:."[27] To "clippers" and "coyners," prisoners in Newgate who feared Newton's rage during interrogations in the Tower, he was a "rogue," and they threatened to shoot him if King James returned.

In the great quarrels which demarcate the periods of Newton's life his major antagonists were invariably more prolific in reporting than he was, so that his behavior during these episodes is reflected chiefly in the distorting mirror of an opponent's anger. Since he had few loves, the portrait of Isaac Newton sometimes becomes thick-laden with the violent colors of hate. The bitterest men were friends later spurned: William Whiston, his successor in the Lucasian Chair at Cambridge, and John Flamsteed, the first Royal Astronomer. They described him in almost identical, unflattering terms as irascible, brooking no criticism, quick with sharp retorts, tolerant only of the darlings who praised him, "fearful, cautious, and suspicious."[28] Jervas painted him as a pompous Royal Society President. In two Vanderbank portraits he appears as a bloated, ill-tempered, and cruel man. There is family anecdotage about his tantrums. In his last years Leibniz considered him underhanded, capable of wicked chicanery, and harped on his reputation for quarrelsomeness. For the astronomer John Keill, on the other hand, he was the "divine Newton";[29] and so he remained for Halley, who called him his *Numen*,[30] not to speak of the lesser favorites in his entourage who owed their advancement to him. Fatio de Duillier, a Swiss disciple, worshiped him like a god, and so did John Conduitt: "Had this great & good man lived in an age when those superiour Genii inventors were Deified or in a country where mortals are canonized he would have had a better claim to those honours than those they have hitherto been ascribed to, his virtues proved him a Saint & his discoveries might well pass for miracles."[31] Great bishops of the realm spoke of Newton's piety with reverence. By the time of his death, a composite official portrait had been created in the public mind—the calm, majestic genius who was above worldly concerns, a paragon of all the virtues of both Christianity and the Enlightenment.[32]

Nothing I shall have to say should be construed as denigration.

Though it departs sharply from the eighteenth-century hagiographical image of Newton, it brings the humanity of genius closer to us and is its own justification. A further reason for concerning ourselves with the life of Newton is, as David Hume would have said, "exposed to some more difficulty": it presumes that science in a given culture has a psychological envelopment, and hence the character components of its great, form-imprinting practitioners are by no means a matter of indifference in understanding the nature of Western science itself. In the present study, there will be occasion to propose congruities between certain of Newton's psychic experiences and his scientific outlook, though this will not be the main thrust of the work. Avenues into his inner life may be opened to enable the eminent historians of science who are today illuminating with scholarly detail so many different phases of his achievement to establish further connexities. I surely must leave to others the identification of Newton's unique mathematical style and its relationship to his person; but where the expressions of his genius were verbal rather than mathematical, it may be possible to propose some correspondences. One has an inkling that a closed scientific system like Newton's, which was consonant with his personality, must in some measure have affected the evolution of Western science by excluding alternatives—the looser models of a Hooke or a Leibniz, for example. The powerful appeal of a total world system for a Christian society that had recently destroyed its traditional guides in science and morals is understandable; but there were other forces in the culture inimical to such a monolithic structure. A sounding into Newton's life history might therefore be useful to those who wish to pursue further the influence of this enigmatic man on the scientific behavior of the century following his death, provided they are not committed to such antediluvian notions as the absolute autonomy of science. When Europe adopted Newtonianism as its intellectual model, something of his character penetrated to the very marrow of the system.[33]

The innermost secrets of Isaac Newton have not been uncovered. Though the curtain may be raised briefly, one goes away burdened with doubt about what has actually been seen in that fleeting moment. And yet the historian can hardly refrain from trying to construct the deeper meaning of acts and words. If the reader can accept an avowal that an element of speculation is consciously interwoven in this portrayal, part of the misunderstanding associated with studies of this character may be dissipated. The goal here is not mathematical truth but general plausibility, which is, after all, what the historian has to offer.

PART ONE

The Lad from Lincolnshire

Chapter **I**

HANNAH AND THE FATHERS

And she said, Oh my lord, as thy soul liveth, my lord, I am the
woman that stood by thee here, praying unto the Lord. For
this child I prayed; and the Lord hath given me my petition
which I asked of him: Therefore also I have lent him to the
Lord; as long as he liveth he shall be lent to the Lord.

—I Samuel 1:26–28

Newton's melancholy temper reflected the emotional climate of
mid-seventeenth-century England, but the Puritan censor merely aggravated his woes. Initially they were inflicted by the one who loved
him most.

The salient facts of Newton's childhood can be briefly narrated.
He was born prematurely on Christmas Day 1642, an hour or two
after midnight at the time of the full moon, in a small manor house
in Woolsthorpe, and was not expected to live. Two women dispatched to Lady Pakenham, one of the local gentry, to fetch some
medicine entertained little hope of finding him alive upon their
return. Under the heading of baptisms for 1642/3, the tiny parish
register at Colsterworth has an entry: "Isaac sonne of Isaac and
Hanna Newton, January 1." The church records bear witness to the
high death rate, particularly among the Newtons, during this period.[1] There was something miraculous about Isaac's survival, a
feeling that was communicated to him early in life and would be
reinforced when he escaped the bubonic plague; like the biblical
Isaac whom he knew so well, Isaac Newton too had been saved at
the last moment by divine intervention. His mother often told him

that at birth he was small enough to fit into a quart pot. Newton also remembered hearing that he was so weak he had to wear a "bolster around his neck to keep his head upon his shoulders" and that "he was very much below the usual size of children."[2] Premature babies often have difficulty in breathing and in holding up their heads during the sucking of the teat, and they require frequent feedings in small quantities. In the fear of suffocation, in the anger generated by insufficient nourishment, may lie the first sources of anxiety. The fact that Newton recalled these stories of his infancy, which he had from his mother, and when he was a very old man recounted them to Conduitt, is some measure of their lasting emotional potency. The shakiness of Newton's self-esteem throughout his life may have one of its origins in an infantile failure to be satiated at the breast and in his littleness.

Newton's father, a yeoman who could not sign his name, had died three months before he was born, and his paternal grandfather, too, was dead. His mother, a gentlewoman, married again on January 27, 1646, probably at about thirty (her date of birth is unknown), when he had just turned three. She went to live about a mile and a half away with her new husband, a man of sixty-three, the rich Barnabas Smith, Rector of North Witham,[3] while Isaac remained in the Woolsthorpe manor with his maternal grandmother, a woman in her fifties, under the legal guardianship of his maternal uncle.[4] When he was about eleven, the Reverend Smith died and Hannah Smith returned to live in Woolsthorpe with the brood of her second marriage, Mary aged about four and a half, Benjamin over two, and Hannah aged one.[5] According to the records, Father Barnabas was still siring children when he was past seventy.

Before her marriage to the Reverend Barnabas Smith, Hannah Ayscough Newton arranged for the repair of the manor house at Woolsthorpe and provided for the acquisition of land to increase Isaac's inheritance. Somebody, either her brother or a schoolmaster at Grantham, was sensible of his genius and, despite her reluctance, got him admitted to Cambridge as a subsizar. There were dangers that she would smother him, retain him by her side as son and elder brother-father to the children she brought from Barnabas Smith. Hannah sacrificed Isaac to the University. In 1665, when he returned home during the plague in Cambridge and was not busy discovering the law of gravity, he still spent some time making out rent receipts for her tenants.[6]

Newton's mother is the central figure in his life. The conventional character-portrait of a strong, self-reliant woman is derived from John Conduitt's account based on his conversations with her son and with a Mrs. Hutton, née Ayscough: "She was a woman of so extraordinary an understanding & virtue that those who . . . think that a soul like Sir Isaac Newton's could be formed by any thing less than the immediate operation of a Divine Creator might be apt to ascribe to her many of those extraordinary qualities with which it was endowed."[7] They were in union with each other during a crucial period, and his fixation upon her was absolute. The trauma of her original departure, the denial of her love, generated anguish, aggressiveness, and fear. After the total possession—undisturbed by a rival, not even a father, almost as if there had been a virgin birth —she was removed and he was abandoned.

Some psychologists report that separation anxiety is most intense when it occurs between the thirteenth and the eighteenth month; others stress an earlier period. Since Newton was already thirty-seven months old at the time of his mother's second marriage, the period of gravest danger was presumably past. But the proximity of his mother's new home may have aggravated rather than mitigated the injury of the loss. The elegant church steeple of North Witham loomed high and could be seen piercing the sky for miles around. Hannah was there, a mere mile and a half away, with the Reverend Smith. She was not gone forever, only for long periods. When would she come to Woolsthorpe and when would she go away? Or was Isaac brought to the rectory for visits and then sent home again, the pain of separation constantly renewed? The child felt blind fury, and a desire was born to destroy his mother and her husband, a murderous obsession of the period before eleven that remained alive in his memory long after Barnabas Smith lay dead, at least until

Newton's twentieth year, when he recorded his guilt as sin number thirteen in the shorthand confession of 1662 in the Fitzwilliam notebook: "Threatning my father and mother Smith to burne them and the house over them." Sin number fourteen, "wishing death and hoping it to some,"[8] a rather obscure sentence which might be interpreted as a suicidal wish as well as an expression of violence, reflects a generalized hostility that could be turned against himself. In confessing such terrible sins—and for a puritanical youth of twenty these are not casual recollections, as they might be in a present-day adolescent—he is trying to cleanse himself of guilt, and it is irrelevant whether the "threat" to his mother and stepfather was ever verbalized or was simply a fantasy.

The loss of his mother to another man was a traumatic event in Newton's life from which he never recovered. And at any moment in his later experience when he was confronted by the possibility of being robbed of what was his, he reacted with a violence commensurate with the terror and anger generated by this first searing deprivation. He saw all his later inventions and acquired dignities as part of himself, and the mere threat of their being torn away overwhelmed him with anxiety. The physical death of his mother in 1679 may have had fewer psychic consequences than the original lapse in the mystical union of mother and child. Her death may even have been in some form a release for Newton, for it was in the early 1680's that, with Halley's aid, the *Principia* was put into final shape during a period of prodigious creativity.

Recovering his mother at the age of eleven, just before puberty, accentuated Newton's possession, and its effect upon his capacity for the sexual love of any other person would be felt throughout his life. The love for Hannah would undergo many transformations, but she would remain the one female figure—the grandmother with whom he lived for eight years left no identifiable trace. In taking another husband Hannah Newton had doubtless been protective of her son—it was a marriage of convenience—but for young Newton her act was a betrayal. On one level of his consciousness, the widowed mother who had rewed was a wicked woman. In his imagination he punished Father and Mother Smith for their sin of a polluted marriage by burning them in the hell of the Puritan sermons. And this wish induced terror, because of a fear that it would be punished by human or divine agency. Nowhere does Newton's ambivalent relationship to his mother emerge with greater poignancy than in a group of words in the Morgan notebook listed under the general rubric "Of Kindred, & Titles." *M* starts with *Marriage,* moves on to *Mother* (so much copied out of Francis Gregory's *Nomenclatura*); it is followed by a word of idealization, *Marquesse,* and then by *Manslayer. Wife, Wedlock, Wooer, Widdow, Widdower* (out of Gregory) are completed by *Whoore.* The letter *F* begins with *Father* (out of Gregory), followed by *Fornicator, Flatterer,* and then two geographic proper nouns with overtones of sin and sensuality to a young puritan, *Frenchman* and *Florentine.* At the end, under *Y,* *Yeoman* stands alone—the status of his true father, who died before he was born.[9] Ambivalence toward his mother would color Newton's whole style of life.

Of the intensity of Hannah Newton's love for her firstborn we have only two bits of evidence: that smidgen of a letter sent to the University in May 1665, in which her love is repeated twice in a few lines—"Isack/ received your leter and I perceive you/ letter from mee with your cloth but/ none to you your sisters present thai/ love to you with my motherly lov/ you and prayers to god for you I/ your loving mother/ hanah"[10]—and her will, in which she made him her sole male heir, Benjamin having been provided for by his father, Barnabas Smith. She commended her soul to God and left her body to be buried as Isaac "shall think fit," and he wrapped it in white wool.[11] Newton, who had come from Cambridge to tend her in 1679 when she caught a fatal fever while ministering to her sick Benjamin in Stamford (Newton told Conduitt that they had exchanged beds), had himself mixed the potions and laid on the poultices. "He attended her with a true filial piety, sate up whole nights with her, gave her all her Physick himself, dressed all her blisters with his own hands, and made use of that manual dexterity for wch he was so remarkable to lessen the pain wch always attends the dressing, the torturing remedy usually applied in that distemper with as much readiness as he ever had employed it in the most delightfull experiments."[12]

The fixation upon his mother may have crippled Newton sexually, but there was a great source of power, strength, and energy in their early, close relationship. His infancy left him with a confused inheritance—reflected in the contradictions of his life—of early maternal warmth and of the primitive distrust and doubt that beset the abandoned one. Both elements are always present in Newton, even though the suspicious, hostile side of his nature is the more profusely documented. It was in his mother's garden in Woolsthorpe that he noticed the apple drawn to the earth—a story to which he frequently adverted in his last years. And a burst of creativity occurred when, during the plague, he returned to his mother from the University. Newton referred to his knowledge and inventions as his "Garden" in the famous letter to Halley where he accused Robert Hooke of pilfering from it. With Hannah, Newton had lived in Eden for a while, a brief blessed while.

Though Newton was befriended by many older men who recognized his genius, there is no sign that he responded by making father surrogates of them; neither his uncles, nor his maternal grandfather, nor the schoolmasters of Grantham, nor his tutor at Cambridge, nor Henry More, nor Boyle, nor even Isaac Barrow ever filled this role. When the child Newton was taught his prayers, his own father had long been in heaven, since almost three months before he was born. The image of this father, the yeoman Isaac Newton, soon fused with the vision of God the Father, and a special relationship was early established between the son and his father. There is a belief among many peoples that a male child born after his father's death, a *posthumous,* is endowed with supernatural healing powers. Conduitt, Newton's echo, recorded that posthumous children were often extraordinary,[13] and the present-day Rector of Colsterworth has attested the survival of this idea in an attenuated form in his own locality, where it is held that such a son is destined to good fortune. Newton's deep sense of being one of the elect was further reinforced by the date of his birth, Christmas Day. Dr. Stukeley reported the popular opinion that it was an omen of future greatness.

Throughout his life Newton arrived at his conclusions, whether in physical science or world chronology, by intuition—by the intrusion of the Holy Spirit—after long concentration upon a single idea; for he was in direct relationship with his father, and things were revealed to him as they had once been to the Hebrew prophets and the apostles and the legendary scientists of the ancient world whom he identified with one another. Though Newton could speak freely in praise of Moses and Toth, Thales, Pythagoras, Prometheus, and Chiron the Centaur, he only rarely had good words to say about either living scientists or his immediate predecessors—and then not without equivocation. History had begun anew with him. Among contemporaries he and he alone had access to the significant truths about God his Father's world. God revealed himself to only one prophet in each generation, and this made parallel discoveries improbable. Despite Newton's lip service to the common promotion of knowledge, he often felt that the findings of his fellow scientists were of no consequence, or only ancillary to his system, or else outright thefts from his "Garden." There was no aspect of creation that would be hidden from him—the inventions of mathematics, the composition of light, the movement of the planets, the elements of chemistry, the history of antiquity, the nature of God, the true meaning of the divine word in Scripture. Newton's occasional denial of his mission, self-disparaging references to his discoveries in natural philosophy and in world history as "divertisements," are only the other side of the coin. Prophets have often tried to escape their destiny, at least since Jonah.

There was only one Father and one Son. Unitarianism, a punishable offense, was not too frequent a religious position in the seventeenth century. Irrespective of the rational and historical basis of Newton's anti-Trinitarian writings, there was an intensity to his secret belief that goes far beyond theological argument and criticism of the proof-texts in John, which he elaborated with scholarly virtuosity in a secret letter of 1690 sent to be printed in Holland and then withdrawn. He was the only son of God and could not endure the rivalry of Christ. At the bottom of a stray folio listing sundry alchemical writings Newton inscribed an anagram of his name, Isaacus Neuutonus—*Jeova sanctus unus.*[14]

Fatherless children are sometimes painfully taunted by their fellows. When a child is told of the death of his father before he was born, an almost metaphysical anguish may seize him. Often the quest for the father continues in a thousand guises through life. Where did he himself really come from? In Newton's case the search would be rendered even more anxious by the absence of his paternal grandfather, who had died in 1641. Newton was absorbed in his genealogy long before he was knighted and had to prepare documents for the College of Heralds. He gave himself strange ancestors—in his last years, if we are to believe the report of the mathematician James Gregory, he claimed that he was descended from a Scottish lord.[15] In the word lists of the Morgan notebook, under the letter *T* in "Of Kindred, & Titles," *Twins* (from Francis Gregory) is followed by *Theife.*[16] Is this an echo of the ancient myth of the abducted child of royalty, of the twin who was humbly reared while his brother inherited the throne? Fantasies of royal and noble birth are common in fatherless children. There are among Newton's euhemeristic historical and chronological papers in Oxford literally scores of genealogies of the gods and of the kings of all nations. In addition to their pragmatic utility for revising world chronology, they may mask an unconscious search for a line of ancestors.

Simultaneous with a sense that it was his father who occupied the heavenly throne, there was doubt and apprehension about his legitimacy. Was his birth tainted? His parents were married in April 1642 and he was prematurely born in late December, possibly within the limits of virtue. But in a manuscript draft of the genealogy he drew up for the College of Heralds at the time of his knighthood, he made an error and pushed back his parents' marriage to 1639.[17] The 1639 date was not haphazard, for it was the year when Newton's grandfather Robert Newton presented the manor in

Woolsthorpe to his son and Hannah Ayscough, apparently in view of their forthcoming marriage.[18] Reasons for the long betrothal are unclear; the actual union did not take place for more than two years. Perhaps in this draft Newton was trying to establish the legitimacy of his birth beyond question. There is no record of the precise date of the wedding in any parish register, and antedating the event, or suppressing the date altogether as he did in the document actually submitted, removed the need for explaining the facts of a premature birth in a formal genealogy. Of course, the whole thing may have been a mere slip.[19]

If Newton felt uneasiness about his lineage, it was reinforced by the ambiguity of his social status. His father Isaac Newton was a yeoman and so were the other Newtons of the area; a century before there had been paternal ancestors of even lower birth.[20] The Ayscoughs from Rutland County were gentlemen and rectors, apothecaries and architects.[21] From the very beginning one has a strong suspicion that there was some misalliance here: on the mother's side a "very ancient family," once wealthy but now apparently on the downgrade, while the Newtons were yeomen coming up. Newton's father, who left about five hundred pounds in "goods and chattles" in addition to property, still called himself yeoman in his will,[22] though the grandfather had already bought a manor and Newton was born lord of the manor—a little one to be sure. The final marriage settlement was made more palatable to the Ayscoughs by the fact that another branch of the Newton family had a baronetcy to which Isaac Newton might conceivably have been an heir—or so his grandmother told him.[23] He entered the University as a poor scholar, a subsizar performing menial tasks. Home from the University in 1666, in the Lincoln visitation he described himself as a gentleman.[24] All his life there was something of the social climber about him, even after he was knighted and took arms: "Sable, two shin bones saltire-wise, the sinister surmounted of the dexter, argent."[25] In another draft of his pedigree he was careful to stress that his maternal grandfather "had arms" and that he himself was kin to "Ld & Captain Sherard and my Lady Ellis."[26] Newton fawned upon worldly aristocrats and admitted more noble nonentities into the Royal Society than had any of his predecessors. He seemed uncomfortable in the presence of the great of the realm and yet he sought their recognition, legitimation. There is, however, a sense in which he always remained a descendant of the earthy, independent yeomanry of the Lincolnshire countryside. His roots were in the land. Though his estate was not vast, he owned substantial property whose administration he controlled himself, even from afar. Throughout his life, this yeoman's son was meticulous in supervising his tenants—no detail escaped him—and he was in the vanguard of local property-holders who pressed for enclosures.

The deprivation of a recognized father in childhood left a mark on Newton and raised the problem of a masculine model for the boy. While the image of his real father was idealized, there could also have been great resentment at his abandonment through death. In Newton's hundreds of manuscripts there is, to my knowledge, only one reference to his father as a person, a passing notice of his death in an affidavit of 1705. If we attach significance to this feeling, it can help to explain his refusal to accept father surrogates and an element of wariness that is detectible in his relationships with the older men who courted and tried to father him.

The substitute, Father Smith, became an object of hatred and a source of guilt feelings, though it could be argued that this hatred of a stepfather was a quasi-legitimate animosity allowable in the culture. What we know of Barnabas Smith comes from the Lincoln diocesan register and the North Witham parish register. At the age of fifteen, in December 1597, he had matriculated at Lincoln College, Oxford. He was instituted to the rectory in North Witham on January 8, 1610, on the presentation of Benedict Smith, probably his father, Rector of South Witham from 1573 to 1635, who had bought the presentation from Sir Henry Pakenham of Belton near Grantham. Of his character in 1611 there is a laconic but pointed entry in the *Liber Cleri* of the bishop of Lincoln's visitation to the effect that he was "of good behaviour, non-resident, and not hospitable."[27] He surely was not hospitable to little Isaac. Barnabas Smith died in 1653; his will was dated August 17 of that year and proved at London February 8, 1654, and again at Lincoln June 11, 1679, presumably at the death of Hannah Ayscough.[28] The document shows him to have been a man of considerable wealth, most of which was left to his son Benjamin. There is no mention at all of Isaac in this will. "All lands and worldly goodes" go to "my only sonne Benjamin" at marriage or at age twenty-one, whichever was first. His daughters Mary Smith and Hannah Smith were each left five hundred pounds to be paid on marriage or on their coming of age, along with a number of houses and sundry objects of value. Provision was made for Hannah Ayscough to be their heir in case of death without issue. Barnabas Smith's gifts to the poor of the local parishes were not munificent: five pounds to those of North Witham and Lobthorpe, two to those of Colsterworth and Woolsthorpe. The witnesses at the probate in Westminster on February 8, 1654, were James Ayscough the elder, Hannah's father, and James Ayscough the younger, her brother, who was Isaac's official guardian. (Neither his maternal uncle nor his maternal grandfather seems to have made any impression on the boy Isaac, though they may have been the men most frequently about when he was growing up.) By the will of Barnabas Smith, Hannah Ayscough was appointed executrix; she thus had two estates from her deceased husbands to administer, in all a sizable amount of property.

Newton's violent hatred of Barnabas Smith crept out in words and phrases in the notebooks and in a homicidal threat. Whatever other considerations made it impossible for Newton to take holy orders during his long years in Cambridge—and he resisted the blandishments of bishops and promises of preferment—the image of his stepfather, the "opulent divine," a scornful phrase from his Latin exercise book, was inhibitory. The Reverend Smith's residence, North Witham, as a place long retained its emotional potency for Newton: half a century later, when he was called upon to pay taxes to that seat in a reorganization of local jurisdictions, he produced a memorandum of protest and denial with his accustomed legalistic acumen. His motives on this occasion are unknowable and may relate to a territorial sensibility, but a deep-rooted antagonism to North Witham because of its painful associations is at least suggested.[29]

Barnabas was not, however, a total loss to his stepson. Though he left Isaac nothing in his will, his library of two hundred-odd works, mostly editions of the Church Fathers and writings of ecclesiastical controversy, was transferred to the study at Woolsthorpe, and Newton's learning in ecclesiastical and general history, the documentation for his unitarianism, was nourished by these works. He may have repudiated Father Smith, but he did not disdain his collection of patristic literature. He also fell heir to his stepfather's large commonplace book of more than a thousand folios, rich with the pompous moral citations of a humanist divine, alphabetically arranged by subject, and it was in this book that Newton wrote notes for many of his mathematical inventions. Barnabas was no ignorant village parson. He quoted profusely from Pliny, Origen, Augustine, Jerome, Ambrose, Eusebius, Bernard, Gregory, the Chronicle of Thomas Walsingham. There are discussions in his commonplace book of spiritual and carnal love and of free will. Under *castigatio* he inclined toward leniency—"castigatio debet esse moderata"[30]— and there is no evidence that he was ever brutal to his stepson. But Isaac Newton saw him with different eyes. He rediscovered the image of Barnabas in many faces, and others paid dearly for his abduction of Newton's mother.

When Father Barnabas died, his son Benjamin was not yet three and he came with his mother to live in Woolsthorpe Manor. In Newton's Latin exercise book there are first intimations of his annoyance with this rival: "I have my brother to entreate."[31] The word associations in the Morgan notebook under the letter *B* of the heading "Of Kindred, & Titles" are quite explicit. *Brother* is followed by *Bastard,* a remarkable coincidence since it is copied out of Gregory's *Nomenclatura;* but then Newton, perhaps stimulated by this chance juxtaposition, let his anger flare: after *Barron* came *Blaspheimer, Brawler, Babler, Babylonian, Bishop, Brittaine, Bedlam, Beggar, Brownist,* and finally *Benjamite.*[32]

There is no recorded emotive reaction to the fact that Newton's mother contracted the fever from which she died in 1679 while tending the sick Benjamin. In the end, a Ben Smith, the son of Benjamin, fell to Newton's care. By all accounts Ben was a wild character, a reprobate, a dilettante, an aesthete who hobnobbed with artists and sojourned in Paris and Rome. For a time he lived in Newton's London house; later, after Newton's death, one of his noble acquaintances got him a miserable living in a country parish, where he referred to his flock as "baptized brutes," a contempt which they reciprocated. At one point Newton had written letters pressing him to choose a profession in "vulgar phraseology" that led the Reverend Sheepshanks, into whose hands the documents eventually fell after Ben Smith's death, to destroy them as a blemish on the name of England's most shining genius.[33] Thus Newton finally vented his spleen upon the rival sibling in the person of his son. But it was a redress of grievances long delayed, and in the course of his life Newton had to appease himself with the slaughter of other rivals, a long and illustrious list. The ironic climax to this relationship came when Newton's *Observations upon the Prophecies of Daniel, and the Apocalypse of St. John* was introduced to the world of letters by this same Ben Smith in a posthumous edition of 1733.

Despite the hurt and anger that were elements in Newton's feeling for his mother, the bond between Hannah and her son was never broken. Eventually his mother's wish was fulfilled and he became the father-master-elder brother of the whole Smith brood. In time of need they turned to him. There is a despairing letter from his half sister Hannah as her husband lay wasting away, and a friendly letter of thanks from his half brother for sending potions to cure his sick wife.[34] After his sisters' husbands were gone he supported them and their sons and daughters. Eight of them, including Benjamin Smith's son, became his legal heirs when he died intestate.[35] In this relationship he had finally supplanted his hated stepfather.

Chapter 2

THE PREGNANCY OF HIS PARTS

Human nature like a plant must have the vital principle in
itself.

       —William Stukeley, *Memoirs of Sir Isaac*
                   Newton's Life

VIRTUALLY all the anecdotes of Newton's boyhood in later biographies are derived from the pages of Dr. Stukeley's letters of 1727 to Dr. Richard Mead, Newton's friend and physician, the memoir of 1752, and Conduitt's notes.

Stukeley knew Woolsthorpe as a hamlet of Colsterworth situated six miles south of Grantham on the great road from London to the north. This observant author of an *Itinerarium Curiosum* through Wiltshire, Gloucestershire, Worcestershire, Herefordshire, Staffordshire, Derbyshire, and Nottinghamshire, who had a way of comparing the virtues of the various counties he explored, has left an enthusiastic description of the countryside around Newton's birthplace.

Wolsthorp is in a pleasant little hollow or convallis, on the west side of the valley of the river Witham, which arises near there; one spring thereof is in this hamlet. It has a good prospect eastward toward Colsterworth. The country hereabout is thought to be the Montpelier of England. The air is exceedingly good; the sharpness of the mediterranean being tempered by the softness of the low parts of Lincolnshire, which makes a fine medium, agreeable to most constitutions. I have seen many parts of England, and think none of a pleasanter view than about Colsterworth, and nothing can be imagined sweeter, than the ride between it and Grantham. This country consists much of open heath, overgrown with the fragrant serpyllum, much like the downs in Wiltshire; differing chiefly in this, that our soil lies upon a white lime stone, good for building, that upon chalk. The valleys are gravelly, very delightful. Woods plentiful. Springs and rivulets of the purest water abound. Such is the place that produced the greatest genius of the human race.[1]

In Woolsthorpe Newton lived on the crossroads between the English agricultural countryside and the small town.[2] His was a middling world, neither aristocratic nor poor. Most of the ordinary occupations he listed in the Morgan notebook under "Artes, Trades, & Sciences" are today outside our experience, the work of artisans replaced in a technological age.[3] There are trades related to coaches, inns, and the care of horses, as one would expect from someone who grew up near Colsterworth, an important stagecoach stop on the road from York to London. Newton was acquainted with many activities of the field, the pasture, the woods, and the shop; the market, the sea, and the road; the inn, the church, and the learned world. Music is a permissible art even among the puritanical, and there is a fiddler, a musician, an organist. A few occupations connected with the stage he may have heard denounced in school or in sermons: stage player, tragedian, comedian. Public officials to keep order are not prominent, though there is a jailer and a hangman.

When Stukeley visited the area in the fall of 1721, five years before his definitive settlement in Grantham, he took a prospect of both the fourteenth-century church at Colsterworth, which has Saxon elements in its walls, and of the manor house at Woolsthorpe.[4] "The house is a pretty good one, built of white stone, which abounds all over this country. They carryed me upstairs and show'd me Sir Isaac's study, in which he used to sit, when he came home from Cambridg to see his mother. The shelves were of his own making, being pieces of deal boxes. There were some years ago 2 or 300 books in it, chiefly of divinity and old editions of the fathers: the library of his father in law [stepfather] Mr. Smith, rector of North Witham. These books Sir Isaac gave to his relation [sic] Dr. Newton of Grantham, who gave some of them to me, when I went to live there."[5]

A substantial part of the Stukeley letter evoked the life of Isaac at the Grantham Grammar School, a sixteenth-century foundation. In this "Town of good resort, adorned with a School built by *Richard Fox* Bishop of *Winchester,* and with a fair Church, having a spire-steeple of a mighty height," the wonders of the boy and the presages of his genius were remembered.[6] His games and pastimes were identified as prefigurations of his future scientific works. The legend, with its measure of profound psychological truth, had already been created. The variety of his activities points to an outgoing curiosity that should serve to amend the stereotype of the dreamy, withdrawn boy; traditional portraiture has tended to be monochromatic.

Sir Isaac, whilst he went to Grantham school, boarded at Mr. Clark's house, an apothecary, grandfather to Mr. Clark, now an apothecary here. 'Twas the next house to George Inn northward in High Street, which was rebuilt about sixteen years ago. Dr. Clark, M.D. brother to Mr. Clark, was usher of the school at this time; he was a pupil of the famous Henry Moore [sic] of Christ College, born in Mr. Bellamy's house over against me. . . . Every one that knew Sir Isaac, or have heard of him, recount the pregnancy of his parts when a boy, his strange inventions, and extraordinary inclination for mechanics. That instead of playing among the other boys, when from school, he always busied himself in making knick-knacks and models of wood in many kinds. For which purpose he had got little saws, hatchets, hammers, and a whole shop of tools, which he would use with great dexterity. In particular they speak of his making a wooden clock. About this time, a new windmill was set up near Grantham, in the way to Gunnerby, which is now demolished, this country chiefly using water mills. Our lad's imitating spirit was soon excited, and by frequently prying into the fabric of it, as they were making it, he became master enough to make a very perfect model thereof, and it was said to be as clean and curious a piece of workmanship, as the original. This sometimes he would set upon the house-top, where he lodged, and clothing it with sail-cloth, the wind would readily take it; but what was most extraordinary in its composition was, that he put a mouse into it, which he called the miller, and that the mouse made the mill turn round when he pleased; and he would joke too upon the miller eating the corn that was put in. Some say that he tied a string to the mouse's tail, which was put into a wheel, like that of turnspit dogs, so that pulling the string, made the mouse go forward by way of resistance, and this turned the mill. Others suppose there was some corn placed above the wheel, this the mouse endeavouring to get to, made it turn.[7]

Newton's way with a mouse later stood him in good stead when he became a great manipulator of men. A psychologist might be tempted to relate the young Newton's concentration upon mechanical objects that he could control with certainty to a flight from intimate human ties where love was either problematical or forbidden. But the play with mechanical instruments was fairly common in this period and we read similar reports in the biographies of Wren, Hooke, and Flamsteed.

A natural mechanical aptitude, an insatiable curiosity, and a capacity to imitate and to innovate were part of Newton from the beginning. Preoccupation with time and motion came early in his life, and Stukeley's narrative includes many stories about his water clocks, ingenious kites, and sundials.[8] The inventions were not all original with him, for some of them are described in works on popular mechanics and artifices with which he was familiar (in the Morgan notebook there are extensive unidentified excerpts in "Old Barley" from John Wilkins' *Mathematicall Magick* and John Bate's *Mysteryes of Nature, and Art*).

Sir Isaac's water clock is much talked of. This he made out of a box he begged of Mr. Clark's (his landlord) wife's brother. As described to me, it resembled pretty much our common clocks and clock-cases, but less; for it was not above four feet in height, and of a proportionable breadth. There was a dial plate at top with figures of the hours. The index was turned by a piece of wood, which either fell or rose by water dropping. This stood in the room where he lay, and he took care every morning to supply it with its proper quantity of water; and the family upon occasion would go to see what was the hour by it. It was left in the house long after he went away to the University. . . .

These fancies sometimes engrossed so much of his thoughts, that he was apt to neglect his book, and dull boys were now and then put over him in form. But this made him redouble his pains to overtake them, and such was his capacity, that he could soon do it, and out-strip them when he pleased; and it was taken notice of by his master. Still nothing could induce him to lay by his mechanical experiments: but all holidays, and what time the boys had allowed to play, he spent entirely in knocking and hammering in his lodging room, pursuing that strong bent of his inclination not only in things serious, but ludicrous too, and what would please his school fellows, as well as himself; yet it was in order to bring them off from trifling sports, and teach them, as we may call it, to play philosophically, and in which he might willingly bear a part, and he was particularly ingenious at inventing diversions for them, above the vulgar kind. As for instance, in making paper kites, which he first introduced here. He took pains, they say, in finding out their proportions and figures, and whereabouts the string should be fastened to the greatest advantage, and in how many places. Likewise he first made lanterns of paper crimpled, which he used to go to school by, in winter mornings, with a candle and tied them to the tails of the kites in a dark night, which at first affrighted the country people exceedingly, thinking they were comets. It is thought that he first invented this method; I can't tell how true. They tell us too how diligent he was in observing the motion of the sun, especially in the yard of the house where he lived, against the walls and roofs, wherein he would drive pegs, to mark the hours and half hours made by the shade, which by degrees from some years observations, he had made very exact, and any body knew what o'clock it was by Isaac's dial, as they ordinarily called it; thus in his youngest years did that immense genius discover his sublime imagination, that since has filled, or rather comprehended the world.[9]

Newton's later manuscripts are graced here and there with sketches and drawings that reveal a measure of artistic sensitivity: there are telescopes, diagrams of optical experiments, alchemical symbols of the human body, anatomical details of men and animals, a ground plan of Solomon's Temple.[10] An early interest in drawing was duly noted by Dr. Stukeley. "Sir Isaac furnished his whole room with pictures of his own making, which probably he copied from prints, as well as from the life. They mention particularly several of the kings heads, Dr. Donne, and likewise his Master Stokes." From Rolf Clark, who later lodged in Newton's room, Stukeley had a description of the plenitude of Newton's creation. The whole wall was "still full of the drawings he had made upon it with charcoal, and so remained till pulled down about sixteen years ago. . . . There were birds, beasts, men, ships, and mathematical schemes, and very well designed."[11] The numerous passages in the Morgan notebook, written in "Old Barley," on the mixing of paints and on sketching excerpted from Bate's *Mysteryes of Nature* support Dr. Stukeley's account. From Bate Newton might also have learned about nude male and female bodies, if other sources had been denied him—the

1654 edition has full-page illustrations of a Herculean man and a Rubens-like woman.[12]

Though he had originally set out to be merely descriptive, Dr. Stukeley's memoir of 1752 tried to establish a connection between Newton's youthful activities and his later scientific discoveries.

It seems to me likely enough that Sir Isaac's early use and expertness at his mechanical tools, and his faculty of drawing and designing, were of service to him, in his experimental way of philosophy; and prepar'd for him a solid foundation to exercise his strong reasoning facultys upon; his sagacious discernment of causes and effects, his most penetrating investigation of methods to come at his intended purpose, his profound judgment, his invincible constancy and perseverance in finding out his solutions and demonstrations, and in his experiments; his vast strength of mind in protracting his reasonings, his chain of deductions; his indefatigable attachment to calculations; his incomparable skill in algebraic and the like methods of notation; all these united in one man, and that in an extraordinary degree, were the architects that raised a building upon the experimental foundation, which must stand coeval with material creation.

A mechanical knack, and skill in drawing, very much assists in making experiments. Such as possess it take their ideas of things incomparably stronger and more perfect than others; it enlarges their view, they see deeper and farther; it maturates and quickens their invention. For want of this handycraft, how many philosophers quietly sit down in their studys and invent an *hypothesis;* but Sir Isaacs way was by dint of experiments to find out *quid Natura faciat aut ferat.*

Philosophers, like great conquerors, or ministers of state, must take into their assistance arts, and helps low and sordid, as success in war depends on the arm of the scum of mankind, as well as on the head of the General. Children are always imitators, and perhaps his being brought up in an apothecarys house might give him a turn towards the study of nature: and undoubtedly it gave him a love for herbarizing. But he was in reality born a philosopher, learning, accident and industry pointed out to his discerning eye, some few, simple and universal truths: these by time and reflexion, he gradually extended one from another, one beyond another; till he unfolded the oeconomy of the macrocosm.[13]

In Stukeley we also find the first version of the stock tales about Newton's evasion of the duties of his estate when his mother withdrew him from school in order to save expenses, intending to make him serviceable to her in management of the farming and country business at Wolsthorpe, and I doubt not but she thought it would turn more to his own account, than being a scholar. Accordingly we must suppose him attending the tillage, grazing, and the like. And they tell us that he frequently came on Saturdays to Grantham market, with corn and other commodities to sell, and to carry home what necessaries were proper to be bought at a market town for a family; but being young, his mother usually sent a trusty old servant along with him, to put him into the way of business. Their inn was at the Saracen's Head in Westgate, where as soon as they had set up their horses, Isaac generally left the man to manage the marketings, and retired instantly to Mr. Clark's garret, where he used to lodge, near where lay a parcel of old books of Mr. Clark's [the memoir says they consisted of "physic," botany, anatomy, philosophy, mathematics, astronomy, and the like], which he entertained himself with, whilst it was time to go home again; or else he would stop by the way between home and Grantham, and lye under a hedge studying, whilst the man went to town and did the business, and called upon him in his return. No doubt the man made remonstrances of this to his mother. Likewise when at home if his mother ordered him into the fields, to look after the sheep, the corn, or upon any other rural employment, it went on very heavily through his manage. His chief delight was to sit under a tree, with a book in his hands, or to busy himself with his knife in cutting wood for models of somewhat or other that struck his fancy: or he would get to a stream and make mill wheels.[14]

Stukeley's memoir of 1752 adds a comical story of Newton's absorption in his thoughts to the neglect of business. "[O]n going home from Grantham, 'tis usual at the town end to lead a horse up Spittlegate hill, being very steep. Sir Isaac has been so intent in his meditations, that he never thought of remounting, at the top of the hill, and so has led his horse home all the way, being 5 miles. And once, they say, going home in this contemplative way, the horse by chance slipt his bridle and went home: but Sir Isaac walked on with the bridle in his hand, never missing the horse."[15]

Stukeley is our sole authority on Newton's relations with a girl who later became Mrs. Vincent, and whose mother, second wife of the apothecary Clark, was a friend of Hannah Newton's. Stukeley's letter of June 26, 1727, is virtually identical with the memoir of 1752, except that the "love" of the early version has for some reason become "passion." Mrs. Vincent's portrait of the boy Isaac is the only intimate one that has survived for posterity.

> She says Sir Isaac was always a sober, silent, thinking lad, and was never known scarce to play with the boys abroad, at their silly amusements; but would rather chose to be at home, even among the girls, and would frequently make little tables, cupboards, and other utensils for her and her playfellows, to set their babys and trinkets on. She mentions likewise a cart he made with four wheels, wherein he would sit, and by turning a winlass about, he could make it carry him around the house where he pleased.[16] Sir Isaac and she being thus brought up together, 'tis said that he entertained a love for her; nor does she deny it: but her portion being not considerable, and he being a fellow of a college, it was incompatible with his fortunes to marry; perhaps his studies too. 'Tis certain he always had a kindness for her, visited her whenever in the country, in both her husbands days, and gave her forty shillings, upon a time, whenever it was of service to her. She is a little woman, but we may with ease discern that she has been very handsome.[17]

Charles Hutton, the late-eighteenth-century compiler of a famous philosophical and mathematical dictionary, who had assembled oral traditions about scientists of the previous age, was reluctant to accept Stukeley's explanation of Newton's failure to consummate this abiding love. Hutton could be crisper than the hagiographers and later Victorian biographers. "These . . . do not appear to be any sufficient reason for his never marrying, if he had an inclination so to do. It is much more likely that he had a constitutional indifference to the state, and even to the sex in general."[18]

On Newton and his peers at school we have no evidence beyond a philosophical reflection by Stukeley and a note in the Conduitt papers. Stukeley's account is the source for the traditional image of the frail, dreamy, solitary lad, afraid of fights and more comfortable with the girls, disliked, who could only excel at a sport through stratagems. "One reason why Sir Isaac did not play much with his schoolfellows, was that generally they were not very affectionate toward him," Stukeley explained in the memoir. "He was commonly too cunning for them in every thing. They were sensible he had more ingenuity than they, and 'tis an old observation, that in all Societys, even of men, he who has most understanding, is least regarded. One instance of Sir Isaacs craft was this:—

"On the day that Oliver Cromwell dy'd, there was a very great wind or tempest over the whole kingdom. That day, as the boys were playing, a sett of them were leaping. Sir Isaac, tho' not otherwise famous for his activity at that sport, yet observing the gusts of the wind, took so proper an advantage of them as suprizingly to outleap the rest of the boys."[19] In later years Newton used to say that this was one of his first experiments.[20] That knowledge might give him the power to outstrip those before whom he felt himself inferior in some respect was not lost on him. The game foreshadows his later contests with his fellow men. Arrogant, he disdains to join with them in their tomfoolery; timid, he fears them. But when he knows the way the wind is blowing, he too can jump and outleap them.

There is no consensus about the length of Newton's schooling at Grantham. Stukeley reckons a total of seven years, with a hiatus when his mother tried to make a "grazier" of him. Conduitt has him attending two little day schools at Skillington and Stoke until he was twelve, when he went to Grantham, was removed, and then returned for only nine months prior to going up to the University in June 1661. If Newton was at Grantham leaping in the direction of the wind on the day Cromwell died he was there in 1658. Further records do not exist.

Stukeley credits Stokes, the schoolmaster at Grantham, with the discovery of Newton's genius and his rescue from a life devoted to managing his mother's and his own estate.

His mother, as well as the servants, were somewhat offended at this bookishness of his: the latter would say the lad is foolish, and will never be fit for business. But his old master, Mr. Stokes, who now became rector of Colsterworth, saw thro', judg'd better, and admir'd his uncommon genius; he never ceas'd remonstrating to his mother what a loss it was to the world, as well as a vain attempt, to bury so extraordinary a talent in rustic business. He at length prevaild with her to send him back to school, that he might fit him for the University; he added that he would make a compliment to her of the 40s. *per annum* paid to the schoolmaster by all foreign lads. He took him home to the school house to bord with him, and soon compleated him in school learning.[21]

Other accounts introduce a mysterious stranger who found Newton reading in a haystack (or chasing sheep) and the maternal uncle, William Ayscough, Rector of Burton Coggles, as the agents who convinced Hannah to give up her son to a higher calling, even as the biblical Hannah had surrendered her son to the priesthood of Israel.[22]

Newton's departure from Lincolnshire aroused contrary feelings at school and in the household. "Upon sending him away from school, we are told, his master who had form'd a just prognostic of his rising abilitys, set him in a conspicuous place in the school, tho' not agreable to the lad's modesty, and made a speech to the boys in praise of him, so moving as to set them a-crying, nor did he himself refrain his tears. However, his mothers servants rejoic'd at parting with him, declaring, he was fit for nothing but the 'Versity."[23] In the last three decades of his life he would prove how wrong they were by becoming a powerful administrator both of the Royal Mint and of English science.

The Conduitt papers do not add much to the Stukeley memoir on Newton's boyhood, but the stories they preserve occasionally have a meaning that transcends the factual material they were intended to convey. Reminiscing to Conduitt, Newton idealized his mother and talked about her strong character; stressed his littleness in anecdotes connected with his birth in contrast with his later great estate; made his survival appear a marvel. Of all the anecdotes he shared with Conduitt, one perhaps is crucial for an understanding of Newton's character; it is about the school bully whom he, though ordinarily passive and fearful, finally worsted and to whom he then meted out punishment. Here is the octogenarian telling himself, Conduitt his worshipful auditor, and through him the world, that this was the way he had become head boy and dealt with his enemies when provoked. The smug satisfaction of his triumph is not limited to the recollection of his adversary's defeat: after reviewing his long life he is contentedly reflecting that in a like manner all his rivals and those who would have injured him have been conquered. It was a story repeated more than once, and Edmund Turnor summarized it from the Conduitt manuscripts. "Sir Isaac used to relate that he was very negligent at school, and very low at it, till the boy above him gave him a kick in the belly, which put him to a great deal of pain. Not content with having thrashed his adversary, Sir Isaac could not rest till he had got before him in the school, and from that time he continued rising till he was the head boy."[24] Spurred on by the schoolmaster's son, who had witnessed the fight, to complete the humiliation of the bully, Newton had dragged him to the church by the ears and rubbed his nose against the wall,[25] a ceremony that he would re-enact on more than one occasion later in life, especially when there were authorities about to give him sanction.

Unfortunately, most of the school anecdotes seem to belong to Newton's later boyhood. For the critical years between his mother's departure for North Witham and her return when he was eleven, during which he lived as a lone child with his grandmother in the Woolsthorpe manor house, there are only two recorded recollections: hearing from his grandmother about his kinship to the Newton family with a baronetcy and threatening to burn Mother and Father Smith. His grandmother remains a figure without substance and their relationship is undefined; there were uncles who visited, but no mother and no father living in the house with him. How absolute was Newton's solitude? Did other children in the area come to play with him? Present-day biographical studies of brilliant mathematicians and physicists commonly tell of their being solitary and of the tardiness of development of those ordinary skills that announce a child's growing mastery of his surroundings. There is frequently a certain initial backwardness in school—Newton had the same experience. A feeling of difference from other boys in Newton's early life is fairly well documented, and this would increase the distance between him and them. One of the stereotypes of his boyhood is his abstracted behavior, a subject of derision among the servants. In loneness a private world can be created from sources in the unconscious—often at the expense of those capacities which allow for an easier coping with everyday reality. The inner visual imagination is alive and the secret language of number can take possession. The sudden bursting forth of Newton's phenomenal inventiveness in the *annus mirabilis* may have had a long preparation originating in the vivid fantasy world of childhood when he was cut off for long intervals from the interplay of more overt and ordinary relations. The language of this secret world remained vital within him even after he learned to communicate with his fellows more freely in their terms and perhaps he had easier access than most men to unconscious processes that symbolize, condense, and displace.

But this psychological foundation for his creative scientific genius might have remained mere narcissistic play if the wider world in which he grew up could not have been assimilated to his inner experience. Newton was saved from the tragedy of a painter in an island of blind men. In the same chapter of the Morgan notebook word list that helps to define the social environment of Newton's boyhood, "Of Artes, Trades, & Sciences," the unusual addition of "Sciences," with a specifically modern meaning, shows a remarkably early interest in the potentialities of this new intellectual domain. It reflects a climate of opinion in the countryside that was unique to England and would not be found elsewhere in the world at this period outside of urban areas. If the scientific genius of a yeoman's son was not to be stifled or die unobserved, at least an embryonic appreciation of the potentialities of science had to be fairly widespread. This involved a different attitude toward new mechanics than prevailed in societies whose upper-class values were purely aristocratic and aesthetic and whose lower-class outlook was traditional and peasantlike. When in 1671 Newton ground lenses for a reflecting telescope for the Royal Society, the first of his achievements to win general acclaim, manual labor was not considered demeaning in a professor of the mathematics; in the puritanical world of his boyhood no disparagement had attached to making things with one's hands. Though John Wilkins, when he wrote his introduction to *Mathematicall Magick,* still needed to justify mechanical experiments with low objects, by the time Newton appeared in the English scientific world the Aristotelian condemnation of manual labor was no longer considered valid in most circles. Experiments were allowable even to the aristocratic Boyle, who wrote in the *Usefulness of Natural Philosophy:* "And though my condition does (God be praised) enable me to make experiments by others' hands; yet I have not been so nice, as to decline dissecting dogs, wolves, fishes, and even rats and mice, with my own hands. Nor, when I am in my laboratory, do I scruple with them naked to handle lute and charcoal."[26] A note by Conduitt says that Newton had carpenter's hands as well as a mathematician's head. Joseph Glanvill proposed experimental science instead of bloody destructive war as a proper avenue to fame and glory.

On the eve of achieving a purpose of high seriousness, science was sometimes still play both at the university and in the countryside. Men like Wren and Hooke were moved in these years by the same curiosity about instruments that were half toys, half useful objects, that piqued Newton as a youth. Puritan educators like Dr. John Wilkins fostered this spirit of inquiry long before it took shape in the "invisible college." When the diarist John Evelyn visited Wilkins at Oxford on July 13, 1654, he was intrigued by a great variety of machines built with Wilkins' mathematical magic. "He [Wilkins] had also contrived an hollow Statue which gave a Voice, & uttered words, by a long & conceald pipe which went to its mouth, whilst one spake thro it, at a good distance, & which at first was very Surprizing: He had above in his Gallery & Lodgings variety of *Shadows,* Dyals, Perspe(c)tives, places to introduce the *Species,* & many other artif(i)cial, mathematical, Magical curiosities: A Way-Wiser, a *Thermometer,* a monstrous *Magnes, Conic* & other *Sections,* a Balance on a demie Circle, most of them of his owne & that prodigious young Scholar, Mr. *Chr: Wren. . . ."*[27]

When new mechanical contrivances made their way into the English countryside in the mid-seventeenth century, their magic aroused wonderment among the young. Books on mechanical inventions and the useful powers of "mathematics" were Newton's favorites. Though we know from the Morgan notebook that he was well acquainted with Wilkins' work on popular mechanics, *Mathematicall Magick,* there is no firm proof that he had also read his earlier and more imaginative *The Discovery of the New World in the Moon* (1638) with its defense of the Copernican system, frequent citations from Galileo and Kepler, and a discussion of a machine which could break through the gravity of the earth, reach a space in which it would be weightless, and land on the moon. The problem of precisely when Newton first became acquainted with the texts of his eminent predecessors still occupies historians of science; but attention might also be directed to works of scientific popularization like those of Wilkins, from which students have always garnered their first notions of the ideas of a previous generation. In the Morgan notebook there are many passages copied out of Wilkins with slight emendations. The adolescent dream of a machine of perpetual motion attracted Wilkins as it had Hartlib, and the young Newton felt the same fascination.

In late adolescence Newton was interested in many cognate problems to which Wilkins had devoted himself—a new philosophical language of notations that would be universally comprehensible, a phonetic system of spelling, various schemes of shorthand and transmission through secret code. Newton's own phonetic system set forth in the Morgan notebook was probably evolved too early to be affected by the Royal Society's committee for improving the English language (1664), and it is certainly prior to Wilkins' *Essay towards a Real Character and a Philosophical Language* (1668), which Newton mentions in a letter of 1679; but many other writers had previously attempted to devise more "rational" systems of spelling and means of communication, particularly in connection with the pansophic movement which Comenius promoted in England by his appearance there during the Commonwealth.

An outgrowth of the Baconian tradition was a widespread desire to encompass all things within an encyclopedia, in a unified system of knowledge, with a common language of symbols for the whole of mankind. These grandiose youthful visions of the new science were harmonious with the young Newton's passion to know all things and to put them into some kind of order, which received expression in the twenty-four hundred-word list in the Morgan Library notebook entitled "The several things contained under these generall heads." The list has been interpreted as relating to Newton's scheme for a rational universal language; while this hypothesis is not excluded, the compilation also reminds one of a common adolescent desire to take stock at some point of what one knows and by recording it all in systematic fashion establish one's mastery over the totality. This great list (written in "Old Barley"), which in its complete form would have embraced the world, still mentions the Protector, pointing to a date not much later than Newton's eighteenth year. From adolescence onward, the pursuit of knowledge as power over things and of knowledge as a revelation of God were both present in Newton, not as sharp contradictory alternatives but often assimilated with one another as they were among other scientists in the West. Newton's profound need for the direct exercise of power lay dormant for years and assumed secret, almost magical, forms in the building of a great system. It finally asserted itself in its nakedness later in life, particularly after the crisis of 1693.

Chapter 3

A MELANCHOLY COUNTENANCE

Have not I Prayed to no purpose, or suffered wandering
thought to eat out my Duties?
Have I redeemed my time from too long or needless Visits,
idle Imaginations, fruitless discourse, unnecessary sleep,
more than needs of the World?

      · · ·

Doth not Sin set light?
Do I live in nothing that I know or fear to be a Sin?
Have not I given way to the workings of Pride, or Passion?
Have I bridled my Tongue, and forced it in?

      · · ·

Have I been diligent in the Duties of my Calling?
Have I dropped never a lye in my Shop or Trade?
      —Joseph Alleine, *Rules for Self-Examination*

Newton's first eighteen years were those of the Civil War, the Commonwealth, and the Protectorate. In 1649, when he had just turned six, a king of England was beheaded. Lincolnshire was an active theater of operations, and a youthful notebook testifies to his awareness of the military presence and his familiarity with contemporary theological and political controversies. We can only guess at the terrors that events of the war in the countryside, the frequent raids and requisitions, may have aroused in him and in his mother.

On May 13, 1643, when Newton was about six months old, there was an engagement in the broad fields near Grantham, a mere ten miles from Woolsthorpe, between the Parliamentary forces and the

Cavaliers. Cromwell was exultant over the miraculous victory of his ragged soldiers:

So soon as we had the alarm, we drew out our forces, consisting of about twelve troops, whereof some of them so poor and broken, that you shall seldom see worse. With this handful it pleased God to cast the scale. For after we had stood a little above musket-shot the one body from the other and the dragooners having fired on both sides for the space of half an hour or more, they not advancing towards us, we agreed to charge them, and advancing the body after many shots on both sides, came on with our troops a pretty round trot, they standing firm to receive us; and our men charging fiercely upon them, by God's providence they were immediately routed, and ran all away, and we had the execution of them two or three miles.[1]

Though we do not know what political side the Newtons and the Ayscoughs took in the civil war, other Lincolnshire property-holders sent petitions denouncing the requisitions made by both parties as the invading armies scoured the countryside for food and fodder. In 1643 *The Protestation and Declaration of Divers Knights, Esquires, Gentlemen, and Freeholders of the Counties of Lincolne and Nottingham Against the unjust oppressions and inhumane proceeding of William Earle of New-castle and his Cavaliers . . .* castigated the outlaws who had "lost the naturall softness of Englishmen and Christians, and degenerated into almost a Turkish inhumanity; our neighbours houses therefore being on fire before our faces."[2] Seven years later Parliament was addressed with *Two Petitions Presented to the Supreme Authority of the Nation, from Thousands of the Lords, Owners, and Commoners of Lincolneshire; against the Old Court-Levellers, or Propriety-Destroyers, the Prerogative Undertakers,* which demanded the restoration of the ancient laws of England, "the benefit whereof our Ancestors enjoyed long before the Conquest, and particularly the Great Charter of Liberties; and that excellent Law (as yourselves call it) of the Petition of Right, with all things therein contained, incident and belonging to the preservation of the Lives, Proprieties, and Liberties of the People; which you there acknowledge, being duely executed, are the most just, free, and equal of any other laws in the world."[3]

After Cromwell's victories Lincolnshire was Roundhead country. The Ayscoughs were gentlefolk, and Newton's stepfather Barnabas Smith was too rich to be identified with the bedraggled soldiers who won Cromwell's first great battle at Winceby, not far from where Newton spent his boyhood; but they were not for popery. Neither his stepfather nor his maternal uncle, who were divines, seem to have been religious militants on either side. They were not removed during the Commonwealth, nor was his uncle ejected with the Restoration (his stepfather had died). A number of divines connected with the church at Grantham and with the school that Newton attended were dismissed as Dissenters during the Restoration, the only indication of a possible sectarian religious influence in Newton's youth.[4] Their supposed effect upon his thinking is not demonstrable, any more than is his "royalism" on the basis of a few lines of poetry on the martyr King, recast from the popular *Eikon Basilike, The Portraiture of His Sacred Majesty in his Solitudes and Sufferings,* which he is said to have penned beneath a drawing of Charles I—that is, if the testimony of a very old lady is credible.[5]

Concealing his anti-Trinitarianism, the precise origins of which are undatable, Newton belonged to the Church of England all his life, and he was carried to his grave in Westminster Abbey by the foremost prelates in the kingdom. His early religious upbringing, however, cannot be adequately defined by the creed of latitudinarian Anglicanism. Though most of his university career spanned the lax years of the Restoration and he rose to great social prominence under a rather licentious Whig hegemony, the moral commandments he absorbed in his boyhood and youth were puritanical in the broad, loose, yet generally understandable, sense of that nettlesome term. Though the word is not meant to evoke the nineteenth-century caricature of the Puritan killjoy, obsessed with sex, who really belongs to the post-Restoration, the world in which Newton was reared, with its strong emphasis on discipline and Bible worship, already bears resemblances to later Puritanism. Irrespective of the shifting religious alignments during this period, the temper of the countryside to which he belonged was becoming puritanical. When he arrived in Cambridge in 1661 and was confronted by the gaming, hard-drinking, lecherous society that went wild during Stourbridge Fair, he withdrew into himself or found solace in the company of Bible-loving John Wickins, who had been equally repelled by his carousing fellow students. (Samuel Pepys has left a memorable description of a visit to Cambridge in February 1660, which consisted largely of drinking "pretty hard."[6]) The Trinity College and Fitzwilliam notebooks reveal the thrifty scholar for whom idleness was vice. Newton put evil behind him—though not without a few visits to the tavern, a wee bit of drinking, some losses at cards, and sundry other such extravagances, all recorded in the money accounts of his early years at Trinity, along with the price of his shoestrings and his laundry bills. While honest pleasures were not denied him by his religion, useless expenditures were rare, treats infrequent, and everything was dutifully entered. He received a fair allowance from his mother, which he managed so carefully that he was able to lend money to his friends.[7] After he became a Fellow and Master of Arts he had more funds at his disposal; he spent substantial sums for clothes and shoes and academic robes, bought new furnishings for his rooms, and continued to have servants to see to his creature comforts. But this measure of ease in living did not fundamentally alter the personality of the young puritan.

The scrupulosity, punitiveness, austerity, discipline, industriousness, and fear associated with a repressive morality were early stamped upon his character[8]—this is the broad conclusion even though our first concrete evidence derives from documents of his adolescence. He had a built-in censor and lived ever under the Taskmaster's eye, as the divines had it. He whom Milton's Eve called "Our great Forbidder"[9] was with him the more constantly because of the very absence of the traditional forbidder in the household. The decalogue he had learned in childhood became an exigent conscience that made deadly sins of lying, falsehood, Sabbath-breaking, egotistic ambition, and prohibited any expressions of violence and breach of control. The Bible was the guide to conduct. Whatever the virtuous characters in the Bible did was allowable and whatever the

Bible failed to mention or specifically interdicted was not. A prohibition against coveting was extended to cover all desires of the flesh, the admonition to honor father and mother made the most minor act of disobedience a religious transgression. By the period of the Restoration the Sabbath was observed with almost rabbinic severity even by members of the Church of England.[10] The Book of Common Prayer reinforced the biblical commandments, which were regularly intoned at ceremonials of baptism, confirmation, and communion and in daily supplications. Newton took these injunctions in deadly earnest—he was a moral puritan, without involvement, of course, in the radical political and social ideas of Puritanism.

An open Bible through which the Holy Spirit revealed itself to each man lay upon the pulpit above the communion table. Throughout life this was Newton's book. He knew it as did few theologians, and he could string out citations from it like a concordance. In his days of prosperity he sent his former Cambridge roommate, John Wickins, Bibles to be distributed among the poor.[11] A "dirty" and well-worn copy is inventoried among Newton's books sold after his death. Since the Bible was not closed to the laity, each individual by himself, independently, had the capacity to find out what the Holy Spirit was saying by wrestling with the text. By extension, more could be learned through grappling with the book of nature in which the Holy Spirit also manifested itself, and the two sources were always consonant with each other. Of course there had to be proofs, specific proofs in the text of Scripture literally and commonsensically interpreted, as there were concrete scientific proofs in repeated experiments. In neither case could there be any sparing of labor, as the proofs were diligently repeated over and over again until there was certainty about God's meaning both in Scripture and in nature. Corruption of a Scriptural text and the faking of an experiment, or slovenliness in its interpretation, were not only violations of scientific method, but sins, like the bearing of false witness. Such lies were in many respects the blackest of crimes because they violated and distorted the truth of God's creation.

When decades later Newton became a friend of men like Pepys, he relaxed somewhat his absolutist moral posture, repairing to coffeehouses after meetings of the Royal Society. But this is the London Newton, a man turned outward. There is not much frivolity in the youth and in the Cambridge scholar. Even late in life John Conduitt never knew him to be unoccupied.[12] Busyness, that false balsam of anxiety, took the form of obsessively copying when there was nothing else to do.

The dominance of the Puritan spirit and its militant anti-Catholicism can be documented in Newton's later chronological works and in his manuscript history of the churches. Behind the hundreds upon hundreds of folios on the revision of ancient chronology, a constant preoccupation of his last forty or fifty years, lies the passion of a Puritan vindication of Israel against the pretensions of heathen Egyptians and Greeks that they were of greater antiquity than the Hebrews and hence closer to the original creation. Throughout his life Newton defined himself and the Christian community to which he belonged as opposite to the Papists, who were idolaters and had denied "Jeova sanctus unus." In the commentaries on the prophecies, the violence of his denunciation of papal iniquities and the description of the imminent vengeance of the Lord upon the Papists were not often surpassed by nonconformist preachers of the seventeenth century:

And because the Church of Rome began now to reign over the ten kings & enticed them to this idolatrous religion & thereby became rich & potent, she is hence forward in this prophecy compared to a woman arrayed in purple & scarlet & decked with gemms, who lives deliciously & sits a Queen upon seven mountains & upon the horned Beast in a spiritualy barren wilderness & commits fornication with the kings of the earth & makes the nations drunk with the wine of her fornication & abounds with gold & silver & pretious stones & pearles & fine linnen & purple & silk & scarlet & all things of price & enriches the merchants of the earth with her costliness . . . and there is no other city beside the great city represented by the whore of Babylon, wch hath committed fornication with all the kingdoms of the world upon the face of the earth.[13]

There were always learned Jesuits about, dead or alive, whom Newton could worst in scientific controversy: the long-deceased chronologist Denis Petau, the aged scientist Francis Hall and his fellow Jesuits of Liège, or the contemporary French scholar Etienne Souciet. Whatever the scientific issues, Newton always took a special delight in defeating and humiliating a Jesuit.

In notebooks whose entries cover the last years in Lincolnshire and the first in Cambridge one can read the fear, anxiety, distrust, sadness, withdrawal, self-belittlement, and generally depressive state of the young Newton. The guilt and the shame doubtless have earlier roots, but here are the first recorded expressions of feelings that would never leave him. When the word and phrase associations in these documents are free, they can, *faute de mieux,* serve as a rather primitive objective personality test, even though the data would hardly lend themselves to refined quantification techniques. No single text in isolation is conclusive, and their evidence is proffered with a measure of skepticism; but in their total effect these records are compelling.

In the Morgan notebook, under the subheading "Of Man, his Affections, & Senses," the word *Dreame* (from Gregory's *Nomenclatura*), is followed by *Doubting, Dispaire, Distrust, Desire, Dread, Displeasure, Discourtesie, Discreadit, Discourse.* A list that begins *Soule* is mostly copied from Gregory's sections "Of the Parts of a Man," "Of the Inward Parts," "Of the Senses," "Of the Understanding, Will and Affections," to which Newton added a sequence of his own: *Sorrow, Subtilness, Slumber, Sobing.* In the same notebook, under "Of Kindred, & Titles," the word *Orphan,* which also comes from Gregory, precedes *Offender,* Newton's self-accusatory association.[14]

The three hundred and fifty-odd phrases of the Latin exercises, which Newton himself made up and translated, or adapted from common adages, or perhaps copied from an unidentified *Sentences for Children,* are corroborative.[15] Among the sentences he composed or chose to reproduce are frequent expressions of self-disparagement and of a sense of insignificance: *A little fellow; My poore help; Hee is paile; There is noe roome for mee to sit.* Juxtaposition of phrases shows a sharp swing from affirmation to profound depression (*In the top of the house—In the bottome of hell*), from command to obedience (*He is the kings counsellor* and *He was thy footeman*). Doubts about his capacities and whether he was good for anything at all beset him: *What imployment is he fit for? What is hee good for?*

A general mood of anxiety predominates. Things and persons are destroyed, disaster and catastrophe loom. *He is broken. This house of youres is like to fall. This pride of hers will come downe. Aboute to fall. The ship sinketh.* Words of fear are frequent: *Hee saith nothing for feare. I am sore affraide. There is a thing which trobelleth mee.* There is dread of punishment, and at the same time recognition of how enticing sin is. *Wee desire those things which hurt us most. Hee cannot forbeare doeing mischeife. The greatest allurement to sin is hope of spareing. Youe are sure to be punisht. Hee should have been punished. At this age I went not a-wenching* may shock at first glance, but contemporary schoolbooks did not shun direct language and words like bawd, whore, cuckold, cuckoldmaker were common.

Authoritarian commands of Newton's elders ring in his ears and they push through his writing. *I will make thee to doe it. Take heede thou dost it not. See thou come backe. Thou maist be gone. Why rise thou not? What hast thou beene doing? Speake out thy words. Show thy selfe a man.* Play and idleness, games, dancing, sport, thriftlessness are frowned upon. *The better gamester the worse man. What else is it to dance but to play the foole? Hee doth nothing but play. Soe much monie soe much credit. He is not able to pay. He is reported to be a spendthrift. He hath not where withall to by a halter to hang himselve.* Pronouncements of distrust and wariness are numerous: *I shall beware of him that hee hurt mee not. You make a foole of mee. You are a foole to believe him. You know what account to make of him. You shall never make mee believe that taile.* There is a pervasive loneliness—*No man understands mee*—and utter despondency: *What will become of me. I will make an end. I cannot but weepe. I know not what to doe.*

In all these youthful scribblings there is an astonishing absence of positive feeling. The word *love* never appears, and expressions of gladness and desire are rare. A liking for roast meat is the only strong sensuous passion. Almost all the statements are negations, admonitions, prohibitions. The climate of life is hostile and punitive. Competitiveness, orderliness, self-control, gravity—these are Puritan values that became part of his being.

The text of Newton's new phonetic system and the stray leaves of the manuscript on a universal language tell the same story.[16] Newton gave numerous examples to illustrate the use of his new signs for vowels and semivowels and his symbols for words. If we exclude the necessarily large number of neutral prepositions and adverbs, the rest principally connote inadequacy, pain, violence, and anger: *lament, taint, hit, folly, fall, fault, mourne, lust, hate, faile, feare, slew, quarrel, woe, yowle, wound, hang't, anguish, kill.* The Hebrew letter *shin* preceded by *t* (which the new system substitutes for *sh* and *ch*) is exemplified by the sequence *child, which, switch;* the sound *ie* by *feare, weane.* According to his own description, in preparation for his system he experimented by putting his lips and tongue and chaps through all manner of trials that recall infantile play, but probably have their origin in a work such as John Wallis' *Grammatica linguae Anglicanae; cui praefigitur, de loquela sive sonorum formatione tractatus grammatico-physicus* (1653).

Thomas Shelton's shorthand books published in the 1640's, which include brief word lists for practice in taking down sermons, resemble in spirit some of Newton's random associations, though they lack their intensity by far.[17] Popular textbooks like Charles Hoole's excerpts from Culman's *Sententiae pueriles,* homilies, and moral treatises, even penmanship books, all betray the same anxious temper in a world of fear and suffering. Children learned to write by copying terrifying poetic effusions from Edward Cocker's *Arts glory: or The Pen-man's treasury:* "Innumerable are man's greate and manifold vexations/ Calamities Enormities and many molestations/ With many Incommodities, and greate Indammadgements;/

With multitudes of greevances Soule-vexing discontents,/ And wranglings notorious which doe attendance give,/ On this vaine transitory Life, so long as here wee live,/ Unlesse by prayer unto the Lord we these greate evills shun/ Or in the way of his most pure Commandements doe runn."[18] Newton abided by the moral values of his puritan world and its repression of instinctual desire. In him, puritan inhibitions were exaggerated with painful consequences.

Newton's formal education at Grantham had concentrated almost exclusively on the Latin classics, as was customary, though there were also Greek and some Hebrew. We have at least two of his books that bear a 1659 date and inscription—some indication that he owned them in Lincolnshire—a Pindar and Ovid's *Metamorphoses,* standard texts in the grammar schools of the day. (In the margin of the third book of Ovid there is a translation into English in minuscule letters of "Old Barley" of the names of Actaeon's many dogs who devoured him after his chance encounter with Diana.)[19] Any boy brought up on the *Metamorphoses* and the Old Testament was well nourished with images of horror, bloodshed, vengeance, punishment, the tearing apart of bodies, the violent rather than the idyllic passions of men and women, gods and goddesses. Did these tales stimulate destructive fantasies, or were they a benign release for them? Throughout his life Newton was an assiduous reader of the Old Testament and of Greek and Roman mythology. The Bible and Ovid were two parallel versions of the creation and Newton later reduced both of them to matter-of-fact history in the euhemeristic fashion of his age. But even though he denatured the myths, depriving them of some of their emotional quality by transforming them into political history and chronology, he was not impervious to their original imagery. For a man denied sexual experience, the reading of cruel, erotic myths of the gods might serve a purpose that was only secondarily related to historical research.

The predominance of crimson in the furnishings of Newton's London chambers, listed in an inventory of his belongings made soon after his death, has been remarked upon: there were crimson mohair hangings, a crimson mohair bed "compleat with case curtains of crimson Harrateen," a crimson settee.[20] A quick inclination to relate this to bloody fantasies should be checked by the realization that crimson was also the color of royalty and the aristocratic status to which this yeoman's son always aspired. Perhaps both elements were at play, and the rival claims of a psychological or a sociological interpretation can be conveniently adjudicated.

Newton's confession of 1662, written sometime around the end of his first year at the University, is by far the most significant document of self-revelation from the period before the explosion of the *annus mirabilis*. Since the sins he committed were divided into two parts, those before and those after Whitsunday 1662, when he was not yet twenty, it is conceivable that the two lists were written at different times. We do not know what religious crisis occurred to bestow special significance upon the date Whitsunday 1662. The confession of guilt after examination of conscience was probably made with the hope of freeing himself of its burden; there may also have been a resolve, on this seventh Sunday after Easter commemorating the descent of the Holy Spirit on Pentecost, to sin no more.[21]

Self-inspection led Newton to discover manifold sins against God and against his fellows. There had been breaches of virtually every one of the Ten Commandments either in deed or thought—and for a man with Newton's censor the distinction between the two was not great. Of the total of fifty-eight sins recorded, only nine after Whitsunday, the overwhelming majority admit failure in his relations with God. He had been commanded not to take the name of the Lord in vain and he found himself guilty of using the word "God" openly. "Thou shalt have no other gods before me" had been flagrantly violated when he turned to the worship of idols instead of God: *Setting my heart on money learning pleasure more than Thee; Caring for worldly things more than God;* relapsing despite his promise; and *A breaking again of my covenant renued in the Lords Supper.* In his heart and conscience he had discovered that he had been wanting in his love for God, nor did he desire His commandments. Sometimes the confession of his alienation from God is dry and formal: *Not craving a blessing from God on our honest endeavors.* But at one point he addresses God directly as *Thee,* enumerating a whole series of infractions: *Not turning nearer to Thee for my affections. Not living according to my belief. Not loving Thee for Thy self. Not loving Thee for Thy goodness to us. Not desiring Thy ordinances. Not long* [longing?] *for Thee in. . . . Not fearing Thee so as not to offend Thee. Fearing man above Thee.*

The scrupulosity and punctiliousness with which Newton recorded every minor breach of the Sabbath that he recollected from his boyhood and youth have to be considered within the context of a religious community where these violations, as in Talmudic Judaism, were not trivial. In the biblical code, punishment for Sabbath-breaking is death; and though even the Puritans did not impose this extreme penalty, the crime was serious. The keeping holy of the Sabbath was an essential part of one's belief in God and submission to His will, for it was His day, set aside for communion with Him. The hallowing of the Sabbath with religious acts rather than fun or relaxation was one of the chief ways of distinguishing the purified reformed Protestant church from lax, idolatrous, pagan Catholicism. The sanctity of the Sabbath and the church was absolute, so that the performance of any secular act, however insignificant, broke the obsessive perfect observance. This was the closed ritualistic world in which Newton was fashioned. And yet it was precisely on the Sabbath that young Newton, free from the rigid discipline of school, might steal off in secret and play with his mechanical devices. His sins included *Eating an apple at Thy house; Making a feather while one* [on] *Thy day; Making a mousetrap on Thy day; Contriving of the chimes on Thy day; Squirting water on Thy day; Twisting a cord on Sunday morning; Putting a pin in John Keys hat on Thy day to pick him.* Such propensities to evil continued at the University, for after Whitsunday 1662, in violation of his resolve, he helped another undergraduate, Valentine Pettit, *to make his water watch at 12 of the clock on Saturday night,* when the Sabbath had already begun. The degree to which all human activities had to be limited to the sacred on the Sabbath is witnessed by the somewhat incomprehensible forty-ninth sin: *Reading the Cn* [Christian?] *champions on Sunday.*

Failure to pray and inattentiveness in church constituted another category of sins against God. *Missing chapel* and *Carelessly hearing and committing many sermons* remind one of the strict regimen that required young men to listen to sermons and learn them by heart. After Whitsunday 1662, Newton's censor concentrated on sins of omission like *Negligence at the chapel; Sermons at Saint Marys 4; Neglecting to pray 3.*

In his relations with his fellowmen Newton had broken the commandment against stealing and then had compounded the felony by lying about it: *Stealing cherry cobs from Eduard Storer; Denying that I did so; Robbing my mothers box of plums and sugar; Denying a crossbow to my mother and grand mother though I knew of it.* The future hangman of "coyners" and "clippers" at the Mint had in his youth been guilty of their crime, albeit on a very small scale: *Striving to cheate with a brass halfe crowne.* The commandment against bearing false witness had been extended in puritan morality to make of any lie a grave offense, and Newton remembered his acts of deception. Not only had he made a feather on the Sabbath but he denied it. The pettiness of the deceits that he felt impelled to confess is a measure of the severe standards by which he judged himself: *Lying about a louse; Deceiving my chamberfellow of the knowledge of him that took him for a sot.*

Loss of control was sinful in and of itself. He called Derothy Rose a jade, he was peevish with his mother and his sister and also at Master Clark's *for a piece of bread and butter.* He had a falling out with servants; he beat Arthur Storer; *Striking many; Punching my sister.* His concupiscence expressed itself in gluttony, which he thrice recorded. And once he made a general confession of lustfulness: *Having uncleane thoughts words and actions and dreamese.* The shame of the masturbator revealed. *Using unlawful means to bring us out of distresses* is simply enigmatic.

Amid these sundry crimes, two stand out. They were sins of an atrocious character and yet they are reported with no greater contrition than an act of disobedience such as *Refusing to go to the close at my mothers command;* or an act of stingy selfishness, *Using Wilford's towel to spare my owne.* The dark deeds drowned in the welter of minor sins were the threats of parricide and matricide and the thoughts of self-slaughter and death to others that dominated him. The recording of these crimes was an attempt to free himself from their toils; but he was never wholly released. In the Judeo-Puritan Deuteronomic code there are gradations of punishment from whipping to death, but any sin is a sign of possession by evil. The devil himself does not figure prominently in Newton's writings, though he can be found lurking among the papers at the Mint at least once.[22] Not the physical reality that he had been for Luther, he had become psychologized into a sense of guilt and sin. To exorcize the devil Newton later had to project onto others the evil, the guilt, the lying, the desire to kill that were in him. For most of his manhood he contained the evil through ascetic behavior enforced with a titanic power of will and, for long periods, by intense concentration on the building of an abstract thought system. But there came a time when the controls collapsed.

There is not much laughter in Newton's life and no echo of "merrie olde England" in his notebooks. He has an image of himself as close to death, tending toward consumption; he doses himself with homemade remedies found in books, mixes powders and balsams. The doctors make their appearance only late in life when he has become a great administrator. Who knows but that his puritan independence and sense of autonomy carried over into medicine saved him from the tender ministrations of many a ruthless bleeder.

A chief source of Newton's desire to know was his anxiety before and his fear of the unknown. When he learned the laws of his God he was able to allay those fears; but his anxiety often kept pace with his discoveries and was perpetually renewed. The intense, personal character of Newton's struggle with nature can be grasped at moments of self-revelation in his manuscripts. His experimental technique in studying colored circles between two contiguous glasses, for example, has dumbfounded commentators. He measured the circles with his naked eye, distinguishing fractions of a hundredth of an inch with unbelievable confidence. He made animated, hostile things of the circles and wrestled with them as if they were evil forces. And he sometimes suffered temporary defeats—"yet many times they imposed upon mee."[23]

The floating anxiety of the puritanical young man may have been reflected in his earliest scientific propositions. Richard Westfall, commenting upon Newton's repudiation of Cartesianism in *De Gravitatione et Aequipondio Fluidorum,* related Newton's conception of absolute space to a metaphysical fear and called it a surrogate for the psychological security lost when the finite universe of Aristotle and the Schoolmen was shattered and men were confronted by the boundless reaches of space.[24] The psychic terrors of the culture channeled through the personal fear of the man brought forth a scientific idea. In the *Principia* Newton's conception received its final form: "Absolute space, in its own nature, without relation to anything external, remains always similar and immovable."[25]

Newton's studies in chronology attempted to resolve problems in the origins of ancient kingdoms, much debated in his age, by establishing dates absolute, fixed through astronomical evidence, for the crucial historical events: the Argonautic expedition and the fall of Troy. He could no more endure the idea of shadowy beginnings for kingdoms than he could for his own antecedents. He had to have precision, assurance, law.

Whatever psychological influences were at play, they operated upon his science within the framework of inherited conceptions such as the infinity of worlds and a heliocentric view of the universe, largely accepted among English scientists by the time Newton went up to the University. But the overwhelming fears, doubts, and insecurities of his early life, which have left indelible telltale marks in the notebooks, gave his science a particular style and on occasion tended to push him in one or another direction.

In Newton overt protestations of principle were often at odds with conduct, let alone inner desire, and some of the contradictions have long been recognized. "Newton's general statements about science, or about the proper kinds of scientific explanation (such as that he framed no hypotheses), are apt to be at considerable variance with his actual practice. In attempts to harmonize the obvious discrepancy, many commentators have produced a tortuous exegesis which requires the omission of many of Newton's major writings," observes I. Bernard Cohen.[26] If one accepts the idea that Newton's moods were subject to wide pendulum swings that had intellectual consequences, scientific contrarieties may be illuminated. Though in most scientific matters his decisions were dictated by new insights and controlled by rigorous experiment, he continued to harbor within him opposing convictions: to believe in a mechanical universe and in miracles, to abhor mystical extravagance and, at the same time, to experience flights of fancy that he would condemn in others; to entertain varying conceptions of the aether; to dedicate years of his life to the alchemical quest and to suffer grave doubts about the possibility of its successful issue; to be committed to the "plain" experimental method and the "plain" historical way of explanation and to be one of the most daring framers of hypotheses in the history of science.

Ambivalent neurotics have a craving for certainty. The more searing the doubt the more profound the need for a safe haven. Newton had two such refuges, a great blessing for a man in his state of everlasting tension: one was the Bible literally interpreted as historical fact, de-allegorized, de-mythisized of everything vague and poetic, reduced to the concrete; the other was mathematical proof. Knowledge that could be mathematicized ended his quandaries. The discovery of his mathematical genius was his salvation; that the world obeyed mathematical law was his security. But there were moments when the mathematical encasement of his thought was not strong enough to preserve him from the volcanic outburst of destructive forces long repressed.

It has not been difficult to identify the sources of mistrust, shame, doubt, guilt, and inferiority in the early stages of Isaac Newton's life, to follow Erikson's schema loosely for the moment. After the accumulation of woes—the raging war, the absconded true father, the physical taint of littleness, the separated mother, the elderly step-father, the returned siblings of another marriage, and the dark side of the puritanical world order—the ratio of "strengths" was hardly favorable. A paradisaical union with the widowed mother in infancy, great natural locomotor initiative and even industry, good masters at school, a social climate benign to scientific genius are on the other side of the balance. But nothing prepares us for the mystery of the creation, the triumphs of 1666.

Chapter 4

TO THE ANNUS MIRABILIS 1666

Fortunate Newton, happy childhood of science! He who has
time and tranquillity can by reading this book live again the
wonderful events which the great Newton experienced in his
young days. Nature to him was an open book, whose letters
he could read without effort. The conceptions which he used
to reduce the material of experience to order seemed to flow
spontaneously from experience itself, from the beautiful experiments which he ranged in order like playthings and describes
with an affectionate wealth of detail. In one person he combined the experimenter, the theorist, the mechanic and, not
least, the artist in exposition.

—Albert Einstein, Foreword to the 1931
edition of the *Opticks*

In 1655 Thomas Fuller described Trinity as "the Stateliest and
most uniform Colledge in Christendom."[1] Though John Evelyn
judged the quadrangle far inferior to that of Christ Church, Oxford,
even he thought the hall ample, the fountain graceful, and the
chapel and the library fair.[2] At the start, Newton's career at this
academic temple of glory was undistinguished from that of other
poor commoners from the country. He was admitted on June 5,
1661, as a subsizar, and matriculated as a sizar in July (the title is
probably derived from "size," a portion of bread and drink received
free). Despite an inheritance, his lowly University status required
the performance of menial services. "He would have been expected
to run errands for his Tutor, fetch his provisions from the buttery
and probably wait on the Fellows at the high table and dine on what

was left over," is the description of his functions by Joseph Edleston, the nineteenth-century editor who was the first to examine the meager official records of Newton's undergraduate days at Trinity.[3] In February 1664 he was elected Scholar and he took his Bachelor of Arts a year later. In 1667 he was a Minor Fellow, in 1668 a Major Fellow and a Master of Arts, and in 1669, upon Isaac Barrow's resignation, he filled the Lucasian Chair of Mathematics—a meteoric rise that left his social position somewhat blurred and confused. If Newton's whole life is viewed from a distant prospect, the two great divides are geographic—the movement from Lincolnshire to Cambridge and from Cambridge to London—and they are, in part at least, due to chance. That he might have lived and died a grazier in his mother's house is not beyond the realm of possibility. Becoming a scholar was embarking on a new way for which he was not destined from birth, and for him there was no security in this role, however early his genius was recognized.

When Newton went up to Cambridge he was not abruptly cut off from his Lincolnshire origins, for prominent older men from the area were resident at the University. Though the orphaned Isaac did not cling to any close relative as an exclusive surrogate father, fostering elders of a lesser order had already made their appearance in Grantham, and their number increased in Cambridge. The young genius was too attractive to be left alone. Though the designation "a genius" with respect to a man of extraordinary mathematical and scientific talent was not yet in general use—in fact the common conception of a scientific genius was probably created by Newton—the boy wonder in Newton was identified early. The first of the fathers had been the apothecary with whom he lodged as a schoolboy; copying remedies into the Morgan notebook and a continuing preoccupation with the mixing of potions, medicinal and alchemical, point to Clark as an early model. Newton was perennially absorbed with maladies and their cures, and he constantly doctored himself and recommended medicines to others—stray sheets of prescriptions in his hand have turned up. The names of the two hundred-odd afflictions he mustered under "Of Diseases" in the Morgan notebook,

THE LAD FROM LINCOLNSHIRE

even if partly drawn from Francis Gregory's *Nomenclatura,* presage
a lifelong immersion in Clark's "physic." The chronic hypochondria, a common symptom of narcissism, anxiety and fear of death,
did not, however, interrupt his work (he may even have sought to
blot out his apprehensions in unremitting labor and busyness). Another protecting father in Grantham had been the schoolmaster
Stokes, but of him we know only the stock anecdote reported by
Stukeley.

The gap between Grantham and Cambridge was first bridged by
Dr. Humphrey Babington, a man with many Lincolnshire ties, whose
name appears a few times in Newton's notebooks. He was related
to the apothecary Clark and was the uncle of Newton's "beloved."
On Newton's arrival Dr. Babington, then a man of forty-six, was
Senior Fellow of Trinity, and Stukeley surmises that his presence
there was the reason Newton entered that College. "The Dr had a
particular kindness for him, owing to his being sensible of the lad's
great merit."[4] Dr. Babington's daybook records small favors performed by Newton as late as 1679, proof of a lasting relationship.
Upon refusing the Commonwealth "Engagement," a formal oath
of allegiance, Babington, along with the poet Abraham Cowley and
other recalcitrants, had been ejected from the University. He was no
great scholar and had held only the degree of Bachelor of Divinity
until he was reinstated with the Restoration and created a doctor
per literas Regias (1669), a reward for his staunch royalism. When
Babington was invited to preach at the Lincoln Assizes in 1678, he
delivered a learned homily with quotations from the Hebrew and
the Targum, the Greek Fathers, Homer, Diogenes Laertius, Cicero,
and Ovid—his only publication, a potpourri of unassimilated erudition.[5] Babington was later elected Vice-master of his College and he
donated to it four additional arches in Neville's Court. Thus at least
one of the persons who "fathered" Newton in Cambridge had been
outspoken on the King's side, and Newton was not without a
prominent protector in Trinity from the moment of his appearance.
A mediocre intellect himself, Babington gazed upon the prodigy
with wonderment. When, a quarter of a century after his arrival in

Cambridge as a subsizar, Newton despatched a copy of the *Principia* to him as a gift, he told the messenger that he would have to study seven years before he comprehended anything of it. During the University's hour of trial in 1687, Newton and his old friend Babington stood shoulder to shoulder before the terrible Judge Jeffreys as delegates from Trinity.

Though as Master of Trinity Dr. John Wilkins, who had left Oxford for Cambridge, had shielded many royalists and was "heartily honored and loved" by men of both parties,[6] with the Restoration he was evicted from the College because his marriage to Oliver Cromwell's widowed sister made him too conspicuous a figure to be overlooked. He was replaced for eighteen months in 1660-1661 by Dr. Henry Ferne, who in 1643 had taken refuge with the Royalists in Oxford after having published a manifesto, *Resolving of Conscience*. In the exercise of his functions he showed moderation, and helped to ease the transition to the new regime during Newton's first year as an undergraduate by obtaining the confirmation of elections to fellowships that had taken place under the Commonwealth. Though Puritan purges were now canceled and Royalists were reinstated, a number of Roundhead Fellows were either retained or readmitted after a short interval. The Act of Uniformity of 1662, however, altered the conciliatory temper in some respects, and in both great universities a retrogressive spirit in philosophy as well as religion became dominant for a time. John Pearson, who followed Ferne in the Mastership of Trinity, announced in his inaugural lecture as Lady Margaret Professor that his method would be that of the Schoolmen, and more particularly Aquinas. Pearson was one of the great worthies of Anglican theology, and who knows but that his *Exposition of the Creed* (1659, revised and enlarged in 1662) drove Newton to secret unitarianism. Despite their religious orthodoxy, however, Ferne, Pearson, and later Isaac Barrow—the first three Masters under the Restoration—were all tolerant of persons and they helped to allay the bitterness of sectarian dissension in academic life.[7]

An intellectual trend from an earlier period contrary to Pearson's traditionalism was allowed to survive. Its outstanding representative at the University was Henry More, another Lincolnshire man, one who had managed to stay on at Cambridge unmolested during both the Commonwealth and the Restoration. Much has been made of More's influence on Newton's thought, but whether there was a strong personal bond with the philosopher of Christ's College when Newton first settled in Cambridge is unknown. More was born in Grantham and one of his students, a Dr. Clark, had been the mathematical usher at the Grammar School when Newton lodged with his brother the apothecary; this might have been the basis for a relationship. The devoted son of a rigid Calvinist, More had turned to Plato as his guide in the *Philosophical Poems* of 1647 and was of the illustrious group of Cambridge Platonists. Before 1662 he had also incorporated into his system the Cartesian philosophy as the "most sober and faithful" in the Christian world, and in *The Immortality of the Soul,* published in 1659 and again in 1662, had advised its study at the universities. There are quotations from the "excellent Dr More in his booke of the soules immortality" in Newton's Cambridge University Library commonplace book under the head "Of Attomes," where the existence of indiscerptible small particles is accepted as "proved beyond all controversie."[8] Late in life Newton confessed to visitors that he had once been a Cartesian— perhaps it was through More's teaching. An aristocratic lawyer, Roger North, who had been a Cambridge undergraduate, recalled in his *Autobiography* that the defense of the French philosopher was a heterodox intellectual position in 1667: "I found such a stir about Descartes, some railing at him and forbidding the reading him as if he had impugned the very Gospel. And yet there was a general inclination, especially of the brisk part of the University, to use him. . . ."[9] That Henry More combined an appreciation of Descartes and Plotinus with a devotion to the Cabala and to the interpretation of the prophecies of Daniel should not astound anyone aware of the intricacies and syncretistic virtuosity of this period in English intellectual life. By 1671, however, in his *Enchiridion Metaphysicum* More had abandoned Descartes, and so had Isaac Newton.

The mystical element that obtrudes into Newton's mechanical philosophy from the very outset of his scholarly career—and it makes an appearance too often to be neglected or reasoned away—was nurtured by Henry More and Cambridge Platonism. Though there is no convincing testimony that Newton ever read Jacob Boehme, More may have been the agent of transmission for notions from the metaphysical German cobbler. Despite Newton's avowed predilection for plain speaking, his world system has a cast that is Platonic rather than Aristotelian, a spirit that may have been strengthened by Henry More. Newton conceived of the ontological problem of causation within a traditional neo-Platonic framework.[10] The doctrine of emanation in More's philosophy, moreover, validated this world as a noble embodiment of God, and the search for Him through a comprehension of the minute details of things He created was more meritorious than the efforts of those who arrogantly sought to know God through direct contemplation alone, a subtle religious apology for the new philosophy.

In Newton's Cambridge University Library notebook of the early 1660's a rich and complex inner life is unfolded that is hidden from us in later writings and rarely breaks through in his correspondence. He muses about the nature of sensation, dreams, fantasy, memory, the imagination, and at one point relates them to invention. Historians of his great physical theories may be interested in his passing reference to Joseph Glanvill's report of an instance of telepathy, demonstrated experimentally to his fellows by a former Oxford student who had learned the art from gypsies. "A man by heitning his fansie & immagination may bind anothers to thinke what hee thinks as in the story of the Oxford scollar in Glanvill Vañ of Dogmatizing."[11] Farfetched as this may now seem, in the thought of the period there was more than a metaphoric affinity among all forms of action at a distance, from God's possession of prophets through ruach to effluvia that emanated from one person to another (as in Quaker belief), cures of wounds at a distance through the application of sympathetic powders to the weapon (Kenelm Digby's fixed idea), the electrical attraction of a magnet, and speculations about the mysterious nature of gravity or the physical attraction of material mass. Our present-day compartmentalization of the phenomena should not be foisted upon the mid-seventeenth century. Newton's mathematicization of knowledge in the wake of Galileo was a powerful influence in accelerating the separation of studies, but the idea of science in his early years was far more fluid.

In Newton's notebooks of the 1660's there is some mark of all the intellectual passions of his later life—optics, astronomy, mathematics, dynamics, chemistry, alchemy. According to the Conduitt memoir to Fontenelle, he always informed himself beforehand of the books his tutor intended to read, and when he arrived at lectures found he knew more of them than the tutor did; his best sources were Sanderson's *Logic* and Kepler's *Optics*. The anecdote is refused by many scholars, though it may well echo the aged Newton in one of his moods of self-inflation.[12] Far from being an engrossment of his old age alone, the common view of *The Chronology of Ancient Kingdoms Amended,* curiosity about world chronology, mythology, and history was born along with his interest in physical science and expressed itself in his very first purchases of books—and he was no casual spender of money. The Trinity notebook records his acquisition of Hall's *Chronicle* (a compilation of English dynastic histories) and Sleidan's *Four Monarchies,*[13] the latter a work based upon the traditional adaptation of Nebuchadnezzar's dream in Daniel as the underlying pattern of universal history. The idea of the four monarchies remained to the very end the structural framework of Newton's understanding of God's way in the historical world. The accounts of the Fitzwilliam notebook for 1667–1669 record the purchase of Bacon's *Miscellany Works,*[14] composed of historical, not philosophical, essays, and that of the *Theatrum Chemicum,* an anthology of alchemical writings.[15] The expenditure of sixteen shillings for Thomas Sprat's *History of the Royal Society*[16] and for the *Philosophicall Intelligences* is concrete proof that Newton early had an inclination toward the new philosophy. Taken together, the notebooks disclose the grand universality of Newton's inquiries,[17] though he has begun to make certain choices: natural philosophy and mathematics rather than psychology or the passions of the soul; alchemy, chemistry, and medicine intermingled, rather than botany. Chronology that relates to exact astronomy has not yet blotted out an interest in the narrative history of England. Traditional theological and philosophical questions about the nature of God, the soul, matter, motion, quantity, quality are frequently posed but they do not emerge as the center of his world—and the philosophical utterances of his middle age will not be counted among his greatest accomplishments. From the beginning there is a certain tendency to denigrate the subjective witness of the senses and to seek refuge in truths derived solely from investigating and measuring the operations of bodies upon each other. He prefers to deal with things and to avoid persons and feelings. This at least is the purport of his reflection upon philosophy in the Cambridge University Library notebook: "The nature of things is more securely & naturally deduced from their operaĉons one upon another ȳ [than] upon o[u]r senses."[18] His general orientation brings him closer to the Puritan scientists and thinkers of the Commonwealth who had invited Comenius to England than to the Anglican theologians and the licentious literary sparks of the Restoration.

During the Revolution, some Puritans had struck at the whole educational system of preparatory schools and universities identified with scholastic theology, ethics learned out of Aristotle, science that quoted him as authority, and a general education based almost exclusively on the classics, whose paganism outraged them. Their anti-Catholic, antipapal animus gave their condemnation of scholasticism a sharp religious bite. Among them were fanatics whose hostility toward the educational strongholds of Anglicanism was so bitter that they favored the outright abolition of all universities, though these extremists were in a minority. The moderate group espoused the new learning, the new science, the practical education of a Comenius, projects for the advancement of natural, instead of scholastic, philosophy. Thus humanist literature and the Schoolmen were generally associated with the conservative Anglican viewpoint, and experimental science, practical knowledge, and Christian (as distinguished from Aristotelian) ethics with the new Puritan out-look.[19] The utopias of Samuel Hartlib and the pansophia of Co-menius espoused physical science in preference to the humanistic study of the ancients. If the Erasmian dispensation of the previous century had called for a synthesis of Christian and classical virtues, which by some moral alchemy turned out to be the same—the iden-tification of Christ and Socrates—the new educational ideal of the Puritan moderates was a synthesis of the values of Christianity and natural philosophy. The Puritans' pejorative view of classical learn-ing, of the Greek and Roman corpus of moral teachings that had once been the heart of the educational reforms proposed by Erasmus and Thomas More, may not have decreed the total abandonment of classical texts and their elimination from the university curriculum, but there developed among them an entirely new way of utilizing and reducing the worth of what had once been prized as humanist culture.

If the classics were not to be a moral inspiration, neither could they serve as models for the expression of thought, as examples of wit and elegance, of style. Many of the Christian scientific virtuosi, both Puritan and Anglican, turned their backs upon the aesthetic values of the classics and rejected their form as well as their moral content. John Wilkins, for example, who made no discoveries him-self but was a great propagandist for the new science, broke with the ornamentation of the wits. The Royal Society made an ideal of setting things forth in a chaste, practical, matter-of-fact language without periphrastic turns, digressions, and elaborations.[20] The Society's motto, *Nullius in Verba,* was primarily a renunciation of the verbal authority of ancient scientists, but there are also overtones of a more general prejudice against literary culture. Wilkins is considered responsible for the initiation of a barebones style, simple, straightforward, to the point, excellent for communicating mathe-matical and physical ideas, for minute and accurate description, but rather inadequate for the rendering of poetical and emotional images or the intricate fabric of feelings. The millions of words

Newton left behind in manuscript are virtually without adjectives, beyond the simple ones that denote quantity and color and are associated with numbers. There is no way of knowing whether he intentionally patterned his style after Wilkins (whose works he read at an early date) or whether his particular mode of expression bespoke a like temper, but the result is the same. In the 1670's there were still signs of elegance in Newton's correspondence; and his early classical education left its mark in hyperbole, even a species of wit on rare occasions, and, mirabile dictu, a simile. By the time we come to the last versions of *The Chronology of Ancient Kingdoms Amended,* we have entered the arid wasteland of Sinai, and this is a work that one reads only for penance.

Preparatory education at the endowed grammar schools like Grantham, which Newton had attended, still concentrated almost exclusively on learning languages through the line-by-line translation of texts, but this Greek and Latin learning was no longer a living source for the study and inculcation of moral values. The Bible and it alone was the fundament of Christian ethics. Since the pagan literary classics, the historians, poets, dramatists, and orators, as distinguished from the Church Fathers, did not provide models for virtuous conduct to a puritanical scientist—and how could they, when their authors were idolaters—and a graceful style was a superfluous, if not irreligious, encumbrance, what use could be made of this literature apart from language exercises? Why was it not abandoned by a man like Newton? Why did he purchase the best sixteenth- and seventeenth-century learned editions of the classics when he had money of his own? Surely not for the pleasure of reading them. The answer is that they contained information, vital grains of useful historical knowledge about God's way in the world, in the midst of all the chaff. Modern literature served no such purpose, and in Newton's library of about eighteen hundred volumes there were virtually no belles lettres and little "vain philosophy." Throughout his life Newton would be suspicious of the poetic and the imaginative in others and in his own nature. Though he referred to certain mathematical proofs as elegant and his mature handwriting is at times beautiful, the aesthetic when related to the sensuous is sternly denied.

On the basis of the same Cambridge University Library commonplace book that affords us glimpses into the diverse objects of Newton's curiosity, a timetable has been drawn up for some major discoveries of that glorious period of creativity, 1664 through 1666, which is usually telescoped into the *annus mirabilis* for commemorative purposes—a succession of triumphs unequaled in the history of scientific invention.[21] The early prismatic experiments and the discovery of the varying refrangibility of colored light, as well as Newton's first observations of comets, have been fixed in the period from 1664 to the spring of 1665. In the autumn of that year came his first attempts to grind lenses of a more complex curvature and a continuation of his prismatic experiments. He completed the theory of colors in the winter of 1666. In his *Annus Mirabilis: The Year of Wonders, 1666* John Dryden celebrated England's naval victory over Holland and London's emergence from the Great Fire, while some miles away the real *annus mirabilis* was being created by the mind of a young man of twenty-three.

The beginning of Newton's exploration of the nature of light and of his searching the sky for comets belongs to the period before the plague. At the University tracking comets kept him awake for nights on end, until he fell ill from exhaustion, he told Conduitt. Newton's eye was his first scientific instrument. A desire to enjoy once more the pleasures of intimate visual exchange which he had experienced when alone with his mother during infancy, before the daily ritual was disrupted by her disappearance, was one of the most powerful psychic drives in his nature and manifested itself in a variety of scientific forms. He re-searches with his eye in strange ways: in the *experimentum crucis* he watches light passing through small holes and refracted by prisms and finds that it consists of "Rays differently refrangible"; he presses and contorts the eye in an effort to generate new sensations of light and color; he boldly stares at the sun and then plunges himself into darkness, hoping for

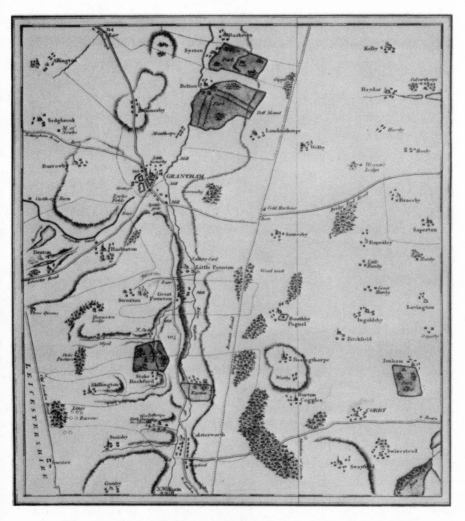

1. The part of Lincolnshire comprehending the Soke of Grantham

The Mannor house of Wulfthorp in the parish
of Colsterworth Lincolnshire, where Sr Isaac
Newton was born: being his own estate.

2. The manor house of Woolsthorpe

afterimages. The experiments open up a world of color as he discovers the infinite gradations between the extremes of red and purple on an ordered scale and offers a solution to the problem of primary colors, which had intrigued mankind for two thousand years. A glimmer of Newton's experience of the wonder of colors as distinct from their measurement can be caught in the plain opening narrative of his letter to Oldenburg on February 6, 1672: "[I]n the beginning of the Year 1666 . . . I procured me a Triangular glass-Prisme, to try therewith the celebrated *Phaenomena of Colours.* And in order thereto having darkened my chamber, and made a small hole in my window-shuts, to let in a convenient quantity of the Suns light, I placed my Prisme at its entrance, that it might be thereby refracted to the opposite wall. It was at first a very pleasing divertisement, to view the vivid and intense colours produced thereby. . . ."[22]

But a passion to see—richly documented in Newton's optical experiments—can be accompanied by a fear of what may be seen, especially if the underlying desire is secret and forbidden. Newton's experiments with light were charged with affect and the publishing of what he discovered would always be fraught with psychic dangers.

From the notebook in the Fitzwilliam Museum and the Buttery Books in Trinity College examined by Edleston, it can be established that on account of the plague Newton left Cambridge for Lincolnshire in June 1665 (the place was "disuniversitied"), not returning until March 20, 1666, when it was believed the epidemic was subsiding. By June he was back again in Lincolnshire because of a new outbreak and there he remained for almost a year, until April 22, 1667.[23] Measures were adopted in the county to isolate the sick, and vagrants were prohibited free movement lest they bear the disease with them. In September 1666 plague-ridden England was shaken by another disaster, the Great Fire of London, in the wake of which riots broke out as far north as Cambridge. Since the year 1666 figured prominently in interpretations of prophecy, Judaic and Christian, as Judgment Day or the Coming of the Messiah, this was truly a year of prodigies. There is something to arouse wonder in Newton's proceeding with his mathematical computations, his theory of colors, and his observations in the garden while the world was coming to an end.

If 1666 is the *annus mirabilis,* most of it was spent in the protective bosom of his mother while the plague raged without—the analogy to their closeness during the civil war years before Newton was three comes to mind. The burst of inventiveness, or at least Newton's feeling that this was the great period of his life, is documented in a nostalgic reflection when he was over seventy. "All this was in the two plague years of 1665 & 1666 for in those days I was in the prime of my age for invention, & minded Mathematicks & Philosophy more then at any time since."[24]

The studies of Derek Whiteside on Newton's first mathematical papers and John Herivel on his early dynamical writings do not fundamentally alter this simple declaration, beyond pushing an opening date back to 1664. Whiteside has corrected Newton's recollections of the early influence of Descartes, Hudde, Barrow, and Wallis, has examined Newton's notes on six standard mathematical texts, and has revised the chronology of what transpired in a month-by-month schematic reconstruction of the growth of Newton's ideas on fluxions during the years 1664–1666, a performance of great virtuosity in which each discrete external stimulus from Newton's reading and each act of autonomous invention has been allotted its appropriate box and date. But for our purposes Newton's summary stands. On the general tone of the papers and style of his life at this time Whiteside writes with warmth: "The papers . . . throb with energy and imagination but yet convey the claustrophobic air of a man completely wrapped up in himself, whose only real contact with the external world was through his books."[25] During the two years following the autumn of 1664, the date of his first entries in the commonplace book of Barnabas Smith, Newton became a mathematical genius the equal of Huygens and James Gregory, his studies reaching a climax in the October 1666 tract on fluxions.[26] The recent publication of Newton's mathematical papers is dramatic witness to the suddenness of the flowering of his inventiveness. "[B]y mid-1665, one short crowded year after his first beginnings, the urge to learn from the work of others was largely abated. . . . It was time for him to go his own way in earnest and thereafter, though he continued to draw in detail on the ideas of others, Newton took his real inspiration from the workings of his own fertile mind."[27] The rest of his creative life was spent in working out in the calculus and in his mathematical thought what had first gushed forth during those years with little or no preparation.

The mathematician Abraham de Moivre's memorandum to Conduitt in 1727 reporting the elderly Newton's reminiscences is the main contemporary source for the chronology of his mathematical awakening—the purchase of a book of astrology at Stourbridge Fair in 1663, then the study of an unidentified book of trigonometry, a Euclid, Oughtred's *Clavis Mathematicae,* Descartes's geometry, Wallis' *Arithmetica Infinitorum,* culminating in the finding of the method of fluxions in 1665 and 1666.

[He] bought a book of Astrology, out of a curiosity to see what there was in it. Read in it till he came to a figure of the heavens which he could not understand for want of being acquainted with Trigonometry.

Bought a book of Trigonometry, but was not able to understand the Demonstrations.

Got Euclid to fit himself for understanding the ground of Trigonometry.[28]

Newton's own manuscript notation, dated July 4, 1699, on a blank sheet in the middle of a leather-bound notebook, runs along the same lines, though it locates early mathematical discoveries more precisely in the summer of 1665. He was not absolutely tied to his mother's umbilical cord during his stay in Woolsthorpe, for he ventured as far as three miles to the northeast, to Boothby Pagnell where Dr. Humphrey Babington was rector and had a library; and there, according to his testimony, he computed "the area of the Hyperbola . . . to two & fifty figures" by the method of infinite series which he had found.[29] Unfortunately, we know virtually nothing about his activities in 1663 and early 1664, the eve of the intellectual explosion, because his account book for those years is lost, though we do have earlier records in the Trinity College note-book and later ones in the Fitzwilliam notebook.[30]

The psychological chronology of this extraordinary period thus has a few relatively secure bench marks. A religious crisis occurred in mid-May 1662, one year after he had left his mother's house for the University. The next date is midsummer 1663 when he visited the Stourbridge Fair east of Cambridge, a sign that he was not com-pletely shut off from the world, and bought the book on astrology. Since his first lively interest in mathematics is datable to September 1664 and in dynamics to January 1665, and in the Cambridge University Library commonplace book there are entries of cometary observations for December 1664 and April 1, 1665, the skies were already opening up for Newton before he returned to Woolsthorpe during the plague; but this in no wise diminishes the significance of the place of the discovery and the person of his mother in that great burst of his genius in 1665 and 1666.[31]

Newton's calculations on the ratios of the force of gravity to the centrifugal forces due to the diurnal and annual motions of the earth were written on the back of a torn piece of legal parchment on which a lease connected with his mother's property was engrossed. After weighing the evidence Herivel judges that these calculations were probably made in 1665 or 1666.[32] The exact nature of what Newton discovered of the "law of gravity" in 1666 is still open to question. Stukeley's story is merely pictorial and introduces the ap-ple in the garden. "After dinner [at Kensington on April 15, 1726], the weather being warm, we went into the garden and drank thea, under the shade of some appletrees, only he and myself. Amidst other discourse, he told me, he was just in the same situation, as when formerly, the notion of gravitation came into his mind. It was occasion'd by the fall of an apple, as he sat in a contemplative mood."[33] Henry Pemberton's account of about the same period—in the last years of Newton's life—is more scientific and has the garden but not the apple:

As he sat alone in a garden, he fell into a speculation on the power of gravity: that as this power is not found sensibly diminished at the remotest distance from the center of the earth, to which we can rise, neither at the tops of the loftiest buildings, nor even on the summits of the highest mountains; it appeared to him reasonable to conclude, that this power must extend much farther than was usually thought; why not as high as the moon, said he to himself? and if so, her motion must be influenced by it; perhaps she is retained in her orbit thereby. However, though the power of gravity is not sensibly weakened in the little change of distance, at which we can place our selves from the center of the earth; yet it is very possible, that so high as the moon this power may differ much in strength from what it is here. To make an estimate, what might be the degree of this diminution, he considered with himself, that if the moon be retained in her orbit by the force of gravity, no doubt the primary planets are carried round the sun by the like power. And by comparing the periods of the several planets with their distances from the sun, he found, that if any power like gravity held them in their courses, its strength must decrease in the duplicate proportion of the increase of distance.[34]

Both Whiston[35] and Pemberton attribute Newton's temporary abandonment of his "postulatum" to his erroneous reckoning that one degree of latitude on the surface of the earth was sixty miles, with the consequence that his computations did not support his insight. The error notwithstanding, Herivel believes, Newton did carry out a test of the inverse square law of gravitation at this time.[36] If his conclusion is valid, 1666 is indeed the *annus mirabilis* when the fundamental law of the universe was both intuited and tested by a young man of twenty-three and a half in a town in Lincolnshire.

To relate the invention of the law of gravity, defining universal attraction, if not yet successfully proving it mathematically, to Newton's psychological history is a hazardous undertaking. It would be the path of prudence to let well enough alone. We have located the discovery in his mother's garden, and from there we should let everyman's fancy roam where it listeth. But somehow the proximity of Newton inspires us to feign the wildest hypotheses.

To assert that the child Newton spent many hours longing for the absent ones, his dead father and his remarried mother, is to affirm something within ordinary experience. To posit a relationship between this longing and a later intellectual structure in which a sort of an impulse or attraction is a key term descriptive of a force is more problematical. In one of the manuscripts of *De Motu Corporum* Newton wrote:

Centripetal force is a certain action or power by which a body is impelled or drawn or in any way tends towards a certain point as if to a centre: of this ilk is the gravity by which a body tends to the centre of the earth, the magnetic force by which iron seeks the centre of a magnet, and that force, whatsoever it may be, by which the Planets are held in their orbits and perpetually restrained from flying off at a tangent. . . . [I] use the words *attraction, impulse,* or *propensity* of any sort towards a centre indifferently and interchangeably one for the other, considering these forces not in the *physical* but only in the mathematical sense. Hence let the reader beware lest he think that by words of this kind I define a type or mode of action or cause or physical reason of any kind.[37]

As gravity was a commonly enough observed phenomenon along with attractions magnetic and electrical, the laws of the *Principia* can be shown to have emerged gradually in the long process of the autonomous development of seventeenth-century science, and their final discoverer could have been any one of a number of men. But the fact is that Newton, who made the last leap, was in a critical period of childhood powerfully drawn to distant persons, that he was hungry for communion with the departed ones in an elementary, even primitive sense. Since this yearning never found an object in sexuality, it could have achieved sublime expression in an intellectual construct whose configuration was akin to the original emotion. That an ardent religious longing for God the Father in the confession of 1662 was one form in which this desire for communion expressed itself is today less preposterous than it might have been before the writings of the great religious mystics were related to the genesis of modern science. An element of religious inspiration in the principle of attraction now has wide, if not universal, acceptance. But the coupling of the emotions of a child being drawn to distant and absent ones with the idea of a natural force that as an adult he could never define cannot be received without a heavy dose of skepticism. Newton knew of the common metaphoric description of the attractive power of a magnet as love and he and others wrote of the "sociability" of liquids in connection with alchemical experiments. But the chasm which most of us would establish between the nature of psychic and physical power did not exist in the mid-seventeenth century. The translation of longing, one's passion for persons, into a systematic inquiry of a mathematical-astronomical character is a giant step; and yet, on one level of existence, Newton lived in an animistic world in which feelings of love and attraction could be assimilated to other forces.

In the Cambridge University Library notebook, Newton described how his curiosity about colors led him to experiment with gazing at the sun and studying its afterimages.[38] Almost thirty years later, in a letter to Locke, he again recounted his experiment. The physiological and scientific consequences concern us less than the performance itself. Newton defiantly and repeatedly stared at the sun in a lookingglass, and then plunged into darkness for three days in order to recover from the "phantasm of the sun" that kept pursuing him. The experimentation with his body, the daring, and the "hazzard" are narrated without affect in the letter to Locke. But one cannot help recognizing that there were other dimensions to this act.

In a few hours I had brought my eyes to such a pass that I could look upon no bright object with either eye but I saw the sun before me, so that I durst neither write nor read but to recover the use of my eyes shut my self up in my chamber made dark for three days together & used all means to divert my imagination from the Sun. For if I thought upon him I presently saw his picture though I was in the dark. But by keeping in the dark & imploying my mind about other things I began in three or four days to have some use of my eyes again & by forbearing a few days longer to look upon bright objects recovered them pretty well, thô not so well but that for some months after the spectrum of the sun began to return as often as I began to meditate upon the phaenomenon, even tho I lay in bed at midnight with my curtains drawn.[39]

Like Jacob, Newton had confronted a god face to face and had been preserved. Isaac Newton had recorded play with his body on other occasions, in particular during the oral contortions incident to his invention of a new orthography.

Though we now possess the witness of great twentieth-century scientists, there is very little from Newton on the psychological experience of inventiveness. In the light of his deep religious commitment, it may be useful to introduce an analogy from another realm, prophetic illumination or communion with God, to supplement the few commonsensical words Newton has left on his own. Bringing all one's powers to bear on a single idea or group of ideas to the radical exclusion of others and then relaxing into passivity is one way of achieving ecstasy or mystical union, and Newton may well have availed himself of such methods in seeking the resolution of major scientific problems. On one occasion he intimated as much when asked how he came to make his discoveries: "I keep the subject constantly before me, and wait till the first dawnings open slowly by little and little into the full and clear light."[40] As a sententious old man he told Conduitt that an irregular life was attended with an irregular head and that truth was "the offspring of silence and unbroken meditation."[41] Mystics who focus upon a single point to prepare for receiving a divine revelation have uttered similar words to describe their preliminary spiritual exercises. In Newton's Cambridge University notebook there is an early realization that physical circumstances could induce or impede a state of creativity. Under "Immagination & Phantasie & invention" he described regimens that would strengthen or disorganize the powers of the intellect.[42]

Though Newton had a consciousness of his special calling as divinely inspired, his insights always had to be verified, even as Maimonides would have the imaginative faculty restrained by the rational in the true prophet as distinguished from the mere enthusiast. The distinction was fundamental for Newton. The scientific notations that follow his illumination are akin to the symbolic acts performed by the prophet in transmitting his message. As a scientist Newton did not dispense with the traditional controls, the lengthy proofs; but at some stage in the process there was a massive, willed concentration that bears at least a kinship to mystic meditation. And his discoveries were often accompanied by a kind of profane exaltation. While the story of the apple dropping in the garden as recounted by the aged Newton is prosaic enough and he lived in apple country, it is impossible to ignore the religious overtones of a theory of the universe called forth by the fruit that at once occasioned man's fall into mortal sin and led to worldly knowledge.

William Whiston is our only outside witness to the operation of what he called Newton's "intuition," though we do not know precisely what he meant by the word. "Sir Isaac in mathematicks, could sometimes see almost by intuition, even without demonstration, as was the case in that famous proposition in his *Principia,* that *all parallelograms* circumscribed about the conjugate diameters of an ellipsis are equal; which he told Mr. Cotes he used before it had ever been demonstrated by any one, as it was afterward. And when he did but propose conjectures in natural philosophy, he almost always knew them to be true at the same time."[43] Such testimony is on a more matter-of-fact level than prophetic inspiration—even of the rational kind that was countenanced by reasonable Anglicans. But the few accounts of Newton's behavior during the Cambridge period when his genius was most productive speak of an indifference to bodily needs and a divorcement from the world which, though hardly equal to the asceticism of mystics in the desert, had something of their denial of the flesh in a holy service.

One is tempted to conjecture further about changes in Newton's life that may have favored the flowering of his natural genius during the period of the *annus mirabilis,* though in an ultimate sense the explanations are feeble when one is confronted with the magnitude of his achievement. If there had been doubts in the family about his fitness for the life of learning, he was vindicated when he was elected Scholar in February 1664 and took his bachelor's degree a year later. The intellectual ferment of the University—despite his revulsion at the coarseness of many undergraduates—the presence of men like Barrow and Henry More, excited the country boy. There is a possibility that he suffered a psychic crisis early in his undergraduate days: witness the confession of 1662 and cloudy references to illness in the notebooks. If the confession lifted the onus of guilt even for a brief period, his energies would find freer play. The significance of the plague in all this is difficult to measure. Though the epidemic was mild by medieval standards, fear of it was widespread. Newton himself later established the temporal association between the plague and the peak of his inventiveness, mentioning them together after many decades. He was surviving, and "survivors" often experience surges of creative power. Maybe in his religious or mythopoeic mind this sparing was a sign of election, of divine grace, of heavenly approbation and blessing that relieved an anxiety intensified by the lack of love or approval from an earthly father. In any event, there was an ordinary external mark of a transformation in his self-appraisal: in 1666 at the Lincoln visitation, when he inscribed himself "Gentleman," he was affirming a new status that was not his father's, even though his manor and Ayscough connections probably entitled him to the designation as a matter of course. He was no longer the pale little boy condemned to be a grazier, but a Bachelor of Arts, a gentleman and a scholar.

PART TWO

The Lucasian Professor

Chapter 5

RESTORATION TRINITY

Trinity College is, God be thanked in peace (I wish all
Christendome were so well) and it is my duty, if I can, to
keep uproars thence.
—Isaac Barrow to John Mapletoft, July 19, 1673

At the University he spent the greatest part of his time in his
closet & when he was tired with his severer studies of Philosophy his only relief & amusement was going to some other study
as History, Chronology Divinity & Chymistry all wch he examined & searched thoroughly as appears by the many papers
he has left on those subjects. . . .
—John Conduitt, Memoir to Fontenelle

Newton's friendship with Isaac Barrow was his most complex
relationship with an older man during his Trinity period.[1] Though
the age difference between them was not too great, a mere
twelve years, Newton outlived Barrow by half a century. This amaz-
ing figure of the first generation of the Royal Society has been
overshadowed by the other Isaac who succeeded him in the Lucasian
Chair of Mathematics at Cambridge. When they first encountered
each other at the University, Barrow already had an adventurous
career behind him. He had entered Trinity College as a pensioner,
one required to pay for lodging, a status between that of fellow-
commoner and sizar, Newton's early rank. In the days of Barrow
and Newton, Trinity had about sixty Fellows, sixty-seven Scholars,
four chaplains, three public professors, and thirteen sizars and sub-
sizars, in addition to about twenty fellow-commoners and some one

hundred and fifty pensioners. Although known for his Cavalier sentiments—his father was draper to King Charles I—Barrow had received his fellowship in 1649. He refused to sign the Engagement to uphold the Commonwealth; but despite the contumely of a Latin oration in the College on November 5, 1651, in which he extolled the King and proclaimed his Episcopalian views, the Master, Thomas Hill, would not eject him. Barrow went on to ridicule the "triumphant barbarism" of the "Saints" and the "fanatic breeds." In public addresses he attacked the pious obscurantism of William Dell, Master of Gonville and Caius College, who had demeaned philosophy and all arts and sciences as totally irrelevant to Christ's kingdom and its ministry. While preserving an admiration for Aristotle, Barrow exposed himself to the new philosophy of Bacon, Descartes, and Galileo at a time when their ideas were as heretical as his religious and political opinions. He was a Christian humanist in the broad style of the Elizabethans.

By 1655 Barrow's position at the University had become untenable, and just before the appearance of the Protector's Commission in Cambridge he managed to secure a travel grant for three years and set off for France. He was required to report to the University, and there is a lively running account in Latin verse of his experiences in the world of the learned Jesuits in Paris, in Florence, in the isles of Greece, in Smyrna, and finally in Constantinople, where he was as interested in the government of the Sublime Porte as in the Greek Fathers, the ostensible reason for his stay. On one occasion he engaged in a hand-to-hand combat with a boisterous Turk and trounced him. Upon his return to Trinity in September 1659, he found tolerant John Wilkins in the Master's Lodge, and since Wilkins was one of the chief Puritan promoters of the new science, Barrow was able to survive the civil war without compromising his religious convictions, which made him persona grata when the Stuart monarchy was restored. He was awarded in turn the Regius Professorship of Greek and the Lucasian Professorship of Mathematics. In midsummer 1662 he was also Gresham Professor of

Geometry, and he was on the first list of Fellows of the Royal Society. The scope of Barrow's studies was phenomenal, and he surely outstripped Newton as a Grecian, a Latinist, and a Hebraist, in addition to having acquired modern languages and some Arabic. He had come to mathematics by a circuitous route. As a divine committed to church history he was led to the study of world chronology, which was clearly dependent upon astronomy—the central proposition of Newton's later revision of world chronology—and from astronomy he had moved to geometry.

The personalities of Isaac Barrow and Isaac Newton were in many respects polar opposites. As a boy Newton did not often engage with his fellows; Barrow took great delight in fighting and he developed a powerful physique. Newton rarely laughed. Barrow spiced his lectures with wit, even self-mockery; "merry and cheerful" is John Aubrey's description of his humor. Newton hardly ever moved outside of Lincolnshire, Cambridge, and London, whereas Barrow undertook a long continental voyage, defended himself valiantly when his ship was attacked by pirates, and traveled to the East. Newton was a Whig and a unitarian, Barrow a Royalist and a devout Anglican in holy orders who became the King's Chaplain when he vacated the Lucasian Chair. Newton rarely used images in his writing and cultivated a sparse style; Barrow's prose is full of conceits and literary inventions, rich with classical allusions which he savored for their own sake. Newton, who was shy in public, was not noted for his oratory; Barrow was one of the great preachers of the Restoration, whose sermons were collected and published in voluminous editions. He was universally loved in the College, unlike his successor, who was never too popular with his colleagues even when they elected him to Parliament. Newton hardly ever acknowledged the intellectual worth of others; Barrow could praise his fellows profusely and with conviction.

Perhaps nothing could more dramatically render the contrast between the solemnity and somberness of Isaac Newton and the natural gaiety of his predecessor than Barrow's oration delivered on the anniversary of his inaugural as Regius Professor of Greek. He had been lecturing to empty halls, and now voiced his satisfaction in a playful academic excursion.

Since you bade me that long farewell a year ago I have sat on my Chair incessantly alone—and I am sure none of you will, as an eye-witness, challenge the accuracy of that statement even if I should be lying—like a Prometheus chained to his rock, or like a supreme judge in that Solipsian State which some one has lately fabricated. I speak not to mountains and woods, but to these walls and benches, murmuring my Greek sentences, figures, phrases and etymologies searched out of every source, just like an Attic owl segregated from other birds. I and my Sophocles have acted on an empty stage, without even his third actor or any chorus, even of boys. There has been no one to accompany the singing or to applaud the dancing or to interrupt the speeches. For if some wandering Freshman or some shipwrecked Sophister was carried by a chance current or an unlucky gale to these coasts—a thing I can hardly remember to have happened—he would scarcely give a glance at the land or listen to more than three words before rushing from my Polyphemus cave, as in dread of being devoured by a barbarous little Grecian, if he should stay.... And why should I blame you for what I esteem a great kindness? ... I have inhabited this large and commodious domicile alone and undisturbed by a jostling and contentious crowd. I have breathed an atmosphere uncontaminated by the foul breath of yawners or by the fetid stench of perspiration. Wearied by no derisive hoots, distressed by no frowning foreheads, far from every fault-finding Momus and every hypercritical Zoilus, in a safe skin, in tranquil peace, and in deep silence I have sat in an easy chair.[2]

Whatever their temperamental differences, Barrow and Newton shared some of the same habits, and it is difficult to know the extent to which Newton came to imitate the older man in personal respects, in addition to following him in the study of the calculus, optics, chronology, and church history. Barrow was notoriously slovenly about his clothes, Aubrey relates: "He was by no means a spruce man, not a Dr. Smirke, but most negligent in his dresse. As he was walking one day in St. James's parke, his hatt up, his cloake halfe on and halfe off, a gent. came behind him and clapt him on the Shoulder and sayd, Well goe thy wayes for the veriest scholar that ever I mett with."[3] Newton's sizar has left a similar sketch: "He very rarely went to dine in the hall, except on some public days, and then if he has not been minded, would go very carelessly, with shoes down at heels, stockings untied, surplice on, and his head scarcely combed."[4] Barrow ate and slept little, as did Newton. Barrow was not one for polishing his scientific works and he had a way of leaving the details of corrections to Newton. When Newton became a renowned scientist, he too entrusted the emendation and publication of his works to disciples. Newton would have scorned the idea that he was patterning himself after another man, but there are too many examples of intellectual inheritance to accept his rare references to Barrow as an adequate measure of the older man's influence.[5] He was not a particularly grateful man, this Isaac son of Isaac who happened to succeed another Isaac in the Lucasian Chair. Though Barrow treated the younger man as a son, giving him presents,[6] Newton's conduct toward him was not without ambivalence. Barrow was a fostering father, but also something of a rival in a covert way.

Upon assuming the Lucasian Professorship in 1669 Newton chose to begin his lectures with optics, conscious that he was about to surpass his predecessor by far. His inaugural made respectful obeisance to Barrow, whose work on colors he could in effect have demolished if he made known his new discoveries, recorded in the University Library notebook.[7]

The late Invention of Telescopes has so exercised most of the Geometers, that they seem to have left nothing unattempted in Opticks, no room for farther Improvements. And besides, since the *Dissertations,* which you have not long since heard from this Place, were composed with so great a Variety of optical Matters, such Plenty of new Discoveries, and that confirmed by accurate Demonstrations; it may seem a vain Endeavour and a useless Labour, if I shall again undertake the handling this Science. But since I observe the Geometers hitherto mistaking in a particular Property of Light, that belongs to its Refractions, tacitly founding their Demonstrations on a certain Physical Hypothesis not well established; I judge it will not be unacceptable, if I bring the Principles of this Science to a more strict Examination, and subjoin, what I have discovered in these Matters, and found to be true by manifold Experience, to what my reverend Predecessor has last delivered from this Place.[8]

Newton's failure to correct flagrant errors in the printed version of Barrow's course, which he supervised, seems a betrayal of confidence that makes him undeserving of the elegant praise lavished on him in the introduction to the text:

For when I resolv'd to publish, I could not bear the Pains of reading over again a great Part of these Things; either from my being tired with them, or not caring to undergo the Pains and Study in new modelling them: But I have done in this as weakly Mothers, who give up their Offspring to the Care of their Friends, either to Nurse and bring up, or abandon to the wide World. One of which (for I think my self bound to Name them) is Mr. Isaac Newton, my Collegue, a Man of great Learning and Sagacity, who revised my Copy and noted such Things as wanted Correction, and even gave me some of his own, which you will see here and there interspersed with mine, not without their due Commendations.[9]

Newton's withholding of his knowledge and allowing some of Barrow's ludicrous mistakes to appear in print might be accounted for by deference, doubt about his own discoveries of the nature of light that ran counter to all contemporary speculations, or a desire not to mix his treasure with Barrow's dross, depending upon how one views the relationship. Contemporaries like Roger North were aware that Newton had failed to bestow much recognition on his predecessor's works, though this did not concern Barrow in the slightest.

The date when Barrow and Newton first met cannot be precisely documented. There is no firm basis for the anecdote that when Barrow examined Newton on Euclid in April 1664 in connection with a Trinity scholarship he found him deficient. Stukeley has it as tradition that when Newton stood for his Bachelor of Arts degree he did not do well and was "put to second posing." His account of subsequent relations with Barrow, whom he calls Newton's tutor, is the only one we have for the early years in Cambridge. "His tutor . . . conceiv'd the highest opinion and early prognostic of his excellence; would frequently say that truly he himself knew something of the mathematics, still he reckon'd himself but a child in comparison of his pupil Newton. He faild not, upon all occasions, to give a just *encomium* of him, and whenever a difficult problem was brought to him to solve, he refer'd them immediately to Newton."[10] Stukeley may be in error and commentators may have exaggerated Barrow's influence on Newton; but I find a recent dismissal of Barrow too sharp a reversal.

From a late manuscript of Newton's we learn that he had attended Barrow's lectures in 1664, but he was vague about their content.[11] Substantiated information about Barrow's active interest in Newton does not appear until 1669, when they were already closely associated. By midsummer of that year Isaac Barrow is enthusiastic in his letters to the mathematician John Collins, to whom he communicates Newton's discoveries like a proud father, referring to him as his "friend," though he is prohibited from naming him. "A friend of mine here, that hath a very excellent genius to those things, brought me the other day some papers, wherein he hath sett downe methods of calculating the dimensions of magnitudes like that of Mr Mercator concerning the hyperbola, but very generall, as also of resolving aequations; which I suppose will please you. . . ."[12] After much persuasion Barrow convinced Newton to let Collins see the papers, but he wanted them back after Collins had perused them, as Barrow wrote on July 31.[13] Finally, on August 20, he revealed the identity of the author and with Newton's permission allowed the papers to be shown to Lord William Brouncker, President of the Royal Society. The barriers of Newton's secretiveness and retentiveness could be breached, but only through the insistent coaxing of admirers. "I am glad my friends paper giveth you so much Satisfaction," Barrow wrote to Collins, "his name is Mr Newton; a fellow of our College, & very young (being but the second yeest [youngest] Master of Arts) but of an extraordinary genius & proficiency in these things." The full text of this letter, now in the Royal Society, hints at a more extensive interchange between Barrow and Newton about his mathematical papers than is allowed by Whiteside: "For the rest which you propound about them I shall discourse with him when I returne, & returne you answer."[14] The absence of Barrow's name in Newton's early papers is not conclusive. There is Flam-

steed's word that Barrow himself proudly carried Newton's telescope to the Royal Society, the first recognition of his worth in the
London scientific world. Newton had access to Barrow's rich private
library of science, theology, and history (the great Trinity Library
had only just been projected), and after Barrow's death he had
something to do with preparing its inventory, which for some unknown reason has ended up in Oxford.[15] Whatever important texts
of the great scientists, ancient and modern, were available in print
at this period were in Barrow's collection, and contemporary philosophers, even the heretical Spinoza and Hobbes, were represented
along with the orthodox divines.

Whether Barrow made way for Newton in the Lucasian Chair
because of a recognition of his superiority, one traditional explanation, or out of a desire to devote himself more completely to his
ministry remains a question. A letter from John Collins to James
Gregory, November 25, 1669, announcing the appointment throws
no light on Barrow's motives, though it is clear that he directed the
choice of his successor, "whom he mentioneth in his Optick Praeface
as a very ingenious person."[16] In 1673 he was back in Cambridge on
Charles II's appointment as Master of Trinity. The Senior Fellows
were delighted, and Newton wrote John Collins with unwonted ex-
uberance: "We are here very glad that we shall enjoy Dr Barrow
again especially in the circumstances of Master, nor doth any rejoyce
at it more then Sr Your obliged humble Servant Newton."[17] But
Barrow's incumbency was brief, for he died in 1676 after having
taken the opium he had learned about in the East during a pulmo-
nary attack.

Dead, Barrow continued to play a significant role in Newton's
career. His letters were the primary testimony to Newton's invention of the calculus. Newton's letter of December 10, 1672, to John
Collins, in which he expressed pleasure that foreign mathematicians
had "falln into the same method of drawing Tangents wth me,"[18]
an early priority claim, was careful to call upon the witness of Isaac
Barrow: "I remember I once occasionally told Dr Barrow when he
was about to publish his Lectures that I had such a method of draw-

ing Tangents but some divertisment or other hindered me from describing it to him."[19]

In addition to Babington, More, and Barrow, Newton had ties with other older men in the 1660's and 1670's; but with the exception of John Wickins, the roommate who remains nothing more than a name, and Francis Aston, a man of small parts, there are no coevals who have left a trace in his life beyond the piddling undergraduate record of his lending them money and their repaying it. The acquaintances and friends are either older or much younger. As they approach his age there is likely to be conflict, especially if they are men of outstanding capacity or merit. John Collins, to whom Barrow had sent Newton's papers, had a wide European correspondence and a passion for seeking out men of genius far superior to himself to serve them. Henry Oldenburg, first Secretary of the Royal Society, not only was a central clearinghouse for scientific papers, but constantly urged publication upon scientists who might otherwise have tended to shut themselves off from their fellows. There were those who charged that he fired jealousies among them in the course of his activities as an intermediary; but his tireless attention to foreign and domestic letters helped to make the Royal Society of London the most prestigious scientific body in the world, and toward Newton at least this heavy activist from Bremen showed a measure of sensitivity.

And there were John Wallis, Savilian Professor of Mathematics at Oxford and a founder of the Royal Society, and Christopher Wren, Savilian Professor of Astronomy. More was born in 1614, Wallis in 1616, Collins in 1624, Oldenburg in 1626, Wren in 1632. All of them were many years Newton's senior and could hardly have been regarded as contemporary rivals. Wallis was old enough to deliver at one point a rather straightforward admonition to Newton that he ought to publish his calculus and his optics after the *Principia*. His letter was couched in terms of such candor that they might have drawn a sharp retort if Newton had not highly esteemed him (he was one of the few men the use of whose mathematical works Newton ever acknowledged).[20] Collins and Oldenburg were ideal scientific friends, not competitive creators, men who nourished Newton's genius with their admiration and encouragement. To accept favors without being able to reciprocate on a quid pro quo basis was difficult for Newton, who had an aversion to being in anyone's debt, and on more than one occasion he was uneasy about receiving Collins' bounty; but generally his relations with these older men were amicable. He confided his plans to them and sometimes followed their paternal advice.

Newton was allowed to retain his Fellowship at Trinity, along with the Lucasian Professorship, despite the fact that he was a layman, because Charles II provided by letters patent that the holder of the chair need not take holy orders. In the period prior to the Restoration men who had a passion for science and were not independently wealthy like Robert Boyle almost invariably became either divines or medical doctors. As divines they usually attached themselves to noble patrons who provided them with a living, and they might go on to high ecclesiastical office. In this respect Newton was of a new breed. There was only a handful of university professorships in mathematics and astronomy, and he had one of them at the age of twenty-seven. The stipend was not munificent, but it allowed for a great measure of independence. Though for decades he inhabited a monastic cell in Trinity, permitting few outsiders to invade his privacy, the isolation was of his own making. These English university chambers—Pearson had allotted him the Spirituall Chamber—had superiorities over the monkish ones. Newton lived there by his own rule, albeit a stricter regimen than prevailed in many a religious order.

If, to pursue the analogy, the Master of a great college was like an abbot, Newton had been fortunate in his first superior, Barrow. The two who followed were insignificant men, who cut no figure in the intellectual world in which he lived. Newton withdrew into himself and paid them virtually no heed. After Barrow's death, there was no one in the Master's Lodge to draw him out of his self-imposed sequestration. The character of the Master of Trinity who succeeded Barrow is well known through the assiduousness of Roger North, whose *Lives of the Norths* (his three brothers), written in a vivid if somewhat esoteric style, is official biography of a peculiar, almost naive frankness. John North, the brother who headed Trinity, is delineated as a man of feeble constitution, inclining to the effeminate. As an undergraduate at the University, "when he was in bed alone, he durst not trust his countenance above the clothes. For some time he lay with his tutor. . . ."[21] Later in life, a divine and a Greek scholar, he indulged in a special "petit entertainment" in his study, "and that was keeping of great house spiders in wide-mouth glasses, such as men keep tobacco in. When he had them safe in hold, he supplied them with crumbs of bread, which they ate rather than starve: but their regale was flies, which he sometime caught and put to them. When their imprisonment appeared inevitable, they fell to their trade of making webs. . . . It pleased him to observe the animals manage their interest in the great work of taking their prey."[22] As Clerk of the Closet to Charles II he had stuck to the view, contrary to general opinion, that the Restoration court could boast as many truly pious and religious people as could be found in any other "resort." John North wrote polemics against Arians and Socinians with the same fervor that Pearson had composed great popular apologies for Anglicanism: little did either of them reckon that in their very midst they harbored a secret enemy of their faith, Isaac Newton.

Though John North was weakly, he looked "vegete and sanguine, and, as some used to jest, his features were scandalous, as showing rather a madam *entravestie*, than a bookworm. . . . And he used his friends as spies upon himself to discover his own failings; and, for that end, used to be very sharp upon the company; and if any one, that he might be free with, had a sore place, he was sure to give it some rubs, and harder and harder, till they must needs feel, and then they fell to retaliating, which was his desire; often saying that he loved, between jest and earnest, to tell people of their faults, that they might pay him in the same coin by telling him his own."[23] To talk about his sadomasochism in the modern manner would seem pallid after the more graphic language of his literary brother.

In his autobiography Roger North chronicled the vain attempts of the family to free the Master of Trinity from his hypochondriacal fixations and the ministrations of his physicians, and he recorded the circumstances of the final collapse in the medical language of the time. "There he fell again to his austerities, rising at five, studying all the morning and afternoon, no refreshment but a dish of coffee, and very anxious about college business, his throat troubling him, physic dispiriting him, the vent of humours that nature had found at his throat stopped, and forced to break open a new channel, whereupon once in a passion with some disorderly scholar which touched the trigger and made the eruption, the humour broke out upon his brain, and he fell down in an apoplexy, which turned to an hemiplegia, in which state he lived miserably three or four years, his condition being fitter for oblivion than history."[24] John North died in 1683 and was at his own request buried in the antechapel where, as he predicted with black humor, "the Fellows might trample upon him dead as they had done living."[25] Newton's relations with him had been amicable enough, though inconsequential. In the one extant letter addressed to him Newton, with perspicacity, caution, and modesty, refrained from elaborate comment upon his elder brother Francis North's *A Philosophical Essay of Musick* (1677), "for want of experiments & skill in Musick," and promised to call at his lodgings.[26]

The Master who followed North was John Montagu, fourth son of the first Earl of Sandwich, who had received his Master of Arts *jure natalium* and his Doctor of Divinity by royal mandate. In 1683 he was appointed Master of Trinity by the Crown, and it was during his incumbency that the creation of the *Principia* took place under the roof of his College. Stories of an even further relaxation of discipline during his tenure are frequent, and his administration enjoyed an ill repute. He was Vice-chancellor of the University in 1687 and 1688 and continued on as Master of Trinity for more than a decade longer. Montagu formally welcomed the Settlement and dutifully wrote Latin verse in honor of William and Mary.

During the rule of North and Montagu as Masters of Trinity the number of elections to Fellowships by royal mandate increased—in violation of ancient statutes—to the point where under James II this was the sole way to preferment. The colleges became a part of the ecclesiastical patronage system in which authority and favor were exercised by the king and his courtiers. By the time of the Glorious Revolution the seniority system had made reform from within virtually impossible, as the place-holding Fellows were reluctant to allow the intrusion of scholars. The solitude of Isaac Newton among these academic mediocrities was rarely broken.

The deterioration continued even after Newton's departure in 1696, until the appointment by a Commission of Bishops (William III cautiously avoided involvement in the selection) of that formidable deus ex machina Richard Bentley, the great pioneer of classical erudition, author of the *Dissertation upon the Epistles of Phalaris,* who initiated his term of office by publicly accusing Fellows and students alike of sloth and drunkenness. Trinity had fallen into low estate, but the greedy, tactless Bentley had no talent for rehabilitating it.[27] For forty years this arrogant, domineering administrator kept the College and the University in continual turmoil, but this was one war in which Newton, who no longer resided in the College, did not actively enlist. Bentley served him in various capacities during his own scientific controversies, and though Newton spoke ill of him on occasion, as he did of virtually all his friends, there was no serious friction between them.

In contrast with the two political purges that had preceded Newton's arrival and the interminable squabbles that harassed Trinity College during Richard Bentley's incumbency, life at the University during the first twenty-five years of Newton's residence there was relatively placid, if dull, especially after Barrow's death. The Lucasian Chair required Newton to give public lectures and those from January 1670 to October 1683 are extant, the number varying from three to ten a year. He had few auditors and hardly any tutees.

Of the few descriptions of Newton's day-to-day behavior at the height of his university career, two come from colorless men, each of whom regarded him by his own feeble light. They caught him at different moments. John Wickins, his roommate for many years, watched him admiringly and even copied papers for him, but left no account himself. About two years Newton's junior, Wickins became a Fellow of the College, and in 1684 was presented to the living of Stoke Edith, near Monmouth. Since they shared quarters from 1665 to 1673 and perhaps longer, the absence of any important recollections from this divine is one of the most unfortunate losses in our portrait. About their relations in Trinity we have nothing but the tradition reported by Wickins' son Nicolas in a letter written in 1728. One day John Wickins retired into the walks and found Newton "solitary & dejected." When both discovered that they disliked their disorderly chamberfellows they decided to room and "chum" together. Nicolas recalls his father's stories about Newton's "forgetfullness of his food, when intent upon his studies; and of his rising in a pleasant manner with the satisfaction of having found out some Proposition; without any concern for, or seeming Want of his Nights Sleep which he was sensible he had lost thereby." Once John Wickins said to Newton that he had turned grey by thirty from deep study, and Newton's reply was touched with a trace of humor: "He would jest with the Experimts he made so often wth Quick Silver, as if from thence he took so soon that Colour." Wickins is also a witness to Newton's hypochondria and self-doctoring; since Newton suspected that he had a tendency to consumption he drank a potion of Lucatellus Balsam which he himself mixed.[28]

Humphrey Newton (no relation), his sizar from 1685 to 1690, had eyes that saw nothing but externals; he was probably intimidated by Newton and noticed little but his austere manner. Humphrey had been sent up to Cambridge from Grantham in the last year of King Charles II's reign to act as Newton's amanuensis. He was with him during the preparation of the *Principia,* which he transcribed for the press, and Newton afterward blamed his ignorance for the many errors in the first edition.[29] More than four decades later, Humphrey Newton put his impressions in writing for Conduitt, and reported them orally to Stukeley. The Newton he described was in his middle forties and is a verbal counterpart of the first portrait, by Godfrey Kneller—though Humphrey's letter is not graced by much penetration or insight. "His carriage then was very meek, sedate, & humble, never seemingly angry, of profound thought, his countenance mild, pleasant, and comely." Just as Mrs. Vincent created the image of the boy Newton, Humphrey Newton is responsible for the stereotype of the absent-minded professor and indefatigable worker.

I never knew him to take any recreation or pastime either in riding out to take the air, walking, bowling, or any other exercise whatever, thinking all hours lost that was not spent in his studies, to which he kept so close that he seldom left his chamber unless at term time, when he read in the schools as being Lucasianus Professor, where so few went to hear him, and fewer understood him, that ofttimes he did in a manner, for want of hearers, read to the walls. . . . So intent, so serious upon his studies that he ate very sparingly, nay, ofttimes he has forgot to eat at all, so that, going into his chamber, I have found his mess untouched, of which, when I have reminded him, he would reply—"Have I!" and then making to the table, would eat a bit or two standing, for I cannot say I ever saw him sit at table by himself. . . . He very rarely went to bed till two or three of the clock, sometimes not until five or six, lying about four or five hours, especially at spring or fall of the leaf, at which times he used to employ about six weeks in his elaboratory, the fire scarcely going out either night or day; he sitting up, one night as I did another, till he had finished his chemical experiments, in the performances of which he was the most accurate, strict, exact. What his aim might be I was not able to penetrate into, but his pains, his diligence at those set times made me think he aimed at something beyond the reach of human art and industry.

Humphrey Newton recorded obsessive little traits. "He was very curious in his garden, which was never out of order, in which he would at some seldom times take a short walk or two, not enduring to see a weed in it." His moderation was proverbial: "I cannot say I ever saw him drink either wine, ale, or beer excepting meals, and then but very sparingly. . . ." His religious observances were limited to Sunday forenoon attendance at St. Mary's Church, and he was seldom seen at chapel. The recluse had few friends. He rarely received visitors or went calling except in the case of two or three persons—a Mr. Ellis (later master of Caius College), a Mr. Laughton who was keeper of the Trinity library, and the Italian chemist John Francis Vigani of Verona, later Professor of Chemistry at Trinity, "in whose company he took much delight and pleasure at an evening when he came to wait upon him." This was the friend whom he later dismissed for telling a joke about a nun. His entertaining was largely limited to the Masters of colleges. "When invited to a treat, which was very seldom, he used to return it very handsomely, freely, and with much satisfaction to himself." A few foreigners had begun to visit him and he received them "with a great deal of freedom, candour, and respect."[30]

Though Humphrey Newton said he had heard him laugh but once, when somebody asked what use and benefit in life the study of Euclid might be, Stukeley later testified that he had often seen him merry and "that upon moderate occasions." He agreed that he was of a "very serious and compos'd frame of mind," but denied that he was morose. "He had in his disposition a natural pleasantness of temper, and much good nature . . . attended neither with gayety nor levity. He usd a good many sayings, bordering on joke and wit. In company he behavd very agreably; courteous, affable, he was easily made to smile, if not to laugh."[31] The two testimonies are not wholly contradictory; smiling may have been an acquired characteristic of Newton's London days.

The first and most famous picture of Isaac Newton is the half-length portrait in the collection of the Earl of Portsmouth painted by Godfrey Kneller in 1689. A three-quarter length version in Kensington Palace is probably from Kneller's studio; Kneller, who was immensely fashionable and was deluged with commissions, often made quick sketches or painted a head, leaving the rest of the work to one of his numerous assistants. Newton, aged about forty-seven, is presented with his own shoulder-length gray hair. A white shirt, open at the neck, is largely concealed by an academic gown from the right sleeve of which spidery fingers emerge. The face is angular, the sharp chin cleft, the mouth delicately shaped. A long, thin nose is elevated at the bridge. Beneath brows knit in concentration, blue, rather protuberant eyes are fixed in a gaze that is abstracted.

The only description of Newton at the height of his powers which really has a third dimension comes from Henry More's sensitive pen and was occasioned by their divergent interpretations of Revelations, differences that now appear esoteric but were matters of profound concern to trained expositors of the word of God. In his latter days More was deeply absorbed in the *Clavis Apocalyptica* of Joseph Mede, a commentator who was also Newton's principal guide to the reading of the prophecy of the weeks in Daniel.[32] In a letter to the famous preacher and divine Dr. John Sharp on August 16, 1680, the aged More, writing affectionately of Newton despite their disagreement, feels hopeful that he will ultimately be persuaded to the truth. In the reflected light of More's gentle and saintly character Newton appears to have a wistful charm, though he preserves his dogged obstinacy.

As Dr Burton [Hezekiah Burton] at the Commencement so I remember you either here at the time or at London before asked me about Mr Newton and my agreement in Apocalyptical Notions. And I remember I told you both, how well we were agreed. For after his reading of the Exposition of the Apocalypse which I gave him, he came to my chamber, where he seem'd to me not onely to approve my Exposition as coherent and perspicuous throughout from the beginning to the end, but (by the manner of his countenance which is ordinarily melancholy and thoughtfull, but then mighty lightsome and chearfull, and by the free profession of what satisfaction he took therein) to be in a manner transported. So that I took it for granted, that what peculiar conceits he had of his own had vanished. But since I perceive he recoyles into a former conceit he had entertained, that the seven Vials commence with the seven Trumpets, which I always look'd upon as a very extravagant conceit, and he will not have the Epistles to the Seven Churches to be a prophecy of the state of the Church from the beginning to the end of the world. He will also have the three dayes and half of the witnesses lyeing slaine, to be three yeares and a half after their mournfull witnessing. Mr Newton has a singular Genius to Mathematicks, and I take him to be a good serious man. But he pronounces of the Seven Churches, not having yett read my Exposition of them, which I wrote by itself on purpose, concerning which another Mathematicall head, noted for that faculty in Cambridge, writ to me, that with Mathematicall evidence I had demonstrated that truth. And I do not doubt but when he shall have read my three fold Appendage to my Prophecyes of Daniell, two parts whereof are, the one to make good that vision of the Seven Churches is such a [prophecy] as I declare, the other to prove that the beasts are all to be [placed] in the seventh Trumpet after the rising of the witnesses (for I find him already something inclinable) that he will be of the same minde with myself. When yett if he be not, it will signify nothing to me. For any divine assent to things from their evidence is antecedent to any others approbation thereof, and not to be thus immediately assured in himself but to expect the voice of another is like that fearfull and unskilfull condition of raw Peter-gunners, that turn their faces [from] their muskets, when they should give fire, and aske their neighbour gunner, does it touch, Tom? So hard a thing [is] it for me not to be merry at the most serious thinges.

Not satisfied with this long-winded defense of his method of interpretation, More returned to it again in a postscript. Throughout, the letter glows with his high regard for Newton. And despite his insistence that a man must follow his own independent insight irrespective of the opinion of others, he is clearly pleased with Newton's praise of his composition in its generality. "When my Exposition of Daniel comes out with this Appendage, I hope you will easily discover that Mr. N. was over sudden in his conceits. I have told him myself of this appendage, and that if he be not convinced thereby, he has free leave from me to enjoy his own opinions. We have a free converse and friendship, which these differences will not disturb. He does still professe that my Exposition is a perspicuous and coherent peece. . . ."[33] Their pleasant relations continued until More's death in 1687, and Newton was bequeathed a funeral ring. With More gone, one of Newton's few personal ties to the University was severed.

The Father Alban Francis case of 1687 was a dramatic episode in Isaac Newton's tranquil and uneventful career as a member of the congregation of the University. The man who had been unconcerned about college affairs and displayed no great interest in students or Fellows suddenly became embroiled in politics. A key to his behavior, which at first sight seems totally out of character, is to be found in that militant, puritan antipapism which runs throughout his life. Here was an opportunity to rise up in righteous indignation against the living embodiment of radical evil, against the Trinitarian idol-worshipers, the defilers, the sensualists, who were the opposite of his image of himself and his people, the true believers in one God the Creator. Though the manner of his protest was juridical, beneath the forms there was genuine passion, even courage and daring, for the dangers of reprisal at the hands of a Papist king were great. This is the one instance of Newton's flagrantly defying recognized authority.

Popery was the bugbear with which English children grew up. Protestants burning at the stake in Foxe's *Book of Martyrs,* tales of the Massacre of St. Bartholomew, and the Great Fire of London were among the heinous crimes for which Catholics were blamed, and more devilish acts were expected from them. On the site in Pudding Lane where the fire had begun, the Lord Mayor had the following words inscribed: "Here by the Permission of Heaven Hell broke loose upon this Protestant City from the malicious hearts of barbarous papists."[34] The royal sons of a Catholic princess, brought up in Catholic courts, could hardly have been expected to share this prevalent feeling, and the chasm between monarchs and subjects was unbridgeable. Charles II tried to compromise, James II was openly Catholic.

In 1686, not long after James had ascended the throne, the Earl of Sunderland, Secretary of State, ordered the Bishop of London to suspend Dr. John Sharp—a friend of More's and an acquaintance, at least, of Newton's—as Rector of St. Giles. Dr. Sharp, a popular preacher who had a reputation for great piety, was considered to have reflected adversely upon the King's religion in one of his sermons. The royal offensive soon shifted from Sharp to the Bishop of London himself, after the appointment of a Court of High Commission for the Inspecting Ecclesiastical Affairs under George, Lord Jeffreys. The dangers of Papist persecution were moving close to persons whom Newton and his friends knew. Henry More's last years were deeply troubled by the fear that James II would return

England to Catholicism. Once Richard Baxter was imprisoned, the author of *A Modest Enquiry into the Mystery of Iniquity* and *The Antidote against Idolatry* could not rest secure.[35] The spirit of toleration that More preached and Locke and Newton both wrote about did not embrace a neutral attitude toward a militant Catholic Church.

It soon became apparent that there would be attempts to use the universities as instrumentalities for the insinuation of Catholic influence. On February 9, 1687, the Vice-chancellor of Cambridge University, Dr. John Pechell (or Peachell), whose principal claim to fame was his bibulousness (his telltale nose was so large that even Pepys shunned his company), received a letter under His Majesty's sign manual ordering that one Alban Francis, a Benedictine monk, be admitted to the degree of Master of Arts without taking the oaths of loyalty to the established Church. The University had occasionally dispensed with the oaths in conferring honorary degrees upon ambassadors and foreign princes (including a Mohammedan), but this new case was seen as part of a plot to infiltrate the University with Papists. The universities were bastions of the Anglican Church, and though their statutes had already been eroded by appointments under royal order, they bridled when it came to allowing a Benedictine monk into their midst. Similar incidents were brewing at Oxford, and all the participants in the contest were aware of the broader implications of this attempt to break down the law that excluded Catholics from Cambridge.[36]

Newton reacted sharply. There is a draft of a letter (in Humphrey Newton's hand) dated February 19, in which his position is set forth with lawyerlike precision and numerous precedents are cited. The Whig theory of the monarchy is succinctly expounded. "Here's a strong report in the Town that a Mandamus has been brought to the Vice-chancellor," he wrote to an unknown correspondent,

to admit one F. Francis a Benedictine Monck to be a Master of Arts, and that the Vicechancellor sent to the Chancellor to endeavour to gett the same recall'd but could not prevail; wch was an error in him, For all honest men are obliged by the Laws of God & Man to obey the King's lawfull Commands.

3. Isaac Barrow, 1676

4. Henry More, 1675

But if his Majesty be advised to require a Matter wch cannot be done by Law, no Man can suffer for neglect of it. The Vice-chancellor cannot by Law admit one to that degree, unless he take the Oaths of Suprem: & allegiance wch are enjoyn'd by 3 or 4 Statutes; & it is not to be said he disobeys the Kings Commands when he is ready to fulfill them if the party be capable to receive the Act commanded: wch this Monk cannot be, & 'tis not probable that a Convocation can be induced to give Grace for the degree to an unqualified Person. And tho it should be expressed in the Mandamus that his Maj. dispenses wth those Oaths, yet that cannot excuse the Vicechancellor for he is no judg thereof, but he knows that the Law of the Land enjoyns the taking of the oaths; & if he admits any one without doing it he is indightable for the same. & if he modestly refuse to admit this person he can run noe risque in it. & if F. Francis be acquainted wth the Obstacles in his way in a decent manner, & is not satisfied therewith, let him take his remedy at Law, & to be sure the V. Chanc. will hear noe more of him. & by civilly standing his ground he will save the University.[37]

There ensued a series of intricate legal maneuvers, through which the members of the University hoped to get the mandamus rescinded without incurring the displeasure of the King. It was suggested that a grace be proposed to a vote of the congregation of the University; but this procedure was dropped because a grace required the unanimous consent of the heads of the colleges and one of them was a Papist. Instead, to avoid a vote, members testified to their concurrence spontaneously and voluntarily, sending a notice verbally to the Vice-chancellor. The Duke of Albemarle, Chancellor of the University, advised a formal petition, and one was adopted by the members of the congregation with only a few dissents, though it was decided to send it by the word of two messengers to avoid any "tumultuary" appearance. The messengers of the University could not gain the Earl of Sunderland's intercession, and on February 24 a second letter from the King arrived warning of the dangers of disobedience. After further petition from the University, bolstered by legal opinions, the Vice-chancellor and deputies of the Senate were ordered to appear before the Lord Commissioners in the Council Chamber on April 21. Henry More was still alive, though ailing, as the Father Francis affair reached this critical juncture. According to the Conduitt papers—which means that Newton still talked of the episode three decades later—he behaved heroically, strengthening the resolve of a vacillating group of delegates when they were prepared to accept a compromise to the effect that Father Francis would be admitted if it were understood that his case set no precedent. On the very eve of publication of the *Principia,* Newton risked his person by appearing as one of the delegates from the University before the redoubtable Lord Jeffreys. Newton's capacity throughout life to compartmentalize his studies and his activities, even to prevent the intrusion of deep anxieties into his work, bespeaks a powerful organization of his person. Only a mighty wave could overwhelm him.

On April 21 a large and noisy crowd were assembled in the Council Chamber. The commissioners who sat in judgment were Lord President Sunderland, Lord Mulgrave, the Earl of Huntington, the Lord Bishop of Durham, the Lord Bishop of Rochester and the Lord Chief Justice Herbert. The chief of the seven commissioners was the notorious George, Lord Jeffreys, fresh from the "bloody assizes" in the north, a drunkard, a master of scurrilous invective, who did James II's bidding to the very end. The representatives of the University were given an opportunity to prepare their answer to the mandamus in writing, and there was a postponement of the case. Among Newton's papers are five drafts, not in his hand, of "The answers to some Questions propounded by the Lord Ch: at the appearance of the Vice ch: and deputies of the senate of the University of Camb. before the Lords Comissioners May 7th 1687." Newton's autograph addendum to one of the texts is so outspoken and vehement that it may not have been submitted, but it is noteworthy as a blunt manifesto of his antipapism, dislike of foreigners, and real concern for "the Nation." He is an Englishman who takes seriously the role of the university in the preservation of his culture. "Men of the Roman ffaith have been put into Masterships of Colleges. The entrance into fellowships is as open. And if forreigners be once incorporated twill be as open to them as others. A mixture of Papist & Protestants in the same University can neither subsist happily nor long together. And if the fountains once be dryed up the streams hitherto diffused thence throughout the Nation must soon fall of. Tis not their preferments but their religion & Church men of conscience are concerned for & if it must fall they implore this mercy that it may fall by the hands of others."[38]

Before the ogre Jeffreys, Dr. Pechell, according to the contemporary historian Gilbert Burnet, put on a pitiable performance. "He was a very honest, but a very weak man. He made a poor defense. And it is no small reflection on that great body, that their chief magistrate was so little able to assert their privileges, or to justify their proceedings. He was treated with great contempt by Jeffreys."[39] When one of the delegates tried to intervene, Jeffreys dismissed him with the sally, "Nay, good Doctor, you were never Vice-Chancellor yet: when you are we may consider you." Another delegate received the same scornful rebuff: "Nay, look you that young gentleman expects to be Vice-Chancellor too, when you are Sir you may speak. Till then it will more become you to forbear." There was much confusion at the trial over why the House had originally taken an informal and unprescribed manner of voicing its opinion, instead of putting the matter to a vote. Newton's name appears as one of those who had intervened with the Vice-chancellor urging defiance of the order until the King had been petitioned.

Pechell was adjudged guilty of "an act of great disobedience"; he was deprived of his Vice-chancellorship and suspended from his Mastership of Magdalene College during the King's pleasure. The delegates reacted to his dismissal with great dignity before the commissioners. Though they insisted that with the elimination of Pechell they no longer represented the Senate, they answered Jeffreys' questions and forcefully demonstrated the legality of the University's action. Unmoved, he sent them packing with a stern injunction: "Gentlemen, the best way will be a ready obedience to his Majesty's commands for the future and by giving a good example to others to make some amends for the ill example has been given you. Therefore I shall say to you what the Scripture says, and the rather because I see most of you are divines. Go your way and sin no more lest a worse thing befall you."[40]

Newton kept a record of the hearings and numerous legal documents in support of the University's position, a sign of his deep commitment. The Alban Francis affair was no minor incident of the last years of the Stuart monarchy. The strong response in the universities forced the King to recede from his position; but he had become too enmeshed with the Papists to save his throne. Ultimately Newton was victorious: two years after the proceedings in the Council Chamber, Lord Jeffreys died ignominiously a prisoner in the Tower and James II was in exile. In 1689 a pamphlet appeared, entitled *The Cambridge Case, being an exact narrative of all the proceedings against the Vice-Chancellour and Delegates of that University, for refusing to admit Alban Francis, a Benedictine Monk, to the degree of Master of Arts, without taking the Oaths,* which accords with the facts in Newton's papers. Though his name is not mentioned, the narrative referring merely to "delegates," he had become a public figure in a minor way, a prominent enemy of Stuart usurpation and papism. The hearing before Judge Jeffreys was also published in *A Complete Collection of State Trials,* where specific reference is made to Newton's role.

Shortly after Newton was sent up to the Convention Parliament in 1688 as a representative of the University, an alteration took place in him. Earlier friendships with two young men, the astronomer Edmond Halley and Charles Montague, a younger son of a noble family, which had begun in Cambridge, flowered in London (Charles Montague's star was rising at court). Ties were also established with Locke and Fatio de Duillier. As a member of the Convention Parliament, although silent during debates, Newton masterminded the transition of the University from the Stuart to the Orange allegiance in a series of letters addressed to Dr. John Covel, Vice-chancellor of the University, on the intricate problems of oath-taking, which troubled the consciences of some members of the congregation. In this situation Newton's legal casuistry was effective, and there were no disturbances.[41] The proclamation of the Vice-chancellor heralded a new spirit under his "Highnesse—the Prince

of Orange—whome God hath chosen—to be the Glorious Instrument—of such inestimable happinesse—to Us and our Posterity."[42]
But in the end there could be no easy return for Isaac Newton from London to a college presided over by an aristocratic nonentity. Something happened to the abstracted professor described by Humphrey Newton that transformed him or at least opened up possibilities of another kind of existence. There was not much to hold him in Cambridge besides the architectural grandeur of the colleges, depicted by David Loggan in *Cantabrigia Illustrata* (1690).

A sketch of the inhabitants of the university town that Newton forsook was drawn by the popular writer Edward Ward in 1700. It is a caricature in Hogarthian style, but other, less dramatic pictures confirm the general impression.

The next place we arriv'd at was our Journeys-end, Cambridge; where Black and Purple Gowns were strolling about Town, like Parsons in a Country Metropolis, during the Bishops visitation; Some looking with as meagre Countenances, as if in search of the *Philosophers-Stone,* they had study'd themselves into a Hypocondriack Melancholly; other's seeming so profoundly thoughtful, as if in pursuance of *Agrippa's* Notions they were studying how to raise Sparagrass from Rams-Horns, or to produce a *Homunculus* as Gardeners do Pumpkins, by burying the Semen in a Dunghil; some looking as Plump and as Jolly as a painted *Bacchus* bestriding a Canary Butt; smiling as he past by, at his own soliloquies, as if he were muttering over to himself some Bacchanalian Ode, he had conceiv'd in Praise of good Clarret; others seeming as Sottishly Sorrowful as if they were Maudlin Fuddl'd, and lamenting the Misfortune of poor *Anacreon,* who Choak'd himself with a Grape-Stone; some strutting along about Eighteen years of Age, in new Gown and Cassock, as if they had receiv'd Orders about two hours before, and were the next Morning to have Institution and Induction, to become the hopeful Guide of a whole Parish; and here and there one appearing so Rakishly Thoughtless, as if Nature, by his empty Looks, had design'd him to grind Mustard, or pick Mushrooms for some Noble-Mans Kitchen: tho' his Parents, in Opposition to his destiny, resolv'd to make him a Scholar. As for the Town it self, it was so abominably dirty, that *Old-street* in the middle of a Winters Thaw, or *Bartholomew-Fair* after a Shower of Rain, could not have more occasion for a Scavenger, than the miry Street of this famous Corporation; and most of them so very narrow, that should two Wheel-barrows meet in the largest of their Thoroughfares, they are enough to make a stop for half an hour before they can well clear themselves of one another, to make room for Passengers.[43]

Once Isaac Newton had been received in London town—the "most August cittie in the World" John Evelyn called it[44]—as an adornment of the new dynasty of William and Mary, the decaying late-seventeenth-century English University, of which he had hardly taken notice during his period of intense creativity, suddenly appeared unattractive to the man approaching fifty.

Chapter 6

GOD AND THE CALLING OF THE NEW PHILOSOPHY

The World was made to be inhabited by Beasts but studied and contemplated by Man: 'tis the Debt of our Reason we owe unto *God,* and the homage we pay for not being Beasts. . . . The Wisdom of God receives small honour from those vulgar Heads that rudely stare about, and with a gross rusticity admire His works: those highly magnifie Him, whose judicious inquiry into His Acts, and deliberate research into His Creatures, return the duty of a devout and learned admiration.
　　　　　　　　　　　—Thomas Browne, *Religio Medici*

DURING the three decades of his fervid intellectual activity in Cambridge, an almost incomparable period of protracted effort, Newton was sustained by a consciousness of the direct personal relationship between himself and God his Father, uninterrupted by a mediator. For His glory he labored without surcease, finding his only "divertisement" in moving from one subject to another. In addition to the optics, the calculus, and the great mathematical and physical synthesis upon which his fame rests secure, in the early seventies he amended and published Varenius' world geography,[1] which stood him in good stead in his later chronological researches. Experiments to lay bare the ultimate unity of the chemical elements and perhaps to discover the very elixir of life were conducted in the Cambridge laboratory whose fires he stoked himself, the last trials taking place on the very eve of his departure for London. In a theology, kept secret, he tackled the awesome problems of the Trinity by analyzing every biblical manuscript he could lay hands on—in any language —that touched upon the divine nature of Christ. And he began to pile up historical writings, comprising an interpretation of mythology, a theory of hieroglyphs, a radical revision of ancient chronology founded upon astronomical proofs, an independent reading of the sense of the Bible, and circumstantial demonstrations of prophecy in the historical world.

In all these works Newton was discharging an obligation to God for his being. The sense of owing to progenitors is deep-rooted in man, and a child has various ways of attempting to requite the debt. But the demands of a father whose face has never been seen are indefinable, insatiable. Since Newton's father was unknown to him and he had not received the slightest sign of his affection, he could never be certain that he had pleased or appeased the Almighty Lord with whom this father was assimilated. Many other puritanical scholars, sons of austere, remote elders, experienced similar feelings toward their exigent Master. The God of Abraham, Isaac, and Jacob whom Newton worshiped had been adored in many ways in the long history of Israel and of the church which had renewed the original covenant; it was given to Isaac Newton to bring Him offerings that surpassed the gifts of all other men. Reasoned, philosophical statements of Newton's religious position come late in his life, in the "Queries" to the *Opticks,* in the General Scholium to the second edition of the *Principia;* but the enduring, emotive relation of his calling to his God, its sacred character, is attested in writings from the confession of 1662 until the year of his death. Newton's devotion to science as a worship accorded with contemporary beliefs about the connections between science and religion in the collegiate bodies to which he belonged, above all the Royal Society. If he differed from his friends it was in the intensity of his religious quest, not its singularity. Though many scientists tended to deemphasize the sectarian character of their religious allegiances and Newton was progressing at an even faster pace than his colleagues toward a divorcement of religion from ritual and dogma, his religious convictions were not the less impassioned.

The beginning of the Stuart Restoration, when young Newton came up to Cambridge University, was a revolutionary moment in the scientific and religious life of England less dramatic but as far-reaching in its consequences as the political upheavals of the preceding two Puritan decades. Recent scholarly discussion over whether the original nucleus of the Royal Society was John Wilkins' scientific club at Oxford, or the London group around John Wallis, or Samuel Hartlib and the Puritan pansophists, or informal meetings in Gresham College, is rather parochial—a number of strands were intertwined.[2] Many men of learning on both sides of the barrier had wearied of the religious controversies of the civil war; and though the spirit of zealotry in defense of a particular form of Catholicism, Anglicanism, or Dissent was by no means dead, there was a growing body of irenic opinion and a tendency to embrace latitudinarian solutions. This does not mean that the prelates and scholars ceased to hold firm beliefs; but many of them were prepared to meet in concert with men of divergent religious views for specific intellectual purposes on noncombatant terms.

The original membership of the Royal Society, which in 1662 received a charter from King Charles II, was a heterogeneous religious assemblage that included both practicing Catholics, like the aristocratic Kenelm Digby, and John Wilkins, Cromwell's brother-in-law. It was from the very beginning clearly understood that religious disputations would be banned; nor would the society entertain political questions that might lead the members into labyrinthine civil debates. In his account of the early meetings before a corporate body was established, written in January 1697, John Wallis, one of the oldest members, recollected their decision to be exclusively absorbed with "the New Philosophy . . . precluding matters of Theology & State Affairs."[3] And Newton later reiterated the doctrine that "religion & Philosophy are to be preserved distinct. We are not to introduce divine revelations into Philosophy, nor philosophical opinions into religion."[4] Thus the neutrality of science was formally proclaimed. It was assumed that there existed a sphere of inquiry to which neither the social status of the scientist nor his

religious convictions were relevant; an area of knowledge unin-
volved with anything but its own concerns was reserved and isolated. This was a comparatively new adventure in Christian Europe,
and many members of the Society were at least vaguely aware of
its unprecedented character. The French Académie des Sciences was
not nearly as free. It may have enjoyed large royal subsidies at an
earlier date than the Royal Society, but its spirit was restricted to
what an absolute Catholic king could endure. When one recalls that
Giordano Bruno was burned in Rome in 1600 and that Galileo recanted before the Inquisition in 1633, the new spirit of English science appears as a unique development, despite recent attempts to
prove that post-Trentine Catholicism did not stifle scientific inquiry.
Acrimonious debates over matters of fact took place at Royal Society meetings, and there were fights a-plenty in this scientific world
but no direct denunciation of another member in the name of God,
however sharply one disagreed with him.

The resolution to avoid religious discrimination was, however,
not quite as firm as the first members of the Royal Society imagined.
At both ends of the spectrum certain religious postures were not
countenanced even in England, though there was never any formal
debate on the subject within the Society. Enthusiasts, men who
spoke with tongues and proclaimed truths by divine inspiration
alone, were to be excluded. The members had no intention of listen-
ing to Quakers who had suddenly been illuminated or to Dissenters of the Leveller and Digger type who were so uncompromising
that as a consequence of direct inspiration from God they would
overturn the whole civil and religious establishment of society. An
individual member of the Royal Society might still experience direct
revelation from God in the secret of his closet, and there is reason
to believe that Newton, after arduous efforts, had occasional visita-
tions; but there is no record of anyone's reporting such an event
to the Society in defense of a scientific proposition.

The rejection of vulgar prophecies and reports of prodigies and
miracles was generally taken for granted. One of the goals that
reasonable Anglican divines hoped the Royal Society would realize

was a purification of true religion from popular superstition and false prognostics that played on the mob's credulity. The separation of the natural and the lawful from the vapors of the religious fanatic would serve to exalt the supernatural by ridding it of nonsense. During Newton's tenure at Cambridge a great Hebraist, John Spencer, was elected Master of Corpus Christi in 1667 and occupied the post with distinction until his death in 1693. The impress of his studies in comparative religion, and especially his important *De Legibus Hebraeorum,* is marked throughout Newton's manuscript renderings of religious history. Spencer was also his guide in interpreting the nature of prophetic revelation, following the Maimonides tradition, which stresses the rigorous rational and moral preparation of the prophet rather than his wild ecstasy. And Spencer was an enemy of modern prophets and enthusiasts, maintaining that the true gift had probably ceased and deriding them as victims of melancholy and hypochondria. "God would no more be look'd for in the whirlwind of raptures, mystical phrases, and ecstatical Orations, but in the *still voice* of a great humility, a sound mind, and an heart reconciled to himself and all the world. . . ."[5] In manifest form and content Newton's interpretations of prodigies and prophecies and their relation to truth revealed by the scientific study of nature were in the same spirit, hostile to mysticism and enthusiasm and the infatuation of the ignorant with phantoms and ghosts as a derogation of true religion. There is even an anecdote of his upbraiding a crowd of agitated undergraduates possessed with the idea that a house was haunted.[6]

If enthusiasm was not allowed a hearing in the Royal Society, neither was clamorous atheism. Skepticism or a form of deism, which was probably the astronomer Edmond Halley's position, was somehow overlooked as long as it kept its mouth shut in public. Private antireligious jokes were frowned upon by Newton, but at least in Halley's case they did not lead to a complete break in friendship, though there was disapproval and censure. Thomas Hobbes, who surely merited a place in the Royal Society by virtue of his once having been in the entourage of Francis Bacon, secular patron saint of the Society from an earlier generation, and who was engaged in violent controversy with Dr. Wallis over mathematical, not political, questions, was not welcomed to the fellowship, probably because of his reputed materialism and atheism and philosophical immorality.[7] When Newton suffered his psychic crisis in 1693, he thought as the most horrible thing imaginable of his dear friend John Locke that he was a Hobbist. For all their sidestepping of religious issues the men of the Royal Society were Christians, and a writer like Hobbes, who was interpreted as maintaining that religion was a mere artifice of the state to hold power more effectively, could not be invited. Usually the Society also drew the line at dogmatic unitarianism and a denial of the divinity of Christ—again if expressed in public. We now know from his manuscripts that Newton was himself a secret unitarian, but he never spread his opinion abroad.

The quality of religious feeling among the scientists cannot be measured by observance and forbearance alone. A willingness to be in the same room with a person of a different religious persuasion is not to be equated with religious lukewarmness. There were surely more and less devout men among members of the Society. Robert Hooke and Edmond Halley would be illustrious examples of the indifferentists. On the other hand, two of the greatest figures of English science in the second half of the seventeenth century, Boyle and Newton, cannot be put into the category of merely formal believers, and theirs is the predominant attitude. Though both were members of the Anglican Church, there was nothing loose or permissive about their personal behavior, as there was among many aristocratic Anglicans of the Restoration whose cavortings enlivened memoirs of court life. Boyle went through an anguished religious crisis in his youth described in his autobiography, and Newton's shorthand confession in 1662 bears witness to a similar event.

Nineteenth-century histories that depicted the agelong war of "rational" science and "irrational" religion made use of generalizations that had served the polemical purposes of Enlightenment anticlerical philosophers like Voltaire and Condorcet, nineteenth-century social thinkers like Saint-Simon and Marx, and the Darwinians who were being attacked by fundamentalist clergymen; but their thesis is not applicable to the relationship of science and religion in seventeenth-century England. In our present-day writing interpretive study has moved in another direction. Instead of seeing the history of the world as a combat between benighted, power-lusting medieval priests and embattled scientists, many thinkers have become aware of the deep religious roots of Western science. The Christian view of a Providence who had established a world order was favorable to the scientific outlook and nurtured it in its infancy, particularly during the age of genius. Discovery of the lawfulness of the world did not exclude the miraculous creation or the unknown end.

Since the sociologist Robert Merton's work in 1938, a peculiar symbiotic relationship has been recognized between Puritanism and science, a parallel to the Weber thesis of a harmony between Calvinism and capitalism. The personal qualities extolled by the Puritan divines would serve an assiduous scientific experimenter well: practicality, orderliness, discipline, scrupulosity, a certain literalness that would apply equally to observing nature and interpreting a biblical text, attention to detail, avoidance of debauch and sensate pleasure, asceticism in the world, utter dedication to one's calling. Perhaps the Merton thesis sometimes overreaches itself (as the Weber thesis did). Other religious sects and even philosophical alchemy could foster the same habits for different theological reasons. But the tendency of the Puritan minority to promote scientific endeavor and to engage in it remains statistically convincing. One did not, of course, have to be an actual member of a dissenter Puritan group to be puritanical—Boyle and Newton, though formally Anglican, lived ascetics in the world.

As the intimate relationship between science and theology in the crucial formative period of modern science has come to be appreciated, it has been easier to reconcile the multifarious activities of Newton's life, and to regard all his works as inspired by the same profound religious sentiment—a position set forth with varying emphasis by Edwin Arthur Burtt and G. S. Brett, by Hélène Metzger, and by Koyré, Léon Bloch, and Adolph Judah Snow. Even Vavilov, the Russian biographer of Newton, took a similar position: "Newton doubtless envisaged the whole of his scientific work from a religious viewpoint. Both of his major works, the *Principia* and the *Opticks,* have religious endings which are written with extraordinary pathos."[8]

Despite difficulties in comprehending Newton's religious expressions over the years—and many of them were not philosophically felicitous—some things can be asserted: he never upheld a simple mechanistic view of the universe, nor was he a partisan of plain deistic natural religion. It may be wicked to quote the devil on the God of Isaac Newton when there are so many pious bishops to bear witness, but Voltaire's report, after conversations with Samuel Clarke, has the virtues of clarity and brevity: "Sir Isaac Newton was firmly persuaded of the Existence of a God; by which he understood not only an infinite, omnipotent, and creating being, but moreover a Master who has made a Relation between himself and his Creatures."[9] The world was not eternal. Creation was a specific act in time by a Lord, even though the process of His labors may perhaps have been more complex than the popular impression of the Mosaic account in Genesis might indicate. The planets had to be distributed in a certain manner by an initial act before the principle of gravity could become operative. Comets were phenomena in whose progress God had to intervene from time to time. A repeopling of the earth after major geological or cosmic catastrophes—and there may have been such incidents in the past—required a divine decree. And as the world had a beginning there was likely to be an apocalyptic end. Every discovery of a scientific principle of matter, every correct reading of a prophetic text, demonstrated the essential goodness and orderliness of the universe that God had created—and what higher praise could be uttered by the religious philosopher, whether Maimonides or Isaac Newton—but this did not signify that He was an absconding Deity. Newton's secret unitarianism was an ardent passion, not the pallid formula of the later Enlightenment.[10]

Newton was not very good at expounding in nonmathematical prose his general ideas about God and the universe, time and space. There was a certain reluctance on his part to philosophize publicly about these ultimate questions, and he usually preferred to let others speak for him on religious subjects, as did Richard Bentley in lectures established by Boyle to combat atheism. Newton was genuinely pleased to have Bentley prove that the world system so marvelously set forth in the *Principia,* far from being inimical to revealed religion, could be used as a mighty bludgeon against atheism. As he said in his famous letter of December 10, 1692: "When I wrote my treatise about our Systeme I had an eye upon such Principles as might work wth considering men for the beleife of a Deity & nothing can rejoyce me more then to find it usefull for that purpose."[11] Newton assured Conduitt that he had written the *Principia* "not with a design of bidding defiance to the Creator but to enforce and demonstrate the power & superintendency of a supreme being."[12] When the Reverend Samuel Clarke defended the Newtonian religious-philosophical views in correspondence with Leibniz and in conversations with Voltaire, he was making explicit what Newton was reticent to say himself, but fervently believed. Newton published nothing significant about God until Clarke's Latin translation of the *Opticks* in 1706, when he carefully worked out his relationship to religion and once and for all refuted the argument that his mechanical philosophy could dispense with an active God.[13] In scientific law he saw His direct and continuous intervention, a traditionalism that separates him sharply from later deist proponents of the mechanical philosophy. Boyle's work *The Christian Virtuoso: shewing that by being addicted to Experimental Philosophy, a man is rather assisted, than indisposed to be a good Christian* (1690, 1691), and other apologiae of science by less prominent men, propagated the same idea—that science was a Te Deum, a laudation, a demonstration of the wonders of God.

There were of course contemporaries who attacked the scientists of the Royal Society on religious grounds, Alexander Ross and Henry Stubbs, for example, themselves not practicing scientists. The arguments of these men—and sometimes Puritan divines like Richard Baxter joined them[14]—were simple and obvious enough, and bore weight. They charged that a concentration of inquiry upon secondary causes, how things worked in the world, would inevitably deflect attention from God as the primary cause. There was a good dose of anti-intellectualism in some of their animadversions against science, reminiscent of one tradition in Christianity that opposed culture and glorified the outpourings of the simple, ignorant, pious heart. A Calvinist could not, after all, maintain that the mysterious gift of grace was more accessible to the learned scientist than to an ordinary man, since it was dependent upon God's arbitrary will. In long terms there was probably some merit to the argument of these mediocre and often venal polemicists against science (Stubbs was paid by the Royal College of Physicians to attack the Royal Society because they feared its competition). But the great seventeenth-century scientists themselves never viewed their activities as a turning away from the love and worship of God.[15] Sir Thomas Browne in the *Religio Medici* (1642/3) had already presented a grand apology for natural philosophy in language that would be repeated with variations for the rest of the century. It was a religious *duty* of the scientist, who was capable of unraveling the wonders of God's creation, to reveal them to mankind. If the scientist failed to acquit himself of this task, he was denying God one form of adoration. Boyle, in the wake of Browne, knew that God would be more gratified by the refined revelations and praise of a sensitive and skillful anatomist than by those of an ignorant butcher. John Ray spent his life unveiling the beauties of the world's flora and fauna that God had made. Even Hooke, perhaps the first to study a flea under a microscope and draw it with intricate detail in his *Micrographia,* pronounced it beautiful in a religious, not an aesthetic, sense.

Seventeenth-century scientists were almost to a man teleologists. They discerned the divine intent in the structure of an animal molar, in the hair of a cheese mite, in the orderly movement of the planets. Everywhere there were traces of divine harmony and perfection. Ray's *Wisdom of God Manifested in the Works of the Creation* and similar justifications of religion reached their epitome in the next generation in the Boyle lectures for 1711 and 1712 on *Physico-Theology: or, a demonstration of the Being and Attributes of God, from his works of creation,* by Newton's friend William Derham, a graduate of Trinity. This work (which saw twelve editions by 1754) makes the traditional argument from design, but now accoutered with voluminous scientific evidence from aspects of the world animal, vegetable, and mineral, and above all from the idea of gravity. On July 18, 1733, William Derham wrote Conduitt of a "peculiar sort of Proof of God, wch Sr Is: mentioned in some discourse wch he & I had soon after I published my Astro-Theology. He said there were 3 things in the Motions of the Heavenly Bodies, that were plain evidences of Omnipotence & wise Counsel. 1. That the Motion imprest upon those Globes was Lateral, or in a Direction perpendicular to their Radii, not along them or parallel wth them. 2. That the Motions of them tend the same way. 3. That their Orbits have all the same or nearly the same inclination."[16]

At other times scientists could relate their discoveries to mundane activities, to the practicalities of British imperial interests and navigation policy. And perhaps in a broad sense the practice of science and its matter-of-factness were consonant with the interests of the new urban economy and with nascent capitalism. But recognition of the utilitarian ends of science—though it would not be phrased in those portentous words—was by no means at variance with a conception of science as an offering to God and a celebration of His perfection. In the 1670's a scientist could assimilate both ideas.

When Newton was named to the Royal Society in 1672 the discoveries about God's world had already begun to multiply. A monotheistic culture, however, must inevitably become engaged in the search for a unifying principle, and can never remain content with the mere amassing of isolated findings and inventions, astonishing as they may be. Newton represents the fulfillment of that quest for underlying unity. "Without Gravity, the whole Universe . . . would have been a confused Chaos," lectured Bentley.[17] The Newtonian system, with its mathematically described force that applied both to the movements of the heavenly bodies and to things on earth, satisfied a religious as well as a scientific need. In chemistry, where Boyle labored, it was difficult if not impossible to find a single mathematical principle. The naturalists were always on the border-line between science and the mere collecting of prodigies—though the Italian Marcello Malpighi, the greatest of them all, corresponded with the Royal Society and presented it with a theory of embryology.[18] In achieving the great synthesis with a law that showed the interrelationship of all parts of creation, at the very moment when it seemed as if science might remain an agglomeration of curiosities and disparate discoveries, Newton overwhelmed his fellow scientists and became the symbol of science in a Christian society.

The mission of science in the realm of the historical, as contrasted with the physical, world was defined in accordance with how the individual scientist saw the moment in time when he lived in the grand design of God's creation. Despite the Society's formal commitment to the promotion of knowledge, which sounds progressive, the ideal of most members, including Newton, has to be sharply distinguished from late-eighteenth- or nineteenth-century conceptions of human perfectibility. In the seventeenth century there was still a pervasive sense of nature's decay, of a steady corruption or running down of its forces. The function of science would then be to try to arrest decay, to restore nature and man, or to slow the process of degeneration. But any remedies applied by art and science would have their limitations because human capacities were not boundless. Bacon's conception of extending man's power over all things possible does not connote the idea of infinitude. The true spirit of the Baconian ideal can be found in his medical reflections: man in this world walks through a vale of tears and we ought to alleviate his anguish. There is no vision here of a perfected new man. John Wilkins' justification of the mechanical philosophy is equally modest—it will help man to regain some of the capabilities lost through the sinfulness of the Fall. In the introductory material to Dalgarno's *Ars Signorum* (1661), a proposal for a universal sign language, there is an appeal from Charles II to support the author's endeavors in "further repairing the Decayes of Nature, untill Art have done its last, or, which is more probable, Nature cease to be, or be Renewed,"[19] a characteristic view that scientific labor is a means of counteracting in some measure the attenuation of nature's force.

The expectation was widespread that ultimately through conflagration or flood, for which the plague and the fire of London were prognostics, the world would be renewed by divine re-creation, or that other worlds would be fashioned.[20] This cyclical conception, which Newton shared with many of his contemporaries, is alien to the canonical eighteenth-century idea of progress. The emotive and intellectual roots of the common seventeenth-century eschatology are to be found in Stoic cyclical theory and in millenarianism, which were united in the conviction that the world was coming to an end. Books on the Second Coming were written by the score during this period, and members of the Royal Society were preoccupied with dating the event. The coming of the Messiah is the subject of a letter from Oldenburg to Manasseh ben Israel, the Amsterdam rabbi, on July 25, 1657.[21] Boyle steadfastly believed that the world would end in annihilation or that it would be totally transformed by a great conflagration which would "destroy the present frame of nature."[22] Newton was convinced that the comet of 1680 had just missed hitting the earth, and in many of his commentaries on Revelations and the Book of Daniel, kept secret during his lifetime, he inclined to the idea that the end of the world in its present form could not be too long delayed, that the times were about to be fulfilled. But neither Boyle nor Newton went ranting about the imminent destruction of London. It would all happen in due course. Perhaps other worlds would be created thereafter. In the meantime, it was given to them as scientists to lay bare the wonders of God's creation in all its intricacy and all its harmonious simplicity, as they waited for the inevitable drawing to a close.

There were of course men like Joseph Glanvill who had a far more expansive view of the practical possibilities of science and dwelt on its creative role, its shining future in this world, if the achievements of the Royal Society continued to accumulate.

Me thinks this Age seems resolved to bequeath *posterity* somewhat to remember it: And the glorious Undertakers, wherewith Heaven hath blest our Days, will leave the world better provided then they found it. . . . Should those Heroes go on, as they have happily begun; they'll fill the world with *wonders.* And I doubt not but posterity will find many things, that are now but *Rumors,* verified into practical *Realities.* It may be some Ages hence, a voyage to Southern unknown Tracts, yea possibly the Moon, will not be more strange then one to America. To them, that come after us, it may be as ordinary to buy a *pair* of *wings* to fly into remotest Regions; as now a pair of Boots to ride a Journey. And to conferr at the distance of the Indies by Sympathetick conveyances, may be as usual to future times, as to us in a litterary correspondence. The restauration of gray hairs to Juvenility, and renewing the exhausted marrow, may at length be effected without a *miracle;* And the turning of the now comparatively *desert* world into a Paradise, may not improbably be expected from late Agriculture.[23]

But though Newton early in his Cambridge career read the book in which these marvels of science were predicted, there is no echo of its exultation in any of his writings. The physical transformations science might work upon the earth did not capture his imagination. For most of his life he saw science in an entirely different light and mundane improvements were hardly worthy of his notice. Science for him was a way of knowing his Father, not a means leading to the multiplication of sinful, sensate pleasures. When in the latter part of his career Newton became involved in the relations of science, the government, and the economy, he was serving purposes that in his creative period he would have frowned upon.

The profession of faith which concluded the second edition of the *Principia* and was retained with some emendations in the third —the General Scholium—was a deliberate effort on Newton's part to distinguish his views from those of atheistic atomists and pantheists and to vindicate himself in the face of insinuations that his doctrine might have irreligious connotations. Though Newton's God was ultimately inscrutable and unknowable, He was not to be identified with the heathen Fates, for He was a ruler, and He had left signs of His Providence throughout His creation.

As a blind man has no idea of colors, so have we no idea of the manner by which the all-wise God perceives and understands all things. He is utterly void of all body and bodily figure, and can therefore neither be seen, nor heard, nor touched; nor ought he to be worshiped under the representation of any corporeal thing. . . . We know him only by his most wise and excellent contrivances of things, and final causes; we admire him for his perfections; but we reverence and adore him on account of his dominion: for we adore him as his servants; and a god without dominion, providence, and final causes, is nothing else but Fate and Nature. Blind metaphysical necessity, which is certainly the same always and everywhere, could produce no variety of things.[24]

What Newton conveyed was a sense of man's puniness before the grandeur and final mystery of God's being, even though men might learn about His governance through the mechanical philosophy, or by resorting to anthropomorphism seek to understand His powers and attributes.

Nothing in the General Scholium represented a novel departure for Newton; he was merely acknowledging publicly the emotions he had experienced throughout his life. God was a lord, a master to be obeyed, not simply a metaphysical entity or a principle arrived at by reasoning. Here lies the powerful and intimate meaning of his exegesis of ordinary religious speech.

This Being governs all things, not as the soul of the world, but as Lord over all; and on account of his dominion he is wont to be called *Lord God* παντοκράτωρ, or *Universal Ruler;* for *God* is a relative word, and has a respect to servants; and *Deity* is the dominion of God not over his own body, as those imagine who fancy God to be the soul of the world, but over servants. The Supreme God is a Being eternal, infinite, absolutely perfect; but a being, however perfect, without dominion, cannot be said to be Lord God; for we say, my God, your God, the God of *Israel,* the God of Gods, and Lord of Lords; but we do not say, my Eternal, your Eternal, the Eternal of *Israel,* the Eternal of Gods; we do not say, my Infinite, or my Perfect: these are titles which have no respect to servants.[25]

If there is support for Newton's assimilation of God with the unknown father to whom it was his duty to submit, before whom he had to become passive, whose yoke he was obliged to bear, it lies in the passionate religious affirmation of the General Scholium. Newton quoted Scripture not only by way of traditional apologetics but to call the witness of mankind to his own feelings.

In a passage of the General Scholium introduced into the third edition of the *Principia,* Newton proffered a psychological interpretation of the anthropomorphic images of God in the Bible that, despite his use of the word *allegory* (in this context he means *analogy*), differs from the Stoic tradition and is closer to ideas secretly diffused in Europe through Spinoza. Newton recognized a "similitude" between the ways of men—their ordinary behavior—and their notions of God. "[B]y way of allegory, God is said to see, to speak, to laugh, to love, to hate, to desire, to give, to receive, to rejoice, to be angry, to fight, to frame, to work, to build; for all our notions of God are taken from the ways of mankind by a certain similitude, which, though not perfect, has some likeness, however."[26] Newton is very far from Hume's or Feuerbach's view of God as created by man in his own image, but he has been pondering the nature of religious emotion in himself and in his fellows and has arrived at the conviction that ideas of God are derived from His relationship to man, not alone from the system of the world.

Chapter 7

ON THE SHOULDERS
OF GIANTS

Bernard of Chartres used to compare us to [puny] dwarfs
perched on the shoulders of giants. He pointed out that we
see more and farther than our predecessors, not because we
have keener vision or greater height, but because we are
lifted up and borne aloft on their gigantic stature.
—John of Salisbury, *The Metalogicon*

Newton's isolation in Cambridge had been relieved by his election
as Fellow of the Royal Society in 1672. If Cambridge after Barrow's
death became an intellectual desert in which a solitary man constructed a system of the world, the scientists of the Society in London were the spiritual brotherhood to which he belonged. Newton
at first looked upon them as a safe haven from the mob he always
feared; but his new ties with this body presented dangers as well as
rewards. With few exceptions, relationships with persons in Cambridge were neutral; there was no great intimacy, with the possible
exception of the nondescript John Wickins, and there was no discord. Though he rarely journeyed to London to attend Royal Society
meetings, his peers were there and once he exposed himself on the
world's "stage"—the image is his—he was caught in an interplay of
competitive ambitions with which he could rarely cope with equa-
nimity. His early life had not trained him to easy converse with
equals. At the very moment when he joined the fellowship he met
a rival, Robert Hooke.

In November 1662, at the age of twenty-seven, Hooke had been chosen the first Curator of Experiments to the newly founded Society. Newton, seven years his junior, still confessing boyhood sins in a little notebook, had not yet found his way. For a decade prior to Newton's election to the Society Hooke was firmly entrenched as its outstanding exemplar of rich and profuse inventiveness, a marvel of the new science, encompassing virtually all fields of knowledge, performing three and four experiments at its weekly meetings. Though mechanics was his favored area, in the course of his life he worked on the theory of light in physics, the theory of combustion in chemistry, respiration in physiology, the cellular structure of plants in biology. He was a great microscopist, whose *Micrographia* (1665), with its engraved magnifications of minute bodies, was a milestone of English science. An erratic genius scurrying from one inquiry to another, he set the thermometrical zero at the freezing point of water and studied the relationship of barometrical readings to changes in the weather; he invented a land carriage, a diving bell, a method of telegraphy, a machine for cutting the teeth of watch wheels; he measured the vibrations of a pendulum two hundred feet long attached to the steeple of St. Paul's and ascertained the number of vibrations corresponding to musical notes. Only a flying machine imitative of muscular movement defeated him. A contemporary physicist has called him the most inventive man that ever was, with a mind "so fertile in expedients, so interrupted at every hour, at every endeavour, by the inrush of new concepts, new projects, that it is hard to disentangle his doings."[1] In his *Brief Lives* Aubrey, the gentleman biographer who espoused Hooke's cause against Newton, credited him with many hundreds of inventions.[2] "[T]he fertility of his Invention . . . hurry'd him on, in the quest of new Entertainments, neglecting the former Discoveries," was the judgment of Richard Waller, the physiologist who was his successor as Secretary of the Royal Society.[3]

While Newton's system ultimately came to represent the English scientific ideal, Robert Hooke still operated in the earlier Baconian tradition, in quest of a plenitude of discoveries rather than a few unifying, mathematical principles. His continuation of Bacon's *New Atlantis,* a utopia published anonymously in 1661 under the initials R. H., Esq., bears witness to his filiation with the past.[4] Newton would never have composed a scientific utopia bustling with myriad simultaneous experiments. His image of perfection was a transcendental symbol, the ancient Temple of Solomon, which in its proportions presaged the heavenly Jerusalem. Hooke's ideal was of this world and his Salomon's House was a great manufactory of scientific novelties for immediate practical application. Behind his enduring interest in the principle of gravity was a plain utilitarian motive: a good theory of planetary motions was needed to resolve the outstanding problem of navigation, how to determine the longitude of a ship's position.[5] The Baconian emphasis upon the conveniences of life and sensate pleasure, fundamentally alien to the puritanical Newton though he gave it occasional lip service, fitted in with Hooke's expansive, pragmatic view of the world. A scientific interpretation of ancient mythology—another object of his curiosity—was consonant with his matter-of-fact spirit; but he was never attracted by the vogue for biblical interpretation, of which Newton was a virtuoso. Hooke might thank God in his diary when he won a lawsuit, but he was far from being possessed by the Holy Spirit.

In Hooke and Newton two different scientific styles confronted each other. While neither devoted his entire life to one subject, their versatility served different ends. Hooke allowed his insights to crowd in upon one another, a Don Juan of science who made quick and easy conquests; Newton, once fixed upon an idea, pursued it relentlessly until it surrendered its full secret or sheer exhaustion forced him to relinquish his hold for a time, when he turned to something else for what he called "divertisement." From the five or six inquiries into which Newton plunged, he returned each time with a heroic discovery; only in alchemy did he fail. Hooke enjoyed many facile victories—his inventions and what are called Hooke's "laws" —but when he died he left no great monument that could be identified as his own, except perhaps his architecture, and even there he was overshadowed by Christopher Wren.[6] Magnificent structures that he built, like Bedlam, have been torn down.

Had Newton ever bothered to consider Hooke's scientific ideal of proliferation he would have been outraged. Hooke not only confessed to his butterfly passion of flitting from flower to flower, but in the preface to his Cutler lectures published in 1679 concocted a theory of sorts to apologize for volatility:

[A]s there is scarce one Subject of millions that may be pitched upon, but to write an exact and compleat History thereof, would require the whole time and attention of a man's life, and some thousands of Inventions and Observations to accomplish it: So on the other side no man is able to say that he will compleat this or that Inquiry whatever it be, (The greatest part of Invention being but a lucky bitt of chance, for the most part not in our own power, and like the wind, the Spirit of Invention bloweth where and when it listeth, and we scarce know whence it came, or whether 'tis gone.) 'Twill be much better therefore to imbrace the influences of Providence, and to be diligent in the inquiry of every thing we meet with. For we shall quickly find that the number of considerable Observations and Inventions this way collected, will a hundred fold out-strip those that are found by Design. No man but hath some luckey hitts and useful thoughts on this or that Subject he is conversant about, the regarding and communicating of which, might be a means to other Persons highly to improve them.[7]

Hooke's manuscripts fell into the hands of Richard Waller, who published a selection of them in 1705 dedicated to—of all people— Isaac Newton, Hooke's inveterate enemy, and thus added a posthumous insult to the injuries Hooke had endured during his lifetime. When Waller died, the remaining documents were passed on to the Reverend William Derham, an old friend of Newton's who took until 1726 to publish another collection, one whose want of consequence he himself pointed out in an introduction. Most of the Hooke papers are now lost, as are the many mechanical instruments that he fashioned with his own hands (they were either stolen or allowed to rust in the rooms of the Society). His portrait has disappeared and his grave is unknown. And there are those who point an accusing finger at his adversary Isaac Newton, the President who severed all ties that bound the Society to the age of Robert Hooke as if he had deliberately set out to expunge the name from the memory of man. Derham once wrote Conduitt that twenty years after Hooke's death Newton still could not speak of him with composure.[8]

Hooke was born on the Isle of Wight, the son of a clergyman, and as a boy was interested, like Newton, in "mathematical magic," mechanical objects, sundials, clocks, water mills, model ships. At Oxford, where he entered a subsizar working his way as a virtual servant, he encountered John Wilkins, William Petty, Christopher Wren, Robert Boyle—a more varied scientific assemblage than awaited Newton at Cambridge, where he had no one but the mathematician Isaac Barrow to whom he could turn. In 1666, after the Great Fire of London, Hooke was appointed one of the surveyors and became a key figure in the rebuilding of the city, earning a vast amount of money which he locked away in an iron chest. He was gregarious, frequenting taverns, founding societies and secret clubs within societies. Though not of the original group of the Royal Society and at first an employee under Robert Boyle's patronage, he was soon elected a Fellow in his own right, and upon Oldenburg's death succeeded him as Secretary.

Richard Waller has left a sketch of Hooke in the introduction to his posthumous works, though he is more generous with particulars about the man who had passed his prime than about the boundlessly energetic promoter who dashed off a record of his multifarious, bewildering activities in a diary of the 1670's.[9]

As to his Person he was but despicable, being very crooked, tho' I have heard from himself, and others, that he was strait till about 16 Years of Age when he first grew awry, by frequent practicing, turning with a Turn-Lath, and the like incurvating Exercises, being but of a thin weak habit of Body, which increas'd as he grew older, so as to be very remarkable at last: This made him but low of Stature, tho' by his limbs he shou'd have been moderately tall. . . .

He was of an active, restless, indefatigable Genius even almost to the last, and always slept little to his Death, seldom going to Sleep till two three, or four a Clock in the Morning, and seldomer to Bed, often continuing his Studies all Night, and taking a short Nap in the Day. His Temper was

Melancholy, Mistrustful and Jealous, which more increas'd upon him with his Years. He was in the beginning of his being made known to the Learned, very communicative of his Philosophical Discoveries and Inventions, till some Accidents made him to a Crime close and reserv'd. He laid the cause upon some Persons, challenging his Discoveries for their own, taking occasion from his Hints to perfect what he had not; which made him say he would suggest nothing till he had time to perfect it himself, which has been the Reason that many things are lost, which he affirm'd he knew.[10]

Hooke had carnal relations with his housekeepers in Gresham College, where he was Professor of Geometry, and he duly recorded his occasional orgasms with the zodiacal symbol Pisces.[11] When his niece, daughter of a brother who had committed suicide, replaced the housekeepers, middle-aged Hooke became the victim of a grand passion, and her unfaithfulness drove him to distraction. (A niece is often as close as a man can get to the image of his young mother.) After her death in 1687, a year already darkened for Hooke by the publication of the *Principia,* he went into a decline, "being observ'd from that time," wrote Waller, "to grow less active, more Melancholly and Cynical."[12] A diary covering the period 1689 to 1693, when he was over fifty and Newton was in the limelight, bears the stamp of a cantankerous, envious, vengeful man, given to outbursts of temper.

The initial encounter with Hooke came early, on February 8, 1672, when Newton's discourse, in which he demonstrated that white light was a composite of the other colors of the spectrum, was read to the Society shortly before his reception as a Fellow. His theory of colors was his first important philosophical paper after the presentation of his reflecting telescope, and he met with a sharp rebuff. No sooner had his letter been received by the Society than Hooke, after faint praise of its "niceness and curiosity," launched into a strong defense of the superiority of his own wave theory of light.[13] Twelve days later he was answered by Newton through a letter to Oldenburg ironically expressing satisfaction that "so acute an objecter hath said nothing that can enervate any part of it [his paper]. For I am still of the same judgment & doubt not but that upon severer examinations it will bee found as certain a truth as I have asserted it."[14] In evaluating his work, Newton had cast aside the cloak of modesty in which he customarily draped himself. He was feeling his oats. From belittling his invention of the new reflecting telescope, for which he had been duly acclaimed by the Society, he had swung to a high point of self-maximization, calling his new discovery of the nature of light "the oddest if not the most considerable detection wch hath hitherto beene made in the operations of Nature."[15]

Four months later, after a progressively acrimonious exchange with Hooke, Newton protested to Oldenburg that he was consciously avoiding the "intermixing of oblique & glancing expressions" in his replies,[16] and on September 21, 1672, he requested that if their correspondence were ever published Oldenburg should "mitigate any expressions that seem harsh."[17] From the beginning Newton was fully aware of his capacity for hurting, and he imposed an external restraint upon himself in the form of Oldenburg's censorship. Hooke was far too powerful a personage, moreover, to be offended with impunity at this early date.

Great stress has been placed upon the barrage of criticism from many quarters foreign and domestic that assailed Newton's theory of colors—Huygens, Hooke, Pardies, and the Jesuits of Liège—as the trauma that inhibited him from publishing his later works. Whatever the merits of that explanation, Newton's immediate responses to his critics were hardly those of a timorous neophyte. He was superior in a letter to Huygens, he demanded public demonstrations of the errors of his lesser critics, and after a while he became so annoyed with the whole business that he impulsively severed relations with the Society, as a pretext relating his decision to his being far removed from London. He wrote to Oldenburg on March 8, 1673: "Sr I desire that you will procure that I may be put out from being any longer fellow of the R. Society. For though I honour that body, yet since I see I shall neither profit them, nor (by reason of this distance) can partake of the advantage of their Assemblies, I desire to withdraw." The real reason for his resignation, however, becomes apparent in a letter to Collins where he complains of the rudeness shown him and resolves to "prevent accidents of that nature for the future."[18] Oldenburg hastened to assuage him, smoothed his ruffled feathers, offered a remission of dues on June 4, 1673, and followed with a testimonial of the general love and esteem in which Newton was held by the Society and an apology for the breach of civility on the part of an unnamed member.[19] Newton was not wholly appeased. He promised to ignore the ill-usage of which he had been a victim, but formally broke with natural philosophy, one of many periodic denials of his destiny: "I intend to be no further sollicitous about matters of Philosophy. And therefore I hope you will not take it ill if you find me ever refusing doing any thing more in that kind, or rather that you will favour me in my determination by preventing so far as you can conveniently any objections or other philosophicall letters that may concern me."[20] A petulant boy is speaking through the mouth of a man of thirty.

If Newton's polemical rejoinders to Hooke and Huygens, as well as to Ignace Pardies and other minor figures, were held within bounds and Newton drew back into his shell for a time to avoid being seen or heard from in further controversy, the controls were not operative during a renewed critical assault from a group of English Jesuits in Liège—ignorant Papists whom he could scorn with impunity on scientific and religious grounds. His counterattacks were emotional outbursts buttressed by brilliant argument. The first antagonist to sally forth was Francis Hall, known as Linus, aged eighty and in his dotage; his charge against Newton in a letter of September 26, 1674, to Oldenburg is generally considered stupid: "From whence I conclude, that the spectrum, this learned Author saw much longer then broad, was not effected by the true sunne beames, but by rayes proceeding from some bright cloud as is sayd: And by consequence, that the Theory of light grounded upon that experiment cannot subsist."[21] When Hall died his place was taken by his colleague John Gascoines and then by Anthony Lucas, who cast doubt on the very worth of an *experimentum crucis*.

Newton reacted with bitter contempt, announced again in two letters to Oldenburg that he would not become a "slave to philosophy" by defending himself, and brushed aside all theoretical objections, insisting that Lucas stick to the facts of the experiment which had been questioned. The second letter, November 28, 1676, affords a more general insight into an aspect of Newton's character—what lies behind his deep fear of publication and of arguing even when he is in the right. He had been accused by Lucas of having erred in describing the length of the image of the spectrum in his first letter on colors; it was not five times longer than broad, Lucas maintained, but only three or three and a half. To be taken to task for "misrepresenting matter of fact" was intolerable to Newton with his fantasies of omnipotence and omniscience and his self-image as the perfect one. If a single mistake in the presentation of his materials was detected, the whole structure would collapse. He conceived of himself as constantly under surveillance by his fellow men who were trying to "trip" him up, to find a flaw; if ever they succeeded in discovering a hidden blemish the magical circle of his infallibility would be broken. Scientific error was assimilated with sin, for it could only be the consequence of sloth on his part and a failure in his divine service. For Newton a sin was not an act of human frailty that could be forgiven, but a sign that the culprit was possessed by evil. In dismay and resentment that his exactness had been challenged, he sent Oldenburg a declaration of loyalty to the rules of empirical science, the absolutism of which has other connotations. His "credit," his reputation for all time, and his person were at stake. "Tis the truth of my experiments which is the business in hand. On this my Theory depends, & which is of more consequence, the credit of my being wary, accurate and faithfull in the reports I have made or shall make of experiments in any subject, seeing that a trip in any one will bring all the rest into suspicion."[22]

There was, of course, good reason for his chariness apart from his mistrustful nature—the scientific brotherhood was peopled by enemies, equally suspicious, who were lying in wait. The early references to Newton in Hooke's private shorthand diary were laconic and for the most part noncommittal, but his watchful eye took careful notice of Newton's rare comings and goings between Cambridge and London. On February 18, 1675, he simply recorded that "Mr. Newton, Cambridge" was in London, and, a few days later, that he met him at Dr. Daniel Whistler's, a professor of geometry at Gresham College. On March 17 he noted "Newton out of towne." But when Hooke was instrumental in forming a secret club within the Royal Society, a sort of hidden box within a box for maximum security in the preservation of scientific arcana, Newton's theory of colors was one of the first papers to be discussed—in his absence. On December 11, 1675: "Mr. Hoskins here, to Joes coffe house where we began New Clubb. Mr. Hill, Hoskins, Lodowick and I, at last Mr. Aubery discoursd about Mr. Newtons new hypothesis." Two weeks later, on New Year, they reinaugurated their "New Philosophicall Clubb" and "Resolvd upon Ingaging ourselves not to speak of any thing that was then reveald *sub sigillo* to any one nor to declare that we had such a meeting at all." As it turned out, the clandestine discussion of this inner group of scientists, which now included Sir Christopher Wren, again revolved around "Mr. Newtons Late Papers." Hooke made the opening move and in the diary minced no words in asserting his priority. "I shewd that Mr. Newton had taken my hypothesis of the puls or wave."[23] From what is known of Hooke's garrulousness and of the scientists' intramural gossiping, it is a fair surmise that despite their solemn pledge of secrecy Newton was immediately apprised of what had transpired at the holy coffeehouse conclave in London and probably given a spiced-up version, though Hooke's naked charge written in his own hand in the diary was grave enough. Twenty days later (January 20) Hooke had Newton's angry riposte, whereupon Hooke in his diary blandly shifted the blame for the dispute onto Oldenburg. "Mr. Auberys papers Read, and some of Mr. Newtons. A letter also of Mr. Newtons seeming to quarrell from Oldenburg fals suggestions. I told them my Experiments about the colours of bodys about the Dark Spot in the middle about the visibleness of glasse." In Hooke's psychic economy the placating of Newton was counterbalanced by an attack on Oldenburg's sinister practices. The composition of Hooke's reply to Newton was an important act signaled with an entry in the diary: "Wrot letter to Mr. Newton about Oldenburg kindle Cole."[24]

The exchange of letters between Hooke and Newton in late January and early February 1676 has been interpreted as an attempt at reconciliation on the part of both, and there are discernible movements in that direction.[25] "These beautiful letters, emulous of good feeling and lofty principle," as the Victorian Sir David Brewster described them, have been far better understood since the twentieth-century commentaries of More and Koyré.[26] Upon further examination the correspondence is found to secrete even more venom than they suspected. Here were two former country boys, now men of genius at the height of their powers, aping the manners of Restoration courtiers—flattering each other, overpraising, scraping and bowing, doffing their scientific plumed hats in grand gestures. At the same time, for all their avowals of respect for each other's persons and of utter devotion to the discovery of truth, they could not refrain from pinpricks and slighting remarks. Hooke and Newton were prodigal with protestations of peaceful intent, of their aversion to public disputes that invariably embittered personal relationships, of their predilection for secret correspondence in which third parties could not intervene to stir up quarrels. Hooke assured Newton:

I do noeways approve of contention or feuding and proving in print, and shall be very unwillingly drawn to such kind of warr . . . I have a mind very desirous of and very ready to imbrace any truth that shall be discovered though it may much thwart and contradict any opinions or notions I have formerly imbraced as such. . . . Your Designes and myne I suppose aim both at the same thing wch is the Discovery of truth and I suppose we can both endure to hear objections, so as they come not in a manner of open hostility, and have minds equally inclined to yield to the plainest deductions of reason from experiment. If therefore you will please to correspond about such matters by private letter I shall very gladly imbrace it. . . . This way of contending I believe to be the more philosophicall of the two, for though I confess the collision of two hard-to-yield contenders may produce light yet if they be put together by the ears of other's hands and incentives, it will produce rather ill concomitant heat which serves for no other use but . . . kindle cole.

And Newton responded in the same spirit.

I was exceedingly well pleased & satisfied wth your generous freedom, & think you have done what becomes a true Philosophical spirit. There is nothing wch I desire to avoyde in matters of Philosophy more then contention, nor any kind of contention more then one in print: & therefore I gladly embrace your proposal of a private correspondence. What's done before many witnesses is seldome wthout some further concern then that for truth: but what passes between friends in private usually deserves the name of consultation rather then contest, & so I hope it will prove between you & me.

Hooke was fulsome in his praise of Newton's genius: "I doe justly value your excellent Disquisitions . . . I judge you have gone farther in that affair much than I did . . . I believe the subject cannot meet with a fitter and more able person to inquire into it than yourself. . . ." In courtly self-depreciation, he denigrated his own abilities as "much inferior." And Newton again replied in kind: "You defer too much to my ability for searching into this subject." He begged for "pertinent Objections," for he knew "no man better able to furnish me wth them then your self."

But interspersed with the baroque compliments are condescending jibes. Hooke, casually alluding to his recognized priority in the field, implied that Newton was merely putting finishing touches on what he had already initiated. He was "extremely well pleased to see those notions promoted and improved which I long since began, but had not time to compleat"; Newton was the ideal person "to compleat, rectify and reform what were the sentiments of my younger studies, which I designed to have done somewhat at myself, if my other troublesome employments would have permitted. . . ." To this blithe assumption of primacy in a historical chain of scientific invention that made of the younger man a mere follower—Hooke was forty and Newton was thirty-three—Newton replied on February 5, 1676, with a timeworn image frequently cited in the literary quarrels of the ancients and the moderns in connection with the idea of progress, an image that harks back at least to John of Salisbury and has since often been quoted out of context, in Newton's name, as proof of his generous appreciation of the work of his predecessors. "If I have seen further it is by standing on the sholders of Giants."[27] Put back where it belongs, in the psychological atmosphere of this correspondence in 1676, the tribute has a far more complicated, even ambiguous meaning; it is a two-edged sword.

The main thrust of Newton's long letter to Oldenburg on January 10, 1676, had been a refutation of Hooke's claim that Newton stole his hypothesis on light from the *Micrographia*. After stoutly denying the allegation, Newton had turned the tables by detailing how many ideas Hooke had lifted from Descartes. "I desire Mr Hook to shew me therefore, I say not only the summ of the Hypothesis I wrote, wch is his insinuation, but any part of it taken out of his *Micrographia:* but then I expect too that he instance in what's his own. It's most likely he'l pretend I had from him the application of vibrations to the solution of the Phaenomena of thin plates. . . . To the things that he has from Des Cartes, pray add this, *that the parts of solid bodies have a vibrating motion* least he should say I had from him what I say about heat."[28] Newton's early acquaintance with the *Micrographia* is amply attested in his extensive critical notes on the work.[29] Far from being impressed with the lavishness of Newton's acknowledgments in the February 5 letter, one is struck by the niggardliness of his praise. "What Des-Cartes did was a good step"—an extravagant eulogy indeed. And as for Hooke, Newton's homage reduces itself to the specific observation: "You have added much several ways, & especially in taking the colours of thin plates into philosophical consideration." Following hard upon such dithyrambs, the image of a dwarf (not mentioned explicitly) standing on the shoulders of a giant sounds like an abrupt shift in tone, until one realizes that there is something devious about Newton's applying this hackneyed simile to his relationship with Hooke. On the face of it Newton appears to be calling Hooke a giant and suggesting that he is a mere dwarf by comparison; but his hyperbole is, after all, addressed to a "crooked" little man, and there is an undertone of contempt here, conscious or unconscious, as in calling a fat man "skinny" and thus underscoring his obesity. Newton did not greatly value Hooke's contribution to the theory of light: he was merely returning an extravagant flourish for Hooke's flattering phrases, laying it on with a trowel, while his real disdain for Hooke as a person and a scientist broke through.

Newton's final dealings with the Jesuits of Liège who had attacked his theory of colors betrayed none of the covert ambiguity of his correspondence with Hooke. A protracted exchange with Lucas and the repetition of experiments at the Royal Society culminated in the drafting of a letter—we are not sure this is the form in which it was sent—on March 5, 1678, the end of which one commentator, perhaps with scholarly license, calls "a scream of rage."[30] Newton's salutation was indeed a snarl: "The stirr you make about your Objections, draws this from me to let you see how easy it was to answer your Letters had not other considerations . . . made me averse from meddling further wth your matters." Francis Hall and Anthony Lucas were not simply wrong or in error, but stood "convicted" of their mistakes by "the tryal of the Royal Society"—the judicial, punitive language would appear again and again in future disputes. There is now evidence that Newton had intended to publish his optical papers along with a complete record of the correspondence with all his critics in order to expose them to public obloquy, to rub their noses against the wall. It is about this time that an accidental fire, which probably destroyed the materials and may have brought on a psychic malaise of which there are rumors in later years, resulted in the abandonment of the publication project for a quarter of a century. Though Newton responded with similar heat to criticisms of other writings, his sensitivity about the theory of light is so acute, his responses so brutally candid, that his behavior seems controlled not by contemporary realities alone but also by events long past.

The great rivals Hooke and Newton kept fencing with each other for years before the final rupture. They made advances, even performed small favors for one another—Hooke sided with Newton in the war against the Jesuits of Liège—but no lasting friendliness eventuated. When Hooke took over the secretaryship of the Royal Society, Newton brought himself to congratulate him.[31] And Hooke again made an effort to get Newton to communicate what he was working on, promising to act as a go-between in keeping him informed of events in the scientific world, which was his appointed function.[32] His inquiring of Newton in a conciliatory letter of November 24, 1679, what he thought about the patently absurd pretensions of one Claude Mallemont de Messanges, a professor of philosophy in the Collège de Plessis who had been pouring out a "new system of the world," was suspect to Koyré, who, in addition to his vast knowledge of their science, had a keen understanding of the intricacies of the exchanges between these two men. Hooke was trying to provoke a reaction, Koyré believed, to his own work on celestial mechanics, *Attempt to Prove the Motion of the Earth from Observations* (1674).[33] Newton's reply of November 28 was rambling and evasive. His mother had been buried on June 4 and he had been away from Trinity for most of six months tending to "Countrey affairs." He then repeated thrice, in various forms, that he had virtually abandoned experimental philosophy: "I had for some years past been endeavouring to bend my self from Philosophy to other studies in so much that I have long grutched the time spent in that study unless it be perhaps at idle hours sometimes for a diversion ... And having thus shook hands with Philosophy, & being also at present taken of wth other business, I hope it will not be interpreted out of any unkindness to you or the R. Society that I am backward in engaging my self in these matters." He might be willing to hear and answer objections to any of his ideas but again only for "divertisment," his affection for philosophy "being worn out, so that I am almost as little concerned about it as one tradesman uses to be about another man's trade or a country man about learning. . . ."[34] That Newton was intentionally putting Hooke off he confessed to Halley a decade later, though this is a retrospective interpretation of his words which does not have to be accepted at face value. "[I]n my answer to his first letter I refused his correspondence, told him I had laid Philosophy aside, sent him only the experimt of Projectiles (rather shortly hinted then carefully described), in complement to sweeten my Answer, expected to hear no further from him."[35]

It was Hooke's misfortune to have Newton as his successor in optics and in dynamics, and in both areas he was so far outstripped that his very existence was for a long time virtually ignored in the history of science. After the failure of an attempt to restore to him far greater weight than his imaginative insights merited,[36] a balance was for a while established by Andrade, Koyré, Herivel, and Rosenfeld; but recently, in a reappraisal of their reappraisal, Westfall has moved in a contrary direction. The latter-day attempt to render historical justice, apportioning the brevets of fame, is an act that neither Hooke nor Newton would have been capable of understanding. They battled over the relative significance of an initial idea and a consummated theory with its mathematical proofs. Koyré held that Hooke had the "idea" as early as 1670 and what he called in 1674 "a system of the world differing in many particulars from any yet known answering in all things to the common rules of mechanical motion" had a striking "near similarity" to Newton's view.[37] Notions of attraction and gravity were common enough in the mid-seventeenth century. Westfall insists that Hooke never had a theory of *universal* gravity, but merely asserted the existence of particular gravities, and that his inverse square relation was a "medley of confusion."[38] Whatever the worth of Hooke's contribution, Newton could not share his birthright with any man—no more with Hooke than with his half brother. Later, in 1686, he executed a maneuver that he had used against Hooke once before: he stated flatly that Hooke had published Giovanni Alfonso Borelli's hypothesis in his own name, an accusation that was quite unacceptable to Koyré. And Newton would repeat the tactic with Leibniz. The idea of a long chain of discovery in which each link adds its own strength was beyond his psychological ken, despite his use of the image from John of Salisbury. If similar wares appeared in the marketplace, then somebody had stolen the original and copied it; and it was easy for Newton to structure a sequence of events that made plagiarism plausible. Once he was embarked upon this line of reasoning, in the heat of controversy the possible was transformed into the probable and the probable into the certain. In his emotional life as in his scientific discoveries Newton "framed" hypotheses. Unfortunately, his psychological conjectures, unlike his inventions, have a way of defying demonstration and proof.

If one follows Koyré—who is quite persuasive—Newton's idea of "sweetening" his answer to Hooke on November 28, 1679, was a bitter pill indeed: a proposal for an experiment that would "prove the motion of the earth by observation," while pretending that he was "unacquainted" with Hooke's "Hypotheses" on celestial motions.[39] Newton's experiment was to provide a solution to the old problem of the trajectory of a heavy body falling to the earth, or to the center of the earth. He suggested offhand as a hypothesis that the trajectory would be a spiral deviating to the east. Whereupon Hooke, in violation of their pact of secrecy, ran to the Royal Society to announce that Newton was wrong: "[H]e shewed, that it would not be a spiral line, as Mr. Newton seemed to suppose, but an excentrical elliptoid, supposing no resistance in the medium: but supposing a resistance, it would be an excentric ellipti-spiral, which, after many revolutions, would rest at last in the centre: that the fall of the heavy body would not be directly east, as Mr. Newton supposed; but to the south-east, and more to the south than the east."[40] Hooke had caught Newton in the trap of an error and was ringing the bells in triumph.

Questions of definition complicate the interpretation of their controversy, but Newton took the position that the fundamental issue was Hooke's conduct: Hooke had presumed to dress him down in public, to maintain that he was wrong, when Newton was merely writing casually about a "fancy." Not only had Hooke "corrected" Newton, an idea that was associated with punishment and mastery over him, but he had exposed him before the Royal Society and the world. Newton still recollected his rage when he described the incident years later in a letter to Halley. "[C]ould scarce perswade my self to answer his second letter, did not answer his third. . . ."[41]

Newton repaid threefold the injury of the "correction" delivered before the Royal Society. On December 13, 1679, he demonstrated in a letter that Hooke was wrong in his conclusion about the path of the trajectory—in the meantime rectifying his own blunder. Newton's reply was tantalizing, beginning with the intimation that he had a full solution to the problem and ending with a teasing remark that it was not worth writing about, sarcastically retracting in advance any mistakes he might be making. The mannerisms of this scientific correspondence, in which the affected style of the great lords is imitated, barely conceal the irony. "Your acute Letter having put me upon considering thus far the species of this curve, I might add something about its description by points *quam proximè*. But the thing being of no great moment I rather beg your pardon for having troubled you thus far wth this second scribble wherin if you meet wth any thing inept or erroneous I hope you will pardon the former & the latter I submit & leave to your correction. . . ."[42] That much for anyone who presumed to "correct" Newton.

The third letter, on January 6, 1680, was the very one in which Hooke solemnly declared his hypothesis on the law of gravity and it became one of the bases of his later claim that he had been robbed of his discovery. Seven years before publication of the *Principia,* Hooke wrote Newton: "But my supposition is that the Attraction always is in a duplicate proportion to the Distance from the Center Reciprocall, and Consequently that the Velocity will be in a subduplicate proportion to the Attraction and Consequently as Kepler Supposes Reciprocall to the Distance."[43] By not responding Newton conveniently blotted out the announcement of a parallel to his great law of the universe.

There is no consistency in Newton's definition of priority of invention. His attitude was flexible and depended upon where he stood in the sequence of events. Was the first generalized conception of an idea an "invention" or was the glory to be conceded only by the man who worked out the abstract intuition in particular experiments verified over and over again along with irrefutable mathematical proofs? Did publication have anything to do with discovery? In answer to Hooke's charge that the *Micrographia* and his conception of gravity had been poached, Newton argued for the completed work, grudgingly conceding some minor influence to his antagonist. To Leibniz, on the other hand, he later maintained that a mere announcement of the existence of a discovery and its recording in an anagram was sufficient to guarantee proprietary rights. Newton was not alone in his anxious concern over priority of discovery. Among the scientists there was great jealousy of the favored one who first saw light pass through the peephole. For many of his contemporaries, and for scientists since, discovery filled profound psychic needs, and total exclusive secret possession was one of them.

In recent years Pope's couplet on Newton, "Nature and Nature's Laws lay hid in night; / God said, Let Newton be!—And all was light," has become unconvincing even as poetic hyperbole. The *Principia* did not spring full-grown like Athena from the head of Zeus. Scholarly analysis of Newton's manuscripts has disclosed that his process of discovery was often tortuous; that while the story of the apple may be true, it was a long way from the initial insight in his mother's garden to the finished mathematical proofs of the *Principia*. The twenty-year interval—long a subject of curiosity among scientists—is explained as much by the persistence of doubts and unresolved technical problems as by his reticence to publish.[44] During these decades the promoting of knowledge had not stopped and other brains, notably Hooke's, were engaged in similar inquiries.[45] Newton wrote a number of versions of the history of his own discovery, but it was difficult for him to allow to others any role in his achievements, and in none of his works was he unstinting in his praise of scientists of the previous generation from whom he inherited. There is a reference to Galileo at the opening of the Scholium to the laws of motion in the *Principia,* but no acknowledgment to Descartes. Newton knew more of Hooke's work than he ever admitted, and even the worshipful Brewster realized that he had not been generous to him in the *Principia*. Newton had a blinding sense of independence and to accept help from others was a defeat; it was tantamount to being subordinate to them. He virtually never reported having been moved to a discovery by what someone else wrote or said, except in the case of Hooke, where the "correction" of Newton's "fancy" acted as a dare, a challenge, a stimulus, a diversion, but not, he insisted, an aid. The mathematical proofs of universal gravity, not the concept or even the formula, were for Newton the crux of the problem. He was indifferent to Hooke's "hypothesis" about gravity; such notions were mere "guesses" like Kepler's. To Fatio, to Derham, to Halley, and who knows to how many others, Newton talked with utter disdain about Hooke's mathematical competence.[46] Hooke was trying to reduce him to a mere arithmetician who had put the finishing touches on an idea of Hooke's invention, whereas he, Newton, and he alone, was the inventor.

According to John Herivel, who has studied the long series of dynamical manuscripts leading to the *Principia,* the first and unsuccessful test of the law of gravity against the moon's motion, which occurred at Woolsthorpe in the summer or autumn of 1666, was followed by a long hiatus from 1667 to 1679 during which Newton was primarily absorbed in other studies. The end of this fallow period coincided with a number of remarkable events: first the death of his mother in June 1679, then six months of business or contemplation in Lincolnshire about which we know little, and finally the provocation of the exchange with Hooke in late 1679, which revived his interest in dynamics and led to the construction of the two propositions corresponding to Kepler's first and second laws of planetary motion, probably before the end of December 1679 —what Herivel calls his "most important single achievement in dynamics."[47]

In the famous account of his discoveries which he drafted for Des Maizeaux around 1718 Newton pushed back the renewal of his interest in planetary motions to 1676–1677, well before the correspondence with Hooke in 1679. "At length in the winter between the years 1676 and 1677 I found the Proposition that by a centrifugal force reciprocally as the square of the distance a Planet must revolve in an Ellipsis about the center of the force placed in the lower umbilicus of the Ellipsis and with a radius drawn to that center describe areas proportional to the times."[48] So minor an antedating of his discovery may be psychologically insignificant and even accidental, for he recognized Hooke's negative role in the resumption of his studies in dynamics and had written as much to Halley; but it may also be a way of eradicating the memory of the enemy. Far more intriguing is the proximity of this crucial discovery to his mother's death. Great moments of creative inspiration as sequels to tragic deprivations have long been commented upon in psychoanalytic literature, from Freud's recounting of his own experiences to recent attempts to characterize such acts as restitutive. The pivotal innovation in the elaboration of Newton's world system following the death of his mother could be another dramatic example of a restorative act after a great loss. John Herivel, though he does not ordinarily deal with psychological phenomena, hints at the possibility: "[W]hen the time was ripe, at the height of his powers, with a mind purged by the most intense emotional experience of his life, he could turn, at Hooke's prompting, to the supreme problem of elliptical motion and find ready to hand just those tools needed to carry the work through to a final conclusion."[49]

The dating of Newton's successful test of the law of gravity and the character of the interruption, from 1680 to 1684, before the final formulation of his fundamental laws are the subject of a number of hypotheses of a technical character beyond the scope of this study. Herivel's revised chronology of the last stages of the *Principia* runs as follows: Halley probably first visited Newton in May 1684, after which he worked out the missing propositions and added a number of new ones. One or more further visits from Halley ensued, and in November 1684 the second version of the tract "De Motu" was sent to London and entered in the Register Book of the Royal Society before February 23, 1685, as "Propositiones de Motu."

Upon the formal presentation of the *Principia* to the Royal Society on April 28, 1686, Hooke directly and publicly accused Newton of plagiarism in connection with the law of gravity. This was the final defy. Though Newton was still in Cambridge, he no longer had to rely upon Oldenburg "kindle Cole" as a reporter of what went on among the scientific elect, for Edmond Halley was in London. Fourteen years Newton's junior, Halley had completely identified himself with the *Principia*. When he first visited Newton in Cambridge he was twenty-eight, and for the rest of Newton's life he served the man whose colossal genius he was great enough to appreciate. Newton's capacity to demonstrate mathematically a law of gravity which he and Wren and Hooke had all intuited in various ways overwhelmed Halley with admiration. It was he who first reported Newton's solution to the Society and he who undertook to bear both the cost and burden of publication when the Society had drained its treasury in printing Willughby's *De Historia Piscium*. For forty-three years Halley, who had a subtle understanding of Newton's character, managed to maintain amicable relations with him, despite occasional reproofs when Halley overstepped the bounds of propriety with raillery in matters of religion. And even after Newton's death he loyally defended the astronomical data in his patron's revision of world chronology, despite the fact that he had more than passing doubts about the validity of the whole system. When Hooke made his charge before members of the Royal Society, Halley was able to report to Newton with sober objectivity, with no incitement, methodically trying to calm down the older man and, moreover, succeeding a good part of the time.

Halley's first report of what had transpired at the presentation of the *Principia* was bland enough. As a great compromiser, he thought that Hooke's claims about the law of gravity could be silenced with an honorable acknowledgment. (Halley's letters to other scientists testify that at this period he had no mean appreciation of Hooke's intuitive genius.[50]) "There is one thing more I ought to informe you of," he began gingerly in his letter of May 22, 1686, from London, "viz, that Mr Hook has some pretensions upon the invention of the rule of the decrease of Gravity, being reciprocally as the squares of the distances from the Center. He sais you had the notion from him, though he owns the Demonstration of the Curves generated therby to be wholly your own; how much of this is so, you know best, as likewise what you have to do in this matter, only Mr Hook seems to expect you should make some mention of him,

in the preface, which, it is possible, you may see reason to praefix."
Like the messenger bearing evil tidings to the king, he feared his
anger and yet he performed his mission with dignity. "I must beg
your pardon that it is I, that send you this account, but I thought it
my duty to let you know it, that so you may act accordingly; being
in myself fully satisfied, that nothing but the greatest Candour imaginable, is to be expected from a person, who of all men has the
least need to borrow reputation."[51]

Newton's reply was immediate, on May 27, 1686, a devastating
denial. He told Halley that in the papers in his hands there was not
a single proposition to which Hooke could lay any claim and he
therefore saw no reason why he should cite him. In those on the
"systeme of the world," he had made reference to Hooke along with
others. Then he laboriously rehearsed the old Hooke-Newton correspondence of 1679–1680 and the history of any ideas on gravity
that may have come from Wren;[52] the account was repeated on June
20 with an elaborate postscript:

Borel did something in it & wrote modestly, he [Hooke] has done nothing &
yet written in such a way as if he knew & had sufficiently hinted all but what
remained to be determined by the drudgery of calculations & observations, ex-
cusing himself from that labour by reason of his other business: whereas he
should rather have excused himself by reason of his inability. For tis plain
by his words he knew not how to go about it. Now is not this very fine?
Mathematicians that find out, settle & do all the business must content themselves with being nothing but dry calculators & drudges & another that does
nothing but pretend & grasp at all things must carry away all the invention
as well of those that were to follow him as of those that went before.

Once Newton was possessed he was prepared to go to any length,
however childish, to injure his enemy. He would under no circumstances engage with Hooke; and if those were the accusations, he
was ready to eliminate the entire third book of the *Principia*. Unless
the whole world would receive the tablets of his law without cavil,
he would smash them, or at least a third of them. "Philosophy is
such an impertinently litigious Lady that a man had as good be engaged in Law suits as have to do with her. I found it so formerly &

now I no sooner come near her again but she gives me warning."[53] At one point he was prepared to suppress the magnificent title itself, refraining only because it would hurt the sale of the book and Halley had risked the investment.

Fear of exposure, with its profound psychic ramifications, is one key to Newton's reluctance to appear before the public eye—already remarked upon in connection with the Lucas correspondence. But there is also a need to withhold, a refusal to surrender what has become part of his being, a game that involves telling others that he has it in him at the same time that he will not separate it from himself. The act of completion was difficult for him because it meant ending, consummating, breaking away. When Newton had the truth he felt no need to share it; he neither received from others nor did he wish to give. The initial insights came easily; they poured out like a flood; and then he let the papers lie about. By the time Halley appeared the most difficult questions in the problem of gravity had been resolved to Newton's satisfaction, and what lay ahead were the elegant systematization, the proofs, and the structuring of the materials into an architectonic whole. But it required young Halley's encouragement and reassuring affection for Newton to surmount the last hurdles.[54] The eighteen months of prodigious labor that preceded the completion of the system are of an order of creativity recalling the *annus mirabilis* of 1665–1666. Newton seems a man transformed—one historian has even noticed that the handwriting of his manuscripts during this period looks different.[55] The *Principia* required Halley's love. In a rare testimonial to a living person, Newton wrote in the preface to the first edition (dated May 8, 1686): "In the publication of this work the most acute and universally learned Mr. *Edmund Halley* not only assisted me in correcting the errors of the press and preparing the geometrical figures, but it was through his solicitations that it came to be published; for when he had obtained of me my demonstrations of the figure of the celestial orbits, he continually pressed me to communicate the same to the *Royal Society*."[56] But the provocation of Hooke, the desire to trounce him, to crush him once and for all, also stung Newton into action. For so great a creation as the *Principia* two midwives were necessary, each assisting at the birth in a unique fashion.

Newton was constantly torn between the dread of involvement in the rough and tumble of conflict with other men and the need to defend his person and what was his, the theoretical structures which he had built around himself. Time and again he would announce that no invention in philosophy was worth contending for and he would abandon the field. For a man of his character there was always the ultimate dangerous enticement of Narcissus, of sinking into a private world and contemplating only for himself and eternity. Through the long years in Cambridge he alternated between escapes into solitude and, when the dikes broke, violent outbursts in which his rage overflowed. When he was aroused beyond control, nothing mattered but defeat of the enemy, and Newton lost sight of the very work he was protecting as he became a hunter seeking to fell his prey, nothing more. It is not uncommon for men who are extremely sensitive to criticism to be blindly injurious to others.

On June 29, 1686, Halley sent Newton a milder version of Hooke's accusation of plagiarism. He was worried that Hooke's conduct had been painted in worse colors than it ought to have been—after all, Hooke had not lodged a formal complaint with the Society demanding that justice be done him nor had he pretended that the whole of the theory was his. At the formal presentation of Newton's book before the Society Hooke had sustained a psychological blow whose full impact Halley sensed. Sir John Hoskins, the Vice-President (one of Hooke's closest friends, whose name is always cropping up in the diary), had been in the chair when Dr. Vincent delivered the encomium of the work, praising both the novelty and the dignity of the subject. Another member had observed that Newton carried the proofs so far that nothing remained to be added. Hoskins had then warmed to the occasion and announced that the *Principia* was the more to be prized because it had been invented and perfected by the same man. Robert Hooke could not endure this public praise of his rival for "invention" from the mouth of his friend Hoskins, who, though privy to his secret ideas about gravity, had not even alluded to him in his remarks. The two, who until then had been almost inseparable cronies, had a falling out and scarcely saw each other thereafter.

The members having adjourned to a coffeehouse after the formal session, Hooke had tried to convince them that he had given Newton the first hint of the "invention"; but, Halley reported, they were all of the opinion that since nothing of Hooke's had appeared either in print or on the books of the Society, Newton alone was the inventor. If Hooke had in fact discovered the law before Newton, he had only himself to blame for not having staked his claim by an overt act. Halley again begged Newton not to "let his resentments run so high" that he would deprive the world of the third book of the *Principia,* introducing the plea with a simple, straightforward affirmation that was meant to allay his indignation: "I am sure that the Society have a very great satisfaction in the honour you do them, by your dedication of so worthy a Treatise."[57]

By this time Newton's temper had subsided, and his letter of July 14, 1686, regretted the postscript of the previous one. He even conceded that there was one fact in Hooke's letters that was new to him: "Twas the deflexion of falling bodies to the south east in our Latitude."[58] But for the rest he continued with the self-justification, which he repeated on July 27. Hooke's pretending to be his "master" had merely irritated him into making his discovery, nothing more. "And thô his correcting my Spiral occasioned my finding the Theorem by wch I afterward examined the Ellipsis; yet I am not beholden to him for any light into that business but only for the diversion he gave me from my other studies to think on these things & for his dogmaticalnes in writing as if he had found the motion in the Ellipsis, wch inclined me to try it after I saw by what method it was to be done."[59] Descartes's errors, he later told Conduitt, made him discover the true system of the world; Hooke too served to goad him on.[60]

During this final ugly episode with Hooke, the third by Newton's count—and he kept a reckoning—no letters passed between them. Hooke's bitterness is recorded in diary entries whenever their paths crossed. The man was beside himself. On February 15, 1689: "At Hallys met Newton; vainly pretended claim yet acknowledged my information. Interest has no conscience; A posse ad esse non valet consequentia." By July 1689 Hooke could not endure Newton's person. On July 3, at the Royal Society meeting: "Hoskins, Henshaw, Hill, Hall: dispute about Newton, of Leibnitz fallere fallentens. Newton & Mr Hamden came in, I went out: returnd not till 7." On August 24: "Newton R"; on August 30: "Newton." On February 3, 1690, Hooke dined with Dr. Busby and reported only: "Dr. Hickman there; sayd Newton the veryest knave in all the Ho:."[61] On September 15, 1689, Aubrey had written the Oxford antiquary and historian Anthony à Wood a letter that was emended by Hooke himself. It supported the charge that Newton had plagiarized Hooke's conception of gravity and praised his friend in extravagant terms: "Mr Wood! This is the greatest discovery in nature, that ever was since the world's creation: it never was so much as hinted by any man before. I know you will doe him right. I hope you may read his hand: I wish he had writt plainer, and afforded a little more paper."[62]

When two powerful figures challenged each other in the small, cramped, scientific societies of the seventeenth century, the clash resounded. There was not room at the head of the Royal Society for both Hooke and Newton. In an almost animal sense one and one only could be the champion of knowledge. Newton was an intruder into a kingdom where Hooke had once reigned supreme, and as the new star rose Hooke lost power and status. He fought for his position, belittling the achievements of the newcomer, repeatedly charging him with plagiarism, clinging tenaciously to his post until his death in 1703—toward the end mere skin and bones. It was only then that Newton assumed the presidency of the Society and became uncontested leader of the herd.

Chapter 8

IN QUEST OF THE GOLDEN FLEECE

Subtle: Sirrah my varlet, stand you forth and speak to him
Like a Philosopher: answer in the language,
Name the vexations, and the martyrizations
Of the metals in the work.
Face: Sir, putrefaction,
Solution, ablution, sublimation,
Cohobation, calcination, ceration, and
Fixation . . .
Subtle: And whence comes vivification?
Face: After mortification.
Subtle: What's cohobation?
Face: Tis the pouring on
Your aqua regis, and drawing him off
To the trine circle of the seven spheres.
—Ben Jonson, *The Alchemist*

THE first dated letter we have from Newton's hand addressed to an actual person was written May 18, 1669, probably to Francis Aston, a Fellow of Trinity who was three years Newton's junior.[1] The salutation is unique in Newton's correspondence: a simple "Fr.," an intimate abbreviation. Though by letters patent Newton was allowed to retain his Fellowship without taking holy orders, the privilege was not extended to Aston, and he went off to Europe on the grand tour. In 1678 he became a member of the Royal Society and was rather frequently of the Council, serving as a joint secretary with Robert Hooke in the early 1680's. During Newton's quarrels with Flamsteed and Leibniz, he was one of that group of intimate followers upon whose unquestioned loyalty Newton could count whenever they were appointed to impartial committees set up to adjudicate the disputes in which he was entangled. Until his death in 1715, Aston remained Newton's friend. He was a relative nonentity, one of those gentleman amateurs of science who comprised more than half the membership of the Society and, in the absence of grants from the Treasury, were a mainstay of the body—Aston bequeathed to it all his property and books.

In about half the letter to Aston, written in response to a request for guidance on the eve of his departure for the Continent, Newton at the age of twenty-six and a half struck a Polonius-like pose, proffering pompous paternal advice to another Fellow on proper worldly behavior in foreign parts. The appointment as Lucasian Professor did not come until later that year, but Newton was already beginning to speak ex cathedra. Though a goodly portion of this letter virtually paraphrases a document written in an unknown hand in 1658 and found among Newton's papers, "An Abridgement of a Manuscript of Sr Robert Southwell's concerning travelling,"[2] such minor literary plagiarism is not to be taken too seriously. (There were petty as well as major cheats in his life, and the brass half crown of his confession of 1662 was followed by other attempts to pass false coin.) Newton delivered a lesson in discretion, counseling his friend to be watchful of a foreign interlocutor's humors, to use insinuation, to avoid quarrels, never to criticize strangers, to overpraise if necessary, to accept an insult rather than bear the marks of a fight throughout one's life—"if you out live it att all." He should at any cost keep reason above passion and exercise self-control. Since young Newton often lived among men as if he were in foreign parts the letter has a measure of psychological interest, for his own behavior is like the model; he constantly admonished himself to forbear when provoked because he knew and feared the consequence of his temper. Until he rose to prominence, Newton made a show of being a careful, prudent man who rarely broke the sententious rules of self-discipline he laid down for Aston, since they were dictated by religion and were the way to get ahead in the world with safety. Newton as a young man is not without guile—though always in a righteous cause.

Having completed his little sermon, Newton proceeded to list matters worth observing when abroad; and the provincial yeoman's son established as a criterion of excellence whether "they" surpassed or came short of "us" in England. Newton remained insular all his life, and though he made exceptions he had no great liking for foreigners. He was surely not curious enough to travel among them. Finally Newton turned to a subject that had just begun to intrigue him, alchemy, and he instructed Aston that if in foreign lands he met with "any transmutations out of one species into another (as out of Iron into Copper, out of any metall into quicksilver, out of one salt into another or into an insipid body &c) those above all others will bee worth your noting being the most luciferous & many times lucriferous experiments too in Philosophy." The Fitzwilliam notebook for April 1669, the month before the letter to Aston, records a two-pound expenditure for "aqua fortis, sublimate, oyle, perle, fine silver, antimony, vinegar, spirit of wine, white lead, allome niter, tartar, salt of tartar, ☿ ," in addition to the payments for furnaces and the *Theatrum Chemicum,* a six-volume compendium of alchemical writings published in Strasbourg by Lazarus Zetzner.[3]

Newton had thus already embarked upon the long alchemical and chemical quest, which he did not abandon until he left for London in 1696 to become Warden of the Mint (even afterward there were intermittent flickers of interest)—a quarter of a century of study and experimentation that yielded one published fragment on acids and a vast accumulation of papers running to about six hundred fifty thousand words, most of them extracts from more than a hundred recondite alchemical treatises. A single alchemical manuscript of his, the "Sententiae notabiles," compiled sometime after 1686, cites seventy-odd references from the literature.[4] When Sir David Brewster found five alchemical treatises copied verbatim in Newton's hand, he brought himself reluctantly to comprehend how a great mind like Newton's might inquire into whether or not the transmutation and multiplication of metals were possible; but that Newton should copy out page after page of "contemptible alchemical poetry" was beyond him. At his death Newton owned about a hundred volumes on alchemy and seventy-five more that have been classified as chemistry and mineralogy, comprising a tenth of his total library; and an inventory of the few effects catalogued after his death lists a "parcel of chymical glasses."[5]

A substantial portion of Newton's manuscripts dealing with alchemy extant at the time of the Sotheby sale are today in King's College, Cambridge. Many are simply transcriptions in his hand of sections of standard alchemical texts; it was a normal practice among his contemporaries to enter into commonplace books long quotations from their reading. Other manuscripts are brief commentaries in which Newton made an effort to analyze and understand the esoteric writers, often comparing and contrasting different opinions about a stage of the traditional alchemical process.[6] One piece, an "Index Chemicus" with its supplement, is an ambitious alphabetical compendium of a hundred and thirteen pages covering the usage of alchemical terms in scores of authors Newton had consulted, along with conscientious citations for each item.[7] Only rarely is there a critical evaluation of what he excerpted and glossed. Zetzner's Latin *Theatrum Chemicum* was combed over and over again, as was the compilation in English made by Elias Ashmole, the *Theatrum Chemicum Britannicum*. The collection in King's College also includes sixteenth- and seventeenth-century manuscripts that are not in Newton's hand but belonged to him.

In 1669 Newton requested Aston to verify a whole series of metallurgical and alchemical hints that he had garnered from the *Symbola Aureae Mensae Duodecim Nationum* (Frankfurt, 1617), another anthology of alchemical authors, edited by the Hungarian alchemist Count Michael Maier.[8] He was particularly curious about rumors connected with a famous charlatan, Giuseppe Francesco Borri. Many of the questions Newton propounded are perhaps metallurgical rather than alchemical, but he was hovering on the ill-defined borderland between the realms.

Whither at Schemnitium in Hungary (where there are Mines of Gold, copper, Iron, vitrioll, Antimony, &c) they change Iron into Copper by dissolving it in a Vitriolate water wch they find in cavitys of rocks in the mines & then melting the slymy solution in a strong fire wch in the cooling proves copper. The like is said to bee done in other places wch I cannot now remember. Perhaps too it may bee done in Italy; For about 20 or 30 years agone there was a certain Vitriol came from thence (called Roman Vitrioll, but of a nobler vertue than that wch is now called by that name) wch Vitrioll is not now to bee gotten becaus perhaps they make a greater gain by some such trick as turning Iron into Copper wth it then by selling it. 2 Whither in Hungary, Sclavonia, Bohemia neare the town Eila, or at the Mountains of Bohemia neare Silesia there be rivers whose waters are impregnated with gold; perhaps the Gold being dissolved by som corrosive waters like *Aqua Regis* & the solution carried along wth the streame that runs through the mines. And whither the practise of laying mercury in the rivers till it be tinged wth gold & then straining the mercury through leather that the gold may stay behind, bee a secret yet or openly practised. . . . 4 There is in Holland one—Bory, who some yeares since was imprisoned by the Pope to have extorted from him some secrets (as I am told) of great worth both as to medicine & profit, but hee escaped into Holland where they have granted him a guard. I think he usually goes clothed in green, pray enquire wt you can of him, & whither his ingenuity bee any profit to the Dutch.

In the same year 1669 there appeared in London a short book with a long title: *Secrets Reveal'd: or An Open Entrance to the Shut-Palace of the King: Containing the greatest Treasure in Chymistry, never yet so plainly Discovered. Composed by a most famous English-Man, styling himself Anonymous, or Eyraeneus Philaletha Cosmopolita who, by Inspiration and Reading, attained to the Philosophers Stone at his Age of Twenty three Years, Anno Domini, 1645, Published for the Benefit of all English-men by W.C. Esq; a true Lover of Art and Nature.* This was one of many volumes of the same character that William Cooper published during the Restoration in an attempt to make available part of the European treasury of alchemical writings.[9] When Newton first acquired the slender volume is unknown, but he filled it with marginalia on almost every page drawn from the numerous alchemical works that he owned. If Philaletha had probed the deep mysteries when he was a young man of twenty-three, could they be withheld from Isaac Newton? The book is written in the symbolic language of the alchemists from which chemists were making an effort to free themselves, an enigmatic vocabulary with which Newton had familiarized himself. On one of the pages of *Secrets Reveal'd*, for example, he commented on the medical uses of alchemical secrets: "Then the Gold dissolving rises by little & little to the top of the water like a white skin or cream scarce distinguishable from the water. This skin Artephius teaches to gather with a feather & after the ☿ is evaporated there will remain a sweet white oyle wch is good for mitigating the pain of wounds, & in wch [philoso]Phers have placed their great secrets for medicine: especially if it be made wth the virgins milk of the ☉ ffor then it is a red fragrant . . . sweet oyle or balsam permiscible in all things, the highest medicine."[10]

That Newton was at one time engaged in a quest for the golden fleece, the alchemical designation for the philosopher's stone, is still doubted by the bowdlerizing rationalists, who summarily dismiss the great pile of alchemical manuscripts in his hand, the reports of secret conversations with adepts, and at least a hundred alchemical volumes in his library, and insist on defining his addiction to this literature as an orthodox scientific interest in chemistry.[11] The image of the golden fleece had a lasting fascination for this grazier's son. When during his London period his private studies in alchemy were replaced by an increasing absorption in chronology, the key date upon which his radical revision of the traditional system rested was the year of the Argonautic expedition, Jason's adventure to possess the golden fleece of Colchis.

A preface to *Secrets Reveal'd* exalts young Philaletha, the only one of his time who among quacks and "false Coiners" had discovered from books the real "Physical Tincture."[12] That all great truths about nature had been recorded somewhere by the ancients is one of the basic postulates of Newton's thought, and it was the duty of the searcher to decipher the hieroglyphs in which ancient wisdom was cast. If Newton could from the symbol of the lyre deduce that Pythagoras had understood the law of gravity, even its mathematical formula, why might not the truth of a universal medium be concealed in one of the many rare alchemical writings he copied, abstracted, studied and explicated? His world was full of hieroglyphs verbal and pictorial, and he believed that the poetry of an alchemist like Thomas Norton or the figures painted upon an arch in St. Innocent's churchyard in Paris and interpreted by Nicholas Flamel could hold the same secret.[13] Elias Ashmole, an original Fellow of the Royal Society, had written of the periodic reappearance through all time of alchemists who possessed the hidden truth—"although the heedlesse world hath seldome taken notice of them."[14] The age of twenty-three was favorable to alchemical discovery. Norton, Theophrastus Paracelsus, and Dionysius Zacharias had all learned of the "gold-making Medicine" when they were quite young. But Philaletha had surpassed them, for while the other adepts had been aided by tutors, he had divined the true elixir from books alone. Almost every page of the preface to *Secrets Reveal'd* was a taunt and a challenge to Newton. To Philaletha "God hath poured down this occult Science . . . through the open windows of Heaven." Newton, too, had had his *annus mirabilis* at the age of twenty-three.

It is not easy to evoke a climate of opinion in which men of such eminence as Robert Boyle, Isaac Newton, John Locke, the King's physician Edmund Dickinson,[15] and Fatio de Duillier could be engaged in alchemical experiments. The alchemist is a stock comic character in Ben Jonson's play, and it seems incongruous that some half century later the procedures he ridiculed were studied and imitated by men of high seriousness. Far from being despised, alchemy experienced something of a revival under the Restoration —witness the number of alchemical treatises which for the first time appeared in English translation.[16] Imagery from this body of esoteric literature in popular poets like Dryden points to a far broader diffusion of alchemical knowledge among ordinary educated men than might be supposed if one focused solely on the mathematical core of the new philosophy.[17] The alchemical substructure of Hermetic, Pythagorean, and neo-Platonic thought was not strange to Newton and his philosophical colleagues in Cambridge. Though the heyday of the Paracelsians under the Commonwealth was passed, there was still support for Van Helmont's reformulation of Paracelsism, emphasizing experimentation and avoiding mere fancies.[18] The new mechanical philosophy pointed in a different direction, but the breach with the past was neither sudden nor universal.

By the time of the Restoration, the alchemist had been divested of his long gown and stripped of his grizzly beard. Despite the statute of Henry IV against "multiplyers," which was in effect until 1689,[19] there were groups of adventurers in London who formed themselves into companies and supported the researches of an "artist" pretending either that he had already discovered, or was about to discover, a technique for transmuting baser metals into more precious ones, above all gold. These men were motivated by greed for money; and their clandestine enterprises do not appear more extraordinary than the hazardous overseas voyages in which similar companies invested their capital. In the dedications of "Englished" alchemical books during this period there are many intimations that eccentric noblemen continued to support alchemist "pretenders" on their country estates in the same style that medieval and Renaissance potentates once had.

By the mid-seventeenth century there was hardly any magic left in alchemical operations, which followed set recipes and were based upon a number of plausible preconceptions: that precious metals grow in the earth in some places and that therefore a way might be discovered to make them grow in the laboratory; that certain earths, especially those of Central Europe, are endowed with unique virtues; that a rearrangement of the atoms in metals by art is conceivable even as, in accordance with the teachings of Epicurus and Lucretius, atoms are continually forming new configurations in nature; that certain metals, especially quicksilver, transfigured into a "subtil" essence through the agency of fire might become the crucial element in the alchemical process.[20]

But in many works on alchemy the ultimate quest took a different turn. Concentration on the production of gold was looked upon as a corruption of the alchemical philosopher's true mission, which was the discovery of a stone or an elixir to cure all the diseases besetting mankind.[21] The concoction of this universal medicine and its distribution to suffering millions was regarded as an act of Christian charity demanded by God of the chosen philosopher whom he had guided to the secret. There are also writings, however, in which the use of the stone for the love of man is subordinated to a diabolical promise that its possession will endow the holder with powers not only remedial but fantastic—seeing at a great distance and forcing others to bow to one's will. While these occult powers of the stone are not stressed in the alchemical treatises, there are manuscripts—one of which Newton transcribed—whose claims can only be called mysterious. Though Newton did not ordinarily move along this path, he was at least curious about such fancies or attracted to them; else why did he copy the texts? It is difficult to imagine what chemical knowledge he could conceivably have gleaned from the following abstract he made out of a manuscript entitled "The Epitome of the Treatise of Health, written by Edwardus Generosus Anglicus innominato who lived Anno Domini 1562":

Edwardus Generosus speaks of 4 stones, the Mineral, Vegetable, Animal & Angelic or the Prospective Stone or divine and magical stone of Moses. The mineral stone is for transmuting metals and hath in him these four natures, that is, he is Animal Vegetable Mineral & Metalline, & yet hath no part of the other 3 stones in him, nor have they any part of his degrees, because they have not any metalline nature or earthly substance in them. This stone is greatly amended by mixture with any of the other three & they are thereby debased. The vegetable stone is of a growing nature & works miraculous effects in vegetables & growing things, as in the nature of man and beast. The Animal is for the animal faculties, the Angelic for magical operations. It keeps mans body from corruption, & endues him with divine gifts & knowledge of things ["to come" is crossed out] by dreams & revelations. By carrying it about wth him he feels most heavenly fragrant beravishing smells. And oftentimes (they say) shall see the apparition of most glorious & blessed Angels. No evil spirit shall endure to come near the bearer thereof, no the fire burn him. Dunstan calls it Angels food because a man may live a long time wthout any food by the tast of this stone. It is an enemy to all corruptibility in mans body. Of some tis called the tree of life. The tree of knowledge. Next under God tis dator annorum. The other two are not to be compared to this. The learned stand in doubt whether a man can dye or not that hath this stone saving that Mors omnibus communis est. Some think that by it the Patriachs [sic] lived long, and Moses the servant of God & Hermes otherwise called Henoch did wonderful things. You may by this prospective stone see whats done in any part of the world & thereby know whether your wife or friend be true to you, who loves or hates you & what shal happen to you before it come to pass. Tis the most fixt resplendent transparent stone in the world, as fixt as ☉ and cast upon him alters him into all manner of resplendent transparent colours.[22]

That Newton might discover an elixir of life which would bestow immortality upon him—if not upon his fellowmen, about whom he had less concern—may be a remote motivation for his search, but one not to be wholly excluded in the light of his hypochondria and his omnipotence fantasies.

Chemical and alchemical curiosity could of course transcend the craving for gold or the universal remedy and relate to the eminently scientific and religious hope that man might fathom the fundamental nature and structure of matter itself. Though this is an area in which Newton's labors through the years did not come to fruition, he left cryptic hints about the nature of the atom in which some commentators have seen foreshadowed the discoveries of a later age. Stukeley reports hearing at one time that Newton had penetrated to the very core of chemistry in a paper "explaining the principles of that mysterious art upon experimental and mathematical proofs and he valued it much, but it was unluckily burnt in his laboratory which casually took fire. He would never undertake that work again, a loss much to be regretted."[23] Vavilov saw in Newton's oracular "Queries" appended to the *Opticks* a belief in some atomic theory in which all elements would be explained as geometrical groupings of a universal atomic substance.

With the possible exception of the plain desire for gain, of which I have discovered little sign in Newton beyond his reference to luciferous experiments in the letter to Aston, he was at one time or another excited by all of the common drives toward alchemical exploration. For him alchemy could serve a multiplicity of purposes:

it could be a source of information for the chemical study of metal alloys; it could spur the search for the basic structure of matter; and it might conceivably reveal the philosopher's stone whose secret lay hidden somewhere in the wisdom of alchemical recipes handed down from ancient times. His faith was not constant, and he vacillated about the chances of success of the alchemical enterprise, but though there was a time when he claimed to have found an irrefutable argument against it, he never let go completely. He could often be galvanized into action by the mere rumor or suspicion that someone else had made a discovery where he had failed or attained only partial fulfillment. The scientific chemists of the seventeenth century were suspicious of the alchemists or self-proclaimed philosophers because of the traditional frauds associated with them and their extravagant pretensions to new discoveries. As Newton wrote in "Sendivogius explained": "Innumerable new things found out by the Ancients are falsely boasted of by Hermetick Professors."[24] But this wariness did not prevent Boyle and Newton from holding secret meetings with them and reading their books while deriding them and warning of their deceits in public. Alchemy as practiced by Newton and Boyle was founded upon the corpuscular theory of matter, but those who depict their writings and experiments in alchemy as mere exercises in this theory have too restricted a sense of the potency of the alchemical world view. There are times when the secret alchemical truth may have appeared to Newton closer to the nature of things than even his great physical laws.

A more intricate question involves alchemical symbolism. One does not have to commit oneself to the philosophical and psychological doctrines of Carl Jung to recognize in the twelve basic procedures outlined in alchemical treatises dramas of mystical communion or of death and resurrection. Newton himself summarized a description of the *Conjunctio viri rubi cum foemina alba* from Flamel— the meaning it had for him unfortunately remains veiled. "Flammel in Chap. 5 paints a man & a woman cloathed in a Orange roab upon a field azure & blew to signify that in this second operation [after putrefaction] you have truly but not yet perfectly two natures conjoyned & married a masculine & a feminine or rather the four elements & these natural enemies begin to approach one another amiably & lay aside the enmity of the old chaos."[25] And who can fathom the import for Newton of a passage headed "Mayer's ffigures praefixed to Basil Valentine's 'Key' "? "Two women cloathed riding on two lyons: each with a heart in her hand. . . . The right hand lyon farts on a company of young lyons behind it & bites the snout of the left hand Lyon & tears him with her paw. This Lyon by her farting (wch signifies her aerial form) & young ones, & being on the side of the hearts next the moon & her biting & tearing the other Lyon signifies the female. Behind the woman on the left hand Lyon is an armed man lifting up a sword as if he would cut of the neck of that woman."[26] Other writers that Newton excerpted contented themselves with less bizarre imagery. In George Ripley's *The Compound of Alchymy,* which Newton encountered in Ashmole's collection, the stages or twelve gates of the alchemical process are headed in the conventional manner: calcination, dissolution, separation, conjunction, putrefaction, congelatyon, cybatyone, sublymation, fermentation, exaltation, multiplycatyon, projectyon;[27] but Newton perceived that, all the same, arcane meanings were locked into the text. In "Notes upon Ripley" he wrote: "In his Gates he describes more openly the operations of nature in the glass, & more secretly hints the operations of the artist."[28]

The curative or regenerative effect of reading narratives of the alchemical drama or of its enactment through firing metals is not determinable, but the accounts of Newton's toiling at his furnace at the spring and fall of the leaf, his staying awake whole nights by the fire, expose a passion that has struck deep roots. Humphrey Newton's prosy sketch only sets the scene for Newton the Alchemist: "About six weeks at spring, and six at the fall, the fire in the elaboratory scarcely went out, which was well furnished with chemical materials as bodies, receivers, heads, crucibles, etc., which was [sic] made very little use of, the crucibles excepted, in which he fused his metals; he would sometimes, tho' very seldom, look into an old mouldy book which lay in his elaboratory, I think it was titled

Agricola de metallis, the transmuting of metals being his chief design, for which purpose antimony was a great ingredient."[29] With his own eyes Newton saw the hot molten liquid flow, the putrefaction and the vivification. There is a stray phrase on one of his papers: "Sowing Gold into the earth, Death & Resurrection."[30] One even wonders what satisfactions he may have derived from what Ben Jonson called the "vexations and martyrizations of metals in the work." The part that fire played in the fantasy of Isaac Newton is only hinted at in his writings. He would "burn" his mother and stepfather; he was always afraid of being "embroiled"; and each autumn, at least when Humphrey Newton was with him, he would stoke his little furnace in the garden. One face of Newton was that of a "philosopher by the fire" in the grand tradition of Jean-Baptiste van Helmont.

Philosophical alchemy had a traditional morality and code of behavior not unlike that of the pious Puritans, and its asceticism was appreciated by Newton. The alchemist or son of Pyrotechny "must resolve to give himself up wholly unto it, and the prosecution of the same, next unto the service of God," wrote George Starkey in *Pyrotechny asserted and illustrated* (1658), a work Newton excerpted. "He must join prayer unto God, with serious meditation, and diligent industrie, this is the way to attain true knowledge. . . . Therefor is true medicine a serious, secret & sacred art, which requires the whole man, and it is to be sought for charitable ends, so is it to be imployed only with designe to glorifie God in doing good."[31] The sins of the alchemist are neglect of God, vicious living, wicked conversation that hinders a man from industrious search, idleness, laziness, pride and conceit among those who straightway think themselves nothing inferior to Hermes or Paracelsus, and finally covetousness. Among Newton's papers are many extracts in his hand in which alchemists pray that they may be granted the discovery of the philosopher's stone as a gift from God, and solemnly engage not to use the knowledge revealed to them for selfish ends or betray the secret to the wicked.[32] Even when Newton was a very old man, John Conduitt heard him speak favorably of the alchemical quest for both moral and scientific reasons: "They who search after the Philosopher's Stone by their own rules obliged to a strict & religious life. That study fruitful of experiments."[33]

In Ashmole's *Theatrum Chemicum Britannicum,* Newton had read the moral imperatives of the English alchemical tradition. The volume began with the stilted rhymes of Thomas Norton's *Ordinall of Alchimy:* "The first chapter shall all Men teache/ What manner People may this Science reache,/ And whie the trew Science of Alkimy/ Is of old Fathers called Blessed and Holy." As in the Cabala, communication of the highest secret was restricted to word of mouth. "For this Science must ever Secret be/ The Cause where of is this as ye may see/ If one evill man had here of all his will/ All Christian Peace he might hastilie spill/ And with his Pride he might pull downe/ Rightfull Kings and Princes of renowne/ Wherefore the sentence of perill and jeopardy/ Upon the Teacher resteth dreadfully."[34] In alchemy as in prophecy one first had to distinguish "fals Men from trew." The alchemical, like the prophetic, preparation was a rigorous one. The masters were aware of the ambiguous nature of their art, and secrecy was imperative to prevent the elixir from falling into the hands of a wicked man. Newton took seriously the warnings of the master alchemists and cabalists that their truths were to be revealed only to those morally prepared and worthy. Secretiveness was deeply embedded in his character; a fear of being seen was the counterpart of a passionate desire to see hidden things. Viewed against this background, his cryptic correspondence with Boyle, Locke, and Fatio about alchemy, which was enveloped with all manner of safeguards against disclosure, becomes more comprehensible. Normally reserved, in dealing with alchemy Newton would double his defenses and look askance upon those who were incautious in their inquiries.

If Isaac Barrow was Newton's original mentor in mathematics, optics, and chronology, Boyle's works, which began to appear when Newton first came up to Cambridge, encouraged the expression of another side of his nature. At this time the practice of multiplication was prohibited by law, and only a man of Boyle's stature and prestige permitted himself public utterances on alchemical subjects. He expressed annoyance with those Paracelsians who claimed to know universal remedies but refused to divulge them, causing pain and suffering to thousands by their reticence. In conversation Boyle could lead Newton to extravagant flights of fancy which he might otherwise have repressed. On September 14, 1673, Boyle dispatched to Newton (through Oldenburg) three copies of his *Several Tracts of the strange Subtilty, Efficacy and determinate Nature of Effluviums,* one for himself and the others to be delivered to Dr. Barrow and Dr. More, along with "his very affectionat service, and assurance of the esteem he hath of your vertue and knowledge."[35] Boyle wanted to approach closer to the rising prodigy and through his overtures a measure of intimacy was established between them. They had private conversations on those rare occasions when Newton went up to London.[36] In his last years Boyle was driven by the same desire to perpetuate his discoveries that Newton would feel when he grew older, and he had great perspicacity in judging the fertility of the soils in which he planted his seed—Robert Hooke and Isaac Newton. But while Hooke gratefully accepted his patronage and fatherhood, Newton was rather standoffish. The earthly pretenders to Newton's fatherhood were often rejected, for he looked to a far more glorious sire.

Boyle was an aristocrat by birth, but of the new Elizabethan creation with origins in business. The Earl of Cork had amassed a vast fortune and his son used part of it to make science respectable even for the upper classes. When Boyle sent his message through Oldenburg he had long been the leading figure of the new science, a man of about forty-six who was already the author of many works on experimental philosophy. Boyle's mother had died when he was a very young child, leaving behind an idealized image: "[H]e would ever reckon it amongst the chief misfortunes of his life, that he did never know her," he wrote in his *Autobiography.*[37] At Eton the reading of Quintus Curtius "conjured up in him that unsatisfied appetite of knowledge, that is yet as greedy, as when it first was raised."[38] While studying at Geneva, awe-inspired by a thunderstorm, he experienced

EDMVND. HALLEIVS LL.D.
GEOM. PROF. SAVIL. & R.S. SECRET.

7. Edmond Halley

8. Nicolas Fatio de Duillier

what he called his conversion, and throughout his life he poured forth scores of religious apologies of science. He was at Florence when Galileo died on January 8, 1642, the year of Newton's birth.

In the summer of 1644, following many adventures, Boyle reached an England in the throes of civil war; his family was generally aligned with the parliamentary side. Settled in London he became part of the Philosophical College, one of the Gresham groups that were antecedents of the Royal Society. In the refuge of his great manor at Stalbridge he worked on chemistry and alchemy, undistinguished from each other, in a state of exaltation: *"Vulcan* has so transported and bewitched me," he wrote his sister, Lady Ranelagh, on August 31, 1649, as to "make me fancy my laboratory a kind of Elysium."[39] When he moved to Oxford, his lodgings became one of the meeting places for another philosophical group composed of Wallis, Wren, Goddard, Wilkins, Seth Ward, and soon Robert Hooke, whom he had engaged as a chemical assistant. Boyle had just published his *New Experiments Physico-Mechanical touching the Spring of the Air and its Effects, made, for the most part, in a new Pneumatical Engine* (1660) when Newton appeared at Trinity, and his early notebooks make frequent reference to the work. Boyle, who was rich and noble and productive, had come to be the model of the new experimental philosopher. In the troubled years between Cromwell's death and the Restoration great laymen with an amateur interest in science, like John Evelyn, sought solace in its study as a way of fleeing the world; and it was to Robert Boyle that Evelyn addressed his scheme for a foundation of adepts of the new philosophy working in monastic isolation.[40] Boyle refused the presidency of the Royal Society, and despite efforts of his many friends to secure a bride for him he remained a bachelor, opening his affections to brilliant men of the younger scientific generation. After he moved to London in 1668 he continued to publish treatises of chemistry, Christian apologetics, and alchemy, until his death in 1691.

To Newton Boyle was a rival as well as an inspiration. In the great alchemical tradition, Boyle had a passionate belief in the transmutability of differing forms of matter by the rearrangement of their particles through the agency of fire. The new mathematics was not within his province, and there is to be found in his writings an occasional denigration of astronomical studies. Though Newton had discovered his fundamental key to the world in mathematics, in his zeal to encompass all branches of science he was also alert for innovations in chemistry and alchemy. At about the same time that Boyle sent Newton his book on effluvia there is a letter from John Collins to James Gregory on October 19, 1675, noting that Newton and Barrow were at least for a time switching their allegiance from mathematics to chemistry. He reported that Newton was intent upon "Chimicall Studies and practises, and both he and Dr Barrow &c beginning to thinke mathcall Speculations to grow at least nice and dry, if not somewhat barren. . . ."[41]

While Newton never published anything on alchemy, accumulating his manuscripts in secret, as far back as 1666 in the *Origin of Forms and Qualities* Boyle had given experimental and "eyewitness proof" from travel literature of water changing into earth, grasshopperlike animals into vegetables, twigs into worms. In the 1670's he came even closer to traditional alchemy, in a statement in the *Philosophical Transactions of the Royal Society* for February 21, 1676, "Of the Incalescence of *Quicksilver* with *Gold.*" Oldenburg as the publisher had warned the readers of this strange document that the author would not answer "Verbal or Epistolary Questions" because he was in some things still enjoined to silence, and Boyle's name was duly disguised under the initials B. R. His problem was crucial to alchemy: "Whether or no there be any such thing as a Mercury that will heat with Gold, that is, which being barely mingled with that mettal reduced to fine parts, will, without the help of external heat, produce upon the commixture of those two Bodies very sensible heat."[42] Boyle confessed to having once been skeptical of the boasts of the alchemists who claimed to have seen the process. Though he had frequented their company and kept abreast of their journeys into foreign parts to collect rare earths, he was wary of their notorious frauds and still doubted whether ordinary mercury would heat gold. But since 1652 he had "by God's blessing" come upon a recipe for an extraordinary mercury which, "purg'd by Sublimations and Distillations," could perform incalescence. Boyle had been so curious that he had searched in the books of those whom "Chymists call Philosophers" and there found similar procedures couched in allegorical language. All purchasers of the *Philosophical Transactions* could now read the great Boyle's witness to a successful trial of alchemical incalescence. What he did not reveal was, of course, the heart of the matter—precisely how he had prepared his strange mercury.

That I might not then be imposed on by others, I several times made trial of our Mercury when I was all alone. For when no Body was by me, nor probably dreamt of what I was doing, I took to one part of the Mercury, sometimes half the weight and sometimes an equal weight of refin'd Gold reduced to a Calx or subtle Powder. This I put into the palm of my left hand, and putting the Mercury upon it, stirr'd it and press'd it a little with the finger of my right hand, by which the two Ingredients were easily mingled, and grew not only sensibly but considerably hot, and that so nimbly, that the Incalescence did sometimes come to its height in about a minute of an hour by a Minute-Clock.

Not content with doing the experiment himself, he gave the ingredients to Lord Viscount Brouncker, President of the Royal Society, and to Oldenburg, both of whom verified the facts. As for the further implications of this "subtil" Mercury for the philosopher's quest he was reluctant to speak; his account had been simply "historical." He nevertheless hazarded the prediction that his mercury would be "of more than ordinary use, both in Physick and Alchymy."[43] To forestall questions as to why he had not made a greater quantity of this "subtil Mercury" he gave a long list of excuses: the death of the only operator he trusted, being diverted by business, removes, and sickness. Boyle had allowed Oldenburg to publish this piece with the proviso that he not have to answer letters because his paralysis prevented him from writing, and in this kind of secret inquiry one could not use an amanuensis. The discovery had left Boyle in a quandary. What if it should fall into "ill hands"? The conclusion of his paper in the *Philosophical Transactions* presented an open question to the "wise and the skillful." What should he do about revealing its details?

It is rare that Newton comments on someone else's work, especially when not asked personally and directly—and even then he is likely to be evasive, refusing to engage. The alchemical writings of Boyle are an exception, and Newton's references to them betray perturbation from the beginning. His letters are full of contradictions. A fear that Boyle might conceivably have made or known of the discovery of the philosopher's stone, as his writings intimated, is apparent and the idea that Newton might be outstripped is intolerable. In a letter to Oldenburg on April 26, 1676, he presumed to answer Boyle's query, raising the prospect of unnamed dangers to mankind if the alchemical truths Boyle was said to possess should ever be announced to the uninitiated. He admonished Boyle—but only through Oldenburg—to keep them secret. In his characteristic manner, he also insisted that his name be withheld: "I have been so free as to shoot my bolt: but pray keep this letter private to your self."[44] Newton was skeptical as to whether this "subtil" mercury would be very significant in either medical or chemical operations, but he nevertheless warned that since "the fingers of many will itch to be at the knowledge of the preparation," it would be prudent not to reveal the details. He did not rule out the possibility that Boyle might have "an inlet to something more noble," but in that event the alchemical tradition ought to be respected because the secret could "not be communicated without immense dammage to the world if there should be any verity in the Hermetick writers." Boyle ought to consult a "true Hermetic Philosopher" whose judgment should be heeded in this regard even if the whole world was of a contrary opinion. Newton was still open on the question of whether there was not something even more important than the transmutation of metals which only the alchemists understood—and then he added, "if those great pretenders bragg not," a complete statement of his persistent doubt and ambivalence toward the quest for the absolute of the secret philosophers, in which he was nonetheless engaged. ("Pretenders" in this context only means aspirants and has no pejorative connotation in itself.)

In 1678, unmindful of Newton's dire warnings—if they had ever been communicated to him—Boyle went further and published "An historical account of a degradation of gold, made by an anti-elixir: A strange chymical narrative," a piece which those who explore only the more rationalist works of the *chymista scepticus* are prone to ignore. It was a fantasy, written as a philosophical dialogue and printed anonymously, but its pretensions were grandiose. Pyrophilus (Boyle) recounted to his friends his meeting with a mysterious stranger who had shown him a packet of paper containing an eighth of a grain of a darkish red powder prepared by an Eastern virtuoso. Before witnesses, Pyrophilus, who had been given the secret packet, mixed the red powder with a concoction of melted gold and produced a little globule that looked not at all yellowish, but like coarse silver. After describing the experiment with the grain of dark reddish powder, Boyle stated the thesis: "For our experiment plainly shews, that gold, though confessedly the most homogeneous, and the least mutable of metals, may be in a very short time (perhaps not amounting to many minutes) exceedingly changed, both as to malleableness, colour, homogeneity, and (which is more) specific gravity." The proof of the transmutation of metals then concluded with a mystification worthy of a gothic novel of the next century. Pyrophilus teased his audience: "[A]s extraordinary, as I perceive most of you think the phaenomena of the lately recited experiment; yet I have not (because I must not do it) as yet acquainted you with the strangest effect of our admirable powder."[45]

A letter of Newton's to Boyle on February 28, 1679, may in part be an answer to Boyle's dialogue. It followed upon months of intense chemical experimentation, of which there is a record in Newton's hand.[46] If Boyle thought he had a secret recipe, Newton knew of a force that was an explanation of the all, to which even the incalescence of gold and the marvelous action of the reddish powder were only corollaries. The letter apparently was inspired also by a conversation about "Physicall qualities" during which Newton had promised to send his "notions" in writing. Boyle stimulated Newton's imaginative powers to roam freely and without restraint, and again, as in the famous letter of 1675 to Oldenburg, Newton made a daring statement of a principle that explained everything in the universe. He had an abiding belief that God expressed Himself in the physical world with divine and elegant simplicity, that there was one "aethereall Nature" in all things, from which all things had originated, a primitive spiritous matter. In a passage of the letter to Oldenburg setting forth the emotive rather than the reasoned side of his theory of light, he had celebrated that universal principle in language of rare poetic beauty. His words pulsate with the rhythms of the pre-Socratic philosophers and of the King James Bible, and are compelling testimony to the identity of his religious and his scientific thought.

For nature is a perpetuall circulatory worker, generating fluids out of solids, and solids out of fluids, fixed things out of volatile, & volatile out of fixed, subtile out of gross, & gross out of subtile, Some things to ascend & make the upper terrestriall juices, Rivers and the Atmosphere; & by consequence others to descend for a Requitall to the former. And as the Earth, so perhaps may the Sun imbibe this Spirit copiously to conserve his Shineing, & keep the Planets from recedeing further from him. And they that will, may also suppose, that this Spirit affords or carryes with it thither the solary fewell & materiall Principle of Light; And that the vast aethereall Spaces between us, & the stars are for a sufficient repository for this food of the Sunn & Planets.[47]

The tenor of Newton's cosmogony in the letters both to Oldenburg and to Boyle is alchemical, founded on the principle of transmutation. "Perhaps the whole frame of Nature," he had written in the same letter to Oldenburg on December 7, 1675, "may be nothing but various Contextures of some certaine aethereall Spirits or vapours condens'd as it were by praecipitation, much after the manner that vapours are condensed into water or exhalations into grosser Substances, though not so easily condensible; and after condensation wrought into various formes, at first by the immediate hand of the Creator, and ever since by the power of Nature, wch by vertue of the command Increase & Multiply, became a complete Imitator of the copies sett her by the Protoplast. Thus perhaps may all things be originated from aether."[48] To Boyle he expounded a variant cosmogony based upon an aethereal substance. "And first I suppose that there is diffused through all places an aethereal substance capable of contraction & dilatation, strongly elastick, & in a word much like air in all respects, but far more subtile."[49] Newton grew more and more excited in the course of composition, to the point where he offered his theory of the aethereal substance that penetrated all matter as "the cause of gravity . . . Imagin now any body suspended in the air or lying on the earth: & the aether being by the Hypothesis grosser in the pores wch are in the upper parts of the body then in those wch are in its lower parts, & that grosser aether being less apt to be lodged in those pores then the finer aether below, it will endeavour to get out & give way to the finer aether below, wch cannot be without the bodies descending to make room above for it to go out into."[50] Reading this letter one feels a powerful primitive animism in which the aethereal substance becomes alive.

With a detail and an openness that is astonishing, in this letter to Boyle Newton had launched a monist theory of the universe: one single force, an aethereal substance, might explain all phenomena, light, chemical operations, and even gravity. Though Newton pulled in the reins on his wild horses and reaffirmations of this belief in the one are rare, the letter bears witness to his need for an absolute unity and for a theory to explain gravity, which he afterward laughed at in his friend Fatio. When later, at the age of seventy, Newton blazoned his defiant *hypotheses non fingo* in the General Scholium to the second edition of the *Principia,* he no longer had any imaginative conjectures to make. He was describing the actual state of his scientific capabilities, as well as enunciating a methodological principle. The authoritative precepts of his scientific method appeared *post festum,* with age and declining imaginative powers. In Hypothesis III of the first edition of the *Principia,* Newton was still asserting that all bodies could be transformed into one another. By the 1690's his early conception of aether was discarded and aether ceased to be the source of all activity and motion in nature; transmutation was limited to the interaction among terrestrial bodies and between these and the vaporous spirit emanating from the tails of comets. Nevertheless there is at least one interpreter who holds that the doctrine of transmutation itself was not completely abandoned, even if in later works it was stripped of its obvious alchemical overtones.[51] The heroic rigor of Newton's experimental philosophy prevented his publishing from hearsay purported alchemical experiments, as Boyle may have done on more than one occasion, but it did not dissuade him from continuing the search for one absolute explanation of all phenomena in byways that later generations of scientists would have frowned upon.

In the General Scholium to the *Principia* there is "a most subtle spirit" that lies hidden in all gross bodies; it accounts for forces acting between particles of matter in bodies and for electrical attraction. The subtle spirit can heat bodies and explains the movement of light; it even penetrates our sensory nerves, creating sensations. In the second English edition of the *Opticks* (1717/1718) this "electric and elastic spirit" seems to have become an all-pervading medium, again called "aether." Far be it from me to attempt to adjudicate among the fine distinctions of meaning that contemporary historians of science have established in their learned accounts of Newton's oscillations with respect to his fanciful subtle matter or aether. In my view of his person, there is no sharp dividing line between the influence exerted on him by the world outlook of philosophical alchemy, with which he was familiar from an early age, and by the later experiments of Francis Hauksbee and John Desaguliers, curators of experiments during his presidency of the Royal Society.

On August 19, 1682, Boyle wrote affectionately in answer to a lost letter of Newton's that expressed approbation of his *Noctiluca,* a work on the phenomena of phosphorescence. Boyle's fond valedictory to Newton is more than mere courtesy. Newton had had a book transcribed for Boyle, and from the cryptic manner in which he refers to it, there is a likelihood that it was alchemical. Boyle, still looking for a disciple, wrote that he would think his pains in composing the *Noctiluca* well employed if Newton would only bestow serious thought upon the subject. The aristocratic scientist, recognizing superior genius, was enthusiastic at the prospect of a visit from Newton. "You much rejoyce me by allowing me the pleaseing expectation of seeing you ere long in this place where we may more commodiously discourse of several things, & I may enjoy the Advantage of a conversation that I was much troubled to be so hastily depriv'd of at your last being in London."[52]

In his final years Boyle became more than ordinarily concerned about his unpublished alchemical papers. A letter of 1689 to an unnamed friend, who may be Locke, communicates his wish that they be printed after his death.

[S]ince I find myself now grown old, I think it time to comply with my former intentions to leave a kind of Hermetic legacy to the studious disciples of that art, and to deliver candidly, in the annexed paper, some processes chemical and medicinal, that are less simple and plain than those barely luciferous ones I have been wont to affect, and of a more difficult and elaborate kind, than those I have hitherto published, and more of kin to the noblest Hermetic secrets, or, as *Helmont* stiles them, *arcana majora.* Some of these I have made and tried; others I have (though not without much difficulty) obtained, by exchange or otherwise, from those, that affirm they knew them to be real, and were themselves competent judges, as being some of them disciples of true adepts, or otherwise admitted to their acquaintance and conversation. Most of these processes are clearly enough delivered; and of the rest there is plainly set down, without deceitful terms, as much, as may serve to make what is literally taught to be of great utility, though the full and complete uses are not mentioned, partly because, in spite of my philanthropy, I was engaged to secrecy, as to some of these uses, and partly because I must ingenuously confess it, I am not yet, or perhaps ever shall be acquainted with them myself. The knowledge I have of your great affection for the public good . . . invites me, among the many virtuosi, in whose friendship I am happy, to intrust the following papers in your hands, earnestly desiring you to impart them to the public faithfully, and without envy, *verbatim,* in my own expressions, as a monument of my good affections to mankind, as well in my chemical capacity, as in the others, wherein I have been sollicitous to do it service. . . .[53]

After Boyle's death on July 26, 1691, his hermetic legacy became the subject of a rather convoluted exchange between Newton and his friend John Locke.[54] Later eighteenth-century anticlerical rationalists for whom these two men were ideal heroes of pure reason would have been incapable of comprehending a relationship in which such dark superstitions as alchemy or interpretation of prophecy and other biblical texts played the central role. Newton had met Locke, returned from his exile in Holland more than two years before, in February 1689, in the Earl of Pembroke's salon where intellectual conversation was the rule; through him he also made the acquaintance of Lord Monmouth. Locke and Newton held similar Whiggish political views and unitarian religious beliefs, and they were naturally drawn to each other. Newton made an effort in March 1690 to initiate Locke into the intricacies of his science by preparing for him a demonstration of planetary motion, but there is no reason to believe that he was any more successful in tutoring his new friend than he would later be with Bentley. Though Locke might not have followed the mathematical argument, he was intrigued by the new discoveries and he extolled the "incomparable Mr. Newton" in the Epistle to the Reader of the *Essay Concerning Human Understanding,* published in 1690. The first letter from Newton to Locke is dated October 28, 1690, and their relationship continued until Locke's death in 1704. One of Newton's rare extended private visits was a sojourn with Locke and his hosts, Lord and Lady Masham, at Oates in February of 1691, and he wrote a lighthearted note of thanks, hoping he had not overstayed his welcome, even allowing a word of self-mockery about his "mystical fansies."[55] This was a friendship in which Newton felt secure, despite interludes that involved prickly subjects which could easily have led to quarrels. Locke, with interests outside of Newton's sphere, was no rival, and he was ever tender and compliant to the genius whose fame he promoted in political and intellectual circles. When Newton had a rare itch to turn literary in an anonymous "Letter to a friend," setting forth the textual arguments against Trinitarianism, Locke offered to have it secretly printed in Holland by Le Clerc; and when Newton took fright and wanted the publication stopped, Locke obeyed immediately and Newton's secret was preserved. In their alchemical correspondence Locke was equally forthright and attentive; and here again Newton was on the rack, plagued with doubts.

At the end of a brief note to Locke about his anti-Trinitarian papers, Newton wrote a seemingly noncommittal postscript. "I understand Mr Boyle communicated his process about the red earth & ☿ to you as well as to me & before his death procured some of that earth for his friends."[56] Letters no longer extant intervened, in which Locke asked Newton how he knew that Locke was informed about the red earth, to which he received a reply in a letter about miracles in the church: "Mr. Paulin told me you had writ for some of Mr Boyles red earth & by that I knew you had the receipt."[57] Locke then sent Newton a liberal quantity of the red earth—more than he had expected, because, as Newton wrote on July 7, 1692, he had no "inclination" to try the process, though he was quite willing to assist Locke if ever he undertook it.[58] It appears that Boyle had a way of giving recipes or parts of them to friends under various restrictions of secrecy. Newton told Locke that he had lost out of his pocket the first and third parts of Boyle's recipe and concluded with a postscript to the effect that when the hot weather was over he intended to perform the first part of the experiment, though he was dubious about its success.

Locke, always more open than Newton, sent him a transcript of the first part of Boyle's recipe as he had found it among the manuscripts, and offered to forward to him the other parts (he and two other executors, Doctors Dickinson and Coxe, had been charged with the inspection of Boyle's papers). Newton replied on August 2, 1692, to dissuade Locke from wasting his time and money on Boyle's recipe, but at the same time he initiated a long, tortuous inquiry about the conditions under which Locke had received the formula. Newton's vacillation about the "red earth" is at its pitch as he changes his mind three times in one note. Apparently he was interested not only in its contents but in whether and why Boyle had been more reserved with him than with Locke. His suspicions of Boyle's candor break through time and time again. At moments in the devious interrogation one hears the rumble of the approaching psychic crisis. There is hardly a sentence in this letter that is not qualified or negated by what follows, as Newton cannot make up his mind definitively about the worth of alchemical science. No one need deny that Newton's chemical experiments recorded in notebooks over the years had a rational scientific purpose even when he used the colorful alchemical vocabulary of the adepts in making notes; but the conclusion that he employed the methods of a skillful chemical experimenter does not exclude other more esoteric goals. The simple and crude alternative of Newton the alchemist or Newton the skeptical chemist is now entertained only by latter-day apologists who refuse to countenance the complexity of his person.

First Newton supposed that the recipe Locke had inherited from Boyle was the very one that had moved him to procure the repeal of the statute against multipliers in 1689. But Newton also concluded from the margin of the paper that this was the recipe for the same mercury that would grow hot in proximity with gold about which Boyle had published a paper sixteen-odd years before in the *Philosophical Transactions*. And yet Newton doubted whether Boyle, despite his published report, had at any time during these two decades ever tried the recipe himself or gotten it performed by anyone else. In fact, when Newton had once expressed his misgivings to Boyle, he "confest" that he had not actually made the experiment himself or seen it tried but insisted that "a certain Gentleman" was now on the way to achieving the results. Newton was willing to admit that by this recipe mercury might change its color and properties, but not that gold could be multiplied. Moreover, he had private evidence that the recipe was ineffective because he knew of a "company" that had used it and had failed, its chief artist having run so far into debt that he had "much ado to live." When taxed with this information, Boyle had admitted that the recipe had been imparted to several chemists.

Following hard upon the opinion that the recipe was worthless was Newton's announcement to Locke that he could not try it in any case because something had been withheld from him by Boyle. "I know more of it then he has told me, & by that & an expression or two wch dropt from him I know that what he has told me is imperfect & useless wthout knowing more then I do." At this point he switched without warning and intimated that he did intend to try making a mercury which would "grow hot with ☉," but before the sentence was finished he added, "if perhaps I shall try that." The more he went on, the more complex the matter became. Boyle had communicated the recipe to Newton under certain conditions that still bound him to secrecy, but if the same reservations had not applied to Locke and if Locke had been told more than he had, then his obligations were void. Nevertheless, Newton reflected, "perhaps I shall be tender by using my liberty." The ending of the letter to Locke is as obfuscatory about his true desires and intentions as Newton can become. It is a bizarre admixture of hurt pride, suspicion, a sense of duty about a promise to a dead man, and a need for secrecy. "I do not desire to know what he has communicated but rather that you would keep the particulars from me (at least the 2d & 3d parts of the ℞.) because I have no mind to be concerned with this ℞ any further then just to know the entrance. I suspect his reservedness might proceed from mine. For when I communicated a certain experimt to him he presently by way of requital subjoined two others, but cumbered them wth such circumstances as startled me & made me afraid of any more." Since Locke was working on the Boyle papers, Newton asked that he publish these two experiments along with the rest; but he insisted that no one should know that they had come through his hands. Finally he offered to send Locke an argument against the multiplication of metals to which he had never found an answer—that is, if Locke would give him his opinion.[59] Unfortunately, there is no extant reply to this letter or treatise from Newton.

Though nothing of consequence ensued from the affair of the reddish powder, Newton was far from done with alchemy. Dated manuscripts are incontrovertible evidence that he continued the search, and the common quest for the secret was one of the links in his friendship with Fatio de Duillier in the 1690's. In October 1689 Newton wrote to Fatio thanking him for an offer to make him acquainted with an alchemist in London.[60] Three years later Newton and Fatio were exchanging alchemical literature—Fatio had lent him the two-volume compendium by William Salmon, *Bibliothèque des philosophes chymiques ou recueil des oeuvres des auteurs* . . . *qui ont écrit de la Pierre Philosophale* (Paris, 1672, 1678). On May 4, 1693, Fatio enthusiastically described for Newton an alchemical experiment. "If You be curious Sir of a metallick putrefaction and fermentation which lasts for a great while and turns to a vegetation producing a heap of golden trees, with their leaves and fruits I can acquaint you with it having seen it and having been told by the owner how he made it."[61] The climax of this particular process was presented by Fatio with a sense of drama and a style often absent from alchemical accounts.

These matters being put in a sealed egg in a sand heat do presently swell, and puff up, and grow black and in a matter of seven days go through the coulours of the Philosophers. After which time there grows a heap of trees out of the matter, which trees change by degrees their colours. They begin now to be near their bottom of a copper colour or violet; the branches are gold and silver. The matters have allready been in digestion for some months. This experiment being noble and exceeding simple seemed to me to be worth your knowing. I have seen to day the vessel, whose sides seem to be full of little drops of ☿ . I believe if that putrefaction be well managed it may be made more lasting: and more mineral bodies may be used to animate the ☿ , and to make it to incorporate better with ⊙. For there is plainly a life and a ferment in that composition.

Later stages involved much grinding. As a philosophical, not only a practical, alchemist, Fatio asked a crucial question: "Is not perhaps heat arising from friction and motion one of the Philosophers fire?"

A fortnight later Fatio was taken with the medicinal potentials of a concoction that entailed a few astrological observations to direct its timing, intermingled with classical alchemical formulas. It had been given him by a friend of a friend: "An Adept knowing my friends charity and generosity gave him the first inlet to the highest Chimistry and one preparation of a ☿ by wch the putrefaction of most mineral bodies becomes easie. He told him that he had enough to go on to the Noblest operations of that Science, thô as I suppose not by the shortest way. His menstruum or ☿ is an ordinary ☿ prepared with boyling it in a wooden vessel exceeding close for several days with some rain gathered while the Sun is in ♈ or ♉ ."[62] Newton may have been disturbed by the magical quality that Fatio introduced into his potion, but he neither broke with the young man nor did he cease performing alchemical experiments and tracking down rumors about them.

After his recovery from the crisis of 1693 Newton returned to his chemical laboratory and continued to welcome adepts or emissaries of adepts until the very eve of his departure for London.[63] On March 2 or 3, 1696, a fortnight before notice of his appointment as Warden of the Mint was conveyed to him by Charles Montague, Isaac Newton received a visit from an unnamed Londoner who had been acquainted with both Boyle and Dr. Dickinson and who reported on alchemical experiments bearing out the writings attributed to Jodocus von Rehe and Basil Valentine. After the guest's departure Newton wrote out a detailed memorandum of their conversation which has since been published. The climax of the intricate procedures the stranger described is recorded without a trace of incredulity. "It [the menstruum] then dissolves and volatizes all metals & gold dissolved & volatized may be digested with it to the end."[64]

There is some evidence that Newton continued to indulge his passion for alchemical literature even after he went up to the Mint in London. Denis Duveen's great collection of alchemical writings includes a copy of Anonymous von Schwarzfus, *Sanguis Naturae. Or, a Manifest Declaration of the Sanguine and Solar Congealed Liquor of Nature* (London, 1696), in which has been inserted a seventeenth-century alchemical manuscript recipe, with a notation in Newton's hand as to where the *Sanguis Naturae,* and presumably other books of this character, could be procured: "at Sowles a Quaker Widdow in White Hart Court at the upper end of Lombard Street."[65] Lists of alchemical writings by "Authores magis utiles, Authores antiquissimi, Authores Arabici" appear on the same folio as a note, "An Account of Gold & Silver moneys coyned since Christmas."[66] It is of course possible that Newton was using old alchemical

papers for more sober business rather than the other way around—
in either case the merchants in the City would have been uneasy at
the discovery.

Newton's alchemical preoccupations are wonderful examples of
the mixture of credulity and sophisticated skepticism that has often
been remarked in great men. Newton was an almost fanatical traditionalist about the ancient word transmitted in the Bible, in the
writings of acceptable Church Fathers and rabbis, in Greek myth, in
the fragments of pre-Socratic philosophers, or in the treatises of
medieval and Renaissance alchemists. And at the same time he was
a most searching and rigorous experimenter, questioning until convinced. One would have imagined that the doubt that possessed him
and his generation about the words of Aristotle and Galen would
be carried over to other ancient texts. Perhaps the matter-of-fact clarity of these scientists led to their outright rejection, while the hieroglyphic quality of the others encouraged the belief that truths were
hidden in their utterances.

There was in Newton simultaneously a longing for the abstract,
for the ineffable, for what he never cast his eyes upon, and an astonishing sense of the real, experimentally wrested from nature by physical actions and controlled by mathematical notations. His greatest
creation has been characterized, perhaps simplistically, as a synthesis
of the abstract and the concrete. One is almost tempted to recognize
in his genius a union of two experiences, his relations with the father
whom he never saw and with his mother whom he possessed with
such intense emotion, whom he saw with his own eyes and always
longed to see again as he had in the early years of infancy—a fantasy
he pursued in vain throughout his life, looking for the image
through peepholes and in "chymical glasses." Newton would doubtless have disapproved of such "mystical fansies" as explanations even
as he derogated them in himself, though he confessed to Locke that
he had them.

Chapter 9

THE APE OF NEWTON:
FATIO DE DUILLIER

O London! London! timely then repent,
And pray God may avert the punishment
Due to thy sins, thou sure deservest more,
Than Sodom or Gomorrah did before.

For they in all their Riot and Excess
Could not out-do thy Pride and Wickedness
I find no sin that's laid to *Sodom*'s charge,
But thou art guilty of the same at large.

Remember the great Plague in Sixty five
Which hardly half thy People did survive;
'Twas for thy Sins that surely on thee fell,
And what is yet behind, no Tongue can tell.

Thou hast by Fire too been once laid waste,
Which counting thy Deserts is but a taste,
Of what we justly may expect remains:
O then Repent, or take it for thy pains.
—A Broadside of November 14, 1707

IsAAC NEWTON died a virgin. The verdict would be upheld in an
English court of law on the word of two witnesses—an elderly relative to whom he confided when already advanced in years that he
had never violated chastity and who whispered intelligence of his
moral victory to the poet Thomas Maude, and Dr. Richard Mead,
his attending physician and friend, interrogated on the subject by
Voltaire who proclaimed it to the world.[1] Those still in doubt about

so positive a judgment with respect to a male child might avail themselves of psychological opinion that the character and strength of Newton's inhibitions probably precluded both cohabitation with women and inversion, though not feelings of tenderness toward a succession of younger men, budding scientists and philosophers. In his relations with Fatio de Duillier, the aristocratic Swiss genius who appeared in England when Newton was about forty-five, these feelings reached a high pitch, posing a threat and creating a demand for repression that was an element in the breakdown of 1693.

Nicolas Fatio de Duillier was born in Basel on February 16, 1664, the seventh child, preceded by five sisters and a brother, to the seigneur of a small fief outside of Geneva, where a rigid Calvinist spirit still prevailed. As a younger son he was at first destined for the ministry, but his extraordinary scientific talents were soon recognized. At seventeen he began communicating astronomical observations—an explanation of Saturn's rings and a theory of zodiacal light —to Cassini at the Royal Observatory in Paris.[2] In the University Library in Geneva there hangs a pastel portrait of him, a frail, rather soft youth with fiery eyes. During the course of his European travels he established intimate scholarly ties with the most eminent scientists of the Continent, the Bernoullis in Basel, the Huygens brothers in Amsterdam, Leibniz in Hannover, de l'Hôpital in Paris,.all of whom were impressed with his precocity. In Holland he informed the exiled Bishop Gilbert Burnet about a plot hatched by one of Louis XIV's agents to abduct William of Orange and put him in the hands of the French.[3] (Late in life, broken and paralyzed, he tried in vain to get a pension from the English Crown as belated recompense for his services.) When he arrived in London in 1687 the learned young man of good family was quickly accepted both by English scientists and members of the aristocracy. Before his coming, Burnet had praised Fatio to Boyle as "one of the greatest men of this age [who] seems born to carry learning some sizes beyond what it has attained."[4] Writing to Christiaan Huygens Fatio debonairly sent the regards of Dr. John Wallis, the venerable Savilian Professor of Mathematics at Oxford. He recommended an acquaintance to Locke and Boyle with the assurance that they were two solid friends on whom he could count.[5] At the age of twenty-four, on May 2, 1688, he was made a member of the Royal Society. Moving freely in diplomatic circles, he had a prospect of becoming secretary to a British ambassador either in Holland or in Spain. But of all his dazzling social triumphs friendship with Newton was the most brilliant.

Fatio's boundless enthusiasm for Newton overflowed in extravagant letters to a professor of philosophy at Geneva, Jean-Robert Chouet, to whom he had once been attached. He would like to settle in England, he wrote in November 1689, and live with Newton, who was not only the greatest mathematician of all time but the most worthy gentleman he had ever known. Descartes's system of the world, so crowded with things one could scarce turn around in it, had become an absurd dream. To exalt his new god, he wove a grandiose fantasy of gilded threads, as befitted a citizen of Geneva. If ever he got hold of an extra hundred thousand *écus* he would erect statues and a monument to his friend, in order to let posterity know that during Newton's lifetime at least one man was capable of appreciating his worth.[6] Fatio was already associating himself with Newton's glory, and maximizing himself through its assimilation.

Fatio had had difficulties with his parents; Newton replaced them, becoming his counsellor and spiritual guide. His mother's constant reproaches over the length of his sojourn in London, his extravagance, his failure to choose a calling, annoyed him. His father, he complained to his elder brother, had denied him love. In letters to the family he described his habitual melancholy and self-torment, and a depressive state that he feared would accompany him to the grave: "The sources of melancholy surround me on all sides. The rivulets . . . flow over me day and night. They follow me everywhere. . . ."[7] Later in life, when he was over fifty, he took to recording his dreams with almost scientific precision, because in their interpretation he expected to find a divine message. While the analysis of dead men's dreams is problematical, the dream of May 10, 1719, points to a lasting preoccupation with themes of the primal scene and of castration. He viewed the world through a barrier and at a distance.

I dreamed last night that looking out of a window I saw a field where there were oxen and cows, some of a monstrous size of about twenty or twenty-five feet in length. There was among others an angry cow which with her horns had lifted into the air a calf to the height of about three stories. She was very much larger than the ordinary cows but much smaller than the oxen of which I have spoken. A man having come to bring her to reason with an iron fork attached to a long handle, I saw that he stuck it into her flanks. She resisted for some time, trying to avenge herself, but he was the stronger and kept himself out of reach with the force of the fork which he held stuck in her flanks. Thus he pushed her head to the ground.[8]

In 1687 Fatio was just twenty-three years old—about Newton's age when he had had the first insights leading to his three great discoveries. Fatio was engaged on the inverse problem of tangents; he was drafting grand plans for new inventions and discoveries in all branches of science; he had studied medicine and knew the properties of herbs and potions. Newton and Fatio had much in common: mathematics, astronomy, classical erudition, exposition of prophecy, alchemical mysteries, the concoction of remedies, perhaps the elixir of life, a mechanical aptitude, even an interest in apples— Fatio later wrote a treatise on pomiculture which appeared with the imprimatur of the Royal Society.[9] His mind had a philosophical bent, and he was confident that he could construct a system that would rival Descartes's. Taking off from the *Principia* he would define the real cause of gravity, a problem Newton tended to shy away from after the publication of the *Principia,* content with the discovery of its mathematical law.

Fatio resembled the young Newton not only in native genius and universal curiosity but in temperament: the hypochondria, the sadness, the secrecy, the pendulum swings between megalomania and self-denigration, the anxiety, the outbursts of anger. Newton became an idol to whom Fatio was ever making symbolic offerings. From Utrecht, where he had gone as a tutor to two young Englishmen, he

wrote to an acquaintance in London: "If I should happen to die before I see you again, I expressly beg you to forward the two smallest
of these boxes to Monsieur Isaac Newton of Trinity College in Cambridge. Thus a mathematician will inherit from a mathematician
papers about which nobody else would care. . . . I have sent you the
keys to my boxes in a sealed packet. It would be a good idea to en-
close the keys in this letter, which takes the place of my will, to be
transmitted sealed to Mr. Newton."[10] Other letters from Utrecht confess to his shyness, his blushing, his "avoiding so much all Com-
panys," and a general discontent with his way of life.[11] During this
stay in Holland he acquired the dark reputation of being a Spinozist,
if the testimony in Edmund Calamy's autobiography is trust-
worthy.[12] When Fatio learned of his mother's death he wrote his
brother on Feburary 3, 1693, a reply full of cryptic reflections about
himself. "My pain comes chiefly from a cause that I cannot explain
here. . . . The reasons I should not marry will probably last as long
as my life."[13]

In Fatio Newton witnessed a re-enactment of his own prodigious
youth. Newton liked talented young people; he sponsored them and
toward them his affective being turned, though his favorites supplanted one another rather rapidly. The narcissistic element in his
friendship for Fatio can be related to an early fixation upon his
mother. If one adopts Freudian imagery, Newton first identified
himself with his mother and took himself as the sexual object; then
he found young men resembling himself and loved them as he would
have had his mother love him. The maternal element in his nature
found reinforcement. When Fatio disappeared for a time in Holland
with his charges, Newton wrote to ask Locke what had become of
him. In another man this would be a fact of no conseqeunce, but
Isaac Newton rarely inquired after anybody, either his person or his
scientific studies; usually he behaved as if he were sufficient unto
himself.

Throughout the 1690's Fatio's name is regularly linked with
Newton's in the international scientific correspondence of Christiaan
Huygens, de l'Hôpital, Leibniz. In a letter to De Beyrie, who was

Counsellor and Resident of Brunswick in London, Leibniz referred to the "liaisons très particulières" between Fatio and Newton and to the great scientific achievements he awaited from their collaboration.[14] With presumption, Fatio wrote to Leibniz in 1694 as if he were an equal member of a partnership: "Nous convenons Monsieur Newton et moi."[15] He boasted that nobody understood the *Principia* as thoroughly as he did and that he expected to prepare the next edition. De l'Hôpital heaped flattery on Fatio and then, aware of his ties with Newton, as if in passing tried to worm out of him what plans were afoot for the publication of the *Opticks*.[16] In his secret diary Hooke coupled Newton and Fatio in reporting attendance at Royal Society meetings, and his bitter enmity toward Newton spilled over onto the favorite. Fatio participated with Locke and Newton in colloquies *à trois*, no mean privilege.

In Newton's friendship with Fatio a passion may have broken through in defiance of the censor. The letters exchanged between Fatio in London and Newton in Cambridge from 1689 through the spring of 1693 glow with a warmth that is absent from Newton's other relationships, except those with his mother and perhaps with Charles Montague. The documents are full of ambiguities, and the nature of their intimacy remains obscure, though it follows the pattern of a middle-aged bachelor's affection for a young replica of himself when a fixation upon the mother underlies his whole emotive structure.

The earliest letter from Newton to Fatio that has been preserved, written from Cambridge October 10, 1689, introduces a relationship that has already been firmly established. In three places of the text, marked by dots of omission in its published form, words have been cut out of the paper by an unknown hand. The topic under discussion patently involves alchemical experiments. Taking young Fatio into his confidence, Newton is critical of the great Boyle for his lack of caution in discussing such arcane matters. The tone of correspondence between the eminent professor of forty-seven and the man of twenty-five is familiar and private, a rarity with Newton. He is putting himself at Fatio's disposition.

I am extreamly glad that you . . . friend & thank you most heartily for your kindness to me in designing to bring me acquainted wth him. I intend to be in London the next week & should be very glad to be in the same lodgings with you. I will bring my books & your letters wth me. Mr Boyle has divers times offered to communicate & correspond wth me in these matters but I ever declined it because of his . . . & conversing wth all sorts of people & being in my opinion too open & too desirous of fame. Pray let me know by a line or two whether you can have lodgings for us both in the same house at present or whether you would have me take some other lodgings for a time till . . . I am Yours most affectionately to serve you. . . .[17]

By 1690 Fatio was in the full swing of English partisan politics of the new reign of William and Mary. A phenomenal linguistic talent helped him to acclimatize himself with relative facility despite his reticence. The letter of February 24 to Newton was written in an ebullient mood, on the upswing, in an almost manic state, in contrast with later ones which sound rather uniformly depressed. Illusions of grandeur about his political influence and scientific capacities sweep through his sentences. He promises to get Locke to intervene with Lord Monmouth on Newton's behalf—proof that Newton has been unburdening himself to the young man about his discontent with his position in Cambridge and that the humiliating quest for a "place" has begun. The letter ends by proclaiming that his own theory of gravity, which he had presented orally to the Royal Society and which had had a somewhat lukewarm reception, was now unexceptionable.[18] A small detail, a casual proposal that they read Huygens' treatise on light together, is a measure of their closeness.

I did see Mr Lock about a week ago, and I desired him that he should speak earnestly of you to Mylord Monmouth. He promised me that he would do it but as from himself not as from you, because said he you had not yet writ to Mylord about a Preceptor for his son, and so it would be improper to speak from you and not mention that. I shall have I think to morrow an exemplar of Mr Hugens his book that he hath sent you. I'll keep it till I know whether or no you would have it sent to Cambridge. It beeing writ in French you may perhaps choose rather to read it here with me. Young Mr Hampden hath mist beeing chosen a member of Parliament the King having desired his Father to order things so that he should not be elected. Mylord M. hath no good reason himself to be satisfyed with the Court and it is plain the King doth wholly give himself up to the high Tory party. Mr Hampden and I had a design to go to see you at Cambridge; but you send me word you will come hither, which I am very glad of. My Theory of Gravity is now I think clear of objections, and I can doubt little but that it is the true one. You may better judge when you see it. I am with all my heart Your most humble and most obedient servant.[19]

The day on which Fatio wrote to Newton, he communicated the substance of his hypothesis on gravity to Christiaan Huygens in Amsterdam with the self-assurance that he was exuding everywhere at this time. Though Huygens and Leibniz were not impressed by his theory, he continued to figure prominently in their correspondence. To continental scientists he acted as if he were not only Newton's official spokesman with respect to corrections for the *Principia,* but a reliable informant about Newton's personal habits. "He has some difficulty understanding French but he manages with a dictionary," he advised Huygens on Newton's handicap in following the argument of the *Traité de la lumière.*[20]

Sometime during the next period there must have been an interruption in the Newton-Fatio relationship, for on October 28, 1690, Newton concluded a letter to John Locke with the remark, "I suppose Mr Fatio is in Holland for I have heard nothing from him the half year."[21] Immediately upon Fatio's return to London from the Continent in the fall of 1691 he wrote Christiaan Huygens that he expected to see Newton in a few days; and David Gregory was quick to signal to Newton Fatio's presence in the city.[22] There is no direct communication from Fatio to Newton until September 17, 1692, almost a year later, when he wrote him a letter from London that confirms the renewal of their friendship—he had been to Cambridge—and at the same time announces a dramatic crisis in his health. Buried amid the tedious clinical facts of his illness is a passage attesting the strong spiritual bond that had been forged between them: Newton had been the cure of his troubled soul. "The Bookseller Lea," he began irrelevantly, "said this morning he had forgot to send you the book of fortifications, which I had bought from him, but that he would certainly send it today, to the Cambridge Coach, at

the black Bull. So mindfull of their promises I am apt to find these
Gentlemen are." Then he delivered the blow:

I have Sir allmost no hopes of seeing You again. With coming from Cambridge I got a grievous cold, which is fallen upon my lungs. Yesterday I
had such a sudden sense as might probably have been caused upon my
midriff/diaphragm by the breaking of an ulcer, or vomica, in the undermost
part of the left lobe of my lungs. For about that place of my midriff/dia-
phragm I felt a momentaneous sense of something bigger than my fist moving
and acting powerfully. That sense was distinct in all that region, but not
troublesome to me, thô my surprise caused my body to bend forwards, as I
was sitting by the fire. What I felt next was only a gentle and easie sense of a
natural heat in that region. My pulse was good this morning; It is now (at
6. afternoon) feaverish and hath been so most part of the day. I thank God
my soul is extreamly quiet, in which You have had the chief hand. My head
is something out of order, and I suspect will grow worse and worse. The
Imperial powders, of which I have taken today four of the weakest sort, and
one of the best sort, have proved quite unsignificant. Which confirms to me
that I have guessed right about the breaking of a Vomica, or else my disease
must be an ague. Were I in a lesser feaver I should tell You Sir many things.
If I am to depart this life I could wish my eldest brother, a man of an extra-
ordnary [sic] integrity, could succeed me in Your friendship. As yet I have
had no Doctor. Perhaps with a paracenthesis they may save my life, which
I am not yet certain is in any danger. Mr Cuningham Sir will acquaint You
with what shall befall me. . . .[23]

The same combination of minute self-observation, physical and spiritual, and a pervasive sense of impending doom characterized the
whole of Fatio's long life—and he lasted for sixty-one years after this
rather confused, anxious report. The offering of his brother to Newton is analogous to a dying woman's bequeathing a successor to her
husband, an act of love which is at the same time a desperate holding
on that eliminates other rivals.

Newton's reply from Cambridge four days later (on September
21, 1692) is touched with more earnest concern than he ever showed
for any other human being in the documents that have been preserved. The peripheral remarks about the book on fortifications and
Fatio's brother hardly disguise what for Newton was profound
emotion.

I have the book & last night received your letter wth wch how much I was affected I cannot express. Pray procure the advice & assistance of Physitians before it be too late & if you want any money I will supply you. I rely upon the character you give of your elder brother & if I find that my acquaintance may be to his advantage I intend he shall have it, & I hope that you may still live to bring it about, but for fear of the worst pray let me know how I may send a letter &, if need be, a parcel to him, & pray let me know his character more fully, & particularly whether his genius lyes in any measure for sciences or only for business of the world.

The closing lines are an unusual commitment from the pen of Isaac Newton, who was ordinarily measured and stiff in his valedictories:

Sr wth my prayers for your recovery I rest Your most affectionate and faithfull friend to serve you.[24]

By the very next day Fatio was sufficiently well to write that the worst of his malady was over and to record every last symptom in detail—the pimples on his lips, the "fomes of an exceeding sharp and troublesome matter, that hath since that time affected now one half of my head and now the other." Among other things Fatio and Newton tell that they have been remembering each other in their prayers—no mere exchange of courtesies but assurances intended literally. The bulk of the letter is devoted to a character of Fatio's brother, which indirectly affords an excellent insight into Fatio himself.

My brother Sir is without exception the most discreet and reserved man I know; even so far as to have been by that reservedness often unkind to me. He is judicious and understands well a great many parts of the Mathematicks, and Algebra itself. He speaks French and German, which will make him able to understand English easily. My father having five daughters, when he had no other Son but him, was too fond of him and suffered him to neglect his studies: so that he left them quite before he understood well the Elements of the Latine tongue. Yet I think he could make a shift to understand some easie sentences of Latin. He hath an extraordinary uprightness and piety. He lived a while with some Merchants, so that he understands trade, tho' he hath not been willing to follow it. He hath a severe and retired conduct. Never seeth any women but my Mother and Sisters; and very seldom any men. He loveth very much books and reading. He is esteemed and respected at Geneva, so that the Soveraignty there gave him some publick and extraordinary marks of their affection. . . . I often spoke with him my thoughts, which he allways took right; and he was the first man whom I persuaded that there were an infinity of sorts of infinits, the one sort infinitly smaller than the next. In a word Sir I do not see his acquaintance can possibly bring You to any manner of trouble or difficultys. He leaveth everybody the liberty of their thoughts, and never hath made any bad use of any mans confidence.[25]

According to Newton's testimony in the fall of 1693, he had felt himself in a state of ill health for the previous twelve months. Whether he was aware of it or not, this period coincided with Fatio's sickness and his long, slow convalescence. Throughout the year 1693 Newton did not leave Cambridge except for periods in June and in the latter part of September (the Buttery Book recorded his exits from the College).[26] During the months from December 1692 through February 1693 the famous letters to Bentley on the religious implications of the Newtonian system were written and they give no indication of a grave psychic crisis. But except for these letters the extended correspondence with Fatio is virtually all that remains of a personal nature for the whole year preceding the outbreak of September 1693. There is a draft of a letter about learned works from Newton to Otto Mencke, the Leipzig philosophy professor and founder of the *Acta Eruditorum,* dated May 30, 1693, but it was probably not sent, for Newton later begged forgiveness for his negligence in not responding to previous correspondence. A letter in Latin from Leibniz written on March 7, 1693, went unanswered for many months, until after the crisis, an omission that could be a symptom of progressive withdrawal on Newton's part.[27] Although the significance of Fatio in the final critical episode is mere inference and might be disputed, the concatenation of events points to him as a major provocation.

In January 1693 a Swiss theologian, Jean Alphonse Turretin, brought Newton word of the halting pace of Fatio's recovery; there followed an exchange of letters about Fatio's health in the course of which Newton proposed that he come to live in Cambridge to escape the London climate, offering him financial support during his stay. Fatio refused the money because he had come into a small competence after his mother's death, but he was quite willing to entertain the idea of residing with Newton. He only pressed his friend to be more explicit. "I do not know but with what my mother hath left me I might live here yet some years, chiefly at Cambridge, and if You wish I should go there and have for that some other reasons than what barely relateth to my health and to the saving of charges I am ready to do so; But I could wish in that case You would be plain in your next letter."[28]

In the same letter of January 30, 1693, Fatio tried to imitate his mentor in the interpretation of Scripture as he had in the sciences, though in fact there was a gulf between their two methods; for while Newton was a scrupulous and literal reader of carefully collated biblical texts even when he used his hieroglyphic key to the language of prophecy, Fatio, the ape of Newton, lacked that element of equilibrium that usually restrained Newton from falling into the abyss of enthusiasm or flying off into the higher realms of mystical experience for more than brief periods. Fatio's letter presaged the unfortunate moment when he would totally break with social reality. "But I am persuaded and as much as satisfyed that the book of Job, allmost all the Psalms and the book of proverbs and the history of the Creation are as many prophecys, relating most of them to our times and to times lately past or to come. That the history of the temptation of Adam and his wife is a Prophecy; the serpent being there the Roman Empire perhaps in conjonction with the eastern Empire, Adam the clergy in them, his wife the Church or people submitted to the clergy &c. That the history of Abel and Cain is a repetition of the same Prophesy." In a reply of February 14 Newton gently but firmly made an attempt to check Fatio's enthusiasm. "I am glad you have taken the prophesies into consideration & I beleive there is much in what you say about them, but I fear you indulge too much in fansy in some things," he tactfully chided.[29]

Newton and Fatio then lapsed into a repetitive discussion back and forth about small debts—a sort of verbal smokescreen for their feelings—with Newton constantly endeavoring to find a pretext to foist money upon his friend and Fatio reluctant to burden him with obligations. Four letters were devoted to the purchase of a remedy they called "Imperial powders," a box of rulers, and two volumes on alchemy—on their face the letters are factual and inconsequential, and yet the trivia do not quite smother the plans for living together and Newton's concern lest Fatio allow an operation for hemorrhoids to be performed on him. On March 7 Newton wrote: "There being 12 doses of your powder for the 1st region in my hand & two books, wch I am to return to you either in specie or in money & apprehending that you will have more occasion for money I have sent you 12£ for them by Mr Purver the Carrier. you put your self to the expence of 5£ for three Rulers wch will now be of no use to you. Possibly they may be sometime or other of use to me & therefore I have sent you 5£ for them if you please to send them to me. For I reccon them bought upon my account. I should be glad of a line or two from you at your best leisure. . . ."[30] The next day Fatio acknowledged receipt of the money, and then on March 9 addressed a pointed question to Newton: "I should be glad to know Sr what prospect You had before You of a way for me to subsist at Cambridge. I must confess that I should like better being there at least for a year than going into my own country; chiefly if it was practicable and proper that I should hire the chambers which You had next to Yours."[31] Newton's response of March 14 reiterates the invitation to return to Cambridge, and is as forthright as he can ever be in a personal relationship.

I have now received the box of rulers, with your receipt of £14. I sent you that money because I thought it was just; and, therefore you compliment me if you reckon it an obligation. The chamber next me is disposed of; but that which I was contriving was, that since your want of health would not give you leave to undertake your design for a subsistence at London, to make you such an allowance as might make your subsistence here easy to you. And, if your affairs in Switzerland be not so pressing but that without damage to them you may stay still some time in England (as your last letter gives me hopes), you will much oblige me by returning hither. I hope you will have good advice before you venture upon the operation you speak of. . . .[32]

After a month's interval Fatio replied on April 11, 1693, that he would have to return to Switzerland at least temporarily to see to his inheritance. He repeated his protestations of affection with the extravagance that was his style. "I could wish Sir to live all my life, or the greatest part of it, with you, if it was possible, and shall allways be glad of any such methods to bring that to pass as shall not be chargeable to You and a burthen to Your estate or family."[33] Most of the letter is devoted to their common alchemical interest in the composition of gold in various parts of the world; but there is one almost playful passage that informs Newton of a visit from Locke to Fatio's chambers in London. Fatio's slightly condescending reference to Locke and the jocular assurance with which he intimates that Locke means to use him as an attraction to lure Newton to Oates in Essex (where Locke was staying with Lady Masham) are the most intriguing aspects of this letter, from which distorted material will emerge during the height of Newton's crisis in a distracted note to Locke. Fatio wrote of Locke: "He is not yet off the fancy to have us to go to Oates. Yet I think he means well & would have me to go there only that You may be the sooner inclinable to come."

The last episode before Newton's psychic collapse is known only through two long, intricate letters from Fatio in May 1693; Newton's responses, if there were any, have been lost. Fatio described alchemical experiments about which there had been previous discussion and then sought advice from the older man on the wisdom of undertaking a new career in medicine with the secret formulas a "friend" had shown him. The letters abound with allusions to esoteric knowledge that they shared, and Fatio made a specific request that Newton burn one of the documents after he had "done with it" (it is still in King's College).[34] Fatio's motives in considering a new calling as a doctor are a peculiar admixture of hunger for money, for his inheritance had turned out to be meager, and a desire to cure the multitudes of disease with an elixir of life which he had tried on himself and which his "friend" had given to above ten thousand persons. "[T]he remedy being exceeding cheap I could cure for nothing thousands of people and so make it known in a little while. After which it would be easie to raise a fortune by it." Though the remedy was "vomitive" he was confident he could overcome that fault.[35] Fatio had embarked upon one of those schemes with which he was from time to time totally possessed and carried away, and it is impossible to distinguish fact from fancy in his reporting of the miraculous cures of his anonymous "friend." Newton was himself engaged in alchemical experiments in his Trinity College laboratory during this same period. Perhaps he became alarmed at Fatio's lack of caution in sending reports on alchemy through the post. When a favorite, however cherished, transgressed the bounds of discretion, Newton had a way of abruptly pulling back. There may have been another reason for withdrawal: Newton's fear of further emotional embroilment with Fatio.

During the anguished autumn of 1693, to our knowledge, not a word passed between Newton and Fatio; in 1694 Fatio wrote Huygens that he had not heard from Newton for more than seven months, which could mean that there was a break around the time of the crisis.[36] Evidence of their later relationship is scanty. Fatio reappears as a character in the Leibniz-Newton quarrel—he may even have sparked it—and Newton publicly calls to witness that he had early laid before him important documents bearing on the priority of discovery of the calculus. There are letters from Fatio to Newton about watchmaking and requests for the endorsement of a new invention, but nothing from Newton's hand can be found. Nevertheless the ties were maintained in some form for a number of years. Fatio entered into a partnership with two French watchmakers in London, obtained a patent in 1704 for an invention related to rubies, and exhibited specimens of watches at the Royal Society in March 1705—a display that could not have taken place without Newton's approval. Though with the turn of the century

David Gregory figures more and more prominently in Newton's company, Fatio is not wholly excluded. An entry of November 15, 1702, in Gregory's diary has Newton promise "Mr. Roberts, Mr. Fatio, Capt. Hally & me to publish his Quadratures, his treatise of Light, & his treatise of the Curves of the 2d Genre." On May 19, 1704, after describing Fatio's improvement of watches, David Gregory further notes: "Mr. Newton has given him a Testimony in writing that he kept two of his watches by him 4 weeks, & that the one kept within one minute of the same."[37] As late as January 1706 Fatio was still active in scientific circles. David Gregory reports under that date: "I saw the schem of M. Fatios Systema Mundi Cometis auctum."[38] Flamsteed met him during one of his trips to London.[39] But after the great scandal of 1707, any relationship with Newton is quite attenuated.

Interpretation of the Book of Daniel and of Revelations commonly interested many of Newton's friends—Henry More, Richard Bentley, William Whiston, John Locke—as it did scores of learned Europeans in the seventeenth century. Newton had devoted himself intermittently to commentary on these texts at least from 1680 on. But when the French Prophets from the Cévennes appeared in London, the preoccupation with difficult passages in Scripture among closeted scholars was overshadowed by the zealotry of Huguenot enthusiasts who ranted in the streets and conducted wild séances during which frenzied men and women prophesied the imminent coming of Judgment Day. Popular attention was more closely riveted to the carryings-on of the Prophets than to the campaigns of Marlborough. The Frenchmen quickly attracted English adherents, one of whom promised to raise the dead. A visionary saw a boat sailing along streets that ran with the blood of the slain. Another predicted that Lord Chief Justice Holt while sitting on the bench would burst with blood flowing from all his veins, head to foot.

The Prophets were mocked by men of common sense in high and low circles. Shaftesbury aimed *A Letter concerning Enthusiasm* against them; at public fairs their contortions were imitated in the-

5. View of Trinity College, 1690

6. Isaac Newton, 1689

atrical booths; and in Thomas D'Urfey's comedy *The Modern Prophets* (1709) Mistress Bicknell played Betty Grey and delighted the sparks by going off into "dainty little agitations" on the stage.[40] Religious and political authorities, alerted by the more staid and respectable French Protestant exiles who feared lest the demonstrations reflect on them, took the fanatics seriously, and their leaders were brought to trial at Guildhall for raising a tumult by foretelling a second burning of London. On November 9, 1707, Offspring Blackall, Bishop of Exeter, preached against them before the Queen at St. James's on *The Way of Trying Prophets*.

This was the sect with which Fatio fell in.[41] In the numerous broadsides directed against the Prophets, Fatio attracted particular attention, for he had become their secretary, taking down their ravings verbatim. While the others could be dismissed as frauds and deluded enthusiasts, this man of learning in geometry and many languages was an anomaly to the most balanced observers who had attended the séances out of curiosity or to expose their deceptions. The author of *Enthusiastick Impostors, no Divinely Inspir'd Prophets, Being a Historical Relation of the Rise, Progress, and Present Practices of the French and English Prophets* has left a circumstantial account of Fatio among the Prophets:

I was so very much dissatisfied with Cavalier's Entertainment that I was surpriz'd to find any Men of sense affected with it; much more to see Mr. Facio so diligent in penning everything that was said, with as much Care as if it had been delivered from Mount *Sinai*. Whereupon I ask'd him, if he had never doubted the Sincerity of these Gentlemen? Who answered me he had, and particularly upon Mr. *Fage's* using strange Words in one of his Extasies, which he thought had no Relation to any Language; but being not present when he spoke them, could not so well judge of them; therefore hearing Mr. Fage say, in an Extasie, that in a short time he should again speak in an Unknown Tongue; tho' Mr. Facio's Esteem of the Prophets began to abate, yet he resolv'd to hear Fage speak in a strange Language. Once after this, Mr. Fage had Warnings of an Extasie; but being awed by the Presence of some Clergymen, he stifled it; but Mr. Facio following him to another House, Fage immediately fell into an Extasie, and spoke to this Effect; Mon Enfant je m'envaie repondre sur les Ennemis mes Jugements terrible, & ma dernier

Sentence sera, Tring, Trong, Swing, Swang, Hing, Hang. Thus in English, My Child, I am going to pour out my terrible Judgments upon my Enemies, and my last Sentence shall be Tring, Trang, Twing, Twang, Hing, Hang. Which unintelligible *Jargon* so stumbled Mr. Facio, that had been conversant in 52 Languages; that he returned home under the greatest Concern imaginable; being under Apprehensions, that hitherto he and his Friends had been scandalously mock'd, abus'd, and impos'd on.

Here he paus'd, and gave me room to ask him, how he surmounted this Difficulty; which he said was by applying himself to Prayer, in which he was directed *not to reject the Prophets:* Besides which solution, he thought the Words, or rather inarticulate Sounds, might allude to the Law among the Jews, not to exceed forty Stripes in punishing some Offences; and tho' he did not count the Blows Fage gave himself, yet he believed they were about that Number, and that the Holy Spirit condescended to express himself by the sound of Blows, as a Man driving a Wedg, cries Ha, Ha, &c.[42]

Before the Prophets were brought to trial, there were attempts on the part of diplomatic representatives of Savoy to save Fatio if he would promise to leave England,[43] but he refused to abandon his fellow-believers and he suffered with them in pillory both at Charing Cross and at the Royal Exchange.[44] News of the disgrace was received at Geneva with consternation, and Fatio's brother tried to argue him out of his fanaticism, warning of the biblical injunction against false prophets; but he could not be budged.[45] Lost to science, he devoted years to the defense of his new friends.

One of the many curious attempts to explain the enthusiasts of the Cévennes lighted on Fatio as the secret mastermind behind the whole movement. The *Clavis Prophetica; or, a Key to the Prophecies of Mons. Marion, and the other Camisars, with some Reflections on the Character of these New Envoys, and of Mons. F their Chief Secretary* (1707) had made inquiries about the brilliant, eccentric mathematician and arrived at a convincing description of his character. He was called a man of good natural parts, but pensive and melancholy; the author was not certain whether his temper derived from his original constitution or was contracted by habit, a question which has by no means been resolved. The reports of Calamy that in Holland he had been a Spinozist or another kind of heretic were confirmed. Failing to find a geometric demonstration of the truth of Christianity, Fatio spoke of it with the freedom of a libertine, singling out one of its chief mysteries for attack—an obvious allusion to his aspersions on the divinity of Christ, by a writer reluctant to mention directly so monstrous a blasphemy. If the allegation was true, there had once been another bond among Newton, Fatio, and Locke: their common secret unitarianism.

The anonymous author had Fatio create a new religion of his own, a "Spiritual Catholicon," since no existing faith was for him the repository of unmixed truth. He knew of Fatio's interest in the medical nostrum about which he had written Newton in 1693 (the great man's name is never mentioned in the pamphlet literature on the Prophets) and supposed that his new religion was meant to effect a similar sovereign cure of all distempers. When the Prophets had suddenly appeared from the Cévennes Fatio had made a deliberate Machiavellian decision, the argument ran, to use the fanatics as instruments for the propagation of his new faith. Proof positive that the whole movement was a contrivance of Fatio's was said to have been discovered at Oxford when, during the appearance of the Prophets there, one of Fatio's letters was purloined and published by a Mr. Thwaites, Fellow of Queen's College and Greek Professor at the University, who aimed to unmask their enthusiasm as a cover for debauchery. The letter from Fatio apparently led Thomas Hearne, the scholarly gossip, to draw a picture of his devious character: "[I]t has been always observ'd of him that he is a Sceptick in Religion, a person of no virtue, but a meer Debauchee. He was formerly a Director to the Duke of Bedford, whilst he was of Magd. Coll. in Oxford, who, by his Means, imbib'd odd Principles, grew a great Gamester and Spend-Thrift. . . . During the time Facio was with him, he got by his Insinuation and cunning a vast sum of Money from the Duke, & made all the Provisions possible for his future Advantage."[46]

There may well be a measure of truth in some of these tales about Fatio. Examination of his papers, however, leads to the belief that his commitment to the Prophets was genuine possession rather than mere simulation. The final pathetic fate of Fatio only increases wonderment at the genius of his idol Newton, who, buffeted by similar destructive forces of massive power, overcame them. Both were born with extraordinary natural endowments and both had access to vast subterranean resources of psychic energy that are beyond ordinary comprehension, but one survived and the other succumbed.

Though Fatio had made the first imputations of plagiarism against him, Leibniz was genuinely concerned when he heard of the public humiliation in the stocks. The philosopher was baffled by the fall into unreason of a promising scientist. On March 16, 1708, he wrote from Hannover: "The affair of the Cévennes Prophets has ended in an unfortunate catastrophe and I am sorry for love of M. Fatio; I do not understand how so excellent a man in mathematics could have embarked on such an affair. The judges were against the men from the Cévennes and if anything had been able to sway people in the other direction it was his reputation. It is as though Cato were taking sides against the gods. They seem to have hoodwinked him for I do not dare doubt his good faith."[47] A few years after Fatio's public chastisement came the ejection of William Whiston from Cambridge University for his vigorous unitarianism. Here was another Newton disciple and mathematician entangled in the thickets of theology. Leibniz had been disturbed when Whiston declared himself a Socinian and at first had mocked his attempt to "use his mathematics on the mystery of the trinity."[48] But when Whiston was punished, Leibniz again wrote with humanity, "I pity the good Mr. Whiston who does himself harm with his excess of zeal."[49] There is charitableness in Leibniz as well as wit, qualities that Newton conspicuously lacked.

When Fatio became publicly identified with the Prophets from the Cévennes, Newton wrapped himself in the official activities of the Mint and, to our knowledge, never raised a finger to save him.[50] And yet there are persistent rumors among eighteenth-century anecdotalists that Newton too had at one time been attracted to the Prophets, and that his friends dissuaded him from going to their sessions lest he be caught up in the same toils as Fatio.[51] That Fatio may have sought his own abasement is consonant with his personality. But when Newton forsook him in his hour of trial, going about his business with routine meetings at the Treasury at the very moment when Fatio was being pelted in pillory, was he re-enacting his own childhood abandonment? Or was he simply the cautious yeoman's son who would not jeopardize his hard-won reputation by identifying himself in any way with a convicted enthusiast?

Fatio, always ailing, lived on for half a century after his humiliation. He traveled to the Continent and was mixed up in the persecutions of the Prophets in Holland. There is a letter to Hans Sloane that refers to a journey to Constantinople in pursuit of his millenarian mission. It is an attempt to convert Sloane, Secretary of the Royal Society, to the religion of the Prophets.[52] A letter to Newton in 1717 discusses a watch he had ordered for Bentley, and another in 1724 requests permission to use Newton's name in a project for increasing the reputation and manufacture of pierced rubies. No replies are extant.[53] Fatio finally settled down in Worcester, and continued to develop his own system of gravity—in everything a caricature of Isaac Newton. After Newton's death, when John Conduitt turned to him for recollections of their common departed god, Fatio produced nothing substantive, though he always insisted that he and he alone had the right to compose Newton's epitaph.[54] But as he grew old he turned upon the memory of his former patron. Standing by itself the *Principia* was grossly inadequate; only *his* system, which explained gravity, was the true system of the world, and only *his* observations could definitively settle the debate over the chronology of ancient kingdoms. He even claimed to have seen written testimony in Newton's hand agreeing with his "cause of gravity."[55] For a prize offered by the French Academy of Sciences he submitted a poem based on the new system that aimed to supplant Lucretius, though he knew that they had secretly reserved the award for a Cartesian. William Whiston, a fellow outcast from the Newton circle, wrote him an occasional letter,[56] but Captain Halley never deigned to answer his long memoranda about new projects for the navy.

When he was struck with paralysis, he abandoned plans to return to Switzerland and became a crank living on the memory of Isaac Newton and writing stray articles for the *Gentleman's Magazine*. His collection of dreams, recorded in almost undecipherable French abbreviations and illustrated with apocalyptic drawings, is the most perplexing of his literary remains. Though he was abandoned in the flesh by his former fellows of the Royal Society, they could not prevent his dreaming about them: once he saw Edmond Halley, hardly renowned for his religious devotion, rise at an open meeting of the assembly and speak with tongues.

Chapter 10

THE BLACK YEAR 1693

Madnesse seemes to be noething but a disorder in the imagination, and not in the discursive faculty.

—John Locke, *Journal*

THE tale that Newton suffered a complete breakdown in 1693 resulting in a permanent deterioration of his faculties was first given wide currency in an account of his life by the French astronomer Jean-Baptiste Biot for the *Biographie universelle* (1821). The idea was circulated in the English-speaking world through Lord Henry Brougham's popular biography of 1829, essentially a translation of Biot.[1] In his monumental *Memoirs of the Life, Writings, and Discoveries of Sir Isaac Newton*, the classical Victorian treatment, David Brewster set out to refute Biot, who had amplified his views in four articles in the *Journal des Savants* for 1836. Brewster took the offensive and associated Biot's opinion with that of his predecessor Laplace, who, according to Brewster, had instructed a Genevan professor to undertake researches in England in order to prove that all of Newton's religious ideas were a consequence of his psychic collapse and were thus to be sharply separated and distinguished from his rational scientific work—a convenient dichotomy for nineteenth-century positivists who saw religion and science in eternal combat and seventeenth-century scientists in their own image.

Reviewing Brewster's work in the *Journal des Savants* for October-November 1855, Biot devoted a whole section to a discussion of Newton's madness and to his works on chronology and theology. After flatly denying the story of the Genevan professor, he went on to present the primary evidence that had persuaded both Laplace and him of Newton's decline: he had seen a manuscript comment in one of Christiaan Huygens' notebooks quoting a young Scotsman about Newton *in phrenesin* for eighteen months. Biot further supported his contention that there had been a mental crisis by quoting from the diary of Abraham de la Pryme, a young Cambridge scholar, and from Newton's letters to Pepys and Locke in 1693. The dates of the illness did not quite coincide in all sources, but the discrepancies, according to Biot, were a result of the changeover in the calendar. In this his second consideration of Newton's works, Biot receded from the extreme position that the mental crisis had spelled the total destruction of Newton's intellectual capacities and said he had never implied that Newton's religious interests and writings were all posterior to 1693, a discreet tactical withdrawal.

Other French astronomers had also been busy spreading rumors about Newton's derangement. Jean-Baptiste Delambre's *Histoire de l'astronomie au dix-huitième siècle* (1827) observed that during the last thirty years of his life Newton had been a mere shadow of his former self.[2] Even in the eighteenth century there had been occasional reflections on Newton's sanity: the editor of Abbé Conti's works remarked that Newton had been touched in the head by the Camisard "Prophets of London."[3]

The bare facts about the crisis are now available in the third volume of the Royal Society edition of Newton's *Correspondence,* and their interpretation is open to every man. Newton may have experienced a number of earlier psychic disturbances—his references to illness are vague—but to our knowledge he sank into delusion only once, during the grave events of September 1693, when he had passed his fiftieth birthday. Then the great man behaved as might any mortal who is struck down. He broke with his friends, crawled into a corner, accused his intimates of plotting against him, and reported conversations that never took place. Newton stands naked before us only at this moment. "Your most humble and most unfortunate servant," he signs himself in a letter to Locke begging his pardon for having wished him dead.

On September 13, 1693, Newton wrote to the diarist Samuel Pepys, during whose tenure of office as President of the Royal Society the *Principia* had been published, abruptly terminating their relationship. As late as January 9, 1692, there had been free converse between them: John Evelyn had been invited to a meeting with Pepys, Dr. Thomas Gale, and Newton, at which they were to "set up" a man in England fit, after Boyle's recent death, to be their Nicholas Peiresc.[4] As one of the reasons for the breach Newton alleged that John Millington, a Fellow of Magdalene College, Cambridge, had importuned him with messages from Pepys and had extorted a promise that he would visit Pepys in London. (From a later letter of Millington to Pepys it is apparent that no such interview had ever taken place.)[5] Newton, aware of his condition, then went on to describe his general state of ill health. "I am extremely troubled at the embroilment I am in, and have neither ate nor slept well this twelve month, nor have my former consistency of mind." The nature of the "embroilment" is difficult to ascertain, though it involves, among other things, the search for a "place." Since Pepys, who had once been charged with complicity in the Popish Plot, was retired and of no influence after the Glorious Revolution, the next phrase in the letter can only be read as a confused outburst of Newton's violent antipopery, an allowable release for his irritability and suppressed anger, which fixed itself on Pepys: "I never designed to get anything by your interest, nor by King James's favour. . . ." But another line in the letter connotes a more dangerous abandonment of the world: "[I] am now sensible that I must withdraw from your acquaintance, and see neither you nor the rest of my friends any more, if I may but leave them quietly."[6]

This strange letter was followed three days later, on September 16, by one to John Locke that was even more enigmatic, written at The Bull in Shoreditch, London. There is nothing to enlighten us about what Newton was doing there; all we know is that it was one of the two periods that year when he was signed out of the University.[7] The handwriting is not as regular as Newton's penmanship usually is in correspondence, and there is an air of untidiness about the letter (now in the Bodleian Library in Oxford); it is soiled with many inkspots. By this time Newton was already beginning to emerge from the acute phase of the episode. The note was at once a confession and a plea for forgiveness, a confession of having entertained evil thoughts, which his censor does not distinguish from acts. The image of embroilment reappears twice, only this time in a somewhat more specific form—he feared entrapment both with "woemen" and the sale of an office, again a possible reference to long pending discussions about preferment. The attack on Locke, for which he begged pardon, the "thought" that he had considered him a "Hobbist" for utterances in the *Essay Concerning Human Understanding,* was of the same order as his implied accusation that Pepys was a Papist. His actually voicing a wish that Locke were dead may or may not have been a fantasy. The letter affords a rare penetration into Newton's psyche during a period of disturbance:

Being of opinion that you endeavoured to embroil me with woemen & by other means I was so much affected with it as that when one told me you were sickly & would not live I answered twere better if you were dead. I desire you to forgive me this uncharitableness. For I am now satisfied that what you have done is just & I beg your pardon for my having hard thoughts of you for it & for representing that you struck at the root of morality in a principle you laid down in your book of Ideas & designed to pursue in another book & that I took you for a Hobbist. I beg your pardon also for saying or thinking that there was a designe to sell me an office, or to embroile me.[8]

For the second time in his life Newton could purge himself with words of confession and apology, a great source of strength.

The letters were also cries for help, and the reactions of Pepys and Locke were in character. Pepys on September 26 wrote to Millington expressing fears for Newton's sanity. This was not his first inquiry about Newton's health; an earlier question had elicited a noncommittal answer. Coming directly to the point, Pepys was concerned that the inconsistency of Newton's letter "arise from that which of all mankind I should least dread from him and most lament for,—I mean a discomposure in head, or mind, or both."[9] His object in writing Millington was not merely to satisfy curiosity;

he wanted to know if he could be of assistance. In a few days Millington put Pepys out of his "generous pain": he had met Newton at Huntingdon, and even before he raised the question of the Pepys correspondence Newton himself had told about "a very odd letter" he had written while "in a distemper that much seized his head, and that kept him awake for about five nights together." Newton was "very much ashamed" of his rudeness to Pepys, who had always so greatly honored him, and asked Millington to convey to him an explanation and apology. Though Millington declared Newton now very well, he described him as "under some small degree of melancholy."[10] A period of depression was the aftermath of the critical fortnight.

A subsequent letter of Pepys to Millington shows his anxious solicitude for Newton's wounded spirit: "And for the kind reflection he has since made upon his letter to me, I dare not take upon me to judge what answer I should make him to it, or whether any or no; and therefore pray that you will be pleased either to bestow on me what directions you see fit for my own guidance towards him in it, or to say to him in my name . . . whatever you think may be most welcome to him upon it, and most expressive of my regard and affectionate esteem of him, and concernment for him."[11] Locke's response to Newton, October 5, 1693, was also full of humanity and forgiveness, a tender witness of his "love and esteem" (the draft, now in the Bodleian, was carefully prepared). He even took seriously Newton's distracted censure that he was a "Hobbist" and asked for the exact passages of the *Essay Concerning Human Understanding* that had provoked his anger, so that he might alter them lest other readers, even for a moment, fall into similar error.[12] A more precise date for the breakdown—if that is the word for it—may be gathered from another of Newton's letters to Locke, written on October 15, 1693. The symptoms had apparently included protracted insomnia and loss of memory for a brief period, though the general malaise was of longer duration. "The last winter by sleeping too often by my fire I got an ill habit of sleeping & a distemper wch this summer has been epidemical put me further out of order, so that when I wrote to you I had not slept an hour a night for a fortnight together & for 5 nights together not a wink. I remember I wrote to you but what I said of your book I remember not."[13]

In the youthful reflections and questionings of his Cambridge University notebook Newton had introspected about the nature of the imagination, fantasy, dreams, and the effect on the rational faculties of prolonged and excessive concentration. "How is it that the Soule so often remembers her dreames by chance otherwise not knowing shee had dreamed, & thence whither she be perpetually employed in Sleepe. whether dreames are of the body or soule. Why are they patched up of many fragments & incoherent passages," he wrote under the heading "Of Sleepe & Dreams."[14] In another notation he betrayed an understanding of psychic dangers: "Phantasie is helped by good aire fasting moderate wine. but spoiled by drunkenesse, Gluttony, too much study (whence & from extreame passion cometh madnesse), dizzinesse commotions of the spirits. Meditation heates the braine in some to distraction in others to an akeing & dizzinesse."[15] But while Newton was aware of psychological disturbances, he considered them, as did most of his intellectual contemporaries, to be disorders akin to physical ailments, with a specific cause and a finite duration. The simple candor of his report about his "distraction" and the responses of his friends are by no means out of the ordinary.

Attacks of deep melancholy in middle-aged men, a sort of male climacteric, are common, and Newton's case assumed a rather severe form. What was oppressing him during this period? A number of things may have upset his tenuous balance, maintained for decades through rigid control. He had written a vehement anti-Trinitarian tract in 1690 and had made a move to get it published by having Locke transmit it to Le Clerc in Holland. Then he took fright lest its author be revealed and withdrew the document. The whole question of the unity of God was troubling him. In search of a place, he had allowed himself to be pushed into the presence of Charles Mordaunt, Lord Monmouth, an influential diplomat who was close to William III and to whom he had been introduced by Locke, and he felt ashamed. He was surrendering his independence, putting himself in the power of others, he whose sense of autonomy was fierce. Seeking honor and neglecting God's work was a sin he had already felt a need to confess in 1662, *Setting my heart on money learning pleasure more than Thee,* and now he had relapsed. The affective relationship to Fatio had approached a climax and the plans to have Fatio reside with him in Cambridge fell through.

When the final explosion, for which there had been a long preparation, occurred in September 1693 and Newton struck out in letters with mad accusations, he chose friends as the objects of his hostility—Locke and Pepys—and he attacked them for evils with which he was himself possessed. If doubts about the nature of God beset him, Locke was called a Hobbist, which meant a materialist and an atheist. If Newton was actively place-seeking, he denounced Pepys for trying to involve him in obligations to the idolatrous Catholic party. If he was conscious of a crisis in his emotional life that was somehow related to Fatio, he charged Locke with trying to "embroil" him with "woemen & by other means. . . ." The last charge is perhaps the most significant because it suggests a distorted rendering of that casual remark of Fatio's in the letter to Newton on April 11, five months before, that Locke was "not yet off the fancy to have us to go to Oates. Yet I think he means well & would have me to go there only that You may be the sooner inclinable to come." That Newton became aware of something sinful in his affection for Fatio which his censor could not cope with is one of the plausible explanations of his flight from reality into illnesss. The feeling of guilt related to this attachment was too great to be contained and endured, and it erupted. He accused his best friends of trying to seduce him and embroil him. They were Papist idolaters and Hobbists who had tempted him with sins of the flesh and denial of God the Father, and he had been contaminated by having converse with them. They had threatened his chastity, his purity, his righteousness —that is the burden of his accusation. But on another level of consciousness, he knew that it was he himself who had been guilty of a sin of the flesh, at least in thought, a sin for which one deserved burning.

Though one is tempted to assign preponderant weight to Fatio in Newton's despondency, the involvement with place-seeking and the humiliation this entailed were no mean shocks to his equilibrium. One could speculate about other contributing irritants. In a more distant way the crisis may be related to the publicaton of the *Principia* itself. After Newton had given birth to the system of the world, what was there left to be achieved? *Post Principia tristis.* A man is commonly not as creative in physics and mathematics after his fiftieth birthday as in his youth. In his undergraduate days, Newton himself had formulated in the psychophysiological language of his time an understanding of the ravages of age: "The boyling blood of youth puts the spirits upon too much motion or else causet too many spirits. but could age makes the brain either two dry to move roundly through or else is defective of spirits. . . ."[16] Newton's scientific wellsprings had by no means been drained; and when later, challenged by a problem Bernoulli had set, he solved it within a day, the continentals quickly recognized the lion among mathematicians by his claw—*tanquam ex ungue leonem.* But there was no longer a flood of new ideas. He was emending, perfecting, restating conceptions which had been generated years before. His growing preoccupation with history and chronology may have been a refuge, and it represents a diminution of his generalizing capacity. To this extent there was a kernel of truth in Biot's analysis of the crisis.

When Newton published the *Principia* and established the laws of the universe he reached the zenith of his genius. He had still not put into print the *Opticks* or his method of the calculus, but he knew his main discoveries were complete. There remained unfinished problems: the perfection of the lunar theory, a revision of world chronology founded on astronomical dating, the discovery of the elusive alchemical principle, the demonstration of the truth of unitarianism on the basis of textual analysis of Scripture. And yet none of these studies entirely absorbed him.

After the Glorious Revolution new worldly opportunities beck-oned Newton and made insupportable the life of a professor at-tached to a college visibly on the decline. The Cambridge scholar who had been possessed by his researches in mathematics, natural philosophy, alchemy, world chronology, Bible commentary, who shunned people, who had no enduring loves and few overt hates, became dissatisfied with his status and his way of life. He had come out into the world during the Father Francis case, while the *Principia* was still in the press. His new interest in public affairs per-suaded him to stand for Parliament from the University, and he was elected. He engaged actively in Whig politics, anticipating a post of authority and power as a reward. Finally he began to taste again the delights of affection, if not of love, some ten years after the death of his mother. When he appeared in London during the Convention Parliament he had Halley and Montague and Locke, even Pepys, as his friends, not to speak of Fatio. No longer was he secluded in Trinity, a professor with no prospect of a mastership because he would not take holy orders. The names of women began to appear in his correspondence—Lady Masham whom he knew at Oates where Locke stayed, her mother Mrs. Cudworth, Lady Mon-mouth. He made an effort to please.

But during this twilight period between the publication of the *Principia* in 1687 and the crisis, he met with defeats. The alchemical experiments yielded nothing, though the record places him in his laboratory in December 1692, January, April, and June 1693, almost on the eve of the crisis.[17] In the confused political situation of the early years of William and Mary the Whigs were not in full con-trol, and no appointment materialized. A proposal to make Newton Provost of King's College came to naught; there were suggestions that he be chosen head of the Charter House but he was unen-thusiastic and they were not acted upon; the comptrollership of the Mint was talked about but not offered. If a casual acquaintance like John Millington could observe that Newton lay "neglected by those in power,"[18] Newton himself would have felt the snub much more keenly. To be rejected when he had risked advances was a terrible blow: such events were easily structured into a pattern that made them appear to be a concerted repudiation of his person. The crisis occurred as his great expectations collapsed and life began to fall back into the old routine.

When word of Newton's distraction spread beyond the shores of England, the cause assigned was either overwork or despair over the loss of manuscripts in a fire. Christiaan Huygens noted in his journal on May 29, 1694: "When he came to see the Archbishop of Cambridge [sic], his conversation was such as to point to his not being in his right mind. At this his friends took him in hand; he was kept at home, and, whether he liked it or not, treatment applied whereby he has now recovered his sanity so far as now again to begin to understand his own book of the Mathematical Principles of Philosophy." Huygens spread the story in so grossly exaggerated a form that his *Schadenfreude* is transparent. He had written to his brother Constantyn on May 26, 1694, that Newton's madness lasted for eighteen months: "There is a man lost and so to speak dead for research, so I believe, which is deplorable."[19] As Huygens passed on the report to Leibniz and de l'Hôpital, it grew in the retelling; a cure had supposedly been effected by "remedies and keeping him shut up."[20] From Leibniz on June 12, 1694, came a straightforward reply to Huygens expressing satisfaction at Newton's recovery and then going on to a puzzling reflection: "It is to men like yourself, sir, and him, that I wish long life and good health, in preference to others, whose loss would not be great, speaking comparatively."[21] For the next few years rumors about Newton's illness kept cropping up, and it is difficult to know whether they were related to the crisis of 1693 or a new sickness. When Dr. Wallis heard a story from the mathematician and philosopher Johann Christoph Sturm in Germany he denied it, but the gossip persisted.[22] In 1695 wild tales in London even had Newton dead.[23]

The story of a fire is printed in the diary of Abraham de la Pryme, a member of St. John's College, Cambridge, who in an entry for February 3, 1693, told of the accidental burning of a manuscript on "colours & light established upon thousands of Experiments" and of Newton's perturbation. "[E]very one thought he would have run mad, he was so troubled thereat that he was not himself for a Month after."[24] Abraham de la Pryme's entry does not seem to allude to a recent event—he is merely recounting an anecdote—and there is no sign of any such catastrophe in Newton's letters to Bentley and Fatio in February 1693. The language of the diary is imprecise and may refer to an earlier incident, the burning of papers on optics in 1678 or a similar occurrence at a later date. Newton told Conduitt that he had lost papers relating to both optics and fluxions by the upsetting of a candle.[25] Newton may have been the victim of many fires, for a good number of his manuscripts are scorched. Whether there was a great conflagration, as Abraham de la Pryme would have it, or merely the loss of several sheets of his optics, as Stukeley reported, we do not know. It is doubtful that a burning of manuscripts was the trauma that led to the crisis of 1693. Nor is imputing the breakdown to overwork a convincing explanation: Newton was always a prodigious researcher and there is no indication that his pace had been accelerated during these months.

Newton's recuperative powers and his resilience were extraordinary. His letters in the last months of 1693 and dated papers in his hand during his final two years in Cambridge give no evidence that there was any recrudescence of his malady. On October 16, 1693, a day after his confession to Locke, Newton sent a belated reply to a letter from Leibniz which, he explained, had slipped from his hands and had been long mislaid among his papers.[26] It is difficult to interpret this document. On the one hand it is full of protestations of friendship and esteem: "I value your friendship very highly and have for many years back considered you as one of the leading geometers of this century. . . . I was however afraid that our friendship might be diminished by silence . . . I hope indeed that I have written nothing to displease you, and if there is anything that you think deserves censure, please let me know of it by letter, since I value friends more highly than mathematical discoveries." The show of humility, asking for "censure," and plea for affection are unwonted. And yet the point of the dagger protrudes: the heart of the letter is a reminder that Newton had once sent Leibniz his method of fluxions through Oldenburg (a fact that Dr. Wallis was about to include in his *History of Algebra*), and there is an implied reprimand that Leibniz had not mentioned Newton's discovery when he published his own version in 1684.

On November 22, 1693, begging pardon of Otto Mencke that his letter of February 1 had "got mislaid among my papers"—the set formula is repeated to cover up the period of his withdrawal from the learned world—he gave him an opinion on a new edition of John Spencer's book on the laws of the Hebrews about which the scholar had consulted him.[27] By this time Newton had obviously recuperated from his depression sufficiently to take care of his long neglected correspondence. And when Pepys on the same day wrote to him about "the Doctrine of determining between the true proportions of the Hazards incident to this or that given Chance or Lot,"[28] Newton answered promptly, and then continued an interchange about gaming and lottery odds until just before Christmas. From a letter to the New Testament scholar John Mill in January 1694, it is clear that he had arranged for the collation of various manuscripts of the Apocalypse, as he had promised some time before;[29] and in early May of that year David Gregory was in Cambridge taking notes of conversations with Newton on a vast variety of subjects physical, mathematical, and theological.[30] Toward the end of the same month Newton wrote a long critical analysis of a new educational scheme proposed for the Mathematical School at Christ's Hospital.[31] He had thus rebounded quite completely by the time international scientists began clucking about an eighteen-month attack of madness, an interlude which, according to Christiaan Huygens, *Messrs. les Anglois* had tried vainly to conceal.

Newton's crisis was followed by a dramatic reorganization of his personality and a rechanneling of his capacities that enabled him to manage his existence successfully for more than three decades. Two and a half years after his malady had subsided, an appointment from the King, a deus ex machina, abruptly changed his whole manner of life. Honors and the symbols of status were awarded him at regular intervals. He was named Warden and soon Master of the Mint; then came the Presidency of the Royal Society, and finally knighthood. The lone scientist became an administrator in London, with power in his hands that was real, palpable, immediate. To say that an aggressiveness which had once been turned inward in self-punitive acts was now allowed to manifest itself outwardly is an oversimplification of his psychological history. The crude description of this reversal does not imply any true emancipation from the ingrained feelings of guilt and unease with which he was possessed. His world was no less hostile because he could dominate it, and at the very apogee of his glory a sense of disappointment and of his own unworthiness rose to the surface. The price he paid for this about-face was to cut himself off in large measure from the boundless inner world which had sustained him with new creations ever since his boyhood. To the extent that he became a successful manipulator of men he was alienated from himself.

PART THREE

In London Town

AMID COINERS AND CLIPPERS

Macheath: That *that* Jemmy Twitcher should peach me, I own surpriz'd me!—'Tis a plain Proof that the World is all alike, and that even our Gang can no more trust one another than other People. Therefore, I beg you, Gentlemen, look well to your selves, for in all probability you may live some months longer.

Matt of the Mint: We are heartily sorry, Captain, for your Misfortune.—But 'tis what we must all come to.

—John Gay, *The Beggar's Opera*, Act III, scene 14

DURING his sojourn in England, Voltaire was entertained by Mrs. Catherine Conduitt, Newton's niece, and the Reverend Samuel Clarke, the disciple who served as a front in Newton's theological controversy with Leibniz; but he was never allowed into the presence of the ailing octogenarian scientist whom he had come to see. From the vivacious lady of the house he garnered anecdotes about Newton's life—the story of the falling apple and instances of Newton's priggishness. The philosophical chaplain, touched with Arianism, translated for him Newton's private views on God and on the atomic tradition, and assured him of Newton's profound admiration for Voltaire's fellow countryman Gassendi. Voltaire requited their hospitality by maliciously proclaiming to the world that Newton owed his appointment at the Mint to the favor Catherine had found in the eyes of the Chancellor of the Exchequer, and not to his scientific eminence alone. "In my youth I thought that Newton had made his fortune by his great merit. I had supposed that the Court and the City of London had named him Master of the Mint by acclamation.

Not at all. Isaac Newton had a very charming niece, Madame Conduitt; she greatly pleased the Lord of the Treasury, Halifax. The infinitesimal calculus and gravity would have availed nothing without a pretty niece."[1] Voltaire could never resist a jest, even at the occasional expense of truth. Newton's warrant of appointment as Warden is dated April 13, 1696, and whatever their subsequent relationship it is highly improbable that Catherine (nee Barton) had even met Charles Montague, later the Earl of Halifax, before she joined her uncle in London when he assumed office. Newton's affectionate ties with Montague date from the young aristocrat's undergraduate days, and there had been protracted discussions about some preferment for the Lucasian Professor of the Mathematics who had sat as a member from Cambridge in the Convention Parliament that brought William III to the throne.

The view once prevailed that the office of Warden was a sinecure.[2] This may have been true for most of the period from before 1600 until the abolition of the post two centuries later. But in the hands of a man with Newton's rigid sense of duty no office could ever be nominal, and the time of his incumbency, 1696 through 1699, marked by a vast increase of business, is an illustrious exception to the perennially low condition of the wardenship. Though documentation is not complete for his entire tenure, his administrative zeal is confirmed statistically by even a partial record. In the nineteen months from June 1698 to Christmas 1699, Newton appeared at the Mint on one hundred twenty-three days to examine two hundred suspects and informers. A peak of activity was reached in the first week of February 1699, when he attended seven times and had ten prisoners in Newgate. His ominous presence rendered the activities of "clippers" and "coyners" peculiarly hazardous. In 1697 there were nineteen executions at Tyburn for coinage crimes in the London area alone,[3] and Newton is credited with a significant reduction in the volume of counterfeiting.[4]

The office of Warden involved a multiplicity of functions, and so did the mastership to which Newton was elevated in 1700, a post he held until his death. His workers melted down plate and turned it into the King's coin; as Master, he was responsible for the purity of the metal at the trial of the pyx. During the recoinage of England's debased currency, a complex, daring undertaking carried out by the Treasury under Charles Montague and actually begun before Newton's arrival, he was a pivotal officer and directed mints in other parts of England as well as in London; in Chester he worked through his friend Halley, who had his difficulties with local officials.[5] (The renovation of the coinage resolved upon in 1695 brought Locke, Newton, and Halley into office at the same time, an intellectual triumvirate the equal of which had rarely been assembled to serve any government, though Philosophy suffered as a consequence.[6]) Where the recoined currency was not available fast enough, public tumults were likely to occur. Under Newton, at the height of the renovation a normal weekly output of fifteen thousand pounds of silver coin was increased to a hundred twenty thousand—witness that he was riding herd and stamping out the monies.

As Warden Newton also fulfilled quasi-judicial functions in tracking down clippers and counterfeiters, organizing a network of agents and informers, interrogating suspects.[7] Later, as Master of the Mint, he waited upon the Lords of the Treasury, and the State Papers record his frequent appearances before them even when he was a very old man. Designs for commemorative medals were prepared by his hand, along with learned commentaries explaining the recondite hieroglyphic symbols that he incorporated into them, often to the embarrassment of his superiors.[8] He composed intricate economic treatises on money in connection with his office, and he is responsible for the establishment of the gold standard, which lasted just about as long as his universal system, a parallel that philosophical Marxists may appreciate.[9] Economic historians have praised his administration. He exercised his trust with impeccable honesty: offered a bribe by a great duchess, he threw the agent out; promised a lucrative pension by Queen Anne, he placed the mastership at the disposal of the Tories but rejected the emolument. He was a great servant of the Crown, who performed his tasks as precisely as he conducted a scientific experiment or interpreted a corrupt text in Scripture. His extraordinary capacity to move from one activity to another with relative ease is dramatically attested by the Mint papers, where theological arguments against the Trinity, animadversions against Leibniz in the controversy over the invention of the calculus, and accounts of plate received in the Tower flow into one another and crisscross on the same page.

But if one inquires what part this new calling played in Newton's psychic economy, rather than in the economy of the realm, attention is drawn to the contents of a manuscript volume in the Royal Mint Library, a Depositions Book covering the years 1697–1704, in which none-too-literate secretaries recorded summaries of hundreds of interrogations, often in the earthy language of the informants and criminals themselves. About two hundred such resumes conclude with Newton's signature and a solemn Latin attestation of his presence. Direct interventions by Newton are frequent.[10] The same book has copies of letters received from prisoners begging favor and, in extremis, mercy.

When Newton embarked upon his pursuit of counterfeiters and clippers, he was thrust into the tumultuous world that John Gay later immortalized in *The Beggar's Opera* (1728)—thieves, beggars, murderers, prostitutes, informers, perjurers. If Newton's acquaintance during his Cambridge period was, by his own choice, rather restricted, when he became Warden of the Mint the range of his associates broadened to include victuallers, bricklayers, cheesemongers, smiths, footmen, cordwainers, barbers, periwigmakers, soldiers, charwomen, distillers, pawnbrokers, solicitors, bailiffs, drunken moneyers, and the wives and mistresses of clippers and coiners from whom he extracted information by bullying them. He learned of bribes to cut off evidence, of secret hideaways in the country, of clandestine meetings in garrets and taverns. He became conversant with men and women of many aliases. The Newton who at the University had driven the chemist Vigani from his presence for telling a joke about a nun sacrificed his innocence in the service of the Crown.

On July 25, 1699, Elizabeth Sutton deposed. "[She] saith that abt a fortnight before she was apprehended she became acquainted with

one Elizabeth Pilkington who took a room in the Mint in South-
wark and sometime after she had taken the said room she came to
this Informant and told her she must raise her bottom. and this Ex-
amt inquiring of the said Pilkington what she meant by those words
she replied she would tell her provided she would not discover what
it was."[11] After much ado it turned out that there were coins hidden
in a napkin. On August 19, 1699, Julian Tuffin accused Ann Pillsbury of passing a bad sixpence. "This informant with others searched
the said Ann Pillsbury and her said little Girle at the said Wardens
of the mint and the informant found wrapt in a paper in the said
Girle 5d worth of farthings & 4 six penies two of which were counterfeit ones."[12] No coin was too small to be sought for and no hiding
place was a sanctuary.

Dealing with criminals involved a measure of risk to Newton's
personal safety, though the bluster and threats of the prisoners, unlike those of the Warden, were rather impotent. On September 16,
1698, Samuel Bond of Ashbourn-in-the-peake in the county of Derby,
a "Chyrurgeon," put him on guard against his enemies.

He sayth that abot a month ago being in Newgate for Debt he there heard
ffrances Ball of Ashbourn aforesaid complain of the Warden of the Mint for
his severity agt Coyners and say Damne my blood I had been out before now
but for him, and Whitfield who was also then in prison made answer that the
Warden of the Mint was a Rogue and if ever King James came againe he
would shoot him and then Ball made answer Goddam my blood so will I
and tho I dont know him yet Ile find him out and the said Whitfield said
further that the Warden had troubled his wife for a little bitt of clippings
found upon her coat and spend 5 hundred Gineas to get her off—And that
abot 3 or 4 days after this the sd Ball and Whitfield having procured an habeas
Corpus in order to be bailed before my Lord Chiefe Justice the Author of
this deposition heard the said Ball say that his father was to be one of their
bayle and went by wrong name and that their bayle was sham bayle. And that
said Ball and Whitfield in talking to one another sayd that the guilding of
pistoles cost them both one G. a piece and that [it] was not the business of
the Warden of the Mint but of the Spanish Embassad. to prosecute men for
counterfeiting them. Jurat . . . coram Is Newton.[13]

At one point in 1696 Newton appeared to weary of the whole
system of prosecuting "coyners" by offering rewards to informers and

defraying costs through forfeitures of the effects of those convicted. "And the new reward of forty pounds per head has now made Courts of Justice & Juries so averse from beleiving witnesses & Sheriffs so inclinable to impannel bad Juries that my Agents & Witnesses," he complained to the Treasury, "are discouraged & tired out by the want of success & by the reproach of prosecuting & swearing for money. And this vilifying of my Agents & Witnesses is a reflexion upon me which has gravelled me & must in time impair & perhaps wear out & ruin my credit. Besides that I am exposed to the calumnies of as many Coyners & Newgate Sollicitors as I examin or admit to talk with me if they can but find friends to beleive & encourage them in their false reports & oaths & combinations against me." But though he formally asked to be relieved of an "undertaking so vexatious & dangerous as this must be whenever managed wth diligence & sincerity,"[14] he really was making a bid for more assistance and an extension of his bureaucratic empire. His protestations of repugnance are of the same order as his avowals of distaste for scientific quarrels and disputations just before he plunges head over heels into a fresh controversy. Newton's efforts were successful, and in about a month he was allowed to appoint an extra clerk in consideration of his duties in prosecuting coinage offenders.[15]

One side of Newton relished these interrogations in the Tower, as he ferreted out criminal evil with perseverance and without pity. The plots against him only whetted his appetite for more quarry. He would prosecute or relent, allow bail or get a man put in chains, threaten recalcitrants with reprisals or dangle the promise of a pardon in exchange for solid information about other rascals. He was like the God of Deuteronomy whom he knew so well: "I kill and I make alive. I wound and I heal." He could rage at prisoners and their wives and mistresses with impunity—all in a holy cause. In the Mint Newton was gratified with the exercise of naked power over fellow creatures. The inquisitor may or may not be relieved of his own guilt by discovering it and punishing it in his victims. There are those who hold that the revelations of the criminal evoke dangerous hidden parallels in the inquisitor and that the expression of righteous indignation is anything but therapeutic for the prosecutor. Newton was not wholly delivered from the bondage of his anger by ranting at prisoners, for there was an inexhaustible font of rage in the man, but he appears to have found some release from its burden in these tirades in the Tower. With such avenues available to him, he never again suffered a psychic breakdown like the one of 1693. He no longer needed to beat his head against the bars of his inner consciousness. There were other human beings upon whom he could vent his wrath.

In modern state bureaucracies a man with the need to act out his aggressiveness is provided with two kinds of objects. There are those hapless outsiders upon whom officialdom operates, the violators of its laws, the miscreants. Then there are the insiders, either rival bureaucrats ready to encroach upon the prerogatives of an office to increase their own power or subordinates seeking a measure of independence from authority. In the exercise of his successive offices of Warden and Master, Newton ferociously fought all enemies both within and without, and came forth gloriously triumphant. He had a "nice" sense of the territorial limits of his jurisdiction and like an animal in the open field he fought tooth and nail against intruders, even surviving a Tory ministry and its circuitous attempts to oust him. After Queen Anne's death he was entrenched for the rest of his life when the war contractors, moneylenders, stockjobbers, and filchers around the Whig ministers who were his friends returned in force.

Potential invaders of Newton's rightful domain as Warden of the Mint were the Comptroller and the Master, the moneyers who had set themselves up as a corporation, and, most dangerous of all, Lord Lucas, the principal governor of the Tower where the Mint was housed. Lines of administrative authority were not always clearly drawn, and during the pre-Newtonian period when the wardenship was a mere sinecure many traditional attributes of the office had been eroded. Newton could be counted upon to seek a restoration of every last one of the former privileges of the post. In his report to the Treasury on "The State of the Mint" in 1696, he was quick to signal invasions of his rights.

[T]he Master & Worker . . . has rejected the Wardens judicial power by endeavouring to have differences referred to the Warden & himself. The Moneyers have also shook off the Wardens authority over them by feigning themselves a Corporation, & the Controller . . . by getting the Office of Master & Worker into his hands . . . hath equalled himself with the Master & Warden. . . . And thus the Wardens Authority which was designed to keep the three sorts of Ministers in their Duty to the King & his people, being baffled & rejected & thereby the Government of the Mint being in a manner dissolved those Ministers act as they please for turning the Mint to their several advantages. Nor do I see any remedy more proper & more easy then by restoring the ancient constitution.[16]

After Newton became Master and Worker at the Mint, it was the smith who worried him, and on August 7, 1711, he appealed to the Lord Treasurer asking that the smith's salary be allocated directly to the Master so that, as he put it, "I may have power over the smith as my servant for carrying on the coynage & dismiss him if he be not of good a bearing."[17] The aging man had a compulsive need for the exercise of direct and absolute authority, and the slightest thwarting of his will was severely punished among his workers and scientific colleagues alike.

But these were minor officials, and Newton in his search for enemies always aimed his sights on lofty targets. Since the Mint and the workers' dwellings were located within the perimeter of the Tower of London, friction was inevitable between the Lord Lieutenant of the garrison and his soldiers on one side and the Warden of the Mint and his civilian workers on the other. They were poised opposite each other like hostile forces. Newton identified himself passionately with the Mint and by extension with its workers, just as he identified himself with the coinage and stood guard against its debasers. If any bureaucratic principle or customary arrangement was violated, the infraction was conceived as an attack directed against his person in an almost literal sense, and he was on the alert to fend off all comers. In July 1697, having been in office for a year, he was already so deeply involved in an altercation with Lord Lucas of the Tower that he appealed for help to the Treasury, where his friend Charles Montague was First Lord. The Mint was not subject to any military power, he proclaimed with assurance. The safety of the coinage depended upon keeping it out of the hands of the garrison. Precedents were being established by this "invasion" of the Mint that he could not abide. Despite royal charters incorporating the workers of the Mint into a body under a warden independent of the government of the Tower, "his" workers were being arrested, their houses searched. If military assaults continued, he could not be responsible for the tools or bullion which lay "scattered about in all the rooms apperteining to the coynage, nor will Merchants & other Importers think their estates secure in the Mint. We were placed in a Garrison that the Exchange & Treasury of the Nation might not be invaded by our Guards but guarded in our custody from all manner of invasion."

"And we further represent that the Centinals begin to be rather a grievance then security to us," Newton complained. When a drunken officer of the guard broke into one of the houses and attacked a servant, the sentinel would not come to the aid of the victim. Lord Lucas had ordered the sentinels "to fire at us"—Newton and the workers united. In the face of Lord Lucas' usurpation of the Warden's prerogatives, puritanical Newton verges on condoning the habitual drunkenness of the workers. He speaks with the voice of gentle reason against severity, a rare posture for him. "For why should we lose a good Artificer upon pretence of his being drunk, when the best are most addicted to that crime & it was never yet made death? Or why should every Centinal be impowered under any feigned pretence to shoot his enemy or any other man that complains, if such bloody discipline may safely be avoyded? Or why should the people who live in the Mint be so terrified as to leave their habitations in it to the neglect of the Kings service & insecurity of the treasure."[18]

Newton worsted his inside bureaucratic competitors in every battle. But before he surrendered the wardenship to become Master of the Mint, he found among the small fry of clippers and coiners an antagonist worthy of him in the person of William Chaloner, notorious and colorful enough to become the subject of a popular biography, *Guzman Redivivus,* published shortly after his hanging in Tyburn on March 22, 1699. "He scorn'd the petty Rogueries of Tricking *single Men,* but boldly aim'd at imposing upon a *whole* Kingdom."[19]

Among the papers at the Royal Mint there is a careful summation of Chaloner's many crimes and felonies, detailed item by item, in the hand of Isaac Newton himself, the draft of a report related to the final trial.[20] The source of each bit of evidence is carefully recorded. In appearance the document resembles a section from *The Original Of Monarchies,* a treatise which Newton had composed about seven years before; only the names of informers now replace biblical and classical citations as marginalia. From this report, the biography, and supplementary evidence in the Depositions Book of the Mint, it is possible to reconstruct the career of William Chaloner the arch-criminal and his ultimate undoing by Isaac Newton. This was Newton's great adventure at the Mint and is a counterpart in miniature of his later pursuit of Leibniz.

About seven years before, Newton relates, Chaloner had been a poor man, a japanner, who wore ragged clothes daubed with colors. Having acquired stamps from one Taylor, he left off his trade, turned coiner, and in a short time was able to put on the habit of a gentleman, take a great house at Knightsbridge, and buy some plate. Originally he had been taught to coin by one Coffee, but the fine points of his art were acquired from Gravener. His first great achievement was a stock of French pistoles, part of which were conveyed into France by a gentleman, the rest being bought up by a variety of fellows, many of whom, under the dire threats of the Warden, ultimately turned against Chaloner. He had, according to his former accomplices, coined some seventeen thousand pistoles and many hundreds of guineas. Thomas Holloway had heard Chaloner boast of his workmanship and had seen the dies in his hands.

When another confederate, Blackford, was caught for passing Chaloner's guineas, he informed and won a brief reprieve. During the interval before Blackford was himself executed Chaloner disappeared from circulation in the London area, though he kept operat-

9. View of the Tower of London, 1707

10. Isaac Newton, 1702

ing secretly with Holloway and Carter at various out-of-the-way places. Once Blackford was dead, Chaloner conceived of an ingenious plan for wiping out any stigma on his person and ingratiating himself with the authorities of the new elective monarchy. He persuaded two printers, "at the expence of several treats and money," to put out forty copies of King James's "Declarations," not for distribution, for that would be treason, but to be sent to some gentleman in the country. As soon as he had the documents, he squealed on the printers to the government and received a reward—he later bragged that he had "fun'd" (cheated, in popular usage) the King out of a thousand pounds.

"A little before May was two years," Newton continues in his memorandum,

he [Chaloner] and some others clipt & filed old hammered money at Mr. Sampsons in a little Alley in Drury Lane leading into Wild Street. And about the same time Gravener & his wife & Carter by the consent of Chaloner coyned at Gravener's house about 60 pounds in half crowns with a pair of stamps made by Chaloner, & Chaloner sent Th. Holloway thither to see them work & learn the art & take away the stamps. . . .

About May was two years Chaloner was accused face to face by Coppinger before the then Lord Mayor Sr. Tho. Stamp and sent to Newgate but saved himself by getting Coppinger hangd out of the way.

Soon after to regain the favour of the Governmt he discovered the plot of cheating the Bank by Orphans Bills cut out of the check book of titles in the Chamber of London & recd of the Bank 200 lb. for a reward.

Chaloner was flying high. Not content with his modest successes, he concocted a grand design to infiltrate the Mint itself with his accomplices at the same time that he publicly attacked its lax administration. But the victim of overweening pride had chosen a formidable opponent, as his anonymous biographer records. "He accus'd that Worthy Gentleman Isaac Newton Esqu; Warden of his Majesties Mint, with several other of the officers thereof, as Connivers (at least) at many Abuses and Cheats there committed."[21]

Newton's report blandly remarks upon Chaloner's brazen intervention into the affairs of the Mint. "And the summer following, that he might have a spy upon the Warden of the Mint for his own safety, recommended to him his intimate friend & fellow coyner T.H. [Thomas Holloway] as a person that could do the Governmt the greatest service by taking up clippers and coyners." Unsuccessful in hoodwinking that "worthy gentleman" in charge of the Mint, Chaloner had recourse to the Parliamentary Committee on the Miscarriages of the Mint, before whom in the early months of 1697 he accused the Mint of coining false money, performed experiments to prove that under the present system it was easy to diminish and counterfeit the coinage, and submitted inventions designed to prevent those abuses. To Newton's chagrin and in despite of his opposition, the committee gave its cachet of approval to Chaloner's inventions, and further resolved to introduce into the House legislation against inefficiencies at the Mint.[22] This was not the first time that Chaloner had tried to win prestige as a cover for his crimes. Pamphlets addressed to Parliament on the reform of the Mint had once flowed freely from his pen. His *Defects in the Present Constitution of the Mint* and *Proposals humbly offered, for passing an Act to prevent clipping and counterfeiting of mony* were works in which a rare technical knowledge of the art of coining was enlivened with historical examples from Roman antiquity.[23] To his cronies Chaloner talked of "funning the Parliament," and he promised Holloway that once he was made supervisor of the Mint "he would then supply him with coyning tools out oth' Tower and teach him how to coyne with blanks. . . . which being soft would easily rise."[24]

Alas for Chaloner, Newton, pursuing him with shrewdness and tenacity, had prevailed upon Thomas Holloway to turn informer, and the machinations of the bold counterfeiter were an open book to the Warden. On suspicion that Chaloner planned further skulduggery, Newton had him committed to Newgate in September, 1697, but Chaloner secured an acquittal by suborning the prosecution's witnesses. Upon his release he forthwith addressed Parliament with a letter seeking redress for his "great sufferings & ruined condition" and charging "some of the Mint" with threatening his life because of his disclosures.[25] Though nothing came of Chaloner's accusations, Newton was affronted and humiliated, obliged to make answer, and vengeance was his. In a memorandum of reply, he refuted Chaloner point by point and testily concluded: "And if he would but let the money & Government alone & return to his trade of Japanning, he is not so far ruined but that he may still live as well as he did seven years ago when he left of that trade & raised himself by coyning."[26]

Throughout his final report Newton, boundlessly curious about all arts and sciences, showed a professional interest in the artifices of Chaloner, who made false gold coins and presumed to succeed where the great scientist in quest of the golden fleece had failed. To Newton the scientist, Chaloner was not only a criminal but a rival, as well as an enemy who had challenged his competence in the administration of the Mint. His doom was sealed. Newton spells out Chaloner's multiple crimes revealed to him by Thomas Holloway in minute detail, recording Chaloner's techniques as well as building up a case against him. As the chase gets hot Newton abandons the formal appellation Warden of the Mint in his memoranda and lapses into the personal pronoun.

Chaloner ordered him [Thomas Holloway] to get two brasses cast by a wooden pattern which he received of Chaloner and shewed me and he did get two brasses cast accordingly and gave them to Chaloner and Chaloner to Hicks to get Peers to file them and Gravener seeing them in the hands of Hicks said I know what those are for those are for casting blanks. . . . The way of using these brasses was also described to me by Tho. Holloway so far as he had learned it of Chaloner. And when Hanwell was newly taken up (viz. Sept 26) he described it to me exactly and said that Chaloner taught it him the winter before with intention that he should work at Holloways house and Chaloner find money and spake of this way as the most profitable.

Once members of Chaloner's gang were caught, the confessions and depositions of informers came thick and fast. Newton operated behind the scenes through a network of agents, as he would later in the Flamsteed and Leibniz quarrels. He was a grand manipulator and kept a tight rein on those who served him. Of course, his creatures worked for different rewards in the various contests in which

he was engaged: the prisoners offered information in exchange for
their lives, to feed their starving children, they said; the young scientists ran interference for Newton out of pride and identification
with his genius or in hope of preferment. Newton's personality is
only vaguely reflected in the reports of his stool pigeons at the Mint,
but he was always at the center of the web and none escaped him.

In November 1698 Chaloner had been arrested on suspicion of
forging malt tickets, and once again imprisoned in Newgate. Pro-
testing in letters addressed directly to Newton that he had not the
talent required for such practices, he rubbed salt into Newton's
wound by observing that the Warden was doubtless "greatly displeased with me abo[u]t the late business in Parliamt. . . ."[27]
Though the ticket forgery charges were dropped, proceedings were
instituted against Chaloner for the far graver offense of counterfeiting coin of the realm.

On January 25, 1699, John Whitfield, a prisoner who had once
cursed him, wrote to Newton at his house near the Tubb Tavern in
German Street offering to inform on Chaloner: "May I humbly begg
the favour of that you will be pleased to remember your promise
which was to my wife. Every day I have thought it a month hoping to
have the honour to have seen you either in passing or in repassing to
the Tower. It lys in your power to admitt me to bayle So good Sr be
pleased to let me know whether I shall send to you or you will be
pleased to call here. . . ."[28] Six days later Thomas Carter gave Newton a circumstantial account of Chaloner's counterfeiting methods.
When confronted with this incriminating testimony, Chaloner
played innocent and tried to turn the tables on Carter by implicating
him in a counterfeiting scheme. Newton had had a clandestine meeting with Whitfield at the Dogg.[29] Chaloner, who was informed by
his agents, too, now became suspicious of Whitfield's fidelity to him
—so Newton was told by Carter.[30]

During the final round of the duel the scales were heavily
weighted in favor of Newton and the Crown. John Ignatius Lawson
came forward to testify that when Chaloner had been his jailmate
that winter he "owned to him that he had coyned 30,000 Gineas or

above." Lawson made regular reports to Newton on the comings and goings in the prison of other confederates of Chaloner's and of their involvement with bailiffs, solicitors, molls, and a parade of shady characters who tried to reassure the great hero caught in Newton's toils. "Hickes's Guang one or other of them come every day to see him. This morning Pearce the Bayliff at the Castle in the New Buildings this evening Scott, Hickes mistriss and Joanna and another woman with Hunt the Solicitor who is with him every day. . . . Gillingham's crew prop him up every day bidding him fear nothing for no one can hurt a hair of his head." Mrs. Coffee had sent Chaloner a secret message about the severity of the Warden's interrogation; wittingly or unwittingly she had betrayed him when she had been brought into Newton's presence. One inevitably thinks of Jenny Diver and Macheath. Newton had pressed her "to discover something of him" but she held out; she later insisted "how she had said nothing but how Mr. Cha: and her husband made ffrench pistoles but nothing of the Gineas and says the Warden was very angery that she would confess no more of him." Chaloner's reaction, reported by Lawson, was unambiguous. "Mr. Ch. says she is a Bitch for he sent to her when he came first into Newgate and that she sent him word she wisht she might be damned if ever she mentioned him."

During the last stages Chaloner played insane; and then, in a final burst of overconfidence, he began to believe that he would again escape the gallows. "Chaloner hath feigned himself mad pulling his shirt to pieces and running stark naked at midnight abot the Ward for ½ an hour togeather afterwards the men bound him hand and foot in his bed but now he seems more rationall and says that he hears very good news that they cannot bring any indictment agt him and he questions not but slip out this sessions as he hath done 5 times before."[31]

On the eve of the execution Chaloner broke, and addressed the Warden with a frantic plea for mercy which went unheeded, like all similar entreaties from his prisoners unless accompanied by a supply of new evidence that would help ensnare other malefactors. Chaloner was abject; too late did he realize that the Warden sitting in justice would exact full retribution for the aspersions Chaloner had once cast upon him. He was caught by surprise when his luck failed him, and he died playacting to the very end. Or was he blubbering with terror? "I am going to be murtherd allthough perhaps you may think not but tis true I shall be murderd the worst of all murders that is in the face of Justice unless I am rescued by your mercifull hands." He had the perfect alibi—he was "out of Towne" at the time. Mrs. Carter had acted out of malice because he had gotten her husband convicted of forgery.

Mrs. Holloway swore false agt me or I desire never to see the Great God and I desire the same if Abbot did not swear false agt me so that I am murderd O God Allmighty knows I am murderd Therefore I humbly begg your Wor[shi]p will considr these Reasons and that I am convicted without Precedents and be pleased to speak to Mr Chancellr to save me from being murthered O Dear Sr do this mercifull deed O my offending you has brought this upon me O for Gods sake if not mine Keep me from being murderd O dear Sr no body can save me but you O God my God I shall be murderd unless you save me O I hope God will move your heart with mercy and pitty to do this thing for me I am

Your near murderd humble Servant

W. CHALONER.[32]

Chaloner, who had been "saucy" in court, had been found guilty of high treason. All his offers to betray confederates were rejected. His anonymous biographer concludes on a note of righteousness that doubtless echoed the sentiments of the Warden: "Justice which often had attempted, and as oft been baffl'd by him, was now ready with her Iron hands to break him to pieces."[33]

Though the Chaloner case was the high point of his career as a prosecutor, up to the very last years of his life, even after John Conduitt had assumed most of the chores of his office, Newton was still consulted about the treatment of criminal counterfeiters. He never flagged in his fierce battle against the falsifiers. For more than three decades the colossal wrath of Isaac Newton found victims in the Tower. At the Mint he could hurt and kill without doing violence to his scrupulous puritan conscience. The blood of the coiners and clippers nourished him.

Chapter **12**

HALIFAX AND LA BARTICA

At Barton's feet the God of Love
This Arrow & his Quiver lays
Forgets he has a Throne above
And with this lovely Creature stays
Not Venus' Beauties are more bright
But each appear so like the other
That Cupid has mistook the right
And takes the Nymph to be his Mother.
—Dryden, *Miscellanies*

THE political, social, and religious worlds through which Newton moved over the years were subject to mercurial change and no shift in his mature life was more abrupt than the passage from Cambridge to London, the largest city in Europe, a metropolis of more than half a million inhabitants. A fixated man and puritanical in spirit, during the early Restoration he immured himself in a monastic university cell. When he emerged to become a protagonist in the war against papism and the Stuarts, he was from the outset an ardent supporter of the House of Orange and he remained consistently Whig until his death, even when others oscillated in their political allegiances. But the Whiggery of the turn of the century and the reign of Queen Anne, though it might raise popular tumults and burn in effigy pope, cardinals, and Dr. Sacheverell,[1] was hardly consonant with a mid-seventeenth-century puritanical morality, not with Somers and Halifax at the helm.

The looseness of society in the reign of Queen Anne and the first George perceptibly modified the outward conduct of Isaac Newton,

245

if not the demands of his austere censor. He was seen more often in coffeehouses after meetings of the Royal Society, he appeared at Court, he even attended an opera—though he left before the end of the performance, saying it was too much of a good thing. His diet was usually Spartan, but on occasion he graced a great dinner with his presence—witness a menu in his hand on one of the stray papers at the Mint for a party at which a galaxy of aristocrats were guests. (A French visitor complained, however, that he served bad wine, mostly palma and madeira he had received as presents.) Until he became ill he lived in the heart of London where the wealthiest and most substantial classes resided. Carried about the city in a sedan chair, he grew quite corpulent. As a public figure he met regularly for business with the corrupt and uninhibited Whig politicians and received foreign noblemen, virtually all of whom were accursed Papists.

At the height of his prestige Newton sat for his portrait to a succession of artists—to Kneller again (1702 and 1720), to Charles Jervas (1703?), to William Gandy (1706?), to Thornhill (circa 1710), and to Thomas Murray (1718). The Jervas, a flat official painting of an "Augustan mask" smothered by a wig, was presented to the Royal Society in 1717 by Newton himself; this was the way he wished to appear in the public eye. He sits stiffly in a high-backed armchair, his left hand on one arm of the chair, his right pointing with a forefinger to a partly hidden book that rests on a table. His eyes look out at the beholder. The white surplice, elegant jacket, loose robe, and satin knee breeches seem more important than the face. The 1720 Kneller, a gift to the Abbé Bignon, is known through a replica in Petworth House; in this representation Newton has moved so far away from his calling that a sword hangs by his side, symbol of his knighthood. The Kneller of 1702 now in the National Portrait Gallery and the two versions of the Thornhill are the paintings most appreciated by present-day art historians. Despite the fact that the Kneller is in external respects conventional, it has been called "as rare an interpretation as any genius can hope for." Newton wears a long curled wig that falls over his bosom, a white pleated shirt unbuttoned at the neck, and a loose, covering robe. His brow is furrowed, his eyes even more protuberant than in the Kneller of 1689. There are lines at the side of the nose and corners of the mouth. The face has become rather square and a second chin is prominent. The Thornhill in Trinity College is described as "that noble Roman presentment of the white-haired seer" and its *contrapposto* is much admired.[2] Though Newton left a meager wardrobe at his death, in these grand portraits he is impressively clad in rich brocades, silks, and velvets.

Newton did not participate in Halifax's orgies nor was he invited to membership in the Kit-Kat Club. He was more likely to be drawn to the millenarian Prophets of London who swallowed up his young friend Fatio than to the witty literary society of Pope, Swift, and Gay. Yet he was no longer ignorant of the ways of the world. In the privacy of his chamber he remained a devout believer, a man of learning, concentrating more and more on history sacred and profane as the final revelation of the divine intent. His absolute, though secret, unitarianism was known only to a few intimates—to William Whiston, to Hopton Haynes, an assistant at the Mint who later published anti-Trinitarian tracts, to John Locke, perhaps to Fatio—not to the bishops and archbishops of the realm who sought out his company and left testimonials to his piety. But his outward style had changed. The break between the public and the private man is now sharp; more than ever he leads a double life. The degree to which in his London period he was prepared to defend some gratification of the senses in an effort to play the man of the world is puzzling unless new colors are introduced into the portrait. In one of his defenses of the reasonable use of paper money, for which there are drafts in the Royal Mint Library dated 1701, Newton countered the argument that this practice would lead to luxurious indulgence with analogies and similes that seem totally alien to his character and would hardly be recognized if not for the handwriting. "But if this be a good objection we must reject wine because it occasions drunkenness & all the best things because by corruption they become the worst. Rather let us suppress drunkenness & keep our wine. But tho Paper credit be a sort of riches we must not use it immoderately. Like vertue it has its extremes. Too much may hurt us as well as too little."[3] Beyond question something happened to the puritanical prig after he left Cambridge. Perhaps this overt transformation helps clarify his relationship to Catherine Barton and Charles Montague, later Lord Halifax, and to their connection with each other, one of the most baffling episodes in his history.

Catherine Barton was born in 1679, the daughter of a country parson, Robert Barton of Brigstock, and Hannah Smith Barton, who was Newton's half sister.[4] A grandfather and an uncle also had been clergymen. Catherine's father died around the time of Newton's crisis in 1693, and when Newton came up to London he took her under his wing and educated her.[5] Our appreciation of Mistress Catherine Barton derives from many contemporary portrayals of her beguiling person. There is a long imaginary conversation with Halifax about Catherine in Mrs. Mary de la Rivière Manley's roman à clef, many references in Swift's *Journal to Stella,* a note about her in a brief official biography of Halifax, heavy compliments in letters of Rémond de Montmort, a member of the French Regency Council,[6] and of Abate Antonio Conti, a Venetian aristocrat, and vignettes in the correspondence of Alexander Pope and histories of London club life.[7] The documents do not, however, resolve the central perplexing problem of the nature of her friendship with Charles Montague. This was no inconsequential private matter to Newton's Victorian biographers, for she lived in his London houses for twenty years, and the sincerity of his puritanical morals was at stake. Hypocrisy cannot be contained as in a cyst. If the shameful allegations that were bruited about were well founded with respect to his private life, the suspicion would always linger that there was a measure of tartuffery in his scientific dealings. The Newtonian world order not only had to be true, it had to be virtuous.

The one remaining letter from Newton to Catherine was written on August 5, 1700, when she was about twenty and had gone into the country to recover from the pox; it has an intimate tone of easy familiarity, is solicitous, discusses homey things, and is signed "your very loving Unkle."

I had your two letters & am glad the air agrees wth you & th[ough the] fever is loath to leave you yet I hope it abates, & that the [re]mains of the small pox are dropping off apace. Sr Joseph [Tily] is leaving Mr Tolls house & its probable I may succeed him[. I]intend to send you some wine by the next Carrier wch [I] beg the favour of Mr Gyre & his Lady to accept of. My Lady Norris thinks you forget your promis of writing to her, & wants [a] letter from you. Pray let me know by your next how your f[ace is] and if your fevour be going. Perhaps warm milk from the Cow may [help] to abate it.[8]

Catherine's description of Newton in the Conduitt papers falls into the common stereotype of the distracted, withdrawn scholar and does not add much to our understanding of him. But she was the only woman who was at all close to him after the death of his mother. The twenty-year-old granddaughter of Hannah, born the year she died, became for him a simulacre incarnate of the lost beloved.[9]

The most extravagant presentation of the relationship between Catherine and Halifax appeared in Mary de la Rivière Manley's *Memoirs of Europe, Towards the Close of the Eighth Century. Written by Eginardus, Secretary and Favourite to Charlemagne; and done into English by the Translator of the New Atalantis* (1710), a book of gossipy and loosely interwoven imaginary tales, the identity of whose chief personages is apparent. This was a sequel to one of the popular novels of the age, *Secret Memoirs and Manners of Several Persons of Quality, of Both Sexes. From the New Atalantis* (1709), which saw seven editions by 1736.[10] To dispel any doubt about the real names of the protagonists, later editions of the *Memoirs of Europe* included a printed key in which "Bartica" was listed as Isaac Newton's niece and "Julius Sergius" as Lord H*f-x. Mrs. Manley was a Tory, a Cavalier's daughter committed to the cause, for whom nothing was too scurrilous to be used against the Whig leaders.[11] The license of her attacks in the original *Secret Memoirs* had been so flagrant that she was arrested and held without bail for about a week.[12] Her apology in court, a playful parade of injured innocence which brought an acquittal, is preserved in the autobiographical *Adventures of Rivella; or, The History of the Author of Atalantis, with Secret Memoirs and Characters of several considerable Persons, her Contemporaries* (1714):

Her defense was with much Humility and Sorrow, for having offended, at the same Time denying that any Persons were concern'd with her, or that she had a farther design than writing for her own Amusement and Diversion in the Country, without intending particular Reflections or Characters: When this was not believ'd, and the contrary urg'd very home to her by several Circumstances and Likenesses; she said then it must be by Inspiration, because knowing her own Innocence she could account for it no other way: The Secretary reply'd upon her, that *Inspiration* us'd to be upon a good Account, and her Writings were stark nought; she told him, with an Air-full of Penitence, that might be true, but it was as true, that there were evil Angels as well as good; so that nevertheless what she had wrote might still be by Inspiration.[13]

While the grand debauches of Lord Halifax did not require Mrs. Manley's novelistic embroidery, the specific accusations leveled at Catherine Barton remain moot. At one point in the *Memoirs of Europe* the flamboyant memorialist introduces a Lucullan feast and wild carousal in the palace of Julius Sergius, in the course of which the drunken host is cannily drawn out about his amours by a foreign count.

I think, my Lord Julius Sergius, continu'd I, addresseing more closely to his Lordship, 'tis hard that of all this heavenly Prospect of Happiness, your Lordship is the only solitary Lover: what is become of the charming *Bartica*? Can she live a Day, an Hour, without you? Sure she's indispos'd, dying, or dead. You call Tears into my Eyes, dear Count, answer'd the Hero sobbing, she's a Traitress, an inconsistent proud Baggage, yet I love her dearly, and have lavish'd Myriads upon her, besides getting her worthy ancient Parent a good Post for Connivance.

The imputation that Newton sold his niece for an office is patently false, though he may still have "connived" at the relationship for other, more subtle reasons. But once Voltaire had put his indelible stamp upon the tale it was impossible to expunge it from "secret histories" for more than a century.

"But, wou'd you think it?" Julius Sergius proceeds,

She has other Things in her Head, and is grown so fantastick and high, she wants me to marry her, or else I shall have no more of her, truly: 'Twas ever a proud Slut; when she pretended most kindness, when she was all over Coquet, and coveted to engage me more and more; when our Intimacy was at the height, she us'd to make my Servants wait three Hours for an Answer to a How-do-ye, or a Letter, which I sent every successive Morn. As to the Letter, interrupted I, there may be some Excuse for that, my Lord: For what Woman, or indeed Man, can dare to write to a Person of your Lordship's Character, the Quintessence of Wit and Politeness, without copy and recopying again? That's true, dear St. Girrone, answer'd his propitious Lordship, then kissing me close, and doing me the Favour of the Glass, to let me know he expected I shou'd follow his Example, he drank deeply, and after cry'd out in an Extasie

And Wit for ever Scarlet
from this Vein shall flow!

Then asking my Excuse, 'twas a Flight of his own Poetry, he presented me the Wine, and continu'd his Indignation against Bartica. He told me, if he pin'd himself to Death, he was resolv'd not to marry her whilst she was so saucy. I don't brag, my dear Count, but methinks I have some Qualifications, besides my Wealth, and being of Consular Dignity, that deserves as good a Wife; my Person is not contemptible, and as to my Wit and Sense, look into the Writing of all those Moderns who durst deliver their Opinions, who durst presume to dedicate to me; see There, what future Ages will think of me.[14]

Grotesque as the caricature may be, it has a measure of verisimilitude. There is other evidence that Montague wore his heart on his sleeve—he surely made no attempt to conceal the friendship. As a member of the Kit-Kat, a Whig club that met in the house of Christopher Cate near Temple Bar and was noted for wit and drinking, Halifax was called upon to toast a favorite. The following verses, incised with a diamond on a wine glass, are attributed to him:

Beauty and wit strove each in vain
To vanquish Bacchus and his train:
But Barton, with successful charms
From both their quivers drew her arms
The roving god his sway resigns
And cheerfully submits his vines.[15]

Brewster, who once had in his possession a photograph of Catherine Barton's miniature, was moved by her beauty,[16] as Rémond de
Montmort had been on the strength of a brief acquaintance during
his visit to London. In a letter to Brook Taylor of the Royal Society,
he left a wildly amatory description.

I am deeply stirred by the honor she does me in remembering me. I have preserved the most magnificent memory of her wit and of her beauty. I loved her
even before I had the honor of seeing her as the niece of Mr. Newton, pre-
disposed by what I had heard of her charms while I was still in France. Ever
since I beheld her, I have adored her not only for her great beauty but for
her lively and refined wit. I believe there is no danger in your betraying me
to her. If I had the good fortune to be near her, I would forthwith become as
awkward as I was the first time we met. My awe and anxiety lest I displease
her would reduce me to silence and I would conceal my feelings. But a
hundred leagues away and separated by the sea, I think a lover can speak
without being judged too bold, and a cultivated woman can tolerate declarations without reproaching herself for being too indulgent.[17]

Halifax was painted a number of times, the most famous portrait
being Kneller's in the celebrated collection of Kit-Kat Club members that had been especially commissioned and is now in the
National Portrait Gallery. Halifax, in full regalia, has a plump,
self-indulgent face, intelligent eyes. Jonathan Swift knew him and
Mistress Barton as well, and they appear rather frequently in his
Journal to Stella, sometimes on successive pages though never in conjunction with each other. One day Swift dines with Lord Halifax at
Hampton Court in the grand manner and the next in pleasant intimacy with Mrs. Barton, but no relationship is suggested. After
Swift had completely broken with the Whigs, he wrote disparag-
ingly of Halifax:

> While Montague, who claim'd the Station
> To be Maecenas of the Nation,
> For Poets open Table kept,
> But ne'er consider'd where they Slept.
> Himself, as rich as fifty Jews,
> Was easy, though they wanted shoes.[18]

He burned all of Halifax's letters but one, which he kept as an admirable example of unfulfilled court promises and professions.[19] Pope was more grateful for Lord Halifax's patronage of his *Homer,* though only to his face: "It is indeed a high Strain of Generosity in you, to think of making me easie all my Life, only because I have been so happy as to divert you an hour or two...."[20] Montague's own poetry, which consists primarily of a circumstantial parody of Dryden written in collaboration with Matthew Prior and entitled "The Hind and the Panther transvers'd to the story of the Country-Mouse and the City-Mouse," won him William III's favor and is memorable only for its inclusion in anthologies. Samuel Johnson in the *Lives of the Most Eminent English Poets* delivered the definitive judgment: "It would now be esteemed no honour, by a contributor to the monthly bundle of verses, to be told, that, in strains either familiar or solemn, he sings like Montague."[21] But Montague was clearly a man of parts as an administrator, and when he visited the Hanoverian court, he impressed even Leibniz with his person and his talents.[22]

Charles Montague was born in 1661, the fourth son of nine children, at Horton in Northamptonshire—virtually condemned to the law or a clerical estate. He married the Countess Dowager of Manchester, many years his senior, and was often ridiculed for making his political career under the tutelage of a venerable matron. In the Treasury his reputation rests on solid accomplishments: he helped establish the Bank of England, saved the currency, invented and circulated Exchequer bills. Under his aegis the recoinage of the debased, clipped English currency was put through, and it was his decision that those who deposited their worn money in the Mint would receive full weight in exchange. Montague displayed a genius for political economy and became the key financial executive of the Whig ministries, the holder of grand offices and the recipient of magnificent titles: Chancellor of the Exchequer in 1694, First Lord of the Treasury in 1697, Baron Halifax of Halifax in 1700 (despite impeachment attacks in the House of Commons), and, in October

1714, First Lord of the Treasury again and Viscount Sunbury and Earl of Halifax. As a great financial and political operator, he was powerful enough to snub even Marlborough, who once complained bitterly that he had been treated like a servant.[23] Though he pops in and out of contemporary memoirs and private correspondence of the great politicians, poets, and writers—he is involved in everything that is going on in the realm, spans two cultures, the scientific and the poetic, is always head over heels in political intrigues, is an orator, guarantor of the established church, rationalist anti-Papist instrumental in assuring the Protestant succession—no full-scale portrait emerges. The Duchess of Marlborough mocked his person. She thought he was a frightful figure yet pretended to be a lover and pursued several beauties, who merely laughed at him. There was nonetheless a rumor that his political difficulties with Queen Anne stemmed from his failure to respond to an amorous signal.

Swift knew Mrs. Manley's "secret memoirs" well (he refers to them in a letter to Addison on August 22, 1710)[24] and in his own peculiar way he was a friend to the Tory lady martyr—he thought she had "very generous principles for one of her sort"[25]—but he never utters a direct word about any liaison between the Chancellor of the Exchequer and La Bartica, a strange reticence, nor does he allude to Newton in connection with them.[26]

From the pages of the *Journal to Stella* there rises a most engaging portrait of Catherine Barton, glimpses of her in the company of Lady Worsley, the great beauty Anne Long, and Lady Betty Germain, daughter of the second Earl of Berkeley, who received such celebrities as Prince Eugene at her assemblies.[27] On September 28, 1710, when Swift dined with Mrs. Barton in her lodgings, she entertained him with slightly prurient stories: from her he heard about a Lady S. who when last in England pretended a tympany, then after vanishing for three weeks returned with tympany gone.[28] Doubtless scandalous rumors about Mrs. Barton had crossed the Irish Sea, for in a November letter Swift playfully upbraided Stella for twitting him about his friend. "I'll break your head in good earnest, young woman, for your nasty jest about Mrs. Barton. Unlucky sluttikin, what a word is there?" And then he became cryptically personal in his usual way: "Faith, I was thinking yesterday, when I was with her, whether she could break them or no, and it quite spoiled my imagination."[29] In December and January he saw her again; and in March 1711 he dined with her "in that genteel manner that MD used when they would treat some better sort of body than usual."[30] On April 3, 1711, he is genuinely effusive about Mrs. Barton. "I love her better than anybody here, and see her seldomer. Why really now, so it often happens in the world, that where one loves a body best—pshah, pshah, you are so silly with your moral observations." On this occasion Mrs. Barton told him another risqué story that he dutifully relayed to Stella. "An old gentle-woman died here two months ago, and left in her will, to have eight men and eight maids bearers, who should have two guineas apiece, ten guineas to the parson for a sermon, and two guineas to the clerk. But bearers, parson and clerk must be all true virgins; and not be admitted till they took their oaths of virginity: so the poor woman still lies unburied, and so must do till the general resurrection."[31] On October 14, 1711, Swift spent the evening with Catherine, the first day she received company after the death of her brother, Colonel Barton, in Canada. "I made her merry enough, and we were three hours disputing upon Whig and Tory. She grieved for her brother only for form, and he was a sad dog."[32] Much of their conversation concerned political differences, with Mrs. Barton playfully defending the Whigs and Swift excoriating them. On October 25, 1711, we learn where these tête-à-têtes were taking place: Swift refers to Mrs. Barton as "my near neighbour," and we know that he had moved to St. Martin's Street, Leicester Fields, a fortnight previously.[33] This was Newton's address, and wherever she may have lived before or after, she was surely in her uncle's house at least part of the time during this period, four years before Halifax's death.[34]

There was a long interruption in the intercourse between Mrs. Barton and Swift—more than two decades—until November 29, 1733, when in reply to a letter she wrote a piece that is touched with a delicate wistfulness. Though she is fifty-three and her beauty has faded, she has not lost her warmth and wit. The letter lends credibility to those witnesses who extolled her charm and intelligence.

I should have guessed your holiness would rather have laid than called up the ghost of my departed friendship, which since you are brave enough to face, you will find divested of every terror, but the remorse that you were abandoned to be an alien to your friends, your country and yourself. Not to renew an acquaintance with one who can twenty years after remember a bare intention to serve him, would be to throw away a prize I am not now able to repurchase; therefore when you return to England I shall try to excel in what I am very sorry you want, a nurse; in the mean time I am exercising that gift to preserve one who is your devoted admirer.[35]

An anonymous biography published shortly after Halifax's death in 1715 makes a valiant attempt to defend Catherine Barton's virtue in the face of the scandalmongers' insinuations, but it only sows more confusion, along with a few patent errors. Toward the end of the slim volume, grandiloquently entitled *The Works and Life of the Right Honourable Charles, late Earl of Halifax. Including the History of his Lordships Times,* there is report of Halifax's resolve after the death of his wife in 1698 to live single thenceforward. But since he needed someone to be "Superintendant of his domestick Affairs," he cast his eye upon the widow of one Colonel Barton, niece of the famous Sir Isaac Newton. (Catherine was no widow and Colonel Barton was her elder brother.) The author then proceeds in the face of calumny to establish the true relationship between Catherine and Halifax. "But as this Lady was young, beautiful, and gay so those that were given to censure pass'd a Judgment upon her which she no Ways merited, since she was a Woman of strict Honour and Virtue; and tho' she might be agreeable to his Lordship in every Particular, that noble Peer's Complaisance to her, proceeded wholly from the great Esteem he had for her Wit and most exquisite Understanding, as will appear from what relates to her in his Will at the Close of these Memoirs."[36]

The codicils to Halifax's will trouble the commentators, for he left Catherine Barton a great fortune. On April 12, 1706, he bequeathed to her all the jewels he had at the time of his death; and, in addition, three thousand pounds, as a "small Token of the great Love and Affection I have long had for her."[37] These were the undisguised sentiments of a man of the world at forty-five about an unmarried woman of twenty-six. On February 1, 1712, the bequest was magnificently enlarged; after a friendly gift to Newton, Halifax made her a great heiress.

[I] do hereby give to Sir Isaac Newton, the Sum of one hundred Pounds, as a Mark of the great Honour and Esteem I have for so Great a Man. And I do likewise give, grant, devise, and bequeath to his Neice, Mrs. Catharine Barton, the sum of five thousand Pounds of lawful Money of *England*. And I do likewise give, devise, and bequeath to her, all the Right, Title, and Interest, I have in a Grant from the Crown of the Rangership and Lodge of Bushy Park, together with all the Household Goods and Furniture belonging to the House, Gardens and Park: To have, hold, and enjoy to her own Use and Benefit. . . . Mrs. Barton to keep the said House and Gardens in Repair and good Order, I do likewise give, grant and bequeath my Manour of Apscourt, in the County of Surry, together with all the Rents, Profits, and Advantages thereunto belonging, to the said Mrs. Catherine Barton during her Life.—These Gifts and Legacies, I leave to her as a Token of the sincere Love, Affection, and Esteem I have long had for her Person, and as a small Recompence for the Pleasure and Happiness I have had in her Conversation. And I strictly charge and command my Executor to give all Aid, Help and Assistance to her, in possessing and enjoying what I have hereby given her, and also in doing any Act or Acts necessary to transfer to her an Annuity of two hundred Pounds *per Annum,* purchased in Sir *Isaac Newton's* Name, which I hold for her in Trust, as appears by a Declaration of Trust in that Behalf.[38]

Isaac Newton could hardly have been astonished by these munificent gifts since he had participated in the annuity arrangements; and in his own hand in King's College there are transcriptions of one of the codicils.[39] The relations between the two men were long and intimate, from the time when Charles Montague was a bright young university undergraduate in 1679 through his death in 1715; and the aged Newton later kept his portrait in his room, according to a visiting French abbé. Montague had been involved with Newton in trying to organize a "Philosophick meeting" at Cambridge in 1685,[40] they had sat together in the Convention Parliament that brought

William III to the throne, and, except for a brief rupture just before Newton's crisis, there was a comfortable understanding between them. Bringing Newton to the Mint was doubtless a move to extricate him from his Cambridge impasse, but his usefulness to Montague during the recoinage was real enough. When Newton stood for Parliament from the University in 1705, he scribbled on the back of chronological manuscripts now in Oxford cold analyses of the chances of "N's" success,[41] notes probably meant for Halifax who, as defeat became likely, sent a breezy letter blaming the "Court" and hinting at intrigues of the inner sanctum. Halifax was aware of Newton's extreme sensitivity to any denial. "I am sorry you mention nothing of the Election, it does not look well," he wrote on May 5, 1705, "but I hope you still keep your Resolution of not being disturbed at the event, since there has been no fault of your's in the Managemt, and then there is no great matter in it: I could tell you some storys where the Conduct of the Court has been the same, but complaining is to no purpose and now the Die is cast, and upon the whole Wee shall have a good Parliamt."[42] Offhand, the idea of a close bond between the stern Newton, son of a yeoman, and the brilliant aristocratic poetaster, Maecenas, parliamentarian, political manipulator, drunkard, and lover seems unlikely; and yet the friendship was one of the ties in Newton's life that lasted, ending only with Halifax's sudden death of a pleurisy. In their correspondence it is not Halifax who adopts a grave philosophical demeanor but rather Newton who is straining to imitate a worldly manner that is alien to him.

The characters of Montague and Halley have something in common: they are brilliant, outgoing activists, with an appreciation of the pleasures of this world. Many of their contemporaries considered them atheists, though they might be classified, in the language of their day, as deists or latitudinarian Anglicans. Both were perhaps at one time hard-drinking men, Montague by common repute, Halley by Flamsteed's not altogether reliable witness that after his command of the scientific expedition to the South Atlantic, as Captain Halley, he took to hard drinking and swearing. Newton entertained an affection for these two wild young men—perhaps at times there was a secret longing for the freedom and ease he had so severely denied himself.

This leads back to the crucial question that so gravely troubled two of Newton's nineteenth-century scientist-biographers, his great apologist David Brewster and Augustus de Morgan, the first to see moral blemishes on Newton's escutcheon.[43] Were Mrs. Mary de la Rivière Manley and Voltaire right? Had Newton knowingly acquiesced in an illicit relationship to the monstrous extent of assenting to legal documents that recompensed his niece for her sin? Was Newton's puritanical morality nothing but a sham when great aristocratic ministers of state were involved? John Conduitt, a wealthy man who married Catherine in 1717, wrote that his wife lived in Newton's house "near twenty years, before and after her marriage." This tells us little about which twenty years and nothing about the relationship with Halifax.

The charge against Mrs. Barton was not confined to hostile political circles, but was generally noised about. The Royal Astronomer, Reverend Flamsteed, to avenge the many insults that Newton had heaped upon him, was quick to light upon that ambiguous eighteenth-century word "conversation," used by Halifax in the second codicil of his will, and to stress its sexual connotations in his correspondence. Newton may have been indifferent to the insinuations of a Tory hack like Mrs. Manley, but not to the unsavory rumors the enemy Flamsteed might spread. It is difficult to imagine that the tale never reached Newton's ears—Flamsteed may even have confronted him with it. Newton's antennae were too numerous to miss defamatory remarks about him and his.

The riddle of the Newton-Catherine-Halifax relationship is insoluble. It has been discussed for more than a century since Augustus de Morgan devoted a little book entirely to the subject of Newton and his niece. A few facts are clear. Newton inhabited the same house with a young lady whose conversation, at least with strangers, was peppered with tales of pregnancy out of wedlock and the rarity of the virginal state. Newton continued to live as a "solitary" in his own apartments much of the time; except for business at the Royal Society and the Mint, he was often alone even in London, and Catherine Barton chose her own style of life and her own associates with little interference. The regular schedule of Newton's domestic existence that Catherine wrote out for her husband is in character. "He was always called a half-hour before dinner, & would let his dinners stand on the table two hours; his gruel, or milk & eggs that was carried to him warm for supper, wd eat cold for breakfast."[44] He had his apartments and Catherine Barton had hers, and she absented herself from time to time to go "into the country," as Swift reports.[45]

For a while Ben Smith, Newton's profligate half nephew, also lived with him in London. With Catherine Barton and the young Ben Smith in the same house, Newton can hardly be said to have dwelt in the odor of sanctity, though Smith in later years was a staunch defender of his cousin's and his uncle's virtue from Voltairean calumny, insisting that Catherine had not yet been born when the appointment to the Mint was made, a gross exaggeration.

Foreigners like Rémond de Montmort and the Abate Conti who called on Newton met and were entertained by Mrs. Barton. Their recollections, plus the concrete evidence that she was Swift's neighbor in 1711, make the notion that she occupied the post of Halifax's "housekeeper" during these years questionable. Even a lady with her enormous gifts could hardly have run the Newton and Halifax households simultaneously. There is also a possibility that for part of the time she lived with the fashionable Anne Long.

Augustus de Morgan, and in his wake the twentieth-century biographer Louis Trenchard More, after much lawyerlike argumentation, opted for a secret marriage between Bartica and Halifax, unable to face the possibility of the chaste Newton's tolerating a sinful relationship between his young friend and patron Halifax and his niece.[46] Did she or not? That was the question that perplexed the eminent Victorian scientists. If she did not, how explain the wills bestowing magnificent properties upon her? And if she did, was Newton, the virtuous Newton, either so blind to reality, so obtuse, or so indifferent to the Holy Commandments that he countenanced a liaison?

Augustus de Morgan's theory of a secret marriage was rejected by Brewster, who wrote him: "I am trying to put together a few pages *re* Halifax, and the wife you have given him. It is the most disagreeable portion of Newton's history. Newton's character is not protected, even if a private marriage could be proved; I have come to the conclusion, on grounds which I fear will not satisfy you, that Mrs. Barton *never lived* in Halifax's house."[47] In the end, Augustus de Morgan's whole case rests upon a phrase in a letter of Newton's dated May 23, 1715, in which he conceivably implies that Halifax's death was that of a relative. "The concern I am in for the loss of my Lord Halifax, and the circumstances in which I stand related to his family, will not suffer me to go abroad till his funeral is over."[48] This is thin evidence indeed upon which to base a secret marriage, especially since the letter itself may no longer be extant. But if the marriage between the great Earl of Halifax and the daughter of a country parson could not be announced during his lifetime for fear of ridicule, why was it kept secret after his death, at the risk of exposing her to public obloquy when the terms of the will became known? Moreover, a sworn allegation preliminary to Catherine's subsequent marriage to Conduitt unequivocally records her status as spinster.[49]

No information has turned up to support the secret marriage though the registers have been combed, or to refute conclusively Brewster's steadfast assertion that the relationship was platonic. But if worthy gentlemen once earnestly debated the existence or the non-existence of a clandestine marriage and the possibility of a fall from chastity, we of another age may divert the inquiry into an entirely different channel. Marriage or no marriage, mistress or virgin, there was a prolonged, intimate friendship between Catherine Barton and Lord Halifax to which Isaac Newton was a third party, an important participant observer. The idea that Newton had simply come to condone the way of the world in the reign of Queen Anne is not convincing. What psychic role did this relationship, consummated

or not, play in his life? Here we are on the bedrock of the unconscious, no longer toying with hypothetical letters whose precise
meaning remains obscure. Victorians could not suffer the intrusion
of illegitimate sex in the family of the hero; and we cannot tolerate
the idea of mere aimless dalliance.

Nothing can be done to clarify the muddle by sticking to the
facts. One can, however, propose a theoretical alternative to explain
the Newton-Barton-Halifax triangle in plausible terms. The interplay among them was possibly more complex than even Voltaire's
nose for a prurient scandal could scent. In the act of fornication between his friend Halifax and his niece was Newton vicariously
having carnal intercourse with his mother? Did he take "the Nymph
to be his Mother" in a sense Dryden never intended? Such a hypothesis can never be verified through traditional historical techniques.
If Newton saw his child-fantasy of desire for his mother consummated through the agency of Halifax making love to Hannah's incarnation in Catherine, it points to a change in his personality. The
relationship with Catherine signifies a movement away from the
perils of Narcissus which had lurked in the ties with Fatio.

On August 26, 1717, Catherine Barton, already a woman of
thirty-eight, married John Conduitt of Cranbury Lodge, Southampton, about nine years her junior, whom she outlived by two
years, dying January 20, 1740.[50] In her last days Catherine Conduitt
showed a meritorious turn toward religion, a subject which had not
always been at the heart of her concerns. A codicil to her will
provided that the eminent Dr. Sykes examine the theological manuscripts of her late uncle with a view to their publication. Unfortunately this part of her last testament is largely unexecuted to this
day; of the hundreds of folios Sir Isaac left to posterity on God,
the nature of the Trinity, the language of prophecy, above all the
early history of the church, many were dispersed during the regret-
table Sotheby sale of the Portsmouth papers in 1936, which netted
the heirs so little, and others lie a-mouldering in various libraries.
A cloud of heresy still hangs over the documents.

This most remarkable woman survived Newton by less than thirteen years. Pope depicts her as still something of a hellion in the 1730's, though according to the uncharitable Swift, who saw her at Court, her beauty had dimmed.[51] Her daughter, the offspring of Catherine and John Conduitt, married the son of one of the great peers of the realm and became Viscountess Lymington. Hannah Ayscough's brood had gone far—with the aid of her son Isaac.

Whatever the secret truth of the relationships among the principals of this story, the bones of all of them now repose in Westminster Abbey: Newton in the middle aisle, Catherine and John Conduitt with their daughter nearby, and the Earl of Halifax in the Duke of Albemarle's vault on the north side of King Henry the VII's Chapel, at a respectable distance.

Chapter 13

THE AUTOCRAT OF SCIENCE

All were like the branches of a tree, deriving their strength
and vigor from the trunk and forming one body with it. The
Royal Society, then at the summit of its intellectual glory, regarded its own fate as indissolubly linked with Newton's. It
interested itself in everything that affected his reputation, and
treated as its own concerns all the disputes that engaged him,
whether about the theory of colors or the invention of the
calculus.

—Paolo Frisi, *Elogio del Cavaliere Isacco Newton*

Had Newton's life been cut off in his fifty-third year, when rumors
of his death had spread in London, the consequences for the long-
range development of Western science would not have been overwhelming. The *Principia* had been published eight years before, the
calculus, at least in its Leibnizian form, had been known since 1684,
and his theory of light, though not in the final version of the *Opticks* (1704), had been communicated to the Royal Society in the
seventies. His alchemical papers, interpretations of prophecy, and
radical revision of world chronology, though they are respectworthy,
rational texts in the spirit of the age, would not, in the long run,
have been missed. And other men would have made the corrections
for the later editions of the *Principia* without his supervision. Nor
would the loss of Newton's "philosophy" recorded in the sibylline
"Queries" to the *Opticks* and the General Scholium to the second
edition of the *Principia* have left a major gap in the annals of
thought.

Newton lived on for more than three decades after the encapsulated psychic episode of 1693 and the mild depression that followed. The royal appointment to the Mint in 1696 made it possible for him to leave the University, alter his whole mode of life and conduct, and give overt expression to a deep need for the exercise of power and to manipulatory skills which had previously been dormant. The massive energy with which he was endowed found new materials to mold in the world of men. A juxtaposition of the first portrait of him by Kneller in 1689 with the late ones by Vanderbank tells at a glance the story of the transformation from a sensitive, melancholy, and troubled scholar clad in black to the heavy, arrogant, irascible administrator in rich brocade and velvet. The exercise of his magistracy at the Mint, which continued to the eve of his death, has disclosed much about his character during this period. The ensuing segment of this portrait focuses on his activities in a second office which he assumed in 1703 and held simultaneously, the presidency of the Royal Society.

During one of the annual November elections of officers of the Society, John Chamberlayne, a Fellow who was a court official under Queen Anne, wrote Newton surrendering to him his vote for members of the Council and voicing a desire to see him made "Perpetual Dictator" of the Society.[1] The sentiment was shared by many others: disciples dedicated their books to the "divine Newton" and outsiders joined the chorus of praise, hoping to attract his attention. Such adulation was more than mere baroque extravagance, for Newton did indeed become the "dictator" of the English scientific establishment, and standing on that solid base he was apotheosized into the symbol of Western science. With more than a soupçon of envy, Laplace later remarked that since there was only one universe it could be granted to only one man to discover its fundamental law. If one remains attuned to the religious as well as the scientific meaning of a law in a Christian society, the divinization of the new Moses by those of his contemporaries, especially the young ones, who were able to read the hieroglyphic tablets of his law is plausible. Could the hunger of Newton for recognition ever be appeased, this was the moment.

A multiplicity of factors contributed to the making of the Newton image—it was not only the work of the later eighteenth-century popularizers of his philosophy. In large measure it was created by Newton himself during the quarter of a century that he ruled the Royal Society. Longevity can be, as we have observed in contemporary politics, an important element in leadership, and Newton lasted long enough to institutionalize himself and his system. Such duration is not necessarily of course an unambiguous good. When the founder of a scientific movement lives on for decades after the spark in him has been extinguished, he may harden and even fossilize the system. His spiritual sons grow up in the shadow of an ancient oak and their own capacities are often stunted.

The creation of the new headship of science involved acts akin to the processes of winning political, military, or religious power. But while primacy in war, politics, and religious movements has been studied critically ever since the Greeks and the Romans, the rise to titular hegemony in science, a more recent phenomenon, has in the nature of things been the subject of relatively little scrutiny. Qualities essential for scientific leadership are not the same in all times and places: the historical situation of Isaac Newton was unique and in some respects his performance was idiosyncratic. But the later Newton, who is usually only of anecdotal interest, emerges from an examination of his doings during this period as the first of a new type in European history, the grand administrator of science.

Scientific truth can speak for itself, but often requires an agency through which it may be amplified and diffused. The practices of Newton himself and the instruments with which he operated in the scientifically less creative part of his life[2] are definable elements among the many social and psychological forces at play in the creation of the "Newtonian world view." His triumph was furthered by a complex of circumstances that did not obtain for either Galileo or Descartes in the previous generation or for his contemporary

Leibniz. The grandeur and genius of the Newtonian synthesis are here taken for granted, as is its emotional appeal to a monotheistic culture not yet divested of the religious swaddling clothes that had protected it in its early years. It has been noted often enough that the growth of a commercial society in a centralized state like England and its consequent concern with the products of "mathematicall magick," the affinity between the precise, methodical behavior of the experimental scientist and the comportment of the self-disciplined, puritanical Protestant, helped fashion a social environment in which science could flourish. The interaction of Protestantism, nascent capitalism, and the new philosophy can be recognized without the establishment of mechanical historical relations of cause and effect among them. Even the most refractory English scientists had been able to survive the civil war: no Bruno had been burned nor had a Galileo recanted and been sequestered. A note by Conduitt echoes the Whiggish sentiments of his idol about the relations of science and English freedom. "Sir I. had the happiness of being born in a land of liberty where he could speak his mind—not afraid of Inquisition as Galileo . . . not obliged as Des Cartes was to go into a strange country & to say he proved transubstantiation by his philosophy."[3] An organized university system had evolved with professorships in mathematics and astronomy, and no major victims had been claimed among the scientists by the purges of the Commonwealth and early Restoration. After the civil war, there was a curious royal court which at least played with science and to which its practitioners had access. The very insularity and provincialism of English scientists provided them with a foundation on which to build a scientific structure, an opportunity denied to those wanderers and exiles, Descartes and Leibniz, without roots in any soil. But when all of the auspicious economic, religious, and social factors are weighed—and there are many more that overdetermine English precedence—it still remains to inquire into the political methods pursued by Isaac Newton in attaining a position of leadership in his own country and in the European world, after the heroic age of the founding fathers of the Royal Society had passed, as had the peak of his own creativity. If one descends from the realm of grand generalizations about the relationships of English science and religion, or English science and social structure, a description of how the first scientific "establishment" in the modern world was organized under Newton's governance is a part of his portrait. There is no presumption that Newton deliberately set himself the task of devising a strategy to capture the Royal Society and transform it into his creature. Viewed retrospectively, however, his tactics and maneuvers show an underlying purposiveness and reveal the functioning of an organizational will.

To secure the ascendancy of his philosophical principles and establish his unquestioned pre-eminence, Newton gathered about him a group of scientific adherents, younger men of varying degrees of talent, joined in absolute loyalty to his person and his doctrine, drawn to him as moths to a flame. There were rivalries among the followers and inevitable ostracisms from the group; but his scientific supremacy was accepted by every one of them. It was a relationship of master and disciples, with all the complexity inherent in that bond. To make the Royal Society a worthy institutional vehicle for the propagation of Newtonian science, over the years he perfected plain administrative methods to bolster the Society through better housekeeping and closer supervision of its operations. Ultimately its unique personality was affirmed in a physical structure, a building all its own, and, in the hope of insuring continuity in scientific work, Newton even drafted a scheme for the introduction of an order of paid pensioners. He was also responsible for weaving a sacred and aristocratic aura around science through the development of ceremonials. Newton's personal ties with the Whig politicians made him the ideal figure to work out a pattern for the role of science in a flexible parliamentary regime, a pattern whose traces have not completely disappeared even in recent years. Science and government came to use and promote each other; but, in contrast with continental models, English science retained a large measure of autonomy. Finally, since no major creation is achieved without negation, Newton waged fierce battles to consolidate his scientific empire and destroy competitive or insubordinate rivals both within and outside the Royal Society. The bitter quarrels with the English Royal Astronomer Flamsteed and with the cosmopolitan philosopher Leibniz, which punctuated the first decade of his presidency and in which he was spectacularly victorious, forcefully demonstrated his authority within the English establishment and in the international scientific world.

For the first half century of its existence the Royal Society had been a rather loose fellowship. Its central figures tended to be the secretaries, who served as a clearinghouse for scientific correspondence. The presidency was largely an honorific office, and though the chair was occasionally occupied by scientists, many of the incumbents were aristocrats and politicians, mere amateurs of science, who often failed to attend either the meetings of the governing Council or the general sessions at which experiments were presented and papers discussed. After the fifteen-year tenure of William, Lord Viscount Brouncker, from 1662 to 1677, there followed a succession of ten presidents, each of whom occupied the office for only a few years. They were intelligent men like Pepys, Montague, and Somers, but with no pretensions to science. No one man dominated the institution until Newton took control. (If any single figure had been outstanding it was Robert Hooke, who had been a mainstay of the Society for forty years, but by the 1690's he was ailing in body and spirit.)

Though Newton was a member of the Council in 1697–1698 and 1699–1700, until he had a clear field he held aloof from the administration of the Society, and he would not accept the presidency as long as his old enemy Robert Hooke was alive. From earliest childhood, he feared and shunned competition: either he dominated a situation totally or he would refuse to play. Immediately upon Hooke's death, however, Newton took over, and he reigned for the rest of his life. Isaac Newton had a way of recasting any office he occupied in his own image. During his years as President he changed the character of the Royal Society, as he did the Mint, and shed upon it the lustre of his own pre-eminence in the world of science.

"The very title was justly rever'd, both at home and abroad. . . . Infinite were the encomiums they received from foreign countrys; in a great measure owing to the superior capacity and unbounded merit of so illustrious a president," wrote William Stukeley.[4]

When Newton assumed the presidency in 1703, at the age of sixty, his genius was universally recognized though his great work was understood by few men and the continental reception of the *Principia* had not measured up to its admiration by the English. Virtually the whole generation of founding fathers of the Society and the second generation to which he belonged had died off. Of the original group only Sir Christopher Wren was still alive (he died in 1723 at the age of ninety-one) and he continued to grace committees with his venerable presence—though he was no longer very active. There were Fellows who would have preferred Wren to Newton, but Wren had insisted on the selection of his colleague. Of Newton's contemporaries there remained Flamsteed and Francis Aston—the latter a compliant agent of no particular distinction, only the former, the stiff-necked Royal Astronomer, a major internal threat to Newton's authority. Sheer longevity combined with political favor and towering achievement had made Newton's position almost unassailable.

Since the Royal Society was Newton's base of operations, the composition of its membership has an intimate bearing on his use of men in the furtherance of his ends. For Newton, persons were usually objects, not subjects. The hundred-odd members of the Society over whom he presided were divided roughly one to two between those with professional competence in science and aristocratic or gentlemanly amateurs. The scientists were in turn concentrated in two major groups, the medical doctors and physiologists and the mathematical-astronomical contingent. The doctors prominent in the Society, men like Hans Sloane, John Arbuthnot, and Richard Mead, were prosperous and influential court physicians who had easy entry to the Palace and the aristocratic houses of the realm; whenever Newton needed something at court, they could serve as convenient bedside intermediaries. Sloane, whom Newton had inherited as Sec-

11. Charles Montague, Lord Halifax, circa 1703–1710

12. Isaac Newton, 1703 (?)

retary of the Society, had begun to resuscitate it after the Glorious Revolution, and he had a penchant for keeping matters in his control during the early years of Newton's tenure. Newton chafed at his behind-the-scenes direction, a hangover from the traditional pattern in which the President was a changing figurehead and the Secretary was the effective officer, and he could be provoked to abusive epithets in denouncing him. With the same persistence with which Newton had secured actual, not merely nominal, control of the Royal Mint, he moved into the Royal Society. Though he used Sloane when he needed him, by 1713 Sloane had been persuaded to withdraw to his house in Chelsea and devote himself to his famous collection of natural curiosities and manuscripts.[5] With Sloane's departure Newton chose as secretaries two men who were of his own creation, Edmond Halley and John Keill, and Sloane did not return to the center of activity until Newton's death, when he succeeded him as President. His eclipse was no great loss to science, since he was an old-fashioned gatherer of nostrums and a purveyor of traditional remedies who stuffed the *Philosophical Transactions* of the Society with his questionable discoveries—though his passion for collecting and preserving things resulted in a massive assemblage of materials that bears his name, now in the British Museum. Mead was a doctor of more philosophical bent and in Newton's last years was his personal physician. Arbuthnot, one of the numerous Scots who made good in the London scientific world, a great wit as his satirical writings show, an innovator in the history of social statistics, a man close to the Prince of Denmark, occupied a pivotal post as physician extraordinary to Queen Anne. When Newton cannily appointed him to committees in both the Flamsteed and the Leibniz contests, he took his functions rather casually, performing in the manner expected of him by the President. With a notable exception, the medical men in the Society caused Newton no serious trouble, and it was one of their number, Dr. William Stukeley, a young man from Lincolnshire, who became a favorite of his old age and his first biographer—though when Stukeley, against Newton's will, ran for office in the Society, he was punished with exile from the presence for several years.[6]

Since they were men of independent means, the doctors were not as beholden to Newton as the young mathematicians and astronomers, but so great was the prestige of his person and his system that they obeyed him and aligned themselves with him in any controversy.

The earnest young men upon whom Newton relied for the energetic building of his fame were the astronomers and mathematicians, who had come to the *Principia* as to a new revelation. They eagerly accepted the role of apostles. A few he had known and favored before he assumed office, others he continued to recruit through the decades of his long tenure, and he even outlived his earlier protégés. By the time of his death the academic map of England and Scotland in the mathematical-astronomical sciences had been completely Newtonized. Year by year as a professorship or a royal office to which a scientist could be appointed became vacant or a new chair was created, he filled it with one of his candidates. They became the king's men in Newton's realm, for there was a secular as well as a spiritual side to his sovereignty. The ties which bound these professors to him were often affective as well as scientific. For the young men, Newton was the father of the clan. The President who had lectured to empty halls during his Lucasian professorship now found himself the head of a scientific family. The old man who had never known woman acquired sons.

David Gregory, who had been one of the first to teach the Newtonian philosophy at Edinburgh in the 1680's, was appointed Savilian Professor of Astronomy at Oxford in 1692, largely through Newton's intervention, after a veritable campaign of ingratiation. Roger Cotes, a mathematician and another of Newton's protégés, became Plumian Professor of Astronomy and Experimental Philosophy at Cambridge in 1706, when he was only twenty-four years old. Newton, who had defined the terms of the new chair himself, as an administrator of science took a very different attitude toward publication than he had in his youth: the Plumian professor would be required to publish regularly either at Cambridge or in the *Philosophical Transactions*. The handsome Cotes was a dearly beloved disciple, at whose premature death in 1716 Newton lamented: "If he had lived we might have known something."[7] William Whiston, who as an undergraduate had heard a few lectures by Newton, first made his acquaintance in 1694. On Newton's nomination he became Lucasian Professor of Mathematics at Cambridge, after having substituted for him when he went up to London. John Keill, a student of David Gregory's, was named Savilian Professor of Astronomy at Oxford in 1712 and gave courses on the new philosophy at the University. He also served as "decypherer" to Queen Anne. Keill was a war-horse whose ardor was so intense that Newton sometimes had to pull in the reins.

The one major scientist who remained by Newton's side throughout the whole period of his tenure as President of the Royal Society was the astronomer Edmond Halley. The nature of their bond may someday be more fully defined if the Halley papers on Newton—which existed at one time—ever turn up. A strange event marks the beginning of their relationship. In 1684, the year that twenty-eight-year-old Halley first visited Newton at Cambridge and received from him the fundamental propositions of the *Principia,* his father had been found dead on the banks of a river near Reading. The coroner's verdict was murder, and a wild insinuation was later made by the academic gossip Thomas Hearne that Halley was implicated in the crime. Hearne also proposed that Newton's death was hastened by a violent scene between him and Halley.[8] But for more than forty years Halley behaved toward Newton with great circumspection: he knew how to mollify him when he was in a wrath, and in the crushing of Newton's enemies he made himself indispensable as chief of staff. During the fight with Hooke he had been a reporter and an agent whose primary function it was to see the *Principia* through the press and keep Newton from destroying the third part in his anger at Hooke's accusation that the law of gravity had been stolen from him. When Newton needed an astronomer to finish and force publication of Flamsteed's star catalogue, Halley was appointed editor. And when in 1712 the Royal Society's *Commercium epistolicum* against Leibniz was to be printed, Halley ran the editorial committee and did all the paper work that was not handled by Newton himself. Newton protected him and, though his reputation for religious skepticism was an impediment to his advancement and Newton occasionally rebuked him, he secured his appointment as deputy comptroller of the Chester Mint in 1696. After a series of scientific voyages, through Newton's assistance he was made Savilian Professor of Astronomy at Oxford in 1703, Secretary of the Royal Society in 1713, and Royal Astronomer in 1721.

By the time Newton became President of the Royal Society, Fatio de Duillier had fallen into disfavor, though he lingered on the sidelines for a few years. Samuel Clarke, who had been converted to the Newtonian philosophy in Cambridge about the same time as William Whiston, had refused a post at the Mint that was in Newton's grant and served as chaplain to the Princess of Wales, from which vantage point he became the expositor of the philosophical and religious conceptions of the Newtonian philosophy in his famous correspondence with Leibniz—but only after careful consultation with Newton himself. Colin Maclaurin and Henry Pemberton and James Stirling were of the second generation of disciples, in the 1720's, after Fatio de Duillier was swallowed up by the Prophets of London, Whiston was estranged, and Gregory and Cotes had died. Maclaurin became Professor of Mathematics at the University of Edinburgh through Newton's sponsorship, and Henry Pemberton ultimately was made Professor of Physic at Gresham College.

Thus were the young mathematicians and astronomers rewarded with chairs in Oxford, Cambridge, and the Scottish universities. Few academic appointments in this field were made without consulting Newton, and his advice was almost always heeded. Sometimes he gave his protégés munificent gifts as well—five hundred pounds went to Clarke, one hundred pounds for each of his children, for his translation of the *Opticks* into Latin. When a minor and rather unreliable disciple, George Cheyne, refused his bounty, he was peremptorily dropped.

Newton usually dealt with people on the basis of "commutation," except on those rare occasions when his tender feelings became involved. He distributed academic posts and royal offices and the beneficiaries acquitted their debts to him through service and loyalty. There is a feudal as well as a paternal cast to his ties with the younger men. They fought his battles and he awarded them university professorships as their fiefs. This formidable man sometimes inspired love, surely in Fatio, perhaps in Halley and Conduitt. More often it is his masterful authority that gives the group of his adherents cohesion.

There was work for the protégés that related directly to Newton's writings. Though before his London period Newton had timorously allowed mathematical papers to be shown only to a few elders like Isaac Barrow and John Collins, once he had stopped creating he granted a number of younger men among his followers freer access to his private mathematical hoard. John Craig, David Gregory, Joseph Raphson, Edmond Halley, Fatio de Duillier, William Jones, John Keill, Henry Pemberton, Abraham de Moivre, Nicholas Bernoulli were among those who enjoyed the occasional privilege. Corrections and emendations of the *Principia* were begun soon after it was published, primarily by Newton himself, who in characteristic fashion blamed all but one of the errors on his ignorant amanuensis. Fatio de Duillier had thought of himself as the only disciple worthy to prepare the second edition, and there are those who consider him by far the most talented mathematician among the disciples. When he went off into the wilderness of religious enthusiasm the mantle fell on Roger Cotes, whose preface (1713) became an integral part of the work, and in popularizations of Newtonianism was usually cited as proof positive that the structure of the universe as revealed by Newton presupposed an infinitely good and wise architect.[9] The third edition thirteen years later was the labor of Pemberton. Throughout this period the disciples busied themselves with teaching the doctrine in the universities and with popularizations, usually with Newton's blessing, though at times accompanied by underground rumor that the new renderings endangered the prestige of the original because they might become more widely diffused than Newton's work, whose grandiose architectural quality and elegant proofs few contemporaries were capable of understanding thoroughly. Whiston, Gregory, Cheyne, Clarke, Maclaurin, Pemberton, Keill, John Theophilus Desaguliers all wrote books on Newtonianism during his lifetime or immediately after his death.[10] Even the doctors and the divines in the Royal Society exerted themselves to apply the Newtonian philosophy in their respective fields, the physicians often producing a literature bordering on the absurd, like Cheyne's proposal for a "Principia Medicinae Theoreticae Mathematica." Men in holy orders, who illustrated the religious nature of the Newtonian philosophy, used its principles as a laudation. John Craig's *Theologiae Christianae Principia Mathematica* (1699) is perhaps the most outlandish example of the Newtonian fashion in religion. The first commentaries of the Newtonian movement were thus written under the watchful eye of the Master, and he allowed its ramifications into the strangest areas without dissent.

While Newton protected his young men and fostered them, he demanded absolute obedience; the father would brook no criticism or opposition or eccentric act that might reflect upon him and jeopardize his position as a Crown official and luminary of the realm. He insisted upon social conformity in their behavior. William Whiston proved to be an incautious man who could not restrain his tongue or mask his views. Differing from Newton over matters of biblical interpretation and chronology, in which he believed himself superior to his patron, he could not withhold his criticism, and such contumely did not sit well with the Master. When Whiston openly expressed Arian convictions that in reality were not very dissimilar from Newton's own secret faith, the lack of prudence was punished.[11] Newton did not lift a finger when Whiston was ousted from the University for religious heterodoxy. And there is anecdotage to the effect that he kept him out of the Royal Society on grounds that he was a heretic, threatening to resign if Halley and Sloane went through with the nomination.[12] Whiston suffered deeply from this rejection, and like a lover denied vented his spleen against those still in the entourage and against Newton's intolerance. He finally settled accounts in his *Memoirs:* "But he then perceiving that I could not do as his other darling friends did, that is, learn of him, without contradicting him, when I differed in opinion from him, he could not, in his old age, bear such contradiction. . . . ."[13] Fatio de Duillier had been excluded when he became involved with the séances of the wild Prophets of London and served as their secretary.

There was one other group in the Royal Society whom Newton befriended by supporting them in more modest positions than university professorships, the Huguenot émigrés. Though he recovered from the more violent seizures of anti-Catholicism which had possessed him and his contemporaries in the 1680's and 1690's, he retained a deep sympathy for the victims of Louis XIV's laws against Protestants, who took refuge in England in a flight reminiscent of the movement out of Germany in the twentieth century. Most of the exiles sought security and respectability in their new home, and were dismayed by the scandal of the Prophets from the Cévennes in which Fatio had become enmeshed. Newton helped the reasonable ones, the mathematician Abraham de Moivre, the translator and compiler of scientific letters Pierre Des Maizeaux, and Desaguliers, who had been brought to England as an infant and became an occasionally paid experimenter of the Royal Society.[14]

Newton kept in close touch with his disciples and his favored Huguenots and met with them regularly. David Gregory has an account of a session with Fatio, Halley, and himself at which Newton unfolded his publication plans.[15] Ralph Thoresby in his diary describes the agreeable Fellows he encountered at the Royal Society and afterward accompanied to the Grecian Coffee-house—President Isaac Newton, attended by the two secretaries Halley and Keill, both his protégés and both professors at Oxford.[16] On many evenings Newton picked up de Moivre at the coffeehouse he frequented, Slaughter's in St. Martin's Lane, and brought him to his own home nearby for philosophical conversation.[17] There was a gentle side to the man that manifested itself in these relationships, but their function was primarily to nourish a scientific movement organized around a doctrine.

Virtually nothing was done in behalf of the Newtonian philosophy without the Master's surveillance and permission. The manuscript legacy of the great controversies in which he was engaged proves that he supervised and usually corrected with his own hand the drafts of whatever the disciples wrote in his defense, but there was a tacit understanding among them that he was never to be exposed. Keill would send a piece for Halley, inviting him and Newton to make changes as they saw fit. Cotes asked Newton to write anything he chose as the polemical, anti-Leibniz preface to the second edition of the *Principia* and offered to append his name to it and defend it as his own. The famous review, or *Recensio,* of the *Commercium epistolicum,* published in the *Philosophical Transactions,* every bit of which Newton himself had composed, was palmed off as Keill's. In Clarke's philosophical interchange with Leibniz, the manuscripts make it abundantly clear that Newton's is the firm guiding hand. And in Des Maizeaux's published collection of documents Newton permitted himself the license of final revisions of his disciples' letters, even after they had been sent off.[18] The Newtonians in the Royal Society—and the collective name had begun to be used—were really what Leibniz called them, Newton's *enfants perdus,* his reconnaissance patrol.[19]

During his tenure as President of the Royal Society Newton adopted a series of measures intended to introduce sound administrative procedures and firm discipline among the members. The meticulous scientist could not tolerate slipshod ways, and the Society would be a mirror of his personality. Under his austere eye, the character of the Council meetings changed markedly, and informal discussions were replaced by complicated rules and frequent ballotings. While previous presidents had appeared at the Society irregularly, according to a count Newton was present at one hundred sixty-one out of a hundred seventy-five sessions of the Council, and in order to participate in the general assemblies, he shifted the weekly meeting from Wednesday to Thursday, a day when he was not occupied at the Mint.[20]

The last decades of the seventeenth century were an especially trying period for the Society as an institution: the membership fell off, dues were in arrears, and changes of officers were unusually frequent. It had not been able to afford the printing of the *Principia,* having exhausted the treasury on Willughby's history of fishes, and for a time the publication of the *Philosophical Transactions* had been suspended. The Society was on the verge of bankruptcy when Newton took over, and he attempted to make it solvent through a reorganization of its finances. In 1706 the Council ordered that before induction every newly elected member should pay his admission fee and give bond that he would make regular weekly contributions. And three years later this measure was strengthened by a Council decision that if in the future a member's dues were two years in arrears and he was not expressly excused, his name would be dropped from the printed list of Fellows. Only a paid-up Fellow, moreover, could become a member of the Council.[21] Newton even tried to jog foreign members into making contributions to the Society on the ground that they were exempt from all the normal fees.[22] When bequests to the Society were contested, he ordered Sloane to "stick at no charge for defending the Legacy," and advanced money until his decision could be ratified by the Council.[23] Not all the efforts made to replenish the treasury were equally felicitous. A cheesemonger to whom the Society had rented its cellar proved to be a nuisance who tenaciously resisted eviction for a decade.[24] In 1723 Newton invested Royal Society funds, along with his own, in the South Sea Company, expecting large profits from an enterprise whose stock was rising spectacularly. This was one occasion, however, when his manipulations failed—though he did not live to see the total debacle.

Newton's psychic owing was boundless, and he could not endure to be obligated or indebted to any man. Whenever it was possible, he tried to substitute paid for volunteer services. He was uncomfortable with anything but a *do ut des* arrangement. In 1720 he had a stipend fixed for the two chief secretaries of the Society as well as for a foreign secretary, a substantial budgetary increase. He was particularly fortunate in his two curators of experiments. Francis Hauksbee, who performed at Newton's inaugural session, served until he died ten years later. His *Physico-Mechanical Experiments on various subjects* (1709), based upon Newtonian conceptions, is now highly appreciated as the work of a precursor in the history of electricity. Scholars recognize a reciprocal relationship between him and Newton and discern his influence in Newton's later reflections on electrical magnetism and his revised theory of the "subtile aether." Early in 1714 Desaguliers appeared to perform before the Royal Society, and upon his appointment as Curator Newton allocated special funds for his work. Newton was no indifferent observer at Desaguliers's trials; he worked out new experiments with the Curator and may have altered his own conjectural physical theory of nature in accordance with them. But in return for his support, Newton insisted that every order of the Council be scrupulously obeyed, and when he felt that Desaguliers was not performing a sufficient number of experiments he had him reprimanded, much to the scientist's dismay.[25]

One of Newton's plans of institutional reform was a *Scheme for establishing the Royal Society* of which there are extant six drafts in his hand.[26] Though the plan did not come to fruition, it tells us a good deal about the authoritarian direction in which he was moving. "Establishing" in this context meant giving the Society's projects a sound financial and organizational frame, though one is tempted to read his meaning as re-establishing the society anew under his aegis. Newton envisaged a system of appointed learned pensioners who would be obliged to attend all sessions of the Society and, if they wished to retain their positions, to produce inventions and discoveries on schedule. The plan classified science into five divisions, into each of which a pensioner would be fitted. Newton's early sense of the fluidity of science—the fantasies of the youth who dabbled freely in all forms of knowledge—has vanished with age. Science is now organized and structural. In this document, the divine consecration of science is strangely absent, as he describes its mission in purely institutional terms. The ultimate goal is secular, to make the Society "famous and lasting"—in one draft he had first written "perpetual," the language of the French Academy.[27] The recluse of Trinity turned administrator was moving along the path of the academies that were agencies of the French crown.

Before Newton's incumbency, the Society had fallen to such low estate that Sloane's "unfit entertainment" became the subject of a public satire. Newton devoted himself to the moral as well as financial renovation of the Society, and made a ceremony of the sessions over which he presided, the first high priest of modern science officiating at its rites. His dread of disorder and tendency to ritualize his own behavior, along with a desire to imitate the elaborate manners of the great, led him to assign specific places to the officers who attended him at meetings like the members of a royal court. The President was to sit at the head of the table, with the secretaries at the lower end, one on each side. The sacred configuration could be altered only to accommodate "some very Honourable Stranger at the discretion of the President."[28] The old porter was pensioned off with a pittance; and a liveried servant installed at the door and carrying a staff that bore the arms of the Society set the tone of the weekly meetings.[29] Only when the President occupied the chair could the mace be laid, no lesser dignitary being permitted to enjoy this distinction—an exclusion that rankled in the bosom of Dr. Hans Sloane, who had it abolished as the first order of business after Newton's death.[30]

Dr. Stukeley, a hushed witness, has left a description of the solemn performances:

Whilst he presided in the Royal Society, he executed that office with singular prudence, with a grace and dignity—conscious of what was due to so noble an Institution—what was expected from his character. . . . There were no whispering, talking nor loud laughters. If discussions arose in any sort, he said they tended to find out truth, but ought not to arise to any personality. . . . Every thing was transacted with great attention and solemnity and decency; nor were any papers which seemed to border on religion treated without proper respect. Indeed his presence created a natural awe in the assembly; they appear'd truly as a venerable *consessus Naturae Consiliariorum*, without any levity or indecorum.[31]

If the solemnity was fractured the culprit was ousted.

In 1710 a famous fracas occurred between the geologist and physician John Woodward, Professor of Physic at Gresham College, notoriously choleric, and Dr. Hans Sloane, who was reading a translation of a French article about bezoars, secretions found in the intestines of goats in Persia and India, which were identified as a type of gallstone and used as an antidote against poison. Woodward kept interrupting the declamation with his dissenting remarks, among them: "Speake Sense or English and we shall understand you. If you understood Anatomy you would know better."[32] Upon Sloane's complaint to the Council that he had been insulted, Woodward countered with the charge that Sloane had been making grimaces at him. Though Sloane formally declared he intended no injury, Woodward refused wholly to retract his statements, and Newton had him removed from the Council to the accompaniment of reflections that he was a good natural but not a good moral philosopher.[33] Woodward's subsequent litigation to regain his place availed him nothing. If an anonymous pamphleteer and an anonymous letter-writer are credited, the incident had many ramifications. It was the open manifestation of "sides" among the Fellows, a partisanship that was exacerbated in a dispute over moving the Society's meeting place. The autocrat had his insurgents to subdue.

The unsigned letter addressed to Newton on March 28, 1710, is a peephole into the backstairs intrigues of the Society at this period. The writer encouraged the President to proceed apace with rehabilitating the Society, assuring him that many members would support him, even as "Dr Sloane, & his Junto of Non-Solvents" aimed to impede and defeat him. Halley, who was in Sloane's camp, was charged with disloyalty: "If Mr Halley would be as forward in that [advancing the Society's honor], as it seems, for Reasons that he best knows, he is, in some other Things that assuredly are not so much for yours or the Society'es Interest, he will tell you how loud Men of Sense all over the Town are in their Complaints, & Men of Wit, in their Railery of the Society on account of Dr Sloanes Management. . . ." The anonymous correspondent, apparently himself a member of the Council, mocked Sloane's communication on bezoars—"I cannot but think a Translation out of a printed French Book a very low, mean, unfit Entertainment for the Royal Society"—and accused Sloane of using Newton as an instrument to avenge himself on Woodward.

Newton was reminded that he had told more than one friend how little qualified Sloane was for the post of secretary and had "freely declared him a *tricking Fellow:* nay *a Villain,* & *Rascal....*"[34]

Whenever Newton was identified with an institution, it became an extension of his person and he sought to protect its position with the same zeal that he would his own. The feeling of identification with Trinity College that he had had during the Alban Francis case, with the Mint in his fight with the Lord of the Tower, he now transferred to the Society. His fierce sense of independence made intolerable the location of the Royal Society, with its museum, meeting room, and library, in the building of Gresham College, where they were subject to the will and pleasure of the Mercers' Company. Moreover, some dissatisfaction had been expressed with their tenancy, and at one point it had required the intercession of the bellicose Dr. Woodward, who was a Gresham professor, to countermand an order to vacate the premises. Newton first tried in vain to obtain a royal grant for a new house, then toyed with a plan for a union of the Queen's Library, the Cotton Library, and the Royal Society, which Halifax supported in the Lords but which came to naught. Newton's final solution was to give the Society "a being of their own," as he phrased it, and he proceeded to find another site, a Dr. Brown's house at 2 Crane Court. Newton threw himself into the business with gusto, haggling over the price, and both Wrens were drawn in to pronounce judgment on the soundness of the structure. Once Newton had made the decision to move, he precipitately called together a meeting of the Fellows, arrogantly refused to explain the reasons for the impending change, "which he did not think proper to be given there," and went ahead despite opposition and in the face of general perplexity as to why the members had been assembled. Like many a modern administrator, he sought democratic assent to his decisions and was resentful when it was not forthcoming. An anonymous pamphlet published after the event records the "surprising Convulsion"—one of the more turbulent episodes of Newton's reign that underscores his arbitrariness in the exercise of power. When dissident Fellows who questioned the wisdom of purchasing the Crane Court house asked for a vote on the matter, the President resorted to a parliamentary maneuver and suddenly raised a doubt about whether a proper meeting had been constituted. "To some of those who had seen with what Resolution, (tho' without any Countenance from the Statutes, or from the Practice of any former *President,* of how great Quality soever,) he had run up the Authority of the Chair (almost every Week for some Months together) in the foregoing Spring (tho' if my Information be right, not once to any of the Just and Wise Ends of his Office) this suddain Scrupulosity was a Subject of Mirth; but to others, a real Grief and Concern, for the condition of that Society, that languish'd under so partial Administration." At a subsequent meeting there were even livelier protests and "some warmth" in the President's answers, until he silenced the Fellows with a decision from the Attorney General that the governance of the Society rested solely in the hands of the Council.[35]

Newton wanted the Society to have a "being of their own," but he equated that being with *his* being. In abandoning the old quarters, he broke completely with the epoch during which Robert Hooke had controlled the Society. As it happened, in the process of transferring from Gresham College, Hooke's portrait—the only one in existence—and many of his instruments disappeared forever.[36] To spruce up Crane Court, the portraits of the other Fellows, Newton commanded, were to be cleaned and identified in gold letters.

When in 1705 Queen Anne knighted the yeoman's son Isaac Newton, the first scientist to be so honored, in a formal ceremony at Trinity College, the bond between science and the Crown was given symbolic representation. For Newton this was a great personal triumph, staged in the College where he had once performed menial duties as a subsizar. In issuing a charter to the Royal Society and in founding the Royal Observatory, Charles II had expressed an interest in the advantages that might accrue to the kingdom through the promotion of scientific discoveries. Under Newton, Master of the Mint and dominant figure of British science, a much closer link was forged between science and the government than had ever existed be-

fore. Since he was frequently summoned by the Lords of the Treasury in his capacity as Master of the Mint, the leading scientist was
no longer looked upon as a closeted Cambridge experimenter, but
as a part of the governmental mechanism. Though his fixing of the
gold standard in 1717 was a function of his office at the Mint, it was
not alien to his long metallurgical and alchemical experiments. Newton always managed to capitalize on his past experience, however remote from current concerns it might appear; nothing seems to have
been lost. Once a member of the government, he began to appear at
court. He was consulted by Caroline, the Princess of Wales, about
the education of her children, and it was to her that he gave the first
copy of his revision of chronology. There are officious little notes to
Sloane instructing him to appear a quarter of an hour early in the
"Ante-Chamber on the Princes side" before a formal reception of the
officers of the Society.[37] Scientific events became matters of national
interest. The intrusion of George I into the Leibniz controversy—
in one case reviewing a reply of Newton's to Leibniz before it was
sent off—even if his purpose was *méchant,* is indicative of the new
status of science.

The Leibniz controversy brought the Royal Society and its President before the eyes of European aristocrats. Those who could not
understand Newton's works were at least able to enjoy the exchange
of insults. The very notoriety of the quarrel gave prestige to science
as the King, his mistress, Princess Caroline, and the whole diplomatic corps took part in reviewing the documents in the case, expressing their opinions of the appropriate tactics to be employed in
its settlement. When science and the Royal Society became fashionable, foreign ambassadors sought membership as one might to an
exclusive club, and many more were admitted in Newton's day than
ever before. The snob in him was not averse to their presence. On
occasion the yeoman's son presided at Royal Society meetings sur-
rounded by European ambassadors like a monarch holding court.
The *Journal Book* describes the occasion when Signor Grimani, the
Venetian Ambassador, Signor Gerardini, Envoy from the Grand

Duke of Tuscany, and the Duke d'Aumont, Ambassador Extraordinary of France, were there together, entertained with experiments on "The productiveness of light by friction; The mutual attraction of the parts of matter . . . preparations . . . of the veins and arteries of a human liver."[38] Newton became a major source of national pride among important segments of the upper classes. In hundreds of eulogies while he was still alive he was hailed as the glory of the English nation, and his science was saluted as an exemplification of the national genius. As a scientist Newton remained an Englishman, and when he was named foreign associate of the French Academy of Sciences he allowed it to be known that he "contemned the distinction," much to the embarrassment of the French.[39]

If in the previous generation the religious nature of scientific inquiry had been given fervid expression—and to the very end science remained for Newton a worship of God—the utility of science was now recognized not only in philosophical works like Bacon's and formal apologies like those of Sprat and Joseph Glanvill, but in practical state measures. As if Marx had been stood on his head, Newton, having devoted the first half of his creative years to the development of a magnificent intellectual superstructure, turned in his latter days to its substructure. In 1709 he accepted offices in the societies of the Mines Royal and the Mineral and Battery Works.[40] Having already given advice on curriculum reform of the Mathematical School at Christ's Hospital in 1694,[41] he turned to plans for reorganizing university education, with greater emphasis on science and upright conduct.[42] The Royal Society became royal not only in name but in fact. It was represented on any governmental body which might remotely be involved with a scientific question; and its advice was sought on any parliamentary bill that concerned invention. Stukeley was proud of the new status: "The Government, the great Council of the nation, paid a distinguished regard to their judgment in all matters of public utility."[43] The relations between the Society and the state were reciprocal. On February 7, 1713, Bolingbroke informed the Fellows that henceforward Her Majesty's envoys to foreign parts would promote the design for which the Society was founded by gathering information and answering inquiries that might be addressed to them by the scientists. (Among the innocent first fruits of this union of science and the state was the despatch to the Society of a giant's tooth discovered near Albany on the Hudson.)[44] Honorific appointments to the Society could serve the simple economic interests of the nation and its traders in foreign parts. Prince Alexander Menshikov, an adviser to Peter the Great, was elected a Fellow on July 29, 1714, at the request of English merchants who sought concessions in Muscovy. And Newton in his own hand carefully prepared three drafts of the letter in response to the Russian nobleman's acceptance, a correspondence that is florid with love for science and humanity.[45]

Charles II was moved to found the Royal Observatory because, in criticizing a charlatan's solution to the problem of longitudes, Flamsteed had pointed out how faulty existing star catalogues were. To say that the growing British Empire was anxious over safe navigation and the prevention of losses at sea is to labor the obvious. The Royal Navy, the merchants of London, and the ships' captains themselves were all vitally concerned. After a petition had been presented to Parliament in May 1714 asking that an award be offered for the discovery of the longitude, a vast committee was appointed with the power to send for persons, papers, and records. Newton appeared at the hearing flanked by his aides Clarke, Halley, and Cotes as might a scientific administrator in a present-day inquiry.[46] The event presages hundreds of similar confrontations between parliamentary committees and the new elite of science. The aged Newton was especially honored with a seat near the committee chairman, and though he would have preferred to limit himself to the scientific analysis of alternative ways of proceeding with the discovery of the longitude, which he read from a prepared paper, neither the chairman nor the committee, it seems, would move the bill until the oracle of science would say that one of the methods currently proposed was likely to be useful. William Whiston, among many other

longitudinarians—as Arbuthnot satirized the profusion of inventors
—had a plan of his own about which Newton was unenthusiastic;
and it was only with great reluctance that he permitted a few words
to be extracted to the effect that Whiston's method might be useful
near the shores. Thereupon a bill passed the committee and the Parliament offering twenty thousand pounds, a huge sum, for a practical
method of determining longitude within half a degree, and a Board
of Longitude was established to sit in judgment on the various proposals and allocate the awards for a full or partial solution. Newton
was of course appointed a member of the Board, and he continued
to receive schemes for the solution of the problem and to evaluate all
of them negatively. The failure of the Board to establish clear-cut
procedures annoyed him and he expressed himself in no uncertain
terms about their incompetence. In a note to the Lords of the Ad-
miralty he intimated that there was not much point in the Board's
meeting until his lunar theory had been made more exact.[47]

Though prominent Fellows of the Society like Arbuthnot had
written about the manifold uses of mathematics for military as well
as civil affairs, and had stressed the need for more widespread mathematical education among officers, Newton himself seems to have
been ambivalent about the scientists' participation in the development of military machines. David Gregory reports Newton's proposal to "cure the Bucking and wideness of touch-hole of great
Gunns" by means of a new metallurgical mixture,[48] another use of
his chemical experiments with alloys, but there is a contrasting story
to the effect that Newton was hostile to the application of science to
warfare. When the disciple's father, also named David, the laird of
Kinairdy, made an invention to improve artillery, Newton urged the
son to destroy the model on the ground that it would soon become
known to the enemy and that it tended to the annihilation rather
than the preservation of mankind.[49]

If scientists aided only sporadically in perfecting military weapons, they gave the government direct assistance in preventing public
disorders. The comet of 1680 had generated a wave of superstition.

In 1715, Halley as Secretary of the Society published a description and a map of the path of the eclipse before it happened on April 22, with a request that curious people note the time and duration of total darkness in their locality with a pendulum clock. What had once been a subject of terror was turned into a mass observation enterprise, whose success the Secretary proudly reported: "Our Astronomy has lost no Credit."[50] The utility of science to civil authority was thus dramatically demonstrated.

In the 1670's John Evelyn dined with Flamsteed, and with veneration referred to him as "the learned *Astrologer* & *Mathematician* whom now his Majestie had established in the new *Observatorie* in *Greenewich* Park, and furnish'd with the choicest Instruments. . . ," as if he were a magus at an Eastern court.[51] By the second decade of the eighteenth century, such individual scientific positions of prestige and influence were virtually eliminated. Newton had systematically consolidated science in one body and under one head, and curtailed the independence of separate scientific agencies. Around him a corporate scientific establishment with an authority of its own had taken shape. It did not enjoy munificent gifts from the Crown and its leading members were fairly independent economically, being supported by university posts or lucrative medical practices or ecclesiastical appointments. But despite its relative autonomy, the activities that involved science with the government were being constantly multiplied. Under Newton they were controlled.

By the early eighteenth century Newtonian science had acquired many faces, and it showed them all: for the young scholars it was a scientific philosophy; for the bishops it was a proof of the existence of God; for the merchants it offered the prospect of reducing losses at sea; for the King it was an embellishment of the throne; for aristocrats it was an amusement. It could be assimilated in many different forms—not excluding a *Newtonism for the Ladies*—[52] a protean quality that is almost a prerequisite for universalist doctrines. The science of Isaac Newton used some of the same mechanisms as a conquering new religion or political ideology in order to secure itself. It triumphed, a truth in its day, but it availed itself of the same apparatus as any other movement. Followers were assembled and bound to an apotheosized leader with ties of great strength. An internal institutional structure was fortified. And the word was propagated by chosen disciples. Since the doctrine was rooted in a national society, its relations with the government gave it special privileges and emoluments. It became the second spiritual establishment of the realm, and at least in its origins presented no threat to the primary religious establishment that it was destined to undermine, and perhaps ultimately to replace. As in many militant doctrinal movements, the truth was not allowed to fend for itself, and on occasion the sacred lie and the pious fraud became means to a higher end.

The content of Newtonian science would have prevailed without the personal force that Newton exerted. But with his extraordinary genius and energy, he was able to impose on the Western world a personal scientific style and a movement that reflected his character. There was validity in Leibniz' prognostication of the imminent decline of English science, for Newton's grip on the establishment did in fact stifle inventiveness for a time: the immediate followers were mere epigones. His great power as both the creator of a closed scientific world view and the organizer of its institutional framework has had analogies in both earlier and later generations and in other fields of endeavor—with similar consequences.

Of the events that established Newton's hegemony, the conflicts with Flamsteed and Leibniz were the most dramatic and the noisiest. The institutionalization of the Newtonian philosophy, like the victory of any great historical doctrine, required the slaughter of enemies both at home and abroad. The quarrels with Flamsteed and Leibniz, though they had earlier origins, really flared up during the period of Newton's presidency. By defeating Flamsteed, Newton established his unquestioned supremacy in the English scientific world; thereafter no competitor dared raise his head during Newton's lifetime. The Leibniz quarrel was the vindication of English science against the "continentals." Once the enemy from without was routed Newtonian science could reign supreme and uncontested, except for the rearguard actions of the French Cartesians.[53] The Leibniz issue was settled by the time Voltaire, that great propagator of the new faith, arrived in London, and his famous eulogy of Newton in the *Letters Concerning the English Nation* perhaps more than any other single document popularized and universalized Newton's image.[54] In *Elements of the Philosophy of Newton* Voltaire became the Paul to Newton's Christ, though it is doubtful that either Newton or Christ would have been satisfied with his respective apostle.

Chapter **14**

TWO HUMBLE SERVANTS
OF THE LORD

I have plowed sowed reaped brought in my Corne, with my own hired Servants & purchased Utensills. Sr I N. haveing been furnished from My Stores would have me thrash it all out my selfe & charitably bestow it on the publick that he may have the prayse of haveing procured it. I am very desirous to supply the Publick wth my Stores if it will but afford me what I have layd out in tillage and harvesting in Utensills & help. & afford me hands to work it up since the labor is both too hard & much for me. for an adequate recompense I doe not expect but I must stand upon a reasonable one since God has blest my labors with large fruites & not to doe it were not to acknowledge his goodness; & my Countries Ingratitude would be attributed, by Sr I N himselfe, to my *Stupidity.*

  —John Flamsteed, a manuscript of May 27, 1707

In the years after 1704, the zenith of his inventiveness long past, the President of the Royal Society was in prime shape for personal and scientific infighting, and he engaged simultaneously with Flamsteed on one flank and Leibniz on the other. There was a difference in the nature of the two contests. Though the battle with Leibniz struck at his vitals, the combatants never confronted each other in person, nor did they exchange insults except through intermediaries. Baroque pomp and circumstance presided over the conduct of the war and grand secular potentates witnessed the fray as amused spectators. Wrangling with Flamsteed—hardly an equal struggle, for the Royal Astronomer was regarded as an eccentric—was of another order.

The conflict between the two officers of the English Crown had a corrosive family intimacy, and their vociferous quarrels at the Royal Society, in the Greenwich Observatory, and in Newton's house afforded Newton an opportunity for the direct release of brutal rage upon another human being. After the turn of the century, intoxicated with power and authority in his dual capacity as Master of the Mint and President of the Royal Society, he allowed his angel of destruction, mightily armed, free rein. While the wearisome mutual recriminations of Newton and Flamsteed over a period of more than two decades are by no means an unprecedented example of science in the service of aggressive needs, Newton's vindictive pursuit of Flamsteed is perhaps more thoroughly documented than most. Unfortunately, as is usually the case, the victim is the one who chronicles the story of his sufferings over and over again, finding a modicum of relief in the obsessive recapitulation of his persecution.

Sixty-year-old John Flamsteed was not unlike Newton in character. He too had suffered a severe psychic trauma in childhood. The death of his mother when he was barely three was an event "my father could so well digest as to accept a second marriage," an acrid comment in his *Self-Inspections of J.F.*, completed when he was twenty-one.[1] A rheumatic ailment at fifteen caused a swelling of his limbs and left him a lifelong cripple. The anguish of his childhood is told by Thomas Hearne, the learned anecdotalist of the academic world. Flamsteed's father was a prosperous maltster, but since the deformed youth was the outcast of the family, he was relegated to carrying out malt with the brewing pan. To alleviate his pains—they made him bear the load on his back—he invented a special wheelbarrow; but this only encouraged his masters to increase the quantity borne away on each trip. Flamsteed came to regret ever having constructed the object, and in later life shrank from the very thought of it. In the pitiless manner of the age, Hearne jocularly described Flamsteed's exit from a tavern with some companions, his toppling into the wheelbarrow that he abominated, then rolling helplessly down the hill.[2] In 1665 Flamsteed journeyed to Ireland to be stroked by the famous Mr. Valentine Greatrackes (the same healer who had been summoned to cure Henry More's friend Lady Conway), but his disability persisted until death.

Once freed from his boyhood servitude, Flamsteed was possessed by a driving passion for the works of science, whose biblical justification he set down at the opening of his autobiography with religious fervor.

God suffers not man to be idle, although he swim in the midst of delights; for when He had placed His own image (Adam) in a paradise so replenished (of his goodness) with varieties of all things, conducing as well to his pleasure as sustenance, that the earth produced of itself things convenient for both,— He yet (to keep him out of idleness) commands him to till, prune, and dress his pleasant verdant habitation; and to add (if it might be) some lustre, grace, or conveniency to that place which, as well as he, derived its original from his Creator. We may suppose man, in his innocency, did strictly prosecute the just injunctions of his Divine Creator; and Scripture shows us that he did retain the pleasure of this gorgeous habitation, till, striving to equal his Creator in knowledge, he lost the pleasure of his paradise, together with the presential knowledge of his Creator. Man's active soul had acted now too far to gain by a recession what his over-active inquisitiveness had induced on him; for he ejected from his pleasant habitation his children, made heirs of the fruits of his fall; and the earth (which formerly produced, of its own accord, sufficient for human necessity) is cursed for his sake, that he might earn his bread forth of his labour, and keep himself from worse employment by his necessary action: for we, who are Adam's heirs by birth, observe that those are generally worst employed who have least to do; and idleness is the prodrome of other evils.[3]

One of the first astronomers to conduct extensive telescopic observations, Flamsteed scanned the heavens through the long, cold nights for half a century as a form of divine service.

The call to astronomy came early. After trying his hand at judicial astrology, as Newton had, he concluded that this study afforded only "conjectural hints," not "perfect declarations"; and for the rest of his life he consecrated himself to tracking the course of celestial bodies, priding himself on his accuracy and distrustful of high-flown theory. As a youthful astronomer self-taught from the almagests of the previous century, he prepared papers that were applauded by the Royal Society. At twenty-four, when he visited London, he was sufficiently respected to be shepherded about the city by Oldenburg and John Collins, the midwives of science. In 1670 a patron appeared in the person of Sir Jonas Moore, the Master of Ordnance, and only then did Flamsteed enter Jesus College, Cambridge. His first observations were published at about the same time that Newton was becoming known for his theory of colors. They were of the same scientific generation in the Royal Society, the first after the founders.

During this period, scientific correspondence among equals was a dangerous game in which elements of cooperation and rivalry were delicately balanced. The participants remained in communication with one another in order to discover what was being accomplished, but were leery lest they divulge more than they learned. Players in this match of wits often ended up complaining that they had been duped, each claiming he had been frank, open, and generous while his opposite number had been guarded and secretive, withholding knowledge. Not all scientists had kindred personalities. Sir Christopher Wren shared his scientific hypotheses casually, since his main interests lay elsewhere; and Leibniz, at least at one time, was rather profligate with his discoveries. Some were not consistent in temper throughout their lives: scientific spendthrifts in their youth, they might become close and tight with age, a rather common regression. Great combats among the old ones often centered around what had happened decades earlier, and men who had once been easygoing and debonair about their work during creative periods now rummaged among their papers, claiming priority in what would not have concerned them in the vigor of their manhood. It could happen that the worth or significance of an early invention was not recognized until years later by the author himself, after others had further developed its consequences. Men whose characters were wary and suspicious, who were retentive, furtive, and afraid of being deceived, were readily given to fantasies that others were plotting to rob them of their ideas. John Flamsteed doubtless fell into this category. As early as November 1673, in a letter to his friend Richard Townley, he was firmly resolved that Giovanni Domenico Cassini, the Italian astronomer who had been invited to the Paris Observatory, would not get any data from him but on terms of "commutation."[4] Since scientific relationships were patterned after other social forms, the scientists behaved at once like businessmen bargaining about their wares, aristocratic heroes competing in a tourney, and servants of the Lord vying for favor in the eyes of God the Father through their strenuous exertions. In a society where the scientist's role was still ill-defined, complex and what might appear to be contradictory motives strove for supremacy in the same person.

Having acquired a master's degree at Cambridge on June 5, 1674, Flamsteed had intended to settle down in a living in his native Derby, when the idea of a royal observatory was urged upon the King by Sir Jonas Moore, Christopher Wren, and Robert Hooke. They agreed upon Greenwich Castle for the site, and Flamsteed was appointed King's Astronomer with an allowance of one hundred pounds a year. Charles II's warrant of June 2, 1675, for the establishment of the Royal Greenwich Observatory stressed its practical uses: "In order to the finding out of the longitude of places for perfecting navigation and astronomy, we have resolved to build a small observatory within our park at Greenwich." Sir Christopher Wren was the architect and the Master of Ordnance directed the construction.[5] After taking holy orders Flamsteed departed for Greenwich equipped to serve both great masters, God and the King. Flamsteed later married, and supplemented the modest royal subsidy with a living at Burstow where he turned up only to bury prominent members of his flock. Thomas Hearne commented sarcastically that "whilst he gazes at the Heavens he neglects to conduct the Souls of his Parishioners thither."[6]

With instruments mostly provided by Sir Jonas Moore, Flamsteed undertook to revise all the tables of the heavenly bodies then in use, to rectify the places of the fixed stars, chiefly those near the ecliptic and "in the Moon's way," he wrote Dr. Seth Ward, the Savilian Professor of Astronomy at Oxford.[7] There was no nobler mission for an astronomer and a divine than the revelation of the absolute truth about God's firmament, cleansing the knowledge of His creation of the flaws, errors, and half-truths of predecessors who had been negligent in their calling, or who had not enjoyed the advantage of the telescope. Flamsteed executed some twenty thousand observations between September 1675 and 1689. With a servant and an "ingenious youth or two" he repeated his observations over and over again. His constant struggle to acquire new instruments raises doubts about the zeal with which the government supported the new science in the 1670's, though they were as aware of its utility for navigation as he was of its sacred purpose.

Reverend Flamsteed's relations with the Royal Society were variable: he was elected a member on February 8, 1677, and he twice served on the Council. During the contest with Newton he allowed his subscription to lapse, and on November 9, 1709, his name was removed from the list of Fellows. A portrait in the Royal Society shows him in his clergyman's gown, a lean face dominated by piercing eyes, with a long prominent nose, a firm chin, a hard mouth—an embittered, intransigent man.

Flamsteed had become acquainted with Newton in the early 1670's. Their relationship at first was amicable, and Flamsteed furnished Newton with many astronomical observations, for which he was later thanked in the *Principia*. In the early months of 1681 an infelicitous incident occurred. Observations on the great comet of November 1680 led Flamsteed to report that the same body which had aroused terror throughout Europe had reappeared after passing the sun. His "brother Mr. Newton," in a friendly controversy, had insisted that there were two different comets. One rarely proved Newton wrong; if one did, retribution, though it might be long delayed, ultimately followed, as both Hooke and Flamsteed learned. For his part Flamsteed kept a careful record of Newton's error and gleefully recalled it decades later in writing to his friend Abraham Sharp.[8]

When in 1705 Flamsteed recapitulated in his notes the events of the 1680's, his jealousy of Newton's triumphs and anger at what he regarded as ingratitude were unconcealed: "1687. His *Principia* published. Little notice taken of Her Majesty's observatory (with very slight acknowledgments of what he had received from the observatory)."[9] By September 1689 Flamsteed had constructed and paid for new instruments—beginning with a seven-foot sextant, he had now acquired a mural quadrant—and from then on his observations attained a level of accuracy unequaled elsewhere in Europe. At this point the interests of the two great English scientists clashed, with little prospect of an easy resolution, over a problem of celestial mechanics translated into human terms: Around whom did the universe revolve? If with Hooke the bone of contention had been the value of an initial scientific insight relative to a mathematically worked out theory, with Flamsteed it was the overall worth of empirical observation relative to theory.

Flamsteed has left many versions of his extended disputes with Newton in diaries and letters, all reasonably consistent with one another. Newton by comparison is silent, though each time he intervenes in public he crushes his opponent. Flamsteed's complaints rose in a crescendo from annoyance that Newton had been niggardly in public acknowledgment of the data he had received from the Observatory, to denunciations of Newton's betrayal in communicating the observations to Halley, to invoking divine punishment upon the transgressor. A suspicious and hypersensitive man, Flamsteed was adept at building elaborate causal structure systems to explain other people's conduct. Obstinate, gnawed by the feeling that he was being persecuted, fiercely independent, terrified lest someone dominate him, he had a sharp and bitter tongue that inflicted injuries where they hurt most. The violent men of wrath, Newton and Flamsteed, always saw themselves aggrieved victims at the very moment when they were delivering the deadliest blows. Quick to discern the signs of a breach of control in each other, they had a way of exacerbating each other's irritability. These depression-prone men habitually employed sarcasm, tearing flesh like dogs, to invoke the meaning of the ancient Greek word. Their self-esteem was fragile—both had sustained incurable wounds in childhood—and they were acutely sensitive to each other's abuse.

At the height of his power Newton behaved toward Flamsteed, four years his junior, his younger brother in the Royal Society, as though he were a menial; and he made no effort to hide his condescension, if not his contempt. This was no schoolboy who was being maltreated, but a member of the Royal Society Council with an extensive correspondence among European scholars, the author of more than twoscore papers in the *Philosophical Transactions,* a man who had devised novel methods of observation and was among the first to use an accurate timepiece and optical means for determining stellar coordinates. While Tycho Brahe, the great Danish astronomer who died in the year 1601, had operated within one degree of accuracy, Flamsteed ultimately reduced errors to the order of ten seconds, a measure of his revolutionary achievement. Flamsteed was as arrogant as Newton, and he dared to talk back to the President of the Royal Society, even to criticize the *Principia,* unpardonable sins. The astronomer boasted that he had provided Newton with the refined gold, his observations, which Newton fashioned into wire. Or he compared his work to the building of St. Paul's: "I had hew'd the Materials out of the Rock, brought them together & formed them but that hands & Time were to be allowed to perfect the building & Cover it." Flamsteed's phrases still rang in Newton's ears when he was a very old man—he never forgot a slight—and Conduitt reports his belated rebuttal: "If Flamsteed dug the ore he [Newton] had made the gold ring."[10] Newton looked upon Flamsteed as nothing more than a convenient source of data for his theories, a tool.

In the 1690's, after Newton had moved to London, he grew dissatisfied with the speed at which lunar observations and calculations were despatched to him from the Greenwich Observatory and offered to pay Flamsteed's servant to copy more diligently,[11] an interference which the Royal Astronomer resented. At one point Flamsteed misinterpreted Newton's promise to gratify him for his pains —by which he meant that he would impart to him the lunar theory as soon as it was completed—as an offer of money, and he was sorely offended at the affront to an independent laborer in the vineyard of the Lord.[12] Despite a relationship of three decades during which Flamsteed had transmitted as many data as his physical handicaps would allow him to accumulate and his retentive character permit him to surrender, Newton's letters became peremptory. Flamsteed always responded in kind—surreptitiously in a diary, in a note scribbled on the face of the insulting letter, in correspondence to his confidant Abraham Sharp, or, when there was occasion, in person. And Flamsteed knew how to shake his adversary: sanctimonious Newton was called venal, virtually an embezzler, and it was intimated that pious Newton's niece, who lived under his roof, was a fallen woman.[13]

Flamsteed had first justified his reluctance to publish his unfinished astronomical data in a letter to Newton on February 24, 1692, when they were still friendly. Humble servant of the Lord, he felt it his duty to proceed with his observations of the constellations as long as he had strength, rather than consume a year transcribing for the press what he had already finished in order "to gain a little present reputation."[14] Flamsteed was being taunted into premature publication by Edmond Halley's mockery,[15] to which he replied with open insults and outright accusations of irreligion.[16] Against young Halley, who had devoted his person and his fortune to the publication of the *Principia,* he wrote Newton a blistering attack: "I have no esteem of a man who has lost his reputation both for skill candor & Ingenuity by silly tricks ingratitude & foolish prate . . . I value not all or any of the shams of him and his Infidel companions being very well satisfied that if Xt and his Appostles were to walk againe upon earth, they should not scape free from the calumnies of their venomous tongues. . . ."[17] Though Flamsteed did not quite believe that he was Jesus Christ he was willing to allow the analogy. The confrontation of a number of Christs in one asylum has been studied by clinicians. Newton and Flamsteed, neither of them psychotic, enacted a similar tragi-comedy on the broader stage of the English scientific world.

For many years Newton avoided taking sides openly in the hostilities between Halley and Flamsteed, both of whom had served him well, and voiced a wish that they might be reconciled;[18] but in the end, since he had to choose between the two astronomers, he could hardly have been expected to prefer a pretentious, critical coeval to the younger man who adored him. Halley, a precocious genius ten years Flamsteed's junior, had once worked at Greenwich with the Royal Astronomer, and in some records their observations are intermingled.[19] Subsequently, he had undertaken a hazardous voyage to St. Helena, where he had plotted the stars of the southern hemisphere and published his findings. He was witty, strikingly attractive as the Royal Society portrait of him as a young man shows, adventuresome, outgoing, a scholar, a drinking man, the sort of person whose rumored affairs with women were the subject of talk at the University.[20] Flamsteed was always on the qui vive lest any of his new Greenwich Observatory data be communicated to Halley when Newton was discussing his new moon theory with him. Halley had once been accused by Flamsteed of buying the papers of Peter Perkins, the Mathematical Master of Christ's Hospital, and publishing material from them as his own—this was at least one of the sources of the bad blood between them. (A modern scientist who has since examined both Halley's paper in the *Philosophical Transactions* and Peter Perkins' manuscripts in the Royal Society considers the charge of plagiarism preposterous.)[21] From the mid-eighties on, there had been a submerged animosity between Halley and Flamsteed that from time to time erupted in charges that they had stolen each other's observations. In Flamsteed's private notes Halley is referred to as "Raymer," the perfidious Nicolaus Raymarus who had disparaged Tycho Brahe after having enjoyed his hospitality.

Beginning in 1694 Newton became increasingly exigent, assuring Flamsteed that when the moon theory was finally published he would be at least as generous in praising the accuracy of Flamsteed's new observations as he had been in the *Principia*—no act of largesse to the astronomer, who considered the thanks perfunctory. It was Newton's plan at this time to announce the theory with Flamsteed's hitherto unpublished observations as empirical support. "For all the world knows," Newton soothed him on February 16, 1695, "that I make no observations my self & therefore I must of necessity acknowledge their Author: *And if I do not make a handsome ac-*

knowledgment, they will reccon me an ungratefull clown." Newton cannily appealed to Flamsteed's self-interest, confronting him with the alternatives of allowing him to publish the observations along with the theory or face the void of oblivion.

And for my part I am of opinion that for your Observations to come abroad thus with a *Theory wch you ushered into the world* & wch by their means has been made exact would be much more for their advantage & your reputation then to keep them private till you dye or publish them wthout such a Theory to recommend them. For such a Theory will be a demonstration of their exactness & make you readily acknowledged the Exactest Observer that has hitherto appeared in the world. But if you publish them wthout such a Theory to recommend them, they will only be thrown into the heap of the Observations of former Astronomers till somebody shall arise that by perfecting the Theory of the Moon shall discover your Observations to be exacter then the rest. But when that shall be God knows: I fear not in your life time if I should dye before tis done. For I find this Theory so very intricate & the Theory of Gravity so necessary to it, that I am satisfied it will never be perfected but by somebody who understands the Theory of gravity as well or better then I do. But whether you will let me publish them or not may be considered hereafter. *I only assure you at present that without your consent I will neither publish them nor communicate them to any body whilst you live, nor after your death without an honourable acknowledgment of their Author.*[22]

This was an unequivocal promise which Newton had already made once before by inscribing on the inside of the back cover of Flamsteed's leather "Diarium Observationum": "Sept. 1. 1694. Received then of Mr fflamsteed two sheets MS of the places of the Moon observed & calculated for years 89 90 & part of 91 wch I promise not to communicate without his consent." Both promises were later broken.[23]

The flattery and cajolery of Newton's letter, practices in which he rarely indulged, as well as the pointed threat that Flamsteed was jeopardizing his own fame by recalcitrance, completely missed their mark. Newton's definition of the relationship made Flamsteed's reputation derive from *him,* an intolerable condition for a man with Flamsteed's fear of dependency. Flamsteed conceived of their partnership the other way around. As he noted on Newton's letter, theories were only probable, whereas the observations themselves were absolute truth; Newton was therefore dependent upon *him*. "He adds a great many words to persuade me that to have the theory of the moon published with my observations, would be a great proof of their accuracy: whereas theories do not commend observations; but are to be tried by them. . . ."[24]

By June 1695, Newton's letters began to show first testiness and then anger at Flamsteed's dilatoriness. He was curt: "I want not your calculations but your Observations only."[25] He spoke ominously of dropping the whole "moon's theory," setting the blame squarely on Flamsteed's shoulders, a recrudescence of the childish petulance he had displayed when Hooke accused him of plagiarism. Just as he had then decided to suppress the third book of the *Principia*—he would not play except on his own terms—he now was prepared to scuttle the moon theory. Eleven days later, on July 9, his ire was still rising: in Flamsteed's three important works he had helped him when he was "stuck" and had communicated matters that were *"of more value then many Observations."* He had been operating on a quid pro quo basis in the exchange and had kept his side of the bargain.[26] Flamsteed's private notes in their turn bristled with a cumulative resentment at the denigration of his observations. He had, moreover, been ill with severe pains in the head. Newton's letter was called "hasty artificiall unkind arrogant."[27] But Newton, for his part, chose to ignore Flamsteed's recriminations; if he suffered from headaches he should follow the example of one Dr. Batteley who used to "bind his head strait with a garter till the crown of his head was nummed."[28]

Once Newton moved to the Mint, Flamsteed began to see enemies everywhere in the Warden's entourage, imputing whatever they did to venality and ambition because of their proximity to Montague. "Dr Gregory is a freind of Mr. Halleys," Flamsteed wrote on the cover of a letter from Dr. Wallis dated December 28, 1698, "tho he was his competitor [over an Oxford professorship] . . .

he is no freind of mine tho I shewd him more freindship then he could reasonably expect on that occasion & Mr Halley as much enmity but he thinkes Mr Halley has an Interest in Mr Newton, & therefore is become his freind, & takes the same courses Hawley did to Ingratiate with him whose favour may be of use to him with Mr. Montague."[29]

Smoldering antagonism between them flared up when Newton wrote Flamsteed a harsh letter on January 6, 1699. Nothing could be so calculated to arouse Newton's indignation as an announcement about a theory that he was in the process of developing prior to his own decision to make it public. He would not countenance Flamsteed's intimation in a letter Dr. Wallis planned to publish in Latin that Newton was working on a lunar theory, even though the "hint" was only an oblique remark that Flamsteed had been transmitting to him observations on the moon from the Observatory. Newton had no desire to expose himself and he spelled out his grounds: what if the theory never materialized, would not people say he had not succeeded? There is a memorandum in almost identical terms about warning Pepys not to spread abroad Newton's ideas for determining longitudes at sea lest he fail to find a solution; and Newton pressed Halley to quash any rumors among Fellows of the Royal Society that he was even occupied with the problem.[30] Newton could not endure public defeat in any matter, scientific or political. (In 1702, he refused to stand for Parliament from the University because his London concerns would have left him little time for campaigning; to "solicit and miss for want of doing it sufficiently, would be a reflection upon me, and it's better to sit still."[31]) As an official at the Mint he had further reason to be secretive, for people might say he was not devoting all of his energies to the recoinage and the pursuit of clippers and counterfeiters. The January letter to Flamsteed was acidulous and authoritarian. If the Royal Astronomer wanted to gain some renown by publishing a few rectifications in Newton's system of the world let him go ahead, but he would not be pushed into revealing his lunar theory. He was in the right and he laid down the law.

I do not love to be printed upon every occasion much less to be dunned & teezed by forreigners about Mathematical things or to be thought by our own people to be *trifling* away my time about them when I should be about the Kings business. And therefore I desired Dr Gregory to write to Dr Wallis against printing that clause wch related to that Theory & mentioned me about it. You may let the world know if you please how well you are stored with observations of all sorts & what calculations you have made towards rectifying the Theories of the heavenly motions: But there may *be cases* wherein your friends should not be published without their leave. And therefore I hope you will so order the matter that I may not on this occasion be brought upon the stage.[32]

Flamsteed reported to Dr. Wallis the receipt of this "very Artificiall" communication from Newton, and agreed to alter the offensive paragraph as he had been instructed.[33] He then proposed to circulate Newton's letter and his own reply among his correspondents. Anyone who executed this sort of maneuver against Newton was laying down the gauntlet and inviting punishment. Flamsteed's answer to Newton was bitter and defiant. He wrote as an equal unimpressed by Newton's exalted political position. Like a paranoid, he even discovered insults where none were intended. He was overinterpreting when he read the word *trifling* as a snide reference to his own work as an astronomical observer, for Newton in that passage was chiefly worried about popular criticism of his neglect of the job at the Mint. Both men were profoundly religious and their works were dedicated to God as a worship. But they were also deeply concerned with what men thought about them, since they lived in a hostile world rendered even more nasty and brutish by their imaginings. Two troubled creatures, one the son of a tradesman, the other the son of a yeoman, now great officers of the Crown and rivals for world fame, they acted out their scientific roles in different ways. Newton felt it incumbent upon him to conceal his researches because he was being paid by the Crown as an administrator. Flamsteed was smarting under the accusation—he never could endure Halley's raillery—that after decades of observation he had not yet produced a great work consolidating his findings, in the tradition of Tycho Brahe and Hevelius. He had seized the opportunity of the "Letter to Wallis" to proclaim that he too had a part in Newton's achievement. Scientific glory was a rather new kind of fame and the contenders did not wholly understand how to divide its rewards.

Throughout Flamsteed's reply to Newton on January 10, 1699, Halley looms in the background as the evil one misleading the good Newton, a friend of younger days whom Reverend Flamsteed might still save from perdition. Flamsteed had done no more than let the world know that the Observatory had furnished Newton with about a hundred fifty places with which to correct the lunar theory, at a time when Halley was freely boasting at the Society and in taverns that Newton had completed the theory and had imparted the great secret to him. How could Flamsteed's act have in any way discomfited Newton since he was merely alluding to what one of his own retinue had already been trumpeting? As for his harassment by curious foreigners, Flamsteed exculpated himself in a direct and forthright manner, putting the blame squarely on "those who think to recommend themselves to you by advanceing the fame of your works, as much as they possibley can." He admitted that he had told scientists the lunar theory required further observations for its perfection; but when they had regarded him as carping, he had become silent. He was deeply hurt at what he conceived to be Newton's denigration of his work as an astronomer, and pictured himself as the tolerant, long-suffering, forgiving Christian who would continue to fulfill his duty despite the wrongs that had been done him.

I wonder that *hints* shoud drop from your pen, as if you Lookt on my business as *trifling* You thought it not soe surely when you resided at Cambridge it's property is not altered; I think it has produced somthing considerable allready & may doe more if I can but procure help to work up the observations I have under my hands *which is one of the designs of my Letter to Dr Wallis was to move for,* I doubt not but it will be of some use to our ingenious travellers and saylers; and other persons, that come after me, will think their time as Little mispent in these Studyes, as those did that have gon before me. The works of the Eternall Providence I hope will be a little better understood through your Labours & mine, then they were formerly. think me not proud for this expression, I Look on pride as the worst of sins, Humility as the greatest virtues, this makes me excuse small faults in all mankind bear great injurys without resentment & resolve to maintain a reale friendship with ingenious men to assist them what Lies in my power without the regard of any interest but that of doeing good by obliging them. . . .[34]

Flamsteed was possessed by ambivalent feelings toward Newton, which produced the admixture of heavy sarcasm and the mouthings of Christian forbearance. There was a tinge of admiration, perhaps even unrequited love, as well as hate. Writing to Sir Christopher Wren on March 28, 1700, Flamsteed again made overtures to Newton: he tried to lure Wren and Newton to Greenwich together where both might examine his papers and perhaps procure him some assistance for publication, which now interested him. He extolled Wren and Newton as the only men with any comprehension of his work.[35] But within several weeks he changed his tune, warning his friend and colleague in the Royal Society, John Lowthorp, to be cautious in his behavior toward Newton. In reporting on a recent hostile personal encounter, Flamsteed recast his conception of their relationship so that Newton's real purpose appeared to be obstructing the independent printing of his lunar observations lest their publication detract from the complete novelty of Newton's theory. At their meeting in Newton's house—our only account is Flamsteed's—they parried. When Flamsteed talked of publishing a "book of tables," Newton "started" and asked "what tables," and if he would publish any for the moon. "My answer was, that she was in his hands, and, if he would finish her, I would lend him my assistance; if not, I would fall upon her myself when I had leisure, and I doubted not of good success; but that the tables I intended were such as I made use of for deducing the places of the stars and planets from my observations with more than usual expedition, and some others that would be of good use. Hereupon he recollected himself and was calm."[36] Flamsteed constantly vacillated between his Christian duty as a clergyman to save Newton from the impious Halley and anger over Newton's conduct. "I believe him to be a good Man at the Bottom," he wrote to his friend Lowthorp, "but through his Naturall temper suspitious & too easy to be possesst with calumnies especially such as are imprest with Raillery."[37] Once, in pursuit of his clerical function as a director of conscience and a curer of souls, Flamsteed slyly acted out a little drama in Newton's house. He had got there before Newton was up, he reported with puritanical self-righteousness, and piously spent his time reading the Bible while he waited. Thoughts of Halley were rankling in him when he suddenly conceived of a way of freeing Newton from that pernicious influence. Taking a sheet of paper he wrote on it a distich from a satire he happened to remember:

> A bantering spirit our men possessed
> And wisdom is become a standing jest.

Then he counseled Newton to read the ninth chapter of Jeremiah up to the tenth verse, a diatribe against deceivers and liars. This piece of paper he left behind, presumably in the Bible, as an admonition. If only Newton would reflect upon what had been written he would find a "seasonable caution" against his credulity and would stop heeding Halley's calumnies. This would instruct him in "the way of the world" better than a play or all of his politics.[38]

In a postscript to the same long-winded letter to Lowthorp, Flamsteed referred to a conversation with an unnamed friend which, had it been reported back to Newton, was no more likely to endear Flamsteed to him than the little morality play that had been staged while Newton slept. The anonymous informant had relayed to Flamsteed the latest gossip from Oxford, that Newton's doctrine of gravity had been so perfected his lunar theory could be derived solely from it and he had no more need of Flamsteed's observations. To which Flamsteed rejoined with indignation that Newton had spent as much time on the moon's motions as he, Flamsteed, had on all the constellations and the planets put together. When Newton worked out lunar tables to fit his preconceived laws they did not square with the facts in the heavens; only after Flamsteed had sent him two hundred observations—the number changes continually—did Newton so alter his theory that it finally suited the observations. If his theory was now correct, it was because he had amended it to accord with the facts.

What Flamsteed was saying in effect was that the lunar theory was a mere derivation, the sort of insinuation Newton had already encountered in his dealings with Hooke in another context. Then, to cap his argument, Flamsteed compared Newton to the atheist Hobbes who had once boasted that his laws were agreeable to those of Moses. Obviously, said Flamsteed, since Hobbes had copied them from the Bible.[39]

Flamsteed's correspondence proudly recites his own foxy tactics in outwitting Newton's supporters. His loyal admirer and former assistant Abraham Sharp is the repository of what Flamsteed fancies to be intricate counterespionage procedures worthy of a wily Roman hero. "My business succeeds, I bless God for it, being well under my hands; but not at that rate that some people, out of a malicious design, represent it. They have emissaries, that understand nothing of the business, that sometimes visit me that they may give them an account of my pains, which they turn as they please. I receive them and use them as Scipio did Hannibal's spies, show them what they desire, dismiss them smiling; for I wish they understood all as well as they would be thought to do."[40] In a letter of July 30, 1702, to the Oxford mathematician John Caswell, he lashed out against Dr. Gregory's book *Elementa Astronomiae,* calling its criticisms of his work attempts to "kill" and "murder" him. As always the ultimate target is Newton, for Gregory was reckoned among his "darlings."[41]

Our most detailed consecutive account of the Newton-Flamsteed quarrel from 1704 to 1716, when it blazed in the open in the scientific and political world, is the "Original Preface" that was suppressed by the editors of Flamsteed's *Historia Coelestis* when the work appeared posthumously. It had been written by Flamsteed in February 1717, and concentrated on Newton's unremitting persecution of the author; one did not cast such aspersions upon the character of the divine Newton with impunity in 1725 and censorship was invoked. The preface presented a lurid picture of Newton as a power-lusting, lying, conniving, treacherous monster, using his influence at court and his intimacy with Lord Halifax to do Flamsteed out of his star catalogue, his money, his independent position as Royal Astronomer.

Flamsteed again depicted himself as a martyr whose devotion to science and the revelation of God's works would not allow him to issue an imperfect star catalogue, a man who was the object of a conspiracy in which hypocritical Newton and atheistical Halley were the prime movers. They had vied for the favor of the Prince of Denmark, Queen Anne's husband, and through chicanery had forced Flamsteed to surrender his manuscripts, making arrangements with booksellers that robbed him of his due, for the Prince had donated twelve hundred pounds for the publication. Flamsteed was the righteous man of God pursued by a political manipulator and a band of adulators constantly singing his praises. Since Flamsteed would not join them he had to be crushed, and each move in the long-drawn-out story of official intrigue was, in Flamsteed's reconstruction of events, consciously planned by the arch-villain.

Despite Flamsteed's obvious exaggerations, the account carries some conviction and cannot be dismissed as nothing more than his wild confabulation. Newton would brook no opposition and was quite capable of destroying a man who crossed him. Flamsteed's version of 1717 is, in much of its detail, corroborated by letters that he wrote to friends at the time the events were taking place, so that if he fantasied, he at least clung more or less closely to the frame of his original imaginings. Nothing in Newton's correspondence contradicts the facts presented, and extant manuscript drafts of agreements and royal orders, in Newton's hand, bolster Flamsteed's central contention that there were intricate behind-the-scenes manipulations and intrigues. In modern bureaucracies scientists are often adept in the art of the cabal, which they quickly learn from their political colleagues when the skill does not come naturally. There is no supporting evidence from independent sources of the evil intent and bad will imputed to Newton, nor any other witness of his vile language and outbursts of rage at formal meetings; these descriptions come from Flamsteed's reports alone. And yet the portrait, if its colors were toned down, would not entirely lack authenticity.

In the suppressed preface, Flamsteed reported that when he and Newton chanced to meet they continued to be civil to each other and that Newton always inquired about the progress of the star catalogue—"as if he were a great master of my methods." In reply the astronomer complained that he needed assistance to carry on his work; but no notice was taken of him until a friend informed Prince George, the royal consort, of his difficulty. Then, and only then, according to Flamsteed, did Newton bestir himself and begin to muscle in on the operation. He came down to Greenwich, examined the half of the catalogue that was finished, along with the books of observations and maps of the constellations that had already been drawn, and offered to recommend its publication to the Prince. Flamsteed was taken by surprise. Here was an attempt to put him in Newton's power and at his mercy. He had long been scrutinizing Newton's character and always found him "insidious, ambitious, and excessively covetous of praise, and impatient of contradiction." Flamsteed remembered the numerous occasions on which he had openly crossed Newton: his pointing out errors in the *Principia* had made Newton ask him why he did not hold his tongue, and his failure to conceal "some truths that are since published in print:, and notoriously known" had aroused ill will. Flamsteed politely declined the offer of Newton's intervention, fearing that once the catalogue was in his hands he would spoil it out of malice and inflate the significance of minor errors. But Newton insisted on talking to the Prince. He took his departure with a benevolent and superior bit of advice, "Doe all the good that lies in your power." When Flamsteed reconstructed this event, thirteen years later in February 1717, he had reason to append an acid comment: "which [advice] it would have been very happy for him if he had followed himself. It has been the rule of my life from my infancy; though I doe not hear that it ever has been of his."[42]

In this retrospective summation of his feelings there is much hindsight, for Flamsteed was writing after the star catalogue had been torn out of his hands at the Queen's command and printed with "distortions" under the direction of his arch-enemy Halley, after another order had placed the Observatory under the supervision of the Royal Society (which in effect meant under Newton's thumb), after Flamsteed had burned three hundred copies of this "false" star catalogue—every book he could lay his hands upon—and while he was desperately struggling in the face of old age and sickness to complete his own version, a work that appeared only after his death. The rumbling jealousy in Flamsteed's story persists to the end. He who had once been favored by Newton had been replaced by ignorant underlings who "understood no more of my works than they did of his book, which they so much cried up."

Flamsteed was moved by a deep dread that he would lose his manhood if he bowed to Newton's will. The images in which he described his predicament in the 1717 preface are graphic; many betray classical symptoms of paranoia.

[H]is design was . . . *to make me come under him* . . . force me to comply with his humours, and flatter him, and cry him up as Dr. G[regory] and Dr. H[alley] did. . . . He thought to work me to his ends by putting me to extraordinary charges. . . . [T]*hose that have begun to do ill things, never blush to do worse and worse to secure themselves.* Sly N had still more to do, and was ready at coining new excuses and pretenses to cover his disingenuous and malicious practices. I had none but very honest and honorable designs in my mind: I met his cunning forecasts with sincere and honest answers, and thereby frustrated not a few of his malicious designs. . . . I would not court him. . . . For, honest Sir Is. N. (to use his own words) would *have all things in his own power,* to spoil or sink them; that he might force me to second his designs and applaud him, which no honest man would do nor could do; and, God be thanked, I lay under no necessity of doing.[43]

Despite Flamsteed's wish to deal directly with the Prince, the Royal Society undertook to recommend the printing of the star catalogue to His Highness, who agreed to subsidize it—Newton so informed Flamsteed in a letter of December 18, 1704, signed "Your very loving friend."[44] For eight years thereafter the President of the Royal Society and the Royal Astronomer proceeded to wrestle for control of the publication. In the Flamsteed case Newton set the pattern for his behavior in the later stages of the Leibniz dispute. He ceased to operate individually and acted only through the agency of a Committee of Referees, nominally appointed by the Prince of Denmark from among the members of the Royal Society, Wren, Roberts, Aston, Gregory, and Arbuthnot, a number of whom would reappear in the committee that condemned Leibniz. In the course of protracted bargaining the committee tried to shackle Flamsteed with legal bonds by getting him to sign "articles," while he invented clever countertricks such as sending them "first night notes" of observations which they misinterpreted, to his unmasked delight. Under the date of November 8, 1704, Flamsteed recorded an example of the bickering about money and authority that characterized every stage of the negotiations between these hard men. "Mr. Newton told me he hoped I would give a note, under my hand, of security for the Prince's money. This I know was to oblige me to be his slave. I answered that I had (God be thanked) some estate of my own, which I hoped to leave, for my wife's support, to her during her life, to my own relations afterwards: that therefore I would not cumber my own estate with impress or security."[45]

If in 1705 there was a superficial accommodation between them, Flamsteed nevertheless remained on guard against Newton, as he wrote Abraham Sharp on the occasion of Newton's knighthood: "I was with him on Saturday last to wish him joy of his honor; he was more than usually gay and cheerful: but I well perceived the same temper that I had always found under it; and therefore took care to be no more open than formerly."[46] In November of that year, when Flamsteed was invited to Newton's house to dine with the Committee of Referees, he finally agreed, with emendations, to the conditions that Newton had drafted—there are many versions among the manuscripts—guaranteeing the respective rights and obligations of the referees, of Flamsteed, and of the printer. This was the last tolerably polite meeting that took place between them.[47]

Newton soon affected the crisp style of the government administrator, writing to Flamsteed on April 9, 1707, as he would to one of his hirelings at the Mint. "The Referees meet on Fryday next at four a clock in the afternoon in Pater-noster Row at the next Tavern to Mr Churchil the Bookseller. You will hear of them at Mr Churchils. I desire you would not fail to meet them because after the Queen returns to Windsor, they will scarce have an opportunity of meeting any more before next winter. And that all things may be now setled & adjusted, I desire that Mr Witty & your Emanuensis may be there & that you will bring your Bill & the three or four folio leaves of MS copy which you had from the Printer."[48]

On May 29, 1707, in the midst of the commotion, a cryptic, puzzling letter was sent by Flamsteed to Sharp. "Worthy Sir I. Newton has twice or thrice been stopping the press: he does all he can to hinder it, or break off, and to perplex me; but an accident has lately happened, that has discovered his proud and insolent temper, and exposes him sufficiently. He has been told calmly of his faults, and could not contain himself when he heard of them. My affair was not forgot. I hope God will turn all to good. This accident was unexpected: and seems to be sent. You shall hear more of it hereafter."[49] What were the "faults" that Newton was charged with and that so disturbed him? What was the providential "accident" to which Flamsteed referred? Was this merely Flamsteed's dream of vengeance? The technicalities of the printing, the stopping of the press because the observations—only part of which had been surrendered by Flamsteed—were condemned as "imperfect," the emendations by Halley, who had been brought in by the referees, and the ambiguities of translations of Ptolemy's star-places into a modern catalogue are a labyrinth of turnings and twistings.[50] Flamsteed was passionate in his outbursts, Halley flippant and witty, Arbuthnot the voice of common sense and reason, and Newton immovable. When there was a change of ministry Newton made a new demarche that forced Flamsteed against the wall. He got Secretary of State St. John (later Viscount) Bolingbroke to issue an order on December 12, 1710, appointing the President of the Royal Society and in his absence the Vice-President, together with "such other as the Council of the said Society shall think fit to join with them, to be constant *Visitors* of the Royal Observatory"[51]—a document for which there are numerous sketches in Newton's hand among his papers. From sometime in March 1711 there is an undated draft of a dire warning to Flamsteed that if he did not supply the rest of the observations for the catalogue he would be guilty of lèse-majesté, contravention of the

Queen's command.[52] At last Newton was "over him" and an explosion was inevitable. The tenacity of English institutions assured the survival of this board, first appointed under such inauspicious circumstances, until very recent years.[53]

In Flamsteed's running diary of the complicated negotiations there is a dramatic passage recounting how he was summoned before the Visiting Committee of the Royal Society and describing the scene that ensued, which quickly degenerated into a fishwives' quarrel. Flamsteed confessed to his own difficulties in remembering parts of the episode because he was so distraught, but even if the narrative is imprecise and confused it rings true. This is one of two closeups we possess of Newton the administrator in action—and the style is the same in both. In Crane Court at the new house of the Royal Society, on Friday, October 26, 1711, Flamsteed and Newton locked horns before witnesses like two old billy goats. Some five months before, it was rumored, Flamsteed had dared accuse Newton of embezzling some of the money provided by the Prince of Denmark for the printing of the British star catalogue. As in all these scientific quarrels, once hostilities were declared the combatants battered each other with any cudgels that lay at hand. The meeting assumed the form of an attempt to administer Royal Society rebuke and punishment: Newton wielded the rod, and obdurate Flamsteed refused to submit. After this clash—even if the diary exaggerates—Flamsteed had to be broken.

"Dr. Halley met me as I entered," Flamsteed relates,

and would have had me drink a dish of coffee with him. I refused: went straight up to the house: my man helped me up stairs, where I found Sir I. Newton, Dr. Sloane, and Dr. Mead. These three were all the Committee that I found there: and the two last, I well knew, were the assertors of the first, in all cases, right or wrong.

After a little pause, Sir I. Newton began; and told me that the Committee desired to know what repairs I wanted, or what instruments in the Observatory? I answered that my repairs were always made by the Office of the Ordnance: that I had applied myself to them; but the season of the year not being fit, it was thought best to forbear them till February next, when I doubted not they would be taken care of. As for the instruments, they were all my own; being either given to me absolutely by Sir Jonas Moore, or made and paid for out of my own pocket. This he well knows, though he dissembles it. He answered, "As good have no Observatory as no instruments." I gave him, hereupon, an account of Sir Jonas Moore's donation, in the presence of Mr. Colwall and Mr. Hanway his son-in-law: how he soon after died, and a controversy about his gift arising betwixt his son Sir Jonas, and myself, we had a hearing before the Board of the Office; whereat Mr. Colwall and Mr. Hanway both attested what I affirmed, that the instruments, books, goods, &c. were given me by Sir Jonas Moore. Whereupon he seemed much moved; and repeated what he had said before, "As good have no Observatory as no instruments;" asked Dr. Mead if it were not so, who assented. I proceeded from this to tell Sir Isaac (who was fired) that I thought it the business of their Society to encourage my labors, and not to make me uneasy for them. He asked Dr. Sloane what I said: who answered, that I said something about encouragement. Whereupon I told him that a frontispiece was engraved for my works, and the Prince's picture (without any notice given me of it), to present to the Queen: and that hereby I was *robbed of the fruits of my labors:* that I had expended above £2000 in instruments and assistance. At this, the impetuous man grew outrageous; and said, "We are, then, robbers of your labors?" I answered, I was sorry that they owned themselves to be so. After which, all he said was in a rage: he called me many hard names; puppy was the most innocent of them. I told him only that I had all imaginable deference and respect for Her Majesty's order, for the honor of the nation, &c.: but that it was a dishonor to the nation, Her Majesty, and that Society (nay, to the President himself), to use me so. At last, he charged me, with great violence (and repeated it), not to remove any instruments out of the Observatory: for I had told him before that, if I was turned out of the Observatory, I would carry away the sextant with me. I only desired him to keep his temper, restrain his passion, and thanked him as often as he gave me ill names: and, looking for the door, told him God had blessed all my endeavors hitherto, and that he would protect me for the future: that the wisdom of God was beyond the wisdom of men; and that I committed my all to Him: or words to that purpose.

I cannot remember everything that was said by the hot gentleman, in its proper place; nor have I given it in its order. I may put it into better, upon recollection, hereafter. . . . He told me, moreover, I had received £3600 of the Government. I answered what had he done for £500 a-year salary that he had, or to that purpose? Which put him to a stand: but, at length, he fell to give me his usual good words: said I was proud and insolent, and insulted him. Dr. Mead said the same thing. I only desired him (as I had often done) to restrain his passion, keep his temper, &c. He said I had called him Atheist.

I never did: but I know what other people have said of a paragraph in his *Opticks*; which probably occasioned this suggestion. I thought it not worth my while to say anything in answer to this reproach. I hope he is none.[54]

In the end Flamsteed had been either persuaded or forced to surrender to the Committee of Referees a record of his original observations and an incomplete set of star-places. Some of the papers had been put under seal in Newton's possession in 1707 and he had broken the bond and released them, Flamsteed later charged. The printing had proceeded haltingly until Prince George's death, when the committee gave Halley—the cruelest cut of all—the task of publishing whatever was in their hands and then filling out the volume with observations of his own. The 1712 edition that was pulled out of this chaos is a veritable hodgepodge because there were numerous unresolved problems of identification when Halley assumed control; and Halley's introduction to Flamsteed's lifework reflected brutally upon the Royal Astronomer's capacities and accuracy. Halley made a laughingstock of Flamsteed by displaying his astronomical records in coffeehouses and taverns. "He has boasted all over the town what Numerous faults he found in it & shewed my Copy amongst his impious associates at Childs all marked" was Flamsteed's bitter plaint.[55]

Ultimately, after King George I succeeded to the throne and the Earl of Halifax died on May 19, 1715, Flamsteed had his primitive revenge in the performance of a grandiose ritual act. A petition to the Lords of the Treasury, who had the legal power to dispose of the 1712 edition of the star catalogue, resulted in the delivery into his hands of three hundred of the four hundred copies printed. What he did with them he solemnly described in the 1717 manuscript:

I brought them down to Greenwich: and, finding both Halley's corrupted edition of my catalogue, and abridgment of my observations, no less spoiled by him, I separated them from my observations: and, some few days after, I made a sacrifice of them to *Heavenly Truth*: as I should do of all the rest of my editor's pains of the like nature, if the Author of Truth should hereafter put them into my power; that none of them but what he has given away and sent into foreign countries may remain to show the ingratitude of two of my countrymen, who had been obliged by me more on particular occasions, than any other of my mathematical acquaintance; and who had used me worse than ever the noble Tycho was used in Denmark. And I should have felt the effects of their malice and envy more had not the good Providence of Almighty God prevented them.[56]

Burning enemies in effigy, in their works or in fantasy, was common to both Flamsteed and Newton.

Because of the Society's relation with the state Newton had ordered Flamsteed to surrender his observations and had gotten them published, not as the isolated astronomer would have had them appear, but as the administrator saw fit. Though he received one hundred pounds a year from the government, Flamsteed still thought of himself as the lone, autonomous servant of God and of his work as an offering. Newton, in the name of the superior interests of organized science and the state, treated him like a rebellious clerk whose idiosyncrasies would not be tolerated. The novelty of this act of intervention and command has been ignored by commentators, though it presaged a new form of scientific organization and control.

In the midst of that humorless band of compulsive geniuses— Hooke, Newton, Flamsteed, and religionists like Whiston and Fatio —Halley appears to be a man of another sort. He is jocular, irreverent, not afraid of physical danger, capable of handling a mutinous mate on the high seas and enduring the hazards of long voyages, of descending to ocean depths in a diving bell, or climbing lofty mountains. He is ingratiating and loyal to a fault where Newton is concerned. He is in fact so generally accommodating that he becomes boon companion to Czar Peter, who spends his nights carousing in the dives and taverns of London. A man who can please both Newton and Peter the Great is flexible, to say the least. In the humiliating preface where he wrote of the Royal Astronomer's errors, Halley emerges as the perfect model of the obedient secretary of a scientific society, eager to do the bidding of the man in power.

After examining the star catalogue "corrupted and spoiled" by Halley, Flamsteed denounced him as a "lazy and malicious thief" in a letter to Abraham Sharp on June 2, 1716.[57] "Dr. Halley has nothing of these," Flamsteed wrote in the following November, rejoicing in the superiority of the true star catalogue he was now working on over "their" false one, "but has wrote a preface only filled with lies and false suggestions against me. God forgive him; I do. But I shall surely let the world know his falsehood and unfitness, both of him and his master, for such an employment; though it is not absolutely necessary: for their late actions in my business have so informed the world of their inabilities, and they have so far ruined their own ill-gotten reputation, that I shall need to say but little in my own vin-dication."[58]

If Flamsteed reports correctly, Newton had impounded the orig-inal sheets sent to him and as late as May 2, 1717, refused to surren-der them, so that Flamsteed had to have them recopied from his "first night notes" for the new publication he was contemplating. But though he could not retrieve the data, Flamsteed reassured his friend Sharp with the exaltation of a dying man: "I shall give you about 12 years' observations more than there are in those sheets Sir I. Newton got into his hands by trick and fraud, and detains by vio-lence."[59]

The annual curt official notices from Crane Court to the Ob-servatory, signed by Halley, kept coming regularly as Flamsteed, hardly able to move about, was slowly sinking into death. On June 7, 1716: "I am commanded by the President, Council, and Fellows of the Royal Society, to put you in mind that you are in arrears to them a copy of your Astronomical Observations for the year 1714; and that those of 1715, ending with December last, are now become due to them: both of which they require you to send them on or before Midsummer Day next, as you are obliged to do by her late Majesty's orders, which constitute them perpetual visitors of the Royal Obser-vatory, and entitle them to the copies they now demand."[60] Flam-steed enveloped himself in silence. On December 31, 1719, in the midst of his efforts to prepare the record of his forty-five years at the Observatory according to his own lights, Flamsteed died at Green-wich and was succeeded by his adversary Edmond Halley. Two friends, Joseph Crosthwait and Abraham Sharp, completed the star catalogue for publication in 1725, a major work in fundamental as-tronomy, while Halley's 1712 edition was consigned to oblivion.[61]

The first volume of this final version of the Flamsteed catalogue was published with a notice to the reader signed—incredible as it may seem—by Francis Roberts, Christopher Wren, Isaac Newton, David Gregory, and John Arbuthnot, the original Committee of Referees, a number of whom were by this time dead. The opening paragraphs described Flamsteed in hyperbolic Latin as "readily the chief astronomer of his century and second to none in previous ages." There followed a dedication to King George I, signed by the widow Margarita Flamsteed and James Hodgson, Flamsteed's assistant. Flamsteed's original *Praefatio* was reduced to a standard history of astronomy since ancient times, with all reference to Newton's persecutions slashed out. Of the whole violent contest not a trace remained; the fratricidal conflict was kept within the family. A few volumes of the Halley edition of the catalogue were in foreign and English libraries and Mrs. Flamsteed wrote to the librarian at Oxford formally requesting that it be removed from the shelves as spurious. To all intents and purposes the affair was decently buried—until the astronomer Francis Baily reprinted a large portion of the Flamsteed correspondence and diaries in 1835, to the utter consternation of Victorian scientists.

Chapter 15

THE DUEL WITH LEIBNIZ

Connais-tu l'animal
Qui inventa le calcul intégral?
—Evariste

In a published series of Latin documents mostly judiciously excerpted translations of letters to and from John Collins in the 1670's, known for short as the *Commercium epistolicum* (1712), a committee of the Royal Society adjudicated a contest over priority in the invention of the calculus in favor of its own President, aged seventy, against one of its oldest foreign members, aged sixty-six.

The Knight from Woolsthorpe and the Freiherr from Leipzig, in a joust over precedence in the new philosophy, had abided by no known set of chivalric rules. At the height of the contest, after repeated letters from Leibniz to Hans Sloane, Secretary of the Society, complaining that Dr. John Keill, a fellow member, had insulted him, Newton the President formally brought together his adherents, under the guise of what he later grandiloquently called "a numerous Committee of Gentlemen of several Nations," to pass upon the merits of Leibniz' accusation. The nations represented on this much-touted impartial committee turned out to be English, Scottish, and Irish, with a Prussian ambassador and a Huguenot émigré later thrown in for continental flavor.[1]

The report of the committee, delivered before the Royal Society on April 24, 1712, insinuated plagiarism on the part of Leibniz, though it was required only to exonerate Keill from the charge that he had injured Leibniz during a polemical exchange, or to confirm it.

We have consulted the letters and letter-books in the custody of the Royal Society, and those found amongst the papers of Mr. John Collins, dated between the years 1669 and 1677 inclusive, and shewed them to such as knew and avowed the hands of Mr. Barrow, Mr. Collins, Mr. Oldenburgh, and Mr. Leibnitz, and compared those of Mr. Gregory with one another, and with copies of some of them taken in the hand of Mr. Collins, and have extracted from them what relates to the matter referred to us, all which extracts herewith delivered to you, we believe to be genuine and authentic; and by these letters and papers we find, 1st. That Mr. Leibnitz was in London in the beginning of the year 1673, and went thence in or about March, to Paris, where he kept a correspondence with Mr. Collins, by means of Mr. Oldenburgh, till about September, 1676, and then returned by London and Amsterdam to Hanover, and that Mr. Collins was very free in communicating to able mathematicians what he had received from Mr. Newton and Mr. Gregory. 2dly, That when Mr. Leibnitz was the first time in London, he contended for the invention of another differential method, properly so called; and notwithstanding that he was shewn by Dr. Pell, that it was Newton's method, he persisted in maintaining it to be his own invention, by reason that he found it by himself, without knowing what Newton had done before, and had much improved it; and we find no mention of his having any other differential method than Newton's, before his letter of June 21, 1677, which was a year after a copy of Mr. Newton's letter of December 10, 1672, had been sent to Paris, to be communicated to him, and above four years after Mr. Collins began to communicate that letter to his correspondents; in which letter the method of fluxions was sufficiently described to any intelligent person. 3dly, That by Mr. Newton's letter of June 13, 1676, it appears, that he had the method of fluxions above five years before the writing of that letter; and by his *Analysis per Operationes numero terminorum infinitas,* communicated by Dr. Barrow to Mr. Collins in July, 1669, we find that he had invented the method before that time. 4thly, That the differential method is one and the same with the method of fluxions, excepting the name and mode of notation, Mr. Leibnitz calling these quantities differences, which Mr. Newton calls moments, or fluxions, and marking them with the letter *d*, a mark not used by Mr. Newton. We therefore take the proper question to be, not who invented this or that method, but who was the first inventor of the method; and we believe that those who have reputed Mr. Leibnitz the first inventor, know little or nothing of his correspondence with Mr. Collins and Mr. Oldenburgh, long before, nor of Mr. Newton's having that method above fifteen years before Mr. Leibnitz began to publish it in the *Acta Eruditorum* of Leipswick.

For which reasons we reckon Mr. Newton the first inventor, and are of opinion that Mr. Keil, in asserting the same, has been no ways injurious to

Mr. Leibnitz; and we submit to the judgment of the Society, whether the extract of the letters and papers, now presented, together with what is extant to the same purpose in Dr. Wallis's third volume, may not deserve to be made public.[2]

Newton was so well protected that publicly the affair appeared to be a Keill-Leibniz controversy; he operated exclusively behind the scenes and with consummate skill. There is only one document in which he took specific personal responsibility for what was said—his reply to Abate Conti in February 1716; for the rest, he was the grand strategist who refused to be revealed. And when he deigned to answer Leibniz through Conti on that occasion, it was by force majeure; for Conti, a Venetian aristocrat sojourning in England, and Princess Caroline of Anspach had playfully decided to act as intermediaries in a reconciliation attempt and he had no choice but to go along with their efforts.

The exchange of letters between Leibniz and Newton through Conti in 1716 only brought into the open a war that had been waged clandestinely since the turn of the century. Two of the greatest geniuses of the European world, not only of their own time but of its whole long history, had been privately belaboring each other with injurious epithets and encouraging their partisans to publish scurrilous innuendoes in learned journals. In the age of reason they behaved like gladiators in a Roman circus. Here were two old bachelors, Leibniz not far from death, Newton with a decade more of life, each fighting for exclusive possession of his brainchild, the right to call the invention of the calculus his own and no one else's. The contest transcended the specific issue of priority of invention to embrace rival conceptions of the nature of matter, substance, the cosmos, God's providence, time, space, miracles. Views of all things in the heavens and on earth became polarized as they stalwartly assumed opposite positions, exaggerating their differences, grossly caricaturing each other's opinions like schoolboys in debate. Their common commitment to advancing the new philosophy was totally forgotten.

For many years others had perpetrated the hostile acts for the principals, who sedulously avoided an open confrontation, though the manuscripts now betray the extent to which they supervised the verbal assaults of their hangers-on, when they did not themselves compose them under the cover of anonymity. Newton had a more numerous troop. He was in London, President of the Royal Society, embattled defender of the English nation in a war where world scientific prestige was at stake. Though Leibniz too had been president of an academy, it was in backwoods Berlin, and his last years were spent as a lonely old man in Hannover writing dynastic history for the head of the House of Brunswick who had become King George I of England.[3] Leibniz had his adherents among the great continental scientists—Johann Bernoulli was a secret ally—but they were leery of engaging with Newton and only reluctantly allowed themselves to be drawn into the fray.

The spectators goaded the contestants on as if they were witnesses at a cockfight. A sophisticated courtier, Leibniz was aware of the indecent delight that aristocratic society, ignorant of mathematics, took in watching the scientists vilify each other. Half mockingly, he resorted to the language of dueling to describe the thrusts and counterthrusts. Newton was affronted by such levity and horrified at the introduction of the style of knight-errantry into serious subjects like mathematics that were matters of fact. His role as king of the hill, a position he had won against many opponents, was now being challenged, and this was no mere romance. George I had a brutal streak in his nature and he looked with satisfaction on the heroes from two parts of his realm inflicting and sustaining grave wounds as they vied for his nod. Princess Caroline was the fluttering heroine in the royal box. And the aged knights, scarred from many a battle, were fighting for her favor too—her soul, they said. Should she believe in the existence of a cosmic vacuum or should she not? That was the question. Her letters to Leibniz, toward whom she leaned at one time,[4] were charming and perceptive, and in many ways she grasped the secret meaning of the quarrel with greater discernment than many later commentators intent on arriving at a simplistic rational verdict of true or false. On April 24, 1716, she told Leibniz of her dismay that learned men of science could not be reconciled, and then sagely reflected: "But great men are like women, who never give up their lovers except with the utmost chagrin and mortal anger. And that, gentlemen, is where your opinions have got you."[5] The great knights hurling instruments from theology and mathematics were worthy opponents; and who knows, as Nietzsche said of other mighty warriors, they may have loved each other in their fashion. But there was also a throng of little squires, some of them contemptible, who sharpened the weapons and from time to time fancied themselves in the center of the field. Above all there was Abate Conti, to whom Newton had bared his breast, to whom he passed secret documents, whom he had entertained in private with his views on science and philosophy, ancient history, and cosmology. Conti was one of those flashy picaresque figures of the eighteenth-century intellectual world, a poetaster, a tragedian, a translator of Racine and Pope, a dabbler in the sciences, a dilettante who intrigued with equal adroitness among princesses and natural philosophers in England, France, Germany, and Italy.

On August 30, 1715, Conti wrote to his friend Rémond de Montmort in Paris, delighted at the manner in which Newton had received him: "I go to Newton's house three times a week and when I return to Paris I know that you will be pleased both with him and with me. You have no idea how learned he is in ancient history and how reasonable and accurate are the reflections he makes on the facts. He has read much and meditated a great deal on the Holy Scriptures, and he speaks about them with great wisdom and good sense, stripping the words of their allegorical meaning and reducing them to history."[6] Conti, who had traveled to England to see Newton and the April eclipse of the sun, was—if he is to be credited—honored by visits from the aged man to his chambers;[7] he was perhaps a temporary replacement for Fatio. Under Newton's sponsorship Conti and the Venetian ambassador were both admitted into the Royal Society.

Abate Conti had a certain hidden disdain for both parties in the priority dispute; as he later confessed, science amused him and gave him pleasure, nothing more.[8] When in 1716 he transmitted a letter from Leibniz exonerating himself from the Royal Society's accusations and counterattacking, Newton was driven into a fury, precisely the kind of response the Venetian would be delighted to report at the King's table[9] or to his friend Lady Mary Wortley Montagu[10] or to Rémond de Montmort, who was, at least for a while, a secret supporter of Leibniz. Rémond de Montmort had written letters of extravagant flattery to Leibniz, which the philosopher, starved for recognition, quoted to his correspondents throughout Europe;[11] but the French aristocrat was no less assiduous in cultivating Newton. These playboys of science often acted as double agents in international espionage, drawing their recompense from both parties.[12] Not until a decade later, during his contest with Nicolas Fréret of the Académie des Inscriptions et Belles-Lettres and with the Jesuit Father Souciet over the unauthorized publication of his revision of chronology, did Newton finally recognize the role enacted by the petty Venetian Iago in stirring him up, and then he loosed against Conti Jovian thunderbolts from the presidency of the Royal Society.

Back in the nineties, Leibniz had been a fervent admirer of English science, and had excitedly inquired from his correspondents about new developments in the Royal Society. "Do me the favor, if you find the opportunity," he wrote to Henri Justel who was in England, "to pay my respects to the Chevalier Boyle, whom I highly esteem, and urge him to give us unstintingly those fine things which he has only half-way hinted at and which he has not yet revealed. Will we have nothing more from the Chevalier Wren, who is so talented a man? Is M. Samuel Moreland back in England? He had promise. What is M. Hooke doing—that marvelously ingenious man? Is Mr. Collins still alive? I once considered him the Mersenne of England. It would be good to get M. Wallis to publish something on the art of deciphering."[13] Leibniz' praises of Newton were frequent and generous. But a decade thereafter the republic of science had become too small for both Newton and Leibniz, as the Royal Society had once been for Newton and Hooke. A quarrel which had its origins in a classical priority fight was fanned into a great conflagration that consumed both of them. Leibniz could look away and jest about the struggle, but he was nonetheless devoured by it. This, rather than the noxious potions he took for the gout, may have killed him. During his lifetime he stood a condemned plagiarist, for who would gainsay the verdict of the Royal Society of London in a judgment that Leibniz himself had demanded? He died alone and virtually nobody but a servant attended his funeral. Newton regurgitated the case repeatedly in Latin and in English, ungallantly pursuing Leibniz beyond the grave—witness the five-hundred-odd folios of manuscript in the University Library in Cambridge devoted to self-vindication, drafts for the *Commercium,* and attacks on the enemy, in addition to stray papers at the Mint and in Shirburn Castle, into all of which his great wrath poured itself.[14] His possession lasted for a quarter of a century, and nowhere are the destructive forces in his character more visibly on the rampage than in this vendetta.

In the 1680's, both Newton and Leibniz had made a reasonable, if tentative, accommodation in their own minds of their respective roles in the invention of various methods in the quadrature of the circle. When Leibniz was informed in a letter from Otto Mencke on July 16, 1684, that the calculus would be publicly attributed to Professor Newton in an English work,[15] his reply was a common-sensical statement of the possibilities of parallel invention.

As far as Mr. Newton is concerned, I have letters from him and the late Mr. Oldenburg in which they do not dispute my quadrature with me, but grant it. Nor do I believe that Mr. Newton will ascribe it to himself, but only some inventions about infinite series which he in part also applies to the circle. Mr. Mercator, a German, first came upon this and Mr. Newton developed it further, but I arrived at it by another way. Meanwhile, I acknowledge that Mr. Newton already had the principles from which he could well have derived the quadrature, but one does not come upon all the results at one time: one man makes one combination, another man another.[16]

Leibniz then enclosed a paper on the rules of differentiation and notation for the differential calculus, which later appeared in the October 1684 number of the Leipzig *Acta Eruditorum.*

In thus publishing his method of the calculus without any public reference to Newton's work Leibniz was disingenuous, for he was aware of the existence of a different method, at least in its generality, though this does not mean that he knew Newton's achievement in any detail, since it had been communicated to him only by means of undecipherable Latin anagrams in a letter to Oldenburg on October 24, 1676, now known as the *Epistola Posterior*. (The briefer of the two will suffice to indicate the measure of their comprehensibility— 6accdae13eff7i3l9r4o4qrr4s8t12vx.) The first edition of the *Principia* has no accusation of plagiarism or trace of enmity on Newton's part, nothing but a favorable, if slightly ambiguous, mention of Leibniz, which he nonetheless appreciated. The Scholium to Book II, Section II, Proposition VII, reads: "In letters which went between me and that most excellent geometer, G. W. Leibniz, ten years ago, when I signified that I was in the knowledge of a method of determining maxima and minima, of drawing tangents, and the like, and when I concealed it in transposed letters involving this sentence . . . that most distinguished man wrote back that he had also fallen upon a method of the same kind, and communicated his method, which hardly differed from mine, except in his forms of words and symbols." As the storm gathered strength, even the great rock of the *Principia* was altered. In the second edition the words "and the concept of the generation of quantities" were added to the last phrase; and in the third edition Leibniz' name was dropped completely from the Scholium.[17]

Though there had been earlier intimations in the writings of John Wallis, the first serious volley of the war was fired in a work published by Fatio in 1699, the *Lineae brevissimi descensus investigatio geometrica duplex,* where the young man, angered by some slight from Leibniz, proposed the dishonorable possibility that Leibniz, the second inventor of the calculus, might have borrowed from the first. In the same passage Fatio boasted of his own mathematical prowess, exalted Newton, and insulted Leibniz. "I now recognize, having been convinced by the evidence itself, that Newton is the first inventor of this calculus, and the earliest by many years; whether

Leibniz, its second inventor, may have borrowed anything from him, I should rather leave to the judgment of those who were shown the letters of Newton and his other manuscripts. Neither the silence of the more modest Newton, nor the eager inclination of Leibniz to claim on any occasion the invention of this calculus for himself, will deceive anyone who examines those records as I have."[18]

When the battle was joined, new charges and countercharges were delivered periodically either by one of Newton's friends or by a friend of Leibniz or by Leibniz writing anonymously in his own behalf. There is no evidence that Newton was responsible for Fatio's first salvo, and there is reason to believe that by this time there was already a growing estrangement between them. (Later, in a letter to John Chamberlayne on May 11, 1714, Newton categorically denied having had anything to do with what Fatio wrote.[19]) But once Leibniz had replied to Fatio in the Leipzig *Acta* in 1700, Newton became totally enmeshed in the tangled skeins of a priority fight. John Keill led the public attack and Newton controlled the written polemics, though the zeal of his defenders sometimes outstripped even his wishes as the lickspittles tried to curry favor with the master. Keill's accusations were crass, and it was at this juncture that Leibniz demanded the Royal Society's intervention. Thereupon Newton took over completely. The committee's membership, its report, and the reviews of the report were all determined by him, down to the last phrase. In the end he trusted no man and felt obliged to oversee every single move. He could no longer rely on intermediaries but had to deliver the body blows himself. Wherever he went, whatever he was doing during these years, his sullen anger at Leibniz dominated him. Newton felt that he had been directly accused of plagiarism,[20] of lying, of being a false prophet—he who never asked or needed the help of any man living or dead, who had discovered everything by concentrated effort and divine inspiration. When the quarrel widened from the priority battle to swallow up the whole Newtonian philosophy, he was in effect called a pagan idolater who would curtail God's omniscience and omnipotence. Newton paraded his old notebooks, papers, and correspondence before every foreign visitor who would look at them; he argued, denounced, set out to take reprisals. The old puritan was fighting for God's truth and his own chosen role in God's world against a prevaricator, a diversionist, and a liar. And despite Newton's disavowal of any complicity in Fatio's charge in 1699, it is the same year in which Newton opened to a blank page in one of his old mathematical notebooks and, seemingly out of the clear sky, wrote a famous passage dating his invention of the calculus to the mid-sixties.

Leibniz too was fighting for his person. The transparent white lies of his "anonymous" publications—he had no Keill or Royal Society as a bulwark—put him in a bad light. An attempt to demonstrate the power of his method of the calculus by having Johann Bernoulli propose to the geometers of the world two problems that he thought could not be solved without it ended in disaster. Newton's solutions within a day, in 1697, with his own system of fluxions, showed that his sovereignty could not be lightly disputed.[21]

A passage in the Leipzig *Acta* for January 1705, reviewing two of Newton's mathematical tracts on curvilinear figures appended to the *Opticks* (1704), would have nettled even a man with a constitution less sensitive to criticism than Newton's. There was deliberate provocation, or at least careless phraseology, in the anonymous contribution which, we now know, was written by Leibniz himself: "Instead of the Leibnizian differences, then, Dr. Newton employs, and has always employed, fluxions [adhibet, semperque adhibuit, Fluxiones], which are very much the same as the augments of fluents produced in the least equal intervals of time; and these fluxions he has used elegantly in his *Mathematical Principles of Nature* and in other later publications, just as Honoratus Fabri, in his *Synopsis of Geometry* substituted [substituit] progressive motions for the method of Cavalieri."[22] Though at one point Newton conceded some ambiguity in these words, he could never free himself from the idea that some readers might believe he had known the differential calculus only since its discovery by Leibniz and had claimed invention of the calculus for himself by simply substituting fluxions for the Leibnizian differences as a cover for his theft. This is the defamatory sense in which the passage was construed in the *Commercium epistolicum*. Leibniz later publicly disavowed any such intention and protested to Conti that his carefully chosen Latin phrases had been misunderstood. "That is the malicious interpretation of a man who was looking for a quarrel. It would seem that the author of the words inserted in the Leipzig *Acts* [Leibniz himself] expressly wished to avoid that meaning by choosing the words *adhibet SEMPERQUE adhibuit,* in order to suggest it was not after seeing my Differences, but before, that he made use of Fluxions. And I defy anyone to give any other reasonable interpretation of the words *semperque adhibuit;* instead of which *substituit* was used when speaking of what Père Fabri had done after Cavalieri."[23]

The explanation is rather lame, especially in the light of the infamously derogatory association of Newton with Fabri, a notorious plagiarist.[24] But Fatio's original provocative allusion to Leibniz in 1699 had been as blunt and unequivocal as Leibniz' was veiled. And in the preface to the *Opticks* in 1704 Newton himself had made reference to the fact that he had mentioned his calculus to Leibniz in a letter of 1676, that he had "lent out a Manuscript containing such Theorems" and that he had since "met with some Things copied out of it. . . ."[25] Though less direct than Fatio's charge, his statement had implications that were sharp enough, for by this time he had become completely convinced of Leibniz's plagiarism and built an airtight case from the evidence. Leibniz retracted his insinuation of plagiarism against Newton, made after the offenses in Fatio's book and in the preface to the *Opticks,* while Newton could never relinquish a construct of events that implied deliberate deceit on Leibniz' part.[26] In some drafts of his reply to Leibniz Newton turned whatever his adversary wrote topsy-turvy. "If he that interpreted the word adhibuit by the word substituit has poisoned this Passage in the Acta by a malicious interpretation the crime is his [his] that wrote the passage."[27] Leibniz was even held responsible for the errors in the *Commercium,* because he had been the first cause.

To call Newton a thief and a liar—and these are the words he heard, whatever Leibniz wrote—was to charge him with religious crimes as well as crimes of honor; and this struck sources of terrible anxiety, for on one level of his consciousness Newton was aware that there were lies in his life. There is another hidden dimension to the attack. Newton was a self-made man, a yeoman's son who had risen to the highest post in the English world of science and fulfilled a major administrative function as an officer of the Crown. The magnificent structure of his public life nevertheless remained shaky because he was a parvenu, a newcomer, a man who had only recently been knighted, and accusations of plagiarism and thievery threatened to pull down the entire edifice. If the contentions of Leibniz were given heed, Newton stood condemned of betraying the two moral codes by which he now lived. The puritan could not shrug off the charge that he had violated the commandment against stealing, and the newly knighted servant of the Crown could never tolerate the affront of being called untruthful and remain a gentleman. Leibniz was, moreover, trying to deprive him of what was rightfully his. If one grants any enduring psychic potency to the idea of deprivation in Newton's life, this is the moment when it must be appreciated.

As the bitterness engendered by the priority fight spilled over onto the whole Newtonian philosophy, Leibniz wrote from Vienna to his Scottish friend the nobleman Thomas Burnet of Kenney on August 23, 1713, after publication of the *Commercium epistolicum,* mocking

the rebirth in England of a theology that is more than papist and a philosophy entirely scholastic since M. Newton and his partisans have revived the occult qualities of the School with the idea of attraction. What you tell me, sir, is so comical it seems that my adversaries in the Royal Society have lately written against me as if I were a Whig rather than a member of their Society. I had believed that M. Newton was somewhat allied with the Whigs; thus I would not have imagined that the spirit of faction would go so far as to spread even into mathematical sciences. These gentlemen who have written against me (quite uncivilly they tell me, for I have not yet seen it) will find themselves caught up by a little reply from one of my friends.

In a postscript Leibniz recalled Newton's other quarrels but still expressed surprise at the onslaught and at his bad faith.

Someone told me that Messrs. Hook and Flamsteed complained of Newton. I would not have believed him capable of maintaining against me what he knows to be false. This gives me a bad opinion of him, and I am equally surprised that M. Halley could do what you report.[28]

The question of God's relationship to the universe, so fervently debated in the Leibniz-Clarke correspondence, with Clarke a mouthpiece for Newton as the manuscripts conclusively demonstrate, was a sideshow.[29] In a letter of March 1716 to Louis Bourguet, a French businessman turned scholar, Leibniz reduced his philosophical differences with Newton to a brief formula. "M. Newton believes that the force of the universe diminishes, like that of a watch, and has to be reestablished by a special action of God, while I maintain that God made things from the beginning in such a way that its force would not be lost. Thus his dynamics are very different from mine and do not in my opinion conform to the perfection of divine operations." These were fighting words: he was in effect saying that Newton was detracting from the absolute perfection of God—no graver accusation could be leveled at a man with an internalized God the Father. In his letter of October 19, 1716, to Rémond de Montmort, Leibniz pithily defined the dispute as revolving around the axiom of "sufficient reason"; it was all or nothing. "If he continues to deny it to me, where is his sincerity? If he accords it to me, adieu the vacuum, the atoms, and the whole Philosophy of M. Newton."[30]

The Newtonians—and they took pride in the collective name—accused Leibniz of refusing to abide by the fundamental principles of experimental philosophy; Leibniz retorted by blaming them for reintroducing scholasticism into science. They charged him with philosophizing without proofs; he countered by forcing into the open the preconceptions of the Newtonian philosophy and then denigrating it as bad metaphysics. The differences between them even had psychological roots: Newton's philosophy of nature now posited a void, a space identifiable with God; Leibniz insisted on a plenum. Apart from the natural tendency to assume an inflexible, contrary position in a quarrel heated by personal animosities, Newton's degradation of matter in his everyday existence and his dread of physical contact are consonant with a view of the world in which space, pure and unsullied, an attribute of God, is preponderant while the material creation is a lesser thing.[31] Leibniz' plenitude is in harmony with his more earthy character. Scholars have sought for the origins of Newton's philosophy of nature in the French philosopher Gassendi and in Henry More (and he knew them both); they might have found them also in a reading and commentary on Genesis, and in Newton's personality.

Leibniz was no innocent, and when he attacked Newton for his revival of scholastic philosophy and his belief in occult qualities he knew the barbs would sting. Like an envious schoolmaster who has been abandoned Leibniz boasted, almost pathetically: "I am surprised that the partisans of Mr. Newton produce nothing to show that their master has communicated a sound method to them. I have been more fortunate in my disciples." He smugly assured Conti that Wren, Flamsteed, Newton, and a few others were all that remained of the scientific "Siècle d'Or d'Angleterre" and that their day would soon be done.[32]

Members of Newton's coterie were under a constant temptation to broadcast what they called the "decision" of the Royal Society, though technically the Society had done nothing except publish a collection of documents and make a finding of fact. Roger Cotes's letter of March 10, 1713, to Richard Bentley, the stormy Master of Trinity, about the second edition of the *Principia* on which they were both engaged is a fair sample of how these righteous men concerted together in the just cause.

As to the Preface I should be glad to know from Sr Isaac with what view he thinks proper to have it written. You know the book has been received abroad with some disadvantage, & the cause of it may easily be guess'd at. The Commercium Epistolicum lately publish'd by order of the R. Society gives such indubitable proof of Mr Leibnitz's want of candour that I shall not scruple in the least to speak out the full truth of the matter if it be thought convenient. . . . If Sr Isaac is willing that something of this nature may be done, I should be glad if, whilst I am making the Index, he would be pleas'd to consider of it & put down a few notes of what he thinks most material to be insisted on. This I say upon supposition that I write the Preface my self. But

13. Isaac Newton, circa 1710

15. Gottfried Wilhelm Leibniz

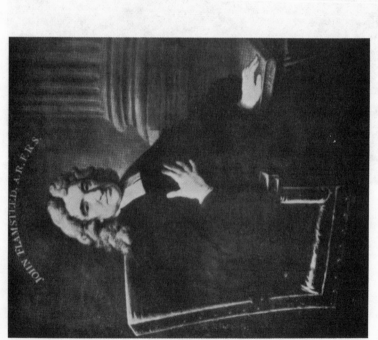

14. John Flamsteed, circa 1712

I think it will be much more adviseable that You or He or both of You should write it whilst You are in Town.

And to avoid any misunderstanding, Cotes volunteered to free Newton from all responsibility for anything he might choose to say in the preface, precisely as John Keill later did for the famous *Recensio*. These professors of astronomy had their own notions of the uses of truth in a holy war. "You may depend upon it that I will own it [the preface] & defend it as well as I can if hereafter there be occasion," Cotes wrote Bentley, assuring him of absolute loyalty.[33] At first Sir Isaac gave him permission to say anything he saw fit about the "controversy of the first Invention," only he was not to be rude and uncivil, and not to name Leibniz directly. Newton and Bentley would of course review the text.[34] Later they revised their plans and limited it to a counterattack against Leibniz' derision of the Newtonian philosophy. Leibniz found the preface "pleine d'aigreur," expressed his astonishment that Newton had approved its discourteous phraseology, and declared that he had no intention of replying to critics who attacked him so boorishly.[35]

When Roger Cotes died prematurely in 1716, the chief Newtonian defenders were reduced to Keill and Halley. On both fronts, the internal one with Flamsteed and the external one with Leibniz, Halley served as grand coordinator. The Royal Society had named a committee of three, Halley, Jones, and Machin, to see the *Commercium epistolicum* through the press; but Halley was the central figure and he left an extraordinary monument to his perseverance and involvement in the cause. The followers vied with each other in serving their leader. John Keill had from the beginning of the controversy placed himself completely at Newton's disposal. "I will observe your orders as far as I can," he wrote on February 8, 1714. "You see we may have what we please printed in these French journals and I am of opinion that Mr Leibnits should be used a little smartly and all his plagiary and blunders showed at large. However Sr. I expect your directions. . . ."[36] When it came to Newton's attention that Leibniz' "anonymous" *charta volans* of July 29, 1713, had been inserted in the Hague *Journal litéraire* for November and December of that year, he moved into action. "I think it requires an Answer," he wrote to Keill on April 2, 1714.

It is very reflecting upon the Committee of the Royal Society, & endeavours to derogate from the credit of some of the Letters published in the Commercium Epistolicum as if they were spurious. If you please when you have it, to consider of what Answer you think proper, I will within a Post or two send you my thoughts upon the Subject, that you may compare them wth your own sentiments & then draw up such an Answer as you think proper. You need not set your name to it. You may write either in English or in Latine & leave it to Mr Johnson to get it translated into French. Mr Darby will convey yor Answer to the Hague.[37]

After having read the pro-Leibniz pieces in the *Journal litéraire*, Keill fully agreed with Newton that retaliation was in order: "I think I never saw anything writ with so much impudence, falsehood and slander as they are both, I am of opinion that they must be immediately answered. . . ."[38] And in a month he produced the response to the challenge: "I leave my whole paper to you and Dr Halley, to change or take away what you please. I only desire that it may be done quickly and sent over. . . ."[39] So impetuous a warrior occasionally had to be held in check or silenced by the master while corrections were being made. If ever Newton slackened in his enthusiasm for the fray, Keill was there to revive his flagging spirits with provocative new intelligence. On June 24, he impatiently reminded Newton of his efforts. "I sent some time agoe to Dr Halley my Answer to Mr Bernoulli and the Leipsick Rogues and desired him to give it you, that you might doe with it as you please."[40] Keill's reply was eventually published in the *Journal litéraire* for July and August 1714.[41]

Of the hundreds of documents on the Leibniz controversy that Newton prepared, the review of the *Commercium epistolicum,* which he himself wrote and published anonymously, reveals the lengths to which he resorted to annihilate a foe. All but three pages of the *Philosophical Transactions of the Royal Society* for the months of January and February 1715 are devoted to this jejune recapitulation of the quarrel, beginning with proof of Newton's first discoveries in the sixties. While the original *Commercium epistolicum* of 1712/1713 had been written in Latin, Newton's review, "An Account of the Book entituled Commercium Epistolicum Collinii & aliorum, De Analysi promota; published by order of the Royal Society, in relation to the Dispute between Mr. Leibniz and Dr. Keill, about the Right of Invention of the Method of Fluxions, by some call'd the Differential Method," is in English. Its text, interspersed with Latin quotations and mathematical proofs, was hardly likely to have great popular appeal, but the sharp polemical passages could now be understood by anyone who perused the volume. Though the piece is unsigned and purports to be a rectification by an editorial "we" of imperfect summaries published abroad, at one point near the end where a solemn warning is issued to Leibniz the author of the "Account" lapses into the singular personal pronoun. His identity is unmistakable. "And in the mean time I take the liberty to acquaint him, that by taxing the Royal-Society with Injustice in giving Sentence against him without hearing both Parties, he has transgressed one of their Statutes which makes it Expulsion to defame them."[42]

Throughout the international disputation, the feeble attempts of the contestants to hide their identities by publishing anonymously were downright childish, and telltale lapses were frequent. In an answer to Keill published in the Leipzig *Acta* for July 1716, the "Epistola pro eminente Mathematico, Dn. Johanne Bernoullio, contra quendam ex Anglia antagonistam scripta," an unacknowledged composition by Bernoulli himself that was published in the third person at his insistence, the author's identity was unwittingly revealed when the editors made a slip and printed *meam formulam* for *eam formulam*—and Newton caught the error.[43] Leibniz, who had few adherents willing to risk their necks for him, had a distinctive style that was easily recognized in his favorable commentaries on his own reviews and in the *charta volans*. Neither Fatio nor John Keill, of course, was ever hesitant to append his name to the cruelest attacks. But of the whole body of literature that poured forth from all sides during the conflict, nothing seems quite so outrageous as that "anonymous" account of 1715 inserted by Newton himself in the *Philo-*

sophical Transactions, translated by de Moivre into the French, prefaced, in a new Latin version, to the 1722 edition of the *Commercium* six years after Leibniz' death, and, to add to the deception, attributed to John Keill.[44]

The review, known as the *Recensio* in the learned literature, is a grandiloquent charge addressed to the whole world, penned by a man in complete control of every jot of manuscript evidence and every polemical document that had passed back and forth across the Channel. Newton laboriously piled up brick after brick to demonstrate that not only was Leibniz a latecomer in the field of the calculus who had access to Newton's prior discovery through its propagation in international scientific correspondence, but he had deliberately and intentionally tried to cover up and distort the facts of how he had arrived at a different method. Leibniz was a plagiarist who had cautiously lain in wait until the old generation of mathematicians like Dr. Wallis were dead before he announced his claim to prior invention. Newton's subtle and eminently persuasive structuring of Leibniz' intentions, the uncovering of a monstrous plagiarist plot, tells far more about Newton than it does about Leibniz, for papers have since revealed that his method was actually inspired by reading some Pascal writings in Paris, as he had testified.[45] Newton hoarded a great part of whatever he wrote and always lived in a circumscribed geographic area, while Leibniz roamed from royal court to royal court, from Muscovy through Berlin, Vienna, Hannover, Paris, in quest of personal preferment and support of his vast projects for the unification of mankind and the promotion of knowledge. In his hour of need he was caught without written proofs, and at the very moment when he hoped to be invited to England as royal historiographer by the head of the House of Brunswick-Hannover, George I, for whose glory he had labored day and night in the archives, he found himself accused of a flagrant falsification of scientific history.

Newton stuck to his contention that he had not been influenced by anybody—"The Progress made by Mr. *Newton* shews that he wanted not Mr. *Mercator's* Assistance"[46]—while the circumstantial evidence assembled with brilliant detail inexorably pointed to the conclusion that Leibniz must have been guided by Newton's discovery. Newton moves relentlessly; he is always quoting chapter and verse, and the scriptural authenticity of his argument is vouched for by documents, open to the perusal of any person of note, while Leibniz has nothing but his own word, his integrity. To Newton's constant refrain, "where is the textual evidence of his invention?" Leibniz could only quote his own assertions in a letter of July 12, 1677, to Oldenburg that he had made the discovery.[47]

Reading the indignant peroration of the *Recensio*'s charge to the jury, one almost forgets that Newton himself is delivering the verdict, that he appointed the committee of the Royal Society, that he edited the documents of the *Commercium,* adding his own footnotes and selecting for publication extracts rather than the full texts, that he interjected numerous unsupported inferences, and that he would in 1722 republish the *Commercium* with further emendations that were not signaled in any preface or introduction. The whole performance has been masterfully analyzed in a nineteenth-century critical edition of the *Commercium epistolicum* by the Frenchmen Biot and Lefort.[48] The preparatory papers in Newton's hand, now assembled in the University Library, Cambridge, and the original collection of letters in the Royal Society reinforce their contentions. At one point in the declamation Newton's censor intruded and forced him to utter an unconscious self-reprimand, even though the words appear to be directed against Leibniz: "But no man is a Witness in his own Cause. A Judge would be very unjust and act contrary to the Laws of all Nations, who should admit any Man to be a Witness in his own Cause."[49] The pompous juridical reflection was a cliché with Newton—he invoked it in his attack upon the Trinitarian Athanasius, one of his historical bêtes noires, with whom Leibniz was assimilated. If it ever occurred to Newton that the sentence was applicable to his own self-righteous conduct, it would only have increased his rage against the enemy.

As long as neither protagonist had spoken in his own name in public, delivered the fatal defy, there was at least the possibility of a truce. Leibniz vouchsafed as much to Caroline on February 25, 1716: "Your Royal Highness shows her kindness towards me and her goodwill to others in wishing to reconcile me with Mr. Newton. I indeed believe that this reconciliation can take place since he has not yet been willing to appear openly against me himself."[50] But once letters were exchanged and spread abroad through the agency of the ubiquitous troublemaker Abate Conti, no compromise was imaginable. Then Newton had to rub his rival's nose against the wall as he once had the bully's in the Grantham Grammar School. This became a war unto the death, and in such combats Newton usually won. He survived Leibniz as he had Barnabas Smith, Robert Hooke, John Flamsteed, and other mortal enemies.

On February 26, 1716, Newton finally condescended to deliver in his own name a letter to Conti that was clearly meant for publication and was in fact printed in 1717, after Leibniz' death.[51] "By the contrivance of some of the Court of Hannover," Newton later explained to the Abbé Varignon, "I was prevailed with to write an answer to a Postscript of a Letter which Mr Leibnitz wrote to Mr l'Abbé Conti that both might be shewed to the King."[52] He referred to the *Commercium epistolicum* as a record of documents in connection with the dispute between Leibniz and Keill, in which he was, so to speak, only an outsider: "I was so far from printing the Commercium Epist. myself that I did not so much as produce the Letters in my Custody . . . least I should seem to make myself a witness in my own cause."[53] But the conclusion to Newton's first overt act acknowledging the existence of his adversary was what Edleston called it, "raking fire."[54] He publicly laid down the gauntlet: "But as he has lately attacked me with an Accusation which amounts to Plagiary; if he goes on to accuse me, it lies upon him by the Laws of all Nations to prove his Accusation on Pain of being accounted guilty of Calumny. He hath hitherto written Letters to his Correspondents, full of Affirmations, Complaints, and Reflections without proving anything. But he is the Aggressor, and it lies upon him to prove his Charge."[55]

Lacking the machinery of the Royal Society (he was refused access to their documents), Leibniz' only recourse in his last years was to unburden himself in letters to sympathetic friends, to Princess Caroline, to anybody who might conceivably tell his side of the story. Playing the courtier, he even wrote a long circumstantial version of the whole controversy to one of the royal paramours, Madame la Comtesse de Kielmannsegge—"the corpulent and ample one." His letter points up the difference in the personalities of the two men. Leibniz had the control of an *honnête homme* who had frequented the antechambers of the great in the capitals of Europe, and though one side of him was totally wrapped up in the dispute, another looked upon it with a pathos of distance that Newton could not feel even for a moment. Leibniz, more experienced with women and the ways of the world, could put on a casual front, step aside and view the episode, as the Hanoverian hangers-on in London did, as something to joke about. Newton was incapable of such detachment. Writing from Hannover Leibniz reassured the Countess that even though she did not understand the calculus she was quite capable of comprehending the history of the controversy. He, Leibniz, was the proud upholder of little Hannover against mighty London. The principality from which she came might have to cede before the metropolis in grandeur and riches, but not in affection for the King, nor in the excellence of its women, nor in geometry. Leibniz was well aware of the mocking delight of the courtiers and after a prolix recounting of the facts in the scientific correspondence he concluded with a witty sally, letting the entourage of the King know that he was cognizant of the real motives behind their sudden preoccupation with learning. He threw a few well-chosen darts at the aristocratic underlings of the monarch who seemed to be siding with his enemy, and he missed no opportunity to call attention to Newton's bad temper, albeit indirectly, by way of an anecdote about the rage of losers in academic disputations at Leyden. "This, Madame, is the history of our controversy and it cannot fail to bore you. But it is impossible to provide you with complete information without going into detail and one cannot avoid making the judges yawn occasionally if they are to understand trials as long drawn out and as important as ours. And if the spectators did not become bored they would be enjoying it too much; they would be entertained at our expense."[56]

The May 18 observations of Newton on Leibniz' final reply were published in London after his death—Newton closed the book with a tedious repetition of the case.[57] If Leibniz had reminded him in almost every letter that on pages 253 and 254 of the first edition of the *Principia* he acknowledged that Leibniz had communicated to him a method not very different from his own, Newton had the last word. In a brief "Remarque" published in Des Maizeaux's compilation, he simply said that he had made the statement in the *Principia* not to honor Leibniz, but to establish his own priority; and in any event, whether Leibniz got the invention from him or discovered it after him was a matter of no importance, because second inventors had no rights whatever.[58] He had already written in the *Recensio:* "The sole Right is in the first Inventor until another finds out the same thing apart. In which case to take away the Right of the first Inventor, and divide it between him and that other, would be an Act of Injustice."[59] And what rights did second sons have? Equally none.

After Leibniz' death Newton continued to pursue him and anyone who had supported him. On December 10, 1716, Conti announced from Hannover, "M. Leibniz is dead and the dispute is over," and then in the next lines assured Newton that since he had access to the papers of the deceased he would be on the lookout for anything related to the quarrel.[60] The world was sharply divided in the manner of Joshua between those who were for "us" and those who were for "our enemies." Any continental like the Abbé Varignon of the French Académie des Sciences who had not spoken out against Newton was embraced.[61] In letters from 1719 through 1722 he rehearsed again and again the story of Johann Bernoulli's perfidy, Leibniz' libel, Bernoulli's attempts to be reconciled to him, new squabbles between Bernoulli and Dr. Taylor. Newton boasted of his own restraint, but was adamant against pardoning Bernoulli until he disavowed Leibniz publicly. The accounts are long-winded, repetitive, and boring, proof of Newton's continued obsession with the shade of the dead Leibniz.

Newton was aware of the mighty anger that smoldered within him all his life, eternally seeking objects, and he made heroic attempts to repress it. Though he protested that he shunned controversies and confrontations—he declared loftily that he left truth to shift for itself—and his censor was commensurate with his other great powers, many were the times when it was overwhelmed and the rage could not be contained. In his adult years, with one known exception—his wishing Locke dead as he had Mother and Father Smith—the anger was always directed into permissible channels. When the enemy was very powerful, as in the case of Robert Hooke, he tended to withdraw, to avoid, to hide away, to bide his time. But entrenched in office, he used virtually every means at his disposal to defeat an antagonist, and he required total submission, public humiliation, annihilation. The inherited morality of the Puritan world, like all Christian morality, prescribed love of God and love of fellowmen, the two principles to which Newton reduced all religion. But Puritanism also ordained the eradication of evil. To love and to destroy—an ambivalent commandment.

It is a commonplace that the scholarly disputations of the seventeenth century were rough. "Dog" and "rat" were among the milder epithets hurled by Richard Bentley at those who crossed him. And Hobbes's rejoinder to the Savilian professors at Oxford, Wallis and Ward, who had brutally demolished his pretensions to mathematics, is memorable: "So go your ways you uncivil ecclesiastics, inhuman divines, dedoctors of morality, unasinous colleagues, egregious pair of Issachers, most wretched Vindices and Indices Academiarum; and remember Vespasian's Law."[62] The bitter contests had not yet been divested of the emotions of religious zealotry. There were notorious enmities in the English scientific world: Flamsteed and Halley, Hooke and Oldenburg, Sloane and Woodward, Woodward and Mead conducted heroic battles that were not limited to mutual accusations of plagiarism, atheism, ignorance, stupidity, and downright fakery, but on occasion assumed the form of physical acts such as making faces at each other during meetings of the Royal Society and drawing swords on the street outside of Gresham College.[63] Written avowals of esteem often concealed barbs manufactured with such superb artistry that only the recipient felt the virulence of the poison in which they had been dipped.

There were also social and political undertones to the controversies that had little to do with the scientific facts or the personalities of the contestants. Disputes sometimes turned into wars between the English and the continentals. On Newton's side were members of the Royal Society and their official organ, the *Philosophical Transactions*. When scientists from Germany, Switzerland, or Holland dared intervene, they had the Leipzig *Acta Eruditorum* and the Hague *Journal littéraire* at their disposal. Embryonic and rather crude national partisanship obtruded into these fights, for there was jealousy over the pre-eminence of English experimental science, and when Leibniz prognosticated its decline in the next generation he betrayed a measure of *Schadenfreude* as well as reasonable accuracy. Occasionally one has the feeling that the English disputants are adopting the freewheeling style of political pamphleteers of the early eighteenth century. Tory and Whig rivals knew virtually no bounds in their mutual attacks and the aggressive party spirit was contagious, setting the tone of social behavior in the scientific establishment.

Priority battles were violent and inconclusive. Was a hint a suggestion or a hypothesis a discovery? Or did publication alone merit that recognition? But in what did publication consist—a letter to a learned society, a letter to a favorite correspondent, a sentence that communciated a new principle by scrambling the Latin characters? The definition usually depended upon who dropped the original idea. In his dispute with Hooke over the law of gravity Newton belittled mere conceptions and insisted upon the significance of working out the laborious computations and publishing them. In the controversy with Leibniz over the invention of the calculus, he stressed with even greater vehemence the initial act of discovery. Scientists protected their wares by writing in shorthand and in cryptograms, which were sometimes totally incomprehensible to the recipient. Newton maintained to the very end that the transmission of the two Latin anagrams plainly established his priority in the invention of the calculus.

In a scientific republic where caution was a common practice, Newton outdid the others. His was a suspicious nature, but his secretiveness, which had psychological as well as social roots, was only more extreme, not really bizarre. Galileo, Hooke, and Fatio resembled him in taking elaborate security measures. Rémond de Montmort agreed to exchange letters with a learned friend only on condition that secrecy be preserved; and he blamed Abate Conti, with his inability to respect confidences, for firing the conflict that embittered the last years of two great scientists.[64] When Newton recorded his invention of the calculus in an anagram which his correspondent could not possibly understand, he was patenting it. Old commonplace books were sometimes adduced as evidence of prior invention, but such proof was, after all, not to be compared to a letter in a rival's hands which had been read by a third party for better assurance and which no one but the author could decipher. Conundrums, riddles, anagrams, hieroglyphs, the secret language of prophecy—all these concealments fascinated Newton and his contemporaries.

In the light of the prevailing combative temper of the age, there may be a tendency to discount the many acrimonious quarrels that engaged Newton during his lifetime. But even if allowances are made for the general truculence of scientists and learned men, he remains one of the more ferocious practitioners of the art of scientific controversy. Genteel concepts of fair play are conspicuously absent, and he never gave any quarter. A fierce independence, a conviction that he was the chosen intermediary between the Creator and mankind, a sense of omnipotence, oscillation between his feelings of grandeur and self-depreciation (which some eighteenth-century and Victorian writers labeled modesty and humility), along with a capacity not unlike that of a paranoid to remain on the look-out for the tiniest weak points in an enemy's ramparts, conspired to make of him a formidable adversary. Anger and suspicion were his constant companions.[65]

When Hooke died and Newton became President and "Perpetual Dictator" of the Royal Society, he moved on to a more elevated plane. He ruled world science; anyone who would not do his bidding was excommunicated. Egged on by his young ones, he destroyed Leibniz. The timing is of some interest. The two quarrels with Hooke and Leibniz spanned virtually the whole of his mature life. (The counterattack on the continentals who had criticized the theory of colors earlier in his career was of a lesser order, though it had involved a great expenditure of psychic energy.) No sooner had the arch-villain Hooke died than the hitherto muted antagonism to Leibniz assumed vast proportions. This was the decisive battle of Newton's life. And when Leibniz was gone, another quarrel erupted, a fracas involving the French academicians and Newton's revision of world chronology.

Almost everybody in Newton's circle felt at least an occasional flick of the whip. The thwarting of his will in the slightest matter was punished with ostracism. Favorites were summarily dropped; they were banished from his presence the way Flamsteed and Leibniz were expunged from later editions of the *Principia*. He had no charitableness, though he distributed charity to relatives for whom he felt responsible; a single fault and a friend was rejected. He had a mission to extirpate evil, and he sat in constant judgment upon his fellowmen. The fonts of love had been all but dammed up. He would not speak with Richard Bentley for a year over differences in the interpretation of Daniel.[66] At one time he had a falling-out with Charles Montague over some unspecified "grudge."[67] He rebuked Hans Sloane over the administration of the Royal Society, and Woodward over his dispute with Sloane. He broke with William Whiston when he dared criticize Newton's chronology, was cold to Dr. Stukeley for a number of years because he stood as a candidate for Royal Society office without Newton's permission, and went to a formal arbitration with his old tenants and friends the Storers over an ill-repaired hut.[68] Even Halley was in disfavor for a while because of his levity in religious matters.[69]

The enemies on whom Newton vented his rage were not confined to the living; they included historical figures and institutions. Once again, commendable devotion to religious truth or chronological fact hid the genesis and real quality of Newton's intemperate anger, resentment, and vengefulness. There had been pagan claims to antiquity and he, Newton, was the defender of the image of Israel —Puritan Israel—against them. Alexandrian chronologists, Eratosthenes and Apollodorus, had lied. And then there was a whole set of Christian liars, beginning with Athanasius, who had falsified the true apostolic tradition and introduced Trinitarianism. Jerome was the next great adulterer of truth. When Newton was castigating Papists, he worked himself into a veritable paroxysm of rage. The catalogue of legitimate, permissible enemies of the Lord and Newton whom it was right to smite, as Saul had been ordered to kill the Amalek, was long. Living and dead, they were all liars, falsifiers, prevaricators, diversionists, impostors, corrupters of the truth. The same phrases occur again and again.

Newton's cunning, structure-making capacity exercised itself in inventing for others a schema of motives from minute details and suppositions or possibilities which then became certainties. Hooke had accused him of plagiarizing his theory of gravity. In fact, Newton maintained, it was Hooke who was the plagiarist, and Newton proposed to Halley how this *might* have happened: after Oldenburg's death, Hooke had possession of the letters of the Royal Society, and since he knew Newton's handwriting he might have read the letters in which Newton first hinted at the theory.[70] Leibniz saw and *could* have deciphered the cryptic letter on the calculus and therefore he certainly plagiarized Newton's method. When Newton analyzes and conjectures and structures the motives of others, he often casts into them the devils that are harassing *him*. He understood the process well enough—in his enemies. During the Leibniz controversy he assailed his rival with the characteristic accusation: "[H]e himself is guilty of what he complains of in others."[71]

The violence, acerbity, and uncontrolled passion of Newton's attacks, albeit directed into socially approved channels, are almost always out of all proportion with the warranted facts and character of the situations. One could, after all, have criticized Manetho's dynastic list without hurling epithets at an Egyptian who had been dead some thousands of years. The case in the Leibniz controversy could have been presented more judicially. Normally, the wardenship of the Mint was a sinecure and did not call for the actual pursuit of criminals into their hangouts and the establishment of a network of informers. All this gives weight to the hypothesis that the source of the rage lies elsewhere, that it accumulated in personal historical situations, that it was the onerous heritage of childhood traumas, beginning with the infant's anxiety after separation from the person who nurtured him—his mother, lost to Barnabas Smith. The rage carried over because it could not be effectively or fully discharged, or it was re-evoked and triggered off by life situations that seemed to reproduce the emotional climate of his boyhood. The lad Newton could not harm his half brother Benjamin or his stepfather Barnabas with impunity; but the great scientist Newton could destroy his rivals and his enemies living and dead. So deep is the hurt and so boundless the anger, however, that he cannot be appeased as long as he lives. His victories do not assuage; his anger is replenished by what it feeds upon.

On occasion the vengefulness assumed monstrous proportions. In his *Historical Memoirs of the Life of Dr. Samuel Clarke,* William Whiston reports in passing: "He [Mr. Jackson] heard Sir Isaac Newton also once pleasantly tell the Doctor [Clarke] that 'He had broke Leibnitz's Heart with his Reply to him.' "[72]

Chapter 16

BAFFLING THE MONSIEURS

The name of Newton raises the image of a profound Genius,
luminous and original. His System of Chronology would alone
be sufficient to assure him immortality.
  —Edward Gibbon, *Remarques critiques sur le nouveau*
  systême de chronologie du Chevalier Newton

The war between Newton and Leibniz has qualities of pathos, if
not tragedy; Newton's final battle with the French scholars is opéra
bouffe.

In the 1720's rumor spread among the antiquarians of Paris that
the elderly Newton, already crowned with the laurels of immortality, had descended from the heavens where he divined the laws of
planetary movement and had deigned to study chronology, mythology, and the revolutions of states and empires. The secret of his
chronological studies was out. The learned abbés of the Académie
des Inscriptions et Belles-Lettres and their secular colleagues were
all agog because it was reported that the conqueror of the physical
universe had devised a system of chronology founded upon novel
principles which disrupted the traditional concordance of ancient
sacred and profane history. The chronologists were at first delighted,
or that at least is the academician de Bougainville's later testimony,
to welcome Newton into their company, as he sought new triumphs
in a savage land where the common herd saw only rocks and thorny
bushes. Mathematics in his hands seemed a universal instrument
capable of resolving all problems. Why should he not free history
from its alloy of mythological fictions?

349

Word went around that the Abate Conte Antonio Conti, who had figured so prominently in the bitter interchange of letters with Leibniz, was in actual possession of an abstract of Newton's chronology which contained the whole system of ancient history in brief. He was said to have acquired a copy of the text in England from Caroline of Anspach, Princess of Wales, who kept the original manuscript among her most treasured possessions.[1] Newton had been persuaded to prepare the abstract when, during a conversation on education with the Princess, he intimated that for many years he had been working on an ancient history with a new plan, though his papers, dating back to Cambridge days, were faulty and in disorder.[2] Sir Isaac granted Conti's request to have a transcript made, with the admonition that it must be kept private. While he habitually enveloped his writings with secrecy and mystification,[3] he was often deceived about the discretion with which they were handled in England. Without his knowledge a number of copies of the abstract had been made, at least three of which are extant: one in King's College Library, Cambridge, its first page decorated with a foliated border and an illuminated initial, two in the British Museum suffixed by polemical appendices from unknown disputants.[4] Of course he himself had written, rewritten, and revised more than a dozen drafts of the abstract, bestowing different names upon the various versions as he went along. The most complete drafts in English are entitled "A short Chronicle from the first memory of things in Europe to the conquest of Persia by Alexander the Great. The times are set down in years before Christ." Latin abstracts sometimes cover a longer period and are called "Rerum ante Imperium Romanorum gestarum Chronicon parvum" or "Rerum ante Imperia quatuor summa gestarum Chronicon parvum." Some of the English drafts occasionally lapse into Latin; and one Latin text includes a number of dates from Chinese history.

Though the Abate Conti in Paris did not surrender his manuscript to a printer, he talked freely about its contents and paraded his intimacy with Newton in the aristocratic and scholarly salons that he frequented. He whetted the appetite of many *érudits;* the text itself he showed only to favorites, among them the Jesuit Father Etienne Souciet, an authority on ancient chronology. The abstract was really nothing more than a chronological index to ancient history, about twenty pages in length, and scholars were left to guess the theoretical basis of the revolutionary system from passing hints. Through the agency of scientists in Newton's circle with whom he had established amicable relations during his sojourn in England, Conti sought clarification of moot points, but he met with a wall of silence; Newton had previously warned him that he would not reply to objections. There seems to have been only one exception to the rule: Father Souciet's learned queries prepared in 1720 were shown to Newton by John Keill, the faithful protégé, himself involved in controversies on the early revolutions of the planet, who received by word of mouth Newton's message that the manuscript in Conti's hands was an abstract of a much longer work, "and he hath not set down the proofs."[5] In another laconic pronouncement Newton casually quoted from memory his source for redating the Argonautic expedition, whose crucial significance for the whole new system of chronology the perspicacious Father Souciet had sensed at once. Keill transmitted the great Newton's oracular answer to Brook Taylor, former secretary of the Royal Society then in Paris, who in turn communicated it to Father Souciet.[6]

Keill's letter released the astronomic key to the mystery of the new chronology even before its publication: the principle of the retrogression of the equinoctial points. "According to his best remembrance he [Newton] found that the ancients had recorded that at the time of the Argonauts Chiron had found the equinoctial points to be in the middle or 15th degree of the constellation Aries. In Meto's time it was found to be in the 8th and in Hipparchus' in the 4th degree of that constellation. Hipparchus reckoned the recession to one degree every seventy-two years [sic] and by that means if we compute we shall find the time of the Argonautical expedition to have fallen out at the time Sir Isaac puts it."[7] The Jesuit chronologist was by no means satisfied with this response to his inquiries, but he maintained "la religion du secret"[8] and published nothing on the subject, though he at once set to work in private to undermine the Newtonian system and to raise his own in its place.

By 1724 the garrulous Conti could restrain himself no longer, and he began passing about the text of the abstract promiscuously among learned men. M. de Pouilly of the Académie des Inscriptions et Belles-Lettres allowed his colleague Nicolas Fréret, a scholar of antiquities then at the height of his powers, to copy and translate the manuscript he had been lent by Abate Conti. When Fréret, who had command of Greek, Latin, Hebrew, and Arabic and could dispute the etymologies of Samuel Bochart and other polyhistors of the previous century, analyzed Newton's text he was aghast. The abstract had cut about four hundred years off the traditional record of Greek history and fixed the Argonautic expedition as late as 936 B.C., telescoping events in an unprecedented manner, and had then slashed even greater chunks of time from the antiquity of the other ancient kingdoms. More than twenty-five years later Jean-Pierre de Bougainville was still apologizing uneasily for the next step taken by his predecessor in the permanent secretaryship of the Academy—the unauthorized publication of the abstract, with a critique. "At the prospect of a revolution about to change the face or at least the perspective of the historical world it was natural, shall we say it was correct, that M. Fréret should become alarmed and that he should move to the frontier to reconnoiter the terrain."[9]

The pirated edition of the *Abstract of Chronology* appeared in 1725;[10] it was then attached as a supplement to the French version in seven volumes of Dean Humphrey Prideaux's *History of the Jews and Neighboring Nations, from the Declension of the Kingdoms of Israel and Judah to the time of Christ*. This was a most unfortunate union, for though the Dean had corresponded with Newton on ancient calendars and there is a British Museum manuscript setting forth Newton's opinions on the subject to the Bishop of Worcester which passed through his hands, Prideaux in the preface to the first London edition of his work (1716) had declared Archbishop Ussher's to be "the exactest and most perfect work of Chronology that hath been published."[11] The two chronologies did not mesh; they flagrantly contradicted each other. Cavelier the printer had prefixed the *Abstract* with a notice which detailed the circumstances of the publication, insisting that a letter from Newton on May 27, 1725, objecting to publication, had arrived too late. He freely admitted that his translator's acquisition of the text might have involved "une infidélité," but that was not his affair—he merely wanted to prove that he had behaved toward M. Newton with scrupulous propriety.

Fréret's remarks appended anonymously (he signed himself the Observator) to the translation of the *Abstract* were on the whole deferential. He pleaded before the public that final judgment be reserved until the appearance of Newton's complete system. For the first time, allusion was made in print to Father Souciet's criticisms, which had been bruited about, and Fréret aligned himself on the Jesuit's side. He questioned two of Newton's fundamental propositions, the advancement of the date of the Argonautic expedition to 936 b.c. and the contention of the great mathematician that the ancients had erroneously reckoned royal reigns as averaging three to a century when the empirical evidence proved that kings lasted on their thrones an average of only eighteen to twenty years. Fréret upheld the antiquity of the Egyptians and their discovery of the arts and sciences on biblical grounds. It seemed to him inconsistent for Newton to brush aside the testimony of Egyptian priests on the beginnings of their culture and yet to accept uncritically the mythic traditions of the Greek poets, certainly less reliable sources. Doubt was cast on Newton's identification of Sesostris and Osiris. Fréret politely praised Newton's ingenuity, then detracted from the purported novelty of many of his findings by noting the priority of John Marsham and the Count de Boulainvilliers.

When word of this illegitimate French publication reached Newton, he was outraged. In high dudgeon he prepared a defense of his system in a paper to the Royal Society, seven separate drafts of which exist,[12] and he created another international scandal.[13] As with his major scientific discoveries, he had been reluctant to publish; but once the die was cast he was passionate in defense of his position. From the presidency of the most august scientific body in the world he denounced the pirated edition and uncovered a plot in which Abate Conti was the mastermind, Fréret his agent, and Cavelier the printer a mere tool.

Newton's strictures on the Observator, known to be Fréret by everyone in Paris, were superior and magisterial. The French critic had completely misunderstood Newton's dating of the Argonautic expedition and had presumptuously undertaken to refute a work whose very principles he did not comprehend. Though it was true, Newton confessed, that in his Cambridge period he had occupied himself agreeably with history and chronology when he was fatigued by other studies, he had never intended to prepare a book on the subject as the Observator announced.

The full barrage of Newton's invective was aimed at his erstwhile friend Conti, who had violated what Newton considered a solemn trust in communicating the manuscript. Newton dismissed the rather flimsy pretext of the printer; a man would have to be completely deprived of his senses to consent that his work be published in a translation he had never seen by a writer with whom he was not acquainted and weighed down with a hostile appendix that was a refutation of his theories. About seven years before, Abate Conti had indeed paid him a visit informing him that a "friend" wished to speak with him about chronology. The "friend" expressed a desire to see what he had composed on the subject, and though he remonstrated that his papers were confused, he finally agreed to present "him" with an abstract if it were kept secret. But once in France, Newton charged, Conti spread copies about indiscriminately and directed a whole cabal.

Fréret was treated mildly in comparison with the formal public denunciation of Abate Conti. This man was a false scientist, an intriguer who under the pretense of mediating the quarrel with Leibniz had tried to entice Newton into further disputations on universal gravitation, the sensorium of God, time, space, the perfection of the universe. Newton disdainfully concluded with the hope that he

354

would no longer be bothered by scientific communications from Conti, any more than by perpetual motion. While the paper inserted in the *Philosophical Transactions of the Royal Society* for 1725 was rational and pointed, it was irascible, not at all in harmony with the image of majestic calm which was the official portrait of Newton toward the end of his life.

Conti refused to be silenced. He published a French translation of Newton's communication along with a rejoinder, *Réponse aux Observations sur la chronologie de M. Newton, avec une lettre de M. l'Abbé Conti au sujet de ladite réponse* (1726).[14] Newton had erred when he claimed that Conti's was the only copy of the abstract; he knew of the existence of three or four others. The promise of secrecy did not preclude criticism, and he had tried in vain to discover the basis for Newton's identification of Sesostris and Osiris. He openly admitted having discussed the system and referred to Father Souciet's attempts to secure further clarification. Newton might have avoided the whole uproar had he condescended to transmit in writing the reply he had just printed. Conti's excuses for his breach of confidence were rather weak. Was it not patent that a work of which there were several other copies would sooner or later be presented in print? Was that a crime which merited a public rebuke? "Anyone but Mr. Newton would have been delighted by the favorable idea I had formed of the merit of his work and by my eagerness to make it known that he was as enlightened in history and criticism as he was profound in Mathematics and in Philosophy." Turning the tables he maliciously reminded his readers that Newton himself had published without permission a letter by Leibniz which Conti had shown him. As for the accusation that he was a perfidious friend, Conti called to witness a galaxy of French learned men and aristocrats in whose presence he had defended the Newtonian system.

The Venetian noble who had been insulted before the whole of Europe could not allow the charges to stand without a counterthrust. "It is astonishing that Mr. Newton, who in Philosophy is only willing to reason on facts, abandons this method in the judgment of human actions. If he persists in his accusations *is he not obliged,* according to his own principle, to prove them, *at the risk of becoming* guilty of calumny? Now how will he demonstrate, as he would a geometric curve . . . my masquerade of friendship, my clandestine intervention, and the other chimeras with which it has suited him to embellish the opinion he has formed of me?" Abate Conti gave vent to a full measure of aristocratic scorn for the commoner, for he was above the pettiness of scientific controversy. "I apply myself to learning neither to make a fortune nor to acquire a great name. I study as I travel, that is to say, for my pleasure." In experimental philosophy and mathematics he had no great involvement, hence Newton's opinion could not touch him. "I like this sort of study very much but it does not at all agitate me. At bottom I do not hold it in any greater esteem than the quadrille or hunting. It all comes to the same when one examines the matter dispassionately. And moreover I am of the opinion that if one should make exception of fifteen or twenty problems useful to the arts and practices of society, all the rest will perhaps one day be as much an object of contempt as certain scholastic problems." With this flippant denigration of science he avenged himself on its most celebrated genius.

After Conti's death the editor of his papers described amicable conversations with Newton in 1715 on ancient history and religion, during which the fundamental principles of the new chronology had been discussed.[15] He suggested direct intent on the part of the French scholars to smoke Newton out and force him into a defense of his system by publishing the *Abstract*. Newton's was the intemperate reply of an old bigot, touched in the head by the Camisard Prophets of London, seeing visions. "In Paris they generally took Conti's side."[16]

Once Fréret had published the text, Father Souciet considered himself absolved of the vow of secrecy. His five mammoth dissertations against the little *Abstract of Chronology* were an avalanche of astronomical, literary, and numismatic evidence presented with logical precision which did not leave a Newtonian date unassailed. The later dissertations had been written after Newton's outburst, and Father Souciet joined the ranks of those in sympathy with his friend and protector Abate Conti. "Good God!" he exclaimed in a most unecclesiastical apostrophe, "How little these gentlemen make use of their Philosophy! Or what a strange Philosophy theirs must be."[17] Defending Conti's integrity and dedicating this work to him, he taunted the Englishman: "But why all this mystery? Does Newton want to repeat with some new Leibniz the scene that was enacted over the infinitesimal calculus?" His conclusion was smug: "M. Newton's Chronology cannot stand . . . he has made an error of about 530 years and . . . mine on the contrary is correct."[18]

Souciet's plan envisaged a complete demolition in four stages. "The first will contain the astronomic proofs that destroy this new system. The second will expound the historical proofs. Those I have drawn from medals will make up the content of the third. And the fourth will refute the changes that Mr. Newton has introduced into the length of a generation." Some of Father Souciet's arguments outdid Newton's wildest conjectures. One was based upon the hypothesis that Columella in his reading of a text of Meton (ix. 14) had confused A, the letter equivalent of number one, with H, the letter for eight, the scribe having somehow opened the two vertical strokes of the letter instead of closing them. Meton had thus really fixed the equinox in the first degree, not in the eighth, and in following Columella Newton had fallen into error.[19]

Souciet was rewarded with the plaudits of his fellow Jesuits. On March 24, 1727, Father Joseph Ignace de Rebeque wrote him: "I have read with pleasure your dissertations against Mr. Newton"; and though he suggested minor rectifications on April 19, 1727, he assured Souciet that nothing would change the correctness of his demonstrations against Newton's system.[20] When John Conduitt heard of Souciet's assault he was so apprehensive about further upsetting the aged scientist with the prospect of another international polemic that he had the main points summarized by a friend, excising the more contentious passages. Much to Conduitt's surprise, when Newton later read the text in full he seemed not at all perturbed, but his opinions remained unaltered; the Jesuit was simply wrong.[21] The scientific war in which eighteenth-century scholars reveled was on, and it continued intermittently for a solid century—theologians, historians, astronomers, and amateur scholars all joined the contest. The battle array was by no means exclusively national,[22] even though there were echoes of the clash between English Newtonians and French Cartesians.

The fight had hardly gathered momentum when its principal contender died and was buried with honors such as had not yet been bestowed upon any European scientist. To the astute Fontenelle fell the task of reading his eulogy before the French Académie des Sciences, which had honored Newton with membership. Primed by memoranda from John Conduitt, Fontenelle delivered a classical panegyric; but he could not avoid reference to the *Abstract,* which had involved a colleague of Fréret's eminence in the "little academy." With tact and adroitness he managed to turn the piracy and critique of the *Abstract* into a compliment to the great deceased. "Does not their very eagerness do honor to Mr. Newton? They quickly seized the chance for the glory of having such an adversary."[23] If Fréret sinned in allowing the *Abstract* to be issued without permission, strange historical vengeance was wrought upon his memory later in the century when the wicked Baron d'Holbach, without leave, printed scurrilous atheist pamphlets as the posthumous works of the renowned permanent secretary of the Académie des Inscriptions et Belles-Lettres.[24]

Abate Conti, pursuing the quarrel with relentless tenacity even after Newton's death, soon discovered a rival Italian system on the early history of mankind to pit against his enemy. Its author was the obscure Giambattista Vico. With pathetic gratitude the unrecognized Neapolitan reproduced favorable letters from Conti in the introduction to the 1730 edition of the *Scienza Nuova.* Conti had sent extracts of the work to Father Souciet in Paris; he had encouraged the impecunious Vico to rearrange his materials and to issue a new version in larger type; above all he praised the originality of his ideas, which even the English would be obliged to concede.[25]

The bombshell that Newton hurled into the staid world of the chronologists largely depended for its effect upon the scientific prestige he had won elsewhere. The idea that the new astronomy could establish a number of irrefutable bench marks in the history of antiquity was in itself a very attractive one, particularly at a time when there were few archaeological monuments which had been dated with any certainty. Newton, if he were right, might rescue history from Baylean skepticism. His work appeared at the very moment when a new group of chronologists like Fréret, who had reviewed the mammoth compendia of the seventeenth century, were themselves troubled by grave doubts about the easy findings of the previous age. It was no passing incident in the lives of the antiquarians when the great Newton was reported to have discovered unimpeachable dates for the major events and when these dates departed substantially from tradition. When it appeared, however, that the system presented in his *Chronology* was dependent not upon pure mathematics but in the last analysis upon the reading of a fragment of the Greek astronomer Eudoxus which might in itself be corrupt, there was disappointment—and secret rejoicing. Newton could not be the arbiter of the historical world, and men would have to proceed with laborious individual studies, making interpretations of myth and early history vested with greater or smaller degrees of probability.

Newton had been greatly wounded by criticism of the *Abstract*. He complained to the Right Reverend Zachary Pearce, Lord Bishop of Rochester, about the "ill-usage" of foreign scholars, and explained his reluctance to publish the full chronology on the ground that "he did not care to give them any further handle for repeating the same ill-usage again." Reverend Pearce believed, nevertheless, that in 1725 he had finally overcome Newton's shyness with the argument that foreign misinterpretations made it imperative for him to leave a true version of his system. When he visited Newton shortly before his death, he witnessed the leave-taking of Mr. Innys the bookseller, who had been discussing the *Chronology* with Newton and later claimed that a firm promise to print it had been given him. As Dr.

Pearce entered Newton's chamber, he found the old man revising the text without spectacles and at a great distance from the window —a little light from the sun upon which he had so long gazed now sufficed him.[26] There is ample corroboration of Newton's preoccupation with the *Chronology* in his last year, when most of his reported conversations centered about ancient history and the beginning of things. On Christmas Day 1725 he showed his friend Stukeley a copy of his drawing of the plan of Solomon's Temple, which became the basis of the fifth chapter in his *Chronology*.[27]

After Newton's death, when executors began to examine and appraise his voluminous manuscripts, they were generally unimpressed with what they found. The greater *Chronology* might have been consigned to oblivion, leaving nothing but the paltry *Abstract,* had it not been for William Whiston's prodding and not disinterested insistence that it be brought out.[28] Whiston had for years stored up rancor against his former patron, and he was chafing at the bit for a chance to destroy the system. Newton's manuscript finally appeared in 1728 as *The Chronology of Ancient Kingdoms Amended,* with a dedication to the Queen by John Conduitt, a bit of florid prose that had benefited from revision by Alexander Pope himself.[29]

Chapter 17

PROPHECY AND HISTORY

The folly of interpreters has been to foretel times and things
by this Prophecy, as if God designed to make them Prophets.
By this rashness they have not only exposed themselves, but
brought Prophecy also into contempt. The design of God was
much otherwise. He gave this and the Prophecies of the Old
Testament, not to gratify men's curiosities by enabling them
to foreknow things, but that after they were fulfilled they might
be interpreted by the event, and his own Providence, not the
Interpreters, be then manifested thereby to the world. For the
event of things predicted many ages before, will then be a
convincing argument that the world is governed by Providence.
    —Newton, *Observations upon the Prophecies
    of Daniel, and the Apocalypse of St. John*

Dᴜʀɪɴɢ the last decades of his life, Newton the scholar, a part of
himself aloof from all worldly agitations, continued to scribble away
industriously in private, and though he never published any of his
historical and theological writings he left a trace of his studies in
the most improbable places. Precisely how and when reflections on
the Cabala, Valentinus, Persian superstition, Christian love, the chronology of Egypt, Assyria, and Greece got on the backs of records of
melted plate dated 1706 or 1714 baffles the investigator. Where were
these notes actually written? Did they fill in intolerable moments of
inactivity at the Mint or did he take the documents home, where he
jotted all over their margins, blank sections, and even narrow inter-
stices? Paper was expensive and like many aging men of his character he could become obsessively stingy about little things. (This is

not contradicted by anecdotes that tell of acts of munificence to relatives or disciples).

The existence of Newton's manuscripts on mythology and theology was known to his Scottish friends David Gregory and Archibald Pitcairne at least as early as 1694–1695. Newton had discussed the prophetic books with the Platonist Henry More in 1680, and at least one manuscript on chronology, which is dated, belongs to that year. A large part of the correspondence with Locke in the nineties is concerned with the meaning of sacred texts and early church history. Though any sequential arrangement of the manuscripts must be conjectural, a great many of them clearly belong to Newton's London period and some can be dated in a general way not only from the occasional unsteadiness of his handwriting but from the contents of letters on whose reverse they were written and from official records at the Mint whose year is known. At the time of the Sotheby sale of Newton's papers from the Portsmouth Collection in 1936, lots totaling close to two hundred thousand words were described as relating directly to chronology, as distinct from what were called the theological writings, which amounted to more than a million words. Most of these papers on what would today be called church history or the history of Christian doctrine rather than theology are now dispersed in various hands throughout the world, though a substantial portion, perhaps the better half, acquired by Lord Keynes, was presented to King's College Library, Cambridge. In addition to manuscripts salvaged from the Portsmouth Collection there are four volumes, about a thousand folios, chiefly on chronology and theology, which the Ekins family gave to New College. Today King's College, Cambridge, owns the greater number of manuscripts on ecclesiastical history and church doctrine; the Bodleian, acting as repository for New College, is richer in chronology and ancient history.

There is little probability that Newton intended to publish during his lifetime any of these manuscripts which had been accumulating for decades, until knowledge of some of the works became public in the 1720's. This was his private world, and he was not grateful to those who, like Conti, brought it into the open. His devotion to these subjects long after his inquiries in natural philosophy and alchemy had virtually ceased poses some problems. That Newton spent a great portion of his time on historical studies, religious and secular, the sheer bulk of the manuscripts he left behind is incontrovertible evidence. Though the memoir that John Conduitt prepared for Fontenelle in October 1727 calls these researches a "divertissement" of his leisure hours and Newton's formal statement before the Royal Society supports him, the ardor with which he defended his chronological system in his last years belies the impression. Newton's own testimony about his works cannot always be accepted at face value; and even at play Isaac Newton was never free from serious purpose. The Crown official was sensitive about public reports of activities that might be construed as deflections from his appointed duties. The little puritanical boy in him was always under the surveillance of some authority.

Viewed in the light of the religious dedication of all his works, Newton's secret researches were a form of daily prayer and communion with God. They are thus not wholly separate from his scientific discoveries; nor should they be strictly compartmentalized into theological, chronological, and mythological studies. History sacred and profane was part of one divine order and the world physical and the world historical were not essentially different in nature. When eighteenth-century philosophes adopted the Newtonian scientific world order as a model for their social and moral systems, they were doing violence to their source in one vital respect. They were banishing the God who was for Newton the immanent power in the whole of existence. The unity of inspiration is incontestable. Newton discovered the impress of the Father whom he never knew everywhere, in nature, history, morals.

Nor were his scholarly studies esoterica. The history of the Creation, the geological transformations of the planet incident to the Flood, the ancient history of mankind, and the interpretation of prophecy were problems commonly discussed in Newton's circle. Many of his closest friends and admirers were at once natural philosophers, chronologists, theologians, and Bible expositors. Though they belonged to the Established Church, they too were in the Puritan tradition in their appreciation of the Bible. And the spirit that animated their Scriptural studies was the same: they all began with the Bible's "true and historical meaning," and their reading remained consistently antiallegorical and antiparabolical. The Bible described events as they had "actually happened" in the commonsense meaning of occurrence; it was the best place to look for historical facts about the objective world.

In a long letter written sometime in January 1681 to Dr. Thomas Burnet, author of the *Telluris Theoria Sacra,* Newton had expressed profound antagonism to the allegorical explanation of the opening Mosaic verses describing the history of Creation. Newton divorced himself from the Renaissance interpreters in the Philonic tradition who looked upon the Bible, as they did upon many pagan myths, as the vehicle for a lofty mystical philosophy. By making a "physica sacra" of these passages Newton gave sanction in advance to the learned conciliations between his system and the text of the Bible which followed in great numbers in the next century.[1] Discovering the principles of modern physics and astronomy in Holy Writ, however, was not allegorizing. He drew a subtle yet fundamental distinction: Moses was popularizing—his was truth for the masses, but nonetheless simple, straightforward, scientific truth, natural history. Newton at first used diffident language: "To answer these things fully would require comment upon Moses whom I dare not pretend to understand . . ."; but then, "by way of conjecture," he gave a circumstantial account of the gravitational forces at play in locating the planets, God's shaping the earth, and slowly accelerating its motion that is hardly to be found in Genesis by the uninitiate. He was merely clarifying the mode of speech, he insisted to Burnet. "[T]he things signified by such figurative expressions are not Ideall or moral, but true. For Moses, accommodating his words to the gross conceptions of the vulgar, describes things much after the manner as one of the vulgar would have been inclined to do had he lived & seen the whole series of wt Moses describes." Moses depicted the historical processes of Creation exactly as they had taken place; his only concession was stylistic. Instead of demarcating the stages of Creation as a trained physical scientist might, Moses, who knew all about vapors and gravity and the Copernican astronomy, reported the events in a manner comprehensible to the ordinary man. Moses was a simplifier, not a falsifier, out of necessity, to improve communication. "To describe them distinctly as they were in them selves would have made the narration tedious & confused, amused the vulgar & become a Philosopher more then a Prophet."[2] This kind of double-truth doctrine with its admonition of discretion to the philosopher was not alien to Newton. To believe the monotheistic truth, but not to publish it in terms that the ignorant would misunderstand, was a practice congenial to his closed nature and his distrust of the mob. Newton had acted from the same motives in the *Principia,* where he intentionally wrote in a cryptic and complicated manner, as he told William Derham, to discourage ignorant quibblers. Moses and he had in common the doctrine that the same ideas could be expressed both in an easy and in an esoteric way. Moses' history of Creation might now require interpretation, but in the direction of the matter-of-fact and the scientific rather than the metaphysical.

For Newton, history and revelation were complementary presentations of the same process. The Book of Daniel and the Apocalypse of St. John were prophetic historical statements which had proved to be factually true down to the minutest detail; they had predicted, described in advance, the early history of Christianity and the history of the great postbiblical monarchies. The fulfillment of prophecy in history was always one of the most convincing proofs of the truth of religion in both the Jewish and the Christian traditions. As Augustine had written in *De Civitate Dei:* "Much of it we see to have come true already, and that gives us firm hope that the rest also must come true."[3] In the *Observations upon the Prophecies* Newton demonstrated that the biblical foretellings had been abundantly fulfilled in Eastern and European history by spelling out the specific events, complete with geographic locations, names of kings, dates of battles, and revolutions of empires, to which they corresponded. "The whole scene of sacred prophecy is composed of three principal parts: the regions beyond Euphrates, represented by the first two beasts of Daniel, the empire of the Greeks on this side of Euphrates, represented by the Leopard and by the He-Goat; and the empire of the Latins on this side of Greece, represented by the beast with ten horns."[4]

Since the prophecies of the Old and New Testaments had to be harmonious one with another, in his commentary on the Apocalypse Newton was at pains to show that John and Daniel foretold the same historical events without inconsistencies. Nebuchadnezzar's dream—of the monstrous image composed of four metals— was for Newton, as it had been for most expositors of prophecy in the Judeo-Christian tradition, the basic framework of world history; it represented the succession of the four monarchies of Babylon, Persia, Greece, and Rome, followed by the barbarian invasions from the north which were signified by the feet and toes of the image. The vision of the four beasts was a recapitulation of the same prophecy. Ten horns of the fourth beast were ten kingdoms in sequence: the Vandals and Alans in Spain and Africa, the Suevians in Spain, the Visigoths, the Alans in Gallia, the Burgundians, the Franks, the Britons, the Huns, the Lombards, and Ravenna. The eleventh horn was none other than the Church of Rome, a kingdom different from all the others because it falsely claimed the universal bishopric: "With his mouth he gives laws to kings and nations as an Oracle; and pretends to Infallibility, and that his dictates are binding to the whole world. . . ."[5] The last chapter of the *Observations upon the Prophecies* used Daniel as the source book for a pejorative history of monasticism, of the growth of saint worship, and of the adoration of relics under the wicked hegemony of the Catholic Church.

The prophecy of the seventy weeks in Daniel was read by Newton, as it had been by many others before him, to prove that the coming of Christ had been foretold in the Old Testament. From Ezra to the death of Christ a period of four hundred ninety years had elapsed, equivalent to seventy weeks if each week were valued at seven years. As for the Second Coming, Newton cautiously avoided the error of the millenarians among his friends who had settled upon

17. Isaac Newton, 1725

16. Isaac Newton, circa 1725

18. Isaac Newton, 1726

a date. "This part of the Prophecy being therefore not yet fulfilled, I shall not attempt a particular interpretation of it. . . ."[6] Fatio de Duillier had been much too certain about the imminent burning of London. Newton always remained firm by the principle that the truth of prophecy could be demonstrated only *after* it had been fulfilled, never before. While he permitted himself to foresee the rebuilding of Jerusalem—"It may perhaps come forth not from the Jews themselves, but from some other kingdom friendly to them, and precede their return from captivity and give occasion to it"—he drew a curtain over the epoch and circumstances of the event. "The manner I know not. Let time be the interpreter."[7] Thus while the books of prophecy were history, the history of things to come, their language could not be truly understood by ordinary men until after the events prophesied had actually happened.[8]

The true meaning of prophecy had revealed itself progressively through time to a long line of interpreters. Newton freely admitted that he had been influenced by the mid-seventeenth-century Puritan expositor Joseph Mede (More's role is somehow never mentioned), and he considered his own commentaries merely another stage in the gradual unfolding of the complete significance of prophetic revelation. But his was a vital addition, perhaps the last one. His lifetime had coincided with a crucial moment in sacred history. "Amongst the Interpreters of the last age there is scarce one of note who hath not made some discovery worth knowing; and thence I seem to gather that God is about opening these mysteries. The success of others put me upon considering it; and if I have done any thing which may be useful to following writers, I have my design."[9]

About one thing Newton had no doubt: God's relationship with the historical world through prophecy was continuous, and He had never abandoned His creatures. Men had not learned from experience about God's unity and the moral laws of behavior; neither were these principles innate. They were truths imparted in a series of *historical* actions, prophecies, which not only forecast the future, but revealed moral laws and bore witness to a steady communication between God and mankind. The mechanics of prophetic revelation had been described over and over again by the chosen ones upon whom the Spirit had descended. Newton's conception of prophecy remained completely in the tradition of Maimonides; it was not wild enthusiasm or mystical illumination, but a granting of truths to men whose striving for the perfection of reason and whose imaginative capacities had, after mighty labors, put them in harmony with the divine will. Newton himself fitted this description perfectly. The first revelation had transmitted elementary rules of human conduct to Noah that remained the essentials of morality for all time. The laws of Noah had been reaffirmed on numerous later occasions by God's appearance to the patriarchs, to Moses, to the prophets, to Christ, to the apostles. These were the great episodes of sacred history. In the pre-Christian history of the Jews there is constant divine surveillance and active intervention; God even resorted to stratagems in dealing with His chosen people as He might with wayward children: "When the Israelites came out of Egypt God led them not through the way of the land of the Philistines although that was near, for God said, Least peradventure the people repent when they see war & they return into Egypt but God led the people about through the wilderness."[10] Divine revelation, which since the patriarchs and the prophets had served as the guide for action in the Jewish commonwealth, rendered the tenor of their history different from that of the Gentiles. The history of the Israelites and of their patriarchal progenitors is the history of a church, not of a kingdom. They were constantly directed by the spirit of prophecy which was denied to the others, a religious fact that established the inferiority of the Greeks and all other pagans.

As a rule Newton's history of the transition from the Jewish to the Christian dispensation tends to minimize rather than to accentuate the break. He is particularly careful when depicting the administration of the early church to demonstrate the gradual transformation of Jewish officers such as presidents of synagogues into bishops. The appearance of Christ and the apostles was the signal for a second covenant and a temporary renewal of prophecy. "At length when a new treaty was to be preached to the Gentiles, namely, *that*

Jesus was the Christ, God sent new Prophets and Teachers: but after their writings were also received and read in the Synagogues of the Christians, Prophecy ceased a second time."[11] From the beginning it had been foreordained that the Christian church like the Jewish should become contumacious—Newton pointed to the establishment of the "fraudulent Catholic religion"—and that the second covenant should not be renewed until many years later, at the time of the Protestant Reformation.

Whenever the prophetic texts were cryptic Newton treated them as "hieroglyphs," a special "secret language" to which he could provide the key by analogies between the "world natural" and "an empire or kingdom considered as a world political."[12] His set of equivalences is elaborately described in the opening of the second chapter of the *Observations upon the Prophecies.*[13] Newton's superb confidence in the superiority of his own method of deciphering the language of prophecy over that of any of his predecessors was rooted in the eminently scientific reflection that his formulas for reading the sacred "hieroglyphs" actually worked in all instances in Scripture where like images were used.

Newton's theory of biblical symbols is precisely the inverse of the Philonic tradition. While neo-Platonic interpretations would read metaphysical and philosophical ideas into the most matter-of-fact descriptions of things—on the presumption that the Bible would not be dealing with ordinary lowly objects—Newton tackled the fantastic symbols in the prophetic texts and found commonplace equivalents in political history for the weird dreamlike visions of Ezekiel, Daniel, and the Apocalypse. Far from subscribing to a cabalistic belief in the special roles of "cherubim" and "seraphim" in the universe, in his manuscripts he treats such words as "hieroglyphs" for plain social groups. Evil spirits simply meant diseases and distempers of the mind, devils were deflated into imaginary ghosts, and "Inchanters, Magicians, Sorcerers, Necromancers & Witches signified deceivers & cheats who by certain forms of words & ceremonies & other juggling tricks pretended to supernatural powers & arts of prognosticating for magnifying themselves among the people."[14]

The *Observations upon the Prophecies* is by no means the best work that Newton left behind on the fulfillment of prophecy. The number of manuscript drafts on the subject indicates that he was engaged in demonstrating the accuracy of the predictions in every verse in Daniel and the Apocalypse through a recounting of Judaic, early Christian, and medieval history down to the Reformation. The *Observations*, which came through his half nephew Ben Smith's hands, is a rather disorderly collection of texts. "The Language of the Prophets," about fifty thousand words long, is a far more complete, better organized, and more consecutive narrative covering the same ground.[15] As a whole, this circumstantial manuscript is a history of the churches Jewish and Christian and their relations with temporal power up to modern times. Nowhere else is Newton so precise in identifying each phrase and image in the prophecies with a specific historical event, justifying the various equivalences with erudite reasons derived from his knowledge of Jewish antiquities and of the classical corpus. And always the tendency is toward reduction to the concrete.

In his interpretation of prophecy Newton made use of numerous "mathematical" calculations which were among the standard techniques of the cabalists: one, known as "gematria," involved the translation of a name or a noun into its numerical equivalent (*A* being equal to *1*, *B* to *2*, and so forth) in order to prognosticate a future date, the coming of the Messiah, for example.[16] While Newton eschewed foretelling, he used similar methods to vindicate past prophecies: "Whence the word ΛΑΤΕΙΝΟϹ is the name of the Western Empire. . . . This name is the proper name of a man & the number of this name is 666 & this is the number of the name of the Beast, as Irenaeus hath long since observed."[17] Newton's rendering (chapter nine of his manuscript) of the prophecy of the "three woes" in chapters eight to thirteen of the Apocalypse is characteristic of his virtuosity in this art of squeezing historical chronology out of what may seem to the untutored to be mysteries or imagistic fantasies. In one passage, for example, Newton's scientific knowledge of the life-span and habits of the locust is the key to his realistic interpretation.

If we date their empire [the Saracen] from that year [637] . . . and if we extend the reign of this monarchy under the Angel of the bottomless pit, from that year inclusively to the end of the year 936, in wch the Chalif lost all his temporal power & ceased to torment the Romans: the whole duration of this great Monarchy will be just 300 years, that is ten prophetick months putting days for years & recconing 30 days to a month. But because there were two successive dynasties of this monarchy the one at Damascus in Syria the other at Bagdad in Chaldea & because the monarchy is represented by Locusts & the nature of Locusts is to live only five months, they being hatched annually by the heat of the sun about a month after the vernal Equinox & laying their eggs & dying about the Autumnal Equinox: the Prophet for the decorum of the type divides the whole time into five months & five months; saying twice, that the Locusts tormented men five months; that is in all ten months. Ffor the repetition is not without a meaning. In this Prophesy there is nothing superfluous. They reigned something less than five months at Damascus & something more at Bagdad; five months at each place more or less; in both places together ten months.[18]

Newton's theological interpretations are always acts of demystification, hieroglyph reading. "It is the temper of the hot and superstitious part of mankind," he wrote in *An Historical Account of Two Notable Corruptions of Scripture*, "in matters of religion, ever to be fond of mysteries; and for that reason, to like best what they understand least. Such men may use the apostle John as they please; but I have that honour for him, as to believe that he wrote good sense; and therefore take that sense to be *his*, which is the best; especially since I am defended in it by so great authority."[19] There are no mystical effusions in Newton's writings on Daniel and the Apocalypse. The chronologist's scientific precision informs even the most sacred historic moments: for example, in the eleventh chapter of the *Observations upon the Prophecies* ("Of the Times of the Birth and Passion of Christ"), after wrestling heroically with the Jewish calendar Newton reached the heterodox conclusion on the basis of textual and astronomical data that the Passion could have occurred only in the year 34.[20]

The historical excluded the metaphysical as well as the mystical. Whatever the more profound psychological reasons for Newton's secret unitarianism, in his private manuscripts he supported his position with an analysis of documentary evidence, not theological argument. His historical study of the dogmatic controversies in the first centuries of the Christian era led him to believe that the doctrine of the Trinity had been introduced many years after the age of the apostles and therefore lacked prophetic authority. Stray manuscript notes which emphasize the "man Christ Jesus" derived their proofs from the purported existence of monotheistic creeds in which the true unadulterated prophetic tradition of the apostles was handed down.[21] *An Historical Account of Two Notable Corruptions of Scripture,* first published posthumously in 1754 in an adulterated version, and a recently printed "Third Letter" on the same subject were attempts to discredit Trinitarian conceptions by setting forth an account of what Newton considered to be false texts.[22] Since he believed in the revelation of God's word through apostolic prophecy as the key to sacred history, the establishment of the authentic word was as relevant to an understanding of truth as was the honest conduct of a scientific experiment.

In purifying the New Testament proof-texts, Newton tracked down the lie by comparing every known printed and manuscript version, demonstrating, sometimes ingeniously and at other times in a dogmatic manner that bears no conviction, that Jerome had purposely corrupted the texts to make them conform to the Trinitarian dogma. "The history of the corruption, in short, is this. First, some of the Latines interpreted the Spirit, Water and Blood of the Father, Son, and Holy Ghost, to prove them One. Then Jerome, for the same end, inserted the Trinity in express words into his version." Much of the method is reminiscent of Richard Simon's in his commentaries on the Old and the New Testament; but, as in all his erudite studies, Newton followed a recognized source for a while and then leaped far beyond the authority on whom he was relying, often proceeding to extremes which would have been summarily rejected. Walton's vast Polyglot Bible,[23] with its texts in Hebrew, Greek, Syriac, Ethiopian (translated into Latin), Chaldee, Samaritan, Arabic, Persian, and Latin, allowed him conveniently to compare the many manuscript versions; it included concordances of all the recognized Greek and Latin variant manuscripts, some of which were in libraries of the colleges in Cambridge. His friend Dr. Covel had still other texts that Newton examined, and he conducted correspondence with eminent scholars in this field, freely exchanging information.[24]

Newton's disclosure of pious fraud was in the grand Renaissance tradition, and his *need* to expose fraud had deep psychological roots. From an analysis of the reports of the church councils, he concluded that the "falsation" of John had occurred in the beginning of the fifth century. Jerome emerged as the villain of the ecclesiastical drama, and Newton adduced evidence against him as if he were in a court of law. "And so, he being called to the bar, we are not to lay stress upon his own testimony for himself (for no man is a witness in his own cause) but laying aside all prejudice, we ought, according to the ordinary rules of justice, to examine the business between him and his accusers by other witnesses."[25] Similarly, the "Paradoxical Questions Concerning the Morals and Actions of Athanasius and his Followers" is a sharply argued historical brief, not untouched by irony, in which St. Athanasius, too, is demonstrated to be a manipulator of sacred records and a bearer of false witness against Arius. Newton's attack on Athanasius took the form of what lawyers call a "consciousness of guilt" argument, designed to show that a series of actions performed by Athanasius were those of a man who knew he had committed a wrong and thereby tacitly admitted it. "[I]f flying from justice and feigning false excuses be arguments of a guilty conscience: we must allow that Athanasius by doing these things has betrayed himself guilty. The very feigning of Letters & stories undermines & overthrows all that was ever said or done for his justification either by himself or others. Ffor it resolves all his defense into a figment; & such a defense when detected is equipollent to a confession of guilt."[26] During much of the discussion of early church history one might well be in doubt as to whether Newton was in a rage against Athanasius or Leibniz or some enemy from his distant past.

As a historian of Christian religion, Newton was committed to two fundamental conceptions: first, that the Christian doctrine was to be identified only in valid, uncorrupted texts written by apostles who were witnesses of Christ, or by an interpretation of Mosaic prophecy, and not through argument or later tradition; second, that originally communion was never refused to anyone who subscribed to a few fundamental beliefs such as the love of one God, abhorrence of lust, and the love of one's neighbors, hence any further restrictions were later impositions irrelevant to the Gospel. Newton's "theology" was therefore historical research concerned with uncovering the true text of the Gospel and demonstrating the latitudinarianism of the primitive church, to which he wanted all men to return. In the light of these fundamental propositions the worship of dead men (saints) and the persecution of heretics were the historical evils of Catholicism. The seven drafts of his "Irenicum, or Ecclesiastical Polity tending to peace" are doctrinal statements (with minor variants) of Newton's reconstruction of true historical Christianity. "The fundamentals of the Christian religion are those & only those things wch the primitive Christians were taught in catechising & instructing them in order to baptism. And those were to forsake the Devil, the lusts of the flesh, the lust of the eye & the pride of life to believe in one God, & one Lord & in the Holy Ghost."[27] Interpreting St. Paul, Newton designated the simple fundamentals of the Christian religion as "milk for babes," the more complex doctrines "strong meats" for older men; for that very reason the difficult and controversial aspects of religion were not to be made requirements for communion. There are passages in the "Irenicum" manuscripts so latitudinarian that the distinction between the Mosaic and the Christian dispensation is virtually abolished. "Christ said the first great commandment was love of the Lord thy God, the second Love thy neighbour as thyself. On these 2 hang all the Law & the Prophets. This was the religion of the sons of Noah established by Moses & Christ & is still in force."[28]

Newton's position naturally delighted the deists and discomfited the Trinitarians when word of his unitarianism leaked out after his death. And yet he was by no means a deist in Toland's or Woolston's sense of the term. He was in agreement with the universalist deist humanitarian moral position and was insistent upon the historical fact that the early church had tolerated a great variety of rites while adhering to "one Faith," but this element in his manuscripts—and it exists—should not be emphasized to the neglect of his paramount interest in the literal interpretation of Old Testament history. The Mosaic dispensation enjoyed an authority in his writings to which few deists would have subscribed, and here again the dominant puritanical influence of his childhood and youth is discernible despite his formal adherence to the Church of England.

Newton's ingenious set of hypotheses fixing the size of the ancient cubit of Memphis as well as the sacred cubit of the Jews, which was studied by the late George Sarton, was not a mere scientific curiosity.[29] His intent was to contribute to an understanding of the exact meaning of the Bible: "To the description of the Temple belongs the knowledge of the Sacred Cubit; to the understanding of which, the knowledge of the Cubits of the different nations will be conducive."[30] It was common in the seventeenth century to draw models of Noah's Ark, the Tower of Babel, the Ark of the Covenant, and the Temple of Solomon, and there were heated debates even among friends (Stukeley and Newton, for example) over the reconstructions.[31] But why this concentration on the smallest detail related to the Temple of Solomon?

The secret purpose of this research is revealed by the Latin and English manuscript in the Sir Isaac Newton Library, Babson Institute, entitled "Prolegomena ad Lexici Prophetici partem secundam, in quibus agitur De forma Sanctuarii Judaici . . . Commentarium." In the same sense that passages in the prophecies of Daniel and St. John were hieroglyphs for the facts of future history, every part of the earthly abode of the Law had its correspondence in the heavenly Jerusalem of the next world. The Temple of Solomon was the most important embodiment of a future extramundane reality, a blueprint of heaven; to ascertain every last fact about it was one of the highest forms of knowledge, for here was the ultimate truth of God's kingdom expressed in physical terms. Thorough knowledge of the structure of the Temple was a prolegomenon to the establishment of the correspondences, and there was no evading this task, any more than it was possible to neglect ferreting out the absolute meaning of every last word in prophecy. In archaic thought temples are conceived to be at the center of the universe, the point of contact between the world of men and the heavens. Newton was not completely divorced from this way of thinking, despite his apparent preference for plain speaking.

The *Chronology of Ancient Kingdoms Amended* and the *Observations upon the Prophecies,* if "connected," constitute a fairly complete universal history of mankind, both sacred and profane, since the Creation—a counterpart to the physical history of the world which the *Principia* had described. The historical events, set into their proper order, disclosed that there was a pattern in the revolutions of empires even as there was a system for the movements of the planets. In the University Library, Cambridge, there is a manuscript of the *Chronology* which ends on an interesting reference to Daniel, supporting the idea that the *Chronology* and the interpretations of prophecy were meant to be related in some fashion. Making an odious comparison between Daniel and the Greek and Roman writers, Newton clearly states his preference for the prophets as a historical source: "And as Daniel has noted the principal action of the Persian Empire so he has noted the principal actions & changes in the Empires of the Greeks & Latins & has done it with more understanding then any Greek or Roman writer ever did, & therefore in the short account & general ideas wch I intend to give of these Empires his descriptions of them deserve to be regarded." The word "intend" is underlined in pencil and there is a note on this page, both probably by John Conduitt, which reads: "This is a proof that he intended his prophecies as a sequel to His Chronology."[32] Moreover—and here there is a striking parallel to Newton's scientific discoveries—the fact that the prophecies had been realized in the past led him to reason, though he refused to lift the veil covering the future, that "in those things which relate to the last times, he [Daniel] must be made the key to the rest."[33] Astronomical calculations were validated by their capacity to predict the movement of the spheres, and so was true prophecy like Daniel's in human affairs. God had revealed himself to Newton not only in the order of nature, which he had interpreted mathematically in his studies of natural philosophy, but also in myth and prophecy. All were traces of one Creator. The histories testify that Newton was pursuing the same fundamental purpose with kindred methods in whatever sphere he labored.

In Newton's new system of chronology the world physical and the world political established a vital point of contact. Knowledge of the divine creation meant above all understanding its history, its movement in time. In this respect there was no sharp distinction in Newton's mind between the physical history of the universe and the history of nations, since both histories could be learned by man and there were continual correspondences between them. In his monist system a chronological event in the history of kingdoms could be translated into an astronomical event in the physical history of the universe and vice versa, for there were parallel histories in the heavens and on earth. Just as the formation of the planetary masses and the regulation of their movements had a temporal beginning, so had there been in the earliest days an "original of monarchies," about which he wrote a treatise. And both worlds were destined to have a consummation as prophesied in the Book of the Apocalypse. The mathematical principles of natural philosophy were the most elegant means known to Newton for describing the history of the planets in the intervening time period between the two absolute poles of creation and destruction.

A cryptic folio, "Of Earth," in Newton's Cambridge University Library notebook illustrates in a single brief passage the harmonious way in which Newton read the Bible and the book of nature, his two equal sources for the knowledge of God and His works. And there is nothing in this note written in his undergraduate days to which he would not have subscribed in his old age. Even the method of exposition was consistent throughout his life—dependence upon painstaking biblical exegesis in the manner of the Talmudic rabbis and Puritan divines for his cosmological and eschatological fantasies. "Its conflagration testified 2 peter 3ᵈ vers 6, 7, 10, 11, 12. The wiked (probably) to be punished thereby 2 Pet. 3 chap. vers 7. The succession of worlds, probable from Pet. 3ᶜ.13ᵛ. in wch text an emphasis upon the word WEE is not countenanced by the originall. Rev 21.ᶜ1ᵛ. Isa. 65ᶜ,17ᵛ.66ᶜ,22ᵛ Days & nights after the Judgmnt Rev 20ᶜ,10ᵛ."[34] Into these terse phrases Newton compressed a wealth of evidence for his belief that the world was inexorably moving toward a cataclysmic end, which would probably be followed by a renewal.

In the first citation the texts of II Peter, chapter three, are interpreted literally from the King James version to prophesy a great conflagration. The Bible reads: "Whereby the world that then was, being overflowed with water, perished: But the heaven and the earth, which are now, by the same word are kept in store, reserved unto fire against the day of judgment and perdition of ungodly men" (verses six and seven). "But the day of the Lord will come as a thief in the night; in the which the heavens shall pass away with a great noise, and the elements shall melt with fervent heat, the earth also and the works that are therein shall be burned up. Seeing then that all these things shall be dissolved, what manner of persons ought ye to be in all holy conversation and godliness. Looking for and hasting unto the coming of the day of God, wherein the heavens being on fire shall be dissolved, and the elements shall melt with fervent heat?" (ten through twelve). Verse seven led Newton to a further deduction: "The wiked (probably) to be punished thereby," an interesting example of the intrusion of an element of doubt—so characteristic of him—in the midst of his religious credulity.

In his third phrase, turning to the problem of whether his was the only world that would ever be, Newton adopted an independent position in his interpretation of the Bible. He accepted outright neither the simple millenarian view that the eternal Sabbath would follow Judgment Day nor the Stoic vision of an infinite succession of worlds ended by conflagrations, but introduced once again the idea of likelihood, supported by subtle traditionalist proofs. The text from II Peter, chapter three, verse thirteen—"Nevertheless we, according to his promise, look for new heavens and a new earth, wherein dwelleth righteousness"—had often been interpreted allegorically to mean a new world for the new Christian man. Rejecting this reading, Newton took the prophecy in a literal, physical sense, for he had checked the text in the Vulgate "in wch text an emphasis upon the word WEE is not countenanced by the originall." His further evidence for a succession of worlds was derived from Revelations and Isaiah: "And I saw a new heaven and a new earth: for the first heaven and the first earth were passed away; and there was no more sea" (Revelations 21:1); "For, behold, I create new heavens and a new earth: and the former shall not be remembered, nor come into mind" (Isaiah 65:17). Here was specific testimony, regarded literally as proof of the same order as scientific fact, that new worlds would be created. Similarly Isaiah 66:22: "For as the new heavens and the new earth, which I will make, shall remain before me, saith the Lord, so shall your seed and your name remain."

Newton's most cogent demonstration, however, came at the end and was based on Revelations 20:10: "And the devil that deceived them was cast into the lake of fire and brimstone, where the beast and false prophet are, and shall be tormented day and night for ever and ever." Though Newton did not spell out his reasoning and merely wrote the phrase "Days & nights after the Judgmnt," the full meaning of this ellipsis would be obvious to anyone who had been subjected to years of exegetical sermons. The basic interpretive rule is that the Bible does not indulge in rhetorical conceits or use any single word or letter to excess, a kind of law of parsimony. Tormenting of the wicked forever and ever is quite comprehensible in itself; but in adding the words "day and night," the prophet made clear that even after Judgment Day there would be a sequence of days and nights. This alternation was inconceivable unless there were other worlds in which the separation of day and night would be marked, and hence Revelations had prophesied a succession of worlds.

There have been attempts to establish what has been called Newton's cycloid conception of the universe upon purely scientific cosmological and physical considerations, when many of his ideas, going back to his youth, were rooted in the first instance in a traditional interpretation of the primary book of God's revelation, the Bible.

To force everything in the heavens and on earth into one rigid, tight frame from which the most minuscule detail would not be allowed to escape free and random was an underlying need of this anxiety-ridden man. And with rare exceptions, his fantasy wish was fulfilled during the course of his lifetime. The system was complete in both its physical and historical dimensions. A structuring of the world in so absolutist a manner that every event, the closest and the most remote, fits neatly into an imaginary system has been called a symptom of illness, especially when others refuse to join in the grand obsessive design. It was Newton's fortune that a large portion of his total system was acceptable to European society as a perfect representation of reality, and his name was attached to the age. That part of the Newtonian system which was related to his puritanical bibliolatry and to his interpretation of prophecy was, of course, rejected by most eighteenth-century intellectuals and for many years was kept hidden as a shameful weakness in their new god. In our own enlightened age, it is now possible to restore to Newton without prejudice the whole of his unified system of the world, both sacred and profane, physical and historical.

In the end, the flights of Newton's religious imagination and the leaps of his scientific inventiveness remain enigmas. Individual elements may be identified in terms of contemporary theological, historical, and scientific preoccupations, but the nature of the whole eludes us. He was the genius architect, putting together ideas from diverse and distant areas in a novel manner to create a grand and original system. But unlike the wanton block-building of the paranoid, which remains centered on himself, Newton's structures were released from this personal imprisonment and attained to the highest levels of abstraction and universal significance.

Chapter 18

THE EVE OF DEATH

Every soul that has perception is, though in different times and
in different organs of sense and motion, still the same indi-
visible person. There are given successive parts in duration, co-
existent parts in space, but neither the one nor the other in the
person of a man, or his thinking principle. . . . Every man,
so far as he is a thing that has perception, is one and the same
man during his whole life, in all and each of his organs of
sense.

—General Scholium to the third edition of the *Principia*

W HEN Isaac Newton reached his eightieth year he was seized with
incontinence of urine, first ascribed to the stone and then thought to
be due to a weakness in the sphincter of the bladder. Dr. Mead advised him to give up his carriage, limit his company, and restrict
his diet.

The word picture of his last years drawn by John Conduitt in his
memoir to Fontenelle does not match the choleric and domineering
temper that can be read in the paintings of Vanderbank in 1725 and
1726. In the first, Newton is dressed in a long velvet coat. He wears
his own hair, has a heavy-jowled face, shaggy eyebrows, and a distracted look. In the second portrait, he sits in majesty in a loose-flow-
ing robe, with a great wig dominating his fat, heavy face, and he has
an aspect at once angry and troubled. It is a formidable visage. On
the wall hangs the symbol of a serpent with its tail in its mouth—
the cycle is complete. In recent years an oil sketch made by Vanderbank in preparation for the 1725 painting has been acquired by the
Royal Society. In many ways it is the most expressive portrait of

Newton. The old man's lips have become loose and almost sensual, the eyes bulge, the face is puffy and creased, the hair is unkempt. If there was cruelty in the man, Vanderbank caught it in this fugitive sketch, which has an authenticity lacking in the finished paintings.

Conduitt's is the more official portrait, though not necessarily a wholly false one.

An innate modesty and simplicity shewed itself in all his actions and expressions. His whole life was one continued series of labour, patience, charity, generosity, temperance, piety, goodness, and all other virtues, without a mixture of any vice whatsoever. . . .

He was blessed with a very happy and vigorous constitution; he was of a middle stature [in the manuscript Conduitt had first written "short" but crossed it out], and plump [the original phrase was "inclining to be fat"] in his later years; had a very lively and piercing eye, and a comely and gracious aspect; had a fine head of hair, as white as silver, without any baldness, and when his periwig was off, was a venerable sight. And to his last illness had the bloom and colour of a young man, and never used spectacles, nor lost any more than one tooth to the day of his death. . . .[1]

The painting in the National Portrait Gallery by an unknown artist, sometimes attributed to Enoch Seeman, catches this softer side of the man.

Francis Atterbury, Lord Bishop of Rochester before his disgrace, took exception to the Newton of Fontenelle's *Eloge,* with his "oeil fort vif & fort perçant," a literal translation of the Conduitt memoir. In the two decades the Bishop had known Newton, he had formed a contrary opinion. "In the whole air of his face and make, there was nothing of that penetrating sagacity which appears in his composures. He had something rather languid in his look and manner, which did not raise any great expectation in those who did not know him."[2]

Conduitt's medical history of Newton's last years is less controversial because it is all we have.

He eat little flesh, and lived chiefly upon broth, vegetables, and fruit, of which he always eat very heartily. In August 1724 he voided, without any pain, a stone about the bigness of a pea, which came away in two pieces; one at some distance from the other. In January 1724/5, he had a violent cough and inflammation of the lungs, upon which he was, with much ado, persuaded to take a house at Kensington, where he had in his eighty-fourth year a fit of the gout, for the second time, having had a slight attack of it a few years before. After which he was visibly better than he had been some years. The benefit he found from the air at Kensington induced him to keep the house till he died. . . . But though he found the greatest benefit from rest, and the air at Kensington, and was always the worse for leaving it, no methods that were used could keep him from coming sometimes to town [the phrase "from coming to town without any real call" was stricken from the manuscript].[3]

Newton still received foreign callers, a number of whom have left their impressions. The Abbé Pierre-Joseph Alari, tutor of Louis XV and an acquaintance of Bolingbroke, was with him in 1725 and a friend has given an account of the visit. The Abbé had gone to his house at nine o'clock in the morning, and Newton began by telling him that he was eighty-three years of age. In his chamber the Abbé saw a portrait of Lord Halifax and one of the Abbé Varignon, of whose geometrical writings Newton had a high opinion. "Varignon," he said, "and Father Sebastien, the Carmelite, are those who have understood best my system of colours." The conversation at last turned on ancient history, with which Newton was then occupied. The Abbé, who was deeply read in Greek and Latin authors, having made himself very agreeable, was asked to dinner. "The meal was awful." Afterward the guest was taken to the Royal Society, where Newton dozed off during the delivery of one of the papers.[4]

Though he was not well, Newton still supervised mathematical appointments in the universities. Having decided upon a third edition of the *Principia,* he was fortunate enough to find as his last young assistant a Dr. Henry Pemberton, who had been working on a popularization of the Newtonian philosophy with the hope of attracting his attention.[5] Newton was swayed less by this performance than by Pemberton's disproof in the *Philosophical Transactions* for April and May 1722 of an Italian mathematician's experiment illustrating the Leibnizian principle of the force of descending bodies. Execration of the dead enemy was still the way to Newton's heart. Delighted with the refutation, Newton called at Pemberton's lodgings, and soon they were engaged in the preparation of the new edition, which came through the press in February 1726, a year before his death. Pemberton's meticulous justification of every one of his emendations has been preserved, and he made no changes without express permission from Newton, including excision of the paragraph favorable to Leibniz which had been preserved in the second edition. Pemberton denied that Newton's intellectual powers had failed. "Though his memory was much decayed, I found he perfectly understood his own writings, contrary to what I had frequently heard in discourse from many persons." Pemberton knew the benign motherly Newton who protected and encouraged his late-born children as he had Fatio. "I only touch upon what I experienced myself," he wrote in the preface to *A View of Sir Isaac Newton's Philosophy* (1728), "during the few years I was happy in his friendship. But this I immediately discovered in him, which at once surprized and charmed me: Neither his extreme great age, nor his universal reputation had rendred him stiff in opinion, or in any degree elated. Of this I had occasion to have almost daily experience. . . . He also approved of the following treatise, a great part of which we read together."

Newton continued to perform his worldly duties to the very end with his wonted austerity, abiding by the rigorous standards that he had established for himself and his fellowmen early in life. When they tried to dissuade him from walking to church in Kensington, he would say: "Use legs and have legs."[6] John Conduitt relieved him of his most onerous burdens at the Mint, an arrangement to which he consented with reluctance, but he still personally examined gold ingots at the Tower in September 1726. He reviewed clemency pleas in behalf of counterfeiters and, as might be expected, denied them. As late as August 25, 1724, there is a note to Lord Townshend about an execution: "I know nothing of Edmund Metcalf convicted at Derby assizes of counterfeiting the coyne; but since he is very evidently convicted, I am humbly of opinion that its better to let him suffer, than to venture his going on to counterfeit the coin & teach others to do so untill he can be convicted again, ffor these people very seldom leave off. And its difficult to detect them."[7]

Once in a great while Newton had a hankering to resume the creative works of science. If he were younger, he told Halley, he would have "another shake at the moon," and to Ben Smith he confided that he would "have another touch at metals"—but these were only passing reflections. When Halley pressed him to complete his lunar theory, he complained it had "made his head ach & kept him awake so often that he would think of it no more."[8]

The last meeting of the Council of the Royal Society over which Newton presided was held a few days before his death. On this occasion he publicly scolded the Royal Astronomer Edmond Halley for his failure to despatch regular reports to the Society on his observations at Greenwich, as provided by royal precept. Halley too was by this time getting on in years—though a mere seventy-one to Newton's eighty-five—and he defended himself on grounds of self-interest. He was not prepared to divulge data that might set someone else upon discovering a method of determining longitudes at sea and thus rob him of the prize offered by Parliament. The *Journal Booke of the Council of the Royal Society* records the last encounter of the two men: "Whereas this precept had not of late been observed it might be of ill consequence to continue in the Neglect of it, And therefore he [Newton] thought it proper to take this opportunity now the Royal Astronomer was present, to put them in mind of the said precept." Halley finally agreed to deliver some observations, but not all, lest "others might take the Advantage of Reaping the benefit of his Labours."[9] *Flamsteed redivivus.*

During his last years Newton's severity sometimes gave way to sentimental outbursts—a polar swing of the compass needle, rather frequent in hard and even punitive characters. According to Conduitt, "A melancholy story would often draw tears from him, and he was exceedingly shocked by any act of cruelty to man or beast; mercy to both being the topic he loved to dwell upon."[10] He commended kindness and humanity and justified his tears with the teleological argument that men had not been endowed with lachrymal glands for nothing.[11] A grandniece of Sir Isaac who had spent whole evenings in his study in St. Martin's Lane remembered him as pleasant and cheerful, able to read small print without spectacles, and "remarkably fond of the company of children."[12] But despite occasional compassionate effusions and affectionate behavior with children, Newton exhibited no great warmth or solicitude for his fellow creatures. His dread of the mob—his schoolmates grown up—was explicit in his early letters to Oldenburg and endured throughout his life. In his final years he wrote profusely about the gospel of love and his abhorrence of religious intolerance over doctrinal matters of no consequence. "Nothing Neither circumcision nor uncircision [sic] nor any thing but the keeping the commandmts of God is of moment to salvation & the chief commandmt is that al belevers love one another: wch certainly those men cannot be said to do who fall out about things that are of an indifferent nature & signify nothing to salvatiō."[13] It is easy to interpret the violent denunciations of Catholic persecutions through the ages in his exposition of the prophecies as a cover for his own vengefulness. But his exhortations to love and fellowship among men are also a sign of his deep yearning for love, a yearning that was never satisfied. He was obeyed and esteemed and often feared; but except for his mother and perhaps Fatio, who dared approach close enough to love his forbidding person? In a longing for warmth he returned to his native county, and at one time he commissioned Stukeley to buy a house for him in Grantham.[14] Like many old men he looked homeward to the place of his birth and would even turn up occasionally at local feasts, sometimes sitting alone until he was recognized. He attended the weddings of his relatives whenever he could, and at these events he would "lay aside gravity, be free, pleasant, and unbended."[15]

There are two witnesses, John Conduitt and Samuel Crell, that a few weeks before his death Newton performed his final rite with fire—he burned some of his manuscripts and perhaps correspondence. What part of his past was he impelled to destroy? If this was a deliberate effort to leave an official portrait behind, why were the alchemical and theological manuscripts preserved, as well as many strange letters from Fatio and Flamsteed? The selection of what he tossed into the flames, one might infer from the papers that have survived, was haphazard, with one exception—there are virtually no letters from his family. All that remain are a charred scrap from his mother, a few lines from his half sister, a message of thanks from his half brother, and a stiff little note from Catherine Conduitt in November 1719 from Cranbury Lodge where she had gone to live after her marriage, inquiring after his health and hoping she would soon be able to pay her duty to him.[16]

John Conduitt is our source for the death scene.

On Tuesday the last of February, 1726-7, he came to town, in order to go to a meeting at the Royal Society. The next day I was with him, and thought I had not seen him better for many years, and he was sensible of it himself, and told me smiling, that he had slept the Sunday before, from eleven at night to eight in the morning, without waking; but his great fatigue in going to the Society, and making and receiving visits, brought his old complaint violently upon him. He returned to Kensington on the Saturday following. As soon as I heard of his illness, I carried Dr. Mead and Mr. Cheselden to him, who immediately said it was the stone in the bladder, and gave no hopes of his recovery. The stone was probably moved from the place where it lay quiet by the great motion and fatigue of his last journey to London, from which time he had violent fits of pain with very short intermissions; and though the drops of sweat ran down from his face with anguish, he never complained, or cried out, or shewed the least signs of peevishness or impatience, and during the short intervals from that violent torture, would smile, and talk with his usual cheerfulness. On Wednesday the 15th of March, he seemed a little better and we conceived hopes of his recovery, but without grounds. On Saturday morning, the 18th, he read the newspapers, and held a pretty long discourse with Dr. Mead, and had all his senses perfect; but that evening at six, and all Sunday, he was insensible, and died on Monday the 20th of March, between one and two o'clock in the morning. He seemed to have stamina vitae (except the accidental distemper of the stone) to have carried him to a much longer age. To the last he had all his senses and faculties strong, vigorous, and lively, and he continued writing and studying many hours every day to the time of his last illness.[17]

Conduitt, who was a bit disturbed that Newton on his deathbed had not asked for the final rites, consoled himself with the pious reflection: "It may be said his whole life was a preparation for another state."[18]

Conduitt was also the rather uncomprehending reporter of some of Newton's last thoughts on the nature of the planetary system and on himself. On Sunday, March 7, 1725, two years before his death, they had a long conversation bearing upon the creation and destruction of planets. Newton imagined that there was "a sort of revolution in the heavenly bodies" and that the comet of 1680 would after five or six more revolutions drop into the sun and so increase its heat that the earth would be burned and none of its animals could survive. Such a catastrophe had probably befallen the world before, and would explain why its inhabitants were of recent date. This was the scientific face of his eschatology, the complement of his biblical interpretation of Doomsday. He held the opinion that all arts and inventions had been discovered within the memory of history, "wch could not have happened if the world had been eternal, & that there were visible marks of ruin upon it wch could not be effected by a flood only, when I asked him how this earth could have been repeopled if ever it had undergone the same fate it was threatned with hereafter by the Comet of 1680, he answered that required the power of a creator." Traditional fancies about the great chain of being flowed freely in his last years. "He seemed to doubt wether there were not intelligent beings superior to us who superintended these revolutions of the heavenly bodies by the direction of the supreme being." Sir Isaac laughed as he explained his unwillingness to publish conjectures; he was the oracular seer again and "had said enough for people to know his meaning."[19]

If a conversation recorded by John Conduitt is authentic, there is a self-image that Newton in his declining years would have liked to see preserved for posterity. And this, too, is a great truth about him. Toward the very end of his life he may have regained, if only for a brief moment, the naive wonderment and engaging simplicity that graced the early reports of his experiments with light. He reflected wistfully to his nephew: "I do not know what I may appear to the world; but to myself I seem to have been only like a boy, playing on the sea shore, and diverting myself, in now and then finding a smoother pebble or a prettier shell than ordinary, whilst the great ocean of truth lay all undiscovered before me."[20]

This guileless and disarming simile may also be his confession. The musings of the aged Newton are the last of his great queries. His life had come full circle to that early period of his childhood when he formulated questions to which there were no answers. His first doubts have not been recorded, and there are historians who, in the absence of written documents, would impose silence upon themselves. But as I listen to the dying man's reminiscences, I hear the echo of his first anguished puzzlement as an abandoned child bewildered about the meaning of his mother's appearances and disappearances. When he learned that his father had died before he was born, he was racked by uncertainty about where his father had gone and whence he, Isaac, had come. All children ask questions; and a part of Newton's native genius lay in his boundless curiosity. But there is a poignancy to his queries that transcends common experience. For more than eighty years he was the great questioner in the face of God, nature, and his own pain.

Newton's undergraduate notebook turns to nature with a long series of "Quaestiones" that have an almost childlike quality. What is light, what is fire, what is motion, what is matter, what is the soul, what is God? The form is not unusual in the scientific literature of the age, but the plain universality of their expression removes them from the current stereotypes. From the early alchemical experiments through the "Queries" of the *Opticks,* from the anti-Trinitarian tract of 1690 to the General Scholium of the second edition of the *Principia* and the *Observations upon the Prophecies,* he asks the primal questions. At times he seemed to find answers: he established the mathematical principles of natural philosophy, wrote out—that is, decided upon—his own genealogy, revised world history and set origins aright for mankind. But doubts persisted and perplexities were renewed to the very end. The ocean of truth lay undiscovered, for all his life he had been merely "diverting" himself, playing at science at the shore's edge. He had never plunged in.

The real answers had eluded him, though his discoveries may have satisfied the world.

The dying man's evocation of himself as a boy playing with seashells is regularly quoted to illustrate his humility before the infinity of truth. On numerous occasions, to friends and enemies alike, Newton disparaged his researches whether in mathematics or chronology as "divertisements." On one level this may have been a mannerism, an affectation of the "gentleman" who was not a gentleman by birth. But it also suggests disappointment that what he found was not what he had been seeking. Perhaps what he was looking for, the great ocean of Mother Truth, was forbidden, and all else had been "divertisement." In his old age Newton saw himself as the little Grantham lad again, his great queries unanswered. To believe that one had penetrated the ultimate secrets of God's world and to doubt it, to be the Messiah and to wonder about one's anointedness, is the fate of prophets.

A passionate intellectual curiosity was the shining countenance of this childhood doubt. But there was another, darker face that showed itself in his relations with men as fear, suspicion, anxiety, mistrust. The plaintive apostrophe of his juvenile Latin exercise book, *What is hee good for?* rings down through the years. His injured self-esteem could never be repaired, not by knighthood nor the presidency of the Royal Society nor the adoration of disciples nor world renown. It demanded a continual bolstering through the elimination of any threat, however remote, to his tenuous security. The memory of the warmth of his mother's bed was a comfort that may have strengthened him, but alas, it was also a polluted bed, for his mother had betrayed him. There were men who overcame his mistrust by devoting themselves totally to him, but one transgression and he thrust them into the ranks of the enemy. He was forever testing them, and there were moments when even the most loyal failed him because they fell short of the perfection he demanded.

There are many other vantage points from which to try to capture the whole person of Isaac Newton. The least rewarding, perhaps, is to see him as a promoter of knowledge in the commonsensical way it was understood by Joseph Glanvill and would soon be identified with scientific progress. Newton was with fair consistency committed to an ahistorical conception of knowledge, sacred and profane. There was one truth, and the ancient prophets as well as the scientist-philosophers of the Greek world and the alchemists of all ages had merely clothed it in different symbolic forms. Recent historians of science have taken literally and not as an offhand conversational boutade Newton's assertions to Fatio and David Gregory and John Conduitt that in the image of the Pythagorean lyre lay hidden the law of gravity.[21] This is a counterpart in the Greek realm to his belief that the "physica sacra" of Moses was communicated to Israel in the popular, unphilosophical language of Genesis. In the end Newton had a profound Baconian respect for the wisdom of the ancients: "The Ancients studied Nature most but we study speculations, whence many of their inventions are lost."[22] Toward the moderns he was less charitable. "Sir I. says he stood on the shoulders of Giants"—the image he had once invoked in writing to Hooke he repeated in his old age to Conduitt. But whenever he became specific his tone changed: Kepler had "whims" and Descartes made "errors."[23]

The more Newton's theological and alchemical and mythological work is studied, the more apparent it becomes that in his moments of grandeur he saw himself as the last of the prophets, living on the eve of the fulfillment of the times. In his generation he was the vehicle of God's eternal truth, the greatest of all time perhaps, for by using new notations and an experimental method he combined the knowledge of Israel's prophets and the Greek mathematicians and the medieval alchemists. From him nothing had been hidden. But Newton's insistence that he was part of an ancient tradition, a rediscoverer rather than an innovator, is susceptible of various interpretations. In manuscript scholia to the *Principia* that date from the end of the seventeenth century he expanded his belief that a whole line of ancient philosophers had held to the atomic theory of matter, a conception of the void, the universality of gravitational force, and even the inverse square law. In part this was euhemeristic interpretation of myth—many of the Greek gods and demigods were really scientists; in historical terms this is a survival of a major topos of the Renaissance tradition of knowledge and its veneration for the wisdom of antiquity. The doctrine may also have served a deep personal need. Newton is so terrified by the hubris of discovery of which he is possessed that, as if to placate God the Father, he assures his intimates and himself that he has broken no prohibitions against revealing the secrets, that he has merely uttered in another language what the ancients had known before him.

There were pure joys in Newton's life, those moments of invention in Cambridge when John Wickins saw him eagerly dashing to a table, despite a sleepless night, to record a new formula; perhaps that day in the garden at Woolsthorpe when the apple fell. There was another kind of pleasure when Anne knighted him on the grounds of the University, the alma mater that had nourished (and sometimes rebuffed) him. But there were also daemonic elements in the man, destructive forces that demanded their toll of human sacrifice, of himself and of his enemies. In his very person he was the great Janus-like symbol for the dual nature of modern science—its capacity for good and evil, its genius for the finding of truth and for lying to protect the truth discovered, its transcendent unworldly quality, free from the lust for possession, and its hoarding of secrets. In the latter part of the twentieth century the faces of Newton and of his science have lost their pure luminousness. The polarities of his nature are paralleled in the ambiguous nature of science itself. On the morrow after he discovered the mathematical expression of matter, he turned to the trivialities of existence and the cruel exercise of dominion, even as some three centuries later the collective discoverers of the infinite potentialities of matter have been first driven to exploit its destructive power. The overwhelming question remains whether Newton's science, which gave him great power and little wisdom, can in some other incarnation bestow that wisdom upon his fellowmen. For the times are not yet fulfilled.

NOTES
INDEX

NOTES

INTRODUCTION

1. For example, eight volumes are projected on the mathematical papers alone; see Derek T. Whiteside, ed., *The Mathematical Papers of Isaac Newton* (Cambridge: Cambridge University Press, 1967——), I, viii. Whiteside is for the first time making known the original texts of Newton's mathematical manuscripts and clarifying the particularities of the seventeenth-century idiom for the modern reader.

2. Frank E. Manuel, *Isaac Newton, Historian* (Cambridge, Mass.: Harvard University Press, 1963).

3. The carving of Newton's name is reproduced by J. A. Holden, "Newton and his Homeland—The Haunts of his Youth," in William J. Greenstreet, ed., *Isaac Newton, 1642–1727, A memorial volume* (London: G. Bell and Sons, 1927), opposite p. 142.

4. Canon C. W. Foster, "Sir Isaac Newton's Family," *Reports and Papers of the Architectural Societies of the County of Lincoln, County of York, Archdeaconries of Northampton and Oakham, and County of Leicester,* XXXIX, part I (1928), 1–62.

5. William Stukeley, *Memoirs of Sir Isaac Newton's Life* . . . *1752; being some account of his family and chiefly of the junior part of his life,* ed. A. Hastings White (London: Taylor and Francis, 1936), p. 23; Stukeley spells the name "Chrichloe."

6. Cambridge, King's College Library, Keynes MS. 136, William Stukeley to Dr. Mead for transmission to John Conduitt, June 26–July 22, 1727. The letter of June 26 was published in Edmund Turnor, *Collections for the History of the Town and Soke of Grantham containing Authentic Memoirs of Sir Isaac Newton* (London, 1806), pp. 174–180. Part of the correspondence was published in the *Gentleman's Magazine* for 1772.

7. William Stukeley, *The Family Memoirs of the Rev. William Stukeley, M.D. and the antiquarian and other correspondence of William Stukeley, Roger & Samuel Gale,* 3 vols. (Durham, London, Edinburgh, 1882, 1883, 1887; Surtees Society Publications, vols. 73, 76, 80).

8. Stukeley, *Memoirs of Newton's Life,* pp. 1, 4.

9. Cambridge, King's College Library, Keynes MS. 130, autograph drafts of portions of John Conduitt's intended life of Newton and disconnected jottings in

small notebooks; Keynes MS. 129A, "Memoirs relating to Sr Isaac Newton sent by me to Monr Fontenelle in Octr. 1727" (a version published in Turnor, *Collections for the History of Grantham*, pp. 158–167); Keynes MS. 129B, drafts of various sections of the "Memoirs relating to Sr Isaac Newton sent to Monr Fontenelle." Conduitt derived many of his anecdotes from his correspondents Stukeley, Abraham de Moivre, William Derham, John Craig, Humphrey Newton, a Mrs. Hutton; but a comparison between what he received and what he wrote to Fontenelle shows that often he treated their information rather cavalierly, embellishing their accounts in the tradition of all those who write lives of saints and heroes. A "Memorandum relating to Sr Isaac Newton given me by Mr Demoivre in Novr 1727" is in private possession in New York and available also in transcription (Cambridge, University Library, Add. MS. 4007, fols. 706–707).

10. The papers of the Morgan and Fitzwilliam notebooks have the same watermark, a cluster of grapes. The Cambridge University Library notebook (Add. MS. 3996) is listed in H. R. Luard *et al., A Catalogue of the Portsmouth Collection of Books and Papers written by or belonging to Sir Isaac Newton* (Cambridge, 1888), p. 47, section VII, no. 8: "A common-place book written from both ends, with 'Isaac Newton, Trin. Coll. Cant. 1661,' in the beginning."

11. Edward Cocker, *Arts glory: or The pen-man's treasury; containing various examples of secretary, text, Roman, and Italian hands* . . . (London, 1659), unpaginated. It was not uncommon to learn both secretary and Italian and to work out an individual hand by combining the letters from both. Chancelleresque or swift Italian was used for business, but was not regarded as beautiful writing. "No hand there is more us'd or necessarie / Than faire Italian mixt with Secretarie."

12. A. N. L. Munby, "The Keynes Collection of the Works of Sir Isaac Newton in King's College, Cambridge," *Notes and Records of the Royal Society of London,* X (1952), 49, notes that Newton's copy of Pindar, now in King's College Library, also has a 1659 inscription.

13. J. A. Comenius, *Orbis sensualium pictus . . . a work newly written by the author in Latin and High Dutch . . . & translated into English by Charles Hoole* (London, 1659); Charles Hoole, trans., *Childrens talke, Pueriles confabulatiunculae Anglo Latinae in varias clausulas distributae* (London, 1659); Charles Hoole, *Maturinus Corderius's School-colloquies, English and Latin, divided into several clauses* . . . (London, 1657).

14. Luard, *Catalogue of the Portsmouth Collection,* p. 30, section V, no. 19, "A bundle containing . . . (3) Attempt to form a universal language. This contains also a genealogical tree of the Newton family, and at the other end an English and Latin phrase-book, not in N's hand." These manuscripts are now in private possession. The *Catalogue* (p. 50, section VIII, no. 25) lists "A Latin phrase-book, under the heads of English words in alphabetical order, the first word *abate,* the last *conduct.* At the end are extracts from Epiphanius, S. Augustine, etc." This list, of a much later date, is in private possession in New York.

15. Sir E. N. da C. Andrade, "Newton's Early Notebook," *Nature,* CXXXV (1935), 360, first noted the derivation of part of the Morgan notebook from John

Bate, *The Mysteryes of Nature, and Art: conteined in foure seuerall Tretises* . . . (London, 1634).

16. Professor David Eugene Smith published parts of the Morgan notebook in Greenstreet, ed., *Isaac Newton,* pp. 17–25, and facsimiles of a number of its leaves on pp. 26–31. He identified three types of handwriting: (1) age 13–16; (2) about 17; (3) age 19–20 (p. 17). I cannot entirely agree with his dating of the different sections. There are two dates in the notebook, the 1659 inscription on the first page, which is not in Newton's hand, and the date of the first year (1662) of the ecclesiastical calendar he computed for a period of twenty-eight years, which leads one to suppose that this leaf was written a year before 1662, or in 1661. The script of the calendar is still "Old Barley" and so is the word list: the *o*-shaped *e* is its most marked distinguishing characteristic. The scheme of reformed spelling, in the "Trinity" hand, is of a later date, as are the astronomical tables, two solutions of triangles, two pages on dialing, and two pages of notes on the Copernican system.

Derek Whiteside (*Mathematical Papers of Newton,* I, 470n) writes of the Morgan notebook that "Newton has inserted the date 1659 on the flyleaf." The entry would appear to be not by Newton but by the witness, Edward Secker. Whiteside's ability to "fix the date of composition of an unexamined portion of autograph manuscript by sight to within half a dozen years (and sometimes even more narrowly still)" (I, xi n. 2) can hardly apply to the manuscripts of the young man under twenty, because they are so rare.

The opening words of the charm in the Morgan notebook are in "Old Barley" longhand.

17. Francis Gregory, *Nomenclatura brevis anglo-Latino in usum scholarum* (the earliest form of this work listed in the catalogue of the British Museum is dated 1654) gives the following "Table of the Heads":

1. Of the true God	18. Of an Hous.
2. Of God the Father	19. Of Houshold-stuff
3. Of God the Son	20. Of a School
4. Of the Holy Ghost	21. Of a Church
5. Of false Gods	22. Of Time
6. Of the Creatures	23. Of the Elements
7. Of Rational Creatures	24. Of Metails
8. Of the Parts of a Man	25. Of Vertues and Vices
9. Of the Inward Parts	26. Of Birds
10. Of the Accidents of the Body	27. Of Beasts
11. Of Diseases	28. Of Fishes
12. Of the Senses	29. Of Husbandry
13. Of Clothing	30. Of Herbs
14. Of Meat	31. Of Shrubs and Trees
15. Of Drink	32. Of a Garden
16. Of the Understanding, Will and Affections	33. Of Arts
17. Of Kindred	

Newton's Morgan Notebook combines Gregory's heads thus:

The Several Things contained under these generall heads
Artes, Trades, & Sciences Chap 1
Birdes Chap 2. vide Nomencleturam, pag: 37

Beasts Chap 3. vide Nomencleturam pag. 39
Cloathes Chap 4
Of a Church Chap 5
Of Diseases Chap 6
Of the Elements Chap 7
Of ffishes Chap 8 Vide Nomencleturam. pag 43 quibus addantur
Of Hearbs & Woodes & fflowers Chap 9
Of a House & Housald-stuffe Chap 10
Of Husbandry Chap 11
Instruments & things belonging to Artes Chap 12
Of Kindred, & Titles Chap 13
Of Man, his Affections, & Senses Chap 14
Of Meate & Drinke Chap 15
Of Mineralls Chap 16

Newton apparently dropped the chapter headings after the letter M.

Ralph W. V. Elliott, "Isaac Newton's 'Of an Universall Language,'" *Modern Language Review*, LII (1957), 1–13, relates the word list to Newton's plan for a universal language. He did not recognize the connection with Gregory's *Nomenclatura*. Foster Watson, *The English Grammar Schools to 1600: their Curriculum and Practice* (Cambridge: Cambridge University Press, 1908), p. 509, notes that Gregory's *Nomenclatura* was mentioned by Charles Hoole in his *New Discovery of the Old Art of Teaching School* (1660).

18. See Ralph W. V. Elliott, "Isaac Newton as Phonetician," *Modern Language Review*, XLIX (1954), 5–12.

19. Isaac Newton, *The Correspondence* (Cambridge: Cambridge University Press, 1959——), I (ed. W. H. Turnbull), 1, Newton to a friend, circa 1661; the signer's initials are printed as "I. N.," I believe erroneously. Henceforward this work will be cited as Newton, *Correspondence*.

20. R. S. Westfall, "The Foundations of Newton's Philosophy of Nature," *The British Journal for the History of Science*, I (1962), 181–182.

21. Most of Newton's papers remained in the hands of the Portsmouth family and were first catalogued in 1888, at which time sections dealing with mathematics, chemistry, and correspondence, plus books, miscellaneous papers, and papers concerning Flamsteed, were given to the Cambridge University Library. In 1936 the remainder of the Portsmouth Collection was put up for auction. Lord Keynes bought personal data, letters, and alchemy, chronology, history, and some theological manuscripts and gave them to King's College, Cambridge. Viscount Wakefield presented the Mint papers to the Mint. Other Newton papers in the Portsmouth Collection have been dispersed. There are four volumes in Oxford (New College MSS. 361, housed at the Bodleian Library), which came through the Reverend Jeffrey Ekins. See also Sotheby & Co., *Catalogue of the Newton Papers sold by order of the Viscount Lymington* (London, July 13–14, 1936). Add. MS. 4007 in the University Library, Cambridge, contains transcripts of letters related to Newton, made by H. R. Luard and J. C. Adams at the time the *Catalogue of the Portsmouth Collection* was being prepared. Some of the original letters have not reappeared since the Sotheby sale, and are known only through these transcripts.

Whiteside has commented on the scorching by fire, the staining by damp, and other soiling of Newton's manuscripts. While I would not presume to reflect upon his critical procedures in editing Newton's mathematical papers, I am puzzled by the forthright affirmation that Newton in his last months burned "a great part of his personal correspondence and, we may suspect, certain inferior technical papers he was unwilling to communicate to his successors" (*Mathematical Papers of Newton*, I, x).

22. Mathurin Veyssière de Lacroze, *Thesaurus Epistolicus Lacrozianus* (Leipzig, 1742), I, 105, Samuel Crell to Lacroze, July 17, 1727: "Paucis ante mortem septimanis non pauca sua manu scripta in ignem coniecit ipse." The letter is cited by David Brewster, *Memoirs of the life, writings, and discoveries of Sir Isaac Newton* (Edinburgh, 1855), II, 390.

23. Keynes MS. 130 (7).

24. See Leon Rosenfeld, "Newton and the Law of Gravitation," *Archive for History of Exact Sciences*, II (1965), 375, where he discusses the current swing from hero-worshiping to hero-debunking of Newton, perceptively adding: "Newton's personality is not easy to understand: secretive and suspicious as he was, one has to catch him, so to speak, in unguarded moments to get a glimpse of his thoughts and of his passions. To reconstruct a coherent portrait from the scraps of evidence gleaned from his papers, his letters and his actions is a hard detective work, but a rewarding one."

25. Stukeley, *Memoirs of Newton's Life*, pp. 68, 69.

26. Peter King, *The Life of John Locke*, 2nd ed. (London, 1830), II, 38, Locke to King, April 30, 1703.

27. See below, p. 159.

28. William Whiston, *Memoirs of the Life and Writings of W. W.* (London, 1749–1750), I, 294: "He was of the most fearful, cautious, and suspicious Temper, that I ever knew: And had he been alive when I wrote against his Chronology and so thoroughly confuted it . . . I should not have thought proper to publish it during his Life Time; because I knew his Temper so well, that I should have expected it would have killed him." This passage was transformed into something even more violent in Jean-Baptiste-Joseph Delambre, *Histoire de l'astronomie au dix-huitième siècle* (Paris, 1827), p. 62, who quotes Whiston on the basis of Bartholomew Prescot, *Inverted Scheme of Copernicus . . . and the doctrine of the formation of worlds out of atoms, by the power of gravity and attraction . . . contrasted with the formation of one world by divine power . . .* (Liverpool, 1822): "Car, d'après la connaissance que j'avais de son caractère, j'aurais dû craindre qu'il ne me tuât."

29. John Ball Keill in the *Introductio ad veram astronomiam*, 2nd ed. (London, 1721), p. vi.

30. Edmond Halley, *Correspondence and papers*, ed. Eugene Fairfield MacPike (Oxford: Clarendon Press, 1932), p. 251, app. XIV, account of his inaugural address as Savilian Professor of Geometry at Oxford. Halley's admiration was also expressed in verse in the introduction to the *Principia*: "Nec fas est propius Mortali attingere Divos."

31. Keynes MS. 130 (14).

32. Alexander Pope, after reviewing the manuscript of Conduitt's "Dedication" for the *Chronology of Ancient Kingdoms Amended,* expressed the desire to see it enlarged with "some Memoirs & Character of him, as a private Man: I doubt not his Life & Manners would make as Great a Discovery of Virtue, & Goodness, & Rectitude of Heart, as his Works have done of Penetration and the utmost Stretch of human knowledge" (Pope, *Correspondence,* ed. George Sherburn [Oxford: Clarendon Press, 1956], II, 459). Conduitt had written him on November 8, 1727, that "the honour of the nation is in some measure concerned in every thing that relates to that great man . . ." (*ibid.,* pp. 457–458).

David Brewster still believed that in Newton's life "the moralist will trace the lineaments of a character exhibiting all the symmetry of which our imperfect nature is susceptible" (*Life of Newton,* I, 3).

33. See I. Bernard Cohen, *Franklin and Newton* (Philadelphia: American Philosophical Society, 1956), pp. 44–45.

PART ONE: THE LAD FROM LINCOLNSHIRE

Chapter 1

HANNAH AND THE FATHERS

1. William Stukeley made a search in Colsterworth and there the Reverend Mason finally came up with a parish register from 1571 through the beginning of 1643, which was intermitted for the years 1630 to 1640; Newton's baptism is among the last entries (Stukeley, *Memoirs of Sir Isaac Newton's Life . . . ,* ed. A. Hastings White [London: Taylor and Francis, 1936], p. 26). For a facsimile of the entry, see Canon C. W. Foster, "Sir Isaac Newton's Family," *Reports and Papers of the Architectural Societies of the County of Lincoln, County of York . . . ,* XXXIX, part I (1928), 19. Many of the baptismal records at Colsterworth for this period omit the parents' names. The register is today preserved in Colsterworth Church.

2. Cambridge, King's College Library, Keynes MS. 130 (2), p. 15.

3. The following story was written to John Conduitt by a Mrs. Hutton, whose maiden name was Ayscough (Conduitt spells it Aiscough):

Mr Smith a neighbouring Clergyman, who had a very good Estate, had lived a Batchelor till he was pretty old, & one of his parishioners adviseing him to marry He said he did not know where to meet with a good wife: the man answered, the widow Newton is an extraordinary good woman: but saith Mr Smith, how do I know she will have me, & I don't care to ask & be denyed; But if you will go & ask her, I will pay you for your day's work. He went accordingly. Her answer was, She would be advised by her Bro: Ayscough. Upon which Mr Smith sent the same person to Mr Ayscough on the same errand, who, upon consulting with his Sister, treated with Mr Smith: who gave her son Isaac a parcel of Land, being one of the terms insisted on by the widow if she married him.

(Keynes MS. 125)

The story is quoted by E. F. King, *A Biographical Sketch of Sir Isaac Newton,* 2nd ed. (Grantham, 1858), p. 6, and Foster, "Sir Isaac Newton's Family," p. 17.

4. There is a record of the marriage of James Aiscoigh and Margery Blyth under date of December 24, 1609. Thus Newton's maternal grandmother, whose birth date we do not know, was probably in her fifties when Newton lived with her (Foster, "Sir Isaac Newton's Family," p. 15).

5. Foster, "Sir Isaac Newton's Family," p. 18, gives the following data about the children of Barnabas Smith. Mary Smith was baptized May 6, 1647, and was married November 22, 1666, at Colsterworth to Thomas Pilkington of Belton, County Rutland. She was thus born when Newton was four and a half. Benjamin Smith was baptized in August 1651, when his stepbrother was nine. Hannah Smith was baptized September 7, 1652, Newton being ten. She became the second wife to Robert Barton of Brigstock, County Northampton. One of her children was the Catherine whom on August 26, 1717, John Conduitt of Cranbury Lodge in the parish of Otterbourne, County Southampton, married. Three children of Benjamin, three of Mary Pilkington, and two surviving children of Hannah were Newton's eight heirs.

6. Cambridge, University Library, Add. MS. 3958B, a rent receipt on behalf of "Hannah Smith of Woolesthorpe," for forty pounds, dated October 30, 1665, in Newton's hand.

7. Keynes MS. 130 (2), pp. 9–10.

8. Richard S. Westfall, "Short-Writing and the State of Newton's Conscience, 1662 (1)," *Notes and Records of the Royal Society of London,* XVIII (1963), 13.

9. New York, The Pierpont Morgan Library, Notebook of Isaac Newton.

10. Newton, *Correspondence,* I, 2, Hannah Ayscough Smith to Newton, May 6, 1665. The preservation throughout his life of the charred scrap now in King's College Library, Cambridge (Keynes MS. 126), may be a witness of his intense feeling, or due to chance.

11. Hannah Ayscough Smith's will, dated 1672, proved June 11, 1679, at Lincoln, reproduced in Foster, "Sir Isaac Newton's Family," pp. 50–53. She left Isaac properties in the fields of Buckminster and in the fields of Woolsthorpe, along with goods and chattels, plus the use and profit of all her other legacies until they became due. This was a substantial bequest.

12. Keynes MS. 130 (2), p. 12, and Keynes MS. 130 (8).

13. Keynes MS. 130 (3).

14. Keynes MS. 13.

15. James Gregory's anecdote is reported in a letter of the Reverend Doctor Thomas Reid of Glasgow to Dr. Gregory of Edinburgh, March 14, 1784:

Mr. Gregory [James Gregory, the mathematician and brother of David Gregory] being at London for some time after he resigned the mathematical chair, was often with Sir Isaac Newton [after October 1725]. One day Sir Isaac said to him, "Gregory, I believe you don't know that I am connected with Scotland."—"Pray how, Sir Isaac?" said Gregory. Sir Isaac said he was told that his grandfather was a gentleman of East Lothian; that he came to London with King James at his accession to the crown of England, and there spent his fortune, as many more did at that time, by which his son (Sir Isaac's father) was reduced to mean circumstances. To this Gregory bluntly replied, "Newton a gentleman of East Lothian? I never heard of a gentleman of East Lothian of that name." Upon this Sir Isaac said, "that being very young when his father died, he had it only by tradition, and it might be a mistake," and immediately turned the conversation to another subject.

The letter is quoted from David Brewster, *Memoirs of the life, writings, and discoveries of Sir Isaac Newton* [Edinburgh, 1855], II, 538. The story was clearly embroidered in the retelling, and a Scotsman who conducted an inquiry found an old knight, Sir John (or Richard) Newton of Newton, either in West Lothian or Mid-Lothian, in whose family there was a tradition that Isaac Newton had written him a letter. There is a slightly altered version of the anecdote in a letter of Dr. Thomas Reid to Professor Robison, April 12, 1792 (*ibid.,* II, 540).

Newton's fantasies about his lofty birth caught on and in 1778 Paolo Frisi wrote in his *Elogio del Cavaliere Isacco Newton,* published in Milan (p. 16): "He was of one of the noblest and most ancient families in the kingdom, which originated in New Town in Lancaster and which had already been in possession of the seigneury of Volstrope [sic] for two hundred years."

16. New York, The Pierpont Morgan Library, Notebook of Isaac Newton.

17. Babson Park, Massachusetts, Babson Institute Library, MS. no. 439, autograph draft of Newton's pedigree, giving his descent from John Newton of Bitchfeild in Lincolnshire. The pedigree filed in the College of Arms, with an accompanying affidavit of November 22, 1705, made by Sir Isaac Newton before a Master in Chancery, was published by Edmund Turnor, *Collections for the History of the Town and Soke of Grantham* (London, 1806), pp. 168–171. In this version, as well as in that given by Stukeley (*Memoirs of Newton's Life,* p. 30), which purports to derive from the copy sent him by Peter Le Neve, Norroy King of Arms, itself presumably a transcript of the pedigree registered at the Heralds' College in London, no date is assigned to the marriage.

Another error in the Babson manuscript genealogy, which reappeared in the document filed at the Heralds' office, involved the death of Newton's mother: he postdated the event by ten years, writing 1689 instead of 1679. According to Le Neve's marginalia on the transcript he sent to Stukeley, Newton merely wrote: "She dyed at Stamford in Lincolnshire . . . day of . . . 1689 buried at . . ." (Stukeley, *Memoirs of Newton's Life,* p. 29). For the error in the year I propose no explanation except perhaps the obvious one that he thus kept her alive for another decade.

There is another autograph pedigree at the University of Texas.

18. Foster, "Sir Isaac Newton's Family," p. 13: "By a deed dated 30 December, 15 Charles I, 1639, which was in Sir Isaac Newton's possession in 1705, Robert settled both these estates [in Woolsthorpe] on his eldest son Isaac Newton and Hannah Ayscough whom Isaac was about to marry. The manor of Woolsthorpe was reckoned to be worth £30 a year. Robert Newton was a churchwarden at Colsterworth. . . ."

19. In Babson Institute MS. no. 439 Isaac Newton also had Robert Newton, his grandfather, die in 1639 (instead of 1641), the same year in which he fixed the marriage of his parents. The error may thus have been based upon the belief that

the bequest of the manor, the marriage, and the death of his grandfather all occurred in the same year.

20. Robert Newton, Sir Isaac's grandfather, was buried at Colsterworth on September 20, 1641, and thus did not live to see married his eldest son and heir, Isaac Newton, baptized on September 21, 1606, at Colsterworth and buried there on October 6, 1642, at the age of thirty-six. This Isaac Newton had two brothers. One was Robert Newton (baptized September 27, 1607), whose family does not seem to have amounted to much. His son John was a carpenter and died in 1725 at the age of sixty (having served as gamekeeper for Sir Isaac). John's son, also John, one of Newton's heirs at law, was a wastrel who met his end when during a drinking bout he fell and a broken pipe-stem lodged in his throat (Brewster, *Life of Newton*, II, 545). The other brother of the elder Isaac was Richard, baptized April 9, 1609, and buried June 23, 1665. His daughter Anne, Sir Isaac Newton's cousin and coeval in Colsterworth, was baptized on September 11, 1642 (Foster, "Sir Isaac Newton's Family," pp. 15, 23, 61, 63). Thomas Maude, in *Viator, a poem; or, A Journey from London to Scarborough by the Way of York. With notes historical and typographical* [and appendix: *Illustrations on the character of Sir Isaac Newton*] (London, 1782), pp. iv-v, has confused traditions about Newton's father, whom he calls John and describes as a "wild, extravagant & weak man."

There is also a tradition that the Newtons originally came from Lancashire, a plausible idea since there was a migration from that county into Lincolnshire in the sixteenth century. By 1524 the family was already settled in the neighborhood: the father of the yeoman Newton recorded at Westby in the time of Henry VIII seems to have been of a humbler social position. For the next century there appears to have been a steady rise in both the status and prosperity of the Newtons (see Foster, "Sir Isaac Newton's Family," pp. 4–5).

21. An Ayscough had built the elegant tower steeple at Great Paunton. James Ayscough, a surgeon and an apothecary in Dr. Stukeley's native town of Holbech, was a cousin of Sir Isaac's mother, "an ingenious man," who used to take Stukeley simpling in Fleetwoods and awakened his interest in medicine (Stukeley, *Memoirs of Newton's Life*, p. 34). See also Reverend John Mirehouse (Rector of Colsterworth) et al., "Pedigree of Newton," and "Newton Family," *Miscellanea Genealogica et Heraldica*, new series, I (1874), 169–176, 191–194.

22. Foster, "Sir Isaac Newton's Family," pp. 45–46, app. 12. The will of Newton's father, after the date October 1, 1642, begins: "I Izacke Newton of Wolsthorpe in the parrish of Coulsterworth in the county of Lincoln yeaman sicke of body but of good and perfect memorie. . . ." He left forty shillings to the poor, ten shillings to repair the village bridge. The "goods and chattles" were valued at some four hundred fifty-nine pounds; there were oxen, corn, hay, and sheep. Apart from some other modest bequests, his estate was left to Hannah Ayscough, his "loveinge wife," whose father James Ayscough and brother William, Rector of Burton Coggles, were declared supervisors. The will is signed "Izacke Newton his X Marke L. S." (the device is a bird).

23. In his affidavit of November 22, 1705, before a Master in Chancery, Newton testified that he had

by tradition from his kindred ever since he can remember, reckoned himself next of kin (among the Newtons) to Sir John Newton's family, and having also, about fifty-four or fifty-five years ago [that is, circa 1650 or 1651, or aetatis 8–9], heard his grandmother Ascough (with whom he lived at Wylstrope aforesaid, alias Woolstrope, till he was about eleven years old, and who at that time frequently conversed with the deponent's great uncle, Richard Newton) say, that he, this deponent, was or had been next heir att law to Mr. Newton, of Hather, until the birth of Mr. Newton's children, who were then two or three infants, and that he and they were cousins two or three times removed, or words to that purpose; and he, this deponent, believing that his said grandmother, upon the marriage of her daughter with his father, might learn the kindred, and that his grandfather Newton, to promote the marriage, might be forward to speak of itt, representing himself cousin once removed, and next heir to the said Mr. Newton, att that time six or seven years under age, afterwards father to Sir John Newton.

(Turnor, *Collections for the History of Grantham*, p. 170)

Though Newton was particularly aware of this relationship, there is no indication of meetings between the two branches of the family until he became famous. He believed he was the closest of kin of Sir John Newton, baronet, and that if he had died without issue would have inherited his fortune. Unfortunately Sir Michael Newton, later Knight of the Bath, was born.

24. Sir Edward Bysshe, *The visitation of the county of Lincoln made by Sir Edward Bysshe, Knight, Clarenceux king of arms in the year of Our Lord 1666*, ed. Everard Green (Horncastle: printed for the Lincoln Record Society by W. K. Morton & Sons, 1917), p. 44. See also Foster, "Sir Isaac Newton's Family," p. 3.

25. Turnor, *Collections for the History of Grantham*, p. 171.

26. Keynes MS. 112.

27. Foster, "Sir Isaac Newton's Family," p. 17.

28. *Ibid.*, pp. 53–54, app. 16.

29. Newton, *Correspondence*, IV (ed. J. F. Scott), 319–320, Memorandum, circa January 18, 1700. The editors of the *Correspondence* remark (IV, 320 n. 1): "For reasons which are not clear, Newton appears to prefer to pay to Colsterworth rather than to Northwitham."

30. Cambridge, University Library, Add. MS. 4004, fol. 127r.

31. Los Angeles, private collection, Latin Exercise Book of Isaac Newton.

32. New York, The Pierpont Morgan Library, Notebook of Isaac Newton.

33. Thomas Dunham Whitaker, *The History and Antiquities of the Deanery of Craven . . .*, 3rd ed. (London, 1878), p. 542.

34. Newton, *Correspondence*, III, 278–279, Hannah Barton to Newton, August 24, 1693; IV, 187, Benjamin Smith to Newton, November 18, 1695.

35. This is a strange fact about a man highly conversant with legal procedures. Was the failure to make a will a denial of death? Or did he refuse to *will* anything to this family, simply allowing the inheritance to happen?

Chapter 2

THE PREGNANCY OF HIS PARTS

1. Cambridge, King's College Library, Keynes MS. 136, Stukeley to Mead for Conduitt, June 26, 1727; printed in Edmund Turnor, *Collections for the History of the Town and Soke of Grantham* . . . (London, 1806), pp. 175–176. (The printed version has been followed in this and later quotations from Stukeley's letters, except in a few instances where it deviates from the original manuscript beyond punctuation and spelling.) A dissenting voice was raised by Thomas Maude in a note to his *Viator, a poem; or, A Journey from London to Scarborough* . . . (London, 1782), p. 16: he thought it a barren, treeless country and concluded that Stukeley "must certainly have been in the best of tempers when the description dropped from his pen."

2. See Christopher Turnor, "The Country-Side in Newton's day," *Reports and Papers of the Architectural Societies of the County of Lincoln, County of York, Archdeaconries of Northampton and Oakham, and County of Leicester,* XXXVIII, part I (1926), 68–71. In Edward Leigh, *England described Or the several Counties & Shires thereof briefly handled* (London, 1659), Lincolnshire is described as a "very large Countrey, reaching almost threescore miles in length, and carrying in some places above thirty miles in bredth: passing good for yeelding of Corn, and feeding of Cattel; well furnished and set out with a great number of Towns, and watered with many Rivers" (p. 118). There was fen country near Grantham in which vast numbers of mallards were caught in nets. Newton probably also knew Boston at the sea, a "commodious Haven" which stood on both sides of the River Witham. In Newton's early notebooks there are references to the sea, and an image of the sea came to the man on the eve of death.

3. New York, The Pierpont Morgan Library, Notebook of Isaac Newton.

4. The manor house in Woolsthorpe is hardly of baronial proportions. It is a solid stone building the size of an average commodious house in an American suburban community. Stukeley, though he could not find in Newton traces of royal blood, did the next best: a leading authority on pre-Norman England, he came up with the idea that the manor of "Wulsthorp" probably belonged to Ulfus, the fourth son of King Harold, and was named after him (*Memoirs of Sir Isaac Newton's Life,* ed. A. Hastings White [London: Taylor and Francis, 1936], p. 35).

5. Stukeley, *Memoirs of Newton's Life,* p. 16.

6. Leigh, *England described,* p. 121.

7. Turnor, *Collections for the History of Grantham,* pp. 176–177.

8. See also J. A. Lohne, "Isaac Newton: The Rise of a Scientist, 1661–1671," *Notes and Records of the Royal Society of London,* XX (1965), 127: "Isaac did not only construct mechanical toys, but also sundials, two of which are still extant. He graduated and engraved the dials himself, but this does not mean that Newton as a boy understood the whole theory of sundials. We are told that he frequently looked at them to learn how late it was. The tip of the gnomon's shadow follows a curved

path (a conic section) on the dial, and Newton's intense occupation with it doubtless gave him an intimate knowledge of the sun's daily path and of its midday elevation at all times of the year." Derek Whiteside (*The Mathematical Papers of Isaac Newton* [Cambridge: Cambridge University Press, 1967], I, 4) detects some "innate geometrical powers" in the Stukeley anecdotes but no arithmetical gifts.

9. Turnor, *Collections for the History of Grantham*, pp. 177–178.

10. For anatomical drawings by Newton, see Cambridge, University Library, Add. MS. 3958, fols. 36v–37r; and for ground plans of Solomon's Temple, MS. no. 434, Babson Institute Library, Babson Park, Massachusetts. See also in Add. MS. 3996, fol. 2, a tree of nature animate and inanimate.

11. Turnor, *Collections for the History of Grantham*, pp. 178, 179–180.

12. A substantial portion of the Morgan notebook is copied or paraphrased from John Bate, *The Mysteryes of Nature, and Art: conteined in foure seuerall Tretises* . . ., which first appeared in London in 1634 and saw subsequent editions in 1635 and 1654. There are passages from pp. 119–128 and 146–148, mostly "Of Drawing." If Newton had access only to the 1634 or 1635 editions he saw illustrations of male and female heads, but no bodies; full naked male and female figures did not appear until the 1654 edition.

13. Stukeley, *Memoirs of Newton's Life*, pp. 54–55.

14. Turnor, *Collections for the History of Grantham*, p. 180.

15. Stukeley, *Memoirs of Newton's Life*, p. 50.

16. Such contrivances were common. They may have derived from Wilkins' *Mathematicall Magick: or the Wonders That may be performed by mechanicall geometry* (London, 1648). In part 2, "Daedalus; or Mechanical Motions," there is a chap. ii entitled "Of a Sailing Chariot, that may without horses be driven on the land by the wind, as ships are on the sea."

17. Turnor, *Collections for the History of Grantham*, p. 179; Stukeley, *Memoirs of Newton's Life*, p. 46.

18. Charles Hutton, *A Mathematical and Philosophical Dictionary*, new ed. (London, 1815; orig. ed. 1795–1796), II, 100.

19. Stukeley, *Memoirs of Newton's Life*, pp. 46–47. The great wind seems to have occurred on August 30, 1658, and was believed by the superstitious to be the devil riding the whirlwind to reclaim Cromwell's black soul; he had been ill of an ague and died on September 3. See John Evelyn, *Diary*, ed. E. S. de Beer (Oxford: Oxford University Press, 1955), III, 220 and n. 2.

20. Keynes MS. 130 (2).

21. Stukeley, *Memoirs of Newton's Life*, pp. 50–51.

22. Oxford, Bodleian Library, New College MSS. 361, IV, excerpt from Thomas Maude: "Sir Isaac when a boy was some times employed in menial offices even to an attendance on the servant. to open gates in carrying corn to Grantham market and catching the sheep in which last occupation tradition says that a gentleman found him near Woolsthorpe looking into a book of the mathematical kind and asking questions perceived such dawnings of genius as induced him to solicit the mother to give her son an University education promising to assist in the youth's

maintenance at College if there was occasion. But whether that necessity took place, is a point, I have not been able to determine."

Reverend William Ayscough, Rector at Burton Coggles, an adjoining parish, held a Master of Arts from Trinity (1637), and it was to that College that his nephew went (Turnor, *Collections for the History of Grantham,* p. 180 n. 1).

23. Stukeley, *Memoirs of Newton's Life,* p. 51.

24. Turnor, *Collections for the History of Grantham,* p. 159 n. 3.

25. Keynes MS. 130 (2), p. 12.

26. Robert Boyle, "The Usefulness of Natural Philosophy," in his *Works* (London, 1744), I, 429.

27. Evelyn, *Diary,* III, 110–111.

Chapter 3

A MELANCHOLY COUNTENANCE

1. Oliver Cromwell, *The Writings and Speeches,* ed. W. C. Abbott (Cambridge, Mass.: Harvard University Press, 1939), I, 230, Cromwell to Sir Miles Hobart, May 13, 1643.

2. *The Protestation and Declaration of Divers Knights, Esquires, Gentlemen, and Freeholders of the Counties of Lincolne and Nottingham Against the unjust oppressions and inhumane proceeding of William Earle of New-castle and his Cavaliers* . . . (London, 1643), p. 7.

3. *Two Petitions Presented to the Supreme Authority of the Nation, from Thousands of the Lords, Owners, and Commoners of Lincolnshire; against the Old Court-Levellers, or Propriety-Destroyers, the Prerogative Undertakers* (London, 1650), p. 7.

4. Herbert McLachlan, in *The Religious Opinions of Milton, Locke and Newton* (Manchester: Manchester University Press, 1941), p. 119, has presented the evidence for the influence of Puritan divines in Grantham.

5. William Stukeley, *Memoirs of Sir Isaac Newton's Life* . . . , ed. A. Hastings White (London: Taylor and Francis, 1936), p. 44. See also Philip A. Knachel, ed., *Eikon Basilike. The Portraiture of His Sacred Majesty in his Solitudes and Sufferings* (Ithaca: Cornell University Press, 1966). Written by the Bishop of Exeter on the basis of texts from the King, the book went through thirty-five editions by 1649.

6. Samuel Pepys, *Diary,* transcribed by the Rev. Mynors Bright, ed. Henry B. Wheatley (London: G. Bell and Sons, 1928–1935), I, 68–73, entry for February 25–26, 1660.

7. The notebook in the Trinity College Library has a long list of his loans, mostly small sums. Under "Otiose & frustra expensa" are: "supersedeas, cherries, Tarte, Custourde, Herbes & washes, Beere, cake, Milke." There is notice of a gift or fine, "To the senior of the pentioners for my long absence." Other extravagances are: "Teniscourt, Wine little, chessmen." Quoted in part in David Brewster, *Memoirs of the life, writings, and discoveries of Sir Isaac Newton* (Edinburgh, 1855), I, 18. During the period of his great discoveries in 1665 and 1666, he lived a frugal

existence whenever he was in residence at Cambridge; his accounts in the Fitzwilliam notebook speak for themselves. (Dates are in Old Style, with New Year's Day on March 25.)

1665

Rd 10 £ May 23d whereof I gave my Tutor 5 £	5 . 0 . 0
Remaining in my hands since the last Quarter .... }	3 . 8 . 4
In all	8 . 8 . 4.
Pd John the Taylor	2 . 0 . 0.
Pd Me. Bychiner	0 . 3 . 6.
To Caverly	0 . 1 . 0.
To my Laundresse	0 . 0 . 6.
To my Bedmaker	0 . 5 . 0.
A paire of Gloves	0 . 2 . 0.
A paire of Stockings	0 . 5 . 4
A hatband	0 . 2 . 0.
Pd Goodwife Powell for my Laundresse .... }	0 . 5 . 0
Gave more to my Tutor	5 . 0 . 0
My Journey to Cambridge Mar 20.	0 . 6 . 6.
In all	8 .10 .10.
Lent Me. Newton	0 .18 . 0
March 25 1666.	
Lent Wilford	0 . 1 . 0.
To the Poore on the fast	0 . 1 . 0.
To Me. Babints: Wom, 6d. Porter 6d	0 . 1 . 0.
Spent wth Rubbins 4d	0 . 0 . 4
Lent to Sr Herring	1 . 6 . 0.
Lent to Sr Drake	1 . 0 . 0.
Payd my Laundresse	0 . 5 . 6.
For a paire of shoos	0 . 4 . 0.
Caverly	0 . 0 . 4.
Payd John Falkoner	0 .11 . 6.
A paire of shooestrings	0 . 0 . 8.
Payd my Bedmaker	0 . 5 . 0.
Dew from John Evans	0 . 1 .10.
	1 .10 . 4.
The summe of my expences +	8 .10 .10
In all	10 . 1 . 2
Dew to mee	3 . 5 .10
More from Me. Guy	0 .10 . 0
Lent in all	3 .15 .10
1665.	
Rd 10 £ March 20th	10 . 0 . 0.
Remaining in my hands	8 . 8 . 4.
In all	18 . 8 . 4
Expences & wt I lent deducted the rest is .... }	4 .11 . 4.

Having studied the same Fitzwilliam accounts as Derek Whiteside for April 1667–April 1669, I cannot quite agree with his picture of a "young man spending his full income in the mild pursuit of luxury and pleasure"; see *The Mathematical Papers of Isaac Newton* (Cambridge: Cambridge University Press, 1968), II, xii.

8. See Michael Walzer, *The Revolution of the Saints: A Study in the Origins of Radical Politics* (Cambridge, Mass.: Harvard University Press, 1965), pp. 199–231.

9. *Paradise Lost,* IX, 815.

10. Christopher Hill, *Society and Puritanism in Pre-Revolutionary England* (London: Secker & Warburg, 1964), p. 215: " 'The profanation of the Lord's Day by open sports and pastimes is by the civil part of the nation accounted scandalous,' said John Corbet in 1660; and by now 'the civil part of the nation' were those who counted. Kings and bishops had to follow them. After some prodding by the House of Commons, Charles II's Worcester House Declaration of October 1660 promised 'to take care that the Lord's Day be applied to holy exercises, without unnecessary divertisements'; and so by implication abandoned his father's Book of Sports." See also pp. 213–214.

11. Brewster, *Life of Newton,* II, 88–90, quoting letter of Nicolas Wickins to Professor Robert Smith, January 16, 1728.

12. Edmund Turnor, *Collections for the History of the Town and Soke of Grantham* . . . (London, 1806), p. 163, John Conduitt to Fontenelle: "[H]e was hardly ever alone without a pen in his hand, and a book before him. . . ."

13. Cambridge, King's College Library, Keynes MS. 5, fols. 119, 120.

14. New York, The Pierpont Morgan Library, Notebook of Isaac Newton.

15. Los Angeles, private collection, Latin Exercise Book of Isaac Newton.

16. See Ralph W. V. Elliott, "Isaac Newton's 'Of an Universall Language,' " *Modern Language Review,* LII (1957), 1–13, and "Isaac Newton as Phonetician," *Modern Language Review,* XLIX (1954), 5–12.

17. Thomas Shelton, *Tachy graphy the most exact and compendious methode of short and swift writing that hath euer yet beene published by any . . . Approoued by both Universities* (London, 1641), "To the Reader," gives as the reason for learning shorthand in the mid-seventeenth century that thousands might enjoy the works of worthy divines which otherwise would have "perished with the breath that uttered them. . . . Besides the priviledge that divers enjoy in forrein parts, by using Bibles & other bookes in this writing, without danger of bloudy Inquisitours."

18. Edward Cocker, *Arts glory: or The pen-man's treasury . . .* (London, 1659), unpaginated.

19. The Pindar is in Cambridge, King's College Library, the Ovid in the Babson Institute, Babson Park, Massachusetts.

20. Richard de Villamil, *Newton: The Man* (London: G. D. Knox, 1931), pp. 46, 51, 52.

21. See R. S. Westfall, "Short-Writing and the State of Newton's Conscience, 1662 (1)," *Notes and Records of the Royal Society of London,* XVIII (1963), 10–16. In 1662 Whitsunday fell on May 18. The catechism in the Book of Common Prayer includes the following: "Question: What is required of them which come to the

Lord's supper? Answer: To examine themselves whether they repent of their former sins, steadfastly purporting to lead a new life."

22. The Royal Mint Library, Newton MSS., V, fol. 33v. On the back of an account, dated April 1715, of silver and gold coined at the Mint from 1713 to 1715, Newton has notes on worshiping the one God in which the devil obtrudes: "By repentance from dead works he means repentance from idolatry ambition covetousness & unchastity. Ffor we promise in baptism to forsake the devil & all his works the pomp & covetous desires of the world & the carnal desires of the flesh. That devil who is opposed to God [who is the father of the wicked and deceived is worshipped by his children & is the father of the wicked & whom they worship] Resist the devil & he will fly from you. God hath commanded that we should have no other Gods than himself that is, in our worship." Words in brackets were stricken out by Newton.

23. Richard S. Westfall, "Isaac Newton's Coloured Circles twixt two Contiguous Glasses," *Archive for History of Exact Sciences,* II (1965), 184, 195.

24. Richard S. Westfall, "Newton and Absolute Space," *Archives internationales d'histoire des sciences,* XVII (1964), 125-126. The "De Gravitatione et Aequipondio Fluidorum," a small book of forty pages in the Cambridge University Library (Add. MS. 4003), was printed in A. Rupert Hall and Marie Boas Hall, eds., *Unpublished Scientific Papers of Isaac Newton* (Cambridge: Cambridge University Press, 1962), pp. 89-156.

25. Newton, *Mathematical Principles of Natural Philosophy* . . . , trans. Andrew Motte, rev. and ed. Florian Cajori (Berkeley, Cal.: University of California Press, 1934), p. 6.

26. I. B. Cohen, *Franklin and Newton* (Philadelphia: American Philosophical Society, 1956), p. 47.

Chapter 4

TO THE ANNUS MIRABILIS 1666

1. Thomas Fuller, *History of the University of Cambridge* (1655) appended to his *Church-history of Britain* (London, 1655), p. 122.

2. John Evelyn, *Diary,* ed. E. S. de Beer (Oxford: Oxford University Press, 1955), III, 136-137, September 1, 1654.

3. Joseph Edleston, ed., *Correspondence of Sir Isaac Newton and Professor Cotes* (London, 1850), p. xli.

4. William Stukeley, *Memoirs of Sir Isaac Newton's Life* . . . , ed. A. Hastings White (London: Taylor and Francis, 1936), p. 52.

5. Humphrey Babington, *Mercy and Judgment. A Sermon preached at the Assises held at Lincolne: July 15, 1678* (Cambridge, 1678).

6. John Wilkins had revived learning at Cambridge by "strickt examinations at

elections," wrote John Aubrey in his *Brief Lives,* ed. O. L. Dick (Ann Arbor, Mich.: University of Michigan Press, 1957), p. 320.

7. The Puritan purges of Royalists had been considerable, amounting perhaps to two thirds of Trinity College; see G. Dyer, *History of the University and Colleges of Cambridge* (London, 1814), II, 297.

8. Cambridge, University Library, Add. MS. 3996, fol. 89r. There is another reference to this work on fol. 108r.

9. Roger North, *Autobiography,* ed. Augustus Jessopp (London, 1887), p. 15.

10. J. E. McGuire and P. M. Rattansi, "Newton and the 'Pipes of Pan,'" *Notes and Records of the Royal Society of London,* XXI (1966), 124–125.

11. Add. MS. 3996, fol. 104, "Of Sensation"; fol. 108, "Of Memory"; fol. 109r, "Immagination & Phantasie & invention"; fol. 109v, "Sympathy & Antipathie"; fol. 130, "Of the Soule"; fol. 132v, "Of Sleepe & Dreams etc." Fol. 109r alludes to Joseph Glanvill, *The Vanity of Dogmatizing: or, Confidence in Opinions Manifested in a Discourse of the Shortness and Uncertainty of our Knowledge, And its Causes: with some Reflexions on Peripateticism; And An Apology for Philosophy* (London, 1661), pp. 198ff.

12. Cambridge, King's College Library, Keynes MS. 129A, p. 3. A. R. Hall questions the anecdotes about Sanderson's *Logic,* Kepler's *Optics,* Euclid, and a book on judicial astrology bought at Stourbridge Fair; see his "Sir Isaac Newton's Note-Book, 1661–1665," *The Cambridge Historical Journal,* IX, no. 2 (1948), 239. G. L. Huxley, "Two Newtonian Studies," *Harvard Library Bulletin,* XIII (1959), 348–361, makes much of the formative influence of Sanderson's classical Aristotelian treatise.

13. Johann Philippson of Sleidan, *The Key of History. Or, A most methodicall abridgement of the four chiefe monarchies* (London, 1631). *Hall's Chronicle* is the work by Edward Hall(e) entitled *The Union of the Two Noble and Illustre Famelies of Lancastre & Yorke* (London, 1548).

14. Francis Bacon, *Certaine Miscellany Works* (London, 1629).

15. I believe Newton is referring here to the *Theatrum Chemicum,* ed. Lazarus Zetzner, 6 vols. (Strasbourg, 1613–1661), and not, as Derek Whiteside has it (*The Mathematical Papers of Isaac Newton* [Cambridge: Cambridge University Press, 1968], II, xii–xiii), to the one-volume *Theatrum Chemicum Britannicum; containing severall poeticall pieces of our famous English philosophers, who have written the Hermetique Mysteries in their owne ancient language . . .* ed. Elias Ashmole (London, 1652). Newton made numerous excerpts from both of these alchemical compilations; the price of the item in the Fitzwilliam notebook (1 pound, 8 shillings) and the omission of the *Britannicum,* make unlikely its identification as Ashmole's work.

16. Thomas Sprat, *History of the Royal Society of London* (London, 1667).

17. Within a few years the attempt to encompass all things was elevated from the boyish cataloguing of objects in the Morgan notebook to a level of abstraction. The index to the Cambridge University Library notebook (Add. MS. 3996, fol. 87), which is really a philosophical commonplace book, reads:

Aer	Memory
Antipathy	Meteors
Asperity	Mineralls

Attoms	Oyles
Attraction { Magnet	Odors
{ Electrical	Opacity
Bodys Conjuntion	Orbes
Comets	Place
Cold	Planets
Colours	Perspicuity
Corruption	Phylosophy
Creation	Quantity
Condensation	Quality
Density	Rarefaction
Ductility	Reflection
Dreames	Refraction
Earth	Soule
Eternity	Sleepe
Fluidity	Starres & Sunnes
Flexibility	Stability & Siccity
Figure	Softness
Fier	Subtility
Flux & Reflux	Smoothnesse
Filtracōn	Salt
Fantacy	Sensacōn
God	Sound
Gravity	Sapors
Hardnesse	Sympathy
Humidity	Time
Hebetude	Tractility
Heate	Touch
Imaginacōn	Vacuum
Invention	Vortex
Levity	Undulation
Light	Vision
1st Matter	Vegitables
Motion	

18. Add. MS. 3996, fol. 101v.

19. There was even an attempt to identify the experimental philosophy with masculinity and to imply that the discursive philosophy was feminine. See Henry Oldenburg, *Correspondence*, ed. and trans. A. Rupert Hall and Marie Boas Hall (Madison and Milwaukee: University of Wisconsin Press, 1965——), I, 287, Oldenburg to Boyle, August 2, 1659 [N.S.] in criticism of the lack of Baconian application in France: "the French naturalists are more discursive, than active or experimentall. In the meane time the Italian proverb is true: Le parole sono femine, le fatti maschii."

20. The Fellows of the Royal Society tried to develop "a close, naked, natural way of speaking; positive expressions; clear senses; a native easiness: bringing all things as near the Mathematical plainness, as they can: and preferring the language of Artizans, Countrymen, and Merchants, before that, of Wits, or Scholars" (Sprat, *History of the Royal Society*, p. 113).

21. Hall, "Newton's Note-Book, 1661-1665," p. 249.

22. Newton, *Correspondence*, I, 92, Newton to Oldenburg, February 6, 1672.

23. Edleston, ed., *Correspondence of Newton and Cotes*, p. xlii.

24. Cambridge, University Lib.ary, Add. MS. 3968.41, fol. 85r, draft of a letter to Des Maizeaux, first printed in H. R. Luard *et al., A Catalogue of the Portsmouth Collection* . . . (Cambridge, 1888), preface p. xviii. See also n. 29 below.

25. D. T. Whiteside, ed., *The Mathematical Papers of Isaac Newton* (Cambridge: Cambridge University Press, 1967——), I, 148.

26. There are extant mathematical manuscripts dated December 1664, May 1665, and November 1665 (Whiteside, ed., *Mathematical Papers of Newton,* I, opposite 268, 378).

27. *Ibid.,* I, 14–15.

28. Cambridge, University Library, Add. MS. 4007B, fol. 706r, quoted in Whiteside, ed., *Mathematical Papers of Newton,* I, 5–6.

29. Cambridge, University Library, Add. MS. 4000, fol. 14v, quoted in Newton, *Correspondence,* IV, 142 n. 10: "July 4th 1699. By consulting an accompt of my expenses at Cambridge in the years 1663 & 1664 I find that in the year 1664 a little before Christmas I being then senior Sophister, I bought Schooten's Miscellanies & Cartes's Geometry (having read this Geometry & Oughtred's Clavis above half a year before) & borrowed Wallis's works & by consequence made these Annotations out of Schooten & Wallis in winter between the years 1664 & 1665. At wch time I found the method of Infinite series. And in summer 1665 being forced from Cambridge by the Plague I computed the area of the Hyperbola at Boothby in Lincolnshire to two & fifty figures by the same method Is Newton." There are equivalent accounts in Add. MS. 3968.41, fols. 76r and 85r, and Add. MS. 4007, fol. 738v, Derham to Conduitt, July 18, 1733. See Whiteside, ed., *Mathematical Papers of Newton,* I, 148–152, app. I, on the chronology of Newton's early researches in the calculus, 1664–1666, put together from fragments of the decade 1711 to about 1720.

30. The Fitzwilliam notebook accounts run from May 23, 1665, to April 1669.

31. The earliest dates in the Waste Book (Add. MS. 4004) are "Jan 20th 1664" (fol. 10r) and "November 1664" (fol. 21r). Derek Whiteside is convinced that the January date is old style, i.e., 1665. The date entries on these folios appear to me to be markedly different from the surrounding notations and could have been inserted shortly afterward or at a considerably later time. January 20, 1664, is the only date among the dynamical entries in the Waste Book and is important for fixing the time of Newton's earliest researches into the problem of collisions between two perfectly inelastic bodies. For the cometary observations, see Add. MS. 3996, fols. 93v and 115r–116v.

Whiteside, in his "Newton's Marvellous Year: 1666 and all that," *Notes and Records of the Royal Society of London* XXI (1966), 32–41, minimizes the import of Newton's stay at Woolsthorpe; but his affirmations are at variance with his own statements, those by John Herivel, and documents cited by both, let alone materials to which no reference is made.

32. John Herivel, *The Background to Newton's Principia. A study of Newton's dynamical researches in the years 1664-1684* (Oxford: Clarendon Press, 1965), p. 183, discusses Add. MS. 3958, fol. 45, in the Cambridge University Library.

33. Stukeley, *Memoirs of Newton's Life,* pp. 19–20.

413

34. Henry Pemberton, *A View of Sir Isaac Newton's Philosophy* (London, 1728), unpaginated preface.

35. William Whiston, *Memoirs of the Life and Writings of W. W.* (London, 1749-1750), I, 35-36.

36. Herivel, *The Background to Newton's Principia,* p. 69. Herivel says that if there was a test of the law of gravitation during the plague years, it was probably in summer or late autumn 1666 (p. 92).

37. *Ibid.,* pp. 318, 319, for translation.

38. Add. MS. 3996, fol. 109.

39. Newton, *Correspondence,* III, 153, Newton to Locke, June 30, 1691.

40. E. F. King, *A Biographical Sketch of Sir Isaac Newton,* 2nd ed. (Grantham, 1858), p. 66. In the December 10, 1692, letter to Bentley he imputed all his merit to "nothing but industry & a patient thought" (*Correspondence,* III, 233).

41. Keynes MS. 130.

42. Add. MS. 3996, fol. 109r.

43. Whiston, *Memoirs,* I, 34-35.

PART TWO: THE LUCASIAN PROFESSOR

Chapter 5

RESTORATION TRINITY

1. On Barrow, see Percy H. Osmond, *Isaac Barrow. His Life and Times* (London: Society for Promoting Christian Knowledge, 1944), and the traditional biography by Abraham Hill, "Some Account of the Life of Dr. Isaac Barrow," in V. de S. Pinto, ed., *English Biography in the Seventeenth Century* (London: G. G. Harrap, 1951).

2. Quoted in Osmond, *Isaac Barrow,* p. 92.

3. John Aubrey, *Brief Lives,* ed. O. L. Dick (Ann Arbor, Mich.: University of Michigan Press, 1957), p. 20.

4. David Brewster, *Memoirs of the life, writings, and discoveries of Sir Isaac Newton* (Edinburgh, 1855), II, 93-94, Humphrey Newton to John Conduitt, January 17, 1728.

5. Derek Whiteside minimizes the influence of Barrow's mathematical teachings and sees Newton as self-taught with the aid of a few books he bought or borrowed. He further observes: "there is here nothing of the cordial intimacy of later anecdote, and not until 1669, when Newton communicated to Barrow his *De Analysi,* do we have formal evidence of personal friendship. Later still, apparently, when Barrow left Cambridge for London the friendship—if indeed it was ever more than a professional relationship—lapsed again" (*The Mathematical Papers of Isaac Newton* [Cambridge: Cambridge University Press, 1967——], I, 11 n. 26).

6. In the Trinity College Library collection of Newton's books—some of which cannot have belonged to him since they were published after his death—there is an autographed Old Testament in Greek (1653 ed.) from Isaac Barrow.

7. See A. R. Hall, "Sir Isaac Newton's Note-Book, 1661–1665," *The Cambridge Historical Journal*, IX, no. 2 (1948), 246.

8. Isaac Newton, *Optical Lectures read in the publick schools of the University of Cambridge, Anno Domini, 1669 . . . Translated into English out of the original Latin* (London, 1728), pp. 1–2. Newton's lectures on optics were deposited in 1674 in the University archives and published in London in 1729 as *Lectiones Opticae, Annis MDCLXIX, MDCLXX, & MDCLXXI in scholis publicis habitae.*

9. Isaac Barrow, *Lectiones XVIII Cantabrigiae in Scholis publicis habitae; in quibus opticorum phaenomenon genuinae rationes investigantur ac exponuntur,* ed. I. Newton and John Collins (London, 1669), "Letter to the Reader." Quoted from the English translation, which appeared as the author's preface in his *Geometrical Lectures,* trans. Edmund Stone (London, 1735), pp. iv–v.

10. William Stukeley, *Memoirs of Sir Isaac Newton's Life . . . ,* ed. A. Hastings White (London: Taylor and Francis, 1936), pp. 53–54.

11. Cambridge, University Library, Add. MS. 3968.5, fol. 21r.

12. Newton, *Correspondence,* I, 13–14, Barrow to Collins, July 20, 1669.

13. *Ibid.,* I, 14, Barrow to Collins, July 31, 1669.

14. *Ibid.,* I, 14–15, Barrow to Collins, August 20, 1669, extract. The full text is in the collection of letters for the *Commercium Epistolicum,* now in the library of the Royal Society.

15. Oxford, Bodleian Library, MS. Rawl. D. 878, fols. 33–59, catalogue of Isaac Barrow's library.

16. Newton, *Correspondence,* I, 15, Collins to James Gregory, November 25, 1669.

17. *Ibid.,* I, 252, Newton to Collins, December 10, 1672.

18. *Ibid.,* I, 247, Newton to Collins, December 10, 1672.

19. *Ibid.,* I, 248, Newton to Collins, December 10, 1672.

20. *Ibid.,* IV, 116–117, Wallis to Newton, April 30, 1695.

21. Roger North, *The Lives of the Norths* (London, 1826), III, 286.

22. *Ibid.,* III, 298–299.

23. *Ibid.,* III, 350, 353–354.

24. Roger North, *Autobiography,* ed. Augustus Jessopp (London, 1887), p. 157. See also p. 218 for a letter from his mother to his sister about John's illness, August 23, 1680.

25. G. M. Trevelyan, *Trinity College: An Historical Sketch* (Cambridge: Cambridge University Press, 1946), p. 48.

26. Newton, *Correspondence,* II, 205, 207, Newton to John North, April 21, 1677.

27. James Henry Monk, *Life of Richard Bentley,* 2nd ed. (London, 1833), I, 143–145.

28. Cambridge, King's College Library, Keynes MS. 137, Nicolas Wickins to Professor Robert Smith, January 16, 1728; printed in Brewster, *Life of Newton,* II, 88–90.

29. See Newton's memorandum on the composition of the *Principia* in Brewster, *Life of Newton,* I, 471.

30. Cambridge, King's College Library, Keynes MS. 135, Humphrey Newton to

Conduitt; printed in Brewster, *Life of Newton*, II, 91ff. Printed version followed, with some corrections from the manuscript.

31. Stukeley, *Memoirs of Newton's Life*, p. 57.

32. Joseph Mede, *The Key of the Revelation searched and demonstrated out of the Naturall and proper Characters of the Visions*, trans. Richard More (London, 1643; 2nd Latin ed. 1632). See Frank E. Manuel, *Isaac Newton, Historian* (Cambridge, Mass.: Harvard University Press, 1963), pp. 175-176.

33. Marjorie Hope Nicolson, ed., *Conway Letters* (New Haven: Yale University Press, 1930), pp. 478-479.

34. Quoted in Arthur Bryant, *Samuel Pepys*, vol. II: *The Years of Peril* (New York: Macmillan, 1935), p. 2.

35. Nicolson, ed., *Conway Letters*, p. 472.

36. Gilbert Burnet, *Bishop Burnet's History of his own Time* (London, 1724-1734), I, 698: "And they knew, all the King's Priests would be let in upon them, which might occasion in present great distraction and contentions among them; and in time they might grow to be a majority in the Convocation, which is their Parliament."

37. Newton, *Correspondence*, II, 467, Newton to [?], February 19, 1687. Newton argued like a lawyer for royal prerogative, when his own interests were involved in the attempt to make him Provost of King's though he was not of the College (Cambridge, King's College Library, Keynes MS. 117, "The Case of King's College").

38. Keynes MS. 116.

39. Burnet, *History of his own Time*, I, 698.

40. L. T. More's account in his *Isaac Newton: A Biography* (New York: Charles Scribner's Sons, 1934), pp. 338-344, based on the manuscripts in King's College and on Burnet, is substantially the same as the record in *A Complete Collection of State Trials*, compiled by T. B. Howell (London, 1816), XI, 1315-1340. Keynes MS. 113, "An Account of the Cambridge cas & all the proceedings therein," is not in Newton's hand.

41. Newton, *Correspondence*, III, 10-24, Newton to Covel, February 10-May 15, 1689.

42. *Ibid.*, III, 11.

43. Edward Ward, *A Step to Stir-Bitch-Fair: with Remarks upon the University of Cambridge* (London, 1700), pp. 12-13.

44. John Evelyn, *Diary*, ed. E. S. de Beer (Oxford: Oxford University Press, 1955), IV, 343, October 4, 1683.

Chapter 6

GOD AND THE CALLING OF THE NEW PHILOSOPHY

1. Bernhard Varenius, *Geographia generalis . . . emendata . . . & illustrata ab Isaaco Newton* (Cambridge, 1672).

2. See Margery Purver, *The Royal Society: Concept and Creation* (Cambridge, Mass.: Massachusetts Institute of Technology Press, 1967).

3. Thomas Hearne, *Works* (London, 1810), III, clxi–clxiv, John Wallis to Thomas Smith, January 29, 1697.

4. Cambridge, King's College Library, Keynes MS. 6, fol. 1r.

5. John Spencer, *A Discourse concerning Vulgar Prophecies. Wherein the Vanity of receiving them as the certain indications of any future Event is discovered; and some characters of Distinction between true and pretending prophets are laid down* (London, 1665), p. 135.

6. Abraham de la Pryme, *The Diary of Abraham de la Pryme, the Yorkshire Antiquary,* ed. Charles Jackson (Durham, 1870; Surtees Society Publications, vol. 54), p. 42.

7. R. S. Westfall, *Science and Religion in the Seventeenth Century* (New Haven: Yale University Press, 1958), p. 20.

8. S. I. Vavilov, *Isaac Newton,* trans. from the Russian (Berlin: Akademie Verlag, 1951), p. 190. See also Robert H. Hurlbutt III, *Hume, Newton, and the Design Argument* (Lincoln, Neb.: University of Nebraska Press, 1965), chap. i, "Newton's Scientific Theism," and chap. ii, "Other Contemporary Scientists."

9. Voltaire, *The Metaphysics of Sir Isaac Newton,* trans. David Erskine Baker (London, 1747), p. 3.

10. Hélène Metzger, *Attraction universelle et religion naturelle chez quelques commentateurs anglais de Newton* (Paris: Hermann et Cie., 1938), part 2, p. 66: "We shall draw the conclusion that Newton's science demands total and passive obedience to suggestions that have been sent to him, that in the first stage he is content to receive, and that then he elaborates with work that is active, no longer passive. We now understand why it can be asserted that Newton's physics was influenced by religious mysticism and Neoplatonism. It is needless to add that once the doctrine was put into the hands of scientists of a completely different upbringing it escaped from the spiritual conditions that gave it birth." See also Gerd Buchdal, *The Image of Newton and Locke in the Age of Reason* (London, New York: Sheed and Ward, 1961), p. 10: "And as we go on we find how the eighteenth-century Enlightenment is steadily squeezing out these spiritual elements—a soul, an immaterial God—and leaving us with a deterministic dance of atoms, as described so powerfully in the popularized versions of these ideas by the celebrated Baron d'Holbach."

11. Newton, *Correspondence,* III, 233, Newton to Bentley, December 10, 1692; the lectures were published in 1693.

12. Cambridge, King's College Library, Keynes MS. 130 (6).

13. In the Latin edition of the *Opticks* (1706) queries of a theological nature appeared among the seven added to the original sixteen, and still others were introduced into the second English edition in 1717/1718.

14. Richard Baxter, *The Reasons of the Christian Religion* (London, 1667), p. 498.

15. The position of Newton's friend John Spencer was in thorough accord with that of the scientists. In the preface to his *Discourse concerning Prodigies,* 2nd ed. (London, 1665) he administered a nice rebuff to those who contended that absorption with secondary causes was unchristian: "[T]he noble attempt to satisfie the subtile

417

Phaenomena in Nature from causes natural and immediate, is thought by some to have so much of the Philosopher, that it hath the less of the Christian therein, and seems to make Natural All. As if to shew how many wheels in some great Engine, move in subordination to the production of some great work, were to obscure and eclypse the art of the Artificer."

See also Leibniz on the religious mission of science and the duty of the divinely endowed scientists to answer the call. "It seems to me that the principal goal of the whole of mankind must be the knowledge and development of the wonders of God, and that this is the reason why God gave him the empire of the globe. And M. Newton, being one of the men on earth who can contribute most to this end it would almost be a crime on his part to allow himself to be distracted by difficulties which are not absolutely insurmountable" (Leibniz, *Die philosophischen Schriften,* ed. C. J. Gerhardt [new ed., Hildesheim, 1960], III, 261: draft of a letter from Leibniz to T. Burnet which was probably not sent; the editor dates it circa 1699-1700).

16. Keynes MS. 133.

17. R. Bentley, *Works,* ed. Alexander Dyce (London, 1838), III, 75, fourth Boyle lecture, June 6, 1692.

18. See Howard B. Adelmann, *Marcello Malpighi and the Evolution of Embryology* (Ithaca: Cornell University Press, 1966).

19. George Dalgarno, *Ars Signorum, vulgo character universalis et lingua philosophica* (London, 1661), preface.

20. See David Kubrin, "Newton and the Cyclical Cosmos: Providence and the Mechanical Philosophy," *Journal of the History of Ideas,* XXVIII (1956), 325-346.

21. Henry Oldenburg, *Correspondence,* ed. and trans. A. Rupert Hall and Marie Boas Hall (Madison and Milwaukee: University of Wisconsin Press, 1965——), I, 123-125, Oldenburg to Manasseh ben Israel, July 25, 1657.

22. Robert Boyle, *The Excellency of Theology compared with Natural Philosophy (As both are Objects of Men's Study) Discoursed of in a letter to a friend. To which are annexed Some Occasional Thoughts about the Excellency and Grounds of the Mechanical Hypothesis (1665)* (London, 1772), p. 11:

And as for the duration of the world, which was by the old philosophers held to be interminible, and of which the Stoicks opinion, that the world shall be destroyed by fire, (which they held from the Jews) was physically precarious; theology teaches us expressly from divine revelation, that the present course of nature shall not last always, but that one day this world, or at least, this vortex of ours, shall either be abolished by annihilation, or, which seems far more probable, be innovated, and, as it were transfigured, and that, by the intervention of that fire, which shall dissolve and destroy the present frame of nature: so either way, the present state of things (as well natural as political) shall have an end.

The third of John Ray's *Three Physico-Theological Discourses,* 3rd ed. (London, 1713), concerned the dissolution of the world and its renewal:

As concerning the future Condition of the World after the Conflagration, I find it the general and received Opinion of the ancient Christians, that this World shall not be annihilated or destroyed, but only renewed and purified. . . . [N]ot only all Animals, but all Vegetables too, yea, and their Seeds also, will doubtless be mortified and destroyed by the

Violence of the Conflagration; but that the same should be restored, and endued with eternal Life, I know no Reason we have to believe; but rather that there should be new ones produced, either of the same with the former, or of different Kinds, at the Will, and by the Power of the Almighty Creator, and for those Ends and Uses for which He shall design them.

(pp. 324, 415)

23. Joseph Glanvill, *The Vanity of Dogmatizing* (London, 1661), pp. 181–182.

24. Newton, *Mathematical Principles of Natural Philosophy* . . . , trans. Andrew Motte, rev. and ed. Florian Cajori (Berkeley, Cal.: University of California Press, 1934), pp. 545–546.

25. *Ibid.*, p. 544.

26. *Ibid.*, p. 546.

Chapter 7

ON THE SHOULDERS OF GIANTS

1. E. N. da C. Andrade, "Robert Hooke," *Proceedings of the Royal Society,* ser. A, CCI (1950), 442.

2. John L. Aubrey, *Brief Lives,* ed. O. L. Dick (Ann Arbor: University of Michigan Press, 1957), p. 166. "He is certainly the greatest Mechanick this day in the World" (p. 165).

3. Robert Hooke, *The Posthumous Works . . . To these discourses is prefixt the author's life . . . Publish'd by Richard Waller . . .* (London, 1705), p. vii.

4. Authorship is considered possible by Edmund Freeman in his article "A proposal for an English Academy in 1660," *Modern Language Review,* XIX (1924), 291–300, and "more than likely" by Geoffrey Keynes, *A Bibliography of Dr. Robert Hooke* (Oxford: Clarendon Press, 1960), pp. 2–4, though rejected by Professor Andrade in a personal communication to Keynes. The evidence seems to me overwhelming in favor of Keynes's viewpoint: the proposal on p. 68 of the *Continuation* for precisely the same microscopic examination of a cheesemite and a louse that appeared in the *Micrographia* (pp. 212–214), published in 1665. Though Hooke before 1660 might conceivably have shown his discoveries to another virtuoso of their intimate circle who subsequently wrote the *Continuation,* it is most unlikely that this putative author would have had the initials R. H.

5. See Leon Rosenfeld, "Newton and the Law of Gravitation," *Archive for History of Exact Sciences,* II (1965), 375.

6. Even here history did not give him his due. Sir Christopher Wren's name has been attached to the Royal College of Physicians in Warwick Lane and Willen Church in Buckinghamshire, which are today acknowledged to be Hooke's work, along with the Merchant Taylors' Hall and Bedlam, whose gate was decorated with statues of madness in different shapes. Entries in the *Diary* about the building of Bedlam run from 1674 to 1678. See M. I. Batten, "The Architecture of Dr. Robert Hooke, F.R.S.," in the *Twenty-Fifth Annual Volume of the Walpole Society, 1936–1937* (Oxford: printed for the Walpole Society, 1937), 83–113.

7. *The Cutler lectures of Robert Hooke* (vol. VIII of Robert W. T. Gunther, *Early Science in Oxford* [London: Hazell, Watson and Viney, 1920–1967]), unpaginated preface.

8. Cambridge, King's College Library, Keynes MS. 133, Derham to Conduitt, July 18, 1733.

9. The events of October 28, 1672, are a fair sample. "Played with Nell—♓. hurt small of Back. A snuff extinguishing stufft my head and made me wake all night, Q. anti-dote. Dind at Lord Salisburys in Shandoes street with Dr. Barrow, Dr. Whitchcot, Mr. Firman, Mr. Hill. Saw Dr. Cudworth's book of philosophy. Discoursd after dinner of new glasses, new theory of musick, Longitude clock. Mr. Lock, Dr. Holder, Dr. Outram, Dr. Beltz there. Visited Dr. Chester. Gave him the *Lacerta Squamosa*. Lems measure of the Colledge. At Garways" (Robert Hooke, *The Diary . . . 1672–1680*, ed. H. W. Robinson and W. Adams [London: Taylor and Francis, 1935], p. 11).

10. Richard Waller, "The Life of Dr. Robert Hooke," in *Posthumous Works of Hooke*, pp. xxvi–xxvii. John Aubrey's description of Hooke in the *Brief Lives* (p. 165) is similar: "He is but of midling stature, something crooked, pale faced, and his face but little belowe, but his head is lardge; his eie full and popping, and not quick; a grey eie. He haz a delicate head of haire, browne, and of an excellent moist curle. He is and ever was very temperate, and moderate in dyet etc."

11. Pisces indicated orgasm, perhaps because of the association of Venus and Cupid in the origin of the symbol. See Hooke, *Diary*, p. 3.

12. Waller, "Life of Hooke," p. xxiv.

13. Hooke's letter to Oldenburg on February 15, 1672, in which Newton's theory is attacked (Newton, *Correspondence*, I, 110–114), is correctly evaluated by R. S. Westfall in his article "Newton's Reply to Hooke and the Theory of Colors," *Isis*, LIV (1963), p. 87: "Hooke did not intend to be insulting, but he wrote with the air of a master—and Hooke surely considered himself to be the master on the topic —addressing a beginner. Pompous, patronizing, the paper adopted an infuriating tone of condescension. It contrived to imply that Hooke had himself performed all of Newton's experiments; and without examining the experiments closely, it asserted that his hypothesis would explain them as well as Newton's. Hooke later wrote to Lord Brouncker that he had only four hours with Newton's paper in which to write his critique."

14. Newton, *Correspondence*, I, 116, Newton to Oldenburg, February 20, 1672.

15. *Ibid.*, I, 82–83, Newton to Oldenburg, January 18, 1672.

16. *Ibid.*, I, 193, Newton to Oldenburg, June 11, 1672. Nevertheless, Westfall has followed in the manuscripts (Cambridge, University Library, Add. MS. 3970, fols. 433–447) Newton's mounting irritation in successive drafts of his reply to Hooke via Oldenburg (Westfall, "Newton's reply to Hooke and the Theory of Colors," pp. 87–88). The first draft had a bland opening, but the letter actually sent read: "The first thing that offers it selfe is lesse agreable to me, & I begin with it because it is so. Mr. Hooke thinks himselfe concerned to reprehend me for laying aside the thoughts of improving Optiques by *Refractions*. But he knows well that it is not for one man

to prescribe Rules to the studies of another, especially not without understanding the grounds on wch he proceeds" (Newton, *Correspondence*, I, 172).

17. Newton, *Correspondence*, I, 238, Newton to Oldenburg, September 21, 1672.

18. *Ibid.*, I, 262, Newton to Oldenburg, March 8, 1673; I, 282, Newton to Collins, May 20, 1673. The incident is reported with a false emphasis by Charles Hutton, *A Mathematical and Philosophical Dictionary*, 2nd ed. (London, 1815), II, 100: "[B]y an order of council, dated Jan. 28, 1675, (which was 3 years after his election into the Royal Society,) it was ordered, that he should be excused from making the usual weekly payments (one shilling per week), on account of his low circumstances, as he represented."

19. Newton, *Correspondence*, I, 284, Oldenburg to Newton, June 4, 1673.

20. *Ibid.*, I, 294-295, Newton to Oldenburg, June 23, 1673.

21. *Ibid.*, I, 318, Linus to Oldenburg, September 26, 1674.

22. *Ibid.*, II, 184, Newton to Oldenburg, November 28, 1676.

23. Hooke, *Diary*, pp. 148, 149, 153, 199-200, 205-206.

24. *Ibid.*, p. 213, January 20, 1676.

25. Newton, *Correspondence*, I, 412-413, Hooke to Newton, January 20, 1676; I, 416-417, Newton to Hooke, February 5, 1676.

26. David Brewster, *Memoirs of the life, writings, and discoveries of Sir Isaac Newton* (Edinburgh, 1855), I, 143; L. T. More, *Isaac Newton: A Biography* (New York: Charles Scribner's Sons, 1934), pp. 177-178.

27. John of Salisbury, *The Metalogicon. A Twelfth-Century Defense of the Verbal and Logical Arts of the Trivium*, ed. and trans. Daniel D. McGarry (Berkeley, Cal.: University of California Press, 1955), p. 167. Robert K. Merton has written what he calls "A Shandean Postscript" on this celebrated saying in his *On the Shoulders of Giants* (New York: Free Press, 1965).

28. Newton, *Correspondence*, I, 408, Newton to Oldenburg, January 10, 1676. The aged Newton, conversing in 1715 with a favorite of the moment, Abate Conti, stressed how much Descartes, too, had borrowed from others. "Mr. Newton told me," Conti wrote in a note, "Descartes was a great man in his day and at the beginning I was a Cartesian, but he is an author who knew how to profit well and to put together well what others discovered. The greatest part of the algebraic things come from Ariotto, and I have shown what he took from Marcantonio de Dominis on colors. The whole rest of his physical theory is based on the idea that matter is extension" (Abate Antonio Conti, *Prose e Poesie* [Venice, 1756], II, 26).

29. A. R. Hall and Marie Boas Hall, eds., *Unpublished Scientific Papers of Isaac Newton* (Cambridge: Cambridge University Press, 1962), pp. 397-413.

30. Newton, *Correspondence*, II, 254-260; Richard S. Westfall, "Newton Defends His First Publication, The Newton-Lucas Correspondence," *Isis*, LVII (1966), 254.

31. Newton, *Correspondence*, II, 239, Newton to Hooke, December 18, 1677.

32. *Ibid.*, II, 297-298, Hooke to Newton, November 24, 1679.

33. Alexandre Koyré, *Newtonian Studies* (Cambridge, Mass.: Harvard University Press, 1965), p. 231.

34. Newton, *Correspondence*, II, 300-303, Newton to Hooke, November 28, 1679.

35. Newton, *Correspondence*, II, 436, Newton to Halley, June 20, 1686.

36. J. Lohne, in his "Hooke versus Newton," *Centaurus*, VII (1960), made a trial out of the Hooke-Newton controversy and after reviewing the documents came to a verdict: "Hooke had for 15 years been speculating and experimenting on gravity and circular motion and had arrived at the principles that govern the fall of a stone and the course of a planet" (p. 50). "For the mechanical system of the world was to a great extent established upon Hooke's principles and erected by means of Newton's methods" (p. 7). See also L. D. Patterson, "Hooke's Gravitation Theory and its influence on Newton," *Isis*, XL (1949), 327-341; XLI (1950), 32-45.

37. Koyré, *Newtonian Studies*, p. 234.

38. Richard S. Westfall, "Hooke and the Law of Universal Gravitation," *The British Journal for the History of Science*, III (1967), 245, 251.

39. Newton, *Correspondence*, II, 302, Newton to Hooke, November 28, 1679; Koyré, *Newtonian Studies*, p. 236. Rosenfeld, "Newton and the Law of Gravitation," p. 374, believes it "outrageously improbable" that Newton had never heard of Hooke's hypothesis about celestial motions.

40. Thomas Birch, *The History of the Royal Society of London* (London, 1756–1757), III, 516.

41. Newton, *Correspondence*, II, 436, Newton to Halley, June 20, 1686.

42. *Ibid.*, II, 308, Newton to Hooke, December 13, 1679.

43. *Ibid.*, II, 309, Hooke to Newton, January 6, 1680.

44. See J. W. Herivel, "Newton's First Solution to the Problem of Kepler Motion," *The British Journal for the History of Science*, II (1965), 350.

45. Derek T. Whiteside, "Newton's early thoughts on planetary motion: a fresh look," *The British Journal for the History of Science*, II (1964), 130-131, thus appraised Hooke's activities:

In England, supremely, Robert Hooke had over twenty years developed his researches into a loose gathering of all the constituents (elliptical planetary orbits round the sun at a focus, deflection of the planet into its orbit from a linear inertial path by a gravitational pull to the sun varying instantaneously as the inverse square of the solar distance) with the exception of Kepler's true areal law—and knowledge, if not acceptance, of that too was becoming increasingly widespread. Unfortunately, too, for Hooke the ultimate fusion needed a mathematical insight surpassing his moderate talents in that field—a point judiciously if heavily made by Newton when he later recalled his own triumph for Halley.

46. William Derham reported that Newton peevishly dismissed Hooke's claim to the discovery of the law of gravity with the remark: "Dr. Hook could not perform that which he pretended to: let him give demonstrations of it. I know he hath not geometry enough to do it" (Cambridge, King's College Library, Keynes MS. 133, Derham to Conduitt, July 18, 1733). For Whiteside's more balanced view of Hooke's mathematical capacities, see his "Newton's early thoughts on planetary motion," p. 131 n. 49.

47. John Herivel, *The background to Newton's Principia; a study of Newton's dynamical researches in the years 1664-1684* (Oxford: Clarendon Press, 1965), pp. 16, 22.

48. Cambridge, University Library, Add. MS. 3968. 41, fol. 85r. First published in H. R. Luard *et al., Catalogue of the Portsmouth Collection* . . . (Cambridge, 1888), p. xiii, where it is suggested that Newton meant 1679–1680.

49. Herivel, *The background to Newton's Principia,* p. 14.

50. Oxford, Bodleian Library, Lister MS. 3, fol. 119, Halley to Dr. Martin Lister, April 9, 1687, reporting on his work in connection with the last book of the *De Systemate Mundi:* "Here he [Newton] falls in with Mr. Hooke, and makes the Earth of the shape of a Compressed Spheroid. . . ."

51. Newton, *Correspondence,* II, 431, Halley to Newton, May 22, 1686.

52. *Ibid.,* II, 433–434, Newton to Halley, May 27, 1686.

53. *Ibid.,* II, 438, Newton to Halley, June 20, 1686.

54. Rosenfeld, "Newton and the Law of Gravitation," p. 379, expresses a similar view.

55. Herivel, "Newton's First Solution to the Problem of Kepler Motion," p. 351 n. 5.

56. Newton, *Mathematical Principles of Natural Philosophy* . . . , trans. Andrew Motte, rev. and ed. Florian Cajori (Berkeley, Cal.: University of California Press, 1934), p. xviii.

57. Newton, *Correspondence,* II, 441–443, Halley to Newton, June 29, 1686.

58. *Ibid.,* II, 445, Newton to Halley, July 14, 1686.

59. *Ibid.,* II, 447, Newton to Halley, July 27, 1686.

60. Cambridge, King's College Library, Keynes MS. 130 (10).

61. Gunther, *Early Science in Oxford,* X (1935), 133, 144, 145, 184.

62. Newton, *Correspondence,* III, 42, Aubrey and Hooke to Anthony à Wood, September 15, 1689. John Aubrey, one of Hooke's few contemporary defenders, reproduced Hooke's argument that he had communicated to Newton "the whole of his Hypothesis" of which Newton only made a "demonstration, not at all owning, he received the first Intimation of it from Mr Hooke. Likewise Mr Newton has in the same booke printed some other theories and experiments of Mr Hooke's . . . without acknowledgeing from whom he had them" (p. 41). For Hooke's further testimony see A. R. Hall, "Two Unpublished Lectures of Robert Hooke," *Isis,* XLII (1951), 225.

Chapter 8

IN QUEST OF THE GOLDEN FLEECE

1. Newton, *Correspondence,* I, 9–11, Newton to Aston, May 18, 1669. While I accept the traditional identification of Newton's correspondent as Francis Aston, made in the *Biographia Britannica* (London, 1760), V, 3241, Whiteside may be right in calling him "unidentified" since the letter exists only in a copy by John Collins; see *The Mathematical Papers of Isaac Newton* (Cambridge: Cambridge University Press, 1968), II, ix. In the *Biographia Britannica* the salutation is "Sir."

2. Cambridge, King's College Library, Keynes MS. 152, "An Abridgement of a Manuscript of Sr Robert Southwell's concerning travelling" (quoted in Newton, *Correspondence*, I, 12).

3. Cambridge, Fitzwilliam Museum, Notebook of Isaac Newton. The list is published in part in David Brewster, *Memoirs of the life, writings, and discoveries of Sir Isaac Newton* (Edinburgh, 1855), I, 33. ☿ = mercury.

4. See F. Sherwood Taylor, "An Alchemical Work of Sir Isaac Newton," *Ambix*, V (1956), 61; Cambridge, King's College Library, Keynes MS. 38, "Sententiae notabiles," published in Taylor, pp. 64–82.

5. R. J. Forbes, "Was Newton an Alchemist?" *Chymia*, II (1949), 29; R. de Villamil, *Newton: The Man* (London: G. D. Knox, 1931), p. 50; H. A. Feisenberger, "The libraries of Newton, Hooke, and Boyle," *Notes and Records of the Royal Society of London*, XXI (1966), 42–55.

6. "The Hunting of the Green Lyon," for example, has a section headed: "In the following notes you have the consent of it with other authors & elucidation thereby" (Keynes MS. 20, p. 5).

7. Keynes MS. 30.

8. Newton had in fact abstracted a passage from Maier, Book XI, pp. 525–526 (Keynes MS. 29, fol. 4); see Newton, *Correspondence*, I, 13.

9. William Cooper prepared the first bibliography of alchemical books in England; it forms a part of *The philosophical epitaph of W. C. Esquire* (London, 1673).

10. Denis I. Duveen, *Bibliotheca alchemica et chemica* (London: E. Weil, 1949), plate XII, fascimile of pp. 90–91 of *Secrets Reveal'd*, with Newton's marginal notations; see also Duveen, p. 470. Artephius was the author of *Liber Secretus nec non Saturni Trismegisti* [2nd ed.; Frankfort, 1685?] and *Clavis Majoris Sapientiae* (Paris, 1609). ☉ = gold.

11. See Marie Boas and A. R. Hall, "Newton's Chemical Experiments," *Archives internationales d'histoire des sciences*, XLIII (1958), 151: "Newton was not in any admissible sense of the word an alchemist; there is no evidence that any of his processes are of the kind necessarily preliminary to the Great Work, or that he ever hoped to fabricate a factitious gold." For the contrary position, see C. H. Josten, ed., *Elias Ashmole, 1617–1692* (Oxford: Clarendon Press, 1966), I, 90: "It should not be forgotten that Sir Isaac Newton and even the sceptical Robert Boyle were in a sense practising alchemists."

12. Eiraeneus Philaletha, *Secrets Reveal'd: or An Open Entrance to the Shut Palace of the King* (London, 1669), unpaginated preface by John Langius.

13. At the Massachusetts Institute of Technology in Cambridge there is a manuscript copy in Newton's hand of Nicholas Flamel, *His Exposition of the Hieroglyphicall Figures which he caused to bee painted upon an Arch in St. Innocents Churchyard in Paris. Together with The Secret Booke of Artephius, And The Epistle of John Pontanus: Concerning both the Theoricke and the Practicke of the Philosophers Stone. Faithfully, and (as the Majesty of the thing requireth) religiously done into English out of the French and Latine Copies* (London, 1624). There are annotations in Newton's hand and his signature on a copy (in the Yale University Library) of a

work by Eugenius Philalethes, *The fame and confession of the fraternity of R. C.* (London, 1652).

14. Elias Ashmole, *Theatrum Chemicum Britannicum; containing severall poeticall pieces of our famous English philosophers, who have written the Hermetique Mysteries in their owne ancient language. Faithfully collected . . . with annotations thereon* (London, 1652), p. 440. On Ashmole, see *Elias Ashmole (1617–1692): His Autobiographical and Historical Notes, his Correspondence and other Contemporary Sources Relating to his Life and Work,* 5 vols., ed. C. H. Josten (Oxford: Clarendon Press, 1966).

15. Edmund Dickinson, the Medicus Regius to Charles II and James II, believed that he knew the secret of transmutation from a French alchemist, Theodore Mundanus. That eminent patron of science, Charles II, is said to have watched his experiments. Dickinson's book, *De Quintessentia Philosophorum,* to which Newton refers in his "Sententiae notabiles," was first published in Oxford in 1686, which helps date Newton's manuscript. At the University of Texas there is an autograph manuscript of sixteen pages by Newton entitled "Ex Epist. Edmundi Dickenson ad Theodorum Mundanum." One part of the manuscript is captioned "Ex Theodori Mundani Responso Del. Parisiis 10 Cal. Octob. 1684," with subheadings such as "De Mecurio [sic] Philosophorum," "De Medicamenta Universal," and "De Patriarchum longaevitae."

16. In Robert Clavell's *General catalogue of books printed in England since the dreadful fire of London 1666. To the end of Trinity-term 1680* (London, 1680), "Physick" (pp. 29–36) is an important category and includes a large number of books that are clearly alchemical. Of course, there were respectable men of science committed to the study of alchemy in the previous generation. See Thomas Browne on the work of Dr. Arthur Dee and his father (Browne, *Works,* ed. Geoffrey Keynes [London: Faber and Faber, 1964], IV, 293–294, 296–298).

17. For example, see the poem by John Dryden, *Annus Mirabilis: The Year of Wonders, 1666:* "Me-thinks already; from this Chymick flame,/ I see a City of more precious mold" (293: 1170).

18. See Allen G. Debus, *The English Paracelsians* (London, New York: Franklin Watts, Inc., 1965) and P. M. Rattansi, "Paracelsus and the Puritan Revolution," *Ambix,* XI (1963), 24–32.

19. Repeal of the statute of 5 Henry IV, 1403–1404, is recorded in *Statutes at Large,* IX (1688–1696), 59–60.

20. Philaletha, *Secrets Reveal'd,* pp. 3–4: " 'Tis likewise evident it is not the vulgar ☿ but the Sophick; because every vulgar ☿ is a Male that is corporeal, specificate and dead: but ours is spiritual, feminine, living and vivifying. Attend therefore to those things that I shall speak of ☿, for as the Philosopher saith, Our ☿ is the Salt of the Wisemen . . . but our ☉ is formed by us, not by creation, but by extracting him out of those things in which he is; Nature co-operating in a wonderful manner, by a witty Art."

21. *Ibid.,* p. 119: "[H]e hath a Medicine Universal, both for prolonging Life, and Curing of all Diseases, so that one true *Adeptist* can easily Cure all the sick People in the World, I mean his Medicine is sufficient."

22. Keynes MS. 38, fol. 9v-10r; printed with some alterations in Taylor, "An Alchemical Work of Newton," pp. 75-76. Keynes MS. 22 is the full treatise of Edwardus Generosus in Newton's hand.

23. William Stukeley, *Memoirs of Sir Isaac Newton's Life* . . . , ed. A. Hastings White (London: Taylor and Francis, 1936), p. 59.

24. Keynes MS. 55, fol. 2r. Michael Sendivogius was the author of *A New Light of Alchymie* (London, 1650).

25. Keynes MS. 40, fol. 20r.

26. Keynes MS. 43, fol. 4.

27. George Ripley, *The Compound of Alchymy* (London, 1591).

28. Keynes MS. 54, fol. 2r.

29. Keynes MS. 135, Humphrey Newton to Conduitt; the printed version (Brewster, *Life of Newton*, II, 95-96) is followed, with corrections from the manuscript.

30. Keynes MS. 43, fol. 4r.

31. George Starkey, *Pyrotechny, Asserted and Illustrated, To be the surest and safest means For Arts Triumph over Natures Infirmities. Being A full and free Discovery of the Medicinal Mysteries studiously concealed by all Artists, and onely discoverable by Fire* (London, 1658), p. 10. This work was dedicated to Robert Boyle.

32. Newton quotes Hermes Trismegistus: "Yet I had this Art and science by the sole inspiration of God who hath vouchsafed to reveal it to his servant. Who gives those that know how to use their reason the means of knowing the truth, but is never the cause that any man follows error & falshood . . ." (Keynes MS. 27, fol. 4). Or again, in a piece entitled "Observations of the matter in the Glass" (Keynes MS. 39, fol. 2r): "so be it far from me to make my self a name or otherwise to use it excessively farther then for competent necessities for my self, but specially for thy honour & glory & maintenance of thy truth, & to the good of the poor fatherless, the poor widdows & all other thy distressed members here on earth."

33. Keynes MS. 130, a Conduitt notebook.

34. Thomas Norton, "The Ordinall of Alchimy," in Ashmole, *Theatrum Chemicum Britannicum*, pp. 10, 14.

35. Newton, *Correspondence*, I, 305, Oldenburg to Newton, September 14, 1673. There exists an inscribed presentation copy to Newton of Boyle's *Essays of the Strange Subtilty/Determinate Nature/Great Efficacy of Effluviums. To which are annext New Experiments To make Fire and Flame Ponderable: Together with A Discovery of the Perviousness of Glass* (London, 1673); see Duveen, *Bibliotheca alchemica et chemica*, p. 94 and plate XIV.

36. Newton, *Correspondence*, I, 393, Newton to Oldenburg, December 14, 1675: "Pray present my humble service to Mr Boyle wn you see him & thanks for the favour of the convers I had wth him at spring."

37. Robert Boyle, "An Account of Philaretus during his Minority" (the autobiography), in *Works* (London, 1744), I, 6.

38. *Ibid.*, I, 8.

39. Thomas Birch, "The Life of the honourable Robert Boyle," in Boyle, *Works*, I, 27.

40. John Evelyn, *Diary and Correspondence*, ed. William Bray (London: H. G. Bohn, 1859), III, 116-117, Evelyn to Boyle, September 6, 1659.

41. Newton, *Correspondence*, I, 356, John Collins to James Gregory, October 19, 1675.

42. Robert Boyle, "Of the Incalescence of *Quicksilver* with *Gold*, generously imparted by B. R.," *Philosophical Transactions of the Royal Society*, X (1675-1676), 517.

43. *Ibid.*, pp. 522-523, 526.

44. Newton, *Correspondence*, II, 1-2, Newton to Oldenburg, April 26, 1676.

45. Robert Boyle, *An historical account of a degradation of gold, made by an anti-elixir: A strange chymical narrative* (1678), in *Works*, IV, 19.

46. Cambridge, University Library, Add. MS. 3973, notes of experiments.

47. Newton, *Correspondence*, I, 366, Newton to Oldenburg, December 7, 1675.

48. *Ibid.*, I, 364, Newton to Oldenburg, December 7, 1675; this is the text as amended in accordance with Newton's letter to Oldenburg, January 25, 1676 (I, 414).

49. *Ibid.*, II, 289, Newton to Boyle, February 28, 1679.

50. *Ibid.*, II, 295, Newton to Boyle, February 28, 1679. See also Cambridge, University Library, Add. MS. 3996, fol. 97r, "Of Gravity & Levity," for an early formulation of this hypothesis.

51. J. E. McGuire, "Transmutation and Immutability: Newton's Doctrine of Physical Qualities," *Ambix*, XIV (1967), 88-89. See also Henry Guerlac, "Newton's optical aether: his draft of a proposed addition to his Opticks," *Notes and Records of the Royal Society of London*, XXII (1967), 45-67; Marie Boas Hall and A. Rupert Hall, "Newton's electric spirit—Four Oddities," *Isis*, L (1959), 473-476; and Alexandre Koyré and I. Bernard Cohen, "Newton's 'Electric and Elastic Spirit,'" *Isis*, LI (1960), 337.

52. Newton, *Correspondence*, II, 379, Boyle to Newton, August 19, 1682.

53. Robert Boyle, "Letter" (circa 1689), in *Works*, I, 82.

54. A recent scholar who has examined Locke's papers found a commonplace book, dated 1693 and written by an amanuensis, full of chemical remedies as well as "fanciful legacies" from his youth such as van Helmont's secret of transposing metals (Oxford, Bodleian Library, MS. Locke c. 44); see Kenneth Dewhurst, *John Locke (1632-1704), Physician and Philosopher. A Medical Biography. With an edition of the Medical Notes in his Journals* (London: The Wellcome Historical Medical Library, 1963), p. 285.

55. Newton, *Correspondence*, III, 147, Newton to Locke, February 7, 1691.

56. *Ibid.*, III, 193, Newton to Locke, January 26, 1692.

57. *Ibid.*, III, 195, Newton to Locke, February 16, 1692.

58. *Ibid.*, III, 215, Newton to Locke, July 7, 1692.

59. *Ibid.*, III, 217-219, Newton to Locke, August 2, 1692.

60. *Ibid.*, III, 45, Newton to Fatio, October 10, 1689.

61. *Ibid.*, III, 265-267, Fatio to Newton, May 4, 1693.

62. *Ibid.*, III, 268, Fatio to Newton, May 18, 1693. ♈ = Aries; ♉ = Taurus.

63. Cambridge, University Library, Add. MSS. 3973 and 3975 include experiments in chemistry and alchemy from December 10, 1678, to February 1696. Boas and Hall,

"Newton's Chemical Experiments," studied these manuscripts, noting intense activity in December 1678 and January 1679, May and June 1681, May–August 1682, April and May 1686.

64. Newton, *Correspondence*, IV, 196–198, Memorandum of March 1696; see also E. D. Geoghegan, "Some Indications of Newton's attitude towards Alchemy," *Ambix*, VI (1957), 106. A short treatise by Jodocus von Rehe is included in *The Last Will and Testament of Basil Valentine* (London, 1671).

65. Duveen, *Bibliotheca alchemica et chemica*, p. 539. The manuscript came from the sale of Viscount Lymington's papers.

66. Keynes MS. 13.

Chapter 9

THE APE OF NEWTON: FATIO DE DUILLIER

1. Thomas Maude, *Viator, a poem; or, A Journey from London to Scarborough* . . . (London, 1782), app., p. vi; Voltaire, *Letters concerning the English Nation* (London, 1733), pp. 116–117.

2. Bibliothèque Publique et Universitaire de Genève, MS. français 602, fols. 43–47, Fatio to Cassini, November 16, 1681.

3. The incident is confirmed by Gilbert Burnet, who reported it to the King:

But I had learned somewhat of the design of a brutal *Savoyard*, who was capable of the blackest things, and who for a foul murder had fled into the territory of *Geneva*, where he lay hid in a very worthy family, to whom he had done some services before. He had formed a scheme of seizing on the Prince, who used to go in his chariot often on the sands near *Schevling* with but one person with him, and a page or two on the chariot. So he offered to go in a small vessel of twenty guns, that should lie at some distance at sea, and to land in a boat with seven persons besides himself, and to seize on the Prince, and bring him aboard, and so to *France*. This he wrote to Mr. *de Louvoy*, who upon that wrote to him to come to *Paris*, and ordered money for his journey. He, being a talking man, spoke of this, and shewed Mr. *de Louvoy's* letter, and the copy of his own: And he went presently to *Paris*. This was brought me by Mr. *Fatio*, the celebrated mathematician, in whose father's house that person had lodged. When I told the Prince this, and had Mr. *Fatio* at the *Hague* to attest it, he was no much moved at it. The princess was more apprehensive.

The quotation is from Gilbert Burnet, Bishop of Salisbury, *Bishop Burnet's history of his own time. With the life of the author by T. Burnet* (London, 1724–1734), I, 689.

4. Gilbert Burnet, *Travels* (London, 1750), p. 14.

5. Bibliothèque Publique et Universitaire de Genève, MS. français 602, fol. 63v, Fatio to M. Huguenin, Utrecht, July 1/11, 1690.

6. Bibliothèque Publique et Universitaire de Genève, MS. français 602, fol. 58, minute of a letter from Fatio to Jean-Robert Chouet, London, November 21, 1689.

7. Bibliothèque Publique et Universitaire de Genève, MS. français 602, fol. 60, minute of a letter of Fatio to his mother, London, February 18, 1690.

8. Bibliothèque Publique et Universitaire de Genève, MS. français 602, fols. 208ff, "Songes de Nicolas Fatio."

9. Fatio's book on fruit trees bore the imprimatur of John Hoskyns, V.P.R.S., August 31, 1698, and a dedication to the Marquis of Tavistock. In addition to the treatise *De la cause de la pesanteur* and the work on pomiculture Fatio's writings included *Epistola N.F.D. de mari aeneo Salomonis ad E. Bernardum . . . in qua ostenditur geometrice satisfieri posse mensuris, quae de mari aeneo in Sacra Scriptura habentur* (Oxford, 1688); *Lettre à Cassini . . . touchant une lumière extraordinaire qui paroît dans le ciel depuis quelques années* (Amsterdam, 1686); *Lineae brevissimi descensus investigatio geometrica duplex. Cui addita est investigatio geometrica solidi rotundi, in quod minima fiat resistentia* (London, 1699); *Four theorems, with their demonstration, for determining accurately the sun's parallax* (London, 1745); *Navigation Improv'd: being chiefly the method for finding the latitude at sea as well as by land, by taking any proper altitudes, together with the time between the observations . . .* (London, 1728).

10. Bibliothèque Publique et Universitaire de Genève, MS. français 602, fol. 63v, minute of a letter from Fatio in Utrecht to Nicolas Tourton in London, June or July 1690.

11. Bibliothèque Publique et Universitaire de Genève, MS. français 602, fols. 68-69v, minutes of letters from Fatio to Richard Hampden, Utrecht, August 7 and September 22, 1690.

12. Edmund Calamy, *An Historical Account of My Own Life* (London, 1829), II, 73-74.

13. Bibliothèque Publique et Universitaire de Genève, MS. français 602, fol. 82v, Fatio to his brother, London, February 3, 1693.

14. Christiaan Huygens, *Oeuvres complètes* (The Hague, Haarlem: M. Nijhoff, 1888-1950), X, 606ff, letters from Huygens to Fatio, 1691-1693; Bibliothèque Publique et Universitaire de Genève, MS. français 602, fol. 5, copy of the postscript of a letter from Leibniz to De Beyrie, 1694. Leibniz wrote of the Newton-Fatio relationship: "I expect great results from this worthy collaboration."

15. Newton, *Correspondence*, III, 308, Fatio to [De Beyrie] for Leibniz, March 30, 1694.

16. Bibliothèque Publique et Universitaire de Genève, MS. français 602, Marquis de l'Hôpital to Fatio, May 15, 1699.

17. Newton, *Correspondence*, III, 45, Newton to Fatio, October 10, 1689.

18. His paper was read to the Society a few days later; see Bernard Gagnebin, ed., "De la cause de la pesanteur. Mémoire de Nicolas Fatio de Duillier présenté à la Royal Society le 26 février 1690. Reconstitué et publié avec une introduction," *Notes and Records of the Royal Society of London*, VI, 2 (1949), 105-160. In the Bibliothèque Publique et Universitaire de Genève, MS. français 603, there is a copy of the treatise on which Newton, Halley, and Huygens had inscribed their signatures.

19. Newton, *Correspondence*, III, 390-391, Fatio to Newton, February 24, 1690.

20. Huygens, *Oeuvres complètes*, IX, 387, Fatio to Huygens, February 24, 1690; reprinted in Newton, *Correspondence*, III, 69.

NOTES TO PAGES 198-207

21. Newton, *Correspondence*, III, 79, Newton to Locke, October 28, 1690.

22. *Ibid.*, III, 168, Fatio to Huygens, September 8/18, 1691; III, 170, David Gregory to Newton, October 10, 1691.

23. *Ibid.*, III, 229-230, Fatio to Newton, September 17, 1692. Double brackets in the original have here been replaced by virgules.

24. *Ibid.*, III, 231, Newton to Fatio, September 21, 1692.

25. *Ibid.*, III, 231-233, Fatio to Newton, September 22, 1692.

26. Joseph Edleston, ed., *Correspondence of Sir Isaac Newton and Professor Cotes, including letters of other Eminent Men* (London, 1850), pp. lxxxvi-xc.

27. Newton, *Correspondence*, III, 270-271, draft of a letter from Newton to Otto Mencke, May 30, 1693; III, 257-258, Leibniz to Newton, March 7, 1693.

28. *Ibid.*, III, 242-243, Fatio to Newton, January 30, 1693. It is possible that the following draft of a letter, penned lengthwise on a closely-written manuscript page, was also intended for Fatio: "I have seen Mr. Craig's new piece but had not time to read it. If yor friend should go into Fflanders or . . . anything else should fall out so that you cannot go to work this winter, what if you should spend the winter here. About a fortnight since I was taken ill of a distemper wch has been here very common, but am now pretty well again . . ." (Oxford, Bodleian Library, New College MSS. 361, III, fol. 33r). A date of 1693 is suggested not only by the content of the letter, but by the fact that John Craig in that year published his piece entitled "Tractatus . . . de Figurarum Curvilinearum Quadraturis et locis Geometricis," important for the development of the theory of fluxions.

29. *Ibid.*, III, 245, Newton to Fatio, February 14, 1693.

30. *Ibid.*, III, 260-261, Newton to Fatio, March 7, 1693.

31. *Ibid.*, III, 262-263, Fatio to Newton, March 9, 1693.

32. *Ibid.*, III, 263, Newton to Fatio, March 14, 1693.

33. *Ibid.*, III, 391, Fatio to Newton, April 11, 1693.

34. *Ibid.*, III, 266, Fatio to Newton, May 4, 1693.

35. *Ibid.*, III, 269, Fatio to Newton, May 18, 1693.

36. Huygens, *Oeuvres complètes*, XII, 162, Fatio to Huygens, sometime in 1694.

37. W. G. Hiscock, ed., *David Gregory, Isaac Newton and their Circle: Extracts from David Gregory's Memoranda, 1677-1708* (Oxford: printed for the editor, 1937), p. 14, November 15, 1702; p. 17, May 19, 1704.

38. *Ibid.*, p. 31, January 1706.

39. Francis Baily, *An Account of the Revd. John Flamsteed, the first Astronomer-Royal* (London, 1835), p. 225. On June 19, 1706, Fatio was still reckoned among the scientists. In his diary the astronomer Flamsteed notes meeting him and sending him observations.

40. James R. Sutherland, *Background for Queen Anne* (London: Methuen and Co., Ltd., 1939), p. 48.

41. Bibliothèque Publique et Universitaire de Genève, MS. français 602, fol. 19, extract from Fatio's journal, November 28, 1706: "Vocation, & engagement solonnel de Jean Daude, Nicolas Fatio, & Charles Portales, avec le Seigneur."

For contemporary literature on the Prophets of the Cévennes, see A. Mazel, *Mémoires inédits d'Abraham Mazel et d'Elie Marion sur la guerre des Cévennes*

1701–1708 (Publications de la Société Huguenote de Londres, vol. 34; Paris: Librairie Fischbacher, 1931); E. Marion, *Nouvelle Prophétie* (1750); E. Marion, *Prophetical warnings* (London, 1707); E. Marion, *An account of the tryal, examination, and conviction of E. Marion and other French prophets* (London, 1707); *Observations upon E. Marion . . . proving this Elias to be a false Prophet* (London, 1707); *An impartial account of the Prophets* (London, 1708); *A reply to the argument in a paper "an impartial acct."* (London, 1708); *The Prophets: An heroick poem* (London, 1708); *A Cry from the Desart: or, Testimonials of the miraculous things lately come to pass in the Cévennes,* tr. by John Lacy *from the originals* (London, 1707); *Examen du Théatre sacré des Cévennes* (London, 1708); *The Cevenois Relieved, or else, Europe Enslav'd* (London, 1703); *The Cevenois request to the King of France, translated from the French* (London, 1704); *A Compleat history of the Cévennes* (London, 1703); *Mélange sur tout ce qui regarde . . . les camisards* (London, 1707).

42. [R. Kingston], *Enthusiastick Impostors, no Divinely Inspir'd Prophets . . .* (London, 1707), pp. 22–23. A letter signed W. C. and dated July 22, 1707, was included in the same account of the Prophets and described an even more tempestuous séance at which Fatio was present (p. 65):

At a Meeting at Sir *Richard Bulkeley's* Chamber in great *Russel-Street,* where were present Mr. *Lacy,* Mr. *Allut,* Mrs. *Allut,* Mr. *Facio,* Mr. *Marion,* Mr. *Cavalier,* and almost the whole Room full of other People; *Betty Grey,* under violent Agitations, personated the great *Whore* of *Antichrist.* Took all the Chairs in the Room, and barricadoed the Door, that no body might come in or go out. This done, she laid aside her *Manteau* and *Night-clothes* tyed up her *Hair* before all the Company, with singular Modesty; then taking a *Peruke* and *Hat* that she found in the Room, put them on her Head, and sat down in an Elbow Chair very Majestically, with her Arms a Kembo: After this she rose out of the Chair, and for about an Hour together, *thump'd* and *beat* with her *Fist* every one in the Room in their Turns, except Mr. *Lacy;* Sir *Richard Bulkeley* hid himself a while in a Corner of the Room, in hopes to avoid the Effects of her Fury, but she finding him out, laid upon him unmercifully, without any regard to his diminutive, infirm *Corps* or his *Quality,* insomuch that he found himself oblig'd to make his escape over the Bed, to shelter himself from the hard Blows of this *Termagant Whore* of *Antichrist;* who, as soon as the Skirmish was over, sat down again in the Elbow Chair, and being still in an *Extasy,* open'd her Mouth, and fell a Ranting at a rate agreeable to her own Character, and the *Whore* she represented.

43. Bibliothèque Publique et Universitaire de Genève, MS. français 602, fol. 32, extract from Fatio's journal.

44. A. Boyer, *The History of Queen Anne* (London, 1735), pp. 316–317, gives a succinct account of the Prophets of the Cévennes in London and describes their punishment:

It being suggested by the Zealots, that they were but the Organs and Instruments of Monsieur Facio, who was shrewdly suspected of Socinianism, and of having form'd a Design to overturn the Christian Religion; Elias Marion, one of the Camisars, John D'Audé and Nicholas Facio, Two of their Abettors, were indicted and prosecuted, at the Charge of all the French Churches in London, as Disturbers of the Publick Peace, and false Prophets; and on the 28th of November, receiv'd their Sentences at the Court of Queen's-Bench Bar: To stand Twice on a Scaffold, with a Paper denothing their Offence; To pay a Fine of Twenty Marks each, and to give Security for their good Behaviour for One Year. According to this Sentence, they were exposed on a Scaffold at Charing-Cross, and the Royal Exchange, the 1st and 2nd of December.

See also a broadside of December 2, 1707, entitled *The English and French Prophets Mad or Bewitcht.*

45. Fatio wrote his brother Jean-Christophe on December 19, 1707, that he had been pilloried unjustly, as time would tell, and asked that he purchase for him a copy of the *Cabbala denudata;* he also noted that he had not been attending sessions of the Royal Society (Bibliothèque Publique et Universitaire de Genève, MS. français 602, fol. 115).

46. Thomas Hearne, *Remarks and Collections* (Oxford: printed for the Oxford Historical Society at the Clarendon Press, 1885–1921), II, 244, August 28, 1709.

47. Leibniz, *Die philosophischen Schriften,* ed. C. J. Gerhardt (Berlin, 1875–1890; reprinted Hildesheim: G. Olms, 1960–1961), III, 316, Leibniz to Thomas Burnet, March 16, 1708.

48. *Ibid.,* III, 313, Leibniz to Thomas Burnet, February 22, 1707.

49. *Ibid.,* III, 324, Leibniz to Burnet, October 18, 1712.

50. In November 1707 Isaac Newton was preoccupied with the Scottish coinage; see his letter, dated November 14, to the Earl of Godolphin (Treasurer of Great Britain) and his correspondence with David Gregory (Newton, *Correspondence,* IV, 500 and 502–506).

51. Rev. Joseph Spence, *Anecdotes, Observations, and Characters, of Books and Men Collected from the Conversation of Mr. Pope, and other eminent persons of his time* (London, 1820), "Ramsay," pp. 56–57:

These were what were then called the French prophets. The great aim of their doctrines was the near approach of the millenary state. Every thing was to be altered, the hierarchy destroyed, and an universal theocracy to obtain on earth. I was then at London, learning the mathematics, under Fatio; and, by his desire, went two or three times with him to hear them. He thought all their agitations the effect of a heavenly inspiration; and actually caught them of them himself.—When that gentleman was speaking, one day, of the cause of attraction, he said (with a confidence unusual to him) that he had absolutely discovered it; that it was the ethereal fluid: "and where," added he very gravely, "do you think I discovered it? I was yesterday at a meeting of the prophets, and whilst I was lost in thought, it struck into my mind, like a sudden gleam of light, all at once."—However this happened, it is the very thing which Sir Isaac Newton has since shown. Sir Isaac himself had a strong inclination to go and hear these prophets, and was restrained from it, with difficulty, by some of his friends, who feared he might be infected by them as Fatio had been.

And, further, "Dr. Lockier, Dean of Peterborough," p. 72: "It is not at all improbable that Sir Isaac Newton, though so great a man, might have had a hankering after the French prophets. There was a time when he was possessed with the old fooleries of astrology; and another when he was so far gone in those of chemistry, as to be upon the hunt after the philosopher's stone."

52. British Museum, Sloane MS. 4043, fol. 307, Fatio to Sloane, October 26, 1714. See also Sloane MS. 4055, fol. 27, for a letter to Sloane in 1736 asking for a subscription so that he might prove the earth as big as Saturn or perhaps Jupiter.

53. Cambridge, King's College Library, Keynes MS. 96.

54. See Nicolas Fatio de Duillier, *Newtonus. Ecloga* (Ghent, 1728).

55. Newton, *Correspondence,* III, 69–70 n. 1.

56. Bibliothèque Publique et Universitaire de Genève, MS. français 603, fol. 270, William Whiston to Fatio, December 5, 1734; "As to your attempt for finding the place of the colours by hypothesis, it is not very unlikely that you may have hit upon Sr I. N. own supposal, when he had a great mind to support the masorete Chronology, which is impossible to be supported."

Chapter 10

THE BLACK YEAR 1693

1. Lord Henry Brougham, *Sir Isaac Newton* (London, 1829).

2. Jean-Baptiste Delambre, *Histoire de l'astronomie au dix-huitième siècle* (Paris, 1927), p. 60.

3. Abate Antonio Conti, *Prose e Poesie* (Venice, 1756), II, 60.

4. Samuel Pepys, *Private Correspondence and Miscellaneous Papers,* ed. J. R. Tanner (London: G. Bell and Sons, 1926), I, 52, Pepys to Evelyn, January 9, 1692.

5. Newton, *Correspondence,* III, 282, Millington to Pepys, September 30, 1693.

6. *Ibid.,* III, 279, Newton to Pepys, September 13, 1693.

7. According to the record of Newton's weekly Buttery bills, October 1686 to February 1694, in 1693 he was not in residence for half of the weeks of June 2, 9, 30, and July 7; also half of the week of September 15, the whole of the week of September 22, and half of the week of September 29. See Joseph Edleston, ed., *Correspondence of Sir Isaac Newton and Professor Cotes* ... (London, 1850), pp. lxxxvi–xc.

8. Newton, *Correspondence,* III, 280, Newton to Locke, September 16, 1693.

9. *Ibid.,* III, 281, Pepys to Millington, September 26, 1693.

10. *Ibid.,* III, 281–282, Millington to Pepys, September 30, 1693.

11. *Ibid.,* III, 282–283, Pepys to Millington, October 3, 1693.

12. *Ibid.,* III, 283–284, Locke to Newton, October 5, 1693.

13. *Ibid.,* III, 284, Newton to Locke, October 15, 1693.

14. Cambridge, University Library, Add. MS. 3996, fol. 132r.

15. Cambridge, University Library, Add. MS. 3996, fol. 109r.

16. *Ibid.*

17. Cambridge, University Library, Add. MS. 3973.

18. Newton, *Correspondence,* III, 282, Millington to Pepys, September 30, 1693.

19. *Ibid.,* III, 369–370 n. 2, Journal of Christiaan Huygens, May 29, 1694. Christiaan Huygens, *Oeuvres complètes* (The Hague, Haarlem: M. Nijhoff, 1888–1950), X, 616, quoted in Newton, *Correspondence,* III, 369.

20. On June 8, 1694, Christiaan Huygens wrote Leibniz: "I do not know if you are acquainted with the accident which has happened to the good Mr. Newton, namely, that he has had an attack of 'frenesie,' which lasted eighteen months, and of which they say his friends have cured him by means of remedies, and keeping him shut up" (*Oeuvres complètes* X, 618).

21. Newton, *Correspondence*, III, 372-373.

22. *Ibid.*, IV, 131, Wallis to Waller, May 31, 1695: "I have been absent from home for some time. I do not hear of any thing there received from you, since I sent you the two Letters for Sturmius & Viviani. I have, since, one from Sturmius, which signifies that he had, some weeks before, received the Book I sent him. He sends me word of a Rumor amongst them concerning Mr Newton, as if his House and Books & all his Goods were Burnt, & himself so disturbed in mind thereupon, as to be reduced to very ill circumstances. Which being all false, I thought fit presently to rectify that groundless mistake. . . ."

23. *Ibid.*, IV, 84, Flamsteed to Newton, February 7, 1695: "The day after I receaved your Last Mr Hanway brought me News from London that you were dead but I shewed him your letter which proved the contrary. he had it from Sr C. Wren to whom he wrote immediately to satisfye him of the falsehood of that report I bless God for your life & pray for your perfect health."

24. *Ibid.*, III, 370, reference to Abraham de la Pryme's diary, February 3, 1693.

25. Cambridge, King's College Library, Keynes MS. 130 (10).

26. Newton, *Correspondence*, III, 285-286, Newton to Leibniz, October 16, 1693.

27. *Ibid.*, III, 291-292, Newton to Otto Mencke, November 22, 1693.

28. *Ibid.*, III, 293, Pepys to Newton, November 22, 1693.

29. *Ibid.*, III, 303-304, Newton to John Mill, January 29, 1694.

30. *Ibid.*, III, 311-344, Memoranda of David Gregory, May 1694.

31. *Ibid.*, III, 357-366, Newton to Nathaniel Hawes, May 25, 1694.

PART THREE: IN LONDON TOWN

Chapter 11

AMID COINERS AND CLIPPERS

1. Voltaire, *Dictionnaire philosophique, in Oeuvres complètes* ([Kehl], 1785), XLII, 165.

On Newton and atomism, see R. H. Kargon, *Atomism in England from Hariot to Newton* (London: Oxford University Press, 1966).

2. For a discussion of Montague's nomination of Newton, see Newton, *Correspondence*, IV, 196 n. 1, and 189-190 n. 4.

3. *Ibid.*, IV, 545 n. 3: "Newton claimed . . . to have inspired the Act of 1697 which made provision or possession of the necessary tools high treason, as counterfeiting the King's coin had been for centuries. The consequent penalty was that the convicted person was dragged on a sledge to the place of execution, but was not drawn or quartered."

4. Sir John H. M. Craig, *Newton at the Mint* (Cambridge: Cambridge University Press, 1946). See also Craig, "Isaac Newton and the Counterfeiters," *Notes and*

Records of the Royal Society of London, XVIII (1963), 136-145, and "Isaac Newton —Crime Investigator," *Nature,* CLXXXII (1958), 149-152.

5. Newton, *Correspondence,* IV, 213, Halley to Newton, November 28, 1696; IV, 230, Halley to Newton, February 13, 1697; IV, 246, Halley to Newton, August 2, 1697.

6. Edmond Halley, *Correspondence and papers,* ed. E. F. MacPike (Oxford: Clarendon Press, 1932), p. 100, Halley to Sloane, November 2, 1696: "Since my last we have been exceedingly prest with the receipt of Clipt moneys, so that I have had little leasure to look after any sort of philosophicall matters. . . ."

7. See, for example, Newton, *Correspondence,* IV, 211, Newton to Prison Keepers, September 7, 1696:

To the Keeper of the Marshalsea. . . . These are therefore in his Maties name to require & command you forthwith upon sight hereof to deliver him the said Charles Ecclestone into the safe custody of the Bearer or Bearers in order to give his evidence at Hicks Hall in St John's street against several persons for coyning & for so doing this shall be your Discharge. . . . To the Keeper of New Prison. . . . Receive herewith sent you into your safe Custody the Body of Charles Ecclestone being charged upon Oath wth High Treason in Counterfeiting the Current Coyne of this Kingdom, & he being now intended for one of his Maties evidences against several clippers & coyners of false & counterfeit money: These are therefore in his Maties name to require you to keep him in safe custody untill further Order & untill he shall be discharged by due course of Law, & for your so doing this shall be your warrant.

8. *Ibid.,* IV, 429, Newton to the Lord Chamberlain (?), November 24, 1704:

Some designes for Medals having been communicated to your Lordship by others, I humbly beg leave to present the enclosed. Her Majesties effigies may be on one side with the usual inscription, & this Designe on the other; & instead of Britannia on a globe the Queen may be placed in a chair.
And if for saving her Majty & your Lordship the trouble of approving Medals your Lordship shall think fit that the Gravers be empowered to make such Medals as I shall approve of under my hand in writing, I am ready to undertake this trust, or otherwise to act in such manner as your Lordship in your great wisdom shall think fit. . . .

In a draft proposal (undated but clearly 1707) for a medal commemorating Queen Anne's uniting of England and Scotland Newton suggested that an emendation of James I's motto (*Faciam eos in gentem unam*) be used: *Feci eos in gentem unam.* "[T]his Motto may at first seem flat, yet being compared with that on the gold coynes of K James I & with the Prophesy of Ezekiel to wch it alludes, it will appear very significant, comprehensive, grave, lively, pious & majestick, & perhaps the most apposite of any that can be thought of" (*ibid.,* IV, 509).

See also Manuel, *Isaac Newton, Historian* (Cambridge, Mass.: Harvard University Press, 1963), pp. 109–111.

9. "Sir Isaac Newton's Mint reports. Hitherto unpublished," in W. A. Shaw, *Select Tracts and Documents Illustrative of English Monetary History, 1626-1730* (London, 1896), pp. 147-204; C. R. Fay, "Newton and the Gold Standard," *Cambridge Historical Journal,* V, no. 1 (1935), 109–117; Anonymous, *A Letter to a friend, occasion'd from what was published in the Daily-courant, on Monday December 30th, by Sir Isaac Newton, relating to coin, etc. Shewing that the value of the*

gold coin, ought not to be lessen'd, but rather the silver be raised (London, 1718). For a negative estimate of Newton as an economist, see G. Findlay Shirras and J. H. M. Craig, "Sir Isaac Newton and the Currency," *The Economic Journal*, LV (1945), 217–241.

10. Sir John Craig, in "Isaac Newton and the Counterfeiters," p. 140, describes Newton's procedure: "He had an informant or criminal brought to the Mint, by force if necessary, cross-examined the witness, and wrote or dictated a statement of what emerged—the first personal pronoun keeps creeping in. The witness could correct or amplify, swore to the result and appended his signature or initial or mark. Newton countersigned as witness."

11. The Royal Mint Library, Depositions Book, no. 233.

12. *Ibid.*, no. 215.

13. *Ibid.*, no. 27.

14. Newton, *Correspondence*, IV, 209–210, Newton to the Treasury, July–August 1696.

15. *Ibid.*, IV, 215 n. 2.

16. *Ibid.*, IV, 207–208, Memorandum, June 1696 (?).

17. The Royal Mint Library, Newton MSS., I, fol. 223, Newton to the Lord Treasurer, August 7, 1711.

18. Newton, *Correspondence*, IV, 242–245, Newton to the Treasury, July 1697.

19. *Guzman Redivivus, A Short View of the Life of Will. Chaloner, The Notorious Coyner, who was Executed at Tyburn on Wednesday the 22d. of March 1698/9: With a Brief Account of his Tryal, Behaviour, and Last Speech* (London, 1699), p. 3. The title derives from Guzman de Alfarache, the "hero" of a popular work whose English title was *The Rogue.*

20. The Royal Mint Library, Newton MSS., I, fols. 501–502.

21. *Guzman Redivivus*, p. 8.

22. For the order of the House of Commons Committee on Miscarriages of the Mint to provide equipment for Chaloner's experiment, see the Royal Mint Library, Newton MSS., I, 506, and Newton, *Correspondence*, IV, 231–232, Arnold to Newton, February 15, 1697. The Committee resolved in favor of Chaloner's methods: "That undeniable demonstrations have been given and shewn unto this committee, by Mr William Challoner, that there is a better, securer, and more effectual way, and with very little charge to his majesty, to prevent either casting or counterfeiting of the milled money, both gold and silver, than is now used in the present coinage. . . . That the house be moved, for leave to bring in a bill, or bills, to prevent the abuses of the officers of the mints, and for the better regulation of the coinage, both in the mint in the Tower, and also in the several mints in the country" (*ibid.*, IV, 232 n. 3).

23. The works of William Chaloner are: *The Defects in the Present Constitution of the Mint. Humbly offered to the consideration of the Honourable House of Commons* [London, 1693?]; *To the Honourable, the Knights, Citizens, and Burgesses in Parliament assembled. Reasons humbly offered against passing an Act . . . to make good the deficiency of the clipt-money, etc.* [London, 1694?]; *To the Honourable, the Knights, Citizens, and Burgesses in Parliament Assembled. Proposals hum-*

bly offered, for passing an Act to prevent clipping and counterfeiting of mony (London[?], 1694).

24. The Royal Mint Library, Newton MSS., I, fols. 501–502.

25. Newton, *Correspondence*, IV, 259–260, Chaloner to Parliament, late 1697.

26. The Royal Mint Library, Newton MSS., I, fol. 498, Memorandum of 1698, quoted in Newton, *Correspondence*, IV, 262.

27. Newton, *Correspondence*, IV, 305–306, Chaloner to Newton, January 20–24, 1699, and n. 2.

28. The Royal Mint Library, Depositions Book, no. 129, John Whitfield to Newton, January 25, 1699.

29. Such meetings were not infrequent and Newton collected his incidental expenses in a lump sum. See Newton, *Correspondence*, IV, 317, Newton to the Treasury, October 1, 1699: "May it please your Lordships/ The prosecution of Coyners during the three last years having put me to various small expenses in coach-hire & at Taverns & Prisons & other places of all wch it is not possible for me to make accompt on oath, your Lordships were pleased to give me hopes of an allowance for the same wch I humbly pray may be an hundred & twenty pounds and that your Lordships will please to direct an Order to the Auditor Mr Bridges for allowing the same in my Accompts. All wch is most humbly submitted to your Lordships great wisdome."

30. The Royal Mint Library, Depositions Book, no. 118, Thomas Carter to Newton, January 31, 1699.

31. *Ibid.*, nos. 131, 134, 165, John Ignatius Lawson.

32. *Ibid.*, no. 205; printed in Newton, *Correspondence*, IV, 307–308, Chaloner to Newton, circa March 6, 1699.

33. *Guzman Redivivus*, p. 10.

Chapter 12

HALIFAX AND LA BARTICA

1. From Jonathan Swift's *Journal to Stella*, ed. H. H. Williams (Oxford: Oxford University Press, 1948), November 17, 1711, it appears that the Whigs had used the anniversary of Queen Elizabeth's birthday to design a mighty procession by midnight and "had laid out a thousand pounds to dress up the Pope, Devil, Cardinals, Sacheverell, etc. and carry them with torches about, and burn them" (II, 415). Catherine Barton made fun of the whole incident, though Swift was quite alarmed in his fashion (II, 417): "I have been so teazed with Whiggish discourse by Mrs. Barton and lady Betty Germain, never saw the like. They turn all this affair of the pope-burning into ridicule; and indeed they have made too great a clutter about it, if they had no real reason to apprehend some tumults."

2. On the 1702 Kneller, see David Piper, *The English Face* (London: Thames and Hudson, 1957), p. 146; on the Thornhill in Trinity, C. H. Collins Baker, "An-

tonio Verrio and Thornhill's Early Portraiture," *Connoisseur,* CXXXI (1953), 11. For a complete review of portraits and sculpture of Newton, see David Piper, *Catalogue of the Seventeenth-Century Portraits in the National Portrait Gallery 1625–1714* (Cambridge: Cambridge University Press, 1963), pp. 248–251.

3. The Royal Mint Library, Newton MSS., II, 614 (dated 1701).

4. See pedigree of the Bartons in Oxford, Bodleian Library, New College MSS. 361, IV, fol. 235v.

5. Newton's sister Hannah bore three children to the Reverend Robert Barton, Hannah who died when she was eight and a half, Robert whom Swift calls a "coxcomb" and who was killed in Quebec, and Catherine. On August 24, 1693, as Newton was approaching his own crisis, his sister wrote him of the hopeless illness of her husband, who was losing his flesh and strength. She was overwhelmed with sorrow and begged to be comforted and advised (Newton, *Correspondence,* III, 278–279, Hannah Barton to Newton).

6. On February 25, 1717, Rémond de Montmort wrote to Newton from Paris thanking him for a gift: "How glorious is it for me! and What Subject of vanity for my Wife to wear ornaments given by Mr Newton and chosen by Mrs Barton, Whose wit and tast are equal to her beauty" (Cambridge, King's College Library, Keynes MS. 101).

7. Stephen Peter Rigaud collected many contemporary references to Catherine Barton in preparation for a biography of Newton (Oxford, Bodleian Library, MSS. Rigaud 50).

8. Newton, *Correspondence,* IV, 349, Newton to Catherine Barton, August 5, 1700. In this connection reference should be made to a letter to Lady Norris, née Elizabeth Read, an oft-widowed lady whose third husband, Sir William Norris, Newton had known at Trinity and who died in 1702. It concerns a marriage proposal and is in John Conduitt's hand with a notation "Copy of a Letter to Lady Norris"; another hand has written the words "A Letter from Sir I. N. to ———." Brewster considered it authentic (see his correspondence with the Reverend Jeffrey Ekins in New College MSS. 361, IV, fols. 159–160, and his *Memoirs of the life, writings and discoveries of Sir Isaac Newton* [Edinburgh, 1855], II, 211–214) because Lady Norris is mentioned as an acquaintance in Newton's letter to Catherine Barton. It is conceivable that fonts of love opened up for Newton in the early years of the eighteenth century, when he was about sixty, but the evidence is flimsy. The style of the letter to Lady Norris does not resemble anything Newton ever wrote—though of course a seizure of love may have momentarily transformed him. Also, the phraseology does not exclude the possibility that the suitor was not the writer of the letter, though Bewster on various grounds dismisses the idea that Sir Isaac was acting in a friend's behalf.

9. Catherine Barton was baptized at Brigstock, November 25, 1679; Newton's mother had been buried the previous June 4.

10. See Gwendolyn B. Needham, "Mary de la Rivière Manley, Tory Defender," *The Huntington Library Quarterly,* XII (1949), 253–288, and "Mrs Manley: an eighteenth century Wife of Bath," *The Huntington Library Quarterly,* XIV (1951), 259–284. In the *Memoirs of Europe,* on the eve of Tory victory, Mrs. Manley let loose

upon Halifax and Newton and his niece without restraint. The book was translated into French. Gwendolyn Needham insists that the "titillating accounts of amorous intrigues often contained a substructure of truth" ("Mary Manley, Tory Defender," p. 261).

It seems that Mrs. Manley had taken Newton's name in vain at least once before. Her story is rather preposterous. If the manuscript key to the Boston Athenaeum copy of her *Secret Memoirs and Manners of several Persons of Quality, of Both Sexes* is correct, Newton had intervened in some intrigue: "Neither did Berintha's [Lady Earnley] Malice stop here (so effectually she pursu'd it) that an old blunt Gentleman [Sir Isaac Newton] (highly scandaliz'd at what he heard) by her Agent's instigation, wrote to Monsieur St. l'Amant [Rich. Cook of Norfolk], whose Friend he was, to advise him to take care of the Baron [Baron de Messaray, Sir Edmund Bacon] and his Wife" (2nd ed. [London, 1709], p. 125).

11. Daniel Defoe has described the savagery of political controversy in the age of Queen Anne: "We fight with the poison of the tongue, with words that speak like the piercing of a sword, with the gall of envie, the venom of slander, the foam of malice" (quoted by E. S. Roscoe, *Robert Harley, Earl of Oxford, Prime Minister 1710–1714. A Study of Politics and Letters in the Age of Anne* [New York and London: Methuen and Co., Ltd., 1902], p. 1).

12. In the *Journal to Stella* (I, 306), July 1, 1711, Swift expressed the hope that the Tories would do something for Mrs. Manley, who had suffered arrest on October 29, 1709, for her *Atalantis* attacks on the Whigs, was admitted to bail a week later and only finally discharged on February 13, 1710.

13. Mary de la Rivière Manley, *The Adventures of Rivella* (London, 1714), p. 113.

14. Mary de la Rivière Manley, *Memoirs of Europe, Towards the Close of the Eighth Century. Written by Eginardus, Secretary and Favourite to Charlemagne; and done into English by the Translator of the New Atalantis*, 2nd ed., corrected (London, 1711), I, 266–267.

15. On the Kit-Kat Club see John Nichols, *Literary Anecdotes of the Eighteenth Century* (London, 1812–1816), I, 294–298. *The Tatler*, no. 24, comments on the custom of inscribing the name of the lady who was the toast of the year on the glasses: "When she is regularly chosen her name is written with a diamond on the drinking-glasses. The hieroglyphic of the diamond is to shew her, that her value is imaginary; and that of the glass to acquaint her, that her condition is frail, and depends on the hand which holds her." See also *Biographia Britannica* (London, 1760), V, 3156 n.

16. Oxford, Bodleian Library, New College MSS. 361, IV, fol. 76, Brewster to Ekins, April 1855.

17. Brook Taylor, *Contemplatio Philosophica* (London, 1793), pp. 93–94, Rémond de Montmort to Taylor, April 12, 1716.

18. Jonathan Swift, *Poems,* ed. Harold H. Williams (Oxford: Oxford University Press, 1937), II, 481, "A Libel on D–D–" (1730).

19. Swift's letter to Halifax on June 13, 1709, is extravagant in its flattery (*Correspondence,* ed. Harold H. Williams [Oxford: Oxford University Press, 1963], I, 142–143). By the fall of 1710, during the period when he was visiting Mrs. Barton,

his attitude toward Halifax was one of critical friendliness. On October 2 he reported: "Lord Halifax [at Hampton Court] began a health to me today: it was the Resurrection of the Whigs, which I refused unless he would add their Reformation too: and I told him he was the only Whig in England I loved, or had any good opinion of (*Journal to Stella*, I, 38–39). On January 24, 1711, he noted that he seldom saw Halifax any longer (*ibid.*, I, 173). Swift felt that promises of preferment made by Halifax had been forgotten, and after Swift joined the Tories he wrote: "I never heard him say one good thing or seem to taste what was said by another" (quoted in Swift, *Correspondence*, I, 143 n). At one point he might have been using Mrs. Barton as an avenue to Halifax' favor. His last judgment was expressed in a letter to Lady Betty Germaine on June 8, 1735 (*ibid.*, IV, 344).

20. Alexander Pope, *Correspondence,* ed. George Sherburn (Oxford: Clarendon Press, 1956), I, 271, Pope to Halifax, December 3, 1714.

21. Samuel Johnson, *The Lives of the Most Eminent English Poets* (London, 1783), II, 284.

22. G. W. Leibniz, *Die philosophischen Schriften,* ed. C. J. Gerhardt (Berlin, 1875–1890; reprinted Hildesheim: G. Olms, 1960–1961), III, 309, Leibniz to Thomas Burnet, July 6, 1706.

23. Sarah, Duchess of Marlborough, *Private Correspondence* (London, 1838), I, 89–90, Duke of Marlborough to the Duchess, May 4, 1707. The Duchess of Marlborough's judgment of Halifax reflects her husband's anger (I, 166): "[T]here is no baseness he is not capable of, for his interest or his gain."

24. Swift had no illusions about the accuracy of Mrs. Manley's memoirs. He wrote to Addison on August 22, 1710: "I read your Charactr in Mrs Manly's noble Memoirs of Europe. It seems to me as if she had about two thousand Epithets, and fine words putt up in a bag, and that she puled them out by handfull, and strewed them on her Paper, where about once in five hundred times they happen to be right. Pray take some Occasion to let my [Lord] Hallifax know the [sense] I have of the Favor he intended me" (Swift, *Correspondence,* I, 170–171).

25. Swift's full description of Mrs. Manley is in the *Journal to Stella,* II, 474, January 28, 1712.

26. In his *Introduction to a Complete Collection of Genteel and Ingenious Conversation, According to the Most Polite Mode and Method now used at Court, and in the Best Companies of England, by Simon Wagstaff Es.* (1728), ed. Eric Partridge (Oxford: Oxford University Press, 1963), p. 41, Swift has a witty passage about Newton:

Some of my Enemies have industriously whispered about, that one Isaac Newton, an Instrument-Maker, formerly living near Leicester Fields, and afterwards a Workman in the Mint, at the Tower, might possibly pretend to vye with me for Fame in future Times. The Man, it seems, was knighted for making Sun-Dyals better than others of his Trade, and was thought to be a Conjurer, because no Body could understand. But, adieu to all noble Attempts for endless Renown, if the Ghost of an obscure Mechanick shall be raised up, to enter into Competition with me, only for his Skill in making Pothooks and Hangers, with a Pencil; which many thousand accomplished Gentlemen and Ladies can perform as well, with a Pen and Ink, upon a Piece of Paper, in a Manner as intelligible as those of Sir Isaac.

27. Swift, *Journal to Stella,* I, 17–18, 172, 238; II, 460.

28. *Ibid.*, I, 3.
29. *Ibid.*, I, 109, November 30, 1710.
30. *Ibid.*, I, 210, March 7, 1711.
31. *Ibid.*, I, 229–230, April 3, 1711.
32. *Ibid.*, II, 383, October 14, 1711.
33. *Ibid.*, II, 395, October 25, 1711; I, 142–143, n. 16.
34. See Walter E. Masters, *The Huguenot Church and Sir Isaac Newton's House, being the History of Orange Street Chapel, known as Leicester Fields Chapel from 1688 to 1775, and of Sir Isaac Newton's House adjoining* (n. p., n. d.). Newton resided there from 1710 until 1725. In 1910, its first floor was used by the Christian Association of London Cabmen, the second floor by actresses and music-hall singers.
35. Swift, *Correspondence*, IV, 214, Mrs. Conduitt to Swift, November 29, 1733.
36. Anonymous, *The Works and Life of the Right Honourable Charles, Late Earl of Halifax. Including the History of his Lordship's Times* (London, 1715), pp. 195–196.
37. Codicil of April 12, 1706, to Halifax' will, in *The Works and Life of the Right Honourable Charles, Late Earl of Halifax*, app., p. iv.
38. Codicil of February 1, 1712, to Halifax' will, in *The Works and Life of the Right Honourable Charles, Late Earl of Halifax*, app., pp. v–vi.
39. Cambridge, King's College Library, Keynes MS. 127.
40. Newton, *Correspondence*, II, 415, Newton to Francis Aston, February 23, 1685.
41. Oxford, Bodleian Library, New College MSS. 361, II, fols. 32, 34.
42. Newton, *Correspondence*, IV, 445, Halifax to Newton, May 5, 1705. An earlier letter had been more sanguine (*ibid.*, IV, 439, Halifax to Newton, March 17, 1705).
43. Augustus de Morgan (1806–1871) was a mathematician.
44. Cambridge, King's College Library, Keynes MS. 130 (5), a note marked "C. C." on Conduitt's manuscript.
45. Swift, *Journal to Stella*, I, 316.
46. Augustus de Morgan, *Newton: his friend: and his niece,* ed. by his wife, Sophia Elizabeth de Morgan, and his pupil A. C. Ranyard (London, 1885), p. 49; L. T. More, *Isaac Newton: A Biography* (New York: Charles Scribner's Sons, 1934), p. 474.
47. De Morgan, *Newton*, p. 110.
48. *Ibid.*, p. 49, Isaac Newton to Sir John Newton, May 23, 1715.
49. Joseph Lemuel Chester, *The Marriage, Baptismal and Burial Registers of the Collegiate Church or Abbey of St. Peter, Westminster* (London, 1876), p. 354 n. 2.
50. One of his name was baptized in St. Paul's on March 8, 1688, which makes him about nine years younger than Catherine. On August 16, 1717, one of his name had a grant of arms "when it was said that he had served as Judge-Advocate of the British forces in Portugal in 1711, and was the next year constituted Captain in the regiment of Dragoons there commanded by Brigadier Hunt Wither" (Chester, *The Registers of St. Peter, Westminster,* p. 348 n. 6).
51. Pope wrote to Hugh Bethel from Southampton on September 28, 1734, that he had enjoyed quiet for some six weeks "till your friend Mrs. Cond. came & put a

Ferment into the Country . . ." (Pope, *Correspondence,* III, 436). In a letter to Lady Worsley on April 17, 1730, Swift commented on the change in Catherine Barton Conduitt (Swift, *Correspondence,* III, 392).

Chapter 13

THE AUTOCRAT OF SCIENCE

1. The Royal Mint Library, Newton MSS., II, fol. 334, John Chamberlayne to Isaac Newton, November 25, 1713: "I beg the Favor of you to mark the inclosed List for me . . . just as you intend to do your own both for New Councilors and New Officers all but one, whom I desire to choose Freely & whom I would make Perpetual Dictator of the Society. . . ."

2. Derek Whiteside believes that Newton's creative mathematical capacities continued almost uninterrupted until he left for London. "Even then his inspiration flickered spasmodically on for another two decades, blazing up from time to time in answer to challenges from Leibniz and Johann Bernoulli and in support of his own claim to priority in systematizing the calculus, and dying out finally only in the very last years of a long life" (*The Mathematical Papers of Isaac Newton* [Cambridge: Cambridge University Press, 1967——], I, xvi).

3. Cambridge, King's College Library, Keynes MS. 130, a Conduitt notebook.

4. William Stukeley, *Memoirs of Sir Isaac Newton's Life* . . ., ed. A. Hastings White (London: Taylor and Francis, 1936), p. 81.

5. Eric St. John Brooks, *Sir Hans Sloane* (London: The Batchworth Press, 1954), p. 202.

6. Cambridge, King's College Library, Keynes MS. 136, Stukeley to Conduitt, June 26, 1727.

7. Newton, *Correspondence,* III, 154–155, Newton to Arthur Charlett, July 27, 1691, recommending David Gregory to the Electors of the Astronomy Professor in Oxford; W. G. Hiscock, ed., *David Gregory, Isaac Newton and their Circle* (Oxford: printed for the editor, 1937), p. 33. There is some evidence of Newton's academic electioneering in behalf of Roger Cotes through the agency of Bentley in an entry in Flamsteed's diary on March 15, 1706: "Met Dr Bently at Garway's Sr Isaack was there. we discourst first about Dr Plumes Astr. professorship. the Dr would have had my hand to a paper for the election of Mr Cotes to be professor I refused till I saw him . . ." ("Extracts from Flamsteed's Diary," in Newton, *Correspondence,* IV, 468). See also Joseph Edleston, ed., *Correspondence of Sir Isaac Newton and Professor Cotes* (London, 1850), p. lxxvii.

8. A broadside had Halley's father barbarously murdered near Rochester in Kent, April 17, 1684. His mother had died in 1672. Thomas Hearne writes: "A Gent., who is very honest, lately told me that he thought what is related in one of these Volumes, viz. that Dr. Halley's Father went in fear of his Life from his own Son, the said Halley, is true. I think Dr. Halley's Father was drown'd"

(*Remarks and Collections* [Oxford: printed for the Oxford Historical Society at the Clarendon Press, 1885–1921], VI [1902], 231, September 25, 1718). Hearne tells of a bitter quarrel on the very eve of Newton's death: "Some time before he died, a great Quarrel happened between him & Dr. Halley, so as they fell to bad language. This 'tis thought so much discomfited Sir Isaac as to hasten his end" (IX [1914], 293, April 4, 1727).

9. See, for example, the preface (unpaginated) to Benjamin Martin, *Philosophia Britannica* (Reading, 1747).

10. George Cheyne, *Philosophical Principles of Natural Religion* (London, 1705); Samuel Clarke, *A Collection of Papers, which passed between the late learned Mr. Leibnitz, and Dr. Clarke . . . Relating to the principles of natural philosophy and religion* (London, 1717); the poem by John Theophilus Desaguliers, *The Newtonian system of the world the best model of government* (Westminster, 1728); David Gregory, *Astronomiae, Physicae et Geometricae Elementa* (Oxford, 1702); John Keill, *Introductio ad veram physicam* (Oxford, 1701); Colin Maclaurin, *An Account of Sir Isaac Newton's Philosophical Discoveries published from the author's manuscript papers* (London, 1748); Henry Pemberton, *A View of Sir Isaac Newton's Philosophy,* 4 vols. (London, 1728); William Whiston, *Praelectiones physico-mathematicae . . . quibus philosophia illustrissimi Newtoni mathematica explicatius traditur et facilius demonstratur* (Cambridge, 1710). According to Whiteside (*Mathematical Papers of Newton,* I, xvi), Newton scorned the publication of his old Lucasian lectures by Whiston in 1707, the *Arithmetica Universalis: sive De Compositione et Resolutione Liber,* and in 1722 issued his own improved edition of the work.

11. Around the turn of the century, Clarke and Whiston, who had been scholars together in Cambridge, began to suspect that the doctrine of the Trinity was not the doctrine of the early ages of Christianity. Whiston did not scruple to announce in 1730 that Newton had entertained that heresy "long before this time" (William Whiston, *Historical Memoirs of the Life of Dr. Samuel Clarke* [London, 1730], p. 12).

12. William Whiston, *Memoirs of the Life and Writings of W. W.,* 2nd ed. (London, 1753), I, 249–250:

On or about the same year, 1720, I take it to have been, that I was refused to be admitted a member of the royal society, by Sir *Isaac Newton:* the case was this; Sir *Hans Sloane,* and Dr. *Edmund Halley,* and myself, were once together at *Child's* coffee-house, in St. *Paul's Church-Yard,* and Dr. Halley asked me, Why I was not a member of that society? I answered, because they durst not choose an *Heretick.* Upon which Dr. *Halley* said to Sir *Hans Sloane,* that if he would propose me, he would second it: which was done accordingly. When Sir *Isaac Newton,* the president, heard this he was greatly concern'd; and, by what I then learn'd, closeted some of the members, in order to get clear of me; and told them, that if I was chosen a member, he would not be president. Whereupon, by a pretence of deficiency in the form of proceeding, the proposal was dropp'd, I not insisting upon it.

13. Whiston, *Memoirs,* 2nd ed., I, 250–251.

14. When Newton's theory of colors was called into question again by Edme Mariotte, Desaguliers reperformed the experiments in 1715 and reported on them

in the *Philosophical Transactions* for 1716 (no. 348); in 1722 he followed the same procedure in reply to Rizzetti. Finally, he published his whole *Course of Experimental Philosophy* (part 1, 1734; part 2, 1745).

15. W. G. Hiscock, ed., *David Gregory, Isaac Newton and their Circle* (Oxford: printed for the editor, 1937), p. 14.

16. Ralph Thoresby, *Diary,* ed. J. Hunter (London, 1830), II, 111, 117.

17. In the preface to *The Doctrine of Chances* (1718), Abraham de Moivre thanked Newton for the honor of having been admitted into his private conversation.

18. Cambridge, University Library, Add. MS. 4007B, fol. 560, Keill to Newton, October 24, 1715. On a copy of a letter from Keill to Sloane (Add. MS. 3968, fol. 338) there are emendations in Newton's hand later printed in the *Commercium Epistolicum*. A letter from Des Maizeaux to Newton, June 4, 1720 (Add. MS. 3968, fol. 507), asked him to read his collection of letters before it appeared.

19. Pierre Des Maizeaux, *Recueil de diverses pièces, sur la philosophie, la religion naturelle, l'histoire, les mathématiques, etc. Par Mrs. Leibniz, Clarke, Newton, & autres autheurs célèbres* (Amsterdam, 1720), II, 48, Leibniz to Conti, April 9, 1716.

20. Sir Henry Lyons, *The Royal Society 1660–1940* (Cambridge: Cambridge University Press, 1944), p. 121.

21. Royal Society of London, Journal Booke of the Council of the Royal Society, February 15, 1682–November 9, 1727 (Council Minutes, II), pp. 137, 159.

22. British Museum, Sloane MS. 3342, fol. 38r (another version of the Royal Society Council Minutes).

23. British Museum, Sloane MS. 4060, fol. 74r, undated note from Newton to Sloane.

24. Royal Society of London, Journal Booke of the Council, p. 273, June 27, 1723.

25. See Henry Guerlac, "Francis Hauksbee: expérimentateur au profit de Newton," *Archives internationales d'histoire des sciences,* XVI (1963), 113–128; Guerlac, "Sir Isaac and the Ingenious Mr. Hauksbee," in *Mélanges Alexandre Koyré,* ed. I. B. Cohen and René Taton (Paris, 1964), I, 228–253; and Roderick W. Home, "Francis Hauksbee's Theory of Electricity," *Archive for the History of Exact Sciences,* IV (1967), 203–217. Desaguliers's letter of self-exoneration, dated April 29, 1725, is preserved in the library of the Royal Society of London (D. 2. 75).

26. Cambridge, University Library, Add. MS 4005, fols. 1–7, "A Scheme for Establishing the Royal Society." One draft reads:

Natural Philosophy consists in discovering the frame & operations of Nature, reducing them (as far as may be) to general Rules or Laws, establishing those Rules by observations & experiments, & thence deducing the causes & effects of things. And for this end it may be convenient that one or two (& at length perhaps three or four) fellows of the R. S. well skilled in any one of the following branches of Philosophy, & as many in each of the rest, be obliged by Pensions & fforfeitures (as soon as it can be compassed) to attend the meetings of the R. S.

The branches are

1. Arithmetick, Algebra, Geometry & Mechanicks with relation to the figures, surfaces, magnitudes, forces, motions, resistances, weights, densities, centers of gravity & percussion, & other mathematical affections of solids & fluids; the composition of forces & motions; the

shock and reflexions of solids; the centrifugal forces of revolving bodies; the motions of pendulous, projectile, & falling bodies; the mensuration of time & distance; the efficacy of the five powers; the running of rivers; the propagation of light & sounds; the harmony & discord of tones & colours: & all such questions about the nature & operations of things as require skill in Mathematicks to resolve them.

2. Philosophy relating to the heavens, the Atmosphere, & the surface of the earth: viz Astronomy, Opticks, Geography, Navigation and Meteorology; & what relates to the magnitudes, distances, motions, densities & centrifugal forces of the heavenly bodies; & to the weight, heat, refraction, height form & motions of the Atmosphere & of the things therein, & to instruments for observing the same: & to the figure magnitude & motions of the earth & sea.

3. Philosophy relating to Animals; viz their species, qualities, passions, anatome, diseases; & the knowledge of their frame & use of their stomachs, entrails, bloodvessels, heart, lungs, liver, spleen, glands, juyces & organs of sensation, motions, & generation.

4. Philosophy relating to vegetables; & particularly to the knowledge of their species, parts, leaves, flowers, seeds, fruits, juyces, vertues & properties; & the manner of their generation, nutrition, & vegetation.

5. Meteorology & Chemistry, & the knowledge of the nature of earths, stones, coralls, Sparrs, metalls, semimetalls, marchasites, Arsnicks, Bitumens, sulphurs, salts, vitriols, rain waters, mineral waters, springs, oyles, tinctures, spirits, vapours, fumes, air, fire, flame & their parts, tasts, smells, colours, gravity, density, fixity, dissolutions, fermentations, coalitions, separations, congelations, liquefactions, volatility, destillation, sublimation, precipitation, corrosiveness, electricity, magnetism & other qualities; & the causes of subterraneous caves, rocks, shells, waters, petrifactions, exhalations, damps, heats, fires, & earthquakes: & the rising or falling of mountains & islands.

To anyone or more of the aforesaid ffellows, such Books, Letters, & Things as deserve it, may be referred by the R. S. at their meetings from time to time. And as often as any such Fellowship becomes void, it may be filled with a Person who hath already invented something new, or made some considerable improvement in that branch of philosophy, or is eminent for skill therein, if such a person can be found. The reward will be an incouragement to Inventors: & it will be an advantage to the R. S. to have such men at their meetings, & tend to make their meetings numerous & usefull & their body famous & lasting.

(fol. 6)

27. Cambridge, University Library, Add. MS. 4005, fol. 3.

28. Royal Society of London, Journal Booke of the Council, p. 184, January 20, 1711.

29. *Ibid.*, p. 248, April 23, 1719.

30. *Ibid.*, p. 302, March 29, 1727.

31. Stukeley, *Memoirs of Newton's Life*, pp. 78-81.

32. Royal Society of London, Journal Booke of the Council, p. 166.

33. On May 14, Halley wrote Sloane that the Council of the Royal Society considered he had been wronged: "[I]t was carried by a great plurality of Voices, that the Dr. had offended, and that the grimaces he sais he apprehended you to make, being subject to a dubious interpretation, and unobserved by my self (who saw you all the while) and severall others present, should first be disowned by you, as to the intention of any looks or actions; and that then the Dr. for his words, which could not be denyed, should begg your pardon before the Society, with a promise not to do the like in the future" (Edmond Halley, *Correspondence and papers*, ed. E. F. MacPike [Oxford: Clarendon Press, 1932], p. 127).

34. Cambridge, King's College Library, Keynes MS. 151, an anonymous letter to Newton, March 28, 1710.

35. Anonymous, *An Account of the Late Proceedings in the Council of the Royal Society, in order to Remove from Gresham-College into Crane-Court, in Fleet-Street. In a Letter to a Friend* (London, 1710), pp. 3, 8-9.

36. A foreign visitor to the Society, the Frankfort traveler Zacharias Conrad von Uffenbach, still noticed the portrait in 1710; see *London in 1710, from the travels of Zacharias Conrad von Uffenbach*, trans. and ed. W. H. Quarrell and Margaret Mare (London: Faber & Faber, Ltd., 1934), p. 102.

37. British Museum, Sloane MS. 4060, fol. 76r, undated note from Newton to Sloane.

38. Charles Richard Weld, *A History of the Royal Society* (London, 1848), I, 419.

39. British Museum, Sloane MS. 4042, fol. 291, undated letter from Etienne François Geoffroy to Sloane.

40. D. Seaborne Davies, "The Records of the Mines Royal and the Mineral and Battery Works," *Economic History Review*, VI (1936), 209-213.

41. Newton, *Correspondence*, III, 357-366, Newton to Nathaniel Hawes, May 25, 1694.

42. Newton, *Unpublished Scientific Papers of Isaac Newton*, ed. A. Rupert Hall and Marie Boas Hall (Cambridge: Cambridge University Press, 1962), pp. 369-373; see also W. W. Rouse Ball, "Isaac Newton on University Studies," *Cambridge Review*, October 21, 1909.

43. Stukeley, *Memoirs of Newton's Life*, p. 81.

44. Weld, *History of the Royal Society*, I, 420-421.

45. David Brewster, *Memoirs of the life, writings, and discoveries of Sir Isaac Newton* (Edinburgh, 1855), II, 257.

46. Great Britain, House of Commons, *Journals*, XVII (1711-1714; reprinted 1803), 641-642 (May 25, 1714), 677-678 (June 11, 1714), 716 (July 3, 1714), 721 (July 8, 1714). See also William Whiston, *Longitude Discovered* (London, 1738), Historical Preface, p. v.

47. Cambridge, University Library, Add. MS. 3972, fol. 35v.

48. Hiscock, ed., *Gregory, Newton and their Circle*, p. 25.

49. Agnes Grainger Stewart, *The Academic Gregories* (New York: Charles Scribner's Sons, 1901), p. 23; Charles Hutton, *Mathematical and Philosophical Dictionary*, 2nd ed. (London, 1815), I, 605.

50. Edmond Halley, "Observations of the late Total Eclipse of the Sun on the 22nd of April last past, made before the Royal Society at their House in Crane-Court in Fleet Street, London," *Philosophical Transactions of the Royal Society*, XXIX, no. 343 (1715), 246.

51. John Evelyn, *Diary*, ed. E. S. de Beer (Oxford: Oxford University Press, 1955), IV, 98, September 10, 1676.

52. See Francesco Algarotti, *Sir Isaac Newton's Philosophy Explain'd for the Use of the Ladies*, trans. Elizabeth Carter (London, 1739); the original Italian version was published in 1737.

53. The English defended Newton, the Germans Leibniz, the French often hedged, conceding Newton's priority but rejecting plagiarism on Leibniz' part. Though the French hailed the *Opticks*, national pride in their own school made it difficult to abandon the Cartesian system of vortices overnight, and many scientists were willing to join Leibniz in an attack upon gravity as an occult quality. But the French were usually rather respectful, and while Brook Taylor conducted a skirmish with Rémond de Montmort over the relative virtues of the Newtonian and the Cartesian systems, they could remain good friends. See Pierre Brunet, *L'Introduction des théories de Newton en France au xviiie siècle* (Paris: A. Blanchard, 1931).

54. Voltaire, *Letters Concerning the English Nation* (London, 1733), Letters XIV-XVII.

Chapter 14

TWO HUMBLE SERVANTS OF THE LORD

1. Francis Baily, *An Account of the Revd. John Flamsteed, the first Astronomer-Royal* (London, 1835), p. 8, "Self-Inspections of J. F." (vol. 32A, fol. 2). Flamsteed's papers are now in the archives of the Royal Greenwich Observatory at Herstmonceux. Throughout this chapter, the printed versions have been followed, corrected from the manuscripts where there were substantive differences; numbers in parentheses refer to the Herstmonceux archives.

2. Thomas Hearne, *Remarks and Collections* (Oxford: printed for the Oxford Historical Society at the Clarendon Press, 1885-1921), V, 130-131, October 31, 1715.

3. Baily, *Flamsteed*, p. 7, "Self-Inspections of J. F."

4. Eugene Fairfield MacPike, *Hevelius, Flamsteed and Halley: three contemporary astronomers and their mutual relations* (London: Taylor and Francis, 1937), p. 20.

5. M. C. Donnelly, *Astronomical observatories in the 17th and 18th centuries* (Brussels: Académie Royale des Sciences, des Lettres, et des Beaux-Arts de Belgique, 1964), p. 15.

6. Hearne, *Remarks and Collections*, I, 294, October 9, 1706.

7. MacPike, *Hevelius, Flamsteed and Halley*, p. 22.

8. Baily, *Flamsteed*, p. 203, Flamsteed to Abraham Sharp, May 30, 1702.

9. *Ibid.*, p. 60 and note.

10. Newton, *Correspondence*, IV, 150, Flamsteed to Newton, July 18, 1695; IV, 332, Flamsteed to Lowthorp, May 10, 1700; Cambridge, King's College Library, Keynes MS. 130, a Conduitt notebook.

11. Newton, *Correspondence*, IV, 156-157, Newton to Flamsteed, July 27, 1695.

12. *Ibid.*, IV, 54-55, Flamsteed to Newton, December 6, 1694; also IV, 58-59, Flamsteed to Newton, December 10, 1694:

But I am displeased wth you not a little for offering to gratifie me for my paines either you know me not so well as I hoped you did or you have suffered your selfe to be possest with that Charecter which the malice & envy of a person from whom I have deserved much better things has endeavord to fix on me. . . . I dare boldly say I was never tempted with Covetousness God allwayes blest me wth more monys then I know well how to dispose of & those that know me even those who calumniate me know how free I have been of it on good occasions. . . . All the return I can allow or ever expected from such persons wth whom I corresponded is onely to have the result of their Studies imparted as freely as I afford them the effect of mine or my paines. I have told you my disposition plainely & if hereafter you offer me any other then this just reward. I shall thinke as meanely of you as I feare you have been persuaded to thinke of mee by false & malitious suggestions.

13. With evident relish Flamsteed wrote his friend Abraham Sharp from the Observatory on July 9, 1715: "I doubt not but you have heard that the Lord Halifax is dead of a violent fever. If common fame speak true, he died worth £150,000; out of which he gave Mrs. Barton, Sir I. Newton's niece, for her *excellent conversation*, a curious house, £5000, with lands, jewels, plate, money, and household furniture, to the value of £20,000 or more. Sir I. Newton loses his support in him; and, having been in with Lord Oxford, Bolingbroke, and Dr. Arbuthnott, is not now looked upon as he was formerly" (Baily, *Flamsteed*, p. 314).

14. *Ibid.*, p. 131, Flamsteed to Newton, February 24, 1692; see also Newton, *Correspondence*, III, 201.

15. Newton, *Correspondence*, III, 202, Flamsteed to Newton, February 24, 1692; IV, 159, Flamsteed to Newton, August 6, 1695: "I know a Sparke is with you that complaines much I have lived here 20 yeares & printed nothing."

16. *Ibid.*, IV, 99, Flamsteed to Newton, March 21, 1695. It was generally held that Halley was a skeptic in matters of religion; see Hearne, *Remarks and Collections*, VI, 132, January 22, 1718: "Dr. Halley hath little or no Religion. The said Dr. Halley defends taking all manner of Oaths, & as soon as ever King George came over, he went to Westminster & took the Oaths publicly, & bragged of what he had done afterwards, in as publick a manner, particularly in the Coffee-Houses."

17. Newton, *Correspondence*, III, 203, Flamsteed to Newton, February 24, 1692. See also IV, 83, Flamsteed to Newton, February 7, 1695:

You know him not[.] I doe and Many of his unsincere & disingenious practises. particularly the best part of that stock of lunar observations where of he boasts are mine & severall things besides he is very unwilling to owne, & hence it comes that he represents me as one so very eager to have acknowledgmts made, as if I required more then was due. I can be content with less, & as for what you have receaved of me I am not sollicitous what you say of them being well assured you will say nothing but what is just & fit & for his aspersions I doe not valew them. I have done with him, who has almost ruined himselfe by his indiscreet behaviour. & you shall hear no more of him from me till wee meet when I shall tell you his history which is too foule & large for a letter.

18. See *ibid.*, IV, 73, Newton to Flamsteed, January 26, 1695.

19. *Ibid.*, IV, 13, Flamsteed to Newton, September 7, 1694: "When Mr. H. shews himselfe as Candid as other men I shall be as free to him as I was the first seven years of our Acquaintance. when I refused him nothing that he desired."

20. On December 18, 1703, Flamsteed wrote to his friend Abraham Sharp that Halley "now talks, swears, and drinks brandy like a sea-captain" (Baily, *Flamsteed*, p. 215). On November 13, 1713, Halley's portrait was placed by the side of Hevelius'

in the gallery of the Bodleian, which provoked Thomas Hearne to comment: "And some Persons say that he is very justly placed by Hevelius, because he made him (as they give out) a Cuckold, by lying with his Wife when he was at Dantzick, the said Hevelius having a very pretty Woman to his Wife, who had a very great Kindness for Mr. Halley, and was (it seems) observed often to be familiar with him. But this Story I am apt to think is false" (*Remarks and Collections,* IV, 257).

21. See MacPike, *Hevelius, Flamsteed and Halley,* p. 92.

22. Newton, *Correspondence,* IV, 87–88, Newton to Flamsteed, February 16, 1695; the italics, which indicate underlining, were probably Flamsteed's.

23. Herstmonceux, Royal Greenwich Observatory, Flamsteed papers, Item 6, "Diarium Observationum." (I am greatly obliged to Mr. Philip S. Laurie, Archivist at the Royal Observatory, for calling this item to my attention and providing me with a slide of the inscription.) It has since been printed in Newton, *Correspondence,* Preface, IV, xvii. See also W. G. Hiscock, ed., *David Gregory, Isaac Newton and their Circle* (Oxford: printed for the editor, 1937), p. 13, November 10, 1702.

24. Flamsteed's note on letter from Newton, February 16, 1695 (Baily, *Flamsteed,* p. 152n).

25. Newton, *Correspondence,* IV, 134, Newton to Flamsteed, June 29, 1695.

26. *Ibid.,* IV, 143, Newton to Flamsteed, July 9, 1695.

27. *Ibid.,* IV, 144, notes by Flamsteed on Newton's letter of July 9, 1695.

28. *Ibid.,* IV, 152, Newton to Flamsteed, July 20, 1695. Even in the midst of their quarrels these old men were often solicitous of each other's health: "I am sorry for your Indisposity & pray God send you your health againe. I can I blesse him for I endure the cold of the nights as well as formerly but I often take cold when [I] sit long to my Numbers within doores & have scarce recovered of one yet that I got in my first days work last week when I was very intent I feare you suffer in the saim manner with my selfe. tis as much requisite to defend our selves against the Injurys of the Air in our studys as on a Jorney our bodys being every day less able to bear the injurys of cold as our days increase. JF:" (IV, 79, Flamsteed to Newton, January 29, 1695).

29. *Ibid.,* IV, 290.

30. *Ibid.,* IV, 194 n. 1: "An undated memorandum by Newton, reproduced in Sotheby's *Catalogue of the Newton Papers* (1936), p. 8, states 'Last Autumn when I was in London Mr Pepys asking me about the possibilities of finding the Longitude at Sea and desiring my leave that he might say that I thought it possible, I desired him not to mention me about it least it might be a means to engage me in it and reflect upon me if I did not compass it.' " See also IV, 193, Newton to Halley, March 14, 1696.

31. *Ibid.,* IV, 383, Newton to [?], 1702.

32. *Ibid.,* IV, 296, Newton to Flamsteed, January 6, 1699.

33. *Ibid.,* IV, 304, Flamsteed to Wallis, January 10, 1699.

34. *Ibid.,* IV, 303, Flamsteed to Newton, January 10, 1699.

35. Baily, *Flamsteed,* p. 173.

36. *Ibid.,* p. 174, Flamsteed to John Lowthorpe, May 10, 1700; this portion of the letter was not reprinted in Newton's *Correspondence.*

37. Newton, *Correspondence,* IV, 332, Flamsteed to Lowthorp, May 10, 1700.

38. Baily, *Flamsteed,* p. 175, Flamsteed to Lowthorp, May 10, 1700.

39. *Ibid.,* p. 176, Flamsteed to Lowthorp, May 10, 1700.

40. *Ibid.,* p. 199, Flamsteed to Sharp, February 6, 1702.

41. *Ibid.,* p. 204, Flamsteed to Caswell, 1702.

42. *Ibid.,* pp. 73–74 (vol. 32C, fols. 76–77). The original preface was printed on pp. 71–105.

43. *Ibid.,* pp. 75–82 *passim* (vol. 32C, fols. 78–82).

44. Newton, *Correspondence,* IV, 432, Newton to Flamsteed, December 18, 1704.

45. Baily, *Flamsteed,* p. 66, Flamsteed's notes of November 8, 1704.

46. *Ibid.,* p. 239, Flamsteed to Sharp, April 24, 1705. For an account of the knighting on April 19, 1705, see the *London Gazette* of April 23.

47. Newton, *Correspondence,* IV, 454, Newton to Flamsteed, November 14, 1705; see also pp. 454–460. For drafts in Newton's hand of articles of agreement, and various orders and decisions from the referees, see Cambridge, University Library, Add. MS. 4006, fols. 8r, 10r, 18r.

48. Newton, *Correspondence,* IV, 484, Newton to Flamsteed, April 9, 1707. Flamsteed's diary and stray manuscripts report on the hostile atmosphere of these meetings ("Further Extracts from Flamsteed's Diary," February 23, 1706–April 15, 1707, in Newton, *Correspondence,* IV, 468, 469, 471).

49. Baily, *Flamsteed,* p. 264, Flamsteed to Sharp, May 29, 1707.

50. Newton's version of the stopping of the press and Halley's intervention is given in a note written late in 1708 on the printing of the *Historia Coelestis Britannica (Correspondence,* IV, 529).

51. Baily, *Flamsteed,* p. 91. See also a copy of the order, with some slight differences of phraseology, among the Newton papers in the Cambridge University Library (Add. MS. 4006, fol. 29).

52. Cambridge, University Library, Add. MS. 4006, fol. 38r, Newton to Flamsteed, circa March 24, 1711: "And if instead thereof you propose any thing else or make any excuses or unnecessary delays it will be taken for an indirect refusal to comply wth her Majts order. Your speedy & direct answer & compliance is expected."

53. See P. S. Laurie, "The Board of Visitors of the Royal Observatory," *Quarterly Journal of the Royal Astronomical Society,* VII (1967), 169–185, and VIII (1968), 334–353.

54. Baily, *Flamsteed,* pp. 228–229 (vol. 33, fols. 104–106).

55. Royal Society Library, Flamsteed to Sharp, November 25, 1712.

56. Baily, *Flamsteed,* pp. 101–102 (vol. 32C, fol. 93). On May 2, 1716, Flamsteed wrote to Sharp: "I committed them to the fire about a fortnight ago. If Sir I. N. would be sensible of it I have done both him & Dr Hally a very great kindnesse" (Royal Society Library).

57. Baily, *Flamsteed,* p. 323, Flamsteed to Abraham Sharp, June 2, 1716.

58. *Ibid.,* p. 326, Flamsteed to Sharp, November [1716].

59. *Ibid.,* pp. 326–327, Flamsteed to Sharp, May 2, 1717.

60. *Ibid.,* p. 324, Halley to Flamsteed, June 7, 1716 (vol. 35, fol. 145).

61. Neither Halley's "Flamsteed" nor the "Flamsteed" prepared by Joseph Crosthwait and Abraham Sharp is free from errors, but the astronomer Baily (*Flamsteed*, p. xlii and note), who reviewed the material in detail, found Halley's allegation in the 1712 introduction a gross exaggeration. The statement that Halley had "corrected errors" in the locations of the fixed stars and had "filled in the by no means few lacunae" (*Historiae Coelestis Libri Duo* [London, 1712], p. iv) was insulting. At the end of the eighteenth century, adaptations of the British star catalogue were still appearing in France and were prized as the best available. See, for example, *Atlas Céleste de Flamsteed, publié en 1776, par J. Fortin, Ingénieur-Mécanicien pour les globes & sphères. Troisième édition, revue, corrigée, augmentée par les Citoyens Lalande & Méchain* (Paris, 1795).

Chapter 15

THE DUEL WITH LEIBNIZ

1. Joseph Raphson, *The History of Fluxions* (London, 1715 [1717]), p. 100, Newton to Conti, February 26, 1716. Edmund Turnor, *Collections for the History of the Town and Soke of Grantham* . . . (London, 1806), p. 185, quoting the Journal Book of the Royal Society, names the original members of the committee: "March 11, 1711/12: Upon account of Mons. Leibnitz's letter to Dr. Sloane, concerning the disputes formerly mentioned, a committee was appointed by the Society to inspect the letters and papers relating thereto, viz. Dr. Arbuthnot, Mr. Hill, Dr. Halley, Mr. Jones, Mr. Machin, and Mr. Burnet, who were to make their report to the Society." Augustus de Morgan, "On a point connected with the dispute between Keil and Leibnitz about the invention of Fluxions," *Philosophical Transactions of the Royal Society*, CXXXVI (1846), 107, states that Robarts (or Roberts) was added on March 20, Bonet the Prussian Minister on March 27, de Moivre, Aston, and Brook Taylor on April 17.

2. Turnor, *Collections for the History of Grantham*, p. 185, quoting the Journal Book of the Royal Society. In the collection of letters, now in the library of the Royal Society, which formed the basis of the *Commercium Epistolicum*, passages that were excerpted are underlined. Only rarely were the full texts printed, and translation from English into Latin is occasionally rather loose.

3. Leibniz, who had worked diligently for the Hannoverian succession, expected to become *Historiographe d'Angleterre*. Rumor had already spread about his presence in England when the King forbade him to come until he had finished the history of the House of Brunswick-Hannover. The correspondence of his last three years has a tragic note: "We dwell here in a kind of solitude since our court has gone to England," he wrote Bourguet in March 1716 (Leibniz, *Die philosophischen Schriften*, ed. C. J. Gerhardt [Berlin, 1875–1890; reprinted Hildesheim: G. Olms, 1960–1961], III, 589). He was obliged to work night and day on this family his-

tory when he believed the time had come to prepare his philosophical synthesis. The King was concerned only that Leibniz would die before finishing his history.

4. *Ibid.*, III, 591, Leibniz to Bourguet, circa March 1716: "Her Royal Highness, who has read my Theodicy with care, has expressed the opinion that my view seems to her to be the more plausible."

5. Leibniz, *Werke*, ed. O. Klopp (Hannover, 1884), XI, 90, Caroline of Anspach to Leibniz, April 24, 1716. Translation quoted from *The Leibniz-Clarke Correspondence*, ed. H. G. Alexander (Manchester: Manchester University Press, 1956), p. 194.

6. Leibniz, *Die philosophischen Schriften*, III, 655, extract from Conti's letter to Rémond de Montmort, August 30, 1715, included in Rémond de Montmort to Leibniz, October 18, 1715.

7. Abate Antonio Conti, *Prose e Poesie* (Venice, 1756), II, 26.

8. Conti, *Réponse* [of Newton] *aux Observations sur la Chronologie de M. Newton, avec une lettre de M. l'Abbé Conti au sujet de ladite réponse* (Paris, 1726).

9. Rémond de Montmort wrote Leibniz from Paris, March 15, 1716: "He [Conti] had the honor of supping with the King of England. . . . His British Majesty wanted to hear from him the history of your quarrel with M. Newton (Leibniz, *Die philosophischen Schriften*, III, 672).

10. Robert Halsband, *The Life of Lady Mary Wortley Montagu* (Oxford: Oxford University Press, 1956), p. 42, notes that Lady Mary found the cosmopolitan abbé stimulating, and addressed to him some letters and a French essay.

11. Leibniz, *Die philosophischen Schriften*, III, 562, Leibniz to Bourguet, January 3, 1714: "M. Rémond in Paris, who I am told is an important personage and one of the chief figures in the Council of the Duke of Orleans, has written me a letter in which he puts my work [the *Theodicy*] on the loftiest pinnacle that a work of this character can be placed." Rémond de Montmort praised Conti to Leibniz in a letter of May 5, 1714: "We have among us M. l'abbé Conti, a Venetian noble of great birth and even greater worth. He has a boundless love for the sciences, and after having meditated on what you have allowed us to see of your system, he offered his views to M. Wolf in a letter sent to M. Hermann under whom I think he studied at Padua. He is one of our closest friends" (*ibid.*, III, 616). Leibniz had been somewhat skeptical about Conti's reputed scientific talents; he wrote Bourguet from Vienna on March 22, 1714: "Others too have, as you, spoken with esteem about M. l'abbé Conti. . . . Provided he some day gives us something fine, one can permit him that incentive to glory, wanting to be original" (*ibid.*, III, 567–568). In a letter to Rémond de Montmort in July of that year he could nevertheless pour on flattery to win adherents: "You are not the first, sir, who has spoken to me of this illustrious abbé as an excellent mind, and I am eager to see his works in order to make use of them, for I do not doubt but that they will serve to enlighten me" (*ibid.*, III, 618–619).

12. Rémond de Montmort to Leibniz, September 4, 1715: "M. l'abbé Conti, who writes often to me, is delighted with that country. It seems that M. Newton keeps nothing hidden from him. I am thus at present very well informed about the private views of the English philosophers. The last pages of M. Newton's book are

rather confused; his conversation is more free and easy" (*ibid.*, III, 650). On October 18, 1715, Rémond sent Leibniz excerpts of Conti's letters from England dated June 30, July 12, and August 30, 1715 (*ibid.*, III, 651-655). Conti's relationship with Rémond de Montmort and Leibniz did not deter him from writing Newton from Hannover, December 10, 1716, after the death of Leibniz: "If anything new develops regarding the Leibniz affair, I shall send you precise details. There is perhaps no one more concerned for your fame than I" (Cambridge, King's College Library, Keynes MS. 140).

13. Leibniz, *Sämtliche Schriften und Briefe* (Berlin, Leipzig: O. Reichl, 1957), ser. I, vol. VI, pp. 266-267, Leibniz to Henri Justel, October 10, 1690.

14. Cambridge, University Library, Add. MS. 3968; documents run to eleven and twelve drafts. H. R. Luard *et al.*, *A Catalogue of the Portsmouth Collection . . .* (Cambridge, 1888), pp. 7 and 8, section I, xi, no. 37, lists several drafts of an intended preface to the *Commercium Epistolicum,* as well as drafts of the *Ad Lectorem* printed in the second edition (no. 21). Augustus de Morgan was the first to note Newton's part in the preparation of the *Commercium Epistolicum.*

15. Leibniz, *Sämtliche Schriften und Briefe,* ser. I, vol. IV (1950), pp. 475-476, Otto Mencke to Leibniz, July 16, 1684.

16. *Ibid.,* ser. I, vol. IV, 477, Leibniz to Otto Mencke [August?] 1684. A variant translation, dated [July?] 1684 is published in Newton, *Correspondence,* II, 399. Leibniz had a profound sense of the long sequence of contributory discoveries in any major innovation. He wrote to Bourguet on March 22, 1714: "It is after all good to study the discoveries of another man so that we may understand the source of his inventions and in a certain sense make them part of ourselves" (Leibniz, *Die philosophischen Schriften,* III, 568).

17. For the anagrams, their solutions, and the translations of their meanings from Latin into English, see Newton, *Correspondence,* II, 115, 129, 134, 153 n. 25, 159 n. 72. Oldenburg transmitted the *Epistola Posterior* to Leibniz on May 2, 1677 (*ibid.*, II, 208). The translation of the Scholium is quoted from Florian Cajori's edition of the *Principia* (Berkeley, Cal.: University of California Press, 1934), pp. 655-656. Leibniz expressed his satisfaction in his letter to Henri Justel on October 10, 1690 (*Sämtliche Schriften und Briefe,* ser. I, vol. VI, 264).

18. Fatio de Duillier, *Lineae brevissimi descensus investigatio geometrica duplex* (London, 1699), p. 18. There is some evidence that after Fatio's insinuation of plagiarism in 1699, Leibniz was on the alert for an opportunity to make reprisals against both Fatio and Newton. Given their intimacy he could not credit Fatio with an independent action. On July 4, 1705, David Gregory reports one such act of malice, or so, at least, was Leibniz' conduct interpreted in the Newton circle. "In a latin book in 8vo, written by one Grononga [Johannes Gröning] or such a name of miscellaneous things & among others of the History of the Cycloid, printed about 1701 or 1702 at Hannover, there is printed a list of Mr. Newtons mistakes in his Princ. Philos. in about 5 or 6 pages. These were communicated by M. Fatio to M. Hugens about the year 1690, and by M. Hugens to M. Libnitz, & after M. Fatio's falling out with M. Libnitz, malitiously published by the contrivance of M. Libnitz. This is M. Fatio's account of the affair this 4 July 1705" (W. G. Hiscock, ed., *David*

Gregory, Isaac Newton and their Circle [Oxford: printed for the editor, 1937], pp. 26–27).

19. Pierre Des Maizeaux, *Recueil de diverses pièces, sur la philosophie, la religion naturelle, l'histoire, les mathématiques, etc. Par Mrs. Leibniz, Clarke, Newton, & autres autheurs célèbres* (Amsterdam, 1720), II, 121, Newton to Chamberlayne, May 11, 1714.

20. The ninth draft of a letter from Newton to Conti, February 26, 1716 (O.S.), quoted by Alexandre Koyré and I. Bernard Cohen, "Newton & the Leibniz-Clarke Correspondence," *Archives internationales d'histoire des sciences*, XV (1962), 112–113, reads in part: "And afterwards I was accused in the Acta Eruditorum & before the Royal Society as a Plagiary who had substituted Fluxions for Differences & thereby taken the Method from Mr Leibnitz. . . . [I]nstead of answering the same in a fair manner, & proving his accusation of plagiary against me, a defamatory Libel was published against me in Germany without the name of the Author or Publisher or City where it was published, & dispersed over Germany France & Italy, & the Libel it self represents that Mr Leibnitz set it on foot."

21. Cambridge, King's College Library, Keynes MS. 129A, Conduitt's memoir to Fontenelle, pp. 10–11: "Sr I. recd the famous problem [sent by Bernoulli in 1697] wch was intended to puzzle all the Mathematicians in Europe at 4 a clock in the afternoon when he was very much tired with the business of the Mint where he had been employd all day, & yet solved it before he went to bed that night." See also Newton, *Correspondence*, IV, 224, Newton to Montague, January 30, 1697, and L. T. More, *Isaac Newton: A Biography* (New York: Charles Scribner's Sons, 1934), pp. 570–571.

22. *Acta Eruditorum*, January 1705, translated in More, *Newton*, p. 578; Guhrauer [Eduard Gottschalk], *Gottfried Wilhelm Freiherr v. Leibniz. Eine Biographie* (Breslau, 1846), I, 311. Aided by Ludovici, Director of the Paulinische Bibliothek, Leipzig, Guhrauer identified the review as Leibniz' through the discovery of the signed manuscript original.

23. Des Maizeaux, *Recueil*, II, 49, Leibniz to Conti, April 9, 1716.

24. More, *Newton*, pp. 580–581.

25. Newton, *Opticks* (1704), "advertisement."

26. In private correspondence, however, Leibniz did not completely surrender his suspicions and claims. See the copy of a letter of April 28, 1714, to Chamberlayne, certified by Richard Waller "and by me Edm. Halley" in the library of the Royal Society (L. 5. 112).

27. Cambridge, University Library, Add. MS. 3968, fol. 420r.

28. Leibniz, *Die philosophischen Schriften*, III, 328–329, Leibniz to Thomas Burnet, August 23, 1713. Burnet was a distant relative of the Bishop of Salisbury and of the scholar Burnet, author of the *Theoria telluris sacra*. He had made Leibniz' acquaintance during a continental tour in 1695 and continued a long correspondence with him.

29. *A Collection of Papers, which passed between the late learned Mr Leibnitz, and Dr. Clarke, in the years 1715 and 1716. Relating to the principles of natural philosophy and religion* (London, 1717). Newton's involvement in the Leibniz-

Clarke correspondence has been conclusively demonstrated by Koyré and Cohen, "Newton & the Leibniz-Clarke Correspondence," pp. 63–126. Leibniz was aware that Clarke was speaking for Newton; he wrote to Rémond de Montmort from Hannover, March 27, 1716 (*Die philosophischen Schriften,* III, 673–674): "Mr. Clarke, the Chaplain of the King of Great Britain, who is attached to Mr. Newton, is engaged in a controversy with me on behalf of his Master, and the Princess of Wales is gracious enough to take cognizance of our dispute."

30. Leibniz, *Die philosophischen Schriften,* III, 590–591, Leibniz to Bourguet, circa March 1716; III, 678, Leibniz to Rémond de Montmort, October 19, 1716.

31. J. E. McGuire, "Body and Void and Newton's De Mundi Systemate: Some New Sources," *Archive for History of Exact Sciences,* III, 3 (1966), p. 227, observes: "Thus in comparison with the necessary existence of Space and God, matter is an entirely impoverished being embodying the lowest degree of reality and perfection. Hence the 'downgrading' of matter is clearly a stated assumption of Newton's position. . . ."

32. Des Maizeaux, *Recueil,* II, 70–71, Leibniz to Conti, April 9, 1716, *apostille.*

33. Joseph Edleston, ed., *Correspondence of Sir Isaac Newton and Professor Cotes* (London, 1850), p. 149, Cotes to Bentley, March 10, 1713.

34. *Ibid.,* p. 150, Bentley to Cotes, March 12, 1713.

35. Leibniz, *Die philosophischen Schriften,* III, 580, Leibniz to Bourguet, August 5, 1715, and Des Maizeaux, *Recueil,* II, 48, Leibniz to Conti, April 9, 1716. See also Edleston, ed., *Correspondence of Newton and Cotes,* p. 154n.

36. Cambridge, University Library, Add. MS. 4007B, fol. 520, Keill to Newton, February 8, 1714.

37. Edleston, ed., *Correspondence of Newton and Cotes,* p. 170.

38. Add. MS. 4007B, fol. 524, Keill to Newton, April 26, 1714.

39. Add. MS. 4007B, fol. 538, Keill to Newton, May 25, 1714.

40. Add. MS. 4007B, fol. 548, Keill to Newton, June 24, 1714.

41. *Journal littéraire,* IV (1714), 319–358.

42. *Philosophical Transactions of the Royal Society,* XXIX no. 342 (1715), p. 221. The personal pronoun is used also where a mathematical demonstration is involved (p. 180).

43. More, *Newton,* pp. 602–603. Edleston, ed., *Correspondence of Newton and Cotes,* pp. 185–186, Newton to Keill, May 2, 1718: "The chief point is that Mr Bernoulli denies that he is the author of the Memoir entituled Epistola pro eminente etc that is inserted in the Acts of Leipsic 1716. The Memoir it self lays it upon Mr Bernoulli by the words *meam solutionem* [sic], & if Mr Bernoulli is injured thereby it is not you but the author of the Memoir who has injured him." The lapse was printed on p. 314 of the *Acta Eruditorum* for July 1716.

44. Newton composed the *Recensio,* the *Ad Lectorem,* and the variants introduced into the 1722 edition of the *Commercium Epistolicum;* the 1712 edition was at least directed by him. The true authorship of these texts, suggested by Biot and de Morgan, has been established since Brewster discovered almost the whole of the *Recensio* and five or six copies of the *Ad Lectorem* in Newton's hand. In the Hague *Journal littéraire,* VII (1715–1716), 114–158, 344–365, the *Recensio* appeared anony-

mously, translated by de Moivre; the Latin translation of 1722 is by Newton. He tried to palm the *Recensio* off on Keill. On October 3, 1715, Halley wrote Keill: "Sr. Isaac is desirous it should be publisht in the Journal Literaire . . . Sr. Isaac is unwilling to appear in it himself for reasons I need not tell you and therefore has ordered me to write to you about it who have been his avowed Champion in this quarrell and he hopes you will gratifie him in this matter by the first opportunity" (E. Halley, *Correspondence and papers,* ed. E. F. MacPike [Oxford: Clarendon Press, 1932], p. 128). To get the review, which had been translated into French, into the *Journal littéraire,* Newton ordered Halley to order Keill to send a letter to them for transmission to Mr. Johnson at the Hague indicating that he thought the review a good summary of the controversy.

45. See the summary in J. E. Hofmann, *Die Entwicklungsgeschichte der Leibnizschen Mathematik während des Aufenthaltes in Paris, 1672–1676* . . . (Munich: Leibniz Verlag, 1949), pp. 194–205.

46. Newton, "An Account of the Commercium Epistolicum," *Philosophical Transactions of the Royal Society,* XXIX, no. 342 (1715), p. 174.

47. Newton, *Correspondence,* II, 231–232, Leibniz to Oldenburg, July 12, 1677.

48. John Collins, *Commercium epistolicum . . . ou Correspondance de J. Collins et d'autres savants célèbres du xviie siècle, relative à l'analyse supérieure. . .* , ed. J. B. Biot and F. Lefort (Paris, 1856). Biot and Lefort collated the texts of the 1712 and 1722 editions, indicating additions, suppressions, alterations, and interpolations in what purported to be merely a new edition of the old *Commercium.*

49. Newton, "An Account of the Commercium Epistolicum," p. 194.

50. Leibniz, *Werke,* ed. O. Klopp, XI, 78, Leibniz to Caroline of Anspach, February 25, 1716. Translation quoted from *The Leibniz-Clarke Correspondence,* ed. H. G. Alexander, p. 193.

51. Koyré and Cohen, "Newton and the Leibniz-Clarke Correspondence," pp. 104–115 (app. I), discuss and reproduce excerpts from the twelve drafts of Newton's letter to Conti, eight of them collected in Cambridge, University Library, Add. MS. 3968, "Papers relating to the dispute respecting the invention of fluxions." For the text of the letter, see Des Maizeaux, *Recueil,* II, 16–25, "Lettre de M. le Chevalier Newton à M. l'Abbé Conti, Servant de Réponse à l'Apostille de M. Leibniz." Raphson, *History of Fluxions,* p. 103, quoted from Newton's letter: "But as he has lately attacked me with an accusation which amounts to Plagiary; if he goes on to accuse me, it lies upon him by the Laws of all nations to prove his Accusation, on Pain of being accounted guilty of Calumny. He hath hitherto written Letters to his Correspondents, full of Affirmations, Complaints and Reflections, without proving any thing. But he is the Aggressor, and it lies upon him to prove his Charge."

When in 1721 Conti heard that Newton was somehow shifting the blame for the whole Leibniz controversy onto his shoulders, he fought back in a long letter of May 22 to Brook Taylor, his version of the denouement of the Leibniz affair. It was Newton, not he, who had made the first move. When Conti had been told to assemble all the foreign envoys in London at the Royal Society solemnly to witness the comparison of papers in the archives with Leibniz' letters, Baron Kielmannsegge openly averred that the available documents were insufficient proof of Leibniz' plagiarism, and advised that Newton write Leibniz a letter demanding specific replies. All the other envoys and the King himself were pleased with the idea. Then it was that Newton wrote Conti the famous letter of February 26. The King's mistress, Baroness Kielmannsegge, had it translated into French, and it was despatched to Hannover—after the King had read and approved it. Conti's accompanying letter to Leibniz had been reviewed by Newton and corrected by de Moivre. Conti faithfully forwarded to Newton copies of any letters that Leibniz sent around in self-justification. A further reply from Newton and the original were printed, along with Leibniz' letters, at the back of Raphson's *History of Fluxions*, without Conti's knowledge, and five years later the whole kettle of fish was reheated and served up again by Des Maizeaux, with further emendations by Newton, in a collection of letters printed in Amsterdam in 1720. In the whole affair Conti, if he is credited, acted only as a postal clerk. See David Brewster, *Memoirs of the life, writings, and discoveries of Sir Isaac Newton* (Edinburgh, 1855), II, 432.

52. Cambridge, University Library, Add. MS. 4007B, fol. 587, draft of a letter from Newton to Abbé Varignon, before November 17, 1718.

53. Add. MS. 4007B, fol. 617, draft of a letter from Newton to Abbé Varignon, after December 21, 1719.

54. Edleston, ed., *Correspondence of Newton and Cotes*, p. 154n.

55. Raphson, *History of Fluxions*, p. 103, Newton to Conti, February 26, 1716.

56. Des Maizeaux, *Recueil*, II, 40, Leibniz to Countess Kielmannsegge, April 18, 1716: "When theses were being disputed at the University the shoemaker of Leyden was never absent from the public debate. Finally someone who knew him asked if he understood Latin. 'No,' he replied, 'and moreover I do not want to bother learning it.' 'Why then do you come so often to this auditorium, where only Latin is spoken?' 'Because I like to judge the blows.' 'And how do you judge without knowing what is being said? 'Oh I have another way of estimating who is right.' 'And what is that?' 'When I notice by somebody's manner that he is annoyed, and that he is getting angry, I judge that he is at a loss for arguments'" (40–41). On George I and Charlotte Kielmannsegge, see J. H. Plumb, *The First Four Georges* (London: Batsford, 1956), p. 40.

57. Des Maizeaux, *Recueil*, II, 75–98.

58. *Ibid.*, II, 106, "Remarque de M. Newton."

59. *Philosophical Transactions of the Royal Society*, XXIX, no. 342 (1715), p. 215. For the aristocratic and even divine connotations of the title "First Finder" ($\pi\rho\tilde{\omega}\tau\sigma s$ 'ευρετής) among the Greeks, see Arnaldo Momigliano, "Time in Ancient Historiography," in *History and the Concept of Time* (*History and Theory*, Beiheft 6; Middletown, Conn.: Wesleyan University Press, 1966), p. 18.

60. Cambridge, King's College Library, Keynes MS. 140.

61. Varignon's Latin letters are in King's College Library (Keynes MS. 142).

62. Quoted in L. T. More, *The Life and Works of the Honourable Robert Boyle* (New York: Oxford University Press, 1944), p. 98.

63. Woodward gave an account of the brawl between Dr. Mead and himself outside Gresham College on June 10, 1719, in the *Weekly Journal* of June 20:

I had by this time drove him from the street quite through the gateway, almost to the middle of the College-yard; when, making another pass, my right foot was stopped by some accident, so that I fell flat down on my breast. In an instant I felt Dr. Mead, with his whole weight upon me. It was then easy for him to wrest my sword out of my hand, as he did; and after that, gave me very abusive language, and bid me ask my life. I told him, I scorned to ask it of one who, through this whole affair, had acted so like a coward and a scoundrel; and at the same time, endeavoured to lay hold of his sword, but could not reach it. He again bid me ask my life. I replied, as before, I scorned to do that, adding terms of reproach suitable to his behaviour. By this time some persons coming in interposed, and parted us. As I was getting up, I heard Dr. Mead, amidst a crowd of people, now got together, exclaiming loudly against me for refusing to ask my life. I told him, in answer, he had shewn himself a coward; and it was owing wholly to chance, and not to any act of his, that I happened to be in his power. I added, that had he been to have given me any of his physick, I would, rather than take it, have asked my life of him; but for his sword, it was very harmless; and I was ever far from being in any the least apprehension of it.

See John Nichols, *Literary Anecdotes of the Eighteenth Century* (London, 1812), VI, 641-642.

64. On January 26, 1737, Rémond de Montmort wrote to a correspondent: "If M. l'Abbé Conti had been of my character one would not have seen two men as great as Newton and Leibniz die enemies after having always lived very peaceably together" (Bibliothèque Nationale, MS. français 24416, fols. 279-280).

65. David Gregory reported his being "offended" and "angry" when anything appeared in the learned world apparently contradictory of any of his propositions. For examples see entry under January 1707 in Hiscock, ed., *Gregory, Newton and their Circle*, p. 40.

66. William Whiston, *Memoirs of the Life and Writings of W. W.*, 2nd ed. (London, 1753), I, 94. These matters of the interpretation of Daniel were of great moment. The same Bentley, a-courting his lady, made her burst into tears by disputing a literal reading of passages in Daniel (I, 95).

67. Newton, *Correspondence,* III, 192, Newton to Locke, January 26, 1692: "Being fully convincd that Mr Mountague upon an old grudge wch I thought had been worn out, is false to me, I have done wth him. . . ."

68. *Ibid.,* II, 502-504, Newton to a friend, January 11, 1688.

69. "He could not bear to hear any one talk ludicrously of religion, often angry with Dr Halley on that score, & lessened his affection for Bentley" (Cambridge, King's College Library, Keynes MS. 130, Conduitt's notes for his life of Newton).

70. Newton, *Correspondence,* II, 438, Newton to Halley, June 20, 1686, postscript: "Mr Hook knowing my hand might have the curiosity to look into that letter & thence take the notion of comparing the forces of the Planets arising from their circular motion & so what he wrote to me afterwards about the rate of gravity, might be nothing but the fruit of my own Garden."

71. See Koyré and Cohen, "Newton and the Leibniz-Clarke Correspondence," p. 109, quoting Add. MS. 3968, fol. 571 (Cambridge, University Library).

72. William Whiston, *Historical Memoirs of the Life of Dr. Samuel Clarke* (London, 1730), p. 132.

Chapter 16

BAFFLING THE MONSIEURS

1. Cambridge, King's College Library, Keynes MS. 129A, Conduitt's memoir to Fontenelle.

2. John Conduitt, Dedication, in Newton, *Chronology of Ancient Kingdoms Amended* (London, 1728), p. v: "For the Chronology had never appeared in its present Form without Your Majesty's Influence; and the Short Chronicle, which precedes it, is entirely owing to the Commands with which You were pleased to honour him, out of your singular Care for the education of the Royal Issue, and earnest desire to form their minds betimes, and lead them early into the knowledge of Truth."

3. William Derham had it from Newton that "he designedly made his Principia abstruse" in order to "avoid being baited by little smatterers in Mathematicks . . ." (Cambridge, King's College Library, Keynes MS. 133, Derham to Conduitt, July 18, 1733). This seems to have determined also the form of the *Short Chronicle*.

4. Conduitt always emphasized that the manuscript prepared for the Princess of Wales was in Newton's hand. Therefore Lord Keynes's conjecture (in a typescript note attached to the manuscript) that the copy he presented to King's College Library (Keynes MS. 139) might be the one used by the Princess is improbable, as the writing is not Newton's. The British Museum manuscripts are: Lansdowne MS. 788, fols. 44–56 (the criticism is entitled *Stricturae quaedam in Newtoni chronologium*), and Sloane MS. 3208, fols. 49–67b.

5. Father Etienne Souciet, *Recueil de dissertations critiques*, vol. II, *Contenant un abrégé de chronologie, cinq dissertations contre la chronologie de M. Newton, une dissertation sur une médaille singulière d'Auguste* (Paris, 1726), p. 56. There was another edition in 1727.

6. David Brewster, *Memoirs of the life, writings, and discoveries of Sir Isaac Newton* (Edinburgh, 1855), II, 304, has noted a reference to the *Chronologie Raisonée* in a letter of January 15, 1724, to Brook Taylor. In the privately printed *Contemplatio Philosophica: a posthumous work of the late Brook Taylor . . . To which is prefixed a life of the author by his grandson, Sir W. Young, Bart.* (London, 1793), pp. 140–141, there is a letter from Count Rémond de Montmort: "They also say that M. Newton is printing his *Chronologie Raisonée.* Everybody is awaiting it with great impatience. Give him my compliments." Brook Taylor was the author of a treatise, *Linear Perspective; or a new method of representing justly all manner of objects as they appear to the eye in all situations* (London, 1715).

7. Souciet, *Recueil de dissertations*, II, 56. Souciet later published *Observations mathématiques, astronomiques, géographiques, chronologiques et physiques, tirées des anciens livres chinois ou faites nouvellement aux Indes et à la Chine par les Pères de la Compagnie de Jésus*, 3 vols. in 2 (Paris, 1729–1732).

8. Souciet, *Recueil de dissertations*, II, 49.

9. Nicolas Fréret, *Défense de la chronologie, fondée sur les monumens de l'his-*

toire ancienne, contre le système chronologique de M. Newton (Paris, 1758), p. x of Preface by Jean-Pierre de Bougainville.

10. *Abrégé de la chronologie de M. le chevalier Isaac Newton, fait par lui-même, & traduit sur le manuscrit anglois* (Paris, 1725). L. T. More, *Isaac Newton: A Biography* (New York: Charles Scribner's Sons, 1934), p. 612, refers to the *Abstract* as *A Short Chronicle from the First Memory of Things in Europe, to the Conquest of Persia by Alexander the Great.* This was the title used in the 1728 edition of the *Chronology,* when the *Abstract* was prefixed to the text. Conduitt in his memoir to Fontenelle (Keynes MS. 129A) wrote of the "abstract of chronology," and Keynes MS. 139 in King's College Library, Cambridge, has the same title.

11. Humphrey Prideaux's work was originally entitled *The Old and New Testament Connected in the History of the Jews and Neighboring Nations, from the Declension of the Kingdoms of Israel and Judah to the time of Christ,* 2 vols. (London, 1716–1718). This edition was in Newton's library. There are more than passing resemblances between Newton's histories and Prideaux's *Connections;* he too has a section on the "Iconography of the Temple of Jerusalem with a Description of the same," and he too demonstrated the fulfillment of the details of Daniel's prophecy through the narrative of historical events (see London, 1749, edition, part I, vol. I, p. 200 and preface pp. xxx–xxxi). His knowledge of the Hebrew chronologists in the original far surpassed Newton's.

12. Isaac Newton, "Remarks upon the Observations made upon a Chronological Index of Sir Isaac Newton, translated into French by the Observator, and publish'd at Paris," *Philosophical Transactions of the Royal Society,* XXXIII, no. 389 (1725), 315–321. The Sotheby & Co. *Catalogue of the Newton Papers sold by order of the Viscount Lymington* (London, 1936) lists seven autograph drafts of this paper, totaling about seven thousand words on twenty-three folio pages, with other autograph notes on the same subject on seven small quarto pages (lot 223). It appeared in French as *Réponse aux observations sur la chronologie de M. Newton* (n.p., n.d.).

13. Abate Antonio Conti, *Prose e Poesie* (Venice, 1756), II, 58.

14. This reply was given circulation by François Granet in the *Journal des érudits* and Père Pierre-Nicolas Desmolets in the *Continuation des mémoires de littérature et d'histoire* (Paris, 1726–1731); see Conti, *Prose e Poesie,* II, 60.

15. Conti, *Prose e Poesie,* II, chap. v, is entitled "Primo viaggio d'Inghilterra, e Prime conversazioni col Newtone, 1715." There is no doubt about the special regard that Newton showed for Conti during their acquaintance. The editor of the second volume of Conti's papers summarized long passages of notes referring to Newton. On one "foglio volante" written some twelve years after his visit to Newton in 1715, that is, at the time of Newton's denunciation, Conti described numerous long conversations during the course of which he was shown manuscripts to which no one else had access, as well as meetings with Cotes and Halley (II, 23–27). According to Conti, the first mathematical work that Newton had ever read was astrological—a detail which reappears in Conduitt's papers. A "carta volante" dated May 21, 1715, from which Conti's editor quotes, further illumines their relationship. "Today Sig. Newton paid me a visit. We talked about virtually everything that concerned philosophy and metaphysics" (II, 26).

16. *Ibid.*, II, 60.

17. Souciet, *Recueil de dissertations,* II, 104–105.

18. *Ibid.*, II, 169. Conti was clearly the center of the cabal. Not only did Father Souciet dedicate his dissertations to him but he called upon him to serve as arbiter. "Decide and favor me with your correction if I have gone astray. One could not choose either a more enlightened or a more talented judge. M. Newton could not wish for a more favorable one, one more disposed in his behalf, nor I a more just one."

19. *Ibid.*, II, 70–71.

20. Bibliothèque Nationale, MS. français 24424.

21. Cambridge, King's College Library, Keynes MS. 129A.

22. A French defender was Louis Jouard de la Nauze, "Lettres au R. P. Souciet, sur ses Dissertations contre le Nouveau Système de M. Newton," in Père Pierre-Nicolas Desmolets, ed., *Continuation des mémoires de littérature et d'histoire,* V, 332–463; VI, 3–72, 373–464. While he did not validate all of Newton's theories he considered criticism of them before final publication of the full chronology premature. He rebutted Souciet point by point and censured his compatriots for their manners (VI, 412).

23. Bernard de Fontenelle, *Eloge de Monsieur le Chevalier Newton* (Paris, 1728), p. 29.

24. Examples of the works published by Holbach's "Synagogue" under Fréret's name were the *Oeuvres philosophiques* (London, 1776); *Examen critique du Nouveau Testament* (London, 1777); *Examen critique des apologistes de la religion chrétienne* (n.p., 1767).

25. Giambattista Vico, *Principi di una Scienza Nuova* (Naples, 1730), pp. vi-viii. Vico quoted from Conti's letter of January 3, 1729: "I was one of the first to appreciate it and to have it appreciated by my friends, all of whom agreed that in the Italian language we do not have a book which contains more erudite and philosophical matters, and the whole original in its theme. I have sent a small extract of it to France to have the French become familiar with it, for it can add to and correct many of their ideas of Chronology, Mythology, no less than Morals and Jurisprudence, all of which they have studied deeply. The English will be obliged to admit the same when they see the book" (p. vi).

26. *The Lives of Dr. Edward Pocock by Dr. Twells; of Dr. Zachary Pearce and of Dr. Thomas Newton by themselves; and of the Rev. Philip Skelton by Mr. Burdy* (London, 1816), I, 433, letter of Dr. Zachary Pearce, August 10, 1754. In the "Life" prefixed to *A Commentary with notes on the Four Evangelists and Acts of the Apostles* . . . (London, 1777), pp. 42–44, Dr. Pearce presented a circumstantial account of Newton's absorbing interest in chronology. Five months before his death Newton had told Pearce that he had spent thirty years, at intervals, in reading over all the authors, or parts of authors, that could furnish any materials for forming a just account of ancient chronology.

According to Conduitt, it was the publication of the pirated *Abstract* that finally determined Newton "to print the work from whence the abstract was made as privately as possible & keep the copies in his own possession (Cambridge, King's College Library, Keynes MS. 129A).

27. Cambridge, King's College Library, Keynes MS. 136, William Stukeley to Dr. Mead for transmission to John Conduitt, June 26, 1727: "I discoursed with Newton this Christmas the twelvemonth about Solomon's temple, having studyd that affair. I find he had formerly drawn it out & considered it. . . . He says it was older than any other great temple, that Sesostris from this model built his temple in Egypt, one in each nome, & that from thence the Greeks borrowed their architecture, as they had their religious rites. I have likewise had some small conference with him about the first plantation of these western parts of the world after the flood & had the satisfaction to find I had fallen into the same notion as he." Entries in Stukeley's diary for April 1 and 15, 1726, are in the same vein; see *The Family Memoirs of Rev. William Stukeley, M.D. and the antiquarian and other correspondence of William Stukeley, Roger & Samuel Gale* (Durham, 1882, Surtees Society Publication no. 73), I, 78.

28. Herbert McLachlan, ed., *Sir Isaac Newton: Theological Manuscripts* (Liverpool: Liverpool University Press, 1950), pp. 2-3.

29. *Sotheby Catalogue,* lot 224a: "Chronology [*The Chronology of Ancient Kingdoms Amended*] Draft in the hand of John Conduitt, of the Dedication to Queen Caroline, with an A.L.s. submitting it to Alexander Pope, and Pope's reply containing criticism and revisions of the Dedication; with a Draft of the Dedication translated into French, and rough proof sheets."

In the meantime an anonymous Gentleman, without taking sides in the contest, in the cause of pure enlightenment so that the public might judge for itself, had published a translation of the *Abstract of Chronology* from the French back into English: *Sir Isaac Newton's Chronology, Abridged by Himself. To which are Added, Some Observations on the Chronology of Sir Isaac Newton. Done from the French, by a Gentleman* (London: J. Peele, 1728), 4to. This work is not in G. J. Gray, *A Bibliography of the works of Sir Isaac Newton* (Cambridge, 1888).

Chapter 17

PROPHECY AND HISTORY

1. By 1774 Herder pretended that he could enumerate fifty systems of *Physiktheologie;* see his *Sämmtliche Werke,* ed. Bernhard Suphan (Berlin, 1883), VI, 202.

2. Newton, *Correspondence,* II, 329-334, Newton to Burnet, January 1681.

3. Augustine, *De Civitate Dei,* X, 32.

4. Newton, *Observations upon the Prophecies,* ed. Bishop Samuel Horsley (*Opera omnia,* V; London, 1785), p. 463.

5. *Ibid.,* pp. 341-342.

6. *Ibid.,* p. 375.

7. *Ibid.,* p. 376.

8. G. S. Brett, "Newton's Place in the History of Religious Thought," in Frederick E. Brasch, ed., *Sir Isaac Newton, 1727–1927: A Bicentenary Evaluation of his Work* (Baltimore: Williams and Wilkins, 1928), p. 262, has felicitously described Newton's treatment of prophecy: "The books seemed to him examples of a method as symbolic as the mathematical. . . . A prophecy was an anticipation which became intelligible after it had been fulfilled."

9. Newton, *Observations upon the Prophecies of Daniel and the Apocalypse of St. John* (London, 1733), p. 253.

10. Oxford, Bodleian Library, New College MSS. 361, II, fol. 118v.

11. Newton, *Observations upon the Prophecies,* ed. Horsley, p. 304.

12. Herbert McLachlan, ed., *Sir Isaac Newton: Theological Manuscripts* (Liverpool: Liverpool University Press, 1950), p. 120.

13. See also McLachlan, ed., *Newton: Theological Manuscripts,* pp. 119–120.

14. Oxford, Bodleian Library, New College MSS. 361, II, fol. 133.

15. Cambridge, King's College Library, Keynes MS. 5.

16. The theoretical basis for gematria in cabalistic literature is set forth in the *Jewish Encyclopedia* (1903 ed.), V, 590.

17. Keynes MS. 5, fol. 32. See Newton, *Observations upon the Prophecies,* ed. Horsley, p. 468, for a similar passage about ΛΑΤΕΙΝΟΣ.

18. Keynes MS. 5, fols. 126–127.

19. Newton, *Correspondence,* III, 108, "An historical account of two notable corruptions of Scripture, in a Letter to a Friend" (John Locke), November 14, 1690. The "account" in fact consisted of two letters that Newton at one time thought of publishing anonymously in Holland, for which purpose he had enlisted Locke's aid (see above, p. 184). The Sotheby & Co. *Catalogue of the Newton Papers sold by order of the Viscount Lymington* (London, 1936) lists as lot 267 a Latin translation of "Two Notable Corruptions of Scripture," in manuscript, dated Amsterdam, 1709, with a few autograph corrections by Newton—proof that he was still committed to its ideas at that time, even though he had suppressed the publication.

20. Newton's final selection of the later of two alternative dates for the Passion was based upon a vivid, down-to-earth re-enactment in his own mind of the homeliest details in the narrative of the Gospels:

Thus there remain only the years 33 and 34 to be considered; and the year 33 I exclude by this argument. In the Passover two years before the Passion, when Christ went thro' the corn, and his disciples pluckt the ears, and rubbed them with their hands to eat; this ripeness of the corn shews that the Passover then fell late: and so did the Passover A.C. 32, *April* 14 but the Passover A.C. 31, March 28, fell very early. It was not therefore two years after the year 31, but two years after 32 that Christ suffered. Thus all the characters of the Passion agree to the year 34; and that is the only year to which they all agree.

(This quotation is from *Observations upon the Prophecies of Daniel* [1733 ed.], pp. 167–168.) It would not have been sensible for the apostles to eat unripe corn.

21. Babson Park, Mass., Babson Institute Library, MS. no. 438.

22. The London, 1754, edition was entitled *Two Letters of Sir Isaac Newton to Mr Le Clerc;* see also n. 19 above. "The Third Letter," dated November [?] 1690, has been printed for the first time in Newton, *Correspondence,* III, 129–146.

23. Brian Walton, Bishop of Chester, *et al.*, *Biblia sacra polyglotta*, 6 vols. (London, 1654–1657).

24. Newton gave a guinea to Samuel Crell, who was a Socinian refugee, as a token of his sympathy. Crell was the author of the pseudonymous *Initium Evangelii S. Joannis Apostoli ex antiquitate ecclesiastica restitutum . . . Per L. M. Artemonium* (London, 1726); there he too demonstrated that the main foundation of the Trinitarian doctrine in Scripture was a corrupt text (Earl Morse Wilbur, *A History of Unitarianism: Socinianism and its Antecedents*, Cambridge, Mass.: Harvard University Press, 1945, p. 576). Newton had several works by Socinians in his library, including Socinus and Crell; see H. John McLachlan, *Socinianism in Seventeenth-Century England* (London: Oxford University Press, 1951), pp. 330–331. On Newton's correspondence concerning various lections of the New Testament see *Correspondence*, III, 305–307, John Mill to Newton, February 21, 1694; III, 289, John Mill to Newton, November 7, 1693.

25. Newton, *Correspondence*, III, 89, "An historical account of two notable corruptions of Scripture."

26. Keynes MS. 10, fols. 23v and 24. McLachlan (*Newton: Theological Manuscripts*, pp. 102–103) altered the orthography slightly.

27. Keynes MS. 3, fol. 43.

28. Cambridge, King's College Library, Keynes MS. 3, fol. 5. One of Locke's papers entitled "Pacific Christians," dated 1688, and drawn up while he resided in Holland, invites comparison with Newton's "Irenicum" (Peter King, *The Life of John Locke*, 2nd ed. [London, 1830], II, 63–67).

29. Despite the fact, wrote Professor George Sarton in his notes "On a curious subdivision of the Egyptian cubit" (*Isis*, XXV [1936], 399), that Newton's argument was based upon three wrong premises, "he found a length which was incredibly close to the correct one." (Newton's value was 527.9 millimeters as against the real length of about 523 to 525 millimeters.) The scale of sacred cubits was used in plate III, p. 346, of Newton's *Chronology of Ancient Kingdoms Amended* (London, 1728).

30. Isaac Newton, "A Dissertation upon the Sacred Cubit of the Jews and the Cubits of the several Nations; in which, from the Dimensions of the greatest Egyptian Pyramid, as taken by Mr. John Greaves, the antient Cubit of Memphis is determined. Translated from the Latin of Sir Isaac Newton, not yet published," in *Miscellaneous Works of John Greaves, published by Thomas Birch* (London, 1737), II, 405.

31. Newton's drawings were ultimately published in *The Chronology of Ancient Kingdoms Amended*. Six sketches and a far more extended commentary, mainly in Latin, are in the Babson Institute Library, MS. no. 434. Stukeley's drawings are mainly in Oxford, Bodleian Library, MS. Top. gen. b. 52; see Stuart Piggott, *William Stukeley: An Eighteenth-Century Antiquary* (Oxford: Clarendon Press, 1950), pp. 23, 40, 130–131, 142, 200, for Stukeley's relations with Newton.

Athanasius Kircher had written an *Arca Noë in tres libros digesta* (Amsterdam, 1675), and a *Turris Babel* (Amsterdam, 1679). Jean Le Pelletier, *Dissertations sur l'Arche de Noé* (Paris, 1700), p. 194, faced a similar problem of measurement in a chapter entitled, "On the quantity of fodder and food which the granary could hold and the quantity which could be consumed in the Ark in a year."

32. Cambridge, University Library, Add. MS. 3987, fol. 123r.

33. Newton, *Observations upon the Prophecies of Daniel* (1733), p. 15.

34. Cambridge, University Library, Add. MS. 3996, fol. 101r.

Chapter 18

ON THE EVE OF DEATH

1. Cambridge, King's College Library, Keynes MS. 129A, pp. 23–24, Conduitt's memoir to Fontenelle; printed in Edmund Turnor, *Collections for the History of the Town and Soke of Grantham* . . . (London, 1806), pp. 165–166. Throughout this chapter the printed version of the memoir is quoted, with corrections from the manuscript.

2. Francis Atterbury, *The Epistolary Correspondence, Visitation Charges, Speeches, and Miscellanies* (London, 1783), I, 180–182, Atterbury to Thiriot, undated.

3. Keynes MS. 129A, pp. 24–26.

4. Henry St. John, Viscount Bolingbroke, *Lettres historiques, politiques, philosophiques et particulières* . . . *Précédées d'un essai historique sur sa vie*, ed. Count H. P. Grimoard (Paris, 1808), I, 156.

5. Pemberton's *View of Isaac Newton's Philosophy* was published in London in 1728, after Newton's death. In the preface Pemberton has left an account of how he became acquainted with his patron:

Mr. Polenus, a Professor in the University of Padua, from a new experiment of his, thought the common opinion about the force of moving bodies was overturned, and the truth of Mr. Libnitz's notion in that matter fully proved. The contrary of what Polenus had asserted I demonstrated in a paper, which Dr. Mead, who takes all opportunities of obliging his friends, was pleased to shew Sir Isaac Newton. This was so well approved of by him, that he did me the honour to become a fellow-writer with me, by annexing to what I had written, a demonstration of his own drawn from another consideration. When I printed my discourse in the philosophical transactions, I put what Sir Isaac had written in a scholium by self, that I might not seem to usurp what did not belong to me. But I concealed his name, not being then sufficiently acquainted with him to ask whether he was willing, I might make use of it or not. In a little time after he engaged me to take care of the new edition he was about making of his Principia.

6. Keynes MS. 130 (6), a Conduitt notebook.

7. Printed in Joseph Edleston, ed., *Correspondence of Sir Isaac Newton and Professor Cotes* (London, 1850), p. 316.

8. Keynes MS. 130 (6).

9. Royal Society of London, Journal Booke of the Council of the Royal Society, February 15, 1682–November 9, 1727 (Council Minutes, II), pp. 300–301, March 2, 1727. See also David Brewster, *Memoirs of the life, writings, and discoveries of Sir Isaac Newton* (Edinburgh, 1855), II, 408n. In 1725 Halley had incurred Newton's

displeasure in connection with tables of the motion of the comet of 1680 to answer some of Flamsteed's observations. Having made an error, Halley quickly wrote to beg pardon as though he were still the young man in awe of his master: "Being yesterday at London I guessed by some symptoms that you take it ill that I have not dispatcht the Calculus I undertook for you, but the aforesd mistake made me dispair of pleasing you in it. Being got home last night I was astonisht to find myself capable of such an intollerable blunder, for which I hope it will be easier for you to pardon me, than for me to pardon myself, who hereby run the risk of disobliging the person in the Universe I most esteem. I entreat therefore that you would not think of any other hand for the computus, and that you please to allow me the rest of this week to do it in, being desirous to approve my self in all things"; published in Edmond Halley, *Correspondence and papers,* ed. E. F. MacPike (Oxford: Clarendon Press, 1932), pp. 131-132, Halley to Newton, February 16, 1725. Newton's reply on March 1 (p. 200) is matter-of-fact and does not respond to Halley's sentiment.

10. Keynes MS. 129A, p. 23.

11. Keynes MS. 130 (6).

12. Oxford, Bodleian Library, New College MSS. 351, IV, fol. 194.

13. Cambridge, University Library, Add. MS. 4005, fol. 73r.

14. William Stukeley, *Memoirs of Sir Isaac Newton's Life . . .,* ed. A. Hastings White (London: Taylor and Francis, 1936), p. 19.

15. *Ibid.,* p. 68. Stukeley tells of Newton's presence at a country affair: "When I went into the dining room upstairs where the better sort of company was, it was talkd that there was an old gentleman belowstairs whom they fancyed to be Sir Isaac Newton. I instantly went down and finding it to be so, sat down with him. They above sent to desire us to walk up into the chief room. I answerd, the chief room was where Sir Isaac Newton was. Upon which the upper room was immediately left to the ordinary company, and the better sort came to us" (pp. 13-14).

16. Keynes MS. 126. Newton scribbled notes on Solomon's Temple on the back of the fragment. J. H. M. Craig, *Newton at the Mint* (Cambridge: Cambridge University Press, 1946), p. 28, quotes a brief undated note from Catherine to Newton, which I have not seen.

17. Keynes MS. 129A, pp. 26-28. Stukeley, though not there, has a slightly emended version of the end, probably from Dr. Mead (Stukeley, *Memoirs of Newton's Life,* pp. 82-83).

18. Keynes MS. 130.

19. Keynes MS. 130 (11). A version of this conversation of March 7, 1725, has been published by Turnor, *Collections for the History of Grantham,* pp. 172-173.

20. *Ibid.,* p. 173 n. 2. The anecdote was sufficiently known to appear among the papers of the Reverend Joseph Spence in 1728-1730; see his *Anecdotes, observations, and characters of Books and Men* (London, 1820), p. 54.

21. Newton was at pains to show that the ancients (Pythagoras, for example) knew not only that gravity was an affection of celestial as well as terrestrial bodies, that the planets were retained in their orbits by the force of gravity, but also "that the Gravity of the Planets towards the Sun are reciprocally as the Squares of their

Distances from it" (discourse inserted in the preface of David Gregory's *The Elements of Physical and Geometrical Astronomy* [London, 1726], p. xii). On Newton's authorship of this section, see David Kubrin, "Newton and the Cyclical Cosmos: Providence and the Mechanical Philosophy," *Journal of the History of Ideas,* XXVIII (1967), 341 n. 65. The Pythagoreans understood the harmony of the spheres, and Apollo's playing upon a harp of seven strings was the appropriate symbol, for the forces "whereby equal Tensions act upon Strings of different Lengths (being equal in other Respects) are reciprocally as the Squares of the Lengths of the Strings" (Gregory, *Elements,* p. x). See also Conduitt's remark: "Sr I. thought Pythagoras's Music of the spheres was intended to typify gravity, & as he makes the sounds & notes to depend on the size of the strings, so gravity depends on the density of matter" (Keynes MS. 130 [7]). The conception of the *prisca sapientia* in Newton's works is admirably developed in J. E. McGuire and P. M. Rattansi, "Newton and the 'Pipes of Pan,'" *Notes and Records of the Royal Society of London,* XXI (1966), 108–143.

22. Keynes MS. 55, "Sendivogius explained," fol. 2r.
23. Keynes MS. 130 (6).

INDEX OF NAMES

INDEX